Procurement and Supply Chain Management

How can businesses marry the short-term advantages of low-cost country sourcing with the longer-term implications of global sustainability? Are we heading for a sustainability crisis? *Procurement and Supply Chain Management: A Sustainability Perspective,* Third Edition, not only fully addresses the environmental, social, and economic challenges of how companies manage procurement and supply chains but also provides coverage of new and emerging concerns including supply chain risk and resilience, transparency, and digital supply chains. In addition to explaining the basic principles and processes of both procurement and supply chain management, the book evaluates how to develop strategic and sustainable procurement and supply chain management.

The authors' key message is that procurement and supply chain management needs to focus on value creation rather than cost cutting. This requires the development of new procurement and supply chain models that involve circular supply structures, supply chain transparency, and collaboration with new stakeholders in traditional sourcing and supply chain settings. Aimed at students, educators, and practitioners the book integrates sustainability into each chapter as a core element of procurement and supply chain management.

This third edition incorporates new examples and case studies from industry throughout, striking a balance between theoretical frameworks and guidelines for implementation in practice.

Thomas Johnsen is Professor of Procurement and Supply Management at Audencia Business School, France, where he also serves as a member of the executive board and acts as the Head of Research for the Information Systems and Supply Chain Management department. He is Associate Editor of the *Journal of Purchasing and Supply Management*.

Joe Miemczyk is Professor of Supply Chain Management at ESCP Europe Business School based at the London, UK campus. He researches sustainable and circular supply chains in a number of sectors, publishing in a variety of supply chain and operations journals.

Leonardo Marques is Associate Professor of Supply Chain Management at Audencia Business School, France, and President of the International Purchasing and Supply Education and Research Association (IPSERA) for the 2023–26 term. His research explores supply chain transparency and digitalization and their relation to social and ecological challenges. He serves as Associate Editor of the *International Journal of Operations & Production Management* and the *Journal of Purchasing & Supply Management.*

Mickey Howard is a University of Exeter Professor Emeritus. After 25 years of working as a UK business school academic, he now spends his time writing about the importance of sustainable supply chains, mentoring the next generation of business leaders, and exploring the high wilderness areas of the world.

This book has been among my resources for teaching different sustainability related courses for the past three years. I am teaching 'Sustainability Oriented Innovation' and 'Business Ethics and Sustainability' for different postgraduate programmes. What I like about the book is that every chapter can be taught separately in a way that reading one chapter and topic is not a prerequisite for the next chapter. I also very much appreciate the case studies where students can work in groups and discuss the case.

Toloue Miandar, *Assistant Professor at the Department of Management of University of Bologna*

Procurement and Supply Chain Management

A Sustainability Perspective

THIRD EDITION

Thomas Johnsen, Joe Miemczyk, Leonardo Marques, and Mickey Howard

Routledge
Taylor & Francis Group
LONDON AND NEW YORK

Designed cover image: Howard (2024), Wiessmies, Switzerland

Third edition published 2026
by Routledge
4 Park Square, Milton Park, Abingdon, Oxon, OX14 4RN

and by Routledge
605 Third Avenue, New York, NY 10158

Routledge is an imprint of the Taylor & Francis Group, an informa business

First edition published by Routledge 2014
Second edition published by Routledge 2018

British Library Cataloguing-in-Publication Data
A catalogue record for this book is available from the British Library

ISBN: 9781032813929 (hbk)
ISBN: 9781032813912 (pbk)
ISBN: 9781003499602 (ebk)

DOI: 10.4324/9781003499602

Typeset in Berling and Futura
by codeMantra

Access the Support Material: www.routledge.com/9781032813912

Contents

Foreword

Procurement has completely transformed from being a tactical function driven by cost savings to a critical partner that adds value to the entire business. Acting as the interface to suppliers, procurement plays a key role in securing critical inputs to production processes whether in the form of raw materials, components or services.

However, the dependence on ever more complex supply chains – or networks – has also brought significant challenges. The dependence on multi-tier, often global, supply networks has made it almost impossible to have full visibility and therefore control over what happens in distant supplier operations. The global drive for cost reduction has occasionally come at the expense of harm to the environment (planet) or labour (people). Consequently, supply chains have to fundamentally change: from linear take-make-waste systems to circular, regenerative systems in balance with the broader eco-system.

Making supply chains more sustainable was why we founded the *Sustainable Procurement Pledge* in 2019. By 2025 more than 25,000 Ambassadors had signed The Pledge showing the global commitment to make Sustainable Procurement the default.

The procurement community has been proactive in grasping the sustainability challenge and sustainable procurement has helped to reinforce the need for procurement to become truly strategic. This has also meant that procurement has emerged as an appealing career path, attracting students to join our thriving procurement community.

Recent geopolitical changes pose a challenge to sustainable procurement and supply chain management. Companies are shifting their attention to the increasing supply chain risks that make our jobs much more interesting as these new challenges must not come at the expense of sustainability. In fact sustainable procurement and supply chains are instrumental to making supply chains more resilient in these changing times.

The third edition of *Procurement and Supply Chain Management: A Sustainability Perspective* continues to place sustainability at the heart of procurement and supply chain management. Instead of looking at supply chains as linear, controllable – "optimizable" – systems, this book looks at supply chains as inherently dynamic and complex: as inter-organizational networks or ecosystems that rely on collaboration with a multitude of stakeholders, such as NGOs.

The new edition of the book picks up on the latest challenges that impact global supply chains. These include the radically changing geopolitical context but also, for example, trends towards digitalization, new regulations and the focus on scope 3 carbon emissions. The book is a great resource for anyone interested in understanding procurement and supply chain management from a sustainability perspective, whether it be students or seasoned practitioners looking for new inspiration.

Thomas Udesen
Group CCO/Member of Executive Board, Aldi South
Co-Founder of the Sustainable Procurement Pledge

Preface to the third edition

First of all, we welcome our new co-author Leonardo Marques to the third edition of our book! Leonardo brings a wealth of experience and insights that we deemed to be critically important in writing the new version of our book. Our objective with the third edition has been to significantly overhaul many parts of the book and inviting Leonardo to join our author team has enabled us to achieve this objective.

When we wrote the second edition of the book (2018) sustainability was already a hot topic and many companies across many industries and countries were embracing the sustainability challenge. This included purchasing and supply chain managers who increasingly saw themselves as integral parts of the transition to a new – sustainable – way of doing business. The impacts of climate change are now all too apparent and global warming has accelerated even since the first edition of our book was published in 2014.

Since the second edition of the book there have been significant developments on several other fronts. The use of digital technologies and especially Artificial Intelligence (AI) are transforming a wide range of business practices and potentially threatening our professional lives. In parallel, law makers have been pushing for legislation for supply chain due diligence, making companies legally responsible for what happens in their extended supply chains. This includes requirements for (large) companies to report the emissions caused by their internal activities as well as those in their supply chains (scope 1–3).

However, we could not possibly have predicted the Covid-19 pandemic and the enormous challenges this presented to global supply chains. Covid-19 was an event that made business leaders begin to rethink many of the best practices that had been taken for granted for decades, most notably lean supply chains relying heavily on global (and in many cases low-cost country) sourcing. In fact, the Covid-19 pandemic seemed only to be the start of a series of crises that disrupted global supply chains. Ongoing wars in Ukraine and Gaza are forcing political leaders to rethink their reliance on supply from – and through – high risk countries and conflict zones.

What we did not foresee either when we embarked on the third edition was the profound change in the geopolitical environment, which is reversing so many of the assumptions of international business (and supply chains), including the global tariff war and the imposed changes in supply chains that we are now witnessing. Coupled with this, some aspects of sustainability are now labelled as "woke", especially – but not limited to – Diversity, Equity, and Inclusion (DEI).[1] What's more, the political debate appears to be crowding out climate targets in favour of how to boost national defence capabilities.

Consequently, we are seeing companies quietly withdrawing their commitments to certain aspects of sustainability. However, these are political tailwinds related to economies under strain and deepening inequalities, and so we believe that while being challenged, sustainability in one form or other will continue to drive change in the long term.

Therefore, it is our firm belief that sustainability will continue to be a core part of purchasing and supply chain management. The language around sustainability may change as will considerations around what drives sustainability. At least some senior executives will want to see a convincing business case before committing to sustainability projects. The business case may be found in cost reduction, value creation, or in supply chain risk and resilience management. For example, creating circular supply chains is one way to tackle the challenges of sourcing of critical raw materials, and localizing sourcing closer to home can help to reduce supply chain risk.

We have not changed the fundamental premise of our view of sustainability, which is that procurement and supply chain managers are in a critically important position to transition towards new sustainable business models. Sustainability is not the responsibility of a few isolated individuals within the company. Instead, it is important that sustainability becomes integrated into the fabric of the firm, as a core part of business strategy, process, and function, with procurement and supply chain management taking a leading role. This is the key procurement and supply chain management challenge we seek to address in this book. If procurement and supply chain managers are to embrace this challenge, they have to change the way they operate. This transition requires new ways of thinking about supply structures, processes, skills, and competencies.

It follows from the above that sustainability is not the responsibility of a few sustainability experts, but a challenge that must be embraced company wide. Sustainability goes beyond the narrow, but crucial, focus of climate change, but addresses broader challenges to the natural world, society, and the economy. It is for this reason that we chose the title '*Procurement and Supply Chain Management: A Sustainability Perspective*', and not 'Sustainable Procurement and Supply Chain Management'. This book is intended as a core textbook for a normal procurement and supply chain management course at university or business school level. The book can also be used for specialized courses in sustainable procurement and supply chain management, but the overall aim of the book is to cover all the most important aspects of procurement, including those aspects of supply chain that concern inter-organizational issues e.g. sourcing and distribution, and to explain how sustainability needs to be taken into account across all of these aspects. Above all, instead of sustainability being treated as one separate lecture or chapter in a procurement or supply chain management course, our intention is that sustainability is considered in the context of each topic.

We did decide to change the book title from '*Purchasing and Supply Chain Management: A Sustainability Perspective*' to '***Procurement** and Supply Chain Management: A Sustainability Perspective*'. Although the meaning of these two closely related terms varies across countries and sectors, it has become clear to us that in practice procurement – and sustainable procurement – has become the dominant term. We expand on definitions in the first chapter.

We sincerely hope that this book will play its part in not only educating but changing the mindsets of current and future procurement and supply chain management professionals.

Thomas Johnsen
Professor of Procurement and Supply Chain Management
Audencia Business School, France

Joe Miemczyk
Professor of Supply Chain Management
ESCP Europe Business School, UK

Leonardo Marques
Associate Professor of Supply Chain Management
Audencia Business School, France

Mickey Howard
Professor Emeritus
University of Exeter, UK

NOTE

1 'Woke' is a term used since the 1930s to refer to racial prejudice and discrimination. It gained popular usage around the 2010s to refer to the broader awareness of social inequalities such as sexism and LGBTQ. In 2014, the phrase 'stay woke' was popularized by Black Lives Matter activists in the wake of police brutality including shootings of African Americans. From 2020 on, the term has increasingly been used sarcastically to disparage leftist or progressive movements as superficial and insincere, particularly over issues of Diversity, Equality, and Inclusion (DEI).

Acknowledgements

This book is written for students, academics, and practitioners. As we have attempted to tackle the double hurdle of academic rigour and practical relevance it has been particularly important to us to discuss ideas with a large number of people that represent both academia and practice. Colleagues and students within the business schools where we are employed, as well as the wider academic communities we form part of, such as the *International Purchasing & Supply Education & Research Association* (IPSERA) and the *Journal of Purchasing & Supply Management* (JPSM) editorial team, have inspired our thinking and development of models and frameworks.

We would like to thank the following colleagues at our own academic institutions: Francois Constant, Mihalis Giannakis, Rhona Johnsen, Osama Meqdadi, Steffen Boehm, Peter Hopkinson, Stefano Pascucci, Roberta De Angelis, Dan Eatherly, and Adam Lumsby. We would also like to thank Anne Touboulic, Morten Møller, Wendy van der Valk, Stefan Seuring, and George Zsidisin for their kind reviews of the previous edition.

From companies/organizations we would like to thank: Tuukka Farin (Head of Procurement Development & Supplier Sustainability, Boliden), Paul Gardner (Incorporated Lead Commercial VP & Chief Procurement Officer, Mars Pet Nutrion), Søren Vammen (ex-CEO, Danish Purchasing & Logistics Forum – DILF), David Dawson (Technology Executive, Rolls-Royce), Tim Engell-Pedersen (Viking Life-Saving Equipment), Stephane Pochat (Evea), Stef Kranedijk (former Chairman of Desso), Jean-Paul Jeanrenaud and Eric Dargent (WWF), Carlos Gomez and David McClintock (EcoVadis).

Many of our academic colleagues have inspired our work: some are, for example, past colleagues, co-authors, or research partners; there are really too many to name all, but we would like to mention (in alphabetical order) Philip Beske-Janssen, Raffaella Cagliano, Richard Calvi, Federico Caniato, Nathalie Fabbe-Costes, Andrew Graves, Christine Harland, Matthias Holweg, Dirk-Jan Kamann, Toloue Miandar, Antonella Moretto, Stefano Ronchi, Richard Lamming, Mike Lewis, Ole S. Mikkelsen, Katia Picaud, Thomas Ritter, Jan Stentoft, Kim Sundtoft Hald, André Sobczak, Mervi Vuori, Andreas Wieland, Helen Walker. Also, we thank our fellow JPSM associate editors and co-editors. Finally, we would like to thank the support team at Routledge especially Jess Harrison and Amy Laurens. Any inaccuracies, of course, are entirely our own responsibility.

CHAPTER 1

Introduction

LEARNING OBJECTIVES:

At the end of this chapter you should be able to:

- Explain the reasons why procurement is no longer an administrative, or clerical, responsibility, but a critical and strategic priority for companies;
- Understand why procurement is now seen as part of supply chain management and the implications of the procurement-supply chain management relationship;
- Define procurement and supply chain management in relation to related concepts such as sourcing and purchasing;
- Evaluate the criticality of the sustainability challenge and how it affects procurement and supply chain management;
- Argue the need for sustainability to become an integrated part of procurement and supply chain management rather than a separate add-on consideration;
- Explain the underlying theoretical perspective and structure of the book;
- Form an overview of the structure of the book.

1.1 INTRODUCTION

Procurement has grown tremendously as a business discipline both in practice and in academia over the past 30 years or so. Many organizations across the private and public sectors worldwide have elevated procurement to a strategic business responsibility; the emergence of the Chief Procurement Officer is a symbol of the rising profile of procurement. The trend towards outsourcing of non-core activities has clearly had a positive impact on the profession as a very high proportion of value adding now stems from suppliers, and many organizations have woken up to this fact and manage procurement accordingly.

However, the elevation of procurement to an important, even strategic, business function is a relatively new development and, in many companies, procurement remains a low priority. Procurement is still often highly driven by achieving low prices from suppliers, regardless of whether or not the company strategy is focused on low cost. So, although

DOI: 10.4324/9781003499602-1

procurement in many companies has become more sophisticated there is much scope for improvement of the profession.

An increasing number of people now choose to develop a career in procurement, but only 20–25 years ago this was by no means a normal choice of career and was often seen as a dubious one. In some ways the emergence of supply chain management has played well into the hands of the procurement profession because procurement is seen as a critical link in the supply chain. But, in other ways the role of procurement in relation to supply chain management is all but clear: some people regard procurement as an integral part of supply chain management whereas others regard it as complementary yet separate.

The recent development of sustainability as a strategic challenge for business and society has boosted the importance of both procurement and supply chain management. A company is no more sustainable than the suppliers it sources from so creating sustainable companies means creating and managing sustainable supply chains. Top management in many companies appear to have grasped this challenge but the often short-term driven, business functions of procurement and supply chain management are not easy to integrate with the challenge of sustainability that by definition requires a long-term perspective. However, this is the challenge taken up by this book: to try to fill the gap of how sustainability affects, and can be incorporated into, procurement and supply chain management decisions. The book is therefore not primarily a book about sustainable procurement and supply chain management but a book that identifies and discusses how sustainability in its various guises is relevant to 'normal' procurement and supply chain management. To paraphrase Kraljic's (1983) message that "procurement must become supply management", the message of this book is: procurement and supply chain management must become *sustainable* procurement and supply chain management.

This chapter begins by tracing the development of procurement from an administrative, tactical function within companies to a managerial, strategic function. The following section introduces the implications of supply chain management for procurement, followed by a section outlining the sustainability challenge and what it means for both procurement and supply chain management. Key concepts are defined and discussed along the way. The chapter concludes with an overview of the structure of the book.

1.2 THE EMERGENCE OF PROCUREMENT AS AN ACADEMIC DISCIPLINE

Compared with other business and management functions, such as marketing, finance, or operations management, procurement is relatively new and under-developed as an academic field of study. The first books and articles that considered purchasing in any detail date back to the 1960s, most notably Robinson et al. (1967), Webster and Wind (1972), and Sheth (1973). This early work focused on explaining organizational buying processes with a view to helping suppliers (sales and marketing people, in other words) to better understand the buying process of their customers, so were not really about purchasing management. In the 1970s the first proper textbooks on purchasing – or procurement – began to appear, including England (1970), Lee and Dobler (1971), and Baily and Farmer (1977). Academically, these can be seen as the foundation stones of purchasing and procurement.

However, it was not until the 1980s and early 1990s that books and articles were published that really sought to promote purchasing as an important business function and therefore as a worthwhile academic field of study. In particular, writers across Europe and North America argued that the position and status of the purchasing function within organizations should be elevated; various maturity models were developed, portraying purchasing as a reactive, passive, and tactical function at one end of the spectrum to an integrative, strategic function at the other, advanced, end of the spectrum (Spekman, 1981; Reck and Long, 1988; Gadde and Håkansson, 1993; Ellram and Carr, 1994).

The lack of academic credibility of procurement until quite recently reflected the fact that purchasing in practice used to be a clerical function focused predominantly on obtaining the lowest possible prices for goods and administrative, mundane, tasks such as record keeping. Around the same time as purchasing began to evolve as a field of study in the late 1980s and early 1990s, companies had embarked on changes in industrial organization, 'farming out' or 'outsourcing' non-core competencies and activities that they used to perform in-house. This trend had major implications for purchasing because it meant that strategically important resources, or complementary competencies (Teece, 1986), had to be sourced – and purchased – from specialized suppliers.

The trend towards outsourcing continues to this day and has even accelerated; over the last decade or so outsourcing has been an integral part of globalization as companies have looked to low cost countries for cheaper sourcing. Outsourcing reflects a deep trend; in addition to a search for low cost sources, outsourcing is part of a wider change process of industrial re-organization in which companies focus on what they do best and connect to the rest through a network of business relationships. Technological innovation is now happening at such a rapid pace that companies can no longer do everything themselves in-house. Even if, ideally, they would prefer to control at least the most important resources and activities by keeping these in-house, they have little choice but to source these from outside companies especially as the most critical resources these days are intangible and knowledge-based.

Consider for example the case of Airbus: despite its history as an aircraft manufacturer Airbus has chosen to outsource the design, development, and manufacture of major aircraft sub-systems to specialized suppliers. As part of the Airbus Power8 rationalization programme, Airbus sought to focus on its core competencies and thereby outsource major aircraft work packages to suppliers, especially those that they term 'risk sharing partners'. For example, approx. 50 per cent of aero-structure work on the Airbus A350 XWB was outsourced. Also, production sites that were previously under Airbus ownership were sold off, including the wing component facility at Filton near Bristol which is now operated by GKN; other sites including some in France followed. At the same time, Airbus sought to reduce the size of its supply base so that it now relies on fewer but more strategic suppliers. These include major industry players such as Rolls Royce, General Electric, and Pratt & Whitney, who assume responsibility for design and build of large aircraft sub-systems. Consequently, Airbus is not really a manufacturer anymore; Airbus relies on its network of suppliers for manufacturing and its role these days is as an aircraft systems integrator rather than a manufacturer.

Indeed, in many industries the proportion of value that stems from the supply chain is almost 80 per cent and in many companies the outsourcing ratio is over 90 per cent. Based on data from 738 UK corporations, Strassmann (2004) calculated the average outsourcing ratio as 78 per cent (revenue/procurement). For example, the outsourcing ratio at British Airways was 77 per cent, at Rolls Royce (aerospace) it was 84 per cent, and at Tesco (supermarket) and Centrica PLC (the energy provider) it was 89 per cent. Examples of relatively low levels of outsourcing include pharmaceutical giants GlaxoSmithKline and AstraZeneca where outsourcing accounts for 'only' 45 per cent but this is still a very significant proportion and is likely to become even higher as the outsourcing trend continues.

The consequence of the outsourcing trend is that companies become heavily dependent on the performance of their suppliers and therefore need to make sure that suppliers are effectively managed as if they were an extended part of their own company: an extended enterprise. As a central function dealing with suppliers, procurement plays a key role in the management of supplier relationships. This role is not only a matter of cost reduction, although saving money remains a priority for any organization, but also about ensuring that the need for a range of criteria, including for example quality, delivery, innovation, and service, are being met by suppliers. The need to procure complex performance (Caldwell and Howard, 2011) requires not only deep collaborative relationships with suppliers, often spanning multiple decades, but also an understanding of how complex outcomes are articulated over time through a combination of contractual incentives and collaborative relationships, requiring new skills and competencies from procurement staff.

It is against this backdrop that the elevation of purchasing from a passive low-level organizational function to a strategic function with corporate visibility and influence needs to be understood. The rise of the executive board position of the Chief Procurement Officer (or CPO) is symptomatic of this trend. Companies increasingly realize the importance of improving their knowledge and competence in procurement. They realize that they need to start filling this knowledge gap and to develop fundamentally new ways of thinking about procurement and its potential contribution to ensure sustained competitive advantage in an increasingly competitive global business landscape.

1.3 TWO DEVELOPMENTS IN PROCUREMENT

Purchasing is in some ways a limited concept and rival terms have emerged, in particular, since the 1980s. In the opening chapter of this book it is important to develop an initial understanding of some of these alternative concepts and how they relate to and impact on purchasing.

The title of this book indicates that two important concepts are to be included alongside procurement: supply chain management and sustainability. Both of these reflect major developments and challenges to procurement theory as well as the procurement profession and they affect the practice of procurement in different ways. The following two sections explore how these are transforming procurement.

1.3.1 Purchasing becomes supply (chain) management

Peter Kraljic's publication in the Harvard Business Review in 1983, 'Purchasing must become Supply Management', was a cornerstone in the rise of purchasing from a tactical to a strategic business function. His most important message, as will be further explored in Chapter 4, was that purchasing should focus more on high value and high supply risk items and that these called for 'supply management' rather than 'purchasing management'. This is a theme that has since been the subject of much debate and the purchasing profession has embraced this fundamental message to the extent that in some parts of the world, most notably North America, purchasing is now simply referred to as supply management or simply 'supply'. Indeed, the need to capture both 'purchasing' and 'supply management' is reflected in the use of the term 'purchasing and supply management' (PSM).

The rise of supply chain management since its early foundations in the 1980s is in many ways a natural extension of this development from purchasing to supply management. Adding the word 'chain' to 'supply management' may seem trivial but is, in fact, significant. The inclusion of the concept of chain hints at the multi-disciplinary genesis of supply chain management, most notably Porter's (1985) value chain (strategic management) and channel management (marketing and distribution). Whereas the focus of purchasing is clearly on supplier relationships, the focus of supply chain management is on the wider business system that includes several layers, or tiers, of suppliers, sub-suppliers, customers, distributors, and so on. In some ways supply chain management has absorbed a number of business functions involved in the process of supply, including purchasing, operations, logistics, and distribution management. Unfortunately, perhaps because of the relatively weak theoretical foundations of supply chain management, this has been a somewhat messy development process so that definitions and boundaries between these remain unclear.

What is without question is the fact that many organizations see their supply chain as a key driver of competitive advantage. As responsible for (or at least instrumental in) the sourcing process, procurement is at the heart of supply chain management but supply chain management shifts the focus from direct, or 'dyadic', relationships between buyers and suppliers towards entire end-to-end supply chains. In many organizations procurement is now an integral part of the supply chain management function, focused on the management of the part of the upstream, supplier-focused, supply chain (sourcing). In view of the changing use of the terms in practice and the generally accepted more comprehensive and strategic nature of the term procurement compared with purchasing, we therefore apply the term procurement in this third edition of the book.

Section 1.4 discusses the varying use of the key terms in more depth but for now the important point is to note that, consistent with the above academic institutions, this book will mostly use the term procurement to capture both non-strategic and strategic purchases.

1.3.2 The rise of sustainable sourcing and supply chain management

The second challenge to procurement is the rapidly rising interest in sustainability. The age of the 'triple bottom line' (Elkington, 1999) is upon us where the assumption is that profit should no longer be at the expense of people (the social dimensions) and planet (the environmental dimension). The pressure on business to deliver economic returns from greener goods is mounting and corporate social responsibility is no longer something that can be dismissed as a fad for environmental fanatics. The planet's resources are in decline and the climate is changing, placing increasing pressures on companies to reduce carbon emissions, recycle or re-use, and to develop clean technologies. Sustainable development i.e. 'development that meets the needs of the present without compromising the ability of future generations to meet their own needs' (World Commission on Environment and Development, 1987) is here to stay and only shows signs of gaining even greater momentum for the foreseeable future. Sustainability therefore implies a long-term perspective which can be divided into three dimensions as shown in Figure 1.1 below.

There has been some criticism of this framework, where some view it as simply a way to manage trade-offs rather than address system change (Elkington, 1999). Taking a systems view, the environmental dimensions of sustainability are now being more accurately measured and planetary risks, or boundaries, identified (Steffen et al., 2015). These nine boundaries (Figure 1.2) show that sustainability actions, including at the company level, are systemic and must go beyond the narrow focus on climate change to address a broader range of issues impacting planetary health. As of 2024, five of these boundaries have been passed already, risking major and irreversible environmental changes (i.e. tipping points) to the climate, nutrient cycles, ecosystems, biodiversity, and water systems, which in turn impact human societies and the economies built by them. While science has advanced sufficiently to track these changes to our planet and their causes rooted in human activity, some, such as the introduction of novel entities, are uncertain. For example, we still do not know the full extent and impact of pollution from micro-plastics in our food chain or so called 'forever chemicals' in the water we drink.

As demonstrated in the triple bottom line perspective, humanity's challenges are also rooted in social issues, hence Kate Raworth (2017) adapted the above framework to include a social foundation as part of the now well-known doughnut model. This foundation comprises 12 societal needs without which societies and economies begin to face material problems including access to energy, water, food, and health services, among others.

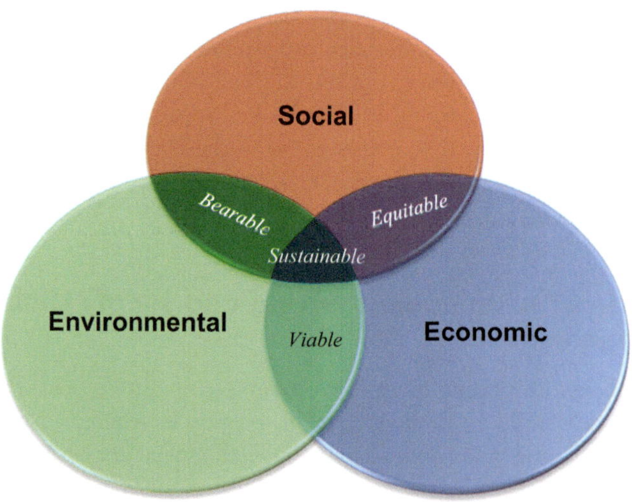

FIGURE 1.1 Three dimensions of sustainability

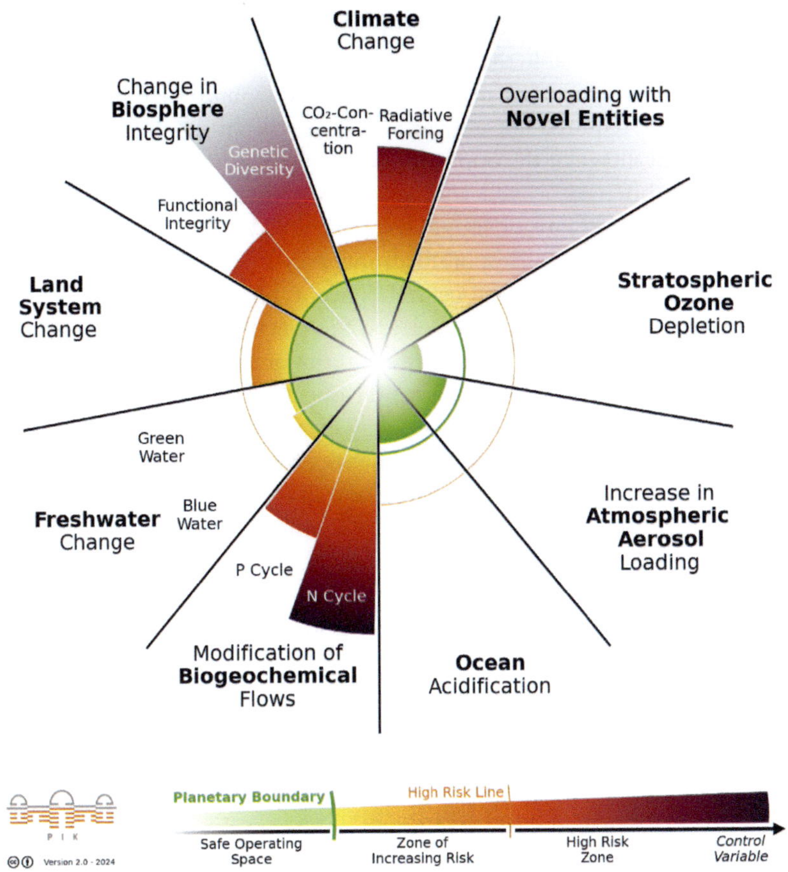

FIGURE 1.2 Planetary boundaries
Source: The Stockholm Resilience Centre, Sweden (2025)

Sustainability, represented by these boundaries and foundations, presents a risk to companies that are unprepared but also an opportunity for companies prepared to embrace the challenge. However, companies cannot tackle sustainability by themselves: implementing sustainability requires systemic change, especially radically overhauled supply models. Paradoxically, the trend towards outsourcing, particularly to low cost countries such as China or India, has exacerbated the sustainable procurement and supply chain management challenge. One of the negative results of global sourcing has been that companies have lost sight of what happens within their extended supply chains and low cost country sourcing sometimes comes at an unexpected price. Consider the problems of the BP oil spill in the Gulf of Mexico in 2010: it shows that companies cannot simply blame its suppliers when environmental disasters happen in the supply chain. Or the collapse of a garment factory in Bangladesh in April 2013 killing over 1,100 factory workers: a supplier of Western fashion companies and retailers looking for low cost sourcing. Companies, including Apple and Nestlé, are rethinking their procurement strategies due to damaging reports of conflict minerals and modern slavery. Again, a key message of this book is that a company is no more sustainable than the suppliers it sources from, putting procurement right at the heart of sustainability implementation. New innovative procurement strategies and methods are required not only to avoid the risks of unethical procurement, but also to fully take advantage of the opportunities posed by sustainability.

Sustainability is often associated with concepts such as corporate social responsibility (CSR), global responsibility, or simply responsibility. While some firms stress sustainable sourcing, others frame it as responsible procurement or CSR in the supply chain. In this book, sustainability remains the central concept, encompassing the TBL approach, planetary boundaries, the doughnut model, and the long-term perspective of the Brundtland Commission (1987). Distinctions between terms are problematic; CSR, for instance, although sometimes extended to environmental aspects, is primarily tied to social responsibility, grounded in ethics and norms, and may even conflict with environmental goals (Markman and Krause, 2016). Criticism highlights CSR as marketing rhetoric decoupled from actual operational change (Matten and Moon, 2008), raising concerns about its legitimacy as so-called private regulation (Bartley, 2007). In our view, a shift from 'do-no-harm' to 'do-good' is needed (Markman and Krause, 2016). In this way companies should go beyond compliance, where true sustainability prioritizes ecology, then society, and finally the economy which is reliant on these first two priorities (Pagell and Shevchenko, 2014; Montabon et al., 2016).

This ecologically dominant view reflects the trend towards the idea of the circular economy that has gained momentum the last decade. The shift in thinking towards the circular economy is reflected in the development of closed-loop supply chains that aim not only to reduce waste through product redesign and extended lifecycles, but to reuse all materials as a positive ingredient or 'nutrient' in supply chains.

The concept of the circular economy as an exciting new business model is rapidly gaining traction in both practitioner and management research communities, offering a vision for the future of production systems as restorative and regenerative by design where ultimately there is no waste or pollution (WEF, 2014; Blomsma and Brennan, 2017). In principle, the circular economy presents an opportunity to address impending global sustainability issues around resource scarcity and environmental degradation, offering the prospect of 'clean growth' to any organization and associated stakeholders who adopt it. Yet progress to date on the actual means or methods of circular economy implementation across all major business sectors has been relatively slow, with less than 7 per cent of the world's resources being circulated (Circle Economy, 2025). Despite recent work of institutions, such as the Ellen MacArthur Foundation (EMF, 2012, 2014) in popularizing the concept, a new British Standard in circular economy, and interest shown by leading multinational brands (e.g. Unilever, Coca Cola, Renault), considerable work remains to make the circular economy a reality.

1.4 VARYING USE OF KEY CONCEPTS: A DISCUSSION

Unfortunately for students of purchasing/procurement and supply chain management there is a plethora of concepts which more or less mean the same thing. Academics as well as practitioners often use these more or less indiscriminately: where some people refer to purchasing, other people refer to procurement, supply management, sourcing, acquisition, or simply buying. What then are the differences?

1.4.1 Purchasing, procurement, supply management, or sourcing?

The following statement of the purpose of purchasing is useful as a starting point: "To purchase the right quality of material, at the right time, in the right quantity, from the right source, at the right price" (Bailey and Farmer, 1977). This classic quote is a useful starting point as it highlights the different objectives, especially as it places price as the last concern, which is often the sole issue that purchasers can think of at the expense of other priorities. As the terms have developed over time, purchasing is increasingly viewed as tied to the transactional processes in connection with making a purchase, with procurement being used to describe a more comprehensive and inclusive concept.

The UK Chartered Institute of Procurement & Supply (CIPS, 2025) defines procurement as:

> The activity overseeing the steps of the procurement cycle, such as market analysis, sourcing, negotiation, contracting and supplier relationship management for goods, works and services, covering both acquisitions from third parties and in-house providers. The process spans the whole procurement cycle from the identification of needs, through to the end of a services contract or the end of the useful life of an asset. It involves options appraisal and the critical "make or buy" decision.

CIPS goes on to distinguish *procurement* from *purchasing*:

> Procurement differs to purchasing in a number of ways. The main difference is that procurement is a long-term approach to acquiring goods and services, and purchasing is the short-term direct purchasing of products and services. Procurement involves sourcing suppliers, negotiating, contract management and supplier development to name a few, and purchasing is fulfilling the transaction only and is very much a reactive and transactional approach.

We would add to this that *supply management* is a widely-used term in North America and in parts of Europe, such as Finland. The use of the term 'supply management' reflects Kraljic's (1983) often-cited argument that "Purchasing must become Supply Management", suggesting that purchasing is tactical as it concerns low value and low risk items, whereas supply management is strategic as it concerns high value and high risk items. The use of the terms is also often sector-specific e.g. the public sector tends to use the term procurement instead of purchasing (Ramsay and Croom, 2008; Rozemeijer, 2008).

Table 1.1 compares some well-known textbook definitions of purchasing and procurement, showing increasingly wide – and long – definitions that seek to capture issues to do with external resource management, strategic contribution, and supplier (relationship) management.

TABLE 1.1 Comparing textbook definitions of purchasing, procurement, and sourcing

	Purchasing	*Procurement*	*Sourcing*
Bailey and Farmer (1977)	To purchase the right quality of material, at the right time, in the right quantity, from the right source, at the right price		
Cousins et al. (2008)	The area of the business that manages the inputs into the organization	Some say that procurement is more strategic while purchasing is a day-to-day activity; others say exactly the reverse. We consider such wordplay specious	
van Weele (2010)	The management of the company's external resources in such a way that the supply of all goods, services, capabilities, and knowledge which are necessary for running, maintaining, and managing the company's primary and support activities is secured at the most favourable conditions	All activities that are required in order to get the product from the supplier to its final destination	Finding, selecting, contracting, and managing the best possible source of supply on a worldwide basis
Farrington and Lysons (2012)	The process undertaken by the organizational unit that, either as a function or as part of an integrated supply chain, is responsible for procuring or assisting users to procure, in the most efficient manner, required suppliers at the right time, quality, quantity, and price and the management of suppliers, thereby contributing to the competitive advantage of the enterprise and the achievement of its corporate strategy	The process of obtaining goods or services by any means	The process of identifying, selecting, and developing suppliers

1.4.2 Supply chain management

The concept of *supply chains* – and, consequently, *supply chain management (SCM)* – was invented in the early 1980s, principally as a method of describing the much more complex concept of a business network. Supply chain management was born as a logistics concept although supply chain management is more than a new name for logistics

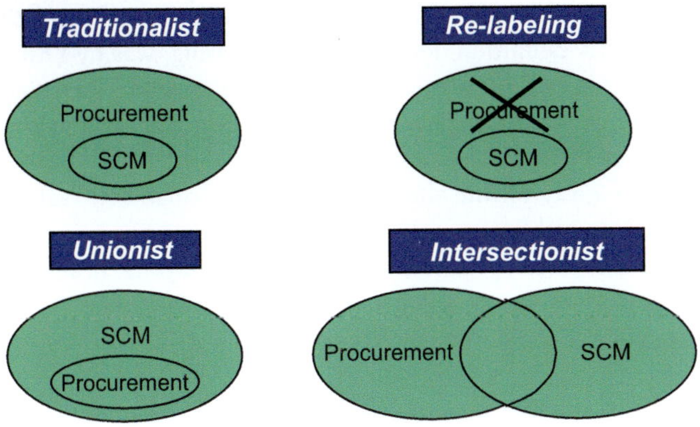

FIGURE 1.3 Procurement in relation to supply chain management
Source: Adapted from Larson and Halldorsson (2002)

(Cooper et al., 1997). Defined as "the management of upstream and downstream relationships with suppliers and customers to deliver superior customer value at less cost to the supply chain as a whole" (Christopher, 1998), SCM is based on the principle that supplier and customer (or simply supply) relationships are all part of a long chain of suppliers to end customers.

If supply chain management is to have meaning beyond simply a wide definition of logistics it must have a foundation in multiple functions related to the process of supply. In terms of intellectual roots, Johnsen et al. (2008) suggest that purchasing and supply management was core to the development of supply chain management as a concept, and that a wide range of other fields, including operations management, logistics, and industrial marketing, played important roles. Larson and Halldorsson (2002) suggest four different views of purchasing in relation to supply chain management: as shown in Figure 1.3, so-called 'unionists' view purchasing as part of supply chain management, whilst others believe that supply chain management has replaced purchasing.

Supply chain management focuses on multiple customer-supplier dyads, ultimately taking in original raw material extractors to final end customers (Harland, 1996). Supply chains tend to be depicted around a focal firm and its upstream and downstream relationships (Christopher, 1998; Lambert et al., 1998) although there has been some debate as to whether supply chains are simple linear structures – chains – or if in reality they are more like 'supply chain networks' (or simply 'supply networks') that include inter-connected supply chains (see e.g. Lamming et al., 2000). The consensus seems to be that supply chains should be understood as the latter but this is a debate we re-examine in more depth in Chapter 7.

1.4.3 Sustainable procurement and sustainable supply chain management

Having considered various definitions of procurement, supply chain management, and related concepts, we can now turn to definitions that specifically link these to sustainability. Many definitions related to sustainable procurement and supply chain management have been proposed but they are often partial, for example, only focusing on environmental issues. One early definition, focusing on purchasing, was by Drumwright (1994) who defined socially responsible organizational buying as attempts to take into account the public consequences of organizational buying or bring about positive social change through organizational buying behaviour.

Building more obviously on the three aspects of sustainability, Walker and Brammer (2009: 128) define sustainable procurement as: "procurement that is consistent with the principles of sustainable development, such as ensuring a strong, healthy and just society, living within environmental limits, and promoting good governance".

In this book sustainable procurement refers to

> the consideration of environmental, social, ethical and economic issues in the management of the organization's external resources in such a way that the supply of all goods, services, capabilities and knowledge which are necessary for running, maintaining and managing the organization's primary and support activities provide value not only to the organization but also to society and the economy.
>
> (Miemczyk *et al.*, 2012: 489)

This definition builds on the definition of purchasing by van Weele (2010), integrating the definition of sustainability as defined by the Brundtland Commission.

However, those definitions essentially concern procurement and not supply chain management. Again, we can identify many different definitions where some focus on specific parts of sustainability, typically the environmental dimension, and other are more inclusive. Two definitions are interesting to note here: Carter and Rogers (2008: 368) define sustainable supply chain management as "the strategic, transparent integration and achievement of an organization's social, systemic coordination of key inter-organizational business processes for improving the environmental and economic goals in the long-term economic performance of the individual company and its supply chains". In a similar vein, Beamon (1999: 337) puts particular emphasis on the need for a closed-loop supply chain by referring to "The fully integrated, extended supply chain contains all of the elements of the traditional supply chain ... but extends the one-way chain to construct a semi-closed loop that includes product and packaging recycling, re-use, and/or remanufacturing operations".

However, it is also relevant to consider an even higher level of analysis in order to fully grasp the implications of sustainability on procurement and supply chain management. In particular when adopting a sustainability perspective it becomes necessary to understand the supply chain as a business system that resembles a complex network of actors or stakeholders that are directly or indirectly involved in the supply process from raw material extractors to end customers/consumers.

We should note that many organizations dedicated to sustainability, such as the World Wildlife Fund (WWF), use the term sustainable sourcing rather than sustainable purchasing or procurement. This reflects the particular focus on sourcing, especially locational issues such as raw material sourced from rainforests and the consequent dangers to wildlife. Nevertheless, the use of the term sourcing by Non-Governmental Organizations

(NGOs) increasingly also covers issues to do with development and management of a global supply base in line with Lysons and Farrington's (2012) definition.

The following section explains the theoretical underpinning – or perspective – of this book, exploring how different levels of analysis help to understand different challenges of sustainable procurement and supply chain management.

1.5 UNDERPINNING THEORETICAL FRAMEWORK OF THE BOOK

In an earlier research project we identified that a significant proportion of sustainable procurement and supply management papers adopt stakeholder theory, institutional theory, and resource-based perspectives (Johnsen et al., 2017). We argued that an inter-organizational perspective, which emphasizes the need for interaction amongst stakeholders, is required. Since then, we have seen the emergence of new theories especially focused on understanding supply chains as complex adaptive systems, that are fundamentally dynamic and difficult to control (see Tate et al., 2022). Whilst this book is influenced by many different theories depending on the subject, a few theories are worth highlighting as especially influential.

A classic 'grand theory' is the resource-based view (RBV), dating back to Wernerfeldt (1984), and later popularized by Prahalad and Hamel's (1990) core competences model and spinning off in various directions such as Teece et al.'s (1997) theory of dynamic capabilities. RBV logic has often been used as the basis for the outsourcing decision, which is fundamental to procurement as it is about what to make in-house and what to buy (from suppliers). Based on RBV and core competence thinking, smart companies have outsourced many resources (and activities) they used to do themselves, making sure that they do not outsource strategically critical resources.

The RBV is therefore a useful theoretical starting point for some procurement and supply chain management analysis. However, rather than the usual resource focus emphasized by RBV, this book adopts a particular resource perspective in two respects:

1 Firstly, given the sustainability perspective, this book relies on a Natural Resource-Based View (NRBV) as first proposed by Hart (1995). This theoretical development builds on the RBV to take into account a focus on the natural environment, especially sustainable development, product stewardship, and pollution prevention. Companies that develop capabilities in establishing a shared vision (a rare skill) are able to accumulate resources necessary for sustainable development; sustainable development strategies focus on new, low-impact technologies and competencies. Product stewardship requires that lifecycle assessment (LCA) be integrated in new product development processes and thereby enables a firm to minimize both economic and environmental/social costs of the product. Finally, pollution prevention can become a causally ambiguous routine that may play a critical role in a company's unique cost reductions as a source of competitive advantage. All three of these strategies require close collaboration with a range of external stakeholders; it becomes a stakeholder-oriented legitimacy-based process.

2 Secondly, it follows from the NRBV that it is absolutely critical how companies can access resources through supplier, and supply chain, relationships and that resources gain social legitimacy through stakeholder collaboration. Therefore, in addition to the NRBV, which highlights the importance of external collaboration, the complementary theories of institutional theory of DiMaggio and Powell (1991), stakeholder theory (Mitchell et al., 1997) and the Industrial Marketing & Purchasing (IMP) Interaction Approach (e.g. Håkansson, 1987) are important influences in this book. These theories emphasize that although it is important to protect internal strategic resources it is increasingly necessary for companies to access important resources through external relationships with other companies. In fact, relationships with other companies, including supply chain partners, can themselves be sources of competitive advantage. On the other hand, many sustainability initiatives are driven by institutional pressures from governments, NGOs, and broader society. These rules of engagement limit what a company can do and may actually prevent differentiated strategies central to the resource-based view.

The NRBV and the IMP Interaction Approach emphasize the role of stakeholders and networks of relationships. Using these approaches enable us to better understand the bigger picture of creating sustainable procurement and supply chain management. Traditionally, much business (or industrial) network theory (e.g. developed by IMP group) has focused on 'business actors', such as manufacturers, suppliers, and distributors. These are typically also the actors considered in supply chain management analysis. However, as companies are seeking to incorporate sustainability into their procurement and supply chain management strategies and practices new forms of actors have to be considered as integral parts of this traditional network picture: NGOs. NGOs play increasingly important roles, for example, in spearheading industry-specific initiatives that concern sourcing and procurement of ingredients or materials linked to pollution, rainforest destruction, or exploitation of labour. As some companies have learned the hard way NGOs can severely work against them, for example by exposing companies in the media. But, NGOs can also engage actively in partnerships with companies, helping companies to monitor and implement sustainability. In short, NGOs are rapidly becoming integral actors, or stakeholders, within supply, or business, networks so are essential to procurement and supply strategy. As Roome (2001: 70) states "we increasingly see ourselves as part of a network society living in a network age", "concerns about complex environmental and social consequences of industrial activity have provoked the need for more frequent and meaningful engagement between companies and stakeholders" and "networks have an identified role in innovation for environmental management and sustainable development", and "knowledge suggests that ecosystems are based on organisms connected through complex networks of energy and material flows".

Drawing on existing classifications of network levels (Harland, 1996; Ritter and Gemünden, 2003; Möller et al., 2005), we distinguish between three levels of procurement and supply chain analysis: dyadic buyer-supplier relationships, supply chains, and networks (Figure 1.4).

	Conventional View	Sustainability View
Dyadic Buyer-Supplier Relationship	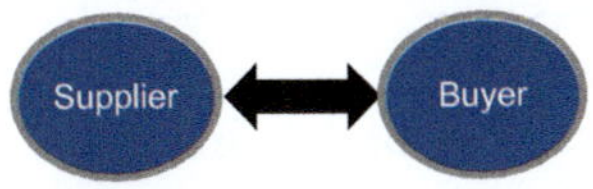 *One-to one buyer-supplier relationships: the building block of supply chains and networks*	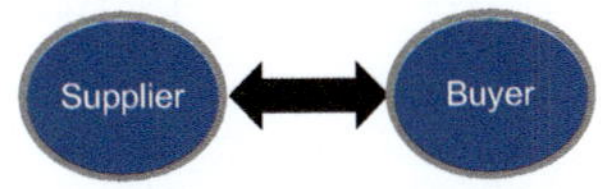 *Same structure but dyadic relationships become more intense as activities are about sustainability rather than purely operational*
Supply Chain	 *Component or product/ service-specific lines of raw material suppliers (RMS), intermediate suppliers (S1), Focal Manufacturer (FM), distributors (D), and end customers (EC)*	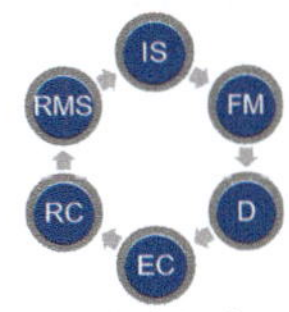 *Closed-loop or circular supply chain where products are recycled (RC) at the end of life/disposal stage and re-enter the supply chain instead of/in addition to new raw materials*
Network	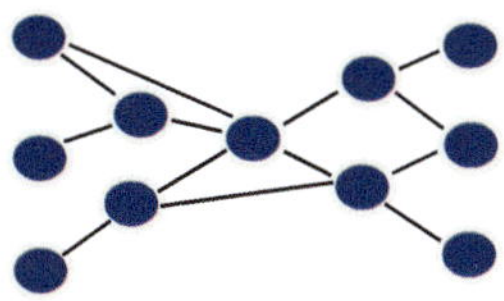 *A set of inter-connected supply chains depicting upstream suppliers and downstream distributors and customers. Mostly vertical connections*	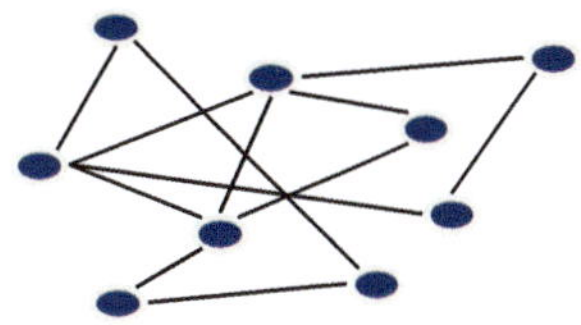 *An ecosystem of vertical supplier, distributor and customer relationships as well as relationships with non-supply chain stakeholders e.g. NGOs, research centres, and regulators*

FIGURE 1.4 A conceptual framework for *Procurement and Supply Chain Management: A Sustainability Perspective*

1.6 BOOK OVERVIEW

As shown in Figure 1.5 the book is divided into three parts that correspond to the levels of analysis illustrated in Figure 1.4.

1.6.1 Part A – Procurement and sourcing

The chapters in the first part of the book focus on dyadic buyer-supplier relationship issues: dyads are the basic building block of supply chains and networks. In order to successfully manage the whole supply chain, companies need to begin by focusing on the relationships with their immediate, direct suppliers (or service providers). Part A therefore concerns the management of the upstream side of the company's supply chain, which is the responsibility of procurement and sourcing management.

Chapter 2 begins by examining the procurement process, that is, the steps that procurement goes through when buying products and/or services from suppliers. The implications of sustainability for each step are discussed. This process is situated within a wider process of a long-term supply base development, involving supplier monitoring, supplier

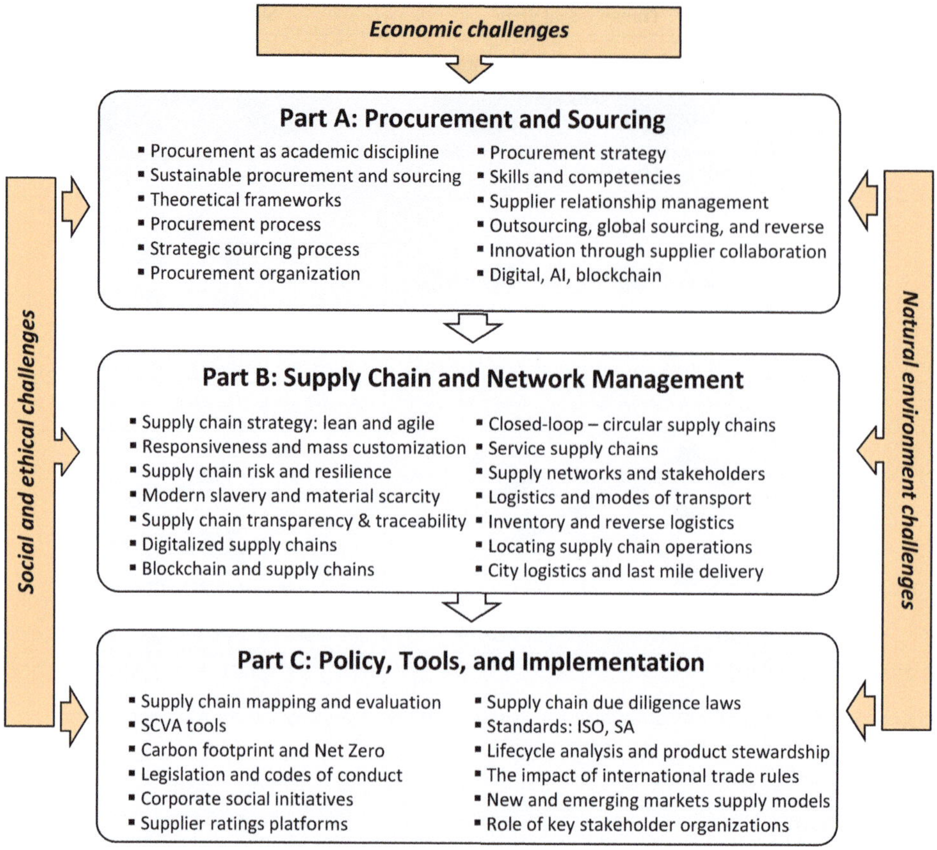

FIGURE 1.5 Book overview

development, and supplier relationship management. Chapter 3 then explains the importance and nature of procurement strategy and explores different procurement organizational structures, skills, and competencies, and again we discuss the implications of sustainability on these. In this third edition of the book we present an overhauled maturity framework that allows the assessment of four different stages of procurement maturity across a range of categorized assessment criteria. Chapter 3 concludes with a section on the particular challenges of procurement within the public sector; public sector cases and examples are also considered throughout the book so the main purpose of this section is to highlight some particular characteristics of public procurement.

Chapter 4 evaluates different sourcing strategies. In tandem with procurement becoming strategic, one of the key changes in sourcing strategy during the previous years was the shift from multi-sourcing strategies, whereby companies maintain a large supply base with suppliers they can play off against each other, towards parallel or single sourcing strategies whereby companies commit to a smaller number of suppliers and in turn become more dependent on the performance of these. However, with the renewed focus on supply chain risk and resilience, this has now changed and we explore these recent changes.

In the second half of Chapter 4 we focus on supplier relationship management. The need for supplier *relationship* assessment (as opposed to *supplier* assessment which is covered in Chapter 13) is discussed as well as the need to develop a portfolio of supplier relationships that are appropriate for different supply situations.

Chapter 5 focuses on outsourcing. The outsourcing decision is examined in terms of the 'make-or-buy' decision, that is, what should a company choose to make in-house and what is better to buy in from suppliers. The outsourcing decision is all too often taken on a simple cost basis. Many companies have realized, especially in recent years, that there are a great many risks associated with outsourcing which therefore needs to take into account a wide range of factors other than cost. Chapter 5 examines some theoretical perspectives that can be used to properly inform the outsourcing decision in order to mitigate these risks. Closely connected to Chapter 5 and the outsourcing question, Chapter 6 focuses on global sourcing, in particular sourcing from low cost countries. Companies have relied extensively on global sourcing but, as frequent reports in the media show, companies across a range of industries have struggled with suppliers located in low cost locations that do not comply with environmental, social, and economic expectations. We discuss the trend away from global sourcing and explore emerging concepts including re-shoring, near-shoring, and friend-shoring.

Part A concludes by focusing on the role of procurement in innovation: although procurement is usually focused on cost reduction it has a critical role to play in value creation by facilitating innovation. Chapter 7 discusses how procurement can facilitate product development and innovation through the involvement of suppliers in new product development projects. Focusing on the development of sustainability-innovations, we explore new practices for scouting for new supply chain partners in wider ecosystems and the application of digital technology in aiding innovation scouting.

1.6.2 Part B – Supply chain and network management

Part B contains four chapters dedicated to procurement and supply issues that concern supply chains and networks. These concern the development, management, and improvement of 'extra-dyadic' issues that go beyond the immediate, dyadic supplier relationships into the extended supply chain or network. Chapter 8 opens this part by examining some fundamental supply chain definitions and models. We explore different supply chain strategies, based on the notion of fit i.e. the need to design supply chains that fit the particular context of the company in terms of the nature of products and market conditions, sometimes dichotomized as lean or agile. We also explore the different ways to implement lean and/or agile supply chains. Furthermore, we challenge the traditional conception of linear supply chains and explore the opportunities for designing a completely different system known as the closed-loop supply chain, fundamental in implementing a cradle-to-grave (or cradle-to-cradle) business philosophy.

As the world is now characterized by changing geo-political conditions and has become truly turbulent with natural disasters, economic tensions, and armed conflicts disrupting supply chains, the issues of supply chain risk and resilience are receiving much attention. Chapter 9 examines frameworks for supply chain risk assessment, including risks categories, drivers, and mitigation strategies. We explore prominent sources of sustainability risk in supply chains, including scarce materials, conflict minerals, and modern slavery.

Chapter 10 is dedicated to another supply chain issue that has seen increasing attention, namely supply chain transparency. Chapter 10 discusses the role of new digital technology, including blockchain, Artificial Intelligence (AI), big data, and Internet of Things (IoT) that are promising to transform supply chain transparency and traceability.

Chapter 11 covers a number of key logistics management topics and shows how logistics and sustainability are inextricably linked, especially from an environmental point of view. Transport is the main issue here, as logistics management is primarily about solving the problem that products are rarely produced where they are consumed. The chapter starts by examining the role of different modes of transport and how transport planning issues can affect environmental impacts. Decisions on inventory also influence the choice of logistics strategy and so this is also dealt with, in particular related to total cost. Location decision making is a third element of logistics management, which is used to help resolve the positioning of producers and customers taking into account transport and inventory. Reverse logistics is also covered as this is an important part of sustainability in supply chains. As much of logistics today is managed by third party providers, the chapter discusses their role in reducing costs and impacts and the final case shows how DHL, one of the largest logistics businesses, has integrated sustainability into their business strategy. As sustainability initiatives in companies are often driven by consumer actions it is important to consider the final customer part of the supply chain. Chapter 11 also examines distribution strategies and how these impact on supply chain structures and processes. Distribution strategies tend to start with marketing channel choices and how to reach consumers. A significant recent development is that companies are heavily influenced by the opportunities of internet-based channels to customers, which in turn affects how products are delivered. This chapter assesses these different channel choices and how they influence the underlying logistics structures and processes. The chapter focuses particularly on the last delivery processes, which are often in urban areas with specific challenges related to sustainable distribution. RFID is discussed in the context of these challenges and particularly with the opportunities of improved traceability. The final case demonstrates how distribution collaboration can be used to minimize the costs and impacts this final delivery part of the supply chain.

Chapter 12 examines the relevance and nature of service supply chains. As competition for products become stronger companies increasingly look to creating competitive advantage on the basis of services. Chapter 12 explores the rise of service operations and business models that move away from product-centred thinking towards models, including procurement of complex performance, servitization, product-service systems, and through-life management. We explore how sustainability impacts on service supply chains, for example through re-manufacturing strategies.

1.6.3 Part C – Policy, tools, and implementation

Part C is more practical in nature than Parts A and B. Part C considers how companies can implement sustainable procurement and supply chain management: this requires a holistic understanding of procurement and supply systems and therefore adopts a higher level of system analysis to examine the role of not only new forms of supply chains but also the need to engage with a range of network actors and stakeholders.

Chapter 13 outlines different methods for mapping and evaluating supply chains, initially those that are not exclusively designed to analyze sustainability. These include methods to analyze processes, flows, systems, and knowledge within supply chains such as value stream mapping tools often used as part of lean supply chain management to identify sources of value and non-value (waste). Methods to analyze various aspects of sustainability are often closely related to lean supply chain mapping methods but adopt a long-term perspective (often a lifecycle). Furthermore, Chapter 13 gives an overview of sustainable supplier and supply chain monitoring processes and examines the role of digital third-party platform providers of supplier and supply chain monitoring services. Finally, we explore the carbon footprint concept and give insights into scope 1–3 measurement and lifecycle assessment (LCA) and discusses whether *lean* is *green*.

Chapter 14 moves on to examining issues concerning legislation, standards, and codes of conduct. The objective to implement sustainability has spurred governments and law makers to introduce a wide range of legislation that companies must comply with, and industry bodies and organizations have developed a myriad of standards, such as ISO14001, SA18000, and eco-labels, that provide guidelines or benchmarks for companies. In addition to guiding the reader through the jungle of standards, Chapter 13 explores the multi-stakeholder standards and guidelines on ethical supplier audits, linking to supplier assessment methods.

1.6.4 How to use this book

The structure of this book is designed so that the chapters can be read either conventionally in the order they appear, or the reader can opt to select topics of particular interest at random. Divided in three main parts, we begin with Part A – Procurement and Sourcing, Part B – Supply Chain and Network Management, and Part C – Policy, Tools, and Implementation. Throughout the book, we have sought to address what we perceive as the prime sustainability challenges facing procurement and supply chain management today, combining social and ethical, economic, and natural environment challenges. Each chapter begins by highlighting which key aspects the reader is expected to understand by the end. Notes are integrated into the text to give further insight into specific issues and give practical examples from industry. At the end of each chapter a longer case study is used to demonstrate core themes and concepts discussed in the book.

1.7 CONCLUSIONS

The first chapter of this book began by outlining the reasons why procurement is no longer simply an administrative, or clerical, responsibility, but a critical and strategic priority for companies. In particular, we emphasized the importance of the trend towards outsourcing: as companies have outsourced a high proportion of production and service activities, procurement plays a key role not only in cost reduction but also in value creation. In many companies the outsourcing ratio is around 70–80 per cent, in some cases even higher, so reducing purchase costs has a direct and significant impact on the bottom line. Furthermore, by helping to ensure that product materials, ingredients, or components, as well as services, are purchased at the right quality and the right time, procurement contributes significantly to the competitive advantage of the company. Ensuring that procurement makes such a contribution to the company requires an understanding of procurement as a strategic value-creating function and not simply a function whose sole aim is to save money.

The concept of purchasing is usually tied to the transactional buying process. In comparison, procurement is viewed as a more strategic and comprehensive concept than purchasing. In view of the changing use of the terms in practice and the generally accepted more comprehensive and strategic nature of the term procurement compared with purchasing, we therefore apply the term procurement in this third edition of the book.

This book is not only about procurement but also about supply chain management, which has a strong foundation in logistics, but is a more holistic concept that spans upstream management of supplier relationships and downstream management of distribution and customer relationships. In this book, where we want to discuss extra-dyadic supply issues, that is, those that concern indirect suppliers (second tier, third tier etc.) and seek to adopt an end customer perspective, we use the concept of *supply chain management*. In other words, our use of the concept of supply chain management implies the perspective of the final end customer and therefore is used to include a long chain of sub-tier suppliers, suppliers, a focal company, and distributors.

Sustainability is a concept with strong implications for procurement and supply chain management, in fact, sustainability is transforming the ways in which we think about and design and manage procurement processes and supply chains. Sustainability is multidimensional, categorizing actions into: the social (people), environmental (planet), and economic (profit); hence profit should no longer be at the expense of people and planet. The sustainability challenge is real: regardless of one's personal feelings towards climate change, the planet's resources are in decline, placing increasing pressures on companies to reduce carbon emissions, recycle or re-use, and to develop green technologies. Moreover, the current model of extensive reliance on global low cost country sourcing is unsustainable, as demonstrated by frequent media reports into, for example, supplier labour violations.

Sustainability presents a risk to companies but also an opportunity for those companies prepared to embrace the challenge. Companies cannot tackle sustainability by themselves: they need to design and manage new sustainable supply chains and networks. Pioneering companies have developed innovative sustainable supply chain models that not only reduce the risks of getting exposed in the media for bad, non-ethical, practice but play a key part in transforming the fortunes of the company. This view of sustainability implies that sustainability needs to become an integrated part of procurement and supply chain management rather than a separate add-on consideration or business function. That is why the title of this book is *Procurement and Supply Chain Management: A Sustainability Perspective* and not just 'Sustainable Procurement and Supply Chain Management'. We consider this as consistent with an ecologically dominant logic rather than sustainability being treated as an add-on or damage limitation.

The chapter also introduced the underlying theoretical perspective and structure of the book. The resource-based view (RBV) is fundamental, because the RBV and its derivative theories provide a foundation for very important, strategic, procurement and supply chain management decisions such as whether to make-or-buy. However, given the sustainability perspective, we rely on a Natural Resource-Based View (NRBV), which takes into account a focus on the natural environment, especially sustainable development, product stewardship, and pollution prevention. Creating a natural resource-based competitive advantage in turn requires close collaboration with a range of external stakeholders; this book therefore explores how companies can access resources through supplier, and supply chain, relationships and how resources can gain social legitimacy through stakeholder collaboration. Therefore, in addition to the NRBV, the complementary theories of institutional theory of DiMaggio and Powell (1991), stakeholder theory of Mitchell et al. (1997), and the Industrial Marketing & Purchasing (IMP) Interaction Approach (e.g. Håkansson, 1987) are important influences in this book. These theories influence the assumption in our approach to purchasing and supply chain management that it is increasingly necessary for companies to access important resources through external relationships with other companies and that supply chain partners can themselves be sources of competitive advantage. Indeed, as companies seek to incorporate sustainability into their purchasing and supply chain management strategies and practices, they need to work with and through a network of actors including Non-Governmental Organizations (NGOs), for example, in helping companies to monitor and implement sustainability in their supply chains. Where Part A of this book focuses on dyadic supplier relationships, Parts B and C shift the focus to supply chains and networks to examine the role of a wider group of stakeholders. Figures 1.4 and 1.5 illustrate the structure of the book in relation to the three levels of analysis.

REFERENCES

Baily P and Farmer D (1977) *Purchasing Principles and Techniques*. London: Pitman.

Bartley T (2007) Institutional emergence in an era of globalization: The rise of transnational private regulation of labor and environmental conditions. *American Journal of Sociology* 113(2): 297–351.

Beamon BM (1999) Designing the green supply chain. *Logistics Information Management* 12(4): 332–342.

Blomsma F and Brennan G (2017) The emergence of circular economy: A new framing around prolonging resource productivity. *Journal of Industrial Ecology* 21(3): 603–614.

Caldwell N and Howard M (eds) (2011) *Procuring Complex Performance: Studies of Innovation in Product-Service Management*. New York: Routledge.

Carter CR and Rogers DS (2008) A framework of sustainable supply chain management: Moving toward new theory. *International Journal of Physical Distribution and Logistics Management* 38(5): 360–387.

Christopher M (1998) *Logistics and Supply Chain Management. Strategies for Reducing Costs and Improving Services*. 2nd edn, London: FT Prentice Hall.

CIPS (2025) What is procurement? https://www.cips.org/intelligence-hub/procurement/what-is-procurement

Circle Economy (2025) Circularity Gap Report 2025: A global call to action. https://www.circularity-gap.world/2025

Cooper MC, Lambert DM and Pagh J (1997) Supply chain management: More than a new name for logistics. *The International Journal of Logistics Management* 8(1): 1–14.

Cousins PD, Lamming RC, Lawson B and Squire B (2008) *Strategic Supply Management: Theories, Concepts and Practice*. Harlow, UK: Pearson Education.

DiMaggio P and Powell WW (1991) *The New Institutionalism in Organizational Analysis*. Chicago: The University of Chicago Press.

Drumwright ME (1994) Socially responsible organizational buying: Environmental concern as a noneconomic buying criterion. *Journal of Marketing* 58(3): 1–19.

Elkington, J (1999) *Cannibals with Forks: The Triple Bottom Line of 21st Century Business*. Springer.

Ellram LM and Carr A (1994) Strategic purchasing: A history and review of the literature. *International Journal of Purchasing and Materials Management* (Spring): 130–138.

Ellen MacArthur Foundation [EMF] (2012) *Towards the Circular Economy Volume 1: An Economic and Business Rationale for an Accelerated Transition*. Cowes, UK: Ellen MacArthur Foundation.

EMF (2014) *Towards the Circular Economy Volume 3: Accelerating the Scale Up Across Global Supply Chains*. Cowes, UK: Ellen MacArthur Foundation.

England W (1970) *Modern Procurement Management: Principles and Cases*. 5th edn, Homewood, IL: Irwin.

Farrington B and Lysons K (2012) *Purchasing and Supply Chain Management*. 8th edn, Harlow, UK: Pearson Education Ltd.

Gadde L-E and Håkansson H (1993) *Professional Purchasing*. London: Routledge.

Håkansson H (ed) (1987) *Industrial Technological Development: A Network Approach*. London: Croom Helm.

Harland CM (1996) Supply chain management: Relationships, chains and networks. *British Journal of Management* 7 (special issue): 63–80.

Hart S (1995) A natural resource-based view of the firm. *Academy of Management Review* 20(4): 986–1014.

Johnsen TE, Lamming RC and Harland CM (2008) Inter-organizational relationships, chains and networks: A supply perspective. In: C Huxham, S Cropper, M Ebers et al. (eds) *The Oxford Handbook of Inter-Organizational Relations*. Oxford: Oxford University Press: 61–87.

Johnsen TE, Miemczyk J and Howard M (2017) A systematic literature review of sustainable purchasing and supply research: Theoretical perspectives and opportunities for IMP-based research. *Industrial Marketing Management* 61: 130–143.

Kraljic P (1983) Purchasing must become supply management. *Harvard Business Review* (Sept–Oct): 109–117.

Lambert D, Cooper M and Pagh J (1998) Supply chain management, implementation issues and research opportunities. *International Journal of Logistics Management* 9(2): 1–19.

Lamming RC, Johnsen TE, Zheng J and Harland C (2000) An initial classification of supply networks. *International Journal of Operations and Production Management* 20(6): 675–691.

Larson PD and Halldorsson A (2002) What is SCM. And where is it? *Journal of Supply Chain Management* 38(4): 36–44.

Lee L Jr and Dobler DW (1971) *Purchasing and Materials Management: Text and Cases.* 2nd edn, New York: McGraw-Hill.

Lysons K and Farrington B (2012) *Purchasing and Supply Chain Management.* 8th edn, Harlow, UK: Pearson.

Markman GD and Krause D (2016) Theory building surrounding sustainable supply chain management: Assessing what we know, exploring where to go. *Journal of Supply Chain Management,* 52(2): 3–10.

Matten D and Moon J (2008) "Implicit" and "explicit" CSR: A conceptual framework for a comparative understanding of corporate social responsibility. *Academy of Management Review* 33(2): 404–424.

Miemczyk J, Johnsen TE and Macquet M (2012) Sustainable purchasing and supply management: A structured literature review of definitions and measures at the dyad, chain and network levels. *Supply Chain Management: An International Journal* 17(5): 478–496.

Mitchell RK, Agle BR and Wood DJ (1997) Toward a theory of stakeholder identification and salience: Defining the principle of who and what really counts. *Academy of Management Review* 22(4): 853–887.

Möller K, Rajala A and Svahn S (2005) Strategic business nets — their type and management. *Journal of Business Research* 58(9): 1274–1284.

Montabon FL., Pagell M and Wu Z (2016) Making sustainability sustainable. *Journal of Supply Chain Management* 52(2): 1–34.

Pagell M and Shevchenko A (2014) Why research in sustainable supply chain management should have no future. *Journal of Supply Chain Management* 50(1): 44–55.

Porter ME (1985) *Competitive Advantage: Creating and Sustaining Superior Performance.* New York: Free Press.

Prahalad CK and Hamel G (1990) The core competencies of the corporation. *Harvard Business Review* (May–June): 71–91.

Ramsay J and Croom S (2008) The impact of evolutionary and developmental metaphors on supply chain practice: A literature critique and pilot study. *Journal of Purchasing and Supply Management* 14(3): 192–204.

Raworth K (2017) A doughnut for the Anthropocene: Humanity's compass in the 21st century. *The Lancet Planetary Health* 1(2): e48–e49.

Reck RF and Long BG (1988) Purchasing: A competitive weapon. *Journal of Purchasing and Materials Management* 24 (Fall): 2–8.

Ritter T and Gemünden HG (2003) Interorganizational relationships and networks: An overview. *Journal of Business Research* 56: 691–697.

Robinson PJ, Faris CW and Wind Y (1967) *Industrial Buying and Creative Marketing.* Boston, MA: Allyn and Bacon.

Roome N (2001) Conceptualizing and studying the contribution of networks in environmental management and sustainable development. *Business Strategy and the Environment* 10(2): 69–76.

Rozemeijer F (2008) Purchasing myopia revisited again? *Journal of Purchasing and Supply Management* 14(3): 205–207.

Sheth JN (1973) A model of industrial buying behaviour. *Journal of Marketing* 37: 50–56.

Spekman R (1981) A strategic approach to procurement planning. *Journal of Purchasing and Materials Management* (Winter): 3–9.

Steffen W, Richardson K, Rockström J, Cornell SE, Fetzer I, Bennett EM, … and Sörlin S (2015) Planetary boundaries: Guiding human development on a changing planet. *Science* 347(6223): 1259855.

Strassmann PA (2004) The economics of outsourcing. *Information Economics Journal* (June): 14–17.

Tate W, Ellram L and Bals L (2022) *A Handbook of Theories for Purchasing, Supply Chain and Management Research*. Edward Elgar. ISBN: 978 1 83910 449 7.

Teece DJ (1986) Profiting from technological innovation: Implications for integration, collaboration, licensing and public policy. *Research Policy* 15: 285–305.

Teece D, Pisano G and Shuen A (1997) Dynamic capabilities and strategic management. *Strategic Management Journal* 18(7): 509–533.

van Weele A (2010) *Purchasing and Supply Chain Management: Analysis, Strategy, Planning and Practice*. 5th edn, London: Thomson Learning.

Walker H and Brammer S (2009) Sustainable procurement in the United Kingdom public sector. *Supply Chain Management: An International Journal* 14(2): 128–137.

Webster FE and Wind Y (1972) A general model of organizational buying behaviour. *Journal of Marketing* 36 (April): 12–19.

World Economic Forum [WEF] (2014) Towards the circular economy: Accelerating the scale-up across global supply chains. WEF report: Ellen MacArthur Foundation and McKinsey & Co.

Wernerfeldt B (1984) A resource-based view of the firm. *Strategic Management Journal* 5: 171–180.

World Commission on Environment and Development (1987) *Our Common Future*. Oxford: Oxford University Press.

PART A

Procurement and sourcing

CHAPTER 2

The strategic procurement process

LEARNING OBJECTIVES:

At the end of this chapter you should be able to:

- Understand the procurement process as a circular process conceptualized as a wheel;
- Describe the main stages of the procurement process;
- Evaluate the differences between detailed and functional specifications and when to use these;
- Explain the management challenges of each stage of the procurement process, especially from a sustainability perspective;
- Examine the key processes required to develop a long-term high-performance supply base;
- Evaluate the different ways to implement supplier monitoring and development.

2.1 INTRODUCTION

This chapter is the first of five chapters that is dedicated to procurement and therefore mostly concerns dyadic buyer-supplier relationships (see Figure 2.1). In other words, Part A focuses on direct supplier relationships, especially how to organize the internal procurement organization and develop a procurement strategy in order to develop and manage these from a sustainability perspective.

Chapter 2 begins by introducing a framework that depicts the procurement process. This framework identifies the main stages of procurement when setting out to buy a procurement item or category, whether a product or a service. This overall procurement process is depicted as circular and divided into sourcing and supply processes.

In parallel with procurement processes, companies should engage in a continuous improvement loop of supplier monitoring, supplier development, and supplier relationship management; these enable companies to build up a long-term supply base.

DOI: 10.4324/9781003499602-3

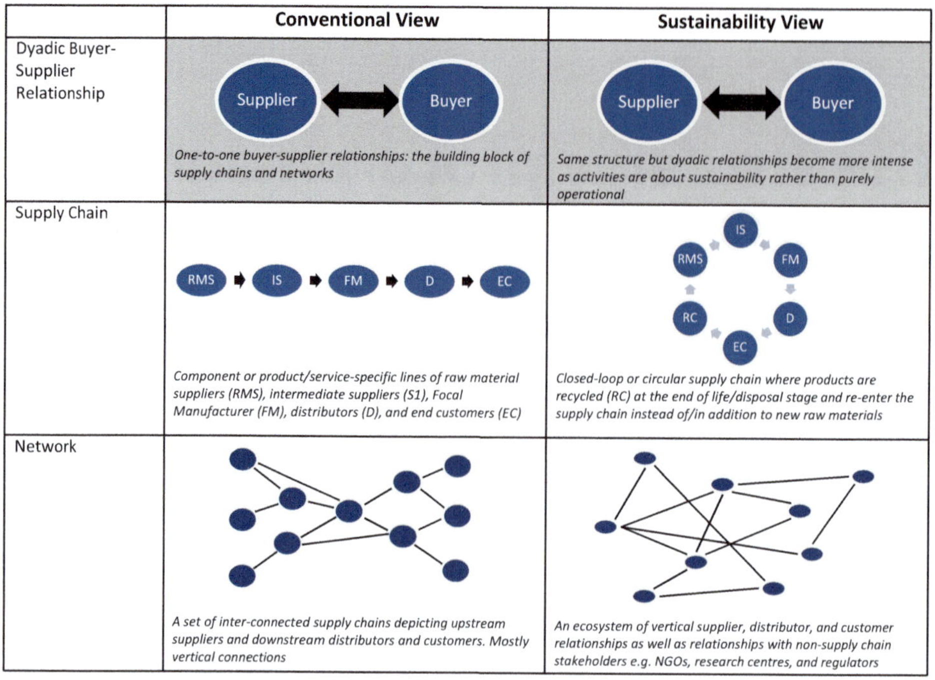

FIGURE 2.1 Level of analysis – Part A

2.2 THE PROCUREMENT PROCESS

As discussed in Chapter 1, there has been much debate and uncertainty over the difference between purchasing and procurement. However, there is now a general consensus that procurement is a wider and more comprehensive process in which purchasing forms a more restricted part. Put differently, the purchasing process is concerned with a specific purchase or transaction where the procurement process takes a longer perspective. Based on the widely applied purchasing process model by van Weele (2010), Figure 2.2 shows six distinct stages in the purchasing process.

The purchasing process is traditionally depicted as a linear process beginning with a specification of the purchase need and ending with an evaluation of the purchase to check that the delivered product or service conforms with the specification and therefore satisfies the expectations. The front end of the purchasing process can be understood as the sourcing process whereas the back end of the process concerns the supply process.

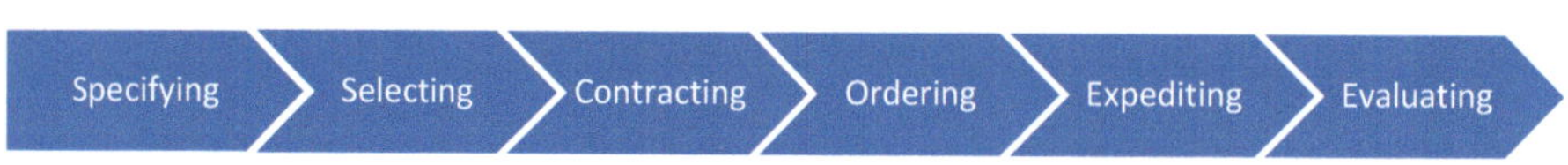

FIGURE 2.2 A linear presentation of the purchasing process

Figure 2.3 illustrates the procurement process as a cycle because it refers to the continuous process that goes beyond any one discrete or individual purchase. This process is more strategic in nature as it forms the basis for the long-term development of a stable and high-performing supply base. The procurement process wheel in this book is inspired by several influential purchasing/procurement/sourcing process models, including the CIPS 'Procurement & Supply Cycle' (2025), van Raaij's 'PSM Process Wheel' (2016), and the '7-step strategic sourcing process' developed by AT Kearney (since 2020 simply known as 'Kearney'). The review of process models by Bäckstrand et al. (2019) was instrumental in gaining an overview of key models produced to date.

The procurement process wheel is divided into stages relating to sourcing and supply processes, and includes at its centre the three processes of supplier monitoring, supplier development, and supplier relationship management. The assumption of the model is that individual purchases do not require starting from scratch but can be initiated on the basis that an existing base of long-term approved and preferred suppliers are available as a safe choice. The company will use these suppliers wherever possible to reduce the (transaction) cost and risk involved in starting all over with new unknown suppliers.

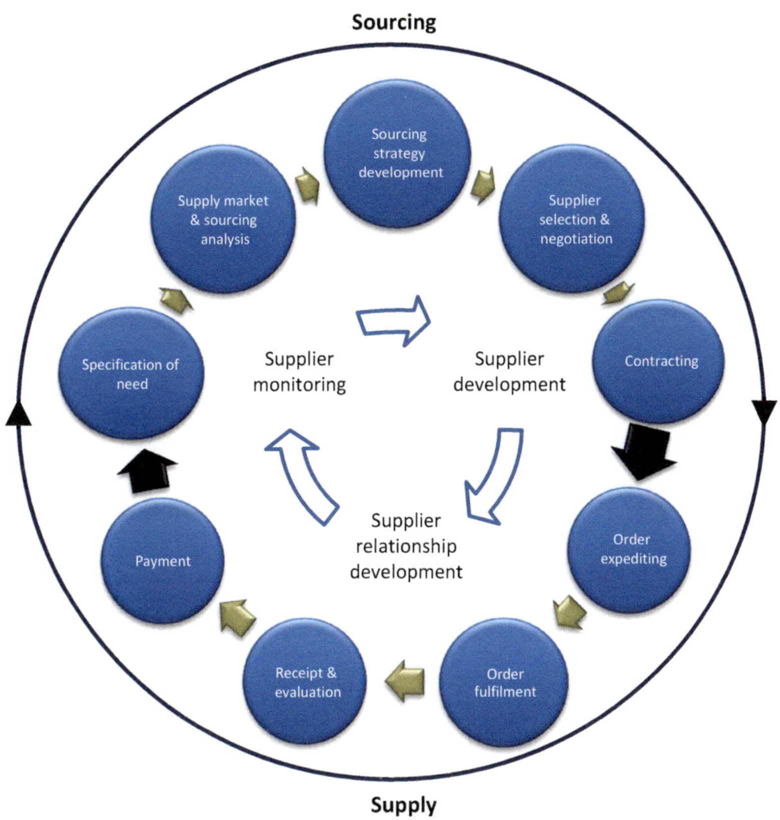

FIGURE 2.3 The procurement process wheel

Procurement staff play a central role in the procurement process, but it is important to note that other functions may also be heavily involved at the different stages. For example, when companies are facing a procurement situation involving a technical product the process is likely to be highly cross-functional. Often, specific stages within the procurement process can in fact be led by functions other than procurement. For example, the engineering, research and development (R&D), or design department often take the lead in the early parts of the process when a company sets out to buy technologically complex components or materials. However, ideally the procurement department should be involved at all stages.

In the following sub-sections we explain each stage in the procurement process in turn, identifying the role of procurement as well as the likely involvement of other functions in the company. In section 2.5 we then take a closer look at the three long-term processes at the heart of the procurement cycle.

2.2.1 Specification of need

The specification 'specifies' the purchase needs and captures these in a document that will serve as a reference point during and at the end of the process. If, at the end of the process, the supplier delivers something that does not satisfy the specification, it indicates a failure, as the company's needs have not been met. Specifications are required to:

- Communicate to the procurement department what to buy;
- Communicate requirements to suppliers;
- Establish tangible goods to be provided;
- Establish intangible services to be provided;
- Establish standards against which inspections, tests, and quality checks are made;
- Balance specification goals of different functions.

Some companies differentiate between specifications and supplier requirements, so that the specifications focus on the purchase item and requirements focus on wider requirements. In any case, as specifications reflect the needs of the company, they should reflect the needs of both the internal customers and, ultimately, the external (end) customers. It is important to match or align the priorities detailed in the specifications with customer needs and requirements. For example, if customers prioritize high quality and innovation, the specification document should reflect those requirements instead of making automatic assumptions about, for example, low cost requirements.

Generally, in order to avoid misunderstanding, it is good practice to provide detailed specifications to suppliers. Especially when dealing with foreign suppliers, there is always a risk of misunderstanding due to language problems or cultural difficulties. When sourcing from other countries, there is a real risk that suppliers do not fully understand specifications and buyers themselves may be unaware of such potential discrepancies in the interpretations of specifications. The use of standard specifications, drawings, and commonly understood and objective terminology helps to reduce the risk of misunderstanding.

Writing a highly detailed specification may leave no scope for misunderstanding, but it may also drastically reduce the number of suppliers capable of meeting the specification; there is a risk that overly-detailed specifications reduce competition. Purchasers

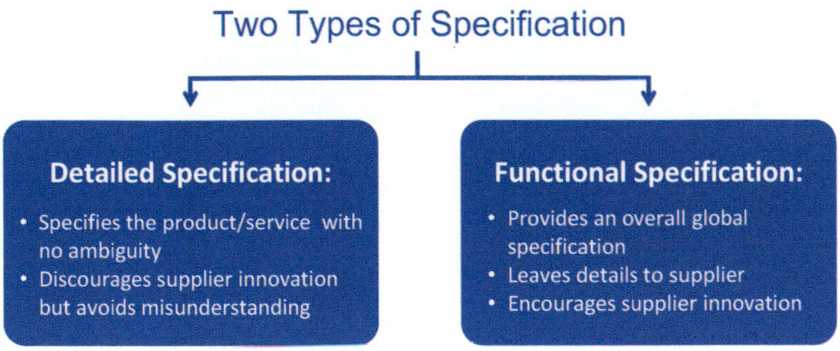

FIGURE 2.4 Detailed and functional specifications

sometimes write specifications with a specific supplier or brand in mind but need to strike a balance between specifying exactly what they require and leaving room for competition between suppliers: on the one hand do not under-specify but on the other hand do not over-specify.

In some situations, it can be difficult for a company to write detailed specifications because the company is not an expert in what it needs. For example, a company may need a technologically complex component: the company knows what function the component needs to fulfil within its product or system, but without being an expert in this component it can be impossible to specify all the technical details. Therefore, it makes sense to employ two different specification strategies, as shown in Figure 2.4.

Detailed (or technical) specifications leave no ambiguity as to what the company requires from the supplier. All areas of uncertainty are explained in clear language and such detail that there is no scope for misunderstanding. In contrast, functional (or global) specifications provide an overall explanation in functional terms, that is, they explain what function the purchase needs to fulfil but not exactly how the supplier should go about achieving the best possible solution. Functional specifications are similar to 'black-box' specifications: the overall outlines are explained but the content is left for the supplier to decide how best to achieve it (Karlsson et al., 1998). The functional specification strategy works on the assumption that the supplier has superior knowledge of its component and that therefore the supplier is best placed to decide what is the best way to meet the customer's requirements. Whereas fully detailed technical specifications leave nothing to chance but therefore also discourage supplier initiative and innovation, functional specifications encourage the supplier to innovate in their pursuit of the best solution.

The specification traditionally details the procurement requirements in terms of technical (e.g. quality) requirements, supply chain (logistics/delivery) requirements, commercial (financial/cost) requirements, and service/maintenance requirements. However, this traditional approach does not take sustainability criteria into account and many companies still do not fully incorporate sustainability criteria into the traditional criteria, instead treating sustainability as a separate process. As argued in this book, the integration of traditional criteria with sustainability criteria is a critical challenge for procurement professionals. Table 2.1 provides an overview of a set of overall criteria and examples of sub-criteria.

Some requirements are objective and relatively easy to specify, but others can be much more difficult to pin down. In general, services are more complex to specify than products,

TABLE 2.1 Criteria and sub-criteria for specification and supplier selection

Overall Criteria	*Examples of Specific Criteria*
Technical requirements	• Technical • Quality: e.g. defect rates, TQM system, 6 sigma
Commercial requirements	• Cost • Payment terms • Liabilities • IPR • Warranty
Supply chain requirements	• Delivery terms • Lead times • Flexibility • IT systems: ERP • Supplier integration capabilities
Service requirements	• Customer service and support • Technical service • Maintenance and repairs
R&D & innovation requirements	• R&D size and budget • Patents • Staff qualifications: no. of qualified engineers, PhDs etc
Sustainability requirements	• Basic qualifying standards: e.g. ISO 14001, SA8000 • Industry specific codes of conduct
Sustainability requirements: environmental	• Environmental requirements • Commitment to environmental protection • Compliance with local laws • Control of emissions/pollution • Protection of biodiversity • Application of life-cycle approach: e.g. use of ISO 14040–14043
Sustainability requirements: employment/social	• Fundamental principles and rights at work: e.g. compliance with International Bill of Human Rights • No child or slave labour • Health and safety at work • Equal opportunities/no discrimination or harassment • Minimum wage • Non-excessive working hours • Employees have written contract • Civil and political rights • Conditions of work and social protection • Human development and training in the workplace
Sustainability requirements: value/collaboration	• Willingness to disclose policies, decisions, and activities: e.g. cooperation with audits/assessment • Behaviour based on honesty, ethics, and integrity: e.g. anti-corruption • Promoting social responsibility in the supply chain • Respect for property rights • Values/standards compatible with those of customer • Accountability

as they are usually highly intangible (see Chapter 12). In any case, in order to avoid ambiguity and ensure that criteria are measurable and thereby comparable, requirements should be considered at an overall level and then be divided into sub-criteria as shown in Table 2.1.

Although procurement should play an important role in developing and communicating specifications as part of the procurement process, other organizational functions often, in reality, take charge of the process. For example, design or engineering departments in manufacturing companies tend to manage specification of parts and materials, whereas procurement often takes the lead for non-complex and indirect purchases (non-components). In many companies, it is critical that procurement and engineering collaborate on specifications; although engineering has the technical knowledge (which purchasers often lack) they may not consider cost or sourcing issues. As Note 2.1 shows, the introduction of 'procurement engineers' was a key factor in the turnaround of American motorcycle company Harley-Davidson.

Note 2.1 Purchasing and engineering collaboration at Harley Davidson

The creation of the *purchasing engineer* role as at Harley Davidson was a forerunner of what since became best practice for ensuring purchasing input into specifications. In the early 1990s Harley Davidson's engineering division was in charge of design and testing activities, and there was little cross-functional collaboration with production and purchasing. Engineers dealt directly with suppliers and relationships with suppliers were poor. Earl Werner, vice-president of engineering, recalled, for example, that if he wanted to develop a new fuel injection system for a motorcycle, the engineering department would have to survey the supply base, identify a supplier who could best make the parts, and then confirm that the supplier had the needed technical capabilities to support the design. "We picked suppliers whose forte was technical innovation", said Werner. "They were low volume and didn't have a high degree of competency on the commercial side. Or they couldn't meet the scheduled requirements for manufacturing". Supplier components arrived late, jeopardizing production.

Traditionally, purchasing had become involved in design and development once engineers had finished their designs. Therefore, there was little room for purchasing to influence supplier selection. Dividing the purchasing division into two functions – operational purchasing and development purchasing – the company enabled part of the purchasing function to focus on the long-term development of the supply base and the integration of suppliers into the product design and development process.

The term 'purchasing engineers' was developed for employees who would work side by side with engineering. "Having engineers in purchasing is critical because they are responsible for translating the technical requirements into a voice for the supplier", said Werner. Jayson Way, a purchasing engineer, says Harley-Davidson learned that when purchasing is not involved in the design process, the company tends to pinpoint parts that can be provided by just one source. By getting purchasing – and thereby multiple suppliers – involved in the design process fosters early competition.

Source: Milligan and Carbone (2000)

Collaboration between engineering and purchasing can also involve value engineering or 'tear-down analysis'. This form of analysis is often carried out for existing products with a view to reducing cost and eliminating bottlenecks caused by the use of highly specialized and difficult-to-source materials. Ideally, this should be considered before products go into production i.e. during the specification stage. Value engineering typically raises questions such as:

- Are there alternative lower cost ways to satisfy need, e.g. copper may substitute silver for use in electrical conductors, or synthetic material may substitute natural textiles/leathers?
- Is it made on correct tooling considering volumes?
- Are limits and tolerances too tight?
- Can we use standard off-the-shelf parts, shared across our product lines?

Many companies deliberately seek to standardize their purchases, especially components, in order to generate economies of scale and thereby achieve purchasing efficiencies. For example, Swedish company IKEA makes extensive use of the same types of screws, bolts, and locks, which are used when customers assemble the IKEA furniture. This not only makes customers familiar with the IKEA assembly process but also helps IKEA procurement achieve economies of scale that are critical to its low cost strategy. It is therefore good practice to use standard – and standardize – specifications wherever possible to reduce cost and improve quality.

2.2.2 Supply market and sourcing analysis

Based on the specification the next step in the procurement process is the analysis of the supply market and the sourcing situation. As an intermediate step, further analysis of the need is often done to categorize the specified product or service. Category management is important here to segment purchases into homogenous groups i.e. those that share characteristics in terms of, for example, similarity in materials, processes, or suppliers. This stage may also involve spend analysis to give further insights into spending patterns and potential areas where savings or other improvement can be achieved.

Supply market research typically involves scouting and scanning for potential suppliers on a global basis. Much of this search can be conducted through internet sources and processes. Trade journals, periodicals, and industry reports provide useful sources. AI can now also be used as a tool, which has the particular advantage that it can widen up global supply markets and help to foster competition. Companies are increasingly applying AI to aid supplier scouting either themselves or by going through service providers. For example, *Scoutbee* offers a search engine to perform wide ranging searches across multiple languages and geographies and get access to suppliers' data including certifications and sustainability scores. Although as Guida et al. (2023) point out, many service providers perform the selection of the best supplier from a list of potential partners already known rather than scouting new suppliers.

The focus should not only be on static analysis of the current situation but also on future trends. What are the technological innovations in the marketplace and are there likely to be significant shifts in the future that might render existing technologies obsolete? Reasons for obsolescence may include phasing out materials due to environmental concerns. It is important to analyze the market dynamics to understand the risks and opportunities that follow from choosing one material over another.

Sourcing teams often carry out supply market analysis using well-known analysis models such as PESTEL (political, economic, social, technological, environmental, and legal factors) that provide insights into opportunities or threats or use Porter's (1980) classic Five Forces model to understand industry dynamics. This can be a critical first step to understand the power dynamics and is often supplemented with models that give insights into the power balance at the category level such as Kraljic (1983) matrix analysis (see also Chapter 4).

2.2.3 Sourcing strategy development

Sourcing strategy is about how you can best source any given purchase item minimizing the cost and risk exposure. This includes the decision concerning the number of suppliers the company prefers for the supply of the item. This is a question of structural sourcing strategy i.e. whether the company is willing to source from a single supplier or preserve the security of having a second source as a backup, or potentially multiple suppliers that it can source from at any given point. In short this is a question between favouring collaboration with one supplier or increasing competition, and thereby spreading risk, by keeping two or more suppliers.

Sourcing strategy should also consider whether the company wants to buy the purchase item from an external supplier or is willing to in-source for increased control. This is the make-or-buy decision, which we discuss further in the chapter on outsourcing. It is a strategically important decision influenced by the perceived risks of having to source from a powerful supplier that puts the company in a position of dependency and therefore risk. The chosen sourcing strategy will depend on the supply market analysis, and not least Kraljic (1983) analysis, as strategic purchase items usually result in a single or dual sourcing strategy where non-critical items often involved keeping multiple suppliers. Please refer to Chapter 4 for further details of sourcing strategy.

2.2.4 Supplier selection and negotiation

Once the supply market research has been carried out and the sourcing strategy decided, the next step in the sourcing process is the supplier selection and negotiation. In principle, the aim is initially to identify a large number of suppliers and then gradually narrow down the field until the selected supplier (or suppliers) remains. For this purpose, it is necessary to write some important documentation to begin what is known as the tender process: initially a request for information (RFI) and subsequently a request for quotation (RFQ) (also known as request for proposal).

Tender documents are issued to suppliers that are invited submit a bid (RFQ or RFP) and constitute the core elements for initiating the tender process. These documents further detail the specifications, breaking down not only pricing, quality, and operational functionality but also the volumes, service level agreements, and terms and conditions.

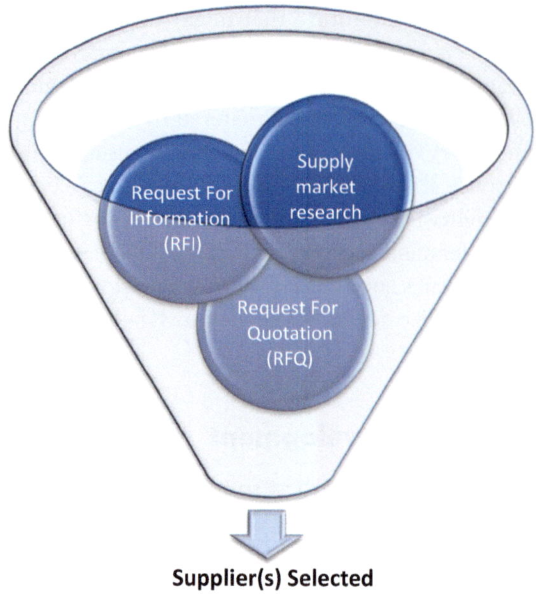

FIGURE 2.5 The supplier selection process: narrowing down the number of suppliers

As with the development of specifications, cross-functional input into the development of tender documents is advisable. At this point, due diligence should be carried out to validate any potential supplier's sustainability compliance. Figure 2.5 illustrates the basic principle of narrowing down during the supplier selection process.

As explained at the beginning of this chapter and shown in Figure 2.5 companies often have an approved list of suppliers that they have purchased from in the past. As the company has previous experience of approved suppliers, trust and confidence have been built up with these suppliers as a result of past performance. Approved suppliers therefore represent lower risk for the company compared with soliciting completely new, unknown suppliers.

Supply market research should result in a 'bidders' long list': a list of potential suppliers that seem to satisfy the basic requirements, but who require further investigation. An RFI is typically produced before an RFQ (or RFP) in order to gather information about the capabilities of potential suppliers. Suppliers may be contacted and visited as part of the RFI and it is often suppliers on the company's approved supplier list that are the main suppliers to be approached for the RFI. This stage should result in elimination of some of the suppliers on the bidders' long list and therefore lead to the bidders' short list. The remaining suppliers on the short list are then issued with the RFQ, which contains more specific information than the RFI. The RFQ serves as the invitation to bid and typically includes details of price and, ideally, the full specifications of the product or service to be purchased. The RFQ could be used later as a legally binding document so it is important that the RFQ captures all the expectations of the purchaser in clear and unambiguous language. An RFQ should also specify a date and time by which suppliers must submit their quote. If an RFQ is issued by a company, suppliers will most likely assume that several suppliers have been invited to bid for the contract so RFQs can be useful in promoting competition amongst suppliers. Full transparency of selection criteria can also be provided as part of the RFQ so that bidding suppliers know the basis on which bids will be evaluated and the contract will be awarded. Indeed, as companies seek to develop more open collaborative supplier relationships, it makes sense for bidding suppliers to have at least some visibility of selection criteria, although it may be appropriate not to divulge too much detail so as to retain negotiation power and discretion in the selection process.

Upon receipt of bids, the procurement department should play a key role in evaluating the bids and in devising a process for the evaluation. For strategic purchases, such as high value and complex technological component systems, it is best practice to form a cross-functional team, including for example procurement, logistics, production, engineering, or quality assurance. Different functions have different priorities so it is important to ensure that these different priorities are reflected in the evaluation and selection process. Many companies have ranking systems where the selection criteria are ranked or given different weightings, and it makes sense to allow each cross-functional team member to score each supplier. When all suppliers have been evaluated the supplier with the most competitive offer will be informed that they have proceeded to the next stage where a contract is ready to be drawn up. Depending on the sourcing strategy more than one supplier can be chosen: it is only for single sourcing that a single supplier will be chosen, whereas in other situations two or more suppliers may be chosen. It is also good practice to inform unsuccessful suppliers that they have not been selected, explaining why their bid was not chosen, as it is likely that the company will want to solicit offers from those suppliers in future.

Negotiation is critically important in order to secure the favourable terms to be formalized in the contract. These concern principally the costs not only from an acquisition but also from a lifecycle and total cost of ownership (TCO) perspective. However, other performance parameters are also critical (quality, delivery, service levels etc.). It is important to aim for a mutual agreement with suppliers to pre-empt any misunderstanding or potential sources of conflict.

The negotiation process is often divided into several stages from preparing (formulating the objectives etc.), over the 'face-to-face' interaction, to finally agreeing and closing the process. The negotiation strategy depends largely on the situation but individual negotiators tend to have their own style i.e. some are naturally deal-minded where others are more implementation-minded, aiming to create a mutual collaborative relationship. The concepts of win-lose or win-win are used to signify a distributive ('zero sum') or an integrative (or 'positive sum') bargaining strategy (Fisher et al., 2011). The win-lose strategy only aims to secure a positive outcome for yourself with the other party losing, whereas the win-win strategy aims for a mutual outcome with both parties winning. Chapter 4 delves into the different types of relationship strategies and the relationship characteristics, such as power and trust, that also impact negotiations.

2.2.5 Contracting

Contracts are essential in order to avoid the risk of non-compliance yet the extent to which extensive formal contracts are required depends on the circumstances. For example, in the public sector the procurement process is governed by a large number of regulations, as will be discussed later, so contracts naturally play an important role in formalizing expectations, and terms and conditions. As explained earlier, some purchasing situations are characterized by a high degree of uncertainty so it is critical to write and negotiate a contract that sets out all the customer's expectations. Consider for example a situation where a European company wants to buy something from a new unknown Asian supplier: due to cultural and language differences there are likely to be different perceptions of the meaning of quality and time, and understandings of property rights (who owns the legal rights to designs, technologies etc.) may also differ; establishing expectations in a formal contract is therefore critical at this stage.

Terms and conditions are at the heart of contracts, which concern, for example, terms of payment and delivery. Although payment should perhaps ideally be upon receipt of goods or services, companies are very sensitive to payment terms as they have to manage their cash-flows and cost of capital. Therefore, most companies want to have the longest possible payment terms without impacting severely on purchase price.

In some cases payments can be made in several instalments. In construction projects for example, the supplier will have to make significant investments a long time before completion of the project and will therefore often insist on payment up front or during the project. It is good practice in such situations to offer partial payment for partially completed work and to withhold the final payment until project completion when the quality of the work has been evaluated (van Weele, 2010).

Procurement should insist that the supplier guarantee the quality and delivery of the work as specified. But how can the purchaser be sure that the supplier will respect the contract and what can they do about it if the supplier delivers something that does not meet the performance requirements? In order to pre-empt this situation contracts should include penalty clauses, such as, say, 10 per cent reduction in the price if the performance requirements are below the expected standard. However, penalty clauses are not always sufficient as it may sometimes be necessary to refuse the work provided by the supplier, if for instance there are serious flaws or it is delivered so late that it is no longer of value to the company. It may also be necessary to specify liabilities for non-conformance, for example, requiring suppliers to compensate direct damages. Therefore, the buyer must incorporate clauses that allow them to reject the supplier's work.

Designing contracts, and agreeing contracts with suppliers, is further complicated by the legal environment. Suppliers will typically have their own terms and conditions and may insist that these apply. It is a critical part of the negotiation process to ensure that the parties agree on whose terms and conditions apply and agree terms and conditions acceptable to both parties. Contracts are also subject to the legal requirements of the country in which the work is delivered and typically the legal rules of the supplier apply, although not always. Again, this will have to be agreed between the parties. International trade terms, such as Incoterms can sometimes be used as a compromise.[1] The example of train buying in Denmark in Note 2.2 below shows the complexities of contracting and the need to ensure that clauses for poor quality and late delivery are fully incorporated into contracts.

Note 2.2 Buying trains: experiences from Denmark

The Danish government landed itself in much trouble when buying trains from an Italian manufacturer. The Danish national train operator, DSB, decided to buy the IC4 trains from AnsaldoBreda following a lengthy procurement process. The trains were supposed to be state-of-the-art inter-city trains and were intended to replace outdated trains. However, long delays and partial deliveries turned the project into a major political issue. The trains were originally scheduled to enter service in 2003 but it was not until June 2007 that the first train entered service. In May 2008, DSB gave Ansaldo Breda an ultimatum: at least 14 trains had to be approved and ready for regular service before May 2009, or the contract would be cancelled and DSB would demand its money back. AnsaldoBreda subsequently agreed to pay DSB a compensation of 2 billion DKr (app. €270 million). Together with previously paid compensation fees this would mean refunding half the original contract value. DSB retained the right to cancel the contract if more than seven trains were delivered more than six months late.

In November 2010, after a seven year delay, DSB finally completed certification of multiple connected IC4 train sets. They were scheduled to enter service in January 2011 but in April 2011, DSB's director stated that further economic sanctions against AnsaldoBreda were likely to be imposed as a result of continuing problems in the quality of the trains delivered. Consequently, the trains had to be upgraded to Danish standards at DSB's own cost. 18 IC4 trains have now been approved for use but some are still not in daily service. In November 2011 two IC4 trains failed to stop at stop signals. This caused the authorities to ban the IC4 from running until the problems had been investigated. The controversy continues.

Contract design is sometimes regarded as so important that it constitutes a *firm capability* (Argyres and Mayer, 2007). Mouzas and Ford (2012: 154) suggest that complex buyer-supplier interactions, information asymmetries, and unforeseen contingencies increasingly lead companies to seek to explicitly state and manifest as joint consent the conditions of business relationships. This implies that contracts are manifestations of agreements that specify how a supplier's resources are acquired, used, or transformed. Naturally, the challenges highlighted by Mouzas and Ford (2012) also make contracting very complex, discouraging some companies from developing detailed contracts, instead preferring so-called 'framework agreements' or 'umbrella contracts' (Mouzas and Furmston, 2008). These are less detailed agreements that place reduced emphasis on what to do if the supplier does not comply with the contract, and more emphasis on the fundamental rules and principles of the relationship, particularly the use of knowledge to create joint gains. Framework agreements are mostly relevant to knowledge-intensive relationships where there is a need for a shared mindset between the parties but can also be used more widely. Clauses in such agreements might include the categories exemplified below:

- Exclusivity: both parties have the right to obtain competitive offers;
- Information: both parties will inform one another if unforeseen circumstances arise;

- Notification: product damages must be communicated with two weeks;
- Subcontracting: must be approved;
- Assignment: must be approved;
- Volume/price: to be agreed;
- Invoicing: monthly basis;
- Re-negotiation: annual;
- Force majeure: parties bear no responsibilities due to war or strikes;
- Guarantee: right to refuse due to poor quality;
- Liability: supplier is also liable for materials supplied by its suppliers;
- Secrecy: all information is confidential;
- Property rights: no transfer of property rights;
- Legal venue: France;
- Amendments: supplier has the right to revoke any orders in writing;
- Business and product continuity;
- Duration: annual;
- Termination: each party has the right to terminate the agreement with two weeks' notice.[2]

Performance-based contracts (PBCs) have become increasingly popular. These are a form of incomplete contract, meaning that they are less prescriptive and allow more freedom and flexibility regarding specific details of the transaction relevant to the contract (Luo, 2002). As a result, PBCs allow suppliers a certain degree of autonomy which can in turn foster innovation (Kim et al., 2007; Ng and Nudurupati, 2010). PBCs are seen as being incomplete since they underline the *outcome* of the transaction rather than prescribing *how* (processes) to deliver it or which resources (inputs) to use. If performance is above-the-baseline it is possible to reward the supplier for the extra performance. Such examples have been reported in the healthcare sector, e.g. for quality of care and treatment outcome (Lindkvist, 1996; Lu et al., 2003), but research into (and therefore knowledge of) such arrangements is scarce.

Service-level agreements (SLAs) are widely used as ways of contracting when buying services. Compared with PBCs, SLAs place much more emphasis on specifying inputs and processes and not just outputs or outcomes. This is because of the difficulty of evaluating the quality of a service which is, by definition, characterized by being intangible. Note 2.3 provides an overview of this problem and the meaning of SLAs and the service issue is discussed in more detail in Chapter 12.

Note 2.3 The service specification and evaluation problem and Service Level Agreements (SLAs)

Services are usually regarded as different from products especially because they are intangible. This creates a number of procurement challenges.

Consider cleaning services: there is no physical product, only an invisible service being delivered. When specifying a physical product (part, component, or material), purchasers can describe in detail what they require in terms of size, weight, technical performance, and so on. The contract with the supplier will reflect these requirements so that when the product is delivered it is evaluated against hard physical evidence; it is possible to evaluate the quality of the product by touching it, visually analyzing it, and taking it apart if necessary. When buying cleaning services, the same logic does not apply, and the evaluation of the quality of the service is likely to be highly subjective, depending on the evaluator's personal expectations and standards.

When buying services, therefore, it is useful to specify, contract, and evaluate in terms of inputs, processes, and outputs. So, continuing with the cleaning services examples:

- Inputs would include the resources to be used, for example, the people carrying out the service and the materials they should use;
- The process might include vacuuming, washing surfaces, polishing windows, dusting etc.;
- The output would include the expected level of cleanliness and could be tested e.g. visually.

Service Level Agreements (SLAs) are often developed around this logic. Typically, they include:

- A basic contract: goal, date, period, parties;
- A service definition;
- Specifications:
  - Coverage and levels of service (no of working days, peak workloads, availability etc.)
  - Actual service: inputs and outputs;
- Manpower and other resources available;
- Reaction times;
- Precision;
- Availability e.g. for problem solving.

In recent years the fundamental difference between products and services have been questioned as there are increasingly examples of offerings that include both rather than one or the other. We discuss this issue in more depth in Chapter 8.

Source: Axelsson and Wynstra (2002)

We might also question whether PBCs are compatible with the need to incorporate sustainability requirements into contracts. In procurement theory this is still a new challenge, but there is little doubt that companies need to find out how they can best include the various dimensions of sustainability in contracts as part of the procurement process. Indeed, specifying resources and how processes should be carried out is important in order to avoid, for example, suppliers using non-sustainable natural resources, polluting production processes, or exploiting labour.

Incorporating sustainability into procurement contracts is complex. Companies will increasingly need to be aware of global regulations such as United Nations (UN) conventions, Organisation for Economic Cooperation and Development (OECD) guidelines, international labour standards as set by the International Labour Organization (ILO), the UN Global Compact, not least its universal declaration on human rights. We expand on issues of legislation, standards, and codes of conduct in Chapter 12.

Finally, it is worth mentioning that various AI solution providers have emerged that aid procurement professionals in contract preparation. For example, *Icertis* provides firms with AI-powered suggestions and insights to optimize contract negotiation, potentially reducing the time spent to manually create long contracts. However, one study indicates that many procurement managers are still sceptical that such a complex task can be transferred to an AI system, believing that human skills are still essential (Guida et al., 2023).

2.2.6 Procurement supply stages: from order expediting to payment

Once a contract is arranged the ordering can take place. In some situations, such as a new-buy situation, the contract itself may constitute the order. In other situations, the contract provides the framework for frequent routine purchases, for example in a high-volume manufacturing operation.

Ordering increasingly takes place through electronic systems that help to automate the process and reduce transaction costs. Materials (or enterprise) resource planning systems (MRP, ERP) can automatically raise orders when the system detects a need. Whether or not the order is raised through an MRP or ERP system, the information should leave no room for ambiguity and should include, typically, an order number, a brief description of the product/service, unit price, number of units required/volume, and expected delivery time and address. Suppliers typically send an order confirmation to confirm the purchase order and its content and this can be automatically directed to the ERP.

Theoretically the system should work smoothly but in practice it is often necessary for the buyer to check that the supplier has understood and delivered the order correctly. A buyer should also make sure that the supplier has not received conflicting instructions from other departments, as for example the instructions to a supplier from the company's procurement department may differ from the instructions issued by the logistics or incoming goods department.

The role of expediting is to secure the quality and timely delivery of goods and components. In a manufacturing context, this involves monitoring the progress of manufacturing at the supplier in terms of quality, packaging, and conformity with standards and lead times. Thus the goal is to ensure that the required goods arrive at the appointed date in the agreed quality at the agreed location.

External or third-party expediters can help to keep track of the process. They can assume responsibility for inspection and notify the involved parties about progress and if any problems are detected. Expediting exists in several levels, e.g.:

- Production control: the expediter inspects to see if the production complies with the required standards;

- Quality control/assurance: the expeditor checks to see if the goods (or components or materials) function as required and if they meet the required standards;
- Packaging/transport: the expeditor checks that the goods are properly packaged and transported to avoid damage during delivery.

2.3 DEVELOPING A LONG-TERM HIGH-PERFORMANCE SUPPLY BASE

As explained at the outset of this chapter, the procurement process wheel illustrates not only those processes involved in a specific procurement project but also a set of long-term processes that aim to build up and maintain a high performing supply base. Typically, companies rely on a fundamental classification or hierarchy of suppliers in which those at the top are viewed as the preferred long-term supply partners. Figure 2.6 illustrates a typical supplier hierarchy as used by many companies, distinguishing between the many potential new suppliers, a relatively smaller number of approved suppliers, and the relatively fewer preferred suppliers that the company has ascertained long-term through rigorous ongoing evaluation and development present little risk: different colours (red, yellow, green) symbolize different perceived risk levels.

Companies invest in their approved suppliers, treating them as long-term relationships and, where appropriate, as partnerships. Companies realize that the process of selecting and evaluating new unknown suppliers is so costly and risky that they prefer to rely on suppliers, whose capabilities have been proven and monitored over a period of time, and whom they therefore trust to fulfil their commitments and promises. In the following we examine the three processes that form the heart of the process of long-term high-performance supply base development: supplier monitoring, supplier development, and supplier relationship management. In the following we delve into the first two of these, leaving the topic of supplier relationship management to Chapter 4.

2.3.1 Supplier monitoring: assessing supplier performance

A core part of the process of investing in relationships with approved and preferred suppliers is ongoing monitoring of suppliers. Supplier assessment is a well-established 'best

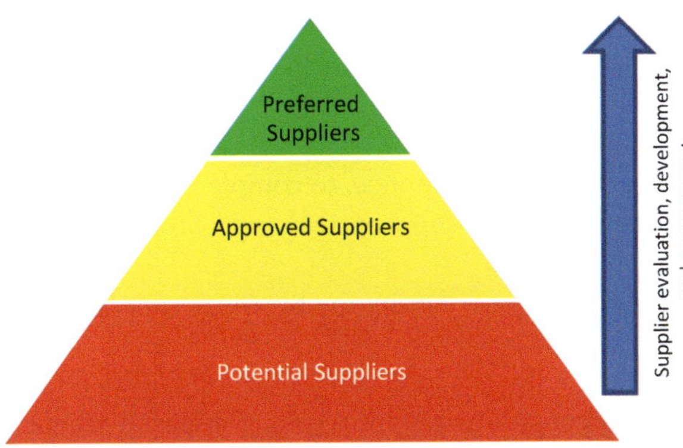

FIGURE 2.6 A supplier hierarchy

practice' and traditionally used to evaluate a supplier's operational performance, especially cost, quality, and delivery performance. Best practice includes designing supplier (or vendor) rating systems and scoring supplier performance. Few companies these days do without structured supplier assessment schemes, even small and medium-sized enterprises (SMEs) have them: one survey of UK SMEs from over 15 years ago (Pressey et al., 2009) showed that almost 50 per cent relied on some form of regular supplier assessment and only 16 per cent made no or very little use of supplier assessment.

Typically, buyers rely on supplier assessment to identify areas where performance is below the expected level and issue penalties accordingly. If supplier performance continues to be below the expected level, companies can decide to fire the supplier and find another supplier. However, companies prefer not to fire suppliers unless absolutely necessary as otherwise all their relationship investment efforts will be lost. In addition to relying on supplier assessment to identifying poor performance, it can also be used to motivate excellent performance. Not only does this enable suppliers to move up into a more strategic relationship category, such as 'strategic supplier' or 'partner', but suppliers can also gain reward for excellent performance. Many companies hold annual supplier award ceremonies where prizes are presented for different categories of performance such as best quality, most innovative, or most improving supplier.

Japanese automotive companies, such as Toyota, are renowned for motivating their suppliers through award ceremonies. In March 2012, Continental Automotive's Chassis and Safety division received an excellence award at Toyota Motor Engineering and Manufacturing North America, Inc.'s (TEMA) Annual Supplier Business Meeting (ABM). This brought together approximately 900 delegates from across North America. On receiving the award, the chief executive officer (CEO) of Continental's NAFTA region, Samir Salman, stated: "We are very proud to be recognized by Toyota for both technology development and quality performance ... We strive every day to exceed our customers' expectations. To be recognized for excellence is certainly gratifying and appreciated". Similar supplier award ceremonies are now common across many industries and are excellent means of stimulating supplier performance.

There are increasing regulatory pressures for companies to carry out supplier assessment or monitoring as a way to demonstrate due diligence. At the time of writing, the much debated European regulation known as the Corporate Sustainability Due Diligence Directive (CSDDD) was still not finally approved. However, many other international regulations have developed in recent years that put the onus on companies to monitor their suppliers for sustainability compliance. We look into regulations in more depth in Chapter 13.

Supplier monitoring typically involves:

- Sending out questionnaires for suppliers to complete known as self-assessment;
- Gathering secondary data on supplier risk and compliance e.g. using AI-enabled platforms;
- Auditing supplier operations either by the buying company itself or through a third party.

Supplier self-assessment questionnaires are typically designed around standards, such as the *International Organization for Standardization* (ISO) or the *Global Reporting Initiative*

(GRI). They can also be designed to cover regulations, such as the French Duty of Care and modern slavery acts (see Chapter 13 for details of supply chain regulations). Questionnaires provide a structured and relatively easy approach as they can be distributed to a large number of suppliers who are then required to complete the questionnaires on their own. Relying on information provided by suppliers in questionnaires can be risky for the buying company as there is little control over whether the information provided is accurate or even falsified. Self-assessment questionnaires are therefore of questionable value unless the information provided is verified by other means. It is good practice to ask for complementary documentation and to cross-check with any publicly available information.

An inherent problem with self-assessment questionnaires is that suppliers are likely to receive a large number of these from all their major customers, taking precious time away from their primary activities that they have been contracted to perform. Suppliers may be wasting time filling in customer questionnaires that may ask for the same information but are usually slightly different. For this reason we have seen the emergence of service providers that offer shared platforms for their clients to assess and rate supplier sustainability risks. One major advantage offered by these platforms is the ability to share supplier data with other platforms member, so that suppliers only have to complete one questionnaire instead of one for each customer. Platform providers also offer a host of other services, such as risk mapping, so-called 360° dashboards and reporting, and corrective action tools for risk mitigation. Chapter 14 delves further into supplier sustainability ratings tools and includes a case study of one of the major platform providers: EcoVadis.

In the last few years a host of procurement and supply chain service provider startups have emerged built around AI-enabled platforms or hubs. These typically rely on AI to collect and analyze vast amounts of secondary data via e.g. company and industry reports, and offer features not only to identify risks but also to assess, prioritize, and mitigate risks. In addition to ongoing supplier monitoring, such data can prove valuable for informing sourcing (or supplier onboarding) processes, and they often have reporting features making them convenient for their clients. In time these platforms may replace the reliance on traditional self-assessment questionnaires.

Supplier audits have long been considered as the best way to follow up initial risk indications. Industry leaders such as Apple, Danone, and Patagonia conduct regular audits of their entire supply bases and publish the results from their efforts in their annual reports.[3] However, audits require significant resources and it can be challenging to uncover activities that are in non-compliance as suppliers may try to hide these in efforts to 'pass' audit visits and providing excess of information may likewise be used as a strategy by the supplier to attempt to dazzle the audit team (Plambeck and Taylor, 2016).

An investigation by the NGO Transparentem (2021) reveals that audit deception is a pervasive problem in apparel supply chains in India, Malaysia, and Myanmar as recruiters and employers conceal labour rights violations. Based on their investigations across nearly 20 garment factories and spinning mills in India, Malaysia, and Myanmar, their report uncovers the use by suppliers of falsifying documents, coaching workers to lie, and hiding workers who appeared to be employed unlawfully. Moreover, they find that observations during site visits are often not representative of typical conditions and that interviewed workers' accounts reveal that many types of labour abuses can be hidden from auditors including:

- Passport retention;
- Wage and hour violations;
- Hazardous working conditions.

Transparentem (2021) recommend that auditors increase worker agency in the assessment process and improve auditing techniques by utilizing fully unannounced audits at times when code violations are most likely to occur, incorporating age-verification techniques (when investigating under-age workers), and providing auditors with proper resources for context-specific audit.

Research by Johnsen et al. (2025) on fashion supply chains reveals that the most advanced fashion companies apply supplier monitoring processes not only to first-tier but also to sub-tier suppliers and disclose in the annual reports the number of first- and sub-tier suppliers being audited annually. They find some of these companies choose to instruct suppliers to cascade requirements to their own sub-tier suppliers. The cascade approach is often applied where there are risks of non-compliance in lower tiers (Villena, 2019) and relies on delegating the responsibility for monitoring from one tier to the next. First-tier suppliers are pressured to cascade requirements to their (sub-) suppliers and the procurement function must play a facilitating role in this process in order for cascading efforts to be successful (Villena, 2019; Johnsen et al., 2022).

First-tier suppliers, therefore, should act as bridge builders (Wilhelm et al., 2016) to ensure that sustainability requirements also reach sub-tier suppliers. A lack of power may prevent companies, such as SMEs, to persuade suppliers to cascade requirements. Much research has shown that more subtle use of power – sometimes called non-coercive power – is more useful when putting pressure on suppliers to monitor their suppliers on a company's behalf (e.g. Wilhelm et al., 2016; Marshall et al., 2019; Meqdadi et al., 2020). For example, awarding suppliers for good performance rather than threatening suppliers with termination of contract is more likely to work especially in situations where suppliers hold the power.

As an alternative to the cascade strategy, companies may choose to audit sub-tier suppliers directly, using an intervention strategy. Put differently, companies may decide to circumvent first-tier suppliers and instead go directly to sub-tier suppliers when carrying out an audit. Clearly, it is not feasible for a company to undertake auditing of all of its suppliers across tiers, so auditing sub-tier suppliers is most likely when this cannot be trusted to a first-tier supplier (Meqdadi et al., 2020).

The end-of-chapter Hugo Boss case, the Danone case in Chapter 4, and the IKEA case in Chapter 6 illustrate how leading companies apply supplier monitoring methods in practice and the challenges they encounter. Monitoring suppliers is a critical part of the process of building up a strong supply base but on its own performance assessment and monitoring does little to improve supplier performance; it is necessary to follow-up such efforts with effective supplier development.

2.3.2 Supplier development: improving supplier capabilities

The practice of supplier development is widely used across industries but it has its origins in the Japanese automotive industry as a natural extension of continuous improvement – or *kaizen*. Supplier development is concerned with improving the suppliers' capabilities. Being closely linked to lean production, two objectives are to:

- root out wasteful (non-value adding) activities;
- achieve long-term improvement of suppliers' quality, cost, and delivery performance.

Sako's (2004) work on the Japanese automotive industry showed how Honda, Nissan, and especially Toyota pioneered supplier development. Toyota stated as early as 1939 that: "Once nominated as Toyota suppliers, they should be treated as part of Toyota ... Toyota shall carry out business with these suppliers without switching to others, and shall make every effort to raise the performance of these suppliers" (Toyota 1939 Purchasing Rules; see Sako, 2004: 286). The logic of supplier development at Toyota, as well as at other lean manufacturers, is that once lean manufacturing has been perfected internally it needs to be cascaded into the supply chain. The Operations Management Consulting Division (OMCD) at Toyota cascades the Toyota Production System (i.e. lean production) to suppliers through lectures, seminars and training courses, individual assistance, and *Jishuken* groups (joint problem-solving supplier groups). Some activities are focused on short-term improvement and problem solving whereas others focus on long-term capability enhancement. Many suppliers in turn have their own OMCD-like operations, cascading their learning further upstream.

Toyota's agreement with suppliers involved in supplier development stipulates that they be allowed to keep the savings resulting from improvement activities. Given the constant cost pressure of Toyota on suppliers, Toyota will naturally benefit from this activity but it is an important part of motivating suppliers to commit to supplier development. As an added benefit, working with suppliers as part of supplier development gives Toyota in-depth insights into supplier cost breakdowns. This means that they gain cost transparency without having to resort to open-book negotiation i.e. asking its suppliers to disclose its books – a practice that often leads to cheating (Lamming et al., 2005).

Following-up on supplier evaluation and monitoring often involves the supplier being required to conduct corrective actions i.e. to eliminate any source of non-compliance. Suppliers may be given a deadline to prove that the problem has been resolved. Many mature companies do not simply leave it to the suppliers to take the necessary corrective actions but try to help them. When dealing with, for example, suppliers in low cost countries this is a critical process of helping suppliers to understand why the corrections are necessary and how to improve their processes: this process is sometimes known as mentoring (Meqdadi et al., 2020). Such processes are known as supplier development and may span operational improvements and/or those related to sustainability.

The need to continue to work with existing suppliers, despite serious ethical supplier problems, is illustrated in the case of Swedish furniture giant IKEA. In May 2007, IKEA's chief executive officer (CEO), Anders Dahlvig, was interviewed by the BBC for its HARDtalk programme. He was presented with serious allegations of child labour and pollution at IKEA's suppliers in India and China. When asked why IKEA continued to source from these suppliers, he answered that IKEA's policy was to continue to monitor and help these suppliers to improve instead of simply getting rid of them. If IKEA had chosen to terminate these supplier relationships it would have meant having to subject the new suppliers to a resource-intensive – and costly – supplier selection and approval process (see the IKEA case study in Chapter 6).

The mentoring approach aims at enhancing the suppliers' sustainability capabilities (Ciliberti et al., 2008) and is based on collaboration and close relationships between customers and suppliers (Vachon and Klassen, 2006). Similarly to traditional supplier development programmes, the mentoring approach focuses on:

- Educating and training supplier personnel;
- Involving suppliers in product design to consider environmental requirements;
- Providing financial assistance for suppliers to improve the environmental performance of their processes, equipment, and materials;
- Mutual problem solving, and knowledge and expertise sharing with suppliers.

The monitoring and control approach requires less time and fewer resources but it does not enable the company to verify suppliers' actual sustainability performance (Vachon and Klassen, 2006). In the worst case this approach may lead to 'green-washing' behaviour i.e. the supplier will cover up the reality and paint a rosy – or rather a green – image. The mentoring approach is more likely to foster real improvement in supplier practices and performance (Seuring and Müller, 2008) but requires significant investment (Rao and Holt, 2005).

Recent trends in practices show that there is convergence between the supplier assessment and development processes and working with stakeholders to help develop capabilities of suppliers especially in the area of sustainability. Gualandris et al. (2015) point to sustainable evaluation and verification processes that are selectively inclusive of different stakeholder groups to leverage their different capabilities. These might include NGOs or other specialists who are able to add to the understanding of a particular issue and might work with suppliers to help improve performance in a certain area (Gualandris and Klassen, 2018). This is particularly the case in developing regions where multinationals are sourcing raw materials for example from agricultural producers, and working with these 'brokers' can help leverage local knowledge and access parts of the supply network which are challenging for Western/Northern companies (Saunders et al., 2019).

Supplier development activities often prioritize first-tier suppliers but may also involve sub-tier suppliers, for example, by sending a team of quality engineers to resolve an urgent problem. Villena and Gioia (2018) found evidence of training of sub-tier suppliers in areas such as health and safety, but they also found that sub-tier suppliers often lack awareness of sustainability requirements from their indirect customers. Villena and Gioia (2018) recommend the use of cascade strategies as it is not feasible for companies to directly monitor and train all of their suppliers across tiers and first-tier suppliers are better placed to deal with their own (second-tier) suppliers as they know these directly.

In many ways the process of defining the performance measures and what you do with it is more important than the measures themselves. The process of defining supplier performance measures should be used to facilitate dialogue with suppliers. Certainly, the data must be shared with suppliers so that suppliers actually know where they stand (Prahinski and Benton, 2004; Modi and Mabert, 2007). That way, the results of the assessment can be used to address problem areas and to improve rather than simply penalize suppliers when performance is below par.

2.4 CASE STUDY: INTEGRATING SUSTAINABILITY INTO SUPPLIER SELECTION AND EVALUATION CRITERIA AT HUGO BOSS

Hugo Boss was founded by Hugo Ferdinand Boss in the town of Metzingen in Germany in 1924 as a small clothing workshop. In the early days, the company produced a wide range of garments by hand including shirts and traditional German loden jackets. It was not until the 1950s that Hugo Boss really began to develop as a fashion company, producing its first men's suits in 1950. The BOSS brand was created in 1970, and was subsequently registered in 1977. By 1985 Hugo Boss was listed on the German Stock Exchange and in later years the company began to diversify notably with production of eyewear, footwear, and watches. The company also strengthened its sponsorships of 'premium' sports, such as motorsports and golf, and arts and launched its womenswear in the late 1990s.

Hugo Boss is now a global leader in the global apparel market, focusing on producing premium fashion and accessories for men, women, and children. Still headquartered in Metzingen, Hugo Boss employs 18,623 employees with sales of EUR 4.3 billion in 2024 (2024 Annual Report). Sales are truly global as collections are sold in 127 countries around the world in Hugo Boss retail stores and shops-in-shops in departments as well as through the online store. The range includes Boss, Boss Green, Boss Orange, and Hugo that each caters for different customer segments. The company highlighted the appointment of English football legend David Beckham in 2024 as their new brand ambassador and 'face', contracting the star for a multiyear design partnership.

As shown in Figure 2.7, the main production sites are located in Turkey, Germany (Metzingen), Poland, and Italy. Accounting for 15 per cent of production volume (2024), Izmir is the largest internal production facility, producing suits, sports jackets, trousers, and shirts as well as women's outerwear. However, around 80 per cent of the production is outsourced to suppliers (or 'partners'). In Western Europe, Italy is a major sourcing country with 26 first-tier suppliers and 195 second-tier suppliers; most of these are located in Northern Italy.

Like other fashion companies, Hugo Boss has traditionally relied extensively on sourcing from Asia. However, in the increasingly uncertain and turbulent global market with risks of large tariffs, particularly between the US, China, and European economies, Hugo Boss now aims to create "a regionally balanced strategic sourcing mix to minimize risks such as local or regional capacity shortfalls" (Hugo Boss Annual Report, 2024: 54). In a move to prioritize nearshoring, sourcing from China

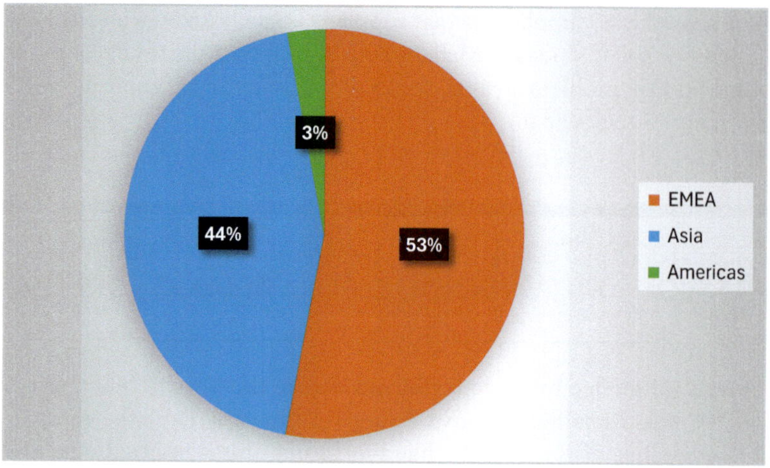

FIGURE 2.7 Hugo Boss global sourcing and production volumes (2024)
Source: Adapted from Hugo Boss Annual Report (2024: 54)

has been reduced to only 7 per cent, down from over 20 per cent a few years ago. Bangladesh (11 per cent) and Vietnam (8 per cent) now represent the largest Asian sourcing markets. Sourcing from Turkey has been further developed and now accounts for about half of the company's European sourcing and thereby by far the largest sourcing market overall. The changing global sourcing strategy also reflects a goal to better align regional sourcing activities with sales markets in order to reduce lead times and improve speed-to-market capabilities.

Hugo Boss prides itself with its dedication to quality, innovation, and responsibility. These three priorities also shape the sustainability strategy. Hugo Boss allocates significant resources to managing the types of sustainability risks that have affected so many fashion and luxury companies in recent years. In fact, the fashion industry has been the target of much criticism over the years as well-known brands have been accused of sourcing from supplier operations that are 'sweat shops' and there have even been cases of slavery in the fashion supply chain.

The company carried out a double materiality assessment in 2024 in preparation for compliance with the European Sustainability Reporting Standard (ESRS). The outcome of this work identified three topics as double material i.e. having high financial impact on Hugo Boss and a high impact on people and the environment: climate change, working conditions in the value chain, and other work-related rights in the value chain.

Complete lists of both first- and second-tier suppliers are shared on Hugo Boss's website (2025). Via *Open Supply Hub*, the company also shares an interactive supplier map. In total, Hugo Boss relies on 271 supplier production sites spread across 36 countries.

Hugo Boss rates suppliers according to four equally weighted criteria:

1 Vendor turnover;
2 Relevance for the company;
3 Management capabilities and country risk;
4 Strategy alignment with regard to ESG.

Suppliers are classified as strategic if they achieve a total result of at least 80 per cent (fulfilment of the minimum requirements in the areas of environment social aspects and corporate governance leads to higher rating in this area). In 2024, 43 suppliers were classified as strategic: these have on average 11-year partnerships with Hugo Boss.

Before suppliers are included in the Hugo Boss supplier portfolio, they must undergo a three-step onboarding process: 1) questionnaires and training; 2) contracts; 3) verification. This means that all active first-tier suppliers are trained on sustainability topics as part of the on boarding process. In addition, all new first-tier and second-tier suppliers have to complete a self-assessment questionnaire on social compliance.

The Hugo Boss Supplier Code of Conduct establishes the standards and expectations of suppliers across operational aspects, with a strong emphasis on social and environmental protection. In 2024, Hugo Boss also developed Responsible Purchasing Guidelines, focusing on equitable partnerships, long-term collaboration, responsible exits, efficient planning, and open communication with suppliers. To support supplier financial stability, a Supplier Financing Programme offers faster access to receivables, helping suppliers stay solvent and meet worker obligations.

The company conducts ongoing social compliance checks of all suppliers. In 2024, 56 audits were carried out, of which 13 per cent were unannounced, identifying 11 supplier violations. These concerned social compliance management and worker issues such as working hours but not forced or child labour. Identified violations against the supplier code of conduct are covered with corrective action plans to be resolved by the supplier. In case of missing cooperation and repeated underperformance in re-audits suppliers will be phased out but only as a last resort. The Fair Labour Association (FLA) independently monitors the company's due diligence efforts by conducting annual audits at selected production sites.

Hugo Boss has set improvement targets for 2025 to source all goods from first-tier suppliers that achieve either 'good' or 'satisfactory' in social compliance performance, verified through audits, self-assessments, or external social compliance certificates. For comparison, in 2024, 93 per cent of goods were sourced from first-tier suppliers that achieved this performance. By 2025 a target of 80 per cent has been set for all goods from first-tier suppliers achieve a 'good' performance (in 2024 65 per cent were rated as 'good').

Hugo Boss organizes supplier training on its Supplier Code of Conduct, offering access to a third-party learning platform with modules on topics like working hours, fair labour practices, and ESG regulations. In 2024 the company conducted ESG training as part of the onboarding process for both new and selected existing suppliers. The company collaborates with partners to improve supply chain standards and digital skills. Employees involved in social compliance receive regular training to help suppliers implement corrective action plans.

Child and forced labour remain significant concerns in the wider fashion industry, especially in upstream raw material production and manufacturing. In addition to working closely with suppliers, Hugo Boss works with a wide range of stakeholders, including NGOs, trade unions, and industry initiatives, to improve labour standards and ensure fair, safe, and equitable working conditions.

Hugo Boss is determined to tackle sustainability risks in its supply chain and a cornerstone in this endeavour is to ensure a rigorous supplier selection process followed up by continuous supplier assessment and development that incorporate a wide range of sustainability standards.

2.5 CONCLUSIONS

This chapter introduced the procurement process wheel, which is divided into stages of sourcing and supply. The framework highlights the importance of building up and maintaining a group of approved suppliers that constitute the company's long-term supply base. Chapter 2 evaluated the main stages of the procurement process, describing each stage and exploring the implications of sustainability for each of these. For example, ways to incorporate sustainability criteria into the specification and supplier selection process were identified.

Chapter 2 examined two critically important processes for long-term supply base development that are essential ways to ensure supplier sustainability compliance: supplier monitoring and development. We took a critical look at the monitoring practices, including self-assessment questionnaires and audit, and explored the use of platforms that provide a collaborative approach to supplier monitoring. Furthermore, we examined the role of supplier development that aims to improve supplier capabilities through, for example, training programmes. Such activities are now viewed as essential ways to demonstrate compliance and due diligence efforts, and we explored how requirements can be cascaded to sub-tier suppliers. We continue in the following chapter by examining procurement strategy and organization, including the notion of procurement maturity models.

NOTES

1 For Incoterms see https://iccwbo.org/?s=incoterms (last accessed 25 February 2025).
2 This example is adapted from Mouzas and Furmston (2008: 44) and concerns a retail environment.

3 See the hyperlinks below for examples of company reports or websites' coverage of sustainable sourcing: Apple: https://www.supplychainreports.apple/home/default.aspx; Danone: http://www.danone.com/en/publications/; Patagonia: https://www.patagonia.com/our-footprint/ (all last accessed 25 February 2025).

REFERENCES

Argyres N and Mayer KJ (2007) Contract design as a firm capability: An integration of learning and transaction cost perspectives. *Academy of Management Review* 32(4): 1060–1077.

Axelsson B and Wynstra JYF (2002) *Buying Business Services*. Chichester: Wiley.

Bäckstrand J, Suurmond R, van Raaij E and Chen C (2019) Purchasing process models: Inspiration for teaching purchasing and supply management. *Journal of Purchasing & Supply Management* 25: 100577.

Ciliberti F, Pontrandolfo P and Scozzi B (2008) Investigating corporate social responsibility in supply chains: A SME perspective. *Journal of Cleaner Production 16*: 1579–1588.

CIPS (2025) Procurement and Supply Cycle. https://www.cips.org/intelligence-hub/procurement/procurement-supply-cycle

Fisher R, Ury W and Patton B (2011) *Getting to Yes: Negotiating Agreement Without Giving In*. 3rd ed, New York: Penguin.

Gualandris J and Klassen RD (2018) Emerging discourse incubator: Delivering transformational change: Aligning supply chains and stakeholders in non-governmental organizations. *Journal of Supply Chain Management* 54(20): 34–49.

Gualandris J, Klassen RD, Vachon S and Kalchschmidt M (2015) Sustainable evaluation and verification in supply chains: Aligning and leveraging accountability to stakeholders. *Journal of Operations Management* 38: 1–13.

Guida M, Caniato F, Moretto A and Ronchi S (2023) The role of artificial intelligence in the procurement process: State of the art and research agenda. *Journal of Purchasing and Supply Management* 29(2): 100823.

Hugo Boss (2024) Annual Report 2024.

Hugo Boss (2025) Our Production Sites. https://group.hugoboss.com/en/sustainability/product/production-suppliers/production-sites

Johnsen R, Johnsen T, Beske-Janssen P and Marques L (2025) Animal welfare in fashion: A typology of transparent, translucent and opaque supply chains. *Supply Chain Management: An International Journal* 30(3): 323–338.

Johnsen TE, Caniato F, Meqdadi O, Miandar T (2022) Swimming against the tide: Supplier bridging roles in diffusing sustainability upstream and downstream in supply networks. *International Journal of Operations & Production Management* 42(10): 1605–1629.

Karlsson C, Nellore R and Söderquist K (1998) Black box engineering: Redefining the role of product specifications. *Journal of Product Innovation Management* 15: 534–549.

Kim S, Cohen MA and Netessine S (2007) Performance contracting in after-sales service supply chains. *Management Science* 53(12): 1843–1858.

Kraljic P (1983) Purchasing must become supply management. *Harvard Business Review* (Sept–Oct): 109–117.

Lamming RC, Caldwell ND, Phillips WE and Harrison D (2005) Sharing sensitive information in supply relationships: The flaws in one-way open-book negotiation and the need for transparency. *European Management Journal* 23(5): 554–563.

Lindkvist L (1996) Performance based compensation in health care – a Swedish experience. *Inquiry – Excellus Health Plan* 43(1): 34–53.

Lu M, Ma CA and Yuan L (2003) Risk selection and matching in performance-based contracting. *Health Economics* 12(5): 339–354.

Luo Y (2002) Contract, cooperation, and performance in international joint ventures. *Strategic Management Journal* 23(10): 903–919.

Marshall D, McCarthy L, Claudy M, and McGrath P (2019) Piggy in the middle: How direct customer power affects first-tier suppliers' adoption of socially responsible procurement practices and performance. *Journal of Business Ethics* 154(4): 1081–1102.

Meqdadi O, Johnsen TE, Johnsen RE and Salmi A (2020) Strategies for diffusing sustainability in supply networks: Case study findings. *Supply Chain Management: An International Journal* 25(6): 729–746.

Milligan B and Carbone J (2000) Harley-Davidson win by getting suppliers on board. *Purchasing* 129(5): 52.

Modi SB and Mabert VA (2007) Supplier development: Improving supplier performance through knowledge transfer. *Journal of Operations Management* 25(1): 42–64.

Mouzas S and Ford D (2012) Contracts as a facilitator of resource evolution. *Journal of Business Research* 65(9): 1251–1253.

Mouzas S and Furmston M (2008) From contract to umbrella agreement. *The Cambridge Law Journal* 67(1): 37–50.

Ng ICL and Nudurupati SS (2010) Outcome-based service contracts in the defence industry – Mitigating the challenges. *Journal of Service Management* 21(5): 656–674.

Plambeck EL and Taylor TA (2016) Supplier evasion of a buyer's audit: Implications for motivating supplier social and environmental responsibility. *Manufacturing & Service Operations Management* 18(2): 184–197.

Porter ME (1980) *Competitive Strategy*. The Free Press.

Prahinski C and Benton WC (2004) Supplier evaluations: Communication strategies to improve supplier performance. *Journal of Operations Management* 22(1): 39–62.

Pressey AD, Winklhofer HM and Tzokas NX (2009) Purchasing practices in small- to medium-sized enterprises: An examination of strategic purchasing adoption, supplier evaluation and supplier capabilities. *Journal of Purchasing and Supply Management* 15: 214–226.

Rao P and Holt D (2005) Do green supply chains lead to competitiveness and economic performance? *International Journal of Operations and Production Management* 25(9): 898–916.

Sako M (2004) Supplier development at Honda, Nissan and Toyota: Comparative case studies of organizational capability enhancement. *Industrial and Corporate Change* 13(2): 281–308.

Saunders LW, Tate WL, Zsidisin GA and Miemczyk J (2019) The influence of network exchange brokers on sustainable initiatives in organizational networks. *Journal of Business Ethics* 154(3): 849–868.

Seuring S and Müller M (2008) From a literature review to a conceptual framework for sustainable supply chain management. *Journal of Cleaner Production* 16: 1688–1710.

Transparentem (2021) Hidden harm: Audit deception in apparel supply chains and the urgent case for reform. https://transparentem.org/project/hidden-harm/

Vachon S and Klassen R (2006) Extending green practices across the supply chain – The impact of upstream and downstream integration. *International Journal of Operations & Production Management* 26(7): 795–821.

van Raaij EM (2016) Purchasing value: Purchasing and supply management's contribution to health service performance. Erasmus Research Institute of Management, Rotterdam.

van Weele A (2010) *Purchasing and Supply Chain Management: Analysis, Strategy, Planning and Practice*. 5th edn, Harlow, UK: Thomson Learning.

Villena VH (2019) The missing link? The strategic role of procurement in building sustainable supply networks. *Production and Operations Management* 28(5): 1149–1172.

Villena VH and Gioia DA (2018) On the riskiness of lower-tier suppliers: Managing sustainability in supply networks. *Journal of Operations Management* 64: 65–87.

Wilhelm MM, Blome C, Bhakoo V and Paulraj A (2016) Sustainability in multi-tier supply chains: Understanding the double agency role of the first-tier supplier. *Journal of Operations Management* 41: 42–60.

CHAPTER 3

Procurement strategy and organization

LEARNING OBJECTIVES:

At the end of this chapter you should be able to:

- Evaluate the changing business context affecting procurement strategy;
- Apply a sustainable procurement maturity model to diagnose how mature procurement is within a given organization;
- Analyze different organizational structures of the procurement function and how these might need to be adapted to better address sustainability requirements;
- Identify skills and competence requirements for the development of the procurement function including those that relate to sustainability;
- Evaluate the particular characteristics of public sector procurement, the complexities of public procurement and how it can be used as a lever for sustainable development.

3.1 INTRODUCTION

Strategy is about setting goals and priorities, typically concentrating on the long term, that is, a 3–5 year horizon. When developing their strategies, business leaders will consider how to create a competitive advantage in the marketplace by offering a distinctive offering in comparison with rivals (Porter, 1996). They will consider their internal resources, especially their core competencies, but more than anything else they will have to consider the external environment in which they operate.

As a business function that works alongside other internal supply chain functions, i.e. manufacturing and logistics, the development of a procurement strategy is to a large extent dictated by the overall corporate strategy and the expectations of top management as to how procurement can add value to the overall organizational performance. Sometimes procurement is part of this strategic decision-making process but other times it is not part of the top management team and will be instructed as to what its priorities should be and the performance metrics that will be applied to measure its success. This will involve

DOI: 10.4324/9781003499602-4

deciding on the competitive priorities, deciding on the relative importance of cost, quality, delivery, innovation, sustainability, and so on.

The principal competitive priority and key performance indicator (KPI) for procurement has historically been closely tied to cost: delivering cost savings. Procurement is perceived by top management as a function whose main job is to reduce the level of expenditure (often simply called 'spend'), and the potential for improving revenue through, for example, sourcing more innovative or sustainable materials often goes unnoticed.

However, with the rapidly shifting business context, the perceptions of procurement's role within organizations are changing. During the last decade the business context has become truly turbulent as a consequence of the global agenda towards green transitioning, the Covid-19 pandemic, and most recently the geopolitical tensions that severely affect global supply chains. Where procurement's role in the past was closely tied to narrow cost savings targets, procurement has to become much more strategic. The procurement community refers to this as growing their maturity.

This chapter, therefore, begins by examining the changing business context and how this alters procurement strategy. This is followed by a presentation of a sustainable procurement maturity model that can be applied as a tool to evaluate the maturity of procurement within a given company. This model incorporates a range of practices that are the subject of other chapters; in this chapter we look at the different ways in which procurement can be organized, centred around the question of centralization, and the skills and competencies required of procurement professionals to thrive in highly demanding procurement functions. The challenge of incorporating sustainability skills into traditional procurement organizations and the need for development of new procurement skills and competencies is explored.

The chapter finishes with an overview of the special challenges related to public sector procurement. In addition to exploring the specific regulatory frameworks that govern public procurement procedures and supplier award decisions, this section discusses how public procurement can be used as a lever for sustainable development.

3.2 BEYOND SAVINGS: CHANGING PROCUREMENT STRATEGIES IN A TURBULENT WORLD

As a point of departure, we consider how the procurement priorities have shifted in recent years. Here it is instructive to look to surveys that are carried out annually by the major management consulting firms that offer procurement consultancy. Collecting data from senior procurement directors, these firms typically ask about the top procurement priorities for the year ahead. Indeed, looking at the last five years, we can see some clear trends where – in addition to the obligatory cost savings – supply chain risk management, sustainability, innovation, and digital transformation take centre stage.

In the aftermath of the Covid-19 crisis the Deloitte 2021 Global Chief Procurement Officer (CPO) Survey showed a strong focus on operational efficiency and cost reduction as companies were clearly having to tighten the belt (Figure 3.1). However, innovation, risk management and CSR (i.e. sustainability) were not far behind.

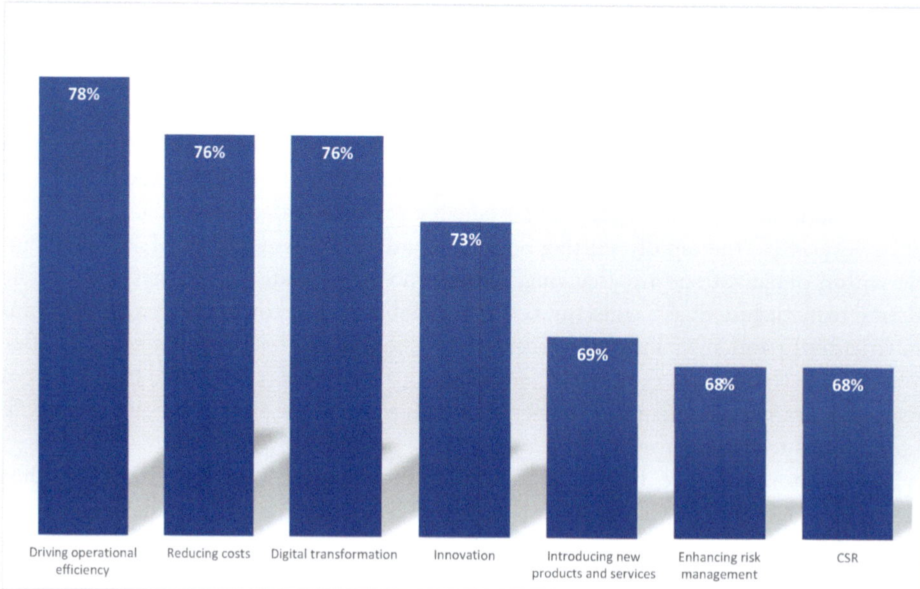

FIGURE 3.1 Top CPO priorities for 2021
Source: Adapted from Deloitte (2021)

Advancing two years to the Deloitte 2023 Global CPO Survey, cost had slightly declined in the ranking of priorities but remained significant, primarily due to concerns over inflation which prevented the realization of anticipated cost savings. In the changing business landscape of 2023 sustainability was now ranked as the second highest priority together with digital transformation, only topped by 'driving operational efficiency'. Not surprisingly considering turbulent supply chain conditions, risk management and supply chain resiliency are also regarded as top priorities. The Deloitte survey further identifies the top strategies to deliver the most value as increasing level of supplier collaboration (61 per cent), investing in digital transformation (42 per cent), enhancing demand management (37 per cent), renegotiation with existing suppliers (36 per cent), addressing total life cycle/ownership costs (29 per cent), and restructuring the supply base (25 per cent).

Coming into power in January 2025, Donald Trump's second US presidency resulted in further geopolitical uncertainty with severe impacts on global trade and supply chains. As a consequence, procurement strategies prioritize supply chain risk and resilience more highly than ever, for example by withdrawing from global sourcing locations that are deemed too high risk. The digital transformation agenda has also become a top priority, especially AI. With the Trump-led US government withdrawing from international climate agreements and European politicians looking to reduce or cancelling sustainability regulations, such as the much touted *Corporate Sustainability Due Diligence Directive* (CSDDD), there are question marks over the future of sustainable business.

Nevertheless, a survey commissioned by *Reuters Events* (Howitt, 2025) indicates that the commitment to sustainability has not dissipated:

- 99 per cent of top 100 US companies publish sustainability reports with 80 per cent requesting scope 3 data from suppliers, 95 per cent report reputational benefits, and 74 per cent link reporting to revenue growth;
- SMEs are actively participating in the sustainability transition;
- To navigate the politicized landscape, companies are rebranding ESG using terms like 'responsiblc growth' or 'sustainability';
- US companies are moving beyond compliance to view sustainability as a strategic imperative;
- Sustainability is being embedded across departments, supported by internal champions and technology;
- 80 per cent of CFOs expect the focus on sustainability to remain steady or grow, even in the face of political headwinds.

Although the future is highly uncertain, it is clear that the current truly turbulent geopolitical environment has changed and will continue to change procurement strategies. Cost reduction remains critically important for many companies that are looking to the procurement function to deliver savings. However, procurement decisions will need to balance a much wider range of objectives, in turn elevating procurement from a tactical to a strategic function.

3.3 STRATEGIC PROCUREMENT: A NEED TO ALIGN PROCUREMENT WITH CORPORATE STRATEGY

A 2023 survey by the Chartered Institute for Procurement and Supply (CIPS) found that 65 per cent believed that the perception of procurement had improved in the past year and 54 per cent believed that procurement is very much valued within their organization. This suggests that procurement has indeed become strategic, but what does *'strategic procurement'* mean?

Fundamentally, the term strategic procurement suggests that procurement contributes to, and is aligned with, the overall corporate and business strategies of the company. In other words, when procurement is strategic it reflects the priorities and goals of the company as a whole. These should be a result of the external environment, especially customer demand and stakeholder expectations, as well as internal resources and capabilities which provide the company with the ability to innovate.

Figure 3.2 shows the logic of these fundamental drivers of strategy development and the logic of alignment of strategies at different levels within the company. The concept of strategic alignment is that strategies of different functions within a company, such as procurement, logistics, marketing, and operations, should be mutually supportive and aim for the same, or at least mutually consistent, objectives. All too often this is not the case in many companies where instead procurement has its own objectives independent of what the company seeks to achieve overall at corporate level.

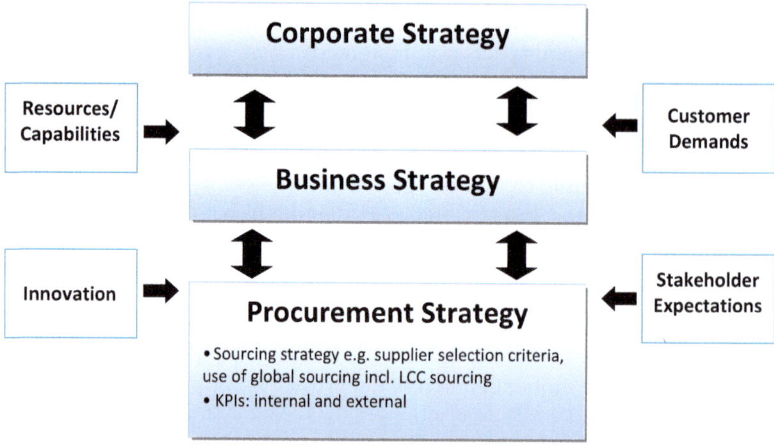

FIGURE 3.2 Strategic alignment of organizational objectives

The important point is that a focus on cost reduction, where cost is the dominant priority, is strategic if the company identifies low cost as a strategic differentiator – a source of competitive advantage. Therefore, for companies competing on low cost, such as discount retailers (Lidl or Aldi), it makes strategic sense if procurement emphasized low cost above everything else. For such companies it would therefore be strategic if sourcing strategy decisions, encompassing supplier selection criteria and the use of global sourcing, prioritized low cost. Furthermore, performance metrics such as Key Performance Indicators (KPIs), used internally for evaluating procurement staff performance and externally for evaluating supplier performance, should likewise be aligned with and therefore prioritize low cost.

However, for companies competing on superior quality, innovation, sustainability, or perhaps a combination of those competitive priorities, it would not be strategic for procurement to prioritize low cost at the expense of these other priorities. Yet, low cost is sometimes disproportionately prioritized in companies whose corporate and business strategies are not about low cost differentiation. Consider for example the focus on cost reduction at the expense of (perceived) quality at Mercedes-Benz in the late 1990s which severely damaged the company's hard-earned reputation for superior quality and reliability. Unfortunately, such misalignment is all too common even in large companies and it means that procurement does not contribute effectively to creating a sustainable competitive advantage for the company. Instead, decisions taken by procurement may undermine what should be a clear strategic business profile.

In general, procurement's visibility and influence depend on a number of factors such as procurement's share in the end-product's cost-price and the extent to which the company is dependent on its supply chain. Put simply, where purchased inputs represent high cost and risk for a company, thus potentially having a strong impact on the bottom-line, procurement is more likely to be viewed as important by senior management. Therefore, procurement is more likely to have a presence at senior management level.

The title of Chief Procurement Officer (CPO) signifies a rise in the status and influence of senior procurement directors with the CPO being part of the executive board of directors whose job it is to develop corporate strategy. If a company has appointed a CPO (or Vice-President for Procurement or similar), it indicates that procurement is seen as an important contributor to overall corporate performance within the company. Nevertheless, not all companies have CPO positions and a CPO position does not always mean that procurement in reality exerts a great deal of influence at a strategic level and the expectation is that procurement simply exists in order to deliver cost savings. This expectation is often the case when procurement reports to the Chief Financial Officer (CFO) rather than directly to the CEO.

As procurement functions mature, they rise within the ranks of the organization. Where procurement in many companies used to have limited visibility and influence, being placed at a low level within the organizational hierarchy, procurement has climbed to the top of the table within many organizations that understand the need for a mature high-performance procurement function.

In sum, the existence, and nature, of a company's procurement strategy is a key ingredient of strategic procurement so formulating a procurement strategy is an essential step in making procurement strategic. Procurement maturity models, discussed in the following section, are used to identify the level of maturity or sophistication of procurement within a company and to show the characteristics of different stages of maturity and to indicate ways to improve.

3.4 A SUSTAINABLE PROCUREMENT MATURITY MODEL

When procurement plays a strategic role within a company it reflects a high degree of procurement maturity. Mature procurement functions are visible and recognized at corporate levels and often exert real influence on strategic decisions within the company. But procurement maturity is also characterized by a range of other factors and procurement maturity models have evolved over the last 40 years or so to help to evaluate the stage of procurement maturity within companies.

There have been many models of procurement management maturity proposed in the past. The model of operations management sophistication developed by Hayes and Wheelwright (1984) clearly inspired the original purchasing maturity model proposed by Reck and Long (1988), which identified four stages: passive, independent, supportive, and integrative. Reck and Long's (1988) model identified a set of characteristics of four stages of maturity, such as the visibility and influence within the company, supplier relationships, supplier evaluation bases, information and communication, and skills. Alternative maturity models have since been developed; these are generally based on the same logic as the original Reck and Long (1988) model, but include more features that characterize modern advanced procurement functions.

Developed on the basis of a synthesis of existing maturity models, from the original to the latest models, our sustainable procurement maturity model is illustrated in Figure 3.3. The model is built on a comprehensive review of maturity models in procurement, supply chain management, and sustainability, elaborated through company case studies, and tested in workshops with procurement professionals spanning multiple industries (see Johnsen et al., 2024 for details).

This model is distinctive from existing models as it incorporates sustainability into all dimensions. The model is designed to evaluate a company's sustainable procurement maturity. It is not intended purely to capture those aspects of procurement that concern sustainability but as a broader assessment of procurement maturity, considering sustainability where appropriate. The model is designed around seven categories and divided into four stages of maturity:

1. *Clerical*: procurement is characterized by a low status as an administrative function driven by a cost savings objective in which supplier relationships are not viewed as sources of value creation or innovation, and with only basic risk and sustainability considerations.
2. *Developing*: procurement has implemented a range of best practices emphasizing centralization, professional qualifications, and growing sustainability awareness. Efforts include supplier questionnaires, audits for compliance, and initiatives like circular procurement. While operational performance and basic risk assessments are in place, there is limited integration of advanced AI technologies and supplier innovation remains in development stages.
3. *Supportive*: procurement strategy is aligned with corporate goals, prioritizing sustainability, and leveraging cross-functional collaboration. Training in sustainability, advanced risk assessment, supplier monitoring, and promoting circular practices. Digital technologies used as enhancement with AI used for operational tasks.
4. *Strategic contributor*: procurement strategy forms an integral part of corporate strategy with sustainability as value driver. Centre-led procurement organization with 360 degree supply chain risk monitoring, extended supply chain visibility, systematic compliance management, ecosystem scouting for (eco)innovations, and the adoption of advanced digital technologies, aiming for strategic integration.

The purpose of the model is to diagnose the level of sustainable procurement maturity in any company. The procurement function within a company may use the model to self-assess each of the criteria, choosing the descriptions that they perceive best characterizes their company. It is always advisable to ensure input from other procurement representatives, for example via workshops, and from other functions that often have different perceptions of the current and potential state of procurement maturity. In addition, the analysis should be complemented with documentary evidence, comprising internal reports such as guidance documents (e.g. codes of conduct and supplier information packs) and company reports, and external reports (e.g. ratings by EcoVadis, Sedex, or other third parties).

The outcome of the analysis is a profile that shows how some categories are less mature than others, thus becoming candidates for improvement. Where maturity models can indicate the current state and potential areas of improvement, they are not designed to provide a detailed roadmap for improvement. They are also not industry- or context-specific so they provide a generic picture in which some descriptions may be inappropriate and therefore require adaptation.

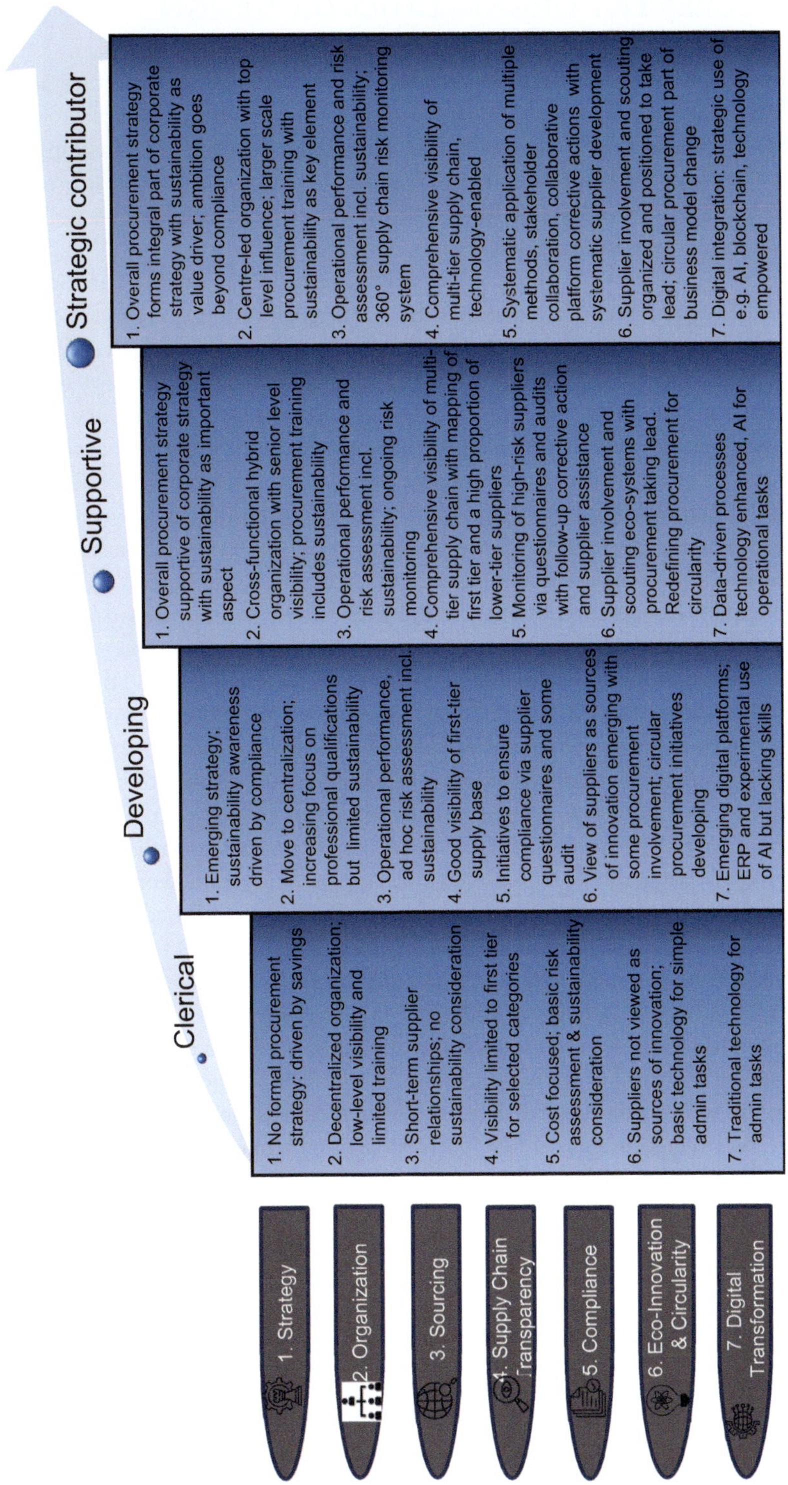

FIGURE 3.3 A sustainable procurement maturity model

3.5 PROCUREMENT ORGANIZATIONAL DESIGN

The organizational design of the procurement department sets the structure and therefore the framework for procurement strategy and the processes that take place within the department. Organizational design therefore plays an important part in implementing procurement strategy and decisions. As discussed in the previous section, if procurement has a position at senior management level within the company it is directly visible at that level and can influence corporate decision-making.

There are many ways of designing organizations, including individual functions such as procurement. Fundamentally, as suggested by contingency theory, organizational design should be appropriate to the particular contingency, or context, of the company. In his *Images of Organization* (1986) Morgan suggested that organizations adapt to the environmental context and as these differ for different companies there is no one best way of organizing. Seeking the most appropriate fit between the circumstances and the company is critical – it is a case of 'horses for courses' (Bowen et al., 2001).

Historically, many large companies used to be structured into multi-layered hierarchies with clear functional departments, such as Production (or Operations), Marketing, Finance, Human Resources (or Personnel), and so on. In fact, traditionally Procurement would not constitute a separate department but would fit underneath another department, typically Production or Finance. Hierarchical structures imply a high degree of centralization and strong departmental boundaries with clearly-defined responsibilities and decision-making processes. But, where organizational designs with fixed, or sometimes rigid, structures used to be seen as appropriate for stable slow-changing environments, much more fluid and dynamic organizational designs are now required for companies to keep up with the constant market and industry changes and increasingly disruptive innovations that can make companies obsolete overnight (Christensen, 1997). Consequently, many companies have made major changes in procurement (and supply chain) frameworks and the trend is away from simple structures towards more complex hybrid ones. Based on responses from nearly 100 CPOs across multiple industries, a report by EY (2022) found that almost 59 per cent of the companies they surveyed are adopting a hybrid model of governance for procurement, building both reactive and proactive capabilities to respond to disruption.

Developing sustainable procurement further adds to the need for complex hybrid organizational structures. In many companies the corporate social responsibility (CSR) or sustainability function exists as a separate department disconnected from procurement (or supply chain management). In fact, both departments may work on similar issues but the structural separation makes it hard to fully integrate sustainability and procurement. Some companies have developed innovative organizational forms to cope with this challenge and we explore examples of interesting solutions at the end of this section.

3.5.1 Centralization or decentralization?

The fundamental question for organizational design of procurement is whether to opt for a high degree of centralization or to pursue decentralization. This is a particularly important question for large companies that operate on an international level and that are therefore likely to have multiple business units such as manufacturing plants and subsidiaries worldwide. Where centralization is about global coordination, integration, and synergy across dispersed organizational units, decentralization implies flexibility and adaptability to local conditions. Figures 3.4 and 3.5 below illustrate how centralized and decentralized procurement organizational structures might look.

Decentralized procurement has many advantages. When procurement decisions are delegated to individual business units it is possible for these to take advantage of local knowledge of supply market conditions and adapt to these. For example, it can be much easier for a local factory to source local material from local suppliers, taking advantage of local opportunities. Financially, sourcing locally may reduce transaction costs and, from a

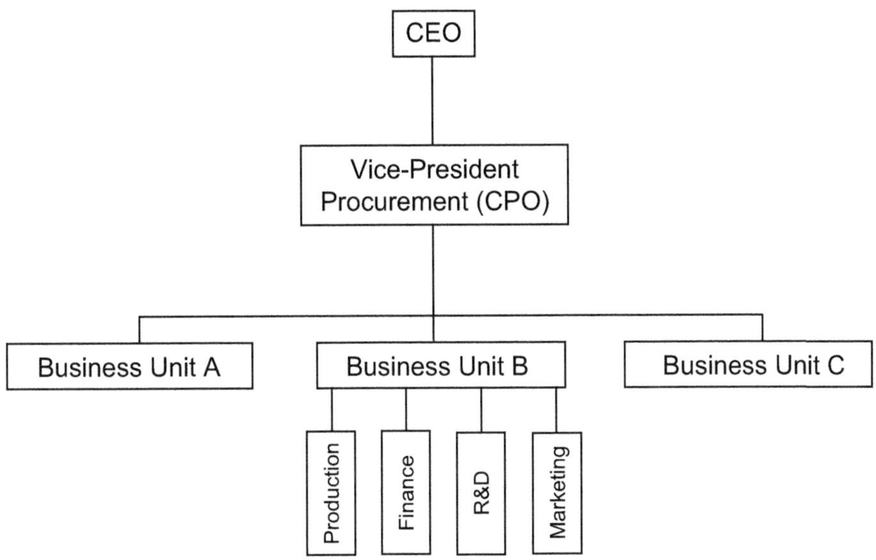

FIGURE 3.4 Centralized procurement organization structure

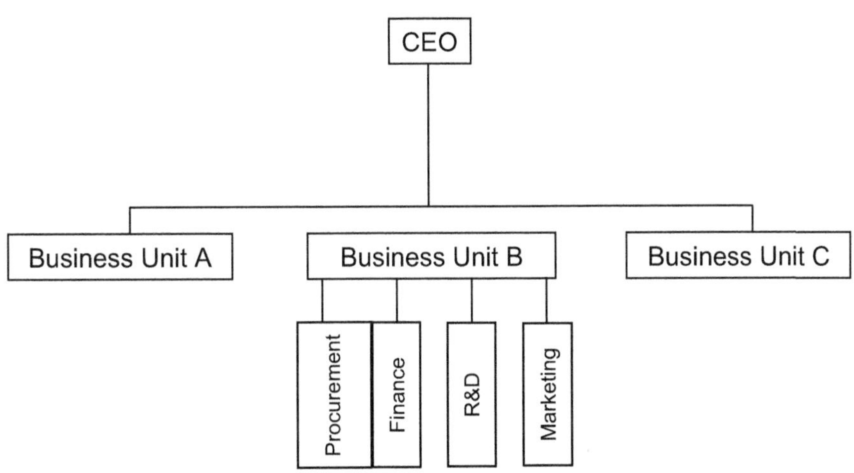

FIGURE 3.5 Decentralized procurement organization structure

sustainability perspective, local sourcing can reduce environmental impacts. Organizations that have a large portfolio of different purchase categories are often reluctant to be dictated to by central procurement management as they believe that they can obtain better deals themselves as they have superior local supply market knowledge. This is often the case in public sector organizations that are naturally decentralized. For example, the UK National Health Service (NHS) consists of a great number of sub-organizations across the UK, including for example hospitals, which are managed by local trusts, doctors' surgeries, and specialist clinics and centres. Traditionally, many procurement decisions have been left to the local units and recent initiatives to impose a central procurement catalogue have met with much resistance (although this has also resulted in substantial savings – see Note 6.1). However, a decentralized organization can easily result in a spirit of competition for resources between units instead of collaboration and synergy.

Achieving synergy across multiple business units is key to centralizing the procurement organization. Procurement synergy can be defined as the increase in performance (efficiencies and effectiveness) resulting from the joining of forces, information, knowledge, and/or the sharing of functional resources of two or more procurement units (Rozemeijer, 2000). Bundling expenditures and suppliers can result in better deals through increased economies of scale and scope (Englyst et al., 2008).

Building on Goold and Campbell (2000) and Rozemeijer (2000) we identify the following forms of synergy that can be achieved through centralization of procurement:

Note 3.1 Procurement consolidation at the UK Police

The UK Police buy a great variety of things including for example: forensic services, aircraft, uniforms, medical services, stationery, catering, IT systems, dog food, insignia, and salvage services. At the beginning of the new millennium the UK Police realized that as each of the 55 regional forces had its own procurement unit there were 55 different procurement units each with different finance and purchase ordering systems and reporting structures. As a result the Police found that procurement was reduced to an administration activity, information about spend was lacking and maverick buying was widespread. Moreover, procurement had little leverage over suppliers and limited scope for economies of scale. As an example, there were no standard specifications for police uniforms so 48 styles of uniforms on 11 different types of cloth purchased around the country. Even with some different regional needs (for example to cater for different climates in the north and south) this was not sustainable.

Realizing that there was much room for improvement, the Police Force created a national strategy for procurement, creating centres of excellence and lead forces that would show other regional forces the best ways forward. Collaborative procurement was also initiated and by 2012 13 police forces in the UK were using a National Police Procurement Hub: an e-procurement platform that provides a portal to a range of approved goods and services online from over 900 suppliers. The Hub is expected to save the police service £69 million over a six year period by supporting collaboration across multiple forces and reducing the cost of purchases through their joint buying power and managing suppliers better. Lee Tribe, director of procurement for the Metropolitan Police said: "The benefits for our suppliers in automating the ordering process will enable them to avoid re-keying Met orders into their sales systems and speed up the end to end process. Users within Met have access to a greater variety of products and services and faster delivery times".

Source: Hastings and Harland (2003)

1 *Pooled negotiation power*: gaining leverage over suppliers by joint buying, reducing the cost and/or improving the quality of the goods purchased. In other words, economies of scale (lower unit costs) can be achieved by increasing market power through volume bundling and standardization of categories (Trautmann et al., 2009). Raw materials, components, and MRO items are often pooled to benefit from synergies. Companies can obtain lower prices by combining orders to a common supplier so as to take advantage of quantity discounts (Tella and Virolainen, 2005). Pooling can also include cooperation with competitors or other companies. In the public sector so-called collaborative procurement initiatives (or collaborative procurement hubs) have become popular ways to pool the procurement power of for example hospitals that belong to the same overall national healthcare service (Bakker et al., 2008). Similarly the concept of consortium procurement or procurement consortia is often used by industrial companies.
2 *Shared resources*: benefits from economies of scale and elimination of duplicated efforts by pooling corporate procurement employees, procurement information and communication systems, corporate management group (overheads), and/or office space and other facilities.
3 *Shared knowledge*: perhaps even more important than shared resources are the benefits associated with the sharing of intangible resources, that is, knowledge and competencies. Examples of knowledge to be shared include procurement strategies and policies, procurement tools, techniques and best practices, procurement skills and competencies, supplier or supply market knowledge. Also, so-called 'economies of process' i.e. establishment of a common way of working can create a globally consistent line of conduct to suppliers, benchmarking procedures and results, and joint training and development (Faes et al., 2000). From a sustainability perspective such benefits are of particular importance as, for example, sharing of sustainability policies, contracts, and codes of conduct needs to be across organizations in order to have serious impact. Furthermore, shared and standardized product specifications are very important drivers of economies of scale, especially in capital intensive industries such as the automotive industry. Companies can also reduce administration and transaction costs, for example, as negotiations are handled by one central unit instead of many decentralized units (Essig, 2000).
4 *Coordinated strategies and policies*: benefits from aligning strategies of two or more businesses e.g. reduced internal competition for the same resources. As explained above, alignment of strategies and policies is of particular importance to implementing sustainable procurement as companies are under pressure to ensure a corporate coherent (Rozemeijer et al., 2003) approach to managing their supplier relationships.

5 *Vertical integration*: benefits from the ability to reduce inventory costs, improve market access, and increase capacity utilization through improved supply chain management.

6 *Combined new business creation*: benefits that stem from the creation of new businesses by combining know-how from different units, by extracting activities from different units to put into a new unit, and by internal joint ventures or alliances between units.

Many organizations have achieved significant savings and value creation through consolidation of fragmented purchases. As discussed in Chapter 2, it makes sense to standardize product components and parts as much as possible, avoiding unnecessary use of different parts where the same parts can be used instead, allowing procurement to obtain economies of scale. Note 3.1 gives an (old but instructive) example of an initiative to consolidate procurement through joint procurement, implementation of collaborative procurement hubs, lead forces, and e-procurement.

The potential benefits of a centralized procurement organization that stem from improved synergies are significant. Often, the theoretical benefits are difficult to implement in practice not least because of internal resistance to comply with centrally-determined decisions. Furthermore, centralizing decision-making means taking away decisions from local procurement teams or individual buyers who used to enjoy a free hand, for example, when it comes to supplier selection or contract negotiation.

The UK National Health Service (NHS) has shifted towards a procurement structure that relies greatly on regional collaborative procurement hubs. Ray Searles, director of procurement at the UK-based North West Collaborative Procurement Hub, which represents 52 NHS trusts, including hospitals and ambulance services, describes how individual members even compete to 'beat the hub' in their own dealings with suppliers: "The benefits in terms of time and in taking to the market a much bigger spend are obvious, but that doesn't stop people pushing against it when they feel their authority is threatened" (Martindale, 2008). Nevertheless, the NHS still face problems of fragmented procurement. As expressed by Jacqui Rock, NHS England Chief Commercial Officer (Ozsevim, 2023):

> We want to focus on eliminating waste, and one of the things that I found really enlightening when I came in here, is that we've got multiple contracts with the same supplier for the same thing, but with lots of variation.

As Note 3.2 reveals, fragmented organizing can lead to so-called maverick buying where buyers bypass formal procedures to make unauthorized purchases. However, maverick buying can also result from centralized procurement as buyers refuse to comply with standard procedures. This type of non-compliance therefore results in 'non-managed spend', which can present a significant proportion of spend in some organizations.

3.5.2 Centre-led procurement

Due to the many problems of centralized procurement, several organizations have moved towards decentralization or a mixture of the two extremes: hybrid organizations that combine the best of both worlds – centre-led procurement in which corporate procurement sets strategies and policies centrally but leaves operational day-to-day decisions to the local level. Typically, centre-led procurement is organized around:

- A central organization handling all purchases with a single upward reporting structure;
- A mixture of centralized and decentralized organization with responsibilities split by function or category;
- A decentralized organization with a centralized coordinating function, e.g. a network of 'lead buyers' reporting to different geographic regions or business units, yet managing categories on behalf of the company as a whole.

Leaving the day-to-day purchases to local teams, the headquarter function of centre-led procurement organizations typically:

- Manages contracts for common requirements;
- Establishes policies, procedures, and systems;
- Participates in system-wide personnel decisions/actions;
- Develops and/or provides training;
- Evaluates or audits unit performance;
- Performs special studies and reports;
- Interfaces with government or industry/professional bodies.

We explained earlier that the right choice of procurement organization structure depends on the circumstances: it is a question of horses for courses (Bowen et al., 2001). Often, the choice of procurement organizational structure depends on two factors (Rozemeijer et al., 2003): procurement maturity and corporate coherence (see Figure 3.6). Indeed, as procurement functions mature the trend is for companies to move away from pure centralized or decentralized models towards hybrid or, ultimately, a centre-led model that combines the best of both worlds. In cases of low procurement maturity and low corporate coherence, decentralized procurement is most likely to be found as central coordination efforts are difficult to achieve. At the opposite end of the scale, where procurement

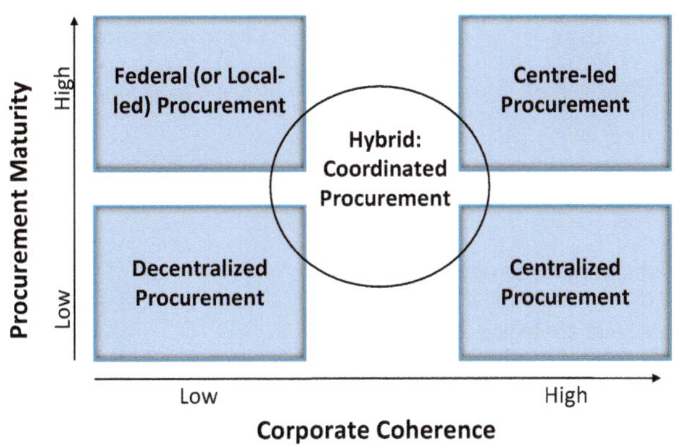

FIGURE 3.6 Corporate procurement organizational models
Source: Adapted from Rozemeijer et al. (2003)

maturity and corporate coherence are high, a centre-led structure is appropriate. Federal (or local-led) procurement is often found in mature procurement functions but clearly reflects low corporate coherence. In this situation corporate procurement staff support autonomous decentralized procurement units in their voluntary efforts to exploit potential synergies (Rozemeijer et al., 2003). In situations of medium procurement maturity and corporate coherence, hybrid structures can be found that combine centralization and decentralization and use voluntary procurement coordination.

A survey by SCM World (now part of Gartner) of almost 500 procurement professionals (John, 2018), indicates that compared with other SCM functions, such as manufacturing and distribution/logistics, procurement is highly centralized. This is particularly the case for procurement of direct materials that are managed by a central team and less so for indirect goods and services. This survey also found that 70 per cent expected procurement to become more centralized over the next five years although CPOs in mature organizations are reportedly moving the 'organizational design pendulum' back towards the middle state. Having moved from decentralized to centralized mature organizations therefore revert back towards a degree of decentralization, adopting a centre-led solution to achieve a more balanced state to be more responsive to business needs.

In summary, there are a number of advantages and disadvantages of pure centralized and decentralized procurement structures and these move companies towards hybrid and centre-led models as they mature and seek corporate coherence. Both of these factors, as discussed, are important from a sustainability perspective, not least to enable the implementation of globally consistent sustainability strategies and policies. Figure 3.6 summarizes the main advantages and disadvantages of decentralized configurations. Generally, the opposite can be assumed for centralized procurement.

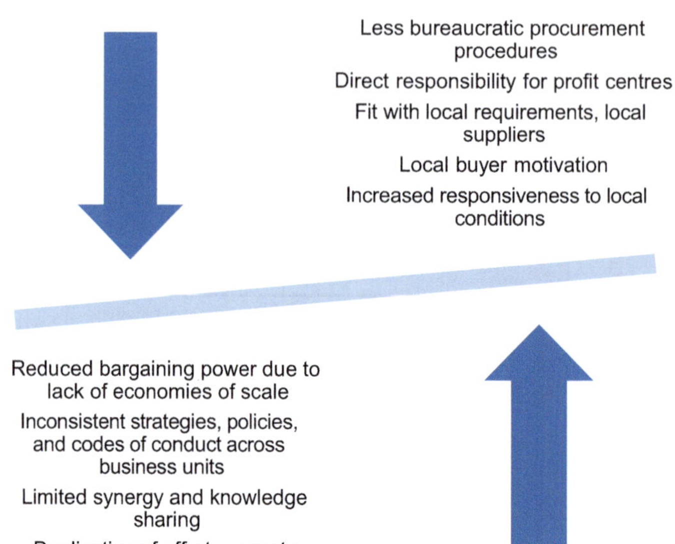

FIGURE 3.7 Advantages and disadvantages of decentralized procurement

3.5.3 Procurement category teams

The degree of centralization is an important starting point in the procurement organization design decision, but there is much more complexity to the modern procurement organization. According to Bals and Turkulainen (2017), companies typically design their procurement organization around the following:

1 Purchasing categories: organizing into category (or commodity) teams e.g. around different direct materials, indirect purchases, and services;
2 Geographic area: organizing according to major regional areas of operation;
3 Product lines: organizing into product line divisions.

The first of these deserves some further insights. Companies buy a vast array of different things, including direct materials, indirect items such as Maintenance, Repair, and Operating materials (known as MRO items: office equipment, spare parts, and so on), and services. Clearly, buying raw materials from commodity markets is entirely different from buying high-tech components, which is again completely different from buying CAPEX and logistics services. This has therefore given rise to *category management* to allow special attention on the unique challenges involved in sourcing and procuring such different purchase categories.

Trautmann et al. (2009) define a category as encompassing a group of similar items that are required for specific business activities of the firm. Put differently, categories share a basic standard, market, or material homogeneity to enable pooling and negotiation across business units (Englyst et al., 2008). Category (or commodity) teams offer a coordination or pooling structure within larger firms that are multinational and consist of a number of individual business units.

Category/commodity teams provide a way to combine centralized and decentralized procurement especially in large multinational/multidivisional companies. However, hybrid organizations imply split organizational responsibilities and companies often encounter problems, for example, to do with personal development and advancement opportunities. To avoid problems of commodity-team commitment and motivation, goals, rewards, and KPIs should be incorporated into commodity-team participation, aligned with the individual team member's career objectives (Englyst et al., 2008).

3.6 PROCUREMENT SKILLS AND COMPETENCIES

As procurement has become more important in companies it is not surprising that the requirements for the skills and competencies of people working in procurement have increased. We saw earlier in this chapter how maturity models show a progression of skills and competencies as procurement functions become increasingly mature and sophisticated: strategic procurement functions require procurement managers and directors to be able to collaborate with a range of other organizational functions, to provide clear leadership, and to act as change managers driving organization-wide changes in their efforts to implement change projects.

Understanding how to integrate the latest digital technologies into procurement tasks whilst engaging with sustainable procurement challenges adds to the increasing complexity of the modern procurement professional. Procurement professionals must not only master traditional procurement skills but also understand how to best exploit emerging digital technologies such as big data analytics, AI, and IoT.

Educational bodies, including universities, business schools, professional bodies/institutes, management consultancies, and training organizations, naturally have their own approaches to and frameworks for identifying sets of skills and competencies. Frameworks can be designed and used to identify gaps within organizations and areas of development. Consequently, there exists a plethora of procurement competence frameworks. One of the oft-cited frameworks is by Tassabehji and Moorhouse (2008), which despite being relatively old, is a useful starting point. This framework identifies five categories of procurement skills as shown below.

Despite the mounting challenges for procurement professionals to understand how to exploit new digital technologies, i.e. demonstrate technical skills, surveys consistently point to the importance of soft skills. In fact, the demand for soft skills has accelerated in recent years as remote working and online meetings have made it even more important to be able to interact with internal teams as well as with external partners such as suppliers.

A survey conducted as part of the 2023 Chartered Institute of Procurement and Supply (CIPS) Salary Guide identifies negotiation (56 per cent), internal stakeholder management (48 per cent), and communication (46 per cent) as the top three skills for procurement professionals across Europe. Figure 3.8 illustrates the top five skills emphasized by procurement recruiters. We should note that skills inevitably depend on the level of seniority: where technical skills concerning, for example, data analytics and tools application are critically important at tactical and operational levels, the required skills for senior procurement professionals are more focused on leadership and influencing skills, change management, and internal stakeholder management.

As the competence profiles of procurement professionals become more demanding so it becomes more challenging to satisfy all the demands. This has implications for education and training but also for recruitment (and for procurement professionals who risk losing their jobs). This creates a need for more talent to come out of universities, and for company training to reskill existing teams for the future of work in procurement (van Hoek et al., 2020). The good news is that these challenges are making qualified candidates highly sought after. As noted by the CIPS CEO Nick Welby:

> The value of procurement and supply professionals continues to strengthen. After years of disruption they are now firmly established as gatekeepers for organisational resilience, continuity and ESG strategies. Managing risk, volatility and supply chain visibility continue to be primary goals, but with global cost pressures weighing heavily on organisations, balancing budget restraints whilst delivering long-term value is paramount. Against this backdrop, perceptions of the profession continue to improve and the most highly qualified individuals are increasingly in demand.
>
> (CIPS/Hays, 2023)

Mounting responsibilities for procurement professionals, therefore, have created what is known as the *talent gap* as organizations are struggling to recruit – and retain – highly competent members of their procurement teams. According to the 2022 Global Chief Procurement Officer Survey by professional services firm EY, two-fifths of companies

TABLE 3.1 Procurement skills framework

Technical skills	• Technical knowledge: e.g., computing, forecasting, e-procurement applications • Basic administration: e.g., legislation, cost analysis, product knowledge, negotiation • Advanced procurement: e.g., category management, global sourcing, project planning
Interpersonal skills	• Oral communication: e.g., listening, persuading, and influencing • Recognize own strengths: e.g., creative thinking, analytical skills, problem-solving, stress management, time management • Leadership: conflict management, decision-making, organization, team building, cross-cultural awareness
Internal enterprise skills	• Organization-wide financial skills • Change management and cultural awareness • Manage internal customers, sales interface, internal motivation • Communicate and sell message/strategy internally, relationship influencing
External enterprise skills	• Cross-functional team working • SRM and SCM • Stakeholder mapping, supplier evaluation, international buying
Strategic business skills	• Demonstrate ability to add value throughout organization • Manage strategic alliances/partnerships • Business skills and risk management

Source: Adapted from Tassabehji and Moorhouse (2008)

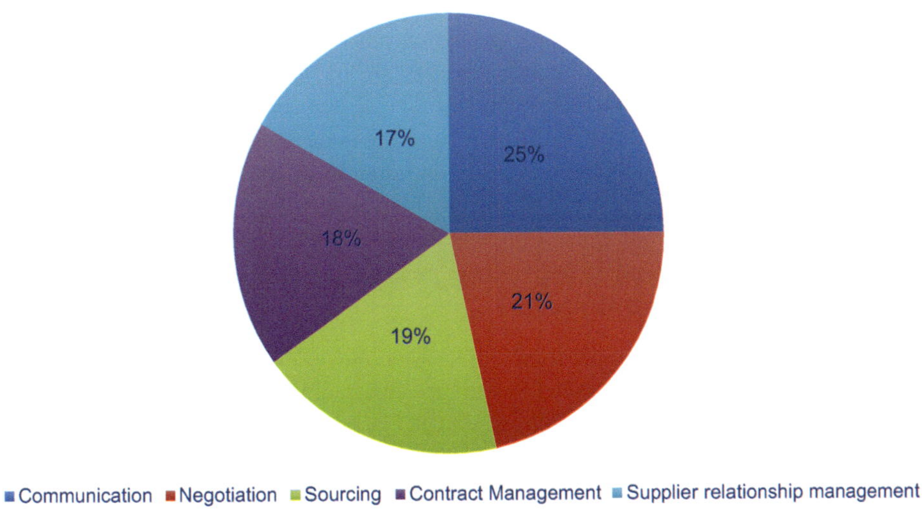

FIGURE 3.8 Top five procurement skills for recruitment
Source: CIPS/Hays 2023

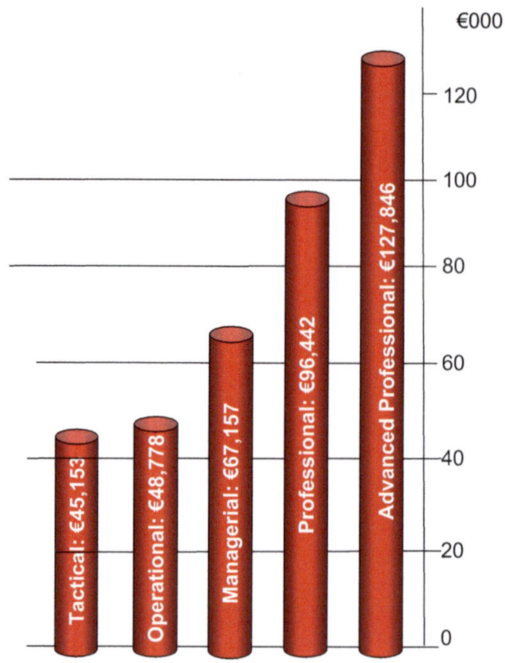

FIGURE 3.9 Average procurement salaries in Europe
Source: Adapted from the CIPS/Hays (2023)

are struggling to find the right talent to support even core procurement capabilities. In realization of this situation, many companies are willing to offer very attractive salaries for procurement and supply talent.

Figure 3.9 shows a snapshot of the salary statistics from the CIPS Salary Survey 2023, which is based on the results from over 5,000 professionals globally. These statistics indicate very competitive and generally rising salary levels for procurement and supply management professionals. Overall, the salary trends are on an upward trend with 63 per cent globally having received a salary increase of 7.2 per cent on average over the last 12 months (CIPS Salary Guide, 2025), reflecting the continued talent gap as companies struggle to recruit people with the right skills and qualifications.

3.6.1 The challenge of integrating procurement and sustainability skills and competencies

The need for procurement people to acquire a wide range of skills and competencies has certainly not decreased with the need to embrace sustainability. Where procurement people have traditionally had good commercial skills, sustainability presents new challenges and new mindsets. In particular, procurement needs to interact with or even integrate with CSR functions. This is a difficult challenge as these two functions involve people that traditionally are likely to have belonged to two different worlds. Leadership, team building, and communication skills are therefore critical to managing this new challenge. Furthermore, procurement and supply management people will need to acquire new skills in learning about a host of environmental and social standards (see Chapter 13) as well as skills related to conducting ethical supplier audits.

This is also emerging in research (Schultze et al., 2019), which suggests that beyond functional-oriented competence new competencies are required to deal with the sustainability challenges facing procurement and supply management professionals. In particular, these include cognition-oriented competencies (e.g. systems thinking), social-oriented competencies (e.g. cross-functional networking and stakeholder communication skills), and meta-oriented competencies (e.g. commitment to change and self-reflection).

The European research project PERISCOPE (n.d.) studied not only new competence requirements for sustainable procurement but also those required for new innovative solutions. In essence, there are two aspects to this challenge: on the one hand new competencies for ensuring compliance and risk management, and on the other hand new competencies for transforming existing business models. The former is about knowing how to manage risks through, for example, developing supplier codes of conduct or carrying out supplier audits, whereas the latter is more about strategic 'big picture' thinking to transition, for example, from linear to circular supply chain models. Figure 3.10 illustrates the PERISCOPE competence framework with the emphasis on holistic procurement competencies required in managing the twin challenges of sustainability and innovation.

As these skills are new to many procurement and supply management professionals it is important to keep up with the development of these: to recruit new people with the right combination of skills and to reskill. There will be a need for companies to attract and recruit people with new skill sets and new perspectives. In-company training may be one option for companies to develop new skills, to develop understanding of the implications of sustainability for procurement and supply management. Perhaps the most difficult challenge will

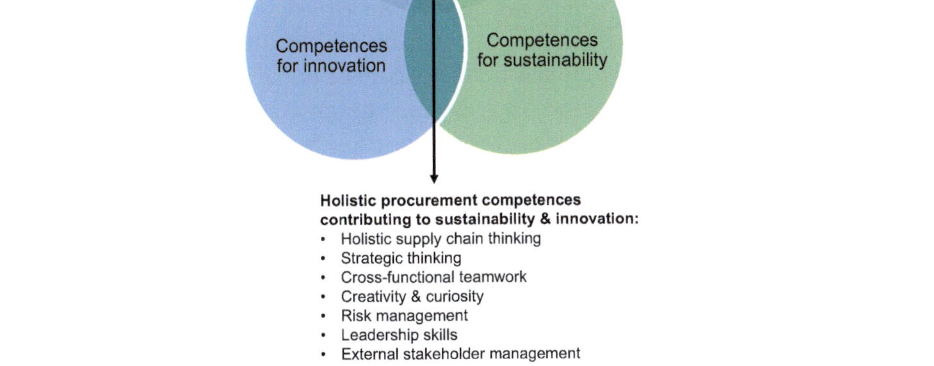

FIGURE 3.10 Procurement competencies for contributing to sustainability and innovation
Source: Adapted from Beske-Janssen et al. (2023)

be the changing of mindsets of traditional procurement and supply employees who may perceive sustainability as a fad or something to which they simply have to pay lip service.

An increasing number of education and training providers, including universities, business schools, professional bodies, non-governmental organizations (NGOs), and management consultancies, offer courses on many aspects of procurement and supply chain management and courses addressing the specific skills that are needed for managing sustainability are beginning to emerge. In fact, this is one of the key trends in education and training and indeed one to which the authors of this book aim to contribute.

3.7 THE SPECIAL CASE OF PUBLIC PROCUREMENT

Procurement in the public sector, usually known as public procurement, is often treated as a special case. In this book we use public sector examples throughout the book but it is useful here to identify some of the particular characteristics and challenges of public procurement, especially those that concern sustainability. In fact, in 2021 public procurement represented approximately 13 per cent of gross domestic product (GDP) in Organisation for Economic Cooperation and Development (OECD) countries (OECD, 2021), making government the single largest customer within many countries. On average across the OECD (2021), healthcare accounts for 31.9 per cent, followed by economic affairs (16.4 per cent), education (10.7 per cent), defence (9.9 per cent), and social protection (9.8 per cent). Following global the political developments in 2025, many countries are boosting their domestic defence capabilities with defence procurement therefore on the increase.

Due to such high levels of spend, governments have realized that they can use their economic influence to drive changes towards growth, innovation, and sustainability. Therefore, governments increasingly seek to deliver policy objectives through public procurement initiatives, for example, by investing in large scale projects to create economic growth during the economic crisis. However, public procurement is a very complex process influenced by extensive regulation and political interests amongst stakeholders.

As a provider of services to the public, public sector bodies are service providers rather than manufacturers but they buy a wide range of goods, works, and services from suppliers. One characteristic of public procurement is the preference for national suppliers as this means support of domestic companies and therefore the national economy. However, if all countries were to follow the same path there would be little scope for open competition amongst international suppliers and the users of public services (i.e. taxpayers) would be worse off, as comparative advantages would be ignored; this would consequently be inconsistent with government objectives of providing best value for money. Various international, regional, and national legislation has been put in place to avoid protectionist behaviour by individual nations and to prescribe fair public procurement procedures. As a fundamental principle, public procurement decisions should not be influenced by national considerations but there are often national pressures to circumvent this principle.

3.7.1 European public procurement regulation and thresholds

The regulations for public procurement within the European Union (EU), as developed by the European Commission (EC), govern EU member states. Many non-EU states are also affected by EC rules, for instance, where the same rules apply under trade agreements with the EC (e.g. Norway and Iceland under the Economic Area Agreement [EAA]) or where states are expected to follow at least the basic principles of EC procurement law under trade agreements. The EC's regime has also influenced the design of other regimes, such as the World Trade Organization's (WTO) Agreement on Government Procurement (GPA). Therefore, it is worth taking a closer look at EC public procurement regulations as an example of a public procurement regulatory regime (Arrowsmith, 2009).

EU member states have signed up to EU procurement law as laid down in the European directives of public procurement. The directives were introduced in the 1970s but have since undergone several revisions. Consistent with the EU principle of free movement of goods and people, the European directives work on the basis of non-discrimination due to nationality, equality, transparency, and proportionality; contracts should not be awarded due to the nationality of the supplier. The European directives prescribe the procedures, with which companies must comply, making public procurement a rather complex and slow process.

The most important specific provisions of the EC Treaty for public procurement are Article 28 on free movement of goods and Article 49 on freedom to provide services. Only in exceptional circumstances can these provisions be circumvented, usually in cases of public security, such as defence procurement from national suppliers to ensure a national defence capability. Discriminatory procurement can be justified on the basis of environmental protection and improvement of working conditions although this remains a grey area. However, purely economic interests can never be used to justify restrictions on trade, and supporting jobs or employment in uncompetitive industries or developing infant industries also cannot be used as a justification (Arrowsmith, 2009: 256).

The EC directives on public procurement regulate the procedures for awarding major contracts and provide the means to enforce these. These procedures are based on the principle of transparency. The Public Sector Directive applies to all entities including state/government departments, local and regional authorities/municipal authorities and federal state governments, associations formed by public bodies, and those bodies governed by public law. The first procurement directives focused on 'works' and 'supply' contracts. These have since been extended to encompass other situations.

The directives apply only to contracts above certain financial thresholds revised every two years (see Table 3.2 for key thresholds). For lower value tenders, only national public procurement rules apply but the general EU principals of transparency and equal treatment should be respected. In principle, the relevant value for determining the threshold is the value of each contract. The EC directives prohibit buyers from dividing contracts in order to bring the value of contracts below the threshold.

The so-called 'light touch' regime for social and other specific services raises the thresholds, for example, to €750,000 in the case of public works contracts. Further exclusions are, for example, contracts governed by different procedural rules connected with joint projects with non-member states, those by international bodies (e.g. the United Nations or the World Bank), and defence contracts.

3.7.2 Public procurement award procedures

Public sector authorities must use one of six types of award procedures. As a general rule the first two of these, open and restricted, should be used; the others require special circumstances (Article 28). In brief, these are:

TABLE 3.2 Thresholds triggering EU-wide rules (Directive 2014/2024/EU)

Central government authorities	Works contracts, subsidised works contracts	€5538000	
	All services concerning social and other specific services listed in Annex XIV	€750000	
	All subsidized services	€221000	
	All other service contracts and all design contests	€143000	
	All supplies contracts awarded by contracting authorities not operating in the field of defence	€143000	
	Supplies contracts awarded by contracting authorities operating in the field of defence	Concerning products listed in Annex III	€143000
		Concerning other products	€221000
Sub-central contracting authorities	Works contracts, subsidized works contracts	€5538000	
	All services concerning social and other specific services listed in Annex XIV	€750000	
	All other service contracts, all design contests, subsidized service contracts, all supplies contracts	€221000	

Source: European Commission (n.d.)

1 Open procedure:

This is a formal tendering (bidding) procedure that requires: clear specifications as the basis for submission of bids; advertisement of the contract in the EU's Tenders Electronic Daily (TED) portal; allowing all interested firms to bid; and evaluation of bids without entering into significant negotiations. The directive specifies minimum time limits for the key phases to ensure suppliers have sufficient time to respond (at least 35 days to tender from the date of dispatch of the contract notice).

2 Restricted procedure:

This is also a formal tendering procedure that again must be advertised in the EU's Tenders Electronic Daily (TED) portal. The main difference from the open procedure is that the public procurement authority can select a limited number to bid from those who express interest. The authority may invite a pre-stated number of firms to bid, although this should be at least five, and it should indicate which evaluation criteria will be used. Authorities must allow at least 37 days for firms to respond and 40 days to bid, although an accelerated version of the procedure (10 and 15 days respectively) is available for cases of urgency.

3 Competitive negotiated procedure:

This is a relatively less structured competitive procedure, requiring advertisement of the contract in the Tenders Electronic Daily (TED) portal and selected participating suppliers but procurement bodies may proceed to select the supplier simply through negotiations. The same award criteria as other procedures must be used, but the directives do not otherwise regulate the process for choosing the best offer. This can only be used in special cases including those where specifications cannot be drawn up with sufficient precision in order to enter formal tendering under the open or restricted procedures, where works are purely for research, experiment, or development purposes, or in exceptional cases where overall pricing is not possible e.g. because of the nature of the works or risks of performance. Examples of this procedure could be the restoration of historical buildings where limited experts are available.

4 Competitive dialogue:

The competitive dialogue procedure was introduced in 2004 to provide more flexibility in awarding complex contracts, especially for major infrastructure projects. It applies to situations where the procurement body is unable to define the technical, financial, or legal aspects of the project, typically because the body does not have the required know-how. The competitive dialogue procedure requires advertisement of the contract in the Tenders Electronic Daily (TED) portal; selection of a limited number of suppliers to participate (minimum three); a dialogue phase to determine proposed solutions; a final tender stage.

5 Innovation partnership:

This process can be used in circumstances where the goods, works, and services to be procured are innovative, and there is an intention to include both the development and purchase elements in the procedure, provided they correspond to agreed performance levels and maximum costs (EC, 2021). This procedure allows for the combination of research, innovation, and procurement and is conducted in three phases. 1) The tendering phase when the suitable partner(s) are selected; 2) the partner(s) develop the new solution in collaboration with the contracting authority (this phase can be divided into sub-stages to gradually reduce the numbers of partners); 3) the commercial phase when the partner(s) provide the results.

6 Design contest:

A design contest is a public promise of a prize issued by a contracting authority to select creative works such as spatial planning, urban design, or architectural designs. The contest enables the authority to evaluate entries for specific projects and may involve negotiating with the winning author for further procurement. Recent updates to public procurement law have expanded its scope to include IT and innovation-focused projects while maintaining the transfer of economic rights from the selected author.

3.7.3 Framework agreements

The principle of open competition is core to EC public procurement regulation but regulation allows for long-term framework agreements, in recognition of the benefits of long-term partnerships that are widely used by private sector companies. Article 1(5) Directive 2004/18/EC defines a framework agreement as

> an agreement between one or more contracting authorities and one or more economic operators, the purpose of which is to establish the terms governing contracts to be awarded during a given period, in particular, with regard to price and, where appropriate, the quantity envisaged.

Framework agreements allow the central negotiation of a contract, while permitting devolved users to manage their spending (Caldwell et al., 2005). Framework agreements are appropriate for repeat purchases, in particular when it is difficult to estimate the timing or quantity of requirements.

Framework agreements involve advertising the requirement and obtaining tenders, selecting a limited number of suppliers (or even a single supplier), and then placing orders on a periodic basis. This avoids the need for a wholly new tendering procedure for every new order. They do not constitute a special type of award procedure, but a variation of the directives' normal procedures.

3.7.4 Rules on specifications and contract award criteria

Article 23(8) prohibits buyers from referring to goods of a specific make or source, or to a particular process, or to trademarks, patents, types, origin, or means of production, where this has the effect of favouring or eliminating certain firms or products. Public procurement bodies must define specifications in one of two ways (or a mixture of the two):

1. By reference to specified European or international standards (e.g. ISO), or if necessary national-level standards. The reference must be accompanied by the words 'or equivalent' and functional equivalents must be accepted.
2. By using performance or functional requirements: when standards do exist authorities can choose either these or performance or functional requirements. When standards do not exist, authorities must use performance or functional specifications.

Contracts must be awarded on either lowest price basis or the most economically advantageous (Article 53). The latter allows consideration of non-price as well as price criteria. In any case the permitted criteria must be linked to the subject matter of the contract. This means, in particular, that authorities cannot take account of social or environmental considerations unconnected with contract performance. The authority must disclose in the advertisement or contract documents the criteria to be used and their relative weighting.

3.7.5 Using public procurement as a lever for sustainable development

This section, 'The special case of public procurement', began by stating that EU member states increasingly use procurement to promote their own policy goals. This remains a controversial issue under the EC procurement regime but an international study of public procurement, documenting procurement changes across 13 countries, found that public procurement is moving towards a policy role enabling alignment of procurement policy with government policy, effectively engaging procurement as a lever of social reform (Harland et al., 2004).

As illustrated in Figure 3.11, sustainable public procurement sits at the interface between sustainable development and public procurement and is a growing trend globally. A survey comparing sustainable procurement practices across 20 countries found that buying from local suppliers, especially small and medium enterprises (SMEs), in ways that protect worker welfare was relatively common in all countries (Brammer and Walker, 2011).

The focus on buying from small and local suppliers, not least in the UK, is at odds with public procurement regulation and could be seen to distort competition. Even more controversial is the way in which governments used public procurement to 'kick start' the economy following the economic recession that began in 2008. Aligning procurement strategy with government strategy is clearly a strategic positioning of procurement, progressing procurement from a transaction and cost-focused function to a strategic

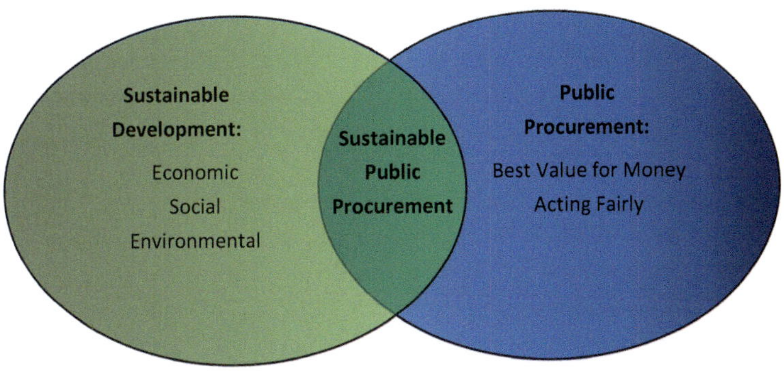

FIGURE 3.11 Sustainable public procurement at the crossroads of sustainable development and public procurement
Source: Adapted from Roos (2012)

contributor, but careful attention must be paid to ensure public procurement regulations are respected.

Public procurement legislation has been continuously adapted worldwide to keep up with best practices and innovation. This is particularly the case in developing countries: recent publications of the OECD-DAC Task Force on Procurement demonstrate progress in strengthening national procurement systems by following a structured approach to procurement reform and capacity development.[1] The EU is increasingly focused on integration of environmental and social criteria into public procurement processes and has set ambitious targets for its member states. The EC public procurement strategy outlines six priorities:

1. To ensure the wider uptake of innovative, green, and social procurement;
2. To professionalize public buyers;
3. To increase access to procurement markets;
4. To improve transparency, integrity, and data;
5. To boost the digital transformation of procurement;
6. To cooperate to procure together.

In addition to the focus on sustainability, the EC public procurement strategy therefore also focuses on innovation in order to support public procurement of innovation. This is part of an ambition to dispense with the bureaucracy and risk avoidance culture that have traditionally hampered public procurement. The move towards public procurement of innovation addresses both the need for innovation in the process and outcomes of innovation. This implies, for example, that public buyers are encouraged to become involved in the research and development of products or services that do not yet exist and to facilitate the success of start-up companies (European Commission, 2017).

The concept of innovation procurement (IP) has emerged, defined as the process by which organizations procure novel solutions to satisfy unmet needs, fostering innovation while delivering better outcomes. Innovation procurement can take two forms:

- Buying the *outcomes* of innovation or *Public Procurement of Innovation* (PPI): Procuring new-to-market solutions with substantially novel characteristics. In PPI, public authorities act as early adopters, leveraging their purchasing power, to shape markets and accelerate the diffusion of innovation.
- Buying the *process* of innovation or *Pre-Commercial Procurement* (PCP): Procuring R&D services to co-develop solutions that do not yet exist. PCP is a specific form of innovation procurement focused on the R&D phase. Buyers describe their needs, prompting businesses and researchers to develop innovative products, services, or processes, which do not yet exist on the market. This enables public buyers to procure R&D services in a phased approach (solution exploration, prototyping, and testing) without acquiring the final product.

Australia, the US, and Japan use similar frameworks and initiatives are spreading to other major emerging economies such as Mexico, Argentina, Brazil, and some developing countries (Roos, 2012).

3.8 CASE STUDY: STRATEGIC PROCUREMENT AT BMW GROUP

3.8.1 Company background

Established in 1916 BMW (Bayerische Motoren Werke AG) is a global car and motorcycle manufacturer. Having started life as an aerospace and automotive engine producer, BMW began making cars in 1928. Over its nearly 100-year long history of car manufacturing, BMW became famous for making sporty cars such as the *Neue Klasse* (New Class) 1500/2000 series of the 1960s and early 1970s, the 3.0 CSL of the 1970s, and the 3-series, 5-series, 6-series, and 7-series, to mention just some of its most well-known cars. The marketing slogan of 'the ultimate driving machine' was created in 1974 and is still central to how the company defines itself relative to the competition.

In 1994 BMW took over the British car company Rover Group, which included several classic British car brands including Rover, Land Rover, MG, Triumph, and Mini. BMW sold the Rover Group in 2000 but retained ownership of the Mini brand and in 1998 the company also acquired Rolls Royce. Although the years of running the Rover Group were problematic, the experience with off-road manufacturer Land Rover was instrumental in BMW's development of its first Sports Utility Vehicle (SUV) the X5 launched in 1999. BMW also retained the popular Mini brand from Rover Group which it has developed into a range of small but stylish vehicles, giving it access to new areas of the market. In 2023 it was the ninth-largest car manufacturer globally and is frequently ranked as the global leader in the premium automotive segment. According to Kantar's 2024 automotive brand valuation, BMW was ranked the third most valuable automotive brand globally only behind Tesla and Toyota.

Like all the other vehicle manufacturers worldwide, BMW has been transforming its powertrains from internal combustion engines (ICE) towards electrification. For a company with a proud history in developing and producing world-leading ICE-engines, this transition has not been easy, yet it was an early mover into electric cars when in launched the battery-electric vehicle (BEV) i3 in 2013, which was the third best-selling EV in 2014 only behind the Nissan Leaf and Tesla Model S. Nevertheless, BMW did not keep up the momentum and ended up having to play catch-up before fully committing to developing a range of BEV vehicles during the last few years. In 2017, when Tesla sold 480,000 Model 3s, BMW's combined sales of BEV cars was 33,676 (BMW Group Report, 2017). BMW did not launch its Tesla Model 3 competitor, the i4, until November 2021.

Despite the delay in rolling out a range of EVs, the company is keen to emphasize its strong dedication to sustainability. The BMW Group Report 2024 includes the following sustainability statement (91):

> The BMW Group believes that its ability to create value and perform at a high level lies in balancing its economic, environmental and social responsibilities. The BMW Group has a long tradition of being responsible and

forward-thinking when it comes to environmental protection, our people and our commitment to society. It is only natural, then, that in recent years we have expanded our focus beyond our own operations to our entire value chain, including our upstream supply chains and the lifecycle of our products after they have been delivered to our customers.

3.8.2 A global production network

BMW Group manufactured 2,513,830 vehicles in 2023. Its production network comprises 33 plants across 16 countries, including Spartanburg in the USA, Dadong and Tiexi in China, Regensburg, Dingolfing, Leipzig, and Munich (Germany), Oxford (UK), and San Luis Potosi (Mexico) to name some of the largest plants. Compared with the likes of Tesla that only makes BEV cars, BMW has decided to pursue multiple powertrain technologies and therefore produce BEV, ICE, and plug-in hybrid (PHEV) cars, and is slowly beginning hydrogen car production. Instead of having dedicated production plants only for BEV cars, BMW Group has a flexible production network that allows for manufacturing of all-electric BEV cars, plug-in hybrid drive cars, and conventional combustion cars on one single line.

The BMW Group sources vehicle parts near its production sites whenever practical, using local purchasing teams in key markets to address regional risks and opportunities quickly. BMW Group sources battery cells near its production sites, following a 'local for local' purchasing strategy. The company evaluates its supply chain for critical components by systematically assessing geopolitical risks and economic efficiency within pertinent regions, aiming to mitigate geopolitical dependencies and associated risks. Figure 3.12 gives an overview of sourcing locations.

3.8.3 Purchasing and supplier network

BMW Group's Purchasing and Supplier Network Division is responsible for global procurement and quality assurance with an annual expenditure of €91.8 billion (2024). In view of this level of purchase spend, top management recognizes that Purchasing and Supplier Network plays a strategically important role in BMW group. Reducing material costs is a key function of the Purchasing Division, achieved through production efficiencies, contract synergies for future projects, and negotiating inflation-related expenses. As of June 2025, Nicolai Martin is the member of the Board of Management responsible for Purchasing and Supplier Network Division.

As a premium vehicle manufacturer quality is paramount. Therefore, the BMW Group has strict measures for quality control and assurance and a focus on continuous improvement. This extends to suppliers that are audited for their quality and receive training on processes such as problem solving and risk assessment. Purchasing's role is cross-functional, assuming a "key role in the interdisciplinary matrix of technology clusters and BMW vehicle production lines, working with other areas to optimize material costs" (BMW Group Report 2024: 65).

Faced with increasing global supply chain risks, maintaining supplies and deliveries to BMW Group plants is a key target of the purchasing strategy. Beyond

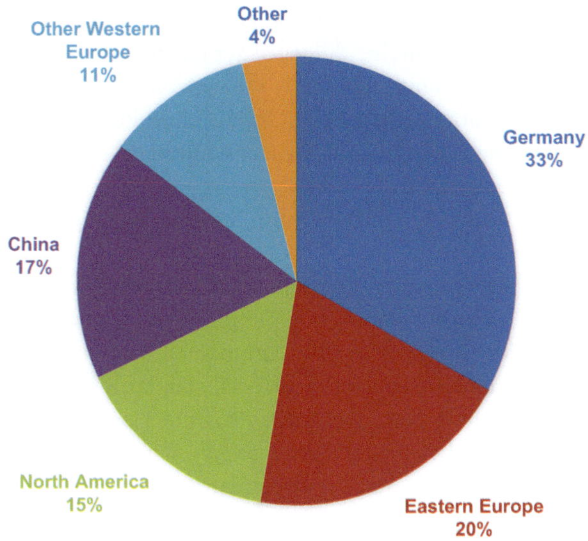

FIGURE 3.12 Distribution of BMW Group purchasing (direct and indirect spend)
Source: Adapted BMW (2024: 63)

challenges like competition and sourcing raw materials, supply chains are increasingly impacted by regulations – including trade restrictions, security concerns, digitalization, sustainability requirements – and by environmental and extreme weather events. The BMW Group IT system *RiskHub* plays a key role in making the company's global supply chains more resilient to external disruptions. This includes the use of AI to detect risks early on and develop mitigation strategies. The Catena-X digital ecosystem is being developed to standardize data exchange across relevant parts of the value chain. Catena-X makes data from sub-tier suppliers available, including information concerning origin, material composition, and recycling. This system enables BMW Group to trace components across multi-tier supply chains.

There has been a concerted effort to improve supply chain risk management. For example, during the global chip shortage (2020–2022), BMW diversified its semiconductor supply to mitigate disruption, including forming closer relationships with multiple chipmakers. BMW now has contracts with multiple battery suppliers (e.g. CATL, Samsung SDI, Northvolt) to secure supplies for its growing EV production.

3.8.4 Sustainable purchasing and supply chain: a critical driver

The company's commitment to sustainability also drives its Purchasing and Supplier Network strategy. The BMW Group Supplier Code of Conduct:

> … sets out the details of the guiding principles listed in the 'Policy Statement on Respect for Human Rights and corresponding Environmental Standards'

> for the global supplier network. These are based on legal regulations, such as the German supply chain due diligence act (Lieferkettensorgfaltspflichtengesetz, LkSG), as well as internationally recognized standards such as the International Bill of Human Rights, the UN Guiding Principles on Business and Human Rights, the OECD Guidelines for Multinational Enterprises, as well as the ILO core labor standards and the principles of the UN Global Compact.
>
> BMW Group Supplier Code of Conduct (2022: 3)

Similarly to the company's quality processes, BMW Group offer courses on sustainability in the supply chain for its internal purchaser staff as well as and suppliers, and it expects first-tier suppliers to offer comparable training for their suppliers. These courses focus on environmental and social standards and BMW group's due diligence measures, teaching participants how to detect and mitigate sustainability risks. The programme *Re:Drive Sustainable Supply Chains* trains purchasing staff and suppliers on environmental and social standards, CO_2 reductions, and the circular economy. Follow-up support is also available to help suppliers implement their measures.

The BMW Group participates in several industry and cross-sector initiatives, including the Sector Dialogue (*Branchendialog Automobilindustrie*), the VDA's Supply Chain Sustainability Working Group, the Responsible Business Alliance (RBA), and Drive Sustainability. These initiatives often involve multiple stakeholders, such as companies, trade unions, and NGOs representing workers' interests. The BMW Group remains actively committed to these efforts. The company aims to benefit local communities by supporting development projects for mica, cobalt, and natural rubber.

The use of secondary materials and the use of electricity from renewable sources e.g. in battery cell production reduces the company's carbon footprint. The BMW Group Circular Economy Strategy not only aims to reduce the use of primary raw materials and thereby lowering the consumption of natural resources, but also aims to strengthen supply chain resilience

3.8.5 Suppliers and startups as sources of innovation

Modern cars are packed with technology and BMW Group wants to be at the forefront of technological innovation to stay one step ahead of competitors in the premium car segment. Prominent examples include new drive technologies for BEV and PHEV powered cars e.g. battery and charging technology, the use of AI in engineering, production, and quality management, and purchasing processes (e.g. an AI tender assistant supporting procurement teams), automated driving, and vehicle connectivity.

BMW Group's innovation strategy is based on open innovation. This means partnering with technology firms and fostering new business relationships, not least startups. *BMW Startup Garage*[2] and *BMW i Ventures* have been created to tap into startups. Where *BMW i Ventures* invests in technology start-ups, the *BMW Startup Garage* is tasked with scouting for innovations; it assesses over 1,000 startups each year. The aim is to evaluate and empower start-ups to become suppliers and partners.

There is also emphasis on collaboration within technology clusters that enable the company to access and develop advanced technologies, supported by ongoing exchanges with strategic suppliers. A central part of ensuring supplier involvement in innovation, BMW Group's Supplier Innovation Awards was established in 2014. The goal is "to inspire suppliers to go beyond their traditional roles and become active participants in shaping the future of automotive technology". Past award winners include:

- CATL (Contemporary Amperex Technologies Co. Ltd.) was recognized in the drive train and e-mobility category for its battery cell and module work. As BMW's strategic partner, CATL helped optimize the battery system, increasing energy content in existing space.
- Continental Automotive GmbH Regensburg and NXP Semiconductors were recognized in the digitalization category for their collaboration on the Ultra-Wideband technology utilized in the BMW Digital Key Plus. This innovation enables drivers to employ their smartphones as car keys, providing enhanced convenience and security relative to alternative wireless technologies.

BMW's Supplier Innovation Award has been instrumental in creating an ecosystem of innovation that extends beyond the company itself and into its supplier network. It is clear that the Purchasing and Supplier Networks Division is integral to ensuring that BMW continues to offer its premium customers the ultimate driving machine in a sustainable and reliable manner. As explained by Alexander Scholz, Head of Digital Supply Chain Projects: "More than 70% of our total value added is generated by our suppliers; this is not only value added from a monetary point of view but also from an innovation point of view" (ASUG, 2024).

3.9 CONCLUSIONS

This chapter has evaluated a wide range of issues concerning procurement strategy and organization. We began by defining strategic procurement in terms of alignment between corporate objectives and procurement objectives. This means that the competitive priorities that drive procurement decisions should support or even drive corporate strategy. We introduced a sustainable procurement maturity model as an analytical model to identify the stage of sustainable procurement maturity within a company.

Surveys show that procurement has become more strategic. The economic crisis in 2008–2009 increased the profile and visibility of procurement as senior executives realized the amount of cost and risk controlled by the procurement function, and therefore the significance of procurement in transforming corporate performance. Recent crises including the Covid-19 pandemic and the changing global geopolitical context radically increase supply chain risks pushing procurement further to the fore.

Chapter 3 also examined different ways of organizing the procurement function. The traditional trade-offs between centralized and decentralized models were discussed, including ways to combine these two extremes into hybrid models. Centre-led (rather than centralized) procurement organizations may be ideally suited to addressing the needs for synergy and corporate coherence while avoiding the traditional drawbacks of centralized structures; centre-led structures are also important to ensure coherent sustainability policies and requirements. Procurement professionals, the people that make up organizations, are increasingly presented with a wider portfolio of challenges, which in turn require different skills and competencies. In addition to functional, or hard, skills such as negotiation and spend analysis, current and future professionals need strong management and leadership skills. The sustainability challenge means that procurement professionals need to learn a host of new skills, such as how to do risk assessments and ethical supplier audits but also how to collaborate with CSR specialists within and outside the company.

Chapter 3 devoted a final section to discussing the particular characteristics of public sector procurement, usually called public procurement, and the complexities of public procurement in particular its regulatory nature. We outlined the most important public procurement regulations, focusing on EC directives, and discussed the background for these and when and how they need to be considered in the procurement process. We concluded this section by exploring how public procurement is increasingly used as a lever for policy changes, not only changes in sustainable development but also innovation: the public sector is striving to change procurement from a transaction and cost-focused function to a strategic contributor playing a key role in sustainable economic development.

NOTES

1 The Organisation for Economic Co-operation and Development (OECD) Development Assistance Committee. See http://www.oecd.org/dac/

2 https://www.bmwstartupgarage.com

REFERENCES

Arrowsmith S (2009) EC regime of public procurement. In: K Thai (ed) *International Handbook of Public Procurement*. Boca Raton, FL: CRC Press, Auerbach Publications Taylor & Francis Group: 251–284.

ASUG (2024) Inside the BMW group's ConnectedProcurement Program: Enhancing efficiency and collaboration with SAP solutions. https://www.asug.com/insights/inside-the-bmw-groups-connectedprocurement-program-enhancing-efficiency-and-collaboration-with-sap-solutions

Bakker E, Walker H, Schotanus F and Harland C (2008) Choosing an organizational form: The case of collaborative procurement initiatives. *International Journal of Procurement Management* 1(3): 297–317.

Bals L and Turkulainen V (2017) Achieving efficiency and effectiveness in purchasing and supply management: Organization design and outsourcing. *Journal of Purchasing Supply Management* 23(4): 256–267.

Beske-Janssen P, Johnsen T, Constant F and Wieland A (2023) New competences enhancing procurement´s contribution to innovation and sustainability. *Journal of Procurement & Supply Management* 29(3): 100847.

BMW (2017) BMW Group Report.

BMW (2022) BMW Group Supplier Code of Conduct.

BMW (2024) BMW Group Report.

Bowen FE, Cousins PD, Lamming RC and Faruk AC (2001) Horses for courses: Explaining the gap between the theory and practice of green supply. *Greener Management International* 35(Autumn): 41–60.

Brammer SJ and Walker HL (2011) Sustainable procurement in the public sector: An international comparative study. *International Journal of Operations and Production Management* 31: 452–476.

Caldwell N, Walker H, Harland C, Knight L, Zheng J and Wakeley T (2005) Promoting competitive markets: The role of public procurement. *Journal of Procurement and Supply Management* 11(5–6): 242–251.

Christensen CM (1997) *The Innovator's Dilemma: When New Technologies Cause Great Firms to Fail*. Boston, MA: Harvard Business School Press.

CIPS (2025) CIPS *Procurement & Supply Salary Guide 2025*. https://www.cips.org/careers/salary-guide

CIPS/Hays (2023) *Procurement Salary Guide 2023*.

Deloitte (2021) 2021 Global Chief Procurement Officer Survey. https://www.deloitte.com/lu/en/services/consulting/research/global-cpo-survey.html

Deloitte (2023) 2023 Global Chief Procurement Officer Survey: Observations, challenges, and trends in procurement. https://www.deloitte.com/us/en/services/consulting/services/procurement-strategy.html

Englyst L, Jørgensen F, Johansen J and Mikkelsen OS (2008) Commodity team motivation and performance. *Journal of Procurement and Supply Management* 14(1): 15–27.

Essig M (2000) Procurement consortia as symbiotic relationships: Developing the concept of consortium sourcing. *European Journal of Procurement and Supply Management* 6: 13–22.

European Commission [EC] (2017) Consultation document on guidance on public procurement of innovation. https://ec.europa.eu/docsroom/documents/25724/attachments/1/translations/en/renditions/native

European Commission (2021) Directorate-General for Internal Market, Industry, Entrepreneurship and SMEs, Innovation partnership – Quick guide from practitioners. *Publications Office of the European Union*. https://data.europa.eu/doi/10.2873/78891.

EY (2022) Global Chief Procurement Officer Survey: The post-pandemic world for procurement.

European Commission (n.d.) Thresholds. https://single-market-economy.ec.europa.eu/single-market/public-procurement/legal-rules-and-implementation/thresholds_en

Faes W, Matthyssens P and Vandenbempt K (2000) The pursuit of global procurement synergy. *Industrial Marketing Management* 29(6): 539–553.

Goold M and Campbell A (2000) Taking stock of synergy: A framework for assessing linkages between businesses. *Long Range Planning* 33(1): 72–96.

Harland CM, Knight LA, Caldwell ND and Telgen J (2004) Government reform and public procurement – Executive report of the first workshop. *International Research Study on Public Procurement*, University of Bath, UK.

Hastings C and Harland C (2003) Radical reform of strategic procurement and supply in complex confederal networks – The case of the police service. CRiSPS Seminar, 29 January, University of Bath, UK.

Hayes RH and Wheelwright SC (1984) *Restoring Our Competitive Edge: Competing Through Manufacturing*. New York: John Wiley.

Howitt R (2025) The state of sustainability reporting by United States business in 2025, Reuters Events. White paper.

John G (2018) The fine art of procurement organization design. https://www.gartner.com/en/supply-chain/insights/power-of-the-profession-blog/fine-art-procurement-organization-design (accessed 19 July 2024).

Johnsen T, Marques L, Miemczyk J, Ritter T and Howard M (2024) Towards a sustainable procurement maturity model: Insights from a 10-year longitudinal case study. IPSERA conference 2024, Rio de Janeiro, Brazil.

Martindale N (2008) Collective action. Supply Business. www.supplybusiness.com

Morgan G (1986) *Images of Organization*. Newbury Park, CA: Sage Publications.

Organisation for Economic Cooperation and Development [OECD] (2021) Public procurement. https://www.oecd.org/en/topics/policy-issues/public-procurement.html

Ozsevim I (2023) Interview Jacqui Rock, NHS England's Chief Commercial Officer. *Supply Chain Digital*. https://supplychaindigital.com/interviews/jacqui-rock

PERISCOPE (n.d.) https://eu-periscope.essca.fr/

Porter ME (1996) What is strategy? *Harvard Business Review* 74(6): 61–78.

Reck RF and Long BG (1988) Procurement: A competitive weapon. *Journal of Procurement and Materials Management* 24(3): 2–8.

Roos R (2012) United Nations Procurement Capacity Building Centre and United Nations Environment Programme: Sustainable public procurement. Briefing note.

Rozemeijer FA (2000) How to manage corporate procurement synergy in a decentralised company: Towards design rules for managing and organising procurement synergy in decentralised companies. *European Journal of Procurement and Supply Management* 6: 5–12.

Rozemeijer FA, van Weele A and Weggeman M (2003) Creating corporate advantage through procurement: Toward a contingency model. *Journal of Supply Chain Management* 39(4): 4–13.

Schultze H, Bals L and Johnsen TE (2019) Individual competences for sustainable purchasing and supply management (SPSM): A literature and practice perspective. *International Journal of Physical Distribution & Logistics Management* 49(3): 287–304.

Tassabehji R, and Moorhouse A (2008) The changing role of procurement: Developing professional effectiveness. *Journal of Purchasing and Supply Management* 14(1): 55–68.

Tella E and Virolainen V (2005) Motives behind procurement consortia. *International Journal of Production Economics* 93–94: 161–168.

Trautmann G, Bals L and Hartmann E (2009) Global sourcing in integrated network structures: The case of hybrid procurement organizations. *Journal of International Management* 15(2): 194–208.

van Hoek R, Sankararaman V, Udesen T, Geurts T and Palumbo-Miele D (2020) Where we are heading and the research that can help us get there – Executive perspectives on the anniversary of the Journal of Purchasing and Supply Management. *Journal of Purchasing and Supply Management* 26: 100621.

CHAPTER 4

Sourcing strategy and supplier relationship management

LEARNING OBJECTIVES:

At the end of this chapter you should be able to:

- Define and evaluate the advantages and disadvantages of a range of sourcing strategies, including single- and multi-sourcing as well as hybrid sourcing strategies including parallel, network, and triadic sourcing;
- Evaluate the appropriateness of different sourcing strategies when facing high risk of supply chain disruption;
- Illustrate and apply sourcing and supplier relationship portfolio models;
- Understand critical relationship constructs including trust and power;
- Explain the concept of dark side relationships;
- Explain the concept of supplier relationship assessment as an alternative to supplier assessment.

4.1 INTRODUCTION

This chapter concerns two important issues in procurement and supply management: sourcing strategy and supplier relationship management (SRM). Sourcing strategy is often used to imply different things. Leaving the major question of where to source from (local or global sourcing) to Chapter 5, this chapter begins by examining three aspects of sourcing strategy. First, the structural decision concerning how many suppliers should be used for the purchase of the same, or very similar, items. We evaluate the strategies known as single sourcing, multi-sourcing, and various forms of hybrid sourcing. Second, we examine sourcing decisions that concern the purchase of items that represent different categories and therefore different procurement and supply chain management challenges. Purchase categories typically concern different types of product (or service) but in addition to category segmentation it is necessary to consider how items differ in terms of cost (or value) and supply market risk and complexity. Third, we evaluate the question of the type of supplier relationship that is appropriate for different supply situations, in particular the

DOI: 10.4324/9781003499602-5

relevance of partnership sourcing compared with more arm's-length adversarial sourcing strategies.

Different sourcing situations call for different supplier relationships and this chapter places particular emphasis on different trends in supplier relationship models. In short, the general trend in recent years has been to rely on fewer but more strategic suppliers; attention is directed towards those suppliers that represent the highest level of risk and value. In general, therefore, we can identify a long-term trend towards more collaborative and strategic supplier partnerships. Nevertheless, recent years have seen many companies shy away from too much dependency on single suppliers as this represents a high risk for companies.

Where companies have an SRM function, suppliers are likely to have their own customer relationship management (CRM), or similar, function in place to manage their customer relationships. This mirror organizational function suggests that both the customer, or purchaser, and the supplier seek to manage what is effectively the same relationship, merely seen from different sides of the relationship. Understanding the interactive nature of customer-supplier relationships is a useful point of departure so after a brief overview of the history of the evolution of customer-supplier relationship models, this chapter examines a model developed in the 1980s, which encapsulated the complex nature of buyer-supplier relationships: the interaction model. This mindset is important as it emphasizes that suppliers need to be treated as active that can – and should – be sources of value to buying companies. We discuss how to assess buyer-supplier relationships and the concept of preferred and attractive customers. We conclude the chapter by reflecting on the use of digital technology SRM solutions.

4.2 SOURCING STRATEGY

The concept of sourcing strategy encompasses several dimensions. In addition to the major, complex issue to do with geographical location, i.e. local or global sourcing, which is separately examined in Chapter 6, one important aspect of sourcing strategy concerns the structural decision of how many suppliers should be used for the purchase of the same, or very similar, items. Another important aspect of sourcing strategy is the need to develop an approach which is appropriate for the particular nature of the purchase item. This decision is about different purchase categories and different purchase situations; it is about finding the appropriate response to different situations that represent fundamentally different challenges.

4.2.1 Structural sourcing options

At the two extremes, procurement and supply chain managers would normally distinguish between a multi-sourcing (or 'multiple') strategy and a single- (or sole) sourcing strategy.

Multi-sourcing is the use of several suppliers for buying the same or very similar products or services. For example, a company can choose to source office stationery from three or four suppliers. These suppliers would offer practically the same products and even if the buyer might choose to buy different types of stationery from the different suppliers, they have the option of switching supplier if necessary. Therefore, the company avoids dependency on any single supplier and spreads the risk as much as possible. Companies can 'play off' suppliers against each other, especially if they are made aware of the presence of the other suppliers. Traditionally, using several suppliers is regarded as good practice because the buyer avoids a high degree of dependency, or 'lock-in', always maintaining alternative supply options. However, multi-sourcing is a strategy that seeks to create and capitalize on an adversarial atmosphere within buyer-supplier relationships; this strategy still has its place but is becoming increasingly outdated as companies require more collaborative supplier relationships.

One of the observations of the superior performing Japanese automotive industry in the 1990s (e.g. Womack et al., 1990; Nishiguchi, 1994) was that, unlike their Western counterparts, the Japanese manufacturers did not multi-source from suppliers – they single-sourced. Instead of focusing on getting the best deal from suppliers by emphasizing competition amongst these, lean Japanese manufacturers used extensive single-sourcing strategies.

Defined as the fulfilment of all corporate requirements for a particular product by one selected supplier (Treleven and Schweikhart, 1988), single sourcing was pursued by lean Japanese automotive manufacturers, especially Toyota, who deliberately adopted a long-term perspective towards operational and supply chain performance improvement. Choosing to accept and manage the risks associated with dependency, Japanese manufacturers chose to increase purchase volumes from fewer suppliers and, perhaps more importantly, to commit to and invest in those suppliers, for example through supplier development programmes. This strategy enabled the single-source suppliers to benefit from economies of scale and helped the Japanese manufacturers to obtain not only lower prices but lower underlying supply chain costs. In other words, where multi-sourcing allows the buyer to reduce the contribution margins of suppliers, single sourcing reduces cost but not necessarily margins. Moreover, keeping a smaller total number of direct suppliers significantly reduces the costs of negotiation with, and managing, a large supply base and therefore transaction costs.

Nevertheless, on further inspection of the Japanese method the reality appeared to be more complex. Research by Richardson (1993) showed that in the 1990s Toyota only single-sourced 28 per cent of their vehicle components. Richardson described how the Japanese did not single-source so much as they used a strategy which he termed 'parallel sourcing' defined as:

> ... two or more suppliers with similar capabilities are concurrently sole-source suppliers for very similar components. While using a sole source for a component, the assembler establishes parallel sources to provide performance comparisons and competitive bidders for the next model cycle.
>
> (Richardson, 1993: 342)

Parallel sourcing, as defined by Richardson (1993), therefore provides a way to maintain competition between suppliers that have similar capabilities and deliver the same type of components. Parallel sourcing is a strategy where the buyer seeks to keep its options open, exploring other sources, and thereby putting pressure on the single-source supplier.

Hines (1995) identified another hybrid sourcing strategy which he called network sourcing. At its core, network sourcing involves using multiple suppliers for groups of similar components and distributing volumes to the best performing supplier. Hines' (1995) network sourcing strategy focuses not only on the dyadic level between the buyer and the direct suppliers but also considers indirect suppliers and how these collaborate amongst themselves.

An alternative hybrid sourcing strategy was later proposed by Dubois and Fredriksson (2008): triadic sourcing. Again, this strategy seeks to capture the best of both worlds of cooperation and competition but "the distinctive feature of triadic sourcing is that the buyer actively creates interdependencies between two suppliers" (2008: 170). In other words, where the operations of the two competing suppliers in more traditional sourcing models, apart from creating a sense of competition for the customer's business, are largely decoupled (Wu and Choi, 2005), triadic sourcing specifically seeks to encourage collaboration amongst the three parties. Based on observations from practices at Volvo Cars, Dubois and Fredriksson (2008) describe how triadic sourcing offers opportunities for creating interdependencies between the suppliers. Volvo deliberately makes two suppliers (seat suppliers Lear and JCI) jointly responsible for developing technically interdependent components. Furthermore, Volvo would allow one supplier to produce what the other has developed and vice versa.

Figure 4.1 illustrates the different structural sourcing strategies and their main characteristics. Single and multi-sourcing are simple to illustrate. Parallel sourcing is similar to dual sourcing although whereas the latter is simply about having two suppliers delivering the same product or service, the dual supplier in parallel sourcing is kept as a backup rather than an ongoing second supplier. The concept of network sourcing shifts the focus from dyadic to supply chain or network: at the dyadic level network sourcing relies extensively

	Multi-sourcing	Parallel sourcing	Single sourcing	Network sourcing	Triadic sourcing
Illustration	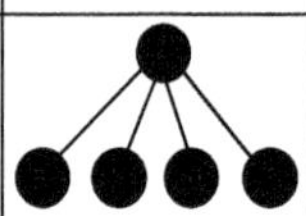	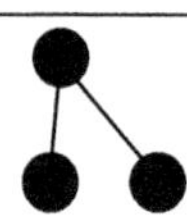		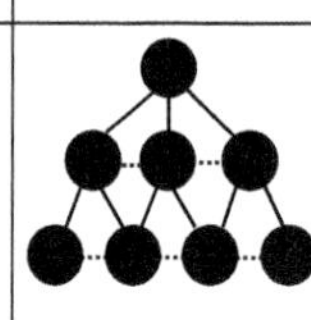	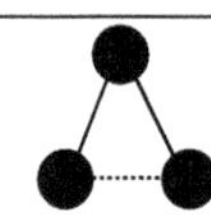
Characteristics	• Competition between suppliers • Spreading risk • Reducing dependency	• Focal firm-supplier collaboration and supplier-supplier competition • Accepting some dependency and risk but backup supplier at hand	• Collaboration between focal firm and supplier • Accepting high degree of dependency • Supplier partnerships	• Focal firm-supplier collaboration • Supplier-supplier collaboration and competition • Delegated tiered supply structure • Parallel/dual sourcing to spread risk	• Collaboration between focal firm and supplier • Competition and facilitated collaboration between suppliers • Reducing dependency

FIGURE 4.1 Sourcing strategies compared

on parallel or dual sourcing and this structure is continued, or cascaded, beyond the dyad into sub-tier suppliers. In addition, suppliers are brought together by the focal firm to share knowledge and transfer best practice. Triadic sourcing again focuses on direct suppliers and does not consider indirect, or sub-tier, suppliers. Like network sourcing, the recent concept of triadic sourcing allows for collaboration between the two dual suppliers but in triadic sourcing this collaboration is taken a step further through focal-firm-initiated interdependencies between the three parties. For example, where in network sourcing there is some sharing of knowledge between suppliers, in triadic sourcing the two suppliers may jointly develop components for (and with) the focal firm and thereby create operational interdependency.

4.2.2 Towards single sourcing – and back to multi-sourcing

A number of empirical studies, most notably part of the International Motor Vehicle Program (IMVP), documented how lean Japanese companies out-performed their Western counterparts in terms of cost, quality, delivery, and innovation advantages. Single and parallel sourcing were seen as an essential explanatory factor in the 'Japanese advantage' (Nishiguchi, 1994); as buyer-supplier collaboration for continuous product development and process improvement was at the heart of this lean supply model (Lamming, 1993), the model was soon labelled as 'partnership sourcing' (Macbeth and Ferguson, 1994) even though the emphasis was on both collaboration and competition.

During the last 15 years or so the Japanese lean supply model has come under scrutiny. Supply chain experts have suggested that some industrial contexts require agile rather than lean practices (e.g. Christopher, 2000). Consequently, question marks over the heavy reliance on single sourcing have been raised as it restricts the ability of companies to cope with radical and unforeseen changes in the environment.

A much-cited example illustrates the risk of single sourcing (Chopra and Sodhi, 2004): when in 2000 lightning hit a power line in Albuquerque (New Mexico), causing a fire at a local plant owned by Dutch electronics giant Philips, two competing Scandinavian mobile phone companies with different sourcing strategies had to take immediate action. Finnish Nokia, which pursued a multi-sourcing strategy, switched its chip orders to other suppliers. Swedish LM Ericsson, which pursued a single-sourcing strategy, was locked in to the one struggling supplier and had no other sources of microchip supply. Ericsson was forced to stop production with very heavy losses (approximately US$400 million). The lesson: in times of stability, where changes are merely small and incremental, single sourcing is a good strategy but in turbulent conditions single sourcing leaves companies at risk.

The global financial crisis, which hit the world in 2008, created such turbulence and uncertainty that companies that had relied on extensive single sourcing found their supply chains unable to cope with the new conditions. With many suppliers struggling to survive, companies faced the problem that their single-source suppliers were unable to supply them on time or even faced bankruptcy.

The Covid-19 crisis sparked even more sourcing disruptions, leading companies to prioritize supply chain risk and resilience. Recent geopolitical changes that have followed in the wake of the war in Ukraine and the global tariff war, have further strengthened this trend. This means that being locked into single source relationships is no longer viewed as desirable. As shown in a survey by McKinsey (2022), many companies have made structural changes to their supply networks by implementing dual or multiple sourcing strategies for critical materials and moving from global to regional networks. 81 per cent of the companies in their survey had implemented dual-sourcing strategies during the past year, up from 55 per cent in 2020. These findings are echoed in other surveys, such as Holgado and Niess (2023), who identified two pre-pandemic recovery sourcing actions:

- Dual- or multiple-sourcing instead of single-sourcing strategies, especially for critical components or materials;
- Local or regional sourcing instead of overseas sourcing.

Procurement managers are therefore becoming much more cautious before entering into single-sourcing agreements. Partnerships with strategic suppliers are still essential but single sourcing implied too high risk. More than ever, a portfolio of different sourcing strategies and different types of supplier relationships is required.

4.2.3 A sourcing portfolio approach

The most widely applied procurement portfolio model is that developed by Kraljic (1983) that specified that purchasing and supply management decisions be taken according to the levels of, first, supply market complexity and, second, importance of the purchase.

1. The first dimension is a key factor in procurement and supply management: it is a measure of the external supply market conditions. As supply markets are becoming increasingly complex, for example, as a result of extensive use of global sourcing, this dimension is as critical as ever.
2. The second measure is another key factor in procurement and supply management: it is a measure of the internal relative importance of the purchase item. Items purchased in high volumes increase the importance of the item.

Later adaptations of the Kraljic model have modified the two dimensions into 'supply risk' and 'profit impact' (e.g. Gelderman and van Weele, 2005), the latter often in practice translated into 'value'. Purchase items should be ranked, e.g. as low and high, or using 1–10 scores on each dimension and then be plotted across the four boxes. Appropriate measures should be identified for the two dimensions. As shown in Figure 4.2 these might be cost and impact on profitability (for the vertical axis) and number of suppliers (low number representing high supply risk) and product novelty or complexity (for the horizontal axis). In addition to emphasizing the need for differentiated strategies for each box, Kraljic (1983) also made the point that whereas companies tend to focus on the non-critical items they should dedicate much more time to the other items which are more challenging, especially strategic items, hence the title of Kraljic's article: 'Purchasing must become supply management'.

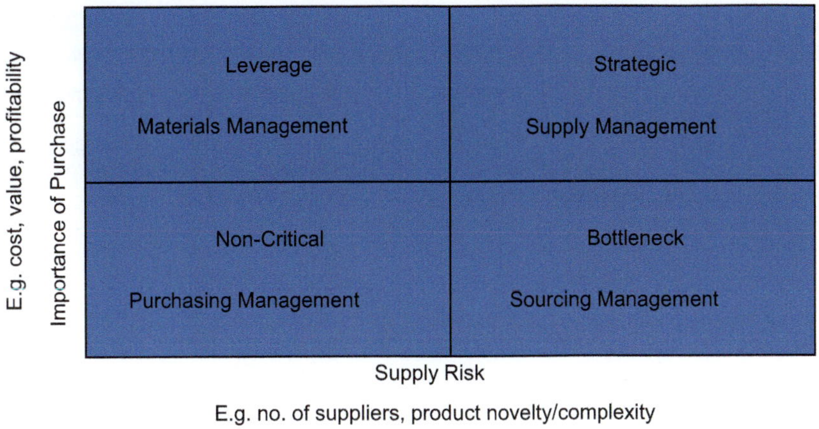

FIGURE 4.2 The Kraljic portfolio model
Source: Adapted from Kraljic (1983)

The four boxes, i.e. purchase situations, require four different strategies, as indicated by each box. Kraljic (1983) suggested that non-critical items were the responsibility of purchasing, bottleneck items needed a focus on sourcing, leverage items required materials management, and strategic items supply management. In his vision, therefore, supply management was a strategic activity; the concept of supply management is used to this day in North America to reflect a strategic function where the combined concept of 'purchasing and supply management' is often used in Europe to encapsulate both tactical and strategic activities. Non-critical items are relatively simple to manage but purchasing managers should be careful not to waste time and money on transactional activities as transaction costs, such as searching for suppliers and negotiating with these, could easily be higher than actual item costs; the focus therefore should be on efficiency. Bottleneck items represent low purchase importance but high supply chain risk. This is a tricky situation because although the item is of low importance it is still likely to create significant problems if it cannot be sourced. The challenge here is therefore to explore alternative sources or to create safety stocks. Finally, leverage items allow for the company to exploit its bargaining power and as these are high cost/value items this is an important task. Whereas Kraljic (1983) basically prescribes diversification for bottleneck items the advice is for full exploitation of power for leverage items. Non-critical and strategic items could be characterized by different buyer-supplier power balances, but again, the buying company should seek a position of power and exploit it where possible. Table 4.1 characterizes each of the four supply situations and typical strategies for managing these.

The Kraljic (1983) model focuses on two variables and so it is perhaps not surprising that the model has been criticized for being over-simplistic (Dubois and Pedersen, 2002). There are also practical implementation problems, such as identifying exactly where to differentiate between categories, category movers, i.e. conditions change over time; it does

TABLE 4.1 Characteristics and appropriate strategies for the four Kraljic categories

	Non-critical	*Leverage*	*Bottleneck*	*Strategic*
Main sourcing focus	Can be multi-sourcing, but focus on efficient processing, reduction of admin cost/time (transaction costs)	Price/cost control Logistics Dual-source LCC sourcing	Secure delivery Reduce dependency and risk: re-source globally Explore alternative designs	Manage TCO Single or parallel source
Make versus buy	Always buy Outsource purchasing	Buy (or make if cost competitive)	Explore options for in-sourcing	Consider in-sourcing (based on strategic core competence analysis)
Number of suppliers	Many but possibly few global service providers	Many approved suppliers (to guarantee competition), few active suppliers	Very few suppliers by definition Constant search for new suppliers	Few suppliers by nature Need to look out for new suppliers
Supplier relationships	Medium to long e.g. framework agreement with full service providers	Competitive bidding short (or medium) term contracts	Long term, nurture relationship	Nurture and develop strategic partnership: trust, commitment, openness...
Price/cost negotiation	Product price is insignificant compared to TCO E-procurement Pool requirements to achieve bargaining power	Constant price reduction pressure Exploit bargaining power, aggressive negotiation E-auctions	Price is not an issue	Open book policy; TCO reduction with risk sharing
Supplier assessment & development policy	Supplier assessment	Supplier assessment Negotiated investment to obtain full benefit	Market/supplier monitoring Limited investment in supplier development	Supplier relationship assessment Co-development and experience sharing with suppliers Invest in supplier development

(*Continued*)

TABLE 4.1 Continued

	Non-critical	*Leverage*	*Bottleneck*	*Strategic*
Early supplier involvement in NPD	No, suppliers can be involved late in NPD	Limited	Purchasing involvement in NPD to avoid bottleneck situation	Yes, as black- or grey-box suppliers
Substitution policy & risk management	No investment Standardization of parts or commodities	Screen the market Cost, productivity & value analysis	Explore product/ supplier substitutes: value analysis Safety stocks, volume insurance (at premium if necessary) Contingency planning	Monitor alternatives: value analysis Risk management
Required information	Good market overview, short-term demand forecast, economic order quantity, inventory levels	Good market data, short to medium term demand planning, accurate vendor data, price / transport rate	Medium term supply/ demand forecasts, very good market data, inventory costs	Long-term supply / demand information, sharing of strategic information e.g. technology roadmaps

Source: Adapted from EFQM (2006)

not take into account that several items representing different boxes may be supplied by the same supplier and that having very different strategies to deal with this supplier is not optimal. Finally, the model focuses on given 'items' and not supplier relationships so it is important to note that it says nothing about how relationships with suppliers might differ even if the different boxes clearly require different types of supplier relationships and that it is strategic items that call for supplier partnerships.

Nevertheless, the model is extensively used by companies around the world to this day and part of its appeal is no doubt its simplicity in application. Some companies encounter the inherent simplicity of the model by having several sophisticated measures of its dimension. Also, by combining different models, for example conducting an initial screening for levels of risk and value, followed by analysis of, say, supplier attractiveness (as suggested by Olsen and Ellram, 1997), may help to avoid being over-simplistic and ignoring important features of the supply situation. This may be an ideal practical method of portfolio model application, however, attempts to over-complicate portfolio analysis arguably imply that they lose their appeal of inherent simplicity (Gelderman and van Weele, 2005).

However, is the Kraljic (1983) model compatible with a focus on sustainability and, if not, how can it be modified? Pagell et al. (2010) evaluated the Kraljic model in light of the need to create sustainable supply chains, suggesting that:

- The horizontal dimension 'Importance of purchase' is purely focused on economic importance. From a sustainability perspective the importance of procurement an item should also include an assessment of importance in terms of its impact on the 'Triple Bottom Line' (TBL): economic, environmental, and social impact.
- The vertical dimension is still a question of supply risk but a TBL focus implies that these are not only economic but also environmental and social. If, for example, a supplier does not comply with the company's standards for labour conditions it indicates a high supply risk. Interestingly, although the supply chain risk literature has grown significantly over the last few years (e.g. Christopher and Lee, 2004; Manuj and Mentzer, 2008; Tummala and Schoenherr, 2011), undoubtedly in response to frequent supply chain disruptions, environmental and social risks tend not to be considered at all or feature at the bottom of the list of priorities. Chapter 7 discusses supply chain risk in more detail.

Figure 4.3 shows the revised Krajlic model where both dimensions focus on sustainability. Non-critical, bottleneck, and strategic remain as in the original model but the assessment of what places items into those categories should depend on the levels of risk and impact from a TBL perspective. The leverage category is divided into three sub-categories:

1. True commodities: basically the same as the original leverage items, although the item has a high impact only on one element of the TBL. Thus, item cost (or price) is still critical although social or environmental issues should also be considered.
2. Transitional commodities: items with temporarily high supply risk, for example, due to lack of compliance with (or lack of information required to assure) the buyer's sustainability requirements. Once corrected through supplier assessment and development these can revert to the true commodity sub-category.
3. Strategic commodities: critical commodities that transcend simple market economics. Strategic commodities have non-economic attributes that could be leveraged into a long-term competitive advantage.

In addressing the same question, Krause et al. (2009: 21) proposed the following for each of the four categories:

1. Strategic items: these items require close supplier partnerships, for example to ensure collaborative product and process development. These efforts should include sustainability. In particular, buying organizations should consider collaborating and cross-fertilizing their know-how with suppliers of strategic items in order to minimize the environmental

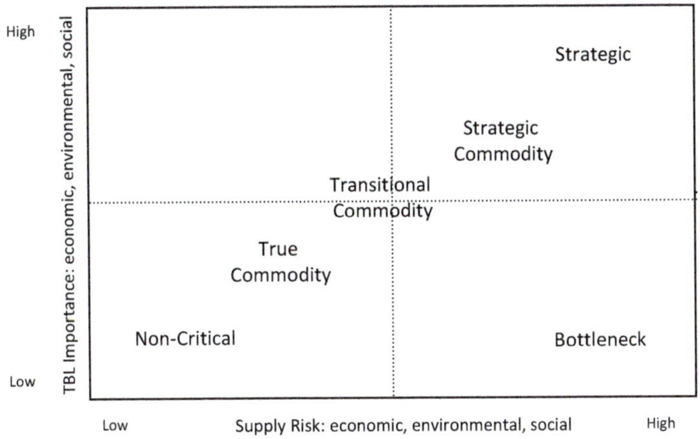

FIGURE 4.3 Revised Kraljic model: a sustainability perspective
Source: Adapted from Pagell et al. (2010)

and social impacts of new products. Supplier partners should be encouraged to adopt sustainability as one of their own competitive priorities.

2 Leverage items: packaging suppliers are typical leverage suppliers. Sustainability should be enforced in such supplier relationships, for example greater emphasis on the use of recyclables and material reduction. Again, these suppliers should place the same requirements on their own suppliers.
3 Bottleneck items: given the high level of supply risk the buyer is likely to be in a position of low power and therefore will find it difficult to influence suppliers; pushing suppliers for sustainability will thus be more problematic. Krause et al. (2009) suggest that in this situation, buyers could instead try to develop or promote industry-wide standards and norms that are conducive to sustainability. One example would be of hospitals pooling their power to certify responsible waste management service companies' processes and equipment. Krause et al. (2009) argue that Kraljic's focus on cost and risk minimization contradicts the idea of sustainability for bottleneck items.
4 Non-critical items: buying companies should use their power to enforce compliance with sustainability criteria. There is likely to be a good choice of suppliers offering items so if any of these do not comply with the buying company's sustainability requirements they should not be retained.

Comparing the suggestions for each category by Krause et al. (2009) with the revised model and suggestions by Pagell et al. (2010), one sees much consistency even if Pagell and his colleagues suggest that leverage items in the traditional sense become rarer and need to be divided into three sub-categories. Overall, the message is clear: fundamentally, Kraljic's (1983) model and the categories still apply from a sustainability perspective but the two dimensions of the model need to consider not only economic but also social and environmental issues. What is more, a focus on sustainable sourcing strategies further emphasizes the need to shift the focus from items or commodities to the suppliers that supply these. The remaining part of this chapter therefore focuses on the role of relationships from a traditional and a sustainability perspective.

4.3 FOUNDATIONAL MODELS OF CUSTOMER-SUPPLIER RELATIONSHIPS

Models of customer-supplier relationships (or 'buyer-supplier relationships') have come a long way since the first models emerged in the 1970s. Summarizing the main thinking behind some of these early developments is a useful starting point for understanding current thinking in SRM. In fact, in order to track down the earliest models of customer-supplier relationships it is necessary to look outside procurement to business-to-business marketing, or as it was known then, organizational buying behaviour. It is only relatively recently that a procurement perspective on supplier relationships has emerged.

4.3.1 Early models of customer-supplier relationships

The organizational buying behaviour theories proposed by Webster and Wind (1972) and Sheth (1973) are sometimes referred to as important starting points for purchasing theory. However, they did not really seek to explain buying behaviour from a buyer perspective but were designed to provide suppliers, or in fact sellers, with a better understanding of the customers' buying organization and processes so that salespeople could better target the right decision makers within the customer organization. The idea that the buying organization might actively seek out suppliers, never mind manage these, was not considered. Instead, buyers were simply seen as passive recipients, almost victims, of sales and marketing activity.

In the 1970s two theories emerged that provided grounding for later models of customer-supplier relationships: inter-organizational theory advanced by, among others, van de Ven (1976) and new institutional economics (Williamson, 1975). Van de Ven's inter-organizational theory focused on relationships between individual organizations and the environment and relationships between groups of organizations. Williamson's theory is also discussed in Chapter 5, focusing on his analysis of alternative forms of vertical organization, i.e. the make-or-buy decision. The main focus in Williamson's models was transactions between companies rather than long-term relationships although in his model relationships build up over time, principally as companies engage in repeat buying and selling transactions.

In the late 1970s and early 1980s a group of researchers known as the Industrial Marketing and Purchasing (IMP) group changed the focus from discrete one-off exchanges or transactions to long-term relationship evolution and processes of institutionalization and adaptation (Ford, 1980). Their model is examined in more depth in the following section.

4.3.2 The interaction model

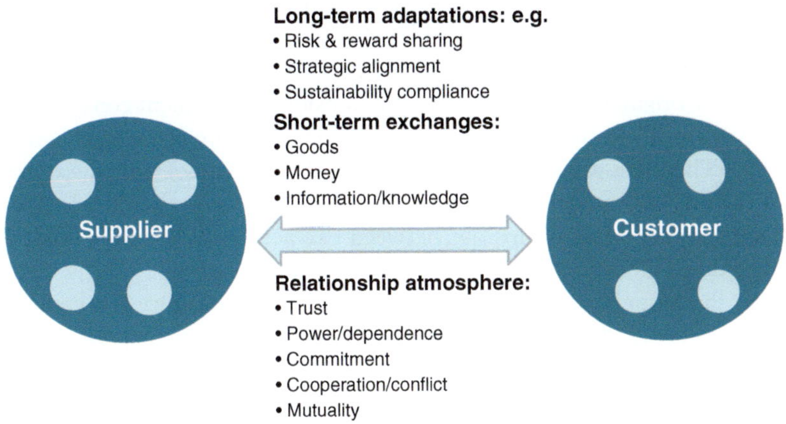

FIGURE 4.4 The interaction model
Source: Adapted from Håkansson (1982)

Figure 4.4 has been adapted from the original model. The main features of the model are identical to the original but some elements have been simplified and examples are consistent with current practice. The model distinguishes between short-term exchanges and long-term exchanges within relationships that institutionalize and adapt to each other (Håkansson, 1982). Short-term exchanges (episodes) can involve product or service, information, financial, and/or social exchange. Long-term adaptations happen, for example, when the two parties develop strategically in the same direction (strategic alignment) or when engaging in long-term sharing of risk and reward sharing arrangements. Adaptations are often highly specific to the counterpart and of little use in other relationships. Institutionalization implies that processes over time become systematized and routinized and in the long run such adaptations and institutionalization may blur the boundary between the two parties as they reflect and resemble each other in many ways. All relationships require investment, not least supplier relationships, and efforts to evaluate and develop supplier capabilities can be seen as part of long-term adaptation and routinization processes. So, a relationship evolves over time as the two parties interact with each other; the exchanges are not discrete and independent but part of a long-term process of relationship creation.

Exchanges take place between two participants or actors; the model differentiates two levels of actors: organization and individual. Clearly, this is a major simplification when considering the number of intra-organizational authorities and stakeholders that characterize complex organizations. But the separation helps one to understand how individuals and sometimes internal departments and functions may have their own aims and experiences, which may affect their behaviour and performance, and in turn pull the relationship in different directions. Although it is possible to describe an overall company-to-company relationship, in reality, relationships are also between the individual employees and departments within the companies.

The interaction model further incorporates a relationship 'atmosphere'. In the original model the atmosphere was described in terms of the power-dependence relationship between the parties, the level of conflict and/or cooperation, overall closeness or distance, and mutual expectations (Håkansson, 1982: 20). In the adaptation of the model shown in Figure 4.4 trust is added as it is now widely considered a critical aspect of relationship atmosphere. The original model included a relationship environment consisting of market structure, dynamism, internationalization, position in the manufacturing channel, and the social system. These are valid to this day although the terminology for these may be different. The interaction model is useful for describing and understanding key features of dyadic buyer-supplier relationships (i.e. between two actors) on the basis that these form the basic building blocks of supply chains and networks.

Although the model does not specifically focus on sustainability the variables of the model could certainly include aspects of sustainability. In particular, when a company requires a supplier to comply with its sustainability requirements it is a form of adaptation and there is clearly a need for institutionalization of sustainability practices within buyer-supplier relationships. Besides, if a company wishes to monitor and implement sustainability practices within a supplier's business it requires the right sort of atmosphere: the company needs to be in a position of power and the two parties need to be willing to share information, which is potentially controversial, so trust and commitment are important. Imposing sustainability on a supplier could, of course, also create friction and conflict, and thereby a very different atmosphere.

4.4 UNDERSTANDING SUPPLIER PARTNERSHIPS

Long-term supplier relationships were labelled 'partnerships' in the 1990s (Carlisle and Parker, 1989; Macbeth and Ferguson, 1994). Inspired by Japanese automotive practices (Womack et al., 1990) supplier partnerships became a popular concept across the world and are generally regarded as a core ingredient of a *lean* supply chain although the term 'partnership' has been criticized for its misleading notion of cosy and non-competitive relationships (Lamming, 1993). Supplier relationships are seen as conduits to supplier capabilities that are essential not only in the company's cost reduction efforts but also in its efforts to continuously improve its products and processes and to come up with innovations.

There are many definitions of partnerships, but the following provides a useful starting point: "an ongoing relationship between two firms that involves a commitment over an extended time period, and a mutual sharing of information and the risks and rewards of the relationship" (Ellram and Hendrick, 1995: 41–42).

In brief, definitions of buyer-supplier partnerships share a number of important ingredients:

- Shared goals: various terms may be used for this, including strategic alignment. A partnership requires that the two parties seek to develop in the same direction.
- Mutual benefit: sometimes expressed as risk and reward sharing. Mutuality concerns the extent to which a company is prepared to relinquish its own goals for the sake of a relationship. Mutuality implies that there are common goals and interests that bind firms in a shared purpose.

- Long-term commitment: the parties stick to the relationship even through difficult times. Commitment implies a lasting intention to build and maintain a long-term relationship.
- Trust and open sharing of information: trust is often regarded as an essential ingredient of successful partnerships but is difficult to define.

4.4.1 The role of trust

Partnerships are based on the existence of several important relationship characteristics, one of which is trust. Without trust one cannot share sensitive information and knowledge. In many ways trust is an underlying and very fragile concept. Trust takes a very long time to develop, usually through demonstrating to the partner that one is trustworthy. Trusting suppliers therefore means that suppliers demonstrate over a period of time that they can deliver according to the specified performance objectives. Also, trust implies not acting opportunistically, for example, taking advantage of knowledge or over-charging the customer. In other words, trust safeguards against opportunistic behaviour – like an informal contract. Without doubt, the quickest way to destroy trust is to act opportunistically, as anyone who has been on the receiving end of opportunistic behaviour will realize. Linking trust to safeguarding against opportunistic behaviour means that trust is a way to reduce and manage risk (Thorelli, 1986; Cousins, 2002).

Sako (1992) distinguishes between three types of trust:

> *Contractual trust*: the trust that the other party will adhere to the explicit and implicit points of the contract as agreed;
> *Competence trust*: the trust that the other party has the ability, or competence, to be able to produce what the contract requires;
> *Goodwill trust*: the trust that the other party will perform tasks in excess of the agreed terms and conditions.

As shown in Figure 4.5, she further suggests that the latter two become more important as the relationship develops over time; initially as a new relationship is explored it is based around compliance with the contract. As the relationships develop the supplier will need to prove that it has the competencies to fulfil its promises, for example, in relation to delivery on time and quality standards. As the relationships mature, and become a partnership, it is the willingness to help each other out of difficulties that counts.

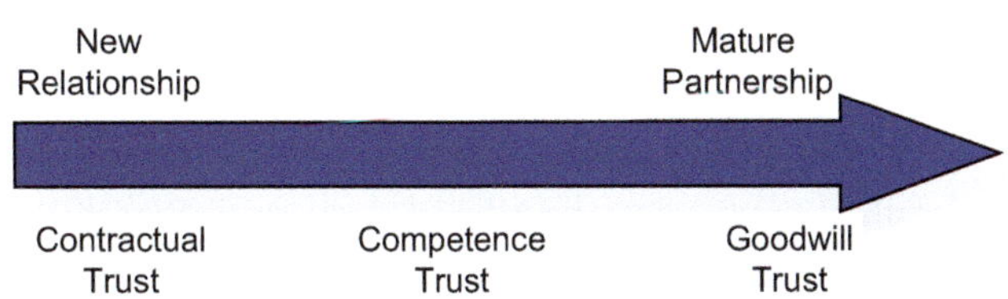

FIGURE 4.5 Progression of trust over time
Source: Adapted from Sako (1992)

Trust can be a difficult concept to apply in a business context where contracts may seem more important. Nevertheless, trust is an important ingredient in successful partnerships and a key factor in preventing opportunistic behaviour by the other party. Where formal contracts provide a legal mechanism for companies to fall back on, trust is an informal and social mechanism. In essence, using a trusted supplier is typically expressed in terms of using a 'safe pair of hands'. As such, trust is equivalent to confidence (Cousins and Stanwix, 2001).

4.4.2 The dark side of supplier relationships: exploiting power, opportunism, and conflict

The Kraljic model shows that multiple strategies need to be applied when managing different supply situations. Where strategic items require long-term supplier relationships that build on openness and trust, leverage items call for use of bargaining power to achieve the desired objectives. Buyers need to try to maximize their power position over suppliers, for example by limiting dependence on single sources, but aggressive exploitation of power in the wrong situation can backfire.

Consider the news reports of UK retailer Tesco in 2014 when *The Independent* newspaper and other media reported procurement practices that could best be described as bullying suppliers to lower their prices (Armitage, 2014). Under pressure to cut costs, Tesco buyers were reportedly treating suppliers with little respect, exploiting their position to demand discounts based on empty promises and delaying payments to deliberately boost Tesco profits. As one supplier said:

> For years we have been bullied and browbeaten by Tesco's buyers, who demand a lowball price for our goods then keep screwing us for more as the contract goes on … Now compare that with Aldi. Don't get me wrong, Aldi drives a very hard bargain, but once you've agreed a deal for a year, it sticks for a year. They don't come back demanding new bonuses, discounts and every other trick.
>
> (Butler, 2016)

Such buying behaviour clearly does not lead to good relationships but is all about seeking short-term gains at the expense of long-term profitability. What is more, re-building supplier trust afterwards, as Tesco has since tried to do, is very difficult. As the Tesco example shows, power and trust can be seen as opposites, as the exploitation of power is detrimental to trust.

But, power comes in different guises and is not necessarily about exploitation. So, what do we mean by power? Someone is powerful when they have an "ability to persuade another person to do something that he/she would not otherwise have done" (Dahl, 1961). However, it is useful to distinguish between coercive power and non-coercive power. Coercive power can be described as "the expectation on the part of P that he will be punished by O if he fails to conform to the influence attempt" (French and Raven, 1959). Non-coercive power is about more subtle ways of using power, for example through being able to offer (and potentially withhold) rewards for good performance or by having expertise or legitimacy to perform certain tasks, such as helping suppliers to improve.

Using power to coerce suppliers to reduce cost against their will can certainly be seen as inconsistent with trying to foster strategic supplier relationships. On the one hand, such use of power does not sit well with attempts to develop a sustainable supply chain and could even make suppliers resist sustainability requirements (Reuter et al., 2010). On the other hand, as explained in relation to Figure 4.3, it may be necessary to enforce sustainability compliance in suppliers (Touboulic et al., 2014). However, it is advisable to use non-coercive power to motivate rather than coerce suppliers, for example, by offering rewards for sustainability performance (Meqdadi et al., 2017).

Buyers may be tempted to abuse power in situations of imbalanced (or asymmetric) power. Suppliers that lack power may have few options but to stay in relationships with powerful customers. However, the unethical exploitation of suppliers may ultimately create significant problems for buyers themselves (Schleper et al., 2017). A whole stream of research has investigated the ethical relationship climates and the so-called dark side of relationships (Johnsen and Lacoste, 2016; Oliveira and Lumineau, 2019). The term 'dark side' has been broadly used to refer to the negative dimensions of inter-organizational relationships. Dark side relationships have been defined as "the set of generally damaging aspects of [inter-organizational relationships]; these aspects can be voluntary or involuntary and are generally driven by competence or integrity issues" (Oliveira and Lumineau, 2019: 232). Examples of damaging aspects include conflict, opportunism, and unethical practices.

Dark side relationships are counter-productive as they result in relationship deterioration and potential failure, for instance following a conflict or perceived opportunistic behaviour by one of the parties. In their review of the field, Oliveira and Lumineau (2019) find that conflict and opportunism can result in ailing relationships, characterized by reduced commitment, satisfaction, and trust. Ultimately, there may be financial consequences of such failings in the form of increased transaction costs or reduced knowledge exchange.

The dark side theme links to the issue of fairness in buyer-supplier relationships (and supply chains), where suppliers are not seen as receiving a fair share of the profits. Milan prosecutors discovered that factories making handbags for Dior and Armani exploited foreign labour to produce luxury goods cheaply. Documents showed Dior paid suppliers €53 per bag, later selling them for €2,600, while Armani bought bags for €93, resold them for €250, and priced them at around €1,800 in stores (Kostov, 2024). Similar disputes occur in relationships between large supermarket chains and farmers.

4.5 A PORTFOLIO OF SUPPLIER RELATIONSHIPS

Whereas the Kraljic (1983) portfolio model provides a way for companies to devise different ways of managing procurement according to purchase items, a related issue is to analyze the portfolio of supplier relationships. Clearly, supplier relationships vary greatly and it is very important not to think of all supplier relationships as partnerships. Only a relatively small proportion of a company's suppliers are usually considered as partnerships, regardless of the label being used to describe these. Companies need to match the desired performance outcome with the appropriate relationship type. Although partnerships are becoming increasingly important, not all relationships will necessarily be long-term or strategic – such as when buying low-value, repeatable commodity items.

It is tempting to consider supplier relationships simply in terms of two extremes: short-term adversarial relationships and long-term partnerships. However, as discussed in this chapter, a range of other relationship dimensions means that relationships vary according to many different dimensions, so any attempt to describe relationships along simple dichotomies would be over-simplistic. Since the early 1980s some companies have therefore implemented relationship portfolio strategies; like Kraljic, they include two dimensions but they focus on relationships instead of items and they may help purchasing and supply managers to avoid falling into the trap of developing the wrong type of relationship in the wrong circumstances, for example to 'over-partner' where not feasible. Relationship portfolios describe multiple relationships along, typically, two dimensions, enabling differentiated relationship management strategies in terms of balancing relationship investment relative to relationship intensity or criticality. Figure 4.6 shows a relationship portfolio model designed around two dimensions: level of confidence and level of dependence.

The horizontal axis is essentially about the level of trust in the supplier, because as discussed earlier trust is equivalent to confidence. Confident signifies a high level of trust, whereas unconfident signifies a low level of trust. The vertical axis is about dependency and therefore also about power. At the top of the model there is a further dimension: one-sided dependency and mutual dependency. If a relationship is one-sided, it means that one party is dependent on the other but not the other way around, so, as suggested in the top left-hand box, this could lead to opportunistic behaviour and therefore a risky situation. If, as suggested by the top right-hand corner, the high level of certainty were combined with mutual dependency this would be an appropriate situation to develop strategic supplier relationships. Interestingly, the boxes end up quite similar to Kraljic but

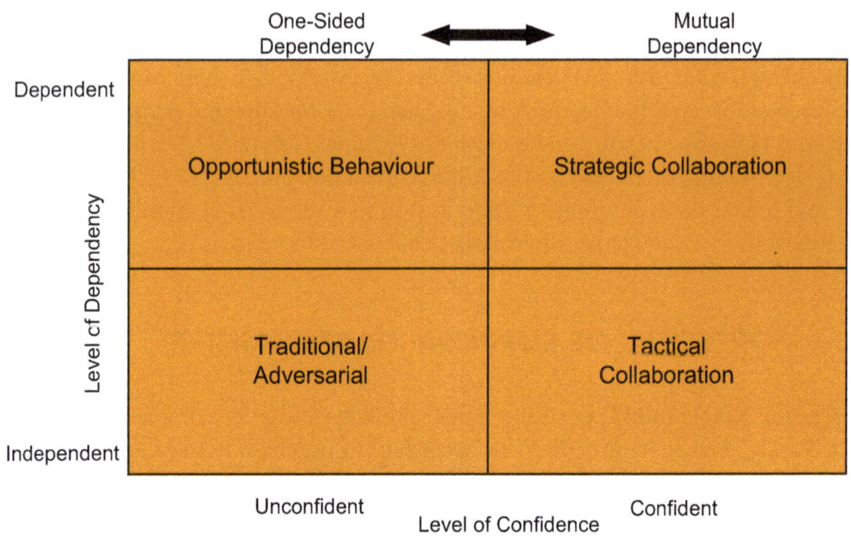

FIGURE 4.6 A relationship portfolio model
Source: Adapted from Cousins (2002)

as a Kraljic analysis would reveal very little about the state of supplier relationships, this model is a useful supplement to a Kraljic portfolio analysis, as it provides further insight into relationship conditions.

4.6 TURNING THE TABLE: RELATIONSHIP ASSESSMENT AND PREFERRED CUSTOMERS

Supplier relationship assessment is closely related to traditional supplier assessment methods (see Chapter 2). Supplier assessment essentially involves the buying company measuring the performance of suppliers. In comparison with traditional applications of supplier assessment, there is now increasing attention on the communication of the results to suppliers, and on providing incentives for suppliers to improve (Prahinski and Benton, 2004; Modi and Mabert, 2007). Some suppliers issue evaluation surveys to their customers, identifying areas in which the customer should improve; it is sometimes due to the customer's own internal processes that the supplier is unable to meet customer expectations. Companies should realize that a supplier's inability to meet its performance expectations might lie within its own company. For example, the expectations, specifications, and performance criteria may not be well communicated and understood by the supplier.[1]

In addition to the two parties measuring one another's performance it is also possible to conceive of an alternative approach to performance measurement, which focuses neither on supplier nor on customer performance, but on *relationship* performance: the health of the relationship (Lamming et al., 1996; Johnsen et al., 2008). This approach considers the supplier relationship as a separate unit of analysis from either the customer or the supplier firm as shown in Figure 4.7.

The argument for relationship assessment instead of supplier assessment is that if companies wish to develop long-term partnerships with some of their suppliers, it makes sense to analyze not only how their supplier performs (a one-way approach to performance assessment) but how the relationship with the supplier performs. At least in the context of strategic partnerships this focus makes good sense.

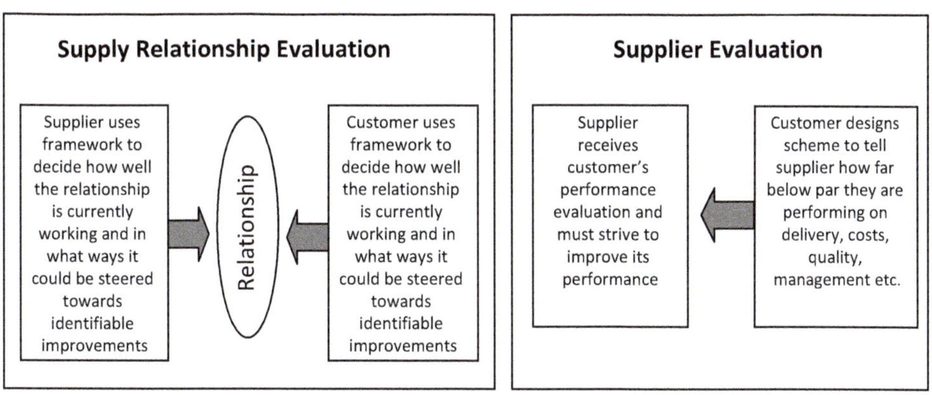

FIGURE 4.7 Supplier assessment and supplier relationship assessment
Source: Johnsen et al. (2008)

The idea of relationship assessment can be traced to the 1990s. Lamming et al. (1996) presented the Relationship Assessment Process (RAP) on the basic argument that supplier (or vendor) assessment exercises often turn into blaming exercises (Figure 4.7 shows the basic logic of this argument), and thus fail to address any root causes of supplier problems (Lamming et al., 1996; Johnsen et al., 2008). Based on this argument, Table 4.2 provides a framework to assess relationship maturity (stages of relationship health or performance) measured through a set of relationship characteristics (Johnsen and Ford, 2008). The purpose of this framework is to map a supplier relationship to see how advanced or mature it is across the different characteristics. Three relationship maturity stages are identified and descriptions of each are provided:

1. Exploration refers to the research and test phase in relational exchange. In the exploratory stage customers and suppliers begin to engage in discussion and negotiation. Customers may test a supplier's potential through small orders and negotiation of terms or product specifications. There may be little mutuality and cooperation at the exploratory stage, but the level of inconsistency may be high as each company is dealing with unknown issues and raising questions.
2. In the developing stage interaction and learning between a customer and supplier grows in terms of intensity and develops through increasing mutuality and growth in commitment. The expansion stage is characterized by continuous improvement in the benefits obtained by the parties, contributing to their increasing interdependence. Customers increase their purchases from suppliers and consider longer-term contracts. Cooperation and trust in the counterpart increases and power becomes increasingly shared.
3. If a relationship reaches the mature stage the parties can benefit from stability, mutual dedication, more balanced power, and established domains of expertise. However, one must also be aware of inertia or lack of initiative during the stable stage. Routines and institutionalization may mean that the relationship is taken for granted and does not reach its full potential. As stable relationships build on trust, commitment, and relationship-specific investments the switching costs at this advanced stage are high.

TABLE 4.2 A framework for evaluating relationship maturity

	Maturity Stage		
	Exploratory & Tactical	*Developing*	*Stable & Strategic*
Mutuality	– Goals differ for each party: no strategic alignment – Win-lose strategy	– Current goals aligned to achieve profitability for both parties – Partial strategic alignment	– Goals for future developed in tandem – Strategic alignment – Win-win: shared risks and rewards
Exclusivity	– Limited adaptation of each party – Limited relative commitment to relationship	– Concessions made by each party for mutual benefit – Security sought through commitment to relationship	– Long-term investment, adaptation, and commitment over and above that of other relationships

(*Continued*)

TABLE 4.2 Continued

	Maturity Stage		
	Exploratory & Tactical	*Developing*	*Stable & Strategic*
Co-operation	– Initial ideas for cooperation explored – Cooperation depends on performance evidence – Limited information sharing: knowledge is power	– Joint projects and plans established to achieve improved capabilities for each party – Parties becoming more open with each other, but still guarded	– Long-term projects for enhancement and achievement of capability development e.g. supplier development programme – Transparency: high level of information sharing
Conflict	– Conflicts arise through lack of knowledge of other party's systems, processes, and responsibilities: destructive conflicts – One-way conflict resolution/blaming	– Disagreements arise over integration of roles, responsibilities, and targets – Partial moves towards joint problem-solving	– Experience of conflict and its resolution enhance debate and depth of understanding: constructive conflicts – Joint problem-solving
Intensity	– No commitment to regular interaction between individuals and teams – Single-interface – Low level operational involvement	– Regular pattern of interaction established with clearly defined roles and routines – More functions involved in relationship – Middle-management involvement	– Friendships and close professional ties underpin long-term interaction and patterns of behaviour/responses – Multi-interface and corporate (director) involvement
Interpersonal Inconsistency	– Different approaches to relationship within each party e.g. across functions – Different approaches to relationship over time creating inconsistent communication	– Common approaches to relationship begin to be defined – Communication patterns become established	– Both parties work to shared principles and patterns for communication – Behaviour and communication consistent over time and across functions

(Continued)

TABLE 4.2 Continued

	Maturity Stage		
	Exploratory & Tactical	*Developing*	*Stable & Strategic*
Power/ Dependence	– One-sided relationship – Stronger party controls strategic and tactical decisions e.g. ordering process, quality, and prices – Weaker party concerned with proving capability/ attractiveness	– Domains of expertise becoming defined and separate – Inter-dependent relationship strategy developing	– Commonly understood and firmly established distribution of power and expertise in different areas – Inter-dependent relationship strategy established
Trust	– Ensuring contractual compliance – Controlling performance through tight measures	– Focus on competence-based trust in defined areas for each party	– Focus on goodwill trust: helping each other out when necessary – Equal commitment to long-term health and growth of relationship

Source: Adapted from Johnsen et al. (2010)

Our discussion of power assumes that the buying company holds the power with the supplier being the less powerful party. This holds true in many sourcing situations but not all. In bottleneck sourcing situations, it is likely that the power balance is reversed. In fact, many companies cannot assume that they hold the power as they may face many suppliers, or they may simply not be an important customer to their suppliers because they account for a small proportion of their turnover. Consider the following quote in the annual survey report on supplier relations in the automotive industry (Plante Moran, 2024): "Suppliers have a choice as to who they work with and can make decisions to manage down business with specific OEMs".

The usual assumption of sourcing from preferred suppliers (see also Chapter 2) can therefore be turned on its head to thinking about how to become a preferred customer. In the current era of heightened supply chain risks and disruptions, customers may find themselves in situations where they have to become the preferred – and attractive – customer (Pulles et al., 2019). Research on customer attractiveness emerged around 25 years ago, revisiting the concept of reverse marketing (Leenders and Blenkhorn, 1988). Findings from this research show that preferred customers stand to benefit by gaining improved supplier commitment (Glas, 2018) and mitigating supplier dependency problems (Schiele and Vos, 2015). Benefits include cost and delivery advantages (e.g. Hald et al., 2009) and preferential access to technological innovation (e.g. Schiele, 2012). Creating supplier satisfaction is seen as a step to become a preferred – and ultimately an attractive – customer.

In addition to accounting for a high proportion of a supplier's business, customers can become attractive to suppliers, for example, by presenting a potential growth opportunity, by being a reliable and supportive customer, or through their operational excellence and innovation potential (Hüttinger et al., 2014). As an example of customer attractiveness, Toyota is consistently ranked as the number one automotive OEM customer by suppliers for its trust and communication with suppliers (Plante Moran, 2024).

4.7 TECHNOLOGY AS ENABLER OF SRM

As a final but important note, we reflect on digital technology-enabled SRM platforms. Increasingly powered by AI, SRM platforms are critically important for enabling SRM programmes, as they act as intelligence hubs to support sourcing (or onboarding) processes, supplier performance monitoring, risk and compliance, supplier collaboration and so on. Having ready access to supplier data can help to better guard against supplier risk and help to improve supply chain resilience. SRM software providers may offer stand-alone SRM solutions or integrated solutions, for example linking with supply chain sustainability (see also Chapter 10 for the topic of digital supply chain applications).

SRM systems can significantly enable and automate SRM processes but they will not completely replace humans (at least for the foreseeable future). Buyer-supplier relationships still involve people and it is no surprise that soft skills continue to be highly valued by procurement and supply chain recruiters.

4.8 CASE STUDY: DANONE[2]

Danone is among the global leaders in the food and beverage sector, committed to creating and sharing sustainable value for all. With global sales totalling €27.4 billion and a work force amounting to 89,528 employees worldwide (2024), Danone relies on three main businesses: Essential Dairy and Plant-Based products (49 per cent of sales); Specialized Nutrition (33 per cent of sales); and Waters (18 per cent of sales). 'Essential Dairy and Plant-Based' products include famous brands like Activia, Oikos, and Danette. Danone is the global market leader in essential dairy and plant-based foods, and number two in packaged waters and early life nutrition.

Danone is known for its strong commitment to sustainability and has been awarded an AAA Morgan Stanley Capital International (MSCI) ESG rating, remains a FTSE4Good Index Series member, and is recognized as a top performer within the industry of food products by *Sustainalytics*. Danone even launched a process in 2015 to become a global B Corp™, and 92.8 per cent of sales are now covered by B Corp™ certification, reflecting the company's high social, societal, and environmental performance. In 2020 the company became the first listed company to adopt the *Société à Mission* status, created by the French 'PACTE' law in 2019.

The *Renew Danone* strategy focuses on enhancing competitiveness and exploring new growth avenues via driving core products and brands through increased support and innovation, diversifying revenue by entering new categories and expanding channel footprints, particularly in digital and out-of-home markets, and the 'Partner for Growth' programme to develop strategic partnerships to "unlock growth opportunities". At the same time, the strategy includes tighter management of Danone's portfolio, divesting underperforming activities such as Michel & Augustin and Horizon Organic.

The *Renew Danone* strategy also expresses a vision of social, societal, and environmental responsibility that the company has upheld for many years. In 2023 Danone reframed its sustainability roadmap as the Danone Impact Journey, based on three pillars: health, nature, and people and communities. This continues its long-term mission to "bring health through food to as many people as possible while driving positive impact".

In 2024 Danone updated its double materiality assessment to identify sustainability impacts, risks, and opportunities to comply with the European Corporate Sustainability Reporting Directive (CSRD). Double materiality assessment considers both impact materiality (effects on people and the environment) and financial materiality (effects on financial performance). This assessment process involved stakeholder consultations and was approved by the Global Engagement Committee. The assessment identified ten relevant sustainability topics with material risks and opportunities with key topics including climate change, pollution, water resources, biodiversity, and resource use. As a business that relies on agriculture, Danone recognizes that its future operations are impacted by climate change, and that activities in the Danone supply chains contribute to global warming through GHG emissions, especially from agriculture. The double materiality assessment identified that extreme weather events could lead to product shortages affecting consumers, and Danone needs to work with suppliers to enhance their preparedness for climate change. In particular, the assessment points to impacts around air, water, and soil pollution (from manure and use of fertilizers); wider ecosystems i.e. from effluents in the natural environment causing health problems for employees and local populations; emissions from logistics and transport; and environmental impact from the use of plastics generated by end-of-life packaging waste.

Reflecting its 'One Planet. One Health' vision, Danone has been working on product re-design and production, reducing the number of ingredients where possible, and proposing new organic and non-genetically-modified (GMO) product lines. Other commitments include promoting sustainable agriculture, conserving water, reducing waste, reducing its carbon footprint, promoting animal welfare, and investing in the community. These initiatives reflect Danone's ambitions around product stewardship and circular economy.

4.8.1 Sustainable sourcing

Danone's name for procurement is Cycles & Procurement. With the Cycles, Danone protects and secures its key resources (milk, water, and plastic) and takes a strategic approach to procurement to support the business and social agenda of Danone. In terms of value, milk represents the main raw material purchased by Danone. Danone sources milk, directly and indirectly, from over 58,000 milk producers in around 16 different countries. A very high proportion of these are small producers located mainly in emerging countries of Africa and Latin America that own fewer than ten cows (so-called 'subsistence farms') or 'family farms' with less than 300 cows. Often, milk is collected from collection centres to which these small producers deliver their production daily. For dairy and beverage products, fruit is another critically-important raw material. Other food raw materials include fruit-based preparations and sugar, and packaging materials, such as plastics and cardboard. Given the nature of these raw materials, supply markets can be volatile.

For milk sourcing, Danone typically enter into agreements with local producers or cooperatives through its operating subsidiaries. Liquid milk prices are set locally, over contractual periods that vary from one country to another. The company aims to ensure a sustainable long-term supply, to minimize risks by optimizing the use of all milk components using new technologies, and to pool the needs among the various businesses.

Danone collaborates with US and European producers to create three-to-five-year contracts that stabilize milk prices and support farmers' financial security. The Cost Performance Model (CPM) contracts, developed with producer input, tie milk pricing to production costs. In 2024, CPM contracts covered 38 per cent of Danone's European and 32 per cent of US milk supply, representing 24 per cent of Danone's total milk collection, with plans for further expansion to strengthen supply chain resilience.

In addition to the operational priorities, Danone's procurement is dedicated to ensuring that the sustainability criteria of the group are respected by all suppliers who are informed of the standards and requirements of Danone from the outset. Sustainability criteria are incorporated into specifications, supplier selection processes, contracts, and ongoing evaluations of supplier performance.

The Sustainability Sourcing Policy (SSP) sets the standards for first-tier suppliers that have a contractual relationship with Danone (i.e. excluding farmers). The SSP outlines Danone's commitments to establish fair, sustainable, and ethical relationships, articulated around three sets of Fundamental Principles on social, environmental, and ethical issues. These in turn are based on the United Nations Guiding Principles on Business & Human Rights (UNGPs), the International Bill of Rights, and the eight core conventions of the International Labour Organization (ILO) as well as Danone's own Code of Conduct for Business Partners.

For each of the fundamental principles the SSP outlines the mandatory requirements that Danone requires suppliers to meet and cascade to their own suppliers, including recommended management systems and advanced practices. The concept of cascading mandatory requirements down through the supply chain means that it is the responsibility of first-tier suppliers to ensure that their suppliers, i.e. second- and sub-tier suppliers, implement these requirements. Danone gives very specific guidelines to suppliers on how they must go about this (2024b: 5):

> Cascading SSP's mandatory requirements (or Suppliers' requirements at least equivalent to SSP) within the extended supply chain requires, without limitation, the following actions: communicating, informing and explaining, monitoring compliance (notably through reporting processes and audits as much as practically possible), sharing significant issues or residual risks with Danone,

and generally enforcing SSP (or Suppliers' requirements at least equivalent to SSP) to the fullest extent possible. We expect all suppliers upstream of Tier 1 suppliers to comply with Danone Code of Conduct for Business Partners as a minimum.

4.8.2 The RESPECT programme for tier one suppliers

The RESPECT programme was originally launched in 2005 and has since undergone iterative changes but the fundamental principle remains the same. The RESPECT programme aims to ensure that suppliers comply with Danone's fundamental social principles that reflect the fundamental rights of ILO conventions and focus on:

1. Child labour;
2. Forced labour;
3. Non-discrimination;
4. Freedom of association and right to collective bargaining;
5. Health and safety at work;
6. Working hours;
7. Pay.

RESPECT applies to first-tier suppliers across all of Danone's purchasing categories except raw milk (covered instead by the Regenerative Agriculture Program), i.e. transformed raw materials (fruit preparations, powdered milk, etc.), packaging, production machinery, and transport and other services. Subcontractors, i.e. suppliers that manufacture finished products on behalf of Danone, are also covered by the RESPECT programme. However, Danone uses very little subcontracting, as the majority of its finished products are produced at its own production sites.

The RESPECT programme is structured around four main pillars:

- ESG risk screening of Tier 1 suppliers;
- Self-assessments;
- On-site assessments commissioned by Danone and performed by third-party experts;
- Ongoing dialogue with suppliers and monitoring of corrective actions.

The figure below illustrates the basic principle of the RESPECT process:

The RESPECT programme in turn is managed through the SEDEX (the Supplier Ethical Data Exchange – a not-for-profit membership organization dedicated to improving responsible and ethical business practices in global supply chains) and EcoVadis platforms. The RESPECT programme focuses on:

- Integrating Danone's Sustainability Principles into supplier contracts and terms and conditions;

- Sharing information through supplier self-assessment concerning their CSR performance, using the SEDEX or EcoVadis platforms shared by consumer goods industry players;
- Auditing CSR performance using the SMETA (Sedex Members Ethical Trade Audit) benchmark for at-risk suppliers (www.sedexglobal.com/ethical-audits/smeta).

By the end of 2024, 3,159 first-tier supplier sites had been registered on the SEDEX or EcoVadis platforms, representing 70.8 per cent of expenditure. Through the AIM Progress consortium for responsible sourcing, Danone can access audits commissioned by its peers on common suppliers, thus reducing the burden of multiple audits. In 2024, Danone had access to 531 SMETA audits of Danone first-tier suppliers, commissioned either by Danone or by peers. The audits are carried out by independent audit companies and evaluate supplier compliance against the four pillars of the SMETA protocol – Labour Rights, Health and Safety, Environment Management, and Business Ethics – that are encompassed in Danone's Sustainability Principles and now in the SSP.

When non-compliance is identified through the audits, the procurement teams verify that the suppliers implement the corrective action plans defined by the auditors. As in previous years, Danone reported that in 2024 most cases of non-compliance (480 reported in total in 2024) concerned health and safety issues (58.3 per cent) or working hours and compensation (28.1 per cent). In July 2017, Danone introduced an indicator to monitor the timely launch of SMETA audits (after the suppliers have been identified as at risk) and the timely closure of the non-compliance: 65 per cent of Danone's suppliers complied with Danone's standards; this rate was 100 per cent for central procurement.

The aim is to eradicate all non-compliances and improve suppliers' sustainability performance; in some cases, there is no alternative but to terminate relationships with suppliers who do not collaborate.

In 2017, Danone launched a process to upgrade RESPECT and evolve towards a due diligence approach, reinforcing a first-tier suppliers approach, covering also its upstream supply chain and focusing in particular on human rights. This process is inspired by the UN Guiding Principles on Business and Human Rights (UNGP) and contributes to the development of a vigilance plan, as required by the 2017 French Corporate Duty of Vigilance Law.

In order to reinforce first-tier supplier assessment, Danone also developed a new approach in 2017 to segment its suppliers according to three levels of priority. Danone determines these levels proactively, using geographical, sector-specific, and trade data. Audits are mandatory for all high priority suppliers. Appropriate assessment measures are taken for medium priority suppliers. In 2024 Danone further reinforced its RESPECT process by introducing a new ESG risk screening tool in order to enable a more tailored and proactive due diligence process, focusing on human rights impacts.

4.8.3 Upstream risk mapping and traceability

Danone maps major potential risks for the most exposed procurement categories. Combined with stakeholder expectations, this risk analysis determines the priority categories of product and service procurements on which Danone will focus its attention. Risks concern workers employed through labour agencies or service providers, and key commodities including palm oil, cocoa, cane sugar, and fruit. The potential risks brought to light are often situated in farms and plantations, located upstream in the supply networks.

Supported by independent experts, Danone has initiated traceability actions on these priority categories. Since 2014, Danone has mapped its palm oil supply chain at least annually, and it can now trace 100 per cent of its palm oil to mills and 98 per cent to plantations. The NGO Earthworm Foundation supports Danone's palm oil traceability efforts, whereas for other categories Danone collaborates with UK-based commodity consultancy 3Keel. Since 2022, 3Keel has been working with Danone to strengthen and implement a traceability process for all priority raw materials of the Renewed Forest Policy (soy, cocoa, paper). With 3Keel's support Danone shifted from annual to semi-annual data collection in 2024, thereby strengthening traceability and improving monitoring of forest policy goals and supplier engagement.

Danone's Renewed Forest Policy aims for traceable, deforestation- and conversion-free supply chains for its main commodities – soya, palm oil, paper and board, cocoa, and animal feed – by 2025. Danone is also using satellite monitoring to enhance traceability, allowing for better detection and verification of deforestation and conversion-free raw materials.

4.8.4 Tackling forced labour

One major risk for Danone concerns forced labour. Workers may end up in this situation through violence or intimidation or by having their identity documents withheld. Especially in the case of migrant workers, workers may be threatened with being reported to immigration officials. Often, workers are forced to pay high recruitment fees which immediately leads them into debt bondage.

In 2016, Danone joined the Consumer Goods Forum's (CGF) collective initiative to eradicate forced labour from global supply chains. CGF members commit to eradicate forced labour drivers from their own operations and global supply chains, based on the three following principles: every worker should have freedom of movement, no worker should pay for a job, and no worker should be indebted or coerced to work.

For several years now, Danone has cooperated with specialized stakeholders to strengthen action to combat the various forms of forced labour in supply chains. For example, to fight informal employment in recycled plastic procurement, Danone has developed cooperatives of waste-pickers with support from local partners, enabling these workers to leave the informal economy and gain access to paid employment, recognized by public authorities, and complemented by social benefits. In 2020,

Danone committed to develop and deploy human rights due diligence systems focusing on the prevention of forced labour in its own and supplier-operated facilities, with the aim of reaching 100 per cent coverage by 2025. Relying on self-assessment and audits, Danone focuses these efforts on high-priority countries i.e. high human rights country risk and the size of the external workforce employed at Danone's sites.

4.8.5 Driving change through industry collaboration

Although auditing and evaluating supplier compliance with Danone's policies is key to Danone's approach to sustainable supply chain development, the company does not see evaluation of compliance as an end in itself; Danone also supports suppliers when non-compliance is identified, engaging with independent organizations in driving sustainability improvement. Through the AIM-PROGRESS group Danone collaborates with other food manufacturers, many of which are competitors, including Nestle, Kraft, Unilever, Diageo, Mars, PepsiCo, and Cadbury. The AIM-PROGRESS group develops common standards on CSR around four pillars – Health and Safety, Labour Standards, Environmental Management, and Business Ethics – with the purpose of mutualizing information and results of audits concerning common suppliers. Members have agreed to share experiences, ideas, and solutions while respecting confidentiality; the idea is that common standards imposed on suppliers by several major food industry members will have greater impact.

4.8.6 Danone controversies

Despite – or perhaps as a result of – its claim to be a sustainable food company dedicated to producing only healthy products, Danone has faced considerable public criticism. In an apparent coup led by two shareholders, former CEO Emmanuel Faber was toppled in 2021 over declining profits. Danone had fallen behind its key competitors Nestle and Unilever and under Faber's leadership the company had announced a restructuring plan laying off 2000 employees, the fifth restructuring in five years. Rumours circulated that shareholders disapproved of Faber's sustainability agenda. He had spearheaded the 'One Planet, One Health' strategy and personally engaged in activist CEO coalitions such as *B Team* and *Business for Inclusive Growth* (B4IG), but financial performance was suffering. Following this event, Danone's commitment to sustainability looked uncertain.

A dispute over sourcing for Volvic bottled water developed in 2023 with accusations of Danone being responsible for drying up water tables in the ecosystems around the Auvergne region. This happened in the middle of many communities facing water use restrictions. Then in September 2024 Danone dropped its Nutri-Score label on drinkable yoghurts such as Actimel, Activia, and Danonino. The decision was taken in light of accusations of the products being overly sugary to warrant a top 'A' score, as Nutri-Scores were updated. Danone's claims of producing healthy foods were beginning to sound hollow, motivating 36 French health specialists to denounce Danone's nutrition and health claims on milk and yogurt-based drinks with added sugars in high quantities (Dongo, 2025).

Danone's packaging efforts have also come under scrutiny, and the company had to settle a plastics transparency lawsuit with an NGO coalition in February 2025. Back in January 2023, the coalition of NGOs took Danone to court alleging that it had violated France's duty of vigilance law because it did not mention its plastic usage in its annual vigilance plan. Following the settlement, the corporation must now publish its use of plastics, strengthen its plastics prevention policy, and attend annual meetings in the coming years.

Danone is not only a leader in many of the markets that it operates within but also in its approach to sustainable sourcing. But this profile sets high expectations and Danone must continue to improve its policies and practices.

4.9 CONCLUSIONS

Fostering and managing collaborative supplier relationships, where extensive information and knowledge are openly shared, is at the heart of successful procurement and supply chain management. As companies have outsourced a high proportion of value-adding activities to suppliers and service providers, they become increasingly dependent on suppliers. The idea of 'partnership suppliers' or 'partnership sourcing' gained popularity from the 1990s onwards, focusing on developing collaborative long-term relationships and often based on single sourcing. This chapter has explored in which circumstances such sourcing models are appropriate, which are those that represent high value and risk but also those in which the right relationship conditions are in place. Various hybrid models that combine the benefits of single sourcing and multi-sourcing while avoiding the limitations of both extremes have been discussed; in general these provide better alternatives to the high-risk single-sourcing strategy.

Supplier relationships are multi-faceted and involve not only collaboration but also potential conflict. Trust is an important feature of relationships but the role of power and dependence should not be under-estimated. Using power is often seen as a negative but is fundamental in order to gain influence over suppliers. In the context of sustainability, using power is important to enforce supplier compliance but companies are advised to use non-coercive power to avoid ruining collaborative relationships. Nevertheless, there is also a dark side to buyer-supplier relationships and abusing power can create serious problems and constrain relationship value creation.

We explored a model of relationship assessment as an alternative or complement to supplier assessment and explored the importance of becoming a preferred and attractive customer to suppliers, especially in times of supply chain risk and disruption. A key message of this chapter is that companies need to develop and invest in relationships with a range of different suppliers that are all unique yet they may share common features. It is through supplier relationships that companies access capabilities that allow them to continuously develop and offer new products and service offerings to their customers.

NOTES

1 Ways to overcome a pure one-way perspective on supplier assessment is discussed further in section 4.2.2 above: 'Towards single sourcing – and back to multi-sourcing'.

2 This case is based on multiple Danone reports (Danone, 2024a, 2024b). In addition, various media and NGO reports have been consulted.

REFERENCES

Armitage J (2014) Tesco crisis: 'They say every little helps, but supermarket's demands are never little'. *The Independent*, 24 September. https://www.independent.co.uk/news/business/analysis-and-features/tesco-crisis-they-say-every-little-helps-but-supermarket-s-demands-are-never-little-9752106.html

Butler S (2016) Tesco delayed payments to suppliers to boost profits, watchdog finds. *The Guardian*, 26 January. https://www.theguardian.com/business/2016/jan/26/tesco-ordered-change-deal-suppliers

Carlisle J and Parker R (1989) *Beyond Negotiation: Redeeming Customer-Supplier Relationships*. Chichester, UK: Wiley.

Chopra S and Sodhi MS (2004) Managing risk to avoid supply-chain breakdown. *MIT Sloan Management Review* 46(1): 53–62.

Christopher M and Lee H (2004) Mitigating supply chain risk through improved confidence. *International Journal of Physical Distribution and Logistics Management* 34(5): 388–396.

Christopher MG (2000) The agile supply chain – Competing in volatile markets. *Industrial Marketing Management* 29: 37–44.

Cousins PD (2002) A conceptual model for managing long-term inter-organizational relationships. *European Journal of Purchasing and Supply Management* 8(2): 71–82.

Cousins PD and Stanwix E (2001) It's only a matter of confidence! A comparison of relationship management between Japanese- and UK non-Japanese-owned vehicle manufacturers. *International Journal of Operations and Production Management* 21(9): 1160–1180.

Dahl RA (1961) Who governs? Democracy and power in an American city, Yale University Press, New Haven.

Danone (2012) Sustainability Report.

Danone (2024a) Universal Registration Document (Annual Financial Report 2024). https://www.danone.com/content/dam/corp/global/danonecom/investors/en-all-publications/2025/registrationdocuments/urd2024accessibleversion.pdf (accessed 16 July 2025).

Danone (2024b) Sustainable Sourcing Policy.

Dongo D (2025) Danone, 'health' claims on drinks full of added sugars. *Food Times*. https://www.foodtimes.eu/consumers-and-health/danone-health-claims-on-drinks-full-of-added-sugars/ (accessed 17 July 2025).

Dubois A and Fredriksson P (2008) Cooperating and competing in supply networks: Making sense of a triadic sourcing strategy. *Journal of Purchasing and Supply Management* 14: 170–179.

Dubois A and Pedersen A-C (2002) Why relationships do not fit into purchasing portfolio models – A comparison between the portfolio and industrial network approaches. *European Journal of Purchasing and Supply Management* 8: 35–42.

Ellram LM and Hendrick TE (1995) Partnering characteristics: A dyadic perspective. *Journal of Business Logistics* 16(1): 41–64.

European Foundation for Quality Management [EFQM] (2006) *The EFQM framework for managing external resources*. ISBN 90–5236–610–1.

Ford ID (1980) The development of buyer-seller relationships in industrial markets. *European Journal of Marketing* 14(3): 72–84.

French JRP Jr and Raven B (1959) The bases of social power. In: D Cartwright (ed) *Studies of Social Power*. Ann Arbor, MI: University of Michigan, Institute for Social Research: 150–167.

Gelderman CJ and van Weele AJ (2005) Purchasing portfolio models: A critique and update. *The Journal of Supply Chain Management* 41(3): 19–28.

Glas AH (2018) The impact of procurement on supplier satisfaction: Service, communication, and speed. *International Journal of Integrated Supply Management* 12(1/2): 90–117.

Håkansson H (ed) (1982) *International Marketing and Purchasing of Industrial Goods: An Interaction Approach*. Chichester: Wiley.

Hald KS, Cordón C and Vollmann TE (2009) Towards an understanding of attraction in buyer-supplier relationships. *Industrial Marketing Management* 38: 960–970.

Hines P (1995) Network sourcing: A hybrid approach. *International Journal of Purchasing and Materials Management* 31(2): 17–24.

Holgado M and Niess A (2023) Resilience in global supply chains: Analysis of responses, recovery actions and strategic changes triggered by major disruptions. *Supply Chain Management: An International Journal* 28(6): 1040–1059.

Hüttinger L, Schiele H and Schröer D (2014) Exploring the antecedents of preferential customer treatment by suppliers: A mixed methods approach. *Supply Chain Management: An International Journal* 18(5/6): 697–721.

Johnsen RE and Ford D (2008) Exploring the concept of asymmetry: A typology for analysing customer-supplier relationships. *Industrial Marketing Management* 37(4): 471–483.

Johnsen TE, Johnsen RE and Lamming RC (2008) Supply relationship evaluation: The relationship assessment process (RAP) and beyond. *European Management Journal* 26: 274–287.

Johnsen TE, Johnsen R and Lee C-J (2010) Towards a managerial model for supplier relationship evaluation. In: *Proceedings of the 26th International Marketing and Purchasing Conference*, 2–4 September, Corvinus University of Budapest, Hungary.

Johnsen RE and Lacoste S (2016) An exploration of the 'dark side' associations of conflict, power and dependence in customer-supplier relationships. *Industrial Marketing Management* 59: 76–95.

Kostov N (2024) Raids find luxury handbags being made by exploited workers in Italy. *Wall Street Journal*, 2 July.

Kraljic P (1983) Purchasing must become supply management. *Harvard Business Review* (Sept–Oct): 109–117.

Krause DR, Vachon S and Klassen RD (2009) Special topic forum on sustainable supply chain management: Introduction and reflections on the role of purchasing management. *Journal of Supply Chain Management* 45(4): 18–25.

Lamming RC (1993) *Beyond Partnership: Strategies for Innovation and Lean Supply*. Hemel Hempstead, UK: Prentice Hall.

Lamming RC, Cousins PD and Notman DM (1996) Beyond vendor assessment: Relationship assessment programme. *European Journal of Purchasing and Supply Management* 2(4): 173–181.

Leenders MR and Blenkhorn DL (1988). *Reverse Marketing: The New Buyer-Supplier Relationship*. New York: The Free Press.

Macbeth D and Ferguson N (1994) *Partnership Sourcing: An Integrated Supply* Chain *Management Approach*. London: Financial Times/Pitman Publishing.

Manuj I and Mentzer J (2008) Global supply chain risk management. *Journal of Business Logistics* 29(1): 133–155.

McKinsey (2022) Taking the pulse of shifting supply chains. https://www.mckinsey.com/capabilities/operations/our-insights/taking-the-pulse-of-shifting-supply-chains#/

Meqdadi O, Johnsen TE and Johnsen R (2017) The role of power and trust in spreading sustainability initiatives across supply networks: A case study of the bio-chemical industry. *Industrial Marketing Management* 62: 61–76.

Modi SB and Mabert VA (2007) Supplier development: Improving supplier performance through knowledge transfer. *Journal of Operations Management* 25(1): 42–64.

Nishiguchi T (1994) *Strategic Industrial Sourcing*. Oxford and New York: Oxford University Press.

Oliveira N and Lumineau F (2019) The dark side of interorganizational relationships. *Journal of Management* 45(1): 231–261.

Olsen RF and Ellram LM (1997) A portfolio approach to supplier relationships. *Industrial Marketing Management* 26(2): 101–113.

Pagell M, Wu Z and Wasserman ME (2010) Thinking differently about purchasing portfolios: An assessment of sustainable sourcing. *Journal of Supply Chain Management* 36(1): 57–73.

Plante Moran (2024) Toyota soars, Ford plummets; Honda, GM, Nissan, and Stellantis makes gains in 2024 Working Relations Study. https://www.plantemoran.com/get-to-know/news/2024/05/2024-working-relations-study

Prahinski C and Benton WC (2004) Supplier evaluations: Communication strategies to improve supplier performance. *Journal of Operations Management* 22(1): 39–62.

Pulles NJ, Ellegaard C, Schiele H and Kragh H (2019) Mobilising supplier resources by being an attractive customer: Relevance, status and future research directions. *Journal of Purchasing and Supply Management* 25(3): 100539.

Reuter C, Foerstl K, Hartmann E and Blome C (2010) Sustainable global supplier management: The role of dynamic capabilities in achieving competitive advantage. *Journal of Supply Chain Management* 46(2): 45–63.

Richardson J (1993) Parallel sourcing and supplier performance in the Japanese automobile industry. *Strategic Management Journal* 14: 339–350.

Sako M (1992) *Prices, Quality and Trust: Inter-firm Relations in Britain and Japan*. Cambridge, UK: Cambridge University Press.

Schiele H and Vos FGS (2015) Dependency on suppliers as a peril in the acquisition of innovations? The role of buyer attractiveness in mitigating potential negative dependency effects in buyer-supplier relations. *Australasia Marking Journal* 23: 139–147.

Schiele H (2012) Accessing supplier innovation by being their preferred customer. *Research Management* 55: 44–50.

Schleper MC, Blome C and Wuttke DA (2017) The dark side of buyer power: Supplier exploitation and the role of ethical climates. *Journal of Business Ethics* 140: 97–114.
Sheth JN (1973) A model of industrial buying behaviour. *Journal of Marketing* 37: 50–56.
Thorelli HB (1986) Networks: Between markets and hierarchies. *Strategic Management Journal* 7: 37–51.
Treleven M and Schweikhart SB (1988) A risk/benefit analysis of sourcing strategies: Single vs. multiple sourcing. *Journal of Operations Management* 7(4): 93–114.
Touboulic A, Chicksand D and Walker HL (2014) Managing imbalanced triadic buyer-supplier-supplier relationships for sustainability: A power perspective. *Decision Sciences* 45(4): 577–619.
Tummala R and Schoenherr T (2011) Assessing and managing risks using the Supply Chain Risk Management Process (SCRMP). *Supply Chain Management: An International Journal* 16(6): 474–483.
van de Ven AH (1976) On the nature, formation, and maintenance of relations among organizations. *Academy of Management Review* 1 (October): 24–36.
Webster FE and Wind Y (1972) A general model of organizational buying behaviour. *Journal of Marketing* 36 (April): 12–19.
Williamson OE (1975) *Markets and Hierarchy: Analysis and Antitrust Implications*. New York: Free Press.
Womack JP, Jones DT and Roos D (1990) *The Machine That Changed the World*. New York: MacMillan International.
Wu Z and Choi TY (2005) Supplier-supplier relationships in the buyer-supplier triad: Building theories from eight case studies. *Journal of Operations Management* 24: 27–52.

CHAPTER 5

Outsourcing

LEARNING OBJECTIVES:

At the end of this chapter you should be able to:

- Define key concepts related to outsourcing;
- Compare transaction cost, resource-based, and network-based perspectives on the outsourcing decision;
- Apply a framework for analyzing 'make, buy, or ally' decisions;
- Evaluate the connections between outsourcing and sustainability.

5.1 OVERVIEW

Outsourcing refers to the practice of contracting out activities or functions to specialized suppliers. It concerns both manufacturing and services and can relate to either domestic or international sourcing markets. In other words, outsourcing is not restricted to moving activities or functions to lower cost or 'best low cost' locations, although in recent years outsourcing has been closely tied to this trend. The outsourcing decision is naturally followed by a sourcing decision, that is, once a company has decided not (or no longer) to perform a component manufacture or service operation in-house, the next immediate challenge is to find a supplier or service provider that can perform this function on its behalf. New terminology has emerged that begins to question the idea of outsourcing such as local supply or 'localization', hinting at the difficulties of monitoring expansion overseas and the competitive advantage of sourcing goods and services from markets nearer to home (Wu and Jia, 2018: 27). Although outsourcing still remains relatively common practice, the increasing cost of labour in low cost countries, risk of supply chain disruption, and concern for the environment means companies are increasingly exploring the possibilities of establishing manufacturing supply chains closer to home (Ellram et al., 2013).

The chapter begins by examining outsourcing decision models by evaluating the so-called 'make-or-buy' decision. In order to understand these, we evaluate and compare some well-known theoretical perspectives including Transaction Cost Economics, the

DOI: 10.4324/9781003499602-6

Resource-Based View (and Natural Resource-Based View), and the Interaction Approach. The final part of this chapter explores the future challenges for outsourcing in terms of the implications for introducing more sustainable approaches.

5.2 OUTSOURCING: 'MAKE-OR-BUY' ANALYSIS

Outsourcing, or 'outside resource using' to use traditional terminology, means contracting out functions or activities outside of the organization. Whereas outsourcing of mundane peripheral activities, such as cleaning, catering, and security, used to be the focus of outsourcing projects, outsourcing increasingly concerns more strategic activities, such as manufacturing, design, and logistics (McIvor, 2008, 2009). This means that whereas in the past outsourcing decisions were relatively easy because they did not touch on the company's strategic activities, outsourcing decisions have become much more complex as companies now fear that by outsourcing a strategic activity they risk losing control of critical strategic assets that constitute sources of competitive advantage.

Many companies used to approach the outsourcing decision from a simple cost-saving perspective: a supplier has offered to take responsibility for an activity cheaper than we can do it ourselves, so why hesitate? Approaching outsourcing from such a simplistic and short-term perspective is one of the reasons why so many outsourcing projects fail (Cox, 2005). Instead, companies need to make a strategic evaluation of what it should make in-house and what should be bought in: the make-or-buy decision. This is a more complex question because it concerns the definition and identity of the company: what are we and what do we do?

The outsourcing decision therefore needs to be approached from a strategic perspective where the key question is: is this core or non-core to our business? In fact, as companies have already outsourced peripheral activities the real question is: how close to the core is this? An underlying theme of a strategic approach to outsourcing is that the boundary between the company and its environment is no longer clear cut. Companies can no longer be experts at everything so are increasingly dependent on specialized knowledge and technologies controlled by suppliers to the extent that we now talk about the borderless organization. Outsourcing stresses the importance of strategic thinking in considering how external resources can reinforce a firm's position in competitive terms. It also emphasizes the potential risks of outsourcing vital public services (e.g. health, welfare, waste management) to private profit-seeking corporations (see Note 5.1).

Arnold's (2000) outsourcing model emphasizes four elements of outsourcing: the outsourcing subject or firm, outsourcing object (i.e. the process, product, or service which might be outsourced, partner, or supplier), and the outsourcing design or 'degree of manufacturing penetration' in terms of core/non-core activities which the supplier may provide (Figure 5.1). Based on a core competence approach (Prahalad and Hamel, 1990) this model provides a useful starting point for identifying what should and should not be outsourced: the closer to a company's core (competence) an outsourcing object gets the higher the risk. Peripheral activities are 'low hanging fruit' that can be outsourced with minimal risk, distinct activities can possibly be outsourced but at higher risk, and core activities (i.e. very close to the company's core) are unlikely to be feasible for outsourcing.

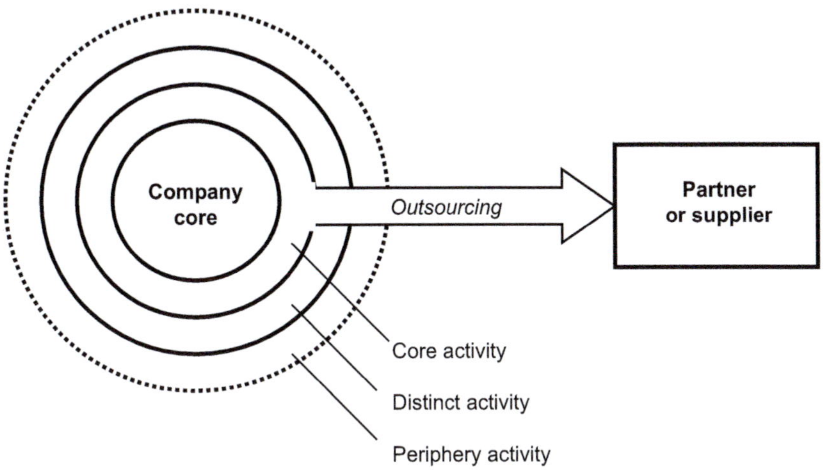

FIGURE 5.1 Outsourcing model
Source: Adapted from Arnold (2000)

As this model indicates, the challenge lies within the close-to-core activities, and it is here that many outsourcing discussions have been focused. In recent years the idea of sustainability competence is also included as part of the company's strategic considerations. Systems thinking, futures anticipation, interpersonal and collaboration are all defined as important core competencies for sustainability (Eizaguirre et al., 2019).

Figure 5.1 suggests that it is not simply a question of make or buy, but that in-between options exist. Some authors have argued that it is a matter of 'make, buy or ally' (Jacobides and Billinger, 2006). 'Ally' implies an alliance-based collaborative approach where suppliers (or outsourcing service providers) make a significant investment in the core operations of the outsourcing company and effectively become an extension of the company, but where the outsourcing provider technically retains its independence from the focal firm. Firms adopting an alliance approach may do so because on the one hand they are unable to produce the required goods or services themselves, for example because they lack the internal technological know-how, but on the other they need more control than a traditional transactional purchasing arrangement allows. An example of the alliance-based approach is Volkswagen investing heavily in Chinese, Korean, Swedish, and German suppliers of lithium ion and other batteries as it seeks to secure its position as a global manufacturer of electric vehicles.

5.3 THEORETICAL PERSPECTIVES INFORMING THE OUTSOURCING DECISION

To consider the make-or-buy decision from a more theoretical perspective it is necessary to explore three important theories: Transaction Cost Economics (TCE), the Resource-Based View (RBV), and the Interaction Approach developed by the Industrial Marketing and Purchasing (IMP) group. Management research examines outsourcing from a theoretical perspective to explain the internal and external dynamics of the firm and to understand what is happening in areas such as core skills, capabilities, and more transient elements such as knowledge. Although TCE and RBV are often presented as conflicting approaches supported by theorists with widely differing views, there are points at which they intersect such as the pursuit of long-term competitive advantage (e.g. Arnold, 2000), even if the means by which this is achieved is not the same. The three theories are now briefly examined in the following sections and then compared in order to identify differences and similarities.

Note 5.1 Outsourcing public services in the UK

Outsourcing is often associated with the practice of handing over public services to be managed by private corporations. The National Audit Office estimates that the UK government spends £187 billion on buying in goods and services every year. Although the reason cited by government is almost always to do with cost saving and capacity constraints, the trend towards ever greater outsourcing is putting vital public services (e.g. health, highways, prisons, waste management) in the hands of potentially unstable, profit seeking conglomerates while still leaving the public sector with the asset risk related to maintaining core infrastructure. Companies such as Serco and G4S are some of the biggest outsourcing firms in the UK who manage hundreds of diverse contracts for national and local government agencies. They are constantly searching for opportunities to find growth and secure profit, which means capturing new contracts and winning renewals in a competitive market. Specialist contracting companies Biffa and Veolia are market leaders in domestic waste collection and are also under pressure to generate financial leverage and boost shareholder returns from contracts with the public sector. Biffa recently had to write down roughly £1 billion of debt to restructure its high level of borrowing. As one of Britain's biggest waste management firms delivering a service once performed by local council workers, it is drawing up plans for a stock market flotation less than three years after financial problems prompted a takeover by its lenders. The move comes as Biffa, which employs more than 6,000 people and operates 2,500 waste collection trucks, some of which are powered by biofuel from waste cooking oil, seeks to take advantage of the growing demand for recycling services in the UK.

Transaction Cost Economics (TCE) is one of the most established economic theories, which underpins not only the concept of outsourcing but also purchasing and supply (chain) management. Although it has its critics (e.g. Ghoshal and Moran, 1996) TCE provides a theory for how production transformation is organized. TCE's chief exponent Williamson (1975, 2005, 2008) puts forward a theory of determining the most economical governance structure for a firm, polarized as to whether the firm decides to be vertically integrated and produce goods in-house or buys from the market. Focusing on transactions (not relationships) as the unit of analysis, Williamson's model of TCE concentrates on minimization of transaction costs as the principal driver of make-or-buy decisions and places much importance on the role of contracts. Williamson's work on transaction costs and how to approach the boundary of the firm is central to the division between the provision and commissioning of goods and services: in other words, the decision over whether a firm will make or buy. To grasp the basic tenets of TCE it is important to understand the following concepts: transaction cost, asset specificity, and opportunism.

- ***Transaction cost*** is the cost incurred in making any economic exchange, for instance when buying or selling goods and services, gathering market information such as price, invoicing and payment, writing a contract, and the whole process of negotiation between buyers and suppliers;
- ***Asset specificity*** is defined as the extent to which the investments made to support a particular transaction have a higher value to that transaction than they would have if they were redeployed for any other purpose. Such assets are specialized and unique to a specific task, for example the production of a certain component may require investment in specialized equipment, e.g. steel tools designed for complex plastic mouldings, or the delivery of a service that requires a particular set of professional skills, e.g. legal advice offered during an industrial dispute. If a supplier makes customized components for a customer there is a high degree of asset specificity as they are specific to that customer;
- ***Opportunism*** means self-interest seeking on the part of an organization involving some kind of guile or deceit, including deliberately withholding or distorting business information, doing less work than agreed, or failing to fulfil formal/informal obligations. It occurs in trading activities where rules are lacking and where the opportunist actor has the power to influence an outcome by the attitude which they choose to take. An example of opportunism is a property maintenance company gradually reducing what it perceives to be 'non-essential' time spent by its ground staff on tending to communal flower beds and tree husbandry. Another example might be a supplier selling its products to a customer despite having promised exclusivity of those products to another customer. Some authors suggest that organizations in business behave in a similar manner to animals in the natural world whereby all are driven to compete for their survival and ultimately to further their own self-interest (Cousins, 2002). This makes the chances of opportunism highly likely between organizations, all of whom may be competing in the same market environment and over the same, often dwindling, pool of natural resources.

TCE makes a number of behavioural assumptions. Firstly, actors are assumed to behave rationally but, as they have neither total information nor perfect information-processing capacities and they have to make decisions within increasingly tight time frames, they behave according to 'bounded rationality' (Simon, 1991). Secondly, business actors are assumed to be profit-driven and the assumption is that if a good opportunity arises they will generally grasp it; opportunism is assumed as standard behaviour and the way to control it is through control and audit. This is opposite to theories such as interaction theory (Håkansson, 1982), where a much greater emphasis is placed on the role of trust and where opportunism is seen as damaging to the development of trust. TCE places much less emphasis on trust and instead argues that significant 'hold-up risks' (for example a supplier playing off two customers against each other) are likely when asset specificity is high, risk of opportunism is high, and there is incomplete contracting. Transactions with highly uncertain outcomes, that occur more frequently and that require higher levels of transaction-specific investments, should be performed within the firm, and therefore not outsourced, because the company cannot safeguard itself against opportunistic behaviour (Guldbrandsen et al., 2009).

Assets that are specific to a transaction are more likely to be internalized within the firm than non-transaction specific assets. Thus, if a supplier delivers parts which are specific to a product then the manufacturer is more likely to seek hierarchical control to reduce opportunism. A particular problem that can occur is opportunistic re-contracting, where either buyer or supplier can act opportunistically when contracts are renewed, for example by increasing prices or decreasing service levels. Nevertheless, Williamson cautions against vertical integration:

> Because added bureaucratic costs accrue upon taking a transaction out of the market and organizing it internally, internal organization is usefully thought of as the organization form of last resort: try markets, try hybrids and have recourse to the firm only when all else fails.
>
> (Williamson, 2008: 9)

When applying TCE during outsourcing decisions, the focus is on ensuring safeguards through control mechanisms rather than relying on trust. TCE has attracted growing criticism over the years because of ignoring the role of capabilities in economic organization, and neglecting issues such as long-term relationships, especially trust and other social elements in buyer-supplier relationships. In the words of Granovetter (1985), Williamson demonstrates an under-socialized view of markets, while holding an over-socialized view of organizations. Furthermore, TCE is concerned with (transaction) cost minimization and so places little emphasis on value creation. A seminal paper by Ghoshal and Moran (1996) even claims TCE to be 'bad for practice' because it fails to recognize the difference between organizations structuring efficient transactions and the marketplace, in other words: the organization cannot simply be viewed as a substitute for the market. Organizations possess unique advantages for governing certain kinds of economic activities which should not be overlooked solely on the basis of transaction cost.

Note 5.2 Common criticisms of TCE

TCE is often criticised because it focuses on cost minimization, leaving no room for the academic or practitioner to consider the positive merits of alternative approaches such as value creation or value capture: both important considerations for example in the design of circular or closed loop supply chains. TCE also understates the cost of organizing and neglect the role of social relationships in economic transactions. This means important ideas around developing managerial trust during the formation of new business relationships are often ignored, which could have serious implications for the focal firm and its suppliers as they seek to transition together towards emerging business models in sustainable business practice, such as carbon net zero, sustainable consumption, and the circular economy.

5.3.1 The Resource-Based View

The Resource-Based View (RBV) of strategic management was proposed in the 1980s and emphasizes the importance of a firm's idiosyncratic attributes to competitive position (Wernerfelt, 1984; Barney, 1991; Teece et al., 1997). RBV focuses on the unique resources and capabilities controlled by the firm as sources of sustainable competitive advantage; the term 'sustainable' (or *sustained*) in this context implies a long-term focus rather than a focus on environmental or social issues.

The central logic of the RBV approach is that a firm's success is determined by the resources it owns and controls. RBV theory has developed in several different directions, the most influential to practitioners being that of core competencies by Prahalad and Hamel (1990) which has clear consequences for the outsourcing question (see Figure 5.1). Identifying core competencies enables the firm to understand its core strengths thereby affecting decisions about activities it seeks to outsource. The underlying focus of RBV is to identify and build sustainable competitive advantage at the level of the firm so from an outsourcing perspective the lesson is to nurture and retain core competencies internally, leaving those that are 'non-core' to be developed and supplied by external companies (Quinn, 1999).

One difficult question is: what qualifies as core competencies? Prahalad and Hamel (1994) argue that core competencies must provide customer value, competitor differentiation (i.e. it must be unique), and form the basis for entry into new product markets (extendibility). This is taken directly from RBV theory which proposes that the basis for firm level competitive advantage lies in the application of a bundle of valuable resources (Wernerfelt, 1984) that meet four different criteria: Valuable, Rare, Inimitable, and Non-substitutable or 'VRIN' (Barney, 1991; Peteraf, 1993). Physical or tangible resources might meet these VRIN conditions, but intangible or 'invisible' (Itami and Roehl, 1987) knowledge-intensive resources, such as capabilities and competencies, are more likely than physical resources to satisfy the VRIN criteria.

Even if the RBV clearly has some very useful implications for outsourcing decisions, particularly in the form of core competence theory, it has been criticized on a number of dimensions. Various observers (e.g. Porter, 1991; Priem and Butler, 2001) have argued that RBV is tautological: the theory identifies criteria that resources must satisfy in order to qualify as sources of sustainable competitive advantage, but provides little guidance on how to *develop* resources that meet these requirements. Most importantly, although RBV provides the foundations for resource accumulation and exploitation, the theory assumes that unique (whether tangible and/or intangible) resources have to exist and be preserved within the boundary of the firm so it underplays the importance of accessing complementary resources/competences outside the company, for example from suppliers. What becomes clear is that firms cannot expect to 'purchase' sustained competitive advantage on open markets. Rather such advantages must be found in the rare, imperfectly imitable, and non-substitutable resources already controlled by a firm (Barney, 1991).

As identified by Ramsay (2001) this assumption is also evident in the core competence theory: "The embedded skills that give rise to the next generation of competitive products cannot be rented in by outsourcing and OEM-supply relationships" (see Prahalad and Hamel, 1990). In addition to a strong internal focus, RBV is a static theory which can sometimes be interpreted as a 'stick to your knitting' approach. In other words, RBV (and core competence) can lead to an assumption that companies should focus on past strengths and therefore not focus sufficiently on developing new strengths. As the pace of innovation across industries is increasing, a competitive advantage could be nullified or even transformed into a weakness i.e. core competencies risk becoming core rigidities (Leonard-Barton, 1992). There are three more recent theoretical developments in RBV which seek to address such criticisms and are discussed further here: dynamic capabilities, Extended Resource-Based View, and Natural Resourced-Based View.

The theory of *dynamic capabilities* extends classic RBV to the realm of evolving capabilities (Teece et al., 1997; Winter, 2003). The important point is not so much whether we talk about capabilities or competencies, but that these are dynamic: viewed as future strengths. Dynamic capabilities are defined as the ability to integrate, build, and reconfigure internal and external processes and competencies to address a rapidly changing environment, where the ability to maintain and adapt these capabilities are the basis of competitive advantage (Teece et al., 1997). The dynamic capabilities theory therefore addresses the danger that RBV and core competence theory might encourage firms to rest on past laurels, accentuating instead the need for firms to change and innovate. The dynamic capabilities theory focuses on the unique, idiosyncratic, and path dependent nature of resources and capabilities: incremental evolution in other words. However, while moderately changing markets tend to rely on existing knowledge and linear execution, higher velocity markets may require disruptive innovation (Eisenhardt and Martin, 2000). Moreover, dynamic capability theory is still predominantly internally focused and provides only a partial account of competitive advantage in interconnected or networks of firms, where unique and difficult to replicate capabilities are those that concern how companies access capabilities through relationships with other companies (Lavie, 2006). These limitations of both RBV and dynamic capability theory have resulted in several complementary theories, suggesting that value lies in the resource configurations and socio-technical interfaces *between* firms, rather than the nature of the capabilities which reside *within* the firm.

The *Extended Resource-Based View* (ERBV) presents the most recent interpretation of classic RBV, conceived where the structure and function of a relationship relates to the specificity of resources to be transferred. ERBV emerges as a response to the development of competitive advantage in situations where resources and capabilities are held beyond the boundary of the firm (e.g. Matthews, 2003; Arya and Lin, 2007). The ERBV focuses on the assumption that strategic resources beyond the boundaries of the firm can be accessed especially given the existence of certain types of inter-firm relationship. Extended resource-based advantage in this context means that the difficulty to replicate stems from the composition of strong collaborative relationships, including those within supply chains and networks.

The ERBV is closely related to the relational view proposed by Dyer and Singh (1998) as part of the growing literature on the importance of trust in and relation building between firms in order to develop competitive – and collaborative – strategic advantage. The relational view argues that relations with outside parties, including suppliers, are essential to developing a sustainable competitive advantage and that it is the relations that constitute the unique and difficult to imitate resources. The focus shifts to *relational competence* (Cox, 1996). Therefore, the nature of the relationship may matter more than the nature of resources (Lavie, 2006). ERBV, therefore, gives structure to the idea of on-going collaboration between organizations across the wider supply network which stimulates resource accumulation and development based on complex interactions and inter-organizational relationships.

The question remains over whether knowledge flowing across the boundary of the firm, e.g. through outsourcing relationships, can be held as proprietary knowledge, or whether knowledge diffusion makes advantage hard to maintain (Lewis et al., 2010). The concept of flowing and diffuse strategic knowledge, and intellectual property, presents a dilemma for firms as on the one hand they need to source critical resources and technologies from outside the company but on the other hand they need to protect these from competitors. TCE advocates formal safeguards, such as control mechanisms and contracts, whereas e.g. the relational view (Dyer and Singh, 1998) emphasizes informal safeguards such as trust and commitment. Arguably, informal mechanisms are much more difficult to imitate because they are socially complex and idiosyncratic to the exchange relationship so have greater potential to deliver superior performance, owing to 1) lower contracting costs, 2) lower monitoring costs, 3) lower adaptation costs, 4) lower recontracting costs, and 5) superior incentives for value-creation initiatives (Dyer and Singh, 1998: 671).

The *Natural Resource-Based View* (NRBV) was introduced in Chapter 1, so will not be repeated in depth here. NRBV is still in its infancy, but we should note this recent development of the RBV as it attempts to build on the RBV to take into account a focus on the natural environment. Hart (1995) argues that sustainable development, product stewardship, and pollution prevention constitute potential sources of sustainable competitive advantage.

All three of these strategies require close collaboration with a range of external stakeholders thus sharing the focus on external resources with the ERBV and the relational view. The NRBV takes this analysis one step further as it suggests that resources gain social legitimacy through stakeholder collaboration. The NRBV therefore relies not only on models of strategic alliances, but on more complex stakeholder or network models. For this reason we turn to the final theory that informs outsourcing decisions and places much importance on collaborative relationships and the embeddedness of these within complex business networks: the Interaction Approach.

Note 5.3 Resources, competitive advantage, and sustainability

The debate around unique, bounded resources and their contribution to competitive advantage is particularly relevant to environmental sustainability. For instance, should the tacit and explicit knowledge of good practice in areas such as low carbon procurement, circular economy, and corporate social responsibility be viewed as a source of sustainable competitive advantage (SCA) available only to a few world-class organizations? Or should such core knowledge be shared with other firms and their suppliers as part of a wider concern over slowing the rate of harmful activities and depletion of non-renewable natural resources which affects the whole planet? Such arguments question the assumptions of classic economic theory and growth around bounded resources as a source of competitive advantage focused at firm level, and gives support to ideas over the Extended Resource-Based View and the benefits of knowledge accumulated from more synergistic or shared supply chain interactions.

The *Interaction Approach* developed by the Industrial Marketing and Purchasing (IMP) group shares many views with the ERBV and relational view, but predates both by around 20 years (e.g. Håkansson, 1987). The Interaction Approach is not a theory of the firm as such and focuses far less on how to achieve a sustainable competitive advantage, but it is relevant here because it is an established buyer-supplier relationship and network theory and it has frequently been relied on by authors in purchasing and supply management including those analyzing the outsourcing question (e.g. Dubois, 1998). The Interaction Approach emphasizes that although it is important to protect internal strategic resources it is increasingly necessary for companies to access important resources through external relationships with other companies; like the relational view (Dyer and Singh, 1998) the Interaction Approach suggests that relationships with other companies, including suppliers, can themselves be sources of competitive advantage. Yet managing the outsourcing relationship requires considerable resources after the decision has been made, where buyer-supplier integration takes time to evolve and is contingent on strategic priorities (Kaipia and Turkulainen, 2017).

However, the view within this school of thought takes the focus on inter-organizational relationships further by challenging the view of boundaries between companies as being separate (Gadde and Håkansson, 2010). Companies are intrinsically interconnected through resource ties, activity links, and actors bonds. So, instead of focusing on where the boundary should be between two firms (as in a typical make-or-buy decision) the firm should understand its multiple boundaries with a range of firms within the wider supply network and its position within this network. The outsourcing decision – moving an activity from inside the firm to another firm within the network – has implications not only on these two actors but on the total pattern of activities: there are network-wide implications that need to be understood (Gadde and Hulthén, 2009). From this perspective, the question of insourcing becomes equally important to the question of outsourcing, where 'make-or-buy' analysis becomes supply network analysis.

There are obvious complementarities between the IMP Interaction Approach and the NRBV as both emphasize the role of stakeholders and networks of relationships. The Interaction Approach has the potential to shed light on the process of implementing sustainability within supply networks yet so far only sporadic attempts at applying an Interaction Approach to sustainable purchasing and supply management (e.g. Crespin-Mazet and Dontenwill, 2012) have been undertaken.

5.4 SYNTHESIS OF THE THEORETICAL APPROACHES TO OUTSOURCING

The discussion of theoretical perspectives that inform the outsourcing decision shows that different theories have different units of analysis and are based on different assumptions. Consequently the recommendations regarding outsourcing differ. The purpose of this section is to try to bring together these differing implications and recommendations for the outsourcing decision, thereby moving from a theoretical to a more practical focus.

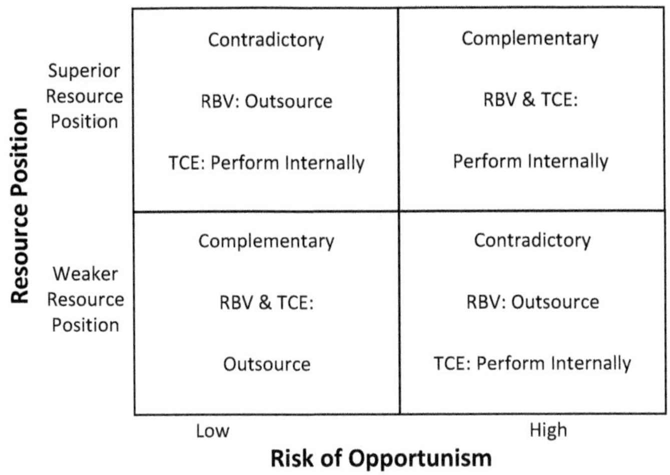

FIGURE 5.2 RBV and TCE prescriptions in outsourcing decisions
Source: Adapted from McIvor (2009)

The main conclusion from TCE is this: the outsourcing decision should be viewed as a strategic make-or-buy decision. Transactions with highly uncertain outcomes, that occur more frequently and that require higher levels of transaction-specific investments, should not be outsourced, because the company cannot safeguard itself against opportunistic behaviour. Companies should focus on minimization of transactions costs as the principal driver of make-or-buy decisions. TCE points to the importance of developing hybrid approaches, but formal safeguard mechanisms are essential to protect the outsourcing company against opportunism.

The main conclusion from traditional RBV theory with obvious implications for outsourcing seems clear: develop and protect strategic resources/core competencies and do not outsource these. In addition, resources and competencies sourced externally do not provide sources of sustainable competitive advantage. Recent spin-offs from the RBV, such as the ERBV and the relational view, state that companies can source critical resources and competencies from strategic partners and that their ability to access these – relational capability – in fact can constitute a source of sustainable competitive advantage. Figure 5.2 captures the two key dimensions from TCE and RBV in a matrix: the resource position and the risk of opportunism. According to this model, TCE and RBV give conflicting recommendations in situations of superior resource position/low risk of opportunism and weaker resource position/high risk of opportunism and it is only in the opposite situations that the two actually agree.

Arnold (2000) provides an alternative framework for reconciling the TCE and RBV recommendations for outsourcing. Figure 5.3 is developed on the basis of his original concept, which in turn draws from Quinn (1999). The framework here is simplified yet incorporates the RBV-VRIN criteria more explicitly and highlights the importance of

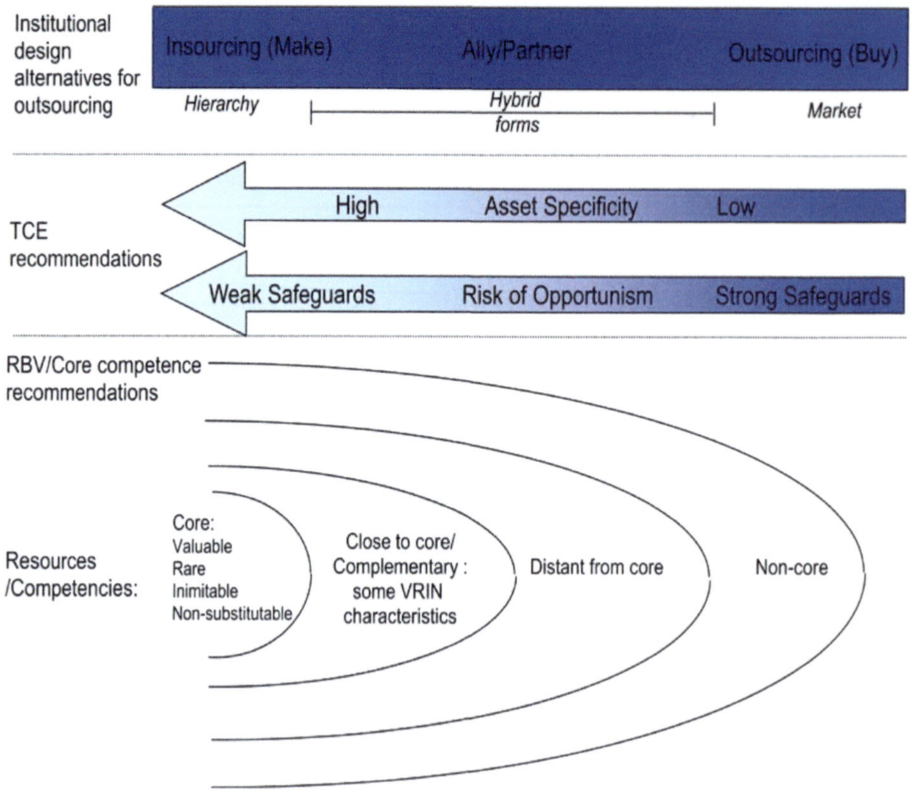

FIGURE 5.3 Combined TCE and RBV outsourcing model
Source: Adapted from Arnold (2000)

safeguard mechanisms. Arnold's model presents the make or buy question as more of a continuum which includes a mid-phase termed 'Ally / Partner' as a possible third option. This suggests that a hybrid approach exists between that of adopting either a pure institutional hierarchy (make) or market based approach (buy). However, although forming an alliance agreement to work with partners such as suppliers may seem a sensible option, this approach to sharing workload may open the firm up to certain risks such as the loss of intellectual property if the relationship deteriorates.

Both NRBV and the Interaction Approach put emphasis on understanding individual companies as parts of complex business networks. Instead of making make-or-buy decisions in isolation companies should understand the network-wide implications of outsourcing decisions. There is therefore a much wider acceptance that critical competencies are not so much core as *distributed* across business/supply networks (Grandstrand et al., 1997). Like the relational view, the Interaction Approach puts more emphasis on relational competencies and the role of informal rather than formal safeguards, including trust, commitment, and mutual dependency.

Understanding whether a firm makes, buys, or opts for some form of hybrid alliance approach, such as developing a (formal or informal) strategic partnership with a supplier, is a complex decision, where much depends on the level of in-house capability and strategic criticality of the component, product, or service in question. Particularly in industries dependent on technological development involving longer lead times, such as the aerospace and pharmaceutical sectors, decisions over inward investment, partnerships, and tactical sourcing from the supply chain are critical in the planning of new products. In the aerospace industry today a considerable proportion of investment by firms such as the engine maker Rolls Royce is spent on tackling how to reduce the weight of components (e.g. use of composites, alloys) as a means of reducing fuel consumption during flight. The development of lighter engines using lightweight components is a source of sustainable competitive advantage to Rolls Royce and one which depends on understanding how to engage with the supply chain and wider market environment.

The analysis matrix in Figure 5.4 gives an example of not only how the firm decides to 'make or buy' based on a sliding scale of firm capability over business criticality, but where the control and protection of key knowledge and skills fit into the overall picture of outsourcing and supply strategy. As Figure 5.4 shows, Rolls Royce considers not only the make/do or buy options, but also options for controlling through licensing agreements and protecting through strategic supplier partnerships. Rolls Royce clearly seeks to make only very little in-house, and accesses everything else through a variety of external sourcing mechanisms.

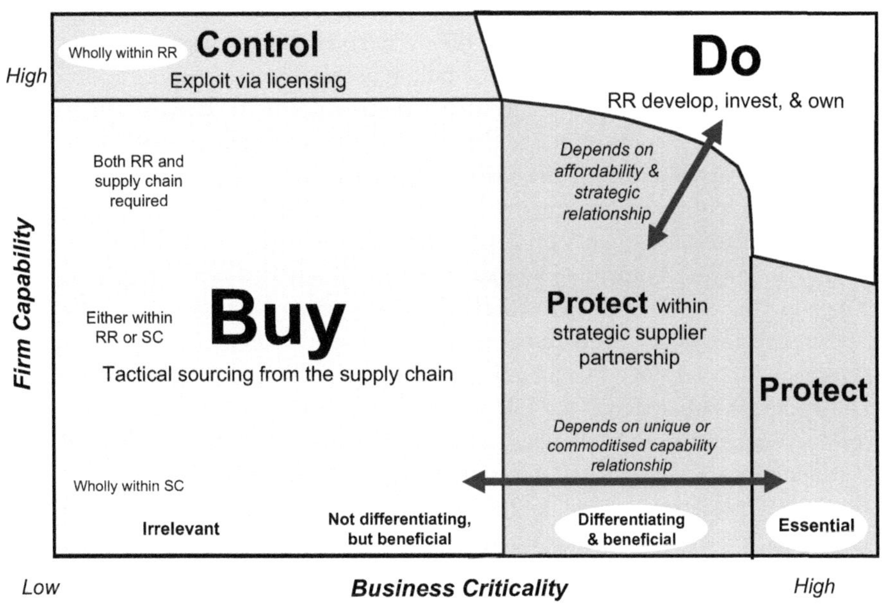

FIGURE 5.4 Business analysis matrix
Source: Adapted from Rolls Royce

5.5 CASE STUDY: OUTSOURCING HOSPITAL CLEANING IN THE UK NATIONAL HEALTH SERVICE

The decision to outsource cleaning contracts was first taken in the 1980s as a means to reduce UK hospital operating costs. Today about 40 per cent of hospitals now use the private sector to provide cleaning services particularly in busy areas such as wards, yet there is evidence that the practice has led to a drop in standards and a rise in infections (Lethbridge, 2012). To underline the seriousness of the issue, in 2008 the Royal College of Nursing conference overwhelmingly voted for a motion proposing an end to the practice of contracting out cleaning to private firms. In response, the government has made cleaning one of its highest priorities to tackle common infections such as MRSA and *Clostridioides difficile*. Yet despite such concerns, the Department of Health claims ensuring hospitals are clean and safe is not as simple as simply bringing all cleaning back in-house to be performed by NHS staff.

This case briefly describes the build-up of events which lead to this difficult decision over the outsourcing of cleaning, and some of the key background information that describes the complexity which surrounds the UK National Health Service (NHS).

The NHS was launched in 1948, born out of a long-held ideal that good healthcare should be available to everyone, regardless of wealth. Apart from charges for prescriptions, optical services and dental services, the NHS today remains free at point of use for all UK residents, which currently stands at more than 64 million people. For the financial year 2015/16, the overall NHS budget was around £116 billion, with NHS England managing £101 billion of this. The structure of healthcare is now devolved in the UK, with England, Northern Ireland, Scotland, and Wales each having their own systems of public healthcare funded by and accountable to separate governments and parliaments, together with smaller private sector and voluntary provision. Each of the four autonomous regions in the UK now has different policies and priorities, resulting in a variety of differences existing between these systems. Yet the challenges of providing a modern and well-equipped health service capable of meeting the demands of a growing population, with a high proportion of elderly people expecting to live well into their 80s and 90s, is taking its toll on NHS hospital capacity and resource planning. Despite this, a 2014 report ranking developed-country healthcare systems, the UK was ranked the best healthcare system in the world overall and in the following categories: Quality of Care (i.e. effective, safe, coordinated, patient-oriented), Access to Care, Efficiency, Equity, and overall palliative care. On the other hand, in 2005–2009 cancer survival rates lagged ten years behind the rest of Europe and, according to the OECD (2015), the UK still has a poor record of preventing ill health where some hospitals remain so short-staffed and underequipped that people are dying needlessly because of lack of investment.

This verdict, of an organization struggling to cope, from the Organisation for Economic Co-operation and Development (OECD) will make embarrassing reading for the UK government, particularly as the so-called 'cash-strapped NHS' (Sabin, 2014) heads for another winter crisis caused by falling temperatures, rising levels of illness in the elderly, and hospital facilities increasingly unable to meet demand.

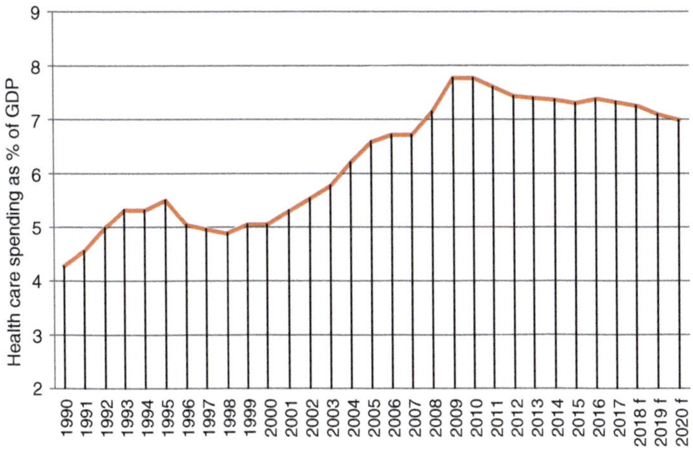

FIGURE 5.5 NHS healthcare spending as percentage of GDP
Source: Adapted from Public spending

MADVERTISINGedical Sstaff are frequently too rushed to improve levels of care that have in many areas fallen below countries such as Turkey and Poland. Almost 75,000 more doctors and nurses are needed to match standards in similar countries, the OECD said in its annual study comparing the quality of healthcare across 34 countries. While access to care is 'generally good', the quality of care in the UK is 'poor to mediocre' across several key health areas as the NHS struggles to get even the basics right such as ward hygiene and cleanliness. Furthermore, the report cites a fundamental lack of investment in hospitals over the last six years and short-term cost cutting as the prime culprit (Figure 5.5).

So, what is to be done over the decision to outsource cleaning services in NHS hospitals? Brought in originally as a means of cutting maintenance costs, the long-term impact has actually increased infection levels on wards, with the effect of raising costs in overall patient care. Yet to reverse the practice of outsourcing and give back cleaning responsibility to nurses now would significantly affect hospital spending, and take many medically trained nurses away from frontline patient care, a duty which is increasingly being entrusted to them as opposed to doctors and consultants. Hospitals taking control of daily in-house cleaning operations would require a major culture shift in an organization that has become used to looking to the outside world for a whole spectrum of medical, technical, and maintenance-related services. With around one fifth of all clinical services being outsourced today by the NHS (CHPI, 2015) such a shift would go against current trends, requiring in-house training and an expansion of ancillary nursing staff, meaning the introduction of further cost commitments into an already struggling UK public health sector. There are around 53,000 contracts now between the NHS and the private sector, where the safety and quality of healthcare is dependent on how these contracts are managed. Hospitals need to recognize that contracting for healthcare can be highly problematic, particularly where "...asymmetry of information makes it impossible for a commissioner of services to know whether a provider is delivering according to the terms of the contract, or is cutting corners or reducing quality in order to gain extra revenue" (CHPI, 2015: 4).

Outsourcing therefore is a challenging activity for the health sector. When executed correctly, it provides organizations with the flexibility to manage their service requirements according to demand over time, and within a defined cost framework. Providing that proper measures can be applied to monitor the quality of essential outsourced services such as hospital cleaning and maintenance, the trend for outsourcing in the NHS is likely set to continue.

5.6 CONCLUSION

The outsourcing decision is highly complex, requiring analysis of a range of issues related to internal and external resource and capability positions, transaction costs (that are often difficult to quantify), and business risks. The outsourcing, make-or-buy, or 'make, buy or ally' decision has significant implications for almost all functions in the company because of the changes working with outside organizations bring to the firm. In simple terms, outsourcing involves asking a series of questions starting with the strategic importance of the activity or function in question, but it also requires assessment of how the relationship with the outsourcing provider (or supplier) is going to be managed and the investment required to develop the relationship and control any business risks. The closer to the core competencies of the company the greater the risks, but the boundaries between the company and its supply network are becoming increasingly blurred as competencies become distributed across multiple supply network actors each with their own specialized competencies. Indeed, managing a network of outsourcing relationships is becoming a core competence in itself.

REFERENCES

Arnold U (2000) New dimensions of outsourcing: A combination of transaction cost economics and the core competence concept. *European Journal of Purchasing & Supply Management* 6(1): 23–29.

Arya B and Lin Z (2007) Understanding collaboration outcomes from an extended resource-based view perspective: The roles of organizational characteristics, partner attributes, and network structures. *Journal of Management* 33(50): 697–723.

Barney JB (1991) Firm resources and sustained competitive advantage. *Journal of Management* 17(1): 99–120.

CHPI (2015) *The contracting NHS – Can the NHS handle the outsourcing of clinical services?* Centre for Health and the Public Interest. www.chpi.org.uk/wp-content/uploads/2015/04/CHPI-ContractingNHS-Mar-final.pdf (accessed 21 April 2016).

Cousins PD (2002) A conceptual model for managing long-term inter-organizational relationships. *European Journal of Purchasing and Supply Management* 8(2): 71–82.

Cox A (1996) Relational competence and strategic procurement management. *European Journal of Purchasing and Supply Management* 2(1): 57–70.

Cox A (2005) Why outsourcing doesn't fly. *CPO Agenda*: 20–29.

Crespin-Mazet F and Dontenwill E (2012) Sustainable procurement: Building legitimacy in the supply network. *Journal of Purchasing and Supply Management* 18(4): 207–217.

Dubois A (1998) *Organising Industrial Activities Across Firm Boundaries*. London: Routledge.

Dyer JH and Singh H (1998) The relational view: Cooperative strategy and sources of interorganizational competitive advantage. *Academy of Management Review* 23(4): 660–679.

Eisenhardt K and Martin J (2000) Dynamic capabilities: What are they? *Strategic Management Journal* 21: 1105–1121.

Eizaguirre A, García-Feijoo M and Laka JP (2019) Defining sustainability core competencies in business and management studies based on multinational stakeholders' perceptions. *Sustainability* 11(8): 2303.

Ellram LM, Tate WL and Petersen KJ (2013) Offshoring and reshoring: An update on the manufacturing location decision. *Journal of Supply Chain Management*, 49(2): 14–22.

Gadde L-E and Håkansson H (2010) *Supply Network Strategies*. Chichester: John Wiley & Sons.

Gadde L-E and Hulthén K (2009) Improving logistics outsourcing through increasing buyer-provider interaction. *Industrial Marketing Management* 38(6): 633–640.

Ghoshal S and Moran P (1996) Bad for practice: A critique of the transaction cost theory. *Academy of Management Review* 21: 13–47.

Granovetter MS (1985) Economics action and social structure: The problem of embeddedness. *American Journal of Sociology* 91(3): 481–510.

Granstrand O, Patel P and Pavitt K (1997) Multi-technology corporations: Why they have 'distributed' rather than 'distinctive core' competencies. *California Management Review* 39(4), Summer: 1–19.

Gulbrandsen B, Sandvik K and Haugland SA (2009) Antecedents of vertical integration: Transaction cost economics and resource-based explanations. *Journal of Purchasing and Supply Management* 15(2): 89–102.

Håkansson H (ed) (1982) *International Marketing and Purchasing of Industrial Goods: An Interaction Approach*. Chichester: Wiley.

Håkansson H (ed) (1987) *Industrial Technological Development: A Network Approach*. London: Croom Helm.

Hart SL (1995) A natural-resource-based view of the firm. *Academy of Management Review* 20(4): 986–1014.

Itami H and Roehl T (1987) *Mobilizing Invisible Assets*. Cambridge, MA: Harvard University Press.

Jacobides M and Billinger S (2006) Designing the boundaries of the firm: From "make, buy, & ally" to the dynamics benefits of vertical architecture. *Organizational Science* 17(2): 249–261.

Kaipia R and Turkulainen V (2017) Managing integration in outsourcing relationship: The influence of cost and quality priorities. *Industrial Marketing Management* 61: 114–129.

Lavie D (2006) The competitive advantage of interconnected firms: An extension of the resource-based view. *Academy of Management Review* 31(3): 638–658.

Leonard-Barton D (1992) Core capabilities and core rigidities. *Strategic Management Journal* (Summer special issue): 111–126.

Lethbridge J (2012) Empty promises: The impact of outsourcing on NHS services. Technical Report. UNISON, London, UK.

Lewis M, Brandon-Jones A, Slack N and Howard M (2010) Competing through operations and supply: The role of classic and extended resource-based advantage. *International Journal of Operations & Production Management* 30(10).

Mathews J (2003) Strategizing by firms in the presence of markets for resources. *Industrial and Corporate Change* 12(6): 1157–1193.

McIvor R (2008) What is the right outsourcing strategy for your process? *European Management Review* 26(1): 24–34.

McIvor R (2009) How the transaction cost and resource-based theories of the firm inform outsourcing evaluation. *Journal of Operations Management* 27: 45–63.

OECD (2015) *Focus on Health Spending: OECD Health Statistics 2015*. www.oecd.org/health/health-systems/Focus-Health-Spending-2015.pdf (accessed 21 April 2016).

Peteraf MA (1993) The cornerstones of competitive advantage: A resource-based view. *Strategic Management Journal* 14: 191.

Porter ME (1991) Towards a dynamic theory of strategy. *Strategic Management Journal* 12(Special Issue): 95–117.

Prahalad CK and Hamel G (1990) Core competence of the corporation. *Harvard Business Review* 68(3): 79–91.

Prahalad CK and Hamel, G (1994) *Competing for the Future*. Harvard Business School Press.

Priem RL and Butler JE (2001) Is the resource-based theory a useful perspective for strategic management research? *Academy of Management Review* 26(1): 22–40.

Quinn J (1999) Strategic outsourcing: Leveraging knowledge capabilities. *Sloan Management Review* 40(4): 9–21.

Ramsay J (2001) The resource based perspective, rents, and purchasing's contribution to sustainable competitive advantage. *Journal of Supply Chain Management* 37: 38–47.

Sabin R (2014) Autumn Statement: Chancellor George Osborne to pledge £2bn boost for cash-strapped NHS. *The Independent*. www.independent.co.uk/news/uk/politics/autumn-statement-chancellor-george-osborne-to-pledge-2bn-boost-for-cash-strapped-nhs-9893409.html

Simon HA (1991) Bounded rationality and organizational learning. *Organization Science* 2(1): 125–134.

Teece D, Pisano G and Shuen A (1997) Dynamic capabilities and strategic management. *Strategic Management Journal* 18(7): 509–533.

Wernerfelt B (1984) The resource-based view of the firm. *Strategic Management Journal* 5(2): 171–180.

Williamson OE (1975) *Markets and Hierarchy: Analysis and Antitrust Implications*. New York: Free Press.

Williamson OE (2005) Transaction cost economics and business administration. *Scandinavian Journal of Management* 21(1): 19–40.

Williamson OE (2008) Outsourcing: Transaction cost economics and supply chain management. *Journal of Supply Chain Management* 44(2): 5–16.

Winter SG (2003) Understanding dynamic capabilities. *Strategic Management Journal* 24: 991–999.

Wu Z and Jia F (2018) Toward a theory of supply chain fields – Understanding the institutional process of supply chain localization. *Journal of Operations Management* 58: 27–41.

CHAPTER 6

Global sourcing

LEARNING OBJECTIVES:

At the end of this chapter you should be able to:

- Define key concepts related to global sourcing;
- Distinguish between international and global sourcing;
- Evaluate the drivers of global sourcing and the limitations of a pure cost focus;
- Explain the trend towards reshoring and nearshoring;
- Analyze the sustainability challenges in the context of global sourcing.

6.1 OVERVIEW

Global sourcing is the practice of contracting out activities or functions to specialized suppliers around the world. The most basic meaning of the term sourcing is 'product searching' and is often associated with the prefix 'global', 'international', or 'strategic'. Whereas Chapter 5 examined outsourcing decision models by evaluating the so-called 'make-or-buy' decision, here we focus on the particular challenges of sourcing from global supply markets, especially Low-Cost Countries (LCCs) such as China, which over the past 30 years have emerged as major supply markets due to significant cost advantages. In short, because of the effects of globalization, global sourcing has become synonymous with standard practice for many companies, whether seeking to source auto parts, computer components, fashion clothing, or relocate call centre services offshore.

A number of consequences have emerged as a result of these low-cost-driven, global supply networks, not just concerning risk and resilience issues of products and services supplied over long distances, but of the challenges associated with supply chain transparency and supplier accountability, particularly in demonstrating a firm's commitment to corporate social responsibility (Walker et al., 2008; Lund-Thomsen and Lindgreen, 2014). One area of major concern for many consumers today is the working conditions of employees in supplier organizations based in developing countries. Modern slavery increased by 10 per cent from 2016 to 2021, affecting over 49 million people, with over 17 million in the

DOI: 10.4324/9781003499602-7

private economy, thus within global supply chains (International Labor Organization et al., 2022). Over the last three decades global brands have been subject to scrutiny including Mattel, Apple, and Nike (Brammer et al., 2011), and many have implemented a major overhaul in supply chain transparency as a response to pressure and criticism (Doorey, 2011).Incidents such as the Rana Plaza have focused the world's attention on Asia (Wang, 2020) and despite alleged changes in their sourcing practices and increased transparency, not rarely the same brands have been re-exposed recently and implicated in forced labour in China (Walden, 2020). More broadly, a number of studies have shown how firms that rely on subminimum wage labour and high levels of outsourcing are likely to be associated with greater modern slavery risks (Caruana et al., 2020).

Public scrutiny and pressure have pushed not only individual companies, but whole sectors such as the fashion industry to re-think their sourcing models. In fact, some companies have begun to reverse their earlier global sourcing decisions, resulting in practices such as 'reshoring' or moving the production of goods and services back towards local sources of supply (Gray et al., 2013; Tate, 2014). These changes in sourcing practice hint at the difficulties of monitoring expansion overseas and the competitive advantage of sourcing from markets nearer to home (Steinle and Schiele, 2008). Local sourcing has also been associated with shifts towards the circular economy, thus addressing not only working conditions, but also environmental impact (Marques and Manzanares, 2023).

Best cost country sourcing (BCCS) is now a term often used instead of low-cost country sourcing, as a means of going beyond evaluating benefit based primarily on labour costs. BCCS seeks to adopt a total cost of ownership approach by including factors such as inflationary pressures on wages in emerging markets, shifting currency values, regulatory compliance, logistics costs, and an increasing focus on greener, more sustainable, and socially responsible supply chains (Dutzler et al., 2011). If reshoring trends have emerged in the early 2000s, they have been accelerated after Covid-19 (van Hoek and Dobrzykowski, 2021). The final part of this chapter explores the future for sustainable global sourcing given the challenges highlighted above.

6.2 INTERNATIONAL AND GLOBAL SOURCING

There is no doubt that a major driver of the increase in outsourcing in recent years has been the opportunity to drastically reduce costs due to low labour costs in developing and industrializing countries such as China and India. In fact, the concept of low-cost country sourcing is often used to reflect this particular form of global sourcing, although global sourcing is not – or should not be – purely a question of accessing low-cost labour. Almost 20 years ago a report by the Boston Consulting Group (BCG, 2007) listed a range of advantages of sourcing from China, including robust product and process innovation, sophisticated and diversified supply bases, low-cost, a highly skilled labour pool that can support production and R&D, low-cost plants and equipment, national and local government incentives, vast and growing domestic market, and in certain sectors e.g. plastics, printing, and electronics also highly developed clusters. However, the report also noted that companies sourcing from China are encountering increasingly tough challenges. A later BCG report (2010) showed that many companies were rethinking LCC sourcing strategies due to growing labour costs, currency fluctuations, volatile commodity prices, quality concerns, labour shortage and double-digit wage inflation, and growing protectionism. These concerns have only risen in recent times.

Best cost country sourcing – or BCCS – is described as the 'next generation' approach to global sourcing, where leading consumer goods and retail companies rank their overseas sourcing initiatives according to their level of maturity: Novice, Progressing, and Best in class (Dutzler et al., 2011). Although cost reductions of between 15–30 per cent in sectors such as textiles and apparel, housewares, injection moulded plastics, and electronics still remain a prime reason for sourcing from Asia, recent scandals mentioned previously, as well as rising inflation in China and India, means companies must revisit their sourcing strategies and re-evaluate the possibility of alternative destinations (e.g. Vietnam, Cambodia, Africa), locating manufacturing closer to the market (e.g. Eastern Europe in the case of European companies), and the need to create a greener, more sustainable strategy by reducing 'merchandising miles'. IKEA, for example, has advanced a plan to double its sourcing volume in India and increase its coverage of retail stores in the country.

This section now explores the rationale for global sourcing in more detail, and then clarifies the meaning of global sourcing compared with international sourcing. A model of different stages of international and global sourcing is presented, where global sourcing is the penultimate stage. However, as is subsequently discussed, there are signs of growing localism, or 'reshoring' which may indicate that the global sourcing trend has peaked.

6.2.1 Why global sourcing?

The traditional motive for global sourcing, especially when it relates to LCCs, would appear to be all about cost, but access to suppliers offering quality components and technology as well as a way to access a new market for sales and marketing purposes, circumventing trade barriers in the process, are also part of the equation (Guinipero and Monczka, 1990; Alguire et al., 1994). Indeed, companies may have little choice but to source from the region in which they wish to expand as local content rules, e.g. in China, often require firms to purchase specified quantities of components from suppliers in the country where the firm opens a manufacturing plant (Munson and Rosenblatt, 1997; Nassimbeni and Sartor, 2007) – see Note 6.1.

Note 6.1 Volkswagen's global sourcing strategy

Europe's largest automaker Volkswagen AG acknowledges that its production plants in western Germany make little profit. The Wolfsburg plant in Lower Saxony, VW's headquarters, is a sprawling 13 square kilometre site employing 48,000 people. Here it takes around 40 hours to build the popular Golf model, with its closest competitor the Renault Megane requiring only 17. With new car enterprises emerging all over China, and China set to overtake Japan as the second largest market after America, the prospect of sourcing cheaper products from the East poses both opportunities and serious threats for VW chiefs over maintaining levels of employment in their home production plants as well as promoting sound corporate social responsibility values in their partner organizations across China. Volkswagen was the first foreign carmaker to invest in China with the joint venture called Shanghai Volkswagen Automotive Company in 1984. With German brands – particularly German automotive brands – highly popular and trusted in China, VW has done well in the region because they know the territory in terms of market trends and regional production capability. They can also compete directly with Chinese competitors and present a better, more reliable image to local customers. However, VW's strategy may backfire in the long term, with foreign automakers only allowed to manufacture cars domestically in China through joint ventures with local partners. The requirement to transfer technology and know-how through forced joint ventures are fundamentally at odds with the commitments China made when it joined the World Trade Organization.

Source: Hawranek (2006); Akan (2017)

Research by Nassimbeni (2006) showed the importance of access to low-cost resources, but also pointed out the significance of access to scarce and distinctive resources. One example here is that rare metal ores and minerals, which are used to produce e.g. mobile phones, computers, and cars, are almost exclusively available from Chinese mines that account for 97 per cent of rare ore and mineral production worldwide. In fact, many companies are increasingly dependent on such critical raw materials that are vital ingredients in green technologies, and efforts are made at political levels to reduce such dependence e.g. the European Union's Critical Raw Materials Act (Hool et al., 2024). Therefore, although access to less expensive resources remains an important driver of global sourcing, it is increasingly considered a source of long-term sustainable competitive advantage (Nassimbeni, (2006: 704). Figure 6.1 provides an overview of global sourcing drivers.

FIGURE 6.1 Key drivers of global sourcing

6.2.2 International and global sourcing: what is the difference?

Often global sourcing is used in the same vein as international sourcing or purchasing, but what are the differences? The important difference is not so much whether we talk about purchasing or sourcing, but the distinction between international and global matters. In short, global sourcing suggests a more advanced stage and tends to imply an integration and coordination of sourcing strategies on a worldwide scale (e.g. Trent and Monczka, 2005; Quintens et al., 2006). A useful definition is provided by Trent and Monczka (2003: 607), describing global sourcing as the worldwide integration of engineering, operations, logistics, procurement, and even marketing within the upstream portion of a firm's supply chain. Where international sourcing implies buying from a foreign supplier on an *ad hoc* basis, global sourcing infers a much more strategically consistent approach (Bozarth et al., 1998).

Capturing the benefits of globalization requires a global sourcing strategy which involves the integration of engineering, operations, and purchasing functions across the global supply network. But, although adopting a global business strategy is seen as critical by companies that wish to expand on a worldwide basis, most firms do not have a well-developed approach to global sourcing in place, with many improvement opportunities left unrealized (Trent and Monczka, 2005). In reality, many companies operate at best an international sourcing strategy as they do not present a coordinated standardized global approach.

6.2.3 The global sourcing process: a stages model

The development of a global sourcing strategy does not happen overnight but tends to evolve over a number of stages, beginning with domestic purchasing and progressing to international purchasing before becoming global. Trent and Monczka's (2005) model (Figure 6.2) suggests a linear progression of increasing excellence in sourcing capability that finishes with the development of a global sourcing strategy integrated across worldwide locations and functional groups.

The distinction between international and global sourcing is therefore one of sourcing strategies: global sourcing is not so much dependent on the number of worldwide sourcing locations; it is the integration and consistency of sourcing strategies across worldwide locations and functional groups. In other words, global sourcing implies a systematic extension of purchasing policy worldwide and a strategic orientation of purchasing activities (Arnold, 1999). Quintens et al. (2006) have identified four dimensions of global purchasing (or sourcing) strategy:

1. Purchasing process configuration;
2. Standardization of global purchasing process;
3. Standardization of product-related characteristics;
4. Standardization of personnel-related characteristics.

Global sourcing strategy decisions therefore concern, in particular, issues of standardization and relate to questions of organizational structure and processes. These decisions are

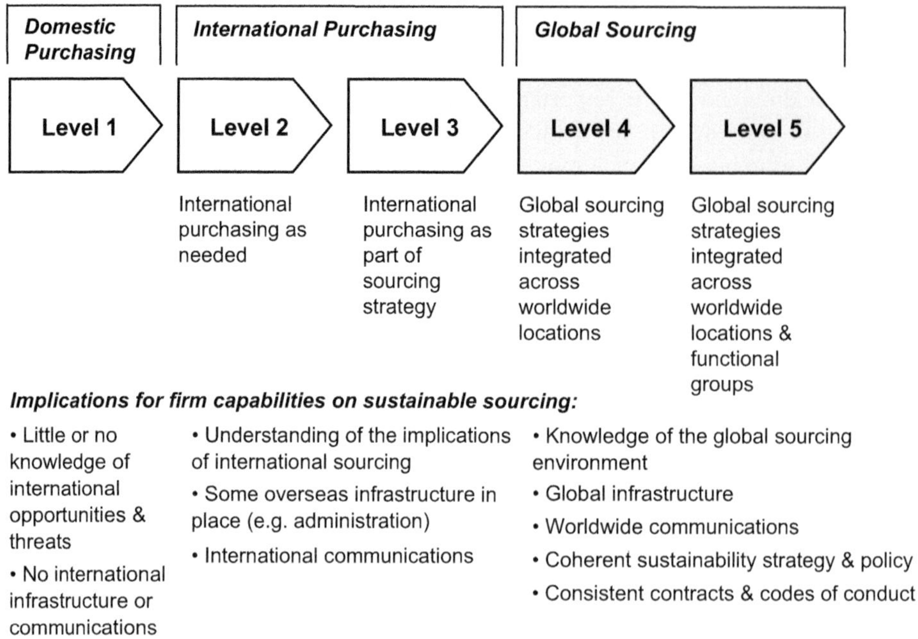

FIGURE 6.2 Progression towards global sourcing
Source: Adapted from Trent and Monczka (2005)

closely tied to the drive for purchasing synergies that were discussed in earlier chapters, for example, using standardized material and component specifications across global locations enables high volumes, improved quality through reduced variety, and even customization. For capital-intensive industries, such as the automotive industry, product architectures increasingly rely on shared platforms and standardized modular components, and it is critical that suppliers worldwide play their part in and comply with these standards.

There are both economies of scale and process (establishment of a common way of working) that are essential in creating a globally consistent line of conduct to suppliers, benchmarking procedures and results, and joint training and development (Faes et al., 2000). A global rather than international sourcing strategy is therefore also critical in order to implement sustainability within the supply network; global sourcing implies a shared sustainability strategy and policies, and shared and consistent contracts and codes of conduct across worldwide locations. SMEs must endure particular challenges when implementing global sourcing strategies. They tend to rely on intuitive global sourcing decisions because they are faced with high time pressure, have limited resources, and source under high levels of uncertainty. Bringing suppliers from jobs in other companies into the SME is a prevalent practice, for example (Ellegaard et al., 2022).

Recent trends in sustainable global sourcing have focused on third-party auditing schemes and emerging technologies as tools to improve monitoring and control of distant suppliers. A recent study by Benstead et al. (2021) suggests that a targeted audit is more likely to identify key indicators of modern slavery, including partnering with a local NGO to empower workers and collaboratively develop suppliers. Findings from Marques et al. (2020) recommend online technology to support knowledge sharing and diffusion of practices in global supply chains. Most recently, blockchain has been proposed as a tool to improve supply monitoring (Benstead et al., 2022), but results at a large scale are still limited and effectiveness has been questioned (Murray et al., 2021; Marques et al., 2024).

Can global sourcing be sustainable? Global sourcing and the lure of low-cost manufacture from overseas suppliers became a trend in the 1990s by Western firms taking advantage of reduced barriers to trade and costs of transportation. Particularly in high-volume, relatively simple goods such as plastic toys, watches, and calculators, the risks involved in setting up the supply chain seemed low in return for such potentially high profits. But it was not until corporations started to outsource more complex components that they began to appreciate the implications of the term 'hidden costs' to their business. Even relatively minor quality issues in electronic equipment, such as wiring harnesses critical to the core function of the motor car, meant prestige brands with strong track records in engineering reliability were forced into sudden and unintended product recalls. Firms caught out by over-stretching their supply chains had to confront the issue that sticking with local suppliers might have been financially more viable in the long run when considering the costs of quality assurance and the resultant impact on product reliability, or brand image, from CSR problems. Global sourcing requires substantial transaction costs, including for example the increased costs of supplier selection, contracting, monitoring, and auditing. In their drive for lower costs, companies have often underestimated these hidden costs instead focusing on the much more obvious lower piece prices. Cost advantages tend to disappear in the total acquisition/landed costs (Steinle and Schiele, 2008).

The argument for reverting to local sourcing, however, is not only based around issues of quality, brand, and total cost. Going local or 'localism' is a term used in conjunction with the protection of more vulnerable cultures or communities (e.g. O'Riordan, 2001) particularly those containing small businesses in developing regions that are threatened by global economic forces. Critical research has recently called attention to dominant supply chain practices, e.g. outsourcing and subcontracting and their impact on working conditions at the supplier base. The study by Meehan and Pinnington (2021) found no examples of firms reporting that they evaluate the extended impacts of their own cost-oriented sourcing practices. Volatile movements in the price of commodities are consequence of the global economy we all live in and yet it is often those upstream, at the end of the supply chain, who are most affected (see Note 6.2 – Fairtrade coffee). Introducing the idea of equity or fairness into purchasing's spectrum of business concerns may seem an odd approach when compared with more traditional portfolio management models, but the rapid uptake of the Fairtrade movement over the past decade with its strong popular appeal to globally aware consumers, demonstrates the power of pledging support to developing regions around the world. Coffee, clothing, and jewellery are now all sold via Fairtrade, one of the first and best-known independent consumer organizations, which guarantees workers in developing countries get a better deal from international trade.

Note 6.2 Fairtrade coffee – telling the local smallholders' story

Coffee is mostly grown by 25–30 million smallholder farms in around 80 countries in the tropical regions of the world. Each smallholder farms between 0.1 and 5.0 hectares of coffee, with most directly depending on the crop as their primary source of income. Between the producer and consumer there is a long chain of traders, exporters, manufacturers, wholesalers, and retailers, each demanding a mark-up on the original price based on kilogram of coffee bean. Located at the end of the supply chain, smallholders are vulnerable to the effects of market fluctuation where oversupply causes prices to drop, which in turn can force them out of business as their small volume does not allow bargaining power and their margins are kept very low.

Fairtrade was launched in 1994 as an independent consumer guarantee for products that enables farmers and workers in developing countries to get a better deal from international trade. Fairtrade describes itself as a "grassroots consumer choice movement that empowers consumers to take responsibility for the role they play when they buy products from developing countries". When shoppers buy a product such as coffee, bananas, wine, or clothing carrying the Fairtrade mark they are the most important link in the supply chain to the producers: an act of solidarity ensures that producers receive extra income through the guaranteed price and additional premium to improve their businesses and develop their local communities. Despite representing an innovative and radical movement in the support of family-owned farms in the developing world, Fairtrade and the principles it supports is not without its critics. Some argue that the fixed price element does not encourage improvements in productivity or quality of the coffee. Others suggest that the rise of 'green' marques such as the Rainforest Alliance is confusing to the consumer and clouds the core message of Fairtrade, which in essence is about the responsibilities of global sourcing.

Source: Fairtrade (n.d.)

6.3 GOING LOCAL: A TREND TOWARDS RESHORING?

The worldwide economic crisis that began in 2008 has further highlighted the need for companies in industrialized countries to question the benefits of global sourcing. The crisis unearthed a wide range of risks that companies expose themselves to when sourcing from offshore locations. In particular, many observers are beginning to question if the benefits in terms of total cost of ownership actually justify the increased risks. Subsequently, some companies have moved back production activities to their home country, i.e. 'reshored' or 'back-shored', and more companies look set to follow (Tate, 2014; Tate et al., 2014). Politically speaking, the bringing back of manufacturing jobs in terms of 'onshoring' or 'nearshoring' is, of course, seen as attractive and important to boost struggling manufacturing sectors in the US as well as parts of Europe (Brandon-Jones et al., 2017). Since the 2000s, many companies have reconsidered LCC sourcing strategies due to growing overseas labour costs, currency fluctuations, volatile commodity prices, and quality concerns. Trends between 2000 and 2025 include 'nearshoring' movements, increasing focus on TCO/landed costs, facing labour shortage and double-digit wage inflation, and growing protectionism (BCG, 2010).

The attraction of drastically lower wages was a significant factor in the offshoring of banking call centre services from Western countries such as the UK and US to Asia (see Note 6.3), enabled by improvements in fibre optic cables and broadband technology, which transferred traditionally localized information-based services to virtually anywhere in the English-speaking world. Although investment in information and communication technology to improve communications between customers and suppliers is one important aspect, of potentially greater significance in terms of long-term resource allocation is the investment in time required to form effective working relationships with other management teams. As can be seen in the example of the UK banking sector's initial decision to offshore its customer service call centres in Note 6.3, the cost benefits can sometimes be outweighed in the long-term over difficulties in transferring core skill sets outside of the focal firm.

Note 6.3 UK banking's decision to offshore (and reshore) customer call centres

The UK banking sector's decision to offshore its customer service call centres began in the 1990s driven by the opportunity to cut operational costs by exploiting drastically lower wages overseas in regions such as India and China. Once a small but significant component of the UK economy, with many customer call centres based in Scotland, such services along with software and back-office IT support now represent 6 per cent of the Indian economy with annual revenues of £49 billion. Yet the offshoring trend in the UK and US has become a controversial issue, not just over growing unemployment, but also service quality issues along with concerns for the welfare of overseas employees who often work long hours for very low pay. Multinational companies may need to think again about offshoring to cheaper locations on the basis that they may not be that much cheaper. In India wages are rising fast, but innovations in productivity means overall benefit is keeping pace. In China manufacturing wages have risen 69 per cent between 2005 and 2010, and if they continue to rise at this rate China's cost advantage over the West could eventually disappear. Santander is the first bank to decide to relocate – or reshore – all of its call centres back to the UK following customer complaints of the services provided from overseas.

Source: BBC (2005)

The perceived difference in cost used to be so significant that shifting manufacturing to a low-cost country location was imperative if cost was high on the agenda. Low labour costs, cheap commodities, and favourable exchange rates ensured that the decision to outsource to global suppliers was seen as fairly straightforward although decisions have often been taken on relatively simple price calculations rather than Total Cost of Ownership (TCO) analysis which often drastically reduce the real cost savings.

Suppliers in historically low-cost countries such as China have been able to offer 'perceived' prices of between 25 to 40 per cent lower than those available onshore: the typical threshold or tipping point for moving offshore (Ferreira and Prokopets, 2009). However, companies have typically tended to underestimate the global sourcing challenge including the hidden costs (e.g. TCO). As Hamid Mughal, executive vice-president of manufacturing, engineering, and technology at Rolls Royce recently said:

> Some of the decisions made in the past few decades by companies to outsource based on unit costs did not take full account of the total costs of putting bases elsewhere, such as inflexibility, lack of responsiveness from very distant plants, and leakage of intellectual property. These are very tangible burdens on companies and, in a hurry to outsource, people forgot that.
>
> (Cooper, 2012)

Companies frequently report on quality problems, longer and more complex supply networks, and loss of intellectual capital as a result of the decision to offshore. Moreover, rooting up suppliers from an established supply base, sometimes within an important industrial cluster, to new suppliers in a distant low-cost location also means that companies may risk losing their ability to innovative in collaboration with their key suppliers (Steinle and Schiele, 2008) and to customize products and services according to customer needs. Offshoring requires shipping container-size minimum orders and months-long order cycle times, thereby reducing supply chain flexibility and responsiveness (Ferreira and Prokopets, 2009). With inflexible supply chains, companies are no longer able to effectively tailor products and services to unique customer and channel needs.

More and more companies now realize that the cost advantages are beginning to erode. Labour costs are rapidly rising each year as are commodity and transportation costs e.g. for ocean freight. Furthermore, many foreign currencies are gaining in value compared to the Western currencies such as the US dollar, the Euro, and the UK pound. Since the early 2010s surveys have captured the intention of US and European companies to relocate manufacturing and sourcing. The further Asian countries improve labour conditions, and establish national minimum wage, the further offshoring advantages erode. In 2012, Mike Wheeler, Managing Director of Auto Styling Truckman, said:

> When we started importing from Thailand in 2003, wages were about $3 a day and they are now $10. It is frightening that workers can live on that little, of course, but it shows the upwards trend. [If] shipping costs continue to go up at the same time as labour costs, it may well become more competitive to manufacture in Britain.
>
> (Cooper, 2012)

Ten years later, the trend continues its course. A 2022 McKinsey survey with 113 supply chain leaders worldwide, representing organizations from a broad range of industries, showed that 44 per cent of respondents said they were developing regionalized supply networks. Moreover, 51 per cent of the respondents expected this momentum to continue in the next years.

Although more and more companies are contemplating reshoring from low-cost country suppliers to domestic or nearby suppliers, one serious obstacle is that in many cases the skills and competence gap has decreased or even reversed. Asian suppliers used to represent low quality but in recent years Asian suppliers have developed tremendously so that these days they are often able to offer superior quality. Manufacturing skills in the US and Europe have declined in recent years partly as a result of these jobs being offshored and many observers believe that it is going to be a hard task to re-create these skills. Daliah Simble, head of sourcing and production for Roland Mouret, the French fashion house, expressed the dilemma:

> I cut my teeth in UK manufacturing in the mid-1990s but I globalised when everyone else did. Over the past five years, however, there has been a swing and I have spent that time rebuilding my UK manufacturing address book. Most factories we are working with are rammed to capacity, but the issue is that the skills are not here anymore.
>
> (Cooper, 2012)

In some cases, diversifying across Asia and reducing dependence on China can be a better economic decision then simply reshoring. For example, China has been losing work to neighbour countries such as Bangladesh, Vietnam, and Cambodia for cheaper, labour-intensive goods like casual clothes, toys, and simple electronics. Li & Fung, a Hong Kong company that handles sourcing and apparel manufacturing for companies like Wal-Mart, reported in the 2010s an increase in volume in their industry plants in Bangladesh four times higher than in China.

Importantly, the supply chain risks associated with sustainability have also caused companies to reconsider their LCC strategies towards BCCS. Activities such as supplier audits and supplier development should now be included in total cost calculations, making LCC sourcing even more questionable. A current trend related to the sustainability dimension that correlates to localism is the circular economy. Often the implementation of circular business models has been associated with local closed loops, although this is not mandatory (Marques and Manzanares, 2023). However, from a broader sustainability perspective, the case is not so clear cut: reshoring (or nearshoring) may reduce one kind of sustainability problem, but also implies removing jobs from developing countries. Global sourcing has been instrumental in the economic boom of developing countries as well as Western countries, so simply stopping this trend may not be the right answer. It is clear therefore that companies engage in global sourcing for a variety of reasons, not only to achieve lower costs or economies of scale, and that given the increasing challenge over issues such as CSR, future considerations will involve greater sharing of knowledge and information, and how to implement best-practice (Trautmann et al., 2009). The case study on IKEA now illustrates some of the challenges of global sourcing, examining the initial rationale for moving away from domestic suppliers in Sweden, towards LCC – and now BCCS – sources. It discusses the sustainability challenges IKEA has encountered, and how it has tried to deal with them.

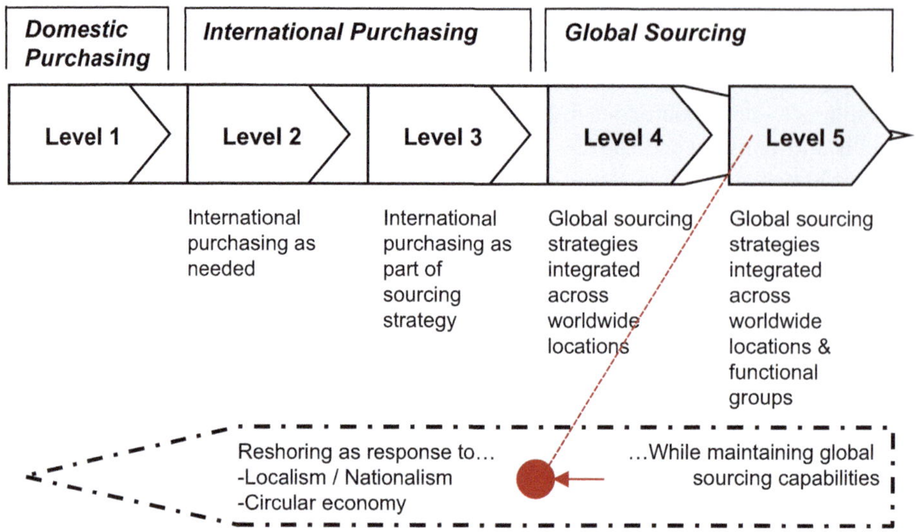

FIGURE 6.3 Pendulum model for global sourcing

In Figure 6.3, we revisit the sourcing model to include the perspectives of reshoring and circularity, picturing the current process as a pendulum that can bounce in-between extreme localism and extreme offshoring.

A recent qualitative study on the reshoring decision-making process during Covid-19 reveals that reshoring is a complex decision process and requires a long-term horizon. As a result, the pandemic might not have led to substantial implementation of reshoring necessarily, but at least reconsideration of sourcing alternatives, and implementation of the dual sourcing strategy as a risk mitigation strategy (van Hoek and Dobrzykowski, 2021). A complementary study looked into data from Bloomberg's Supply Chain Function on direct suppliers of 30 of the largest American manufacturers in terms of market capitalization (2014–2020). The study shows that American manufacturers are progressively reducing the geographical dispersion of their supply chain, concentrating purchase spend to fewer suppliers. Contrary to the aims of governmental policies, American manufacturers increased their dependence on foreign suppliers and reduced their dependence on local ones (Chakkol et al., 2023). One thing seems certain: companies will continue to move their supply chains away from low-cost countries if these do not continue to offer significant cost advantages. Moving activities home may be one option, but another option is simply to look for alternative, BCCS, or 'best cost' locations, especially if labour costs still constitute a significant proportion of the cost basis. Thus, the offshoring versus reshoring debate is in fact more complex than most would like to frame. At any point in time, we will witness multiple trends and shifts, like a pendulum that floats to each side over time … but never settles at one extreme.

6.4 CASE STUDY: GLOBAL SOURCING AT IKEA – BALANCING LOW-COST STRATEGY AND SUSTAINABLE SOURCING

The Swedish home furnishing giant IKEA was founded by Ingvar Kamprad in the region of Småland in Sweden in 1943. The first IKEA store was opened in Älmhult, Sweden, in 1958. The first store outside Sweden was established in Norway in 1963 and the first store outside Scandinavia was established in Switzerland in 1973. The business idea that has driven the firm throughout the years has been to offer affordable home furnishings at prices that make it possible for as many people as possible to afford them and to grow through duplication of a global market offering.

IKEA's ground-breaking idea of involving customers in the value adding process, by flat packing pieces of furniture that are then assembled by customers, has been a key characteristic of IKEA's business model. In fact, a key component in the low-cost strategy at IKEA has been to own only a small proportion of the means of production. In addition, IKEA has developed a wide product range based around highly standardized components, including screws, bolts, nuts, and locks. The high volumes of such componentry coupled with the assembly are critical factors in IKEA's low-cost strategy and its successful growth over several decades.

In 2024, IKEA's annual turnover reached €45.1 billion and the number of IKEA stores worldwide, including those run by franchisees, reached 485 stores in 63 markets in June 2025. The number of IKEA 'co-workers' count 216,000 (2024): 'co-workers' include employees working for all the different IKEA companies including non-owned stores. IKEA products are all principally the same in IKEA stores around the world: same design and same Swedish names that ensure customers come away from shopping trips with a Swedish experience that even extend to the iconic meatballs served in the IKEA restaurants. Products that are sold across IKEA stores, including well-known products like the BILLY bookcase, the PAX wardrobe, and the SULTAN bed are to a large extent sourced from a global supply network.

The initial development of sourcing outside the Nordic countries and later in Eastern Europe was the result of a ban on supplying IKEA by the Swedish furniture trade organization (Hultman et al., 2012). IKEA founder Ingvar Kamprad famously said:

> It was our first contacts with the Poles. We knew that [Poland] had a big furniture industry. But back then, focus was on quantity rather than quality. [...] I often wonder if IKEA would exist today without all those difficulties. The reason we turned to Denmark and to Poland, and abroad at all, was the enormous blockade that we faced.

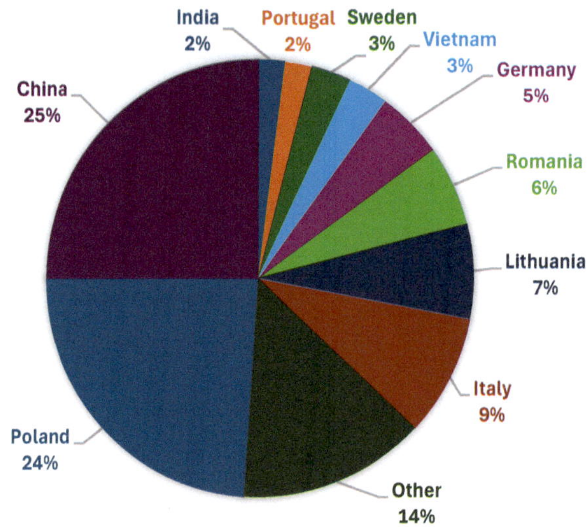

FIGURE 6.4 IKEA sourcing market distribution
Source: Adapted from IKEA (2024: 39)

The conflict between IKEA and the Swedish furniture industry was a result of the persistent search for cost reductions by IKEA which the Swedish industry was not ready to adopt at the time. However, the establishment of supplier relationships in Poland and in other parts of Eastern Europe enabled IKEA to develop and sustain its position as a low-cost alternative in the market for home furnishing. The establishment of Poland as a sourcing market was the beginning of an expansion of sourcing markets that has continued ever since. The development of supply chains in low-cost countries outside the immediate sales markets in the mid-1960s, when IKEA sold primarily to the domestic and Nordic market, initially took place in other parts of Eastern Europe (e.g. Czechoslovakia, Romania, and Hungary), and later in more distant locations (e.g. China, Indonesia, and Malaysia).

Figure 6.4 illustrates IKEA's current sourcing market distribution (based on percentages of volumes purchased). It should be noted that in the case of wood sourcing Poland accounts for an even higher percentage (29 per cent) with Lithuania counting for 13 per cent and Sweden and China both counting for 10 per cent.

One major driver of global sourcing has, of course, been the continuous search for low cost but also to secure capacity as the business has expanded rapidly to become truly global. Considering the global nature of IKEA's operations, we take a closer look at its governance and structure.

6.4.1 Corporate governance and structure

In 2016 IKEA initiated changes in its governance structure. Inter IKEA Holding BV (located in the Netherlands) is the new holding company for all IKEA related businesses. Globally, a large number of companies operate under the IKEA trademarks. Inter IKEA Group and INGKA Group (one of twelve franchisees) have the same founder, and a common history and heritage, but have operated under different owners and management since the 1980s. Within Inter IKEA Group there are the following important organizational units:

Retail Concept: All IKEA franchisees are independent of Inter IKEA Group although a large group of franchisees are owned and operated by INGKA Group. Part of Inter IKEA Systems B.V. in the Netherlands, Retail Concept develops and implements the IKEA Concept globally. Retail Concept also includes subsidiaries, such as IKEA Marketing & Communication AB, which creates IKEA communication content.

IKEA Range is responsible for designing and developing the global IKEA product range, including home furnishings, food, and packaging solutions. With almost 12,000 products in total IKEA's product range is very large. Product development centres in Delhi and Shanghai support the product development and design in Älmhult, Sweden. What is more, IKEA introduces around 2,000 new products each year. IKEA product development is based on the concept of 'Democratic Design' which seeks to develop better products at lower costs. When developing new products, IKEA designers focus on form, functionality, quality, sustainability, and, of course, low price. Working on innovations in materials and process technology to reduce dependency on raw materials, IKEA is increasingly dedicated to sustainability. The product range includes, notably, products for living room and workspace, bedroom and bathroom, kitchen and dining, lighting and home smart, textiles, cooking, eating and decoration, food.

IKEA Supply: Based in Switzerland, IKEA Supply AG owns the goods in the distribution centres and is responsible for cross-border flows and replenishment of goods throughout the IKEA network of retailers and wholesalers. IKEA Supply AG is the focal actor in the IKEA supply chain, managing its network of wholesale subsidiaries, transport service providers, warehouse providers, and customs brokers. IKEA Supply AG also encompasses IKEA Industry, which produces around 10 per cent of the product range focusing mainly on wood-based furniture with the remaining 90 per cent sourced from suppliers worldwide. The largest producer of wooden furniture in the world, IKEA Industry has more than 30 production units, across 18 sites in seven countries: Poland, Slovakia, Portugal, Sweden, Lithuania, China, and Hungary. IKEA Industry produces furniture in solid wood and light-weight or board-based wood. As a division of IKEA Supply AG, IKEA Components AB is responsible for developing, sourcing, packaging, and supplying various components, including screws and wooden dowels, utilized in the assembly of IKEA furniture.

6.4.2 A closer look at IKEA Supply AG

IKEA Supply AG's particular focus is on efficient production and logistics. The aim is to be lean and economical with resources, finding more efficient ways to manufacture products and striving to make more from less. IKEA co-locates supply networks, production facilities, and sales markets, and strategically plans the locations of distribution units. More than 60 per cent of products are shipped directly from suppliers to the IKEA stores.

Purchasing operations and business development teams are located in 24 offices, within nine Purchasing Operations Areas: South Europe, Southeast Europe, North Europe, Northeast Europe, Central Europe, Americas, South Asia, Southeast Asia, and East Asia. Likewise, logistics operations have a global presence which spans Global Distribution Network Design, Global Goods Flow and Capacity Planning, Global and Regional Transport Purchasing and Operations, Regional Supply Teams in Europe, Asia Pacific, and North America, Regional Quality Support Centres, and Customs Service Centres.

Where in the past IKEA had a larger supply base and a more aggressive approach to supplier management, fewer and long-term supplier relationships now appear to be the norm. In the mid-1990s IKEA had more than 2,000 suppliers, but in 2010 the company decided to reduce its supply base to around 1,200 suppliers despite increasing sales volumes as part of a consolidation strategy to build secure capacity for continued growth. By 2024 the number of suppliers has expanded to around 1,500 in total, for categories as diverse as home furnishing, transport, logistics and distribution services, components, and food. IKEA prides itself that the average supplier relationship lasts for 11 years. The operational relationships with suppliers are operated through purchasing offices, ensuring close proximity to suppliers.

Over the past several years, there has been a continuous rise in raw material and commodity prices, along with transportation and logistics costs. However, 2024 witnessed a swift downward trend, leading to a significant reduction in sourcing and supplying costs for products to IKEA franchisees. Despite the diminished impact of logistics disruptions in 2024, they continue to pose a risk and remain a point of concern as they affect product availability for customers. 2024 saw a strong decrease of cost of raw materials and consumables (-11.4 per cent compared to 2023).

As a result of global supply chain disruptions, caused by e.g. the Covid-19 pandemic, port strikes, the Suez Canal incident, and the Red Sea crisis, IKEA experienced container shortages and transport constraints which posed major challenges to replenish inventory. 2022–2023 therefore saw unusually high inventory levels that have since been brought down. The geopolitics continue to cause significant uncertainty and disruptions. In addition to the wars in Ukraine and the Middle-East and trade restrictions, extreme weather events are heavily affecting IKEA's global supply chain. Consequently, the focus on supply chain risk has gained prominence.

6.4.3 Committing to a sustainable supply chain

IKEA has built a reputation for supplying flat pack domestic furniture which is cheap, yet at the same time stylish and sturdy, supported by a network of suppliers located across the world. But this business model has also been labelled 'fast furniture', likening IKEA to the inherently wasteful fast fashion industry. Whilst interested in the principles of sustainable living for several decades and mindful of the public scrutiny from NGOs, by 2000 IKEA launched a sustainability code of conduct named 'IWAY' to complement its approach to global sourcing.

'IWAY' is short for IKEA's WAY on Purchasing Home Furnishing Products. The corporation understands that while some of its suppliers are located in countries where the environmental and social issues have been a high priority for many years, it also works with many suppliers where the agenda is only just emerging. IKEA recognizes that negative publicity over environmental or social conditions of its suppliers could damage the IKEA brand considerably. IWAY defines a code of conduct of supplier responsibilities in approved areas such as legal requirements, working conditions, wages and working hours, child labour, environmental improvements, emissions, discharge and noise, discrimination, harassment, fire prevention, wood procurement, and forestry management. To implement the code of conduct, IKEA has established a set of procedures for suppliers worldwide where all potential partners are informed about its sustainability requirements. On-site audits by IKEA auditors are conducted after a supplier has been selected and before the first delivery. Using the principles established by IWAY, a typical audit takes around two days and involves interviews of randomly selected employees and management representatives, as well as observations of factory working conditions and checks of employment contracts, levels of pay, and factory conditions.

IKEA's strategy of engaging in long-term relationships with suppliers means that in the event of non-compliance with the IWAY code of conduct, it does not break off relations with a supplier that shows willingness to improve. IKEA requires suppliers to prepare an action plan for all failed items and specify in writing how the areas of non-compliance will be rectified. For example, issues over waste-water treatment might involve a change in the supplier's attitude, an alteration to existing procedure, and possibly investment in the plant's infrastructure. IKEA requires corrective action to be carried out within a period of 24 months, where suppliers continue to be audited on a regular basis with the same team of internal auditors working with the supplier for periods of up to five years. Once a supplier is IWAY approved, the IKEA purchasing team follow up with regular contact to ensure that the code of conduct remains a high priority.

IKEA's reputation amongst suppliers as a 'tough customer' ultimately benefits successful suppliers who have achieved IWAY and are provided with a strong reference when applying for work with new customers. IKEA constitutes an important customer for many of its suppliers who strive to fulfil the requirements both in terms of product specification as well as the sustainable code of conduct. Given IKEAs size and reputation, suppliers cannot afford to give IWAY low priority as this might cause a termination of their relationship with the global furniture firm, which in turn would be very damaging to their business.

6.4.4 Accusations of unethical wood sourcing

Despite IKEA's long-term commitment to sustainable global sourcing, the company has been accused of unethical or even ruthless sourcing practices. Much of the criticism has centred on the enormous quantities of wood that IKEA requires as a result of almost 60 per cent of its products being made of wood: to put this into perspective, IKEA is the largest buyer of wood on the planet consuming 21 million cubic metres of wood (2019 figure), and one tree is logged every second for an IKEA product (Earthsight, 2021). In fact, IKEA sources one per cent of global lumber production.

Perhaps, therefore, it should come as no surprise that IKEA is constantly on the lookout for sources of wood. In one TV documentary, 'IKEA loves wood' by Danish national broadcaster *Danish* Radio (2024), the company was accused of destroying woodlands, including Europe's last remaining old-growth forests – the Carpathian Forest in Romania. In another report, the NGO *Earthsight* (2021) found that IKEA was responsible for illegally felling trees in the forests of the Ukrainian Carpathians which is home to endangered lynx and bear. The report said this was enabled by the corrupt state-owned forestry enterprises and that failings of the *Forest Stewardship Council* (FSC) allowed the wood to carry the certification label. IKEA also got into a dispute with the Lithuanian government over its aggressive logging practices.

IKEA has even been taken to court in Brazil for causing ecological damage. IKEA is accused of hiding behind contractors, but this has become untenable as IKEA is viewed as ultimately responsible. Even IKEA's homeland of Sweden has been losing its primary forests at an alarming rate as almost one-fourth of the remaining unprotected old-growth forests were logged between 2003 and 2019.

6.4.5 Taking sustainable global sourcing to the next level

In view of the latest sustainable sourcing challenges, IKEA continues to rely on the IWAY system to set out its sustainability agenda across the global supply networks. In its most recent iteration IWAY is not only IKEA's supplier code of conduct and monitoring system but also a development programme. IKEA prides itself that 2024 saw IKEA supporting suppliers with more than 1,240 implementation activities. This includes training on internal auditing, health and safety, and responsible recruitment.

The bottom line remains compliance with IWAY requirements and over 790 verification activities were performed in the Inter IKEA Group supply chain in 2024. In cases of non-compliance IKEA stipulates corrective actions and phases out suppliers that fail to address the issues; the focus on sub-tier suppliers has become an increasing priority. In 2024 these activities covered any remaining board mills, papermills, and verification of compliance with IWAY requirements at critical third-tier subcontractors. Supply chains are being 'mapped to the forest roadside' i.e. right down to raw material extraction, and verification of compliance with IWAY is ensured at critical sub-contractors. In turn, IKEA suppliers are requested to communicate the IWAY requirements to their employees and sub-tier suppliers, ensuring that all required measures are implemented at their own operations.

In addition to focusing on supplier compliance across tiers, IKEA is dedicating its efforts to reducing resources and a stronger focus on circularity. Furniture recycling is not only seen as part of its corporate responsibility, but also as adding commercial value. For example, using the 'Furniture Reuse Network', UK customers can have their old sofas collected from home for free and assessed by IKEA for possible refurbishment and redistribution or, if in very poor condition, dismantling into its constituent parts. Using fewer resources and raw materials means a lower environmental impact but has the added advantage of lower costs. IKEA even replaced wooden pallets with paper pallets and loading ledges. This change increases sustainability, improves filling rates, and reduces handling material costs.

Increasing stakeholder scrutiny and regulatory requirements concerning human rights and ethical sourcing, i.e. the EUDR, CSRD, and CSDDD, are forcing IKEA to demonstrate due diligence and to further improve supply chain transparency. At the COP15 conference IKEA launched an initiative to fast-track biodiversity assessments of FSC-certified forests in Brazil, Finland, and Sweden in collaboration with FSC and WWF. This new Forest Management certification contributes to biodiversity conservation in Brazil, Finland, and Sweden.

However, there are continuing concerns over the company's policies and its sourcing of wood is at the heart of the company's challenges. Despite its claims to be committed to no deforestation by 2026, having developed a strategy to become 'forest-positive' by becoming one of the largest private landowners of forests worldwide and 'to improve forest management worldwide by 2030', some observers label this as 'forest colonisation' (see Hruza, 2024).

But IKEA remains committed to sustainable sourcing. In the words of IKEA's Chief Sustainability Officer, Karen Pflug:

> We firmly believe sustainability and affordability must go hand-in-hand, so during this year we launched our Sustainable Living Shops online and continued to scale up our circular services by piloting IKEA Preowned, our new peer-to-peer second-hand marketplace, to enable customers to buy and sell used IKEA furniture at even lower prices.
>
> (Downes, 2025)

6.5 CONCLUSION

The adoption of a global sourcing strategy has been a long-term trend where Western firms for decades have taken advantage of significantly lower costs in developing regions of the world through LCC sourcing. However, in addition to ever diminishing cost advantages from LCC sourcing strategies, companies are increasingly realizing the importance of best cost country sourcing or BCC, described as where leading companies rank their overseas sourcing initiatives according to a range of factors which includes managing the ethical supply risks that come with the territory. Companies have to invest in the monitoring of supplier compliance in areas such as workforce rights, protection of natural habitats, and emission of toxic substances, particularly at sub-tier supplier level, which is more difficult to police and susceptible to 'public outings' as the result of investigation by NGOs. These policing activities all represent costs that are difficult to calculate and easy to underestimate. So, there are signs of a rethink of LCC sourcing strategies: not only is the difference in labour costs between East and West diminishing, resulting in some sectors such as banking services beginning to reshore, but there is an increased awareness of the total costs of conducting business worldwide, a factor which is persuading some managers to reconsider their global sourcing strategy altogether, particularly those that rely on an LCC strategy. Continuing concern over the world economy is a major factor in growing protectionism of home markets and the susceptibility of foreign firms to increases in barriers to trade. Pressures related to political nationalism and the circular economy add further pressure towards localism and reshoring. While many corporations have announced their intentions towards becoming more sustainable, more circular, and have begun to take the first steps in reviewing their global sourcing strategy, few have translated this into a coherent, end-to-end supply chain policy that includes long-term prospects for both local sources of production as well as safeguarding the regions around the world in which they operate.

REFERENCES

Akan E (2017) How China made Volkswagen the world's biggest carmaker. *The Epoch Times*. http://www.theepochtimes.com (accessed 5 May 2017).

Alguire MS, Frear CR and Metcalf LE (1994) An examination of the determinants of global sourcing strategy. *Journal of Business and Industrial Marketing* 9(2): 62–74.

Arnold U (1999) Organization of global sourcing: Ways towards an optimal degree of centralization. *European Journal of Purchasing and Supply Management* 5(3/4): 167–174.

BBC (2005) HSBC bank 'to offshore more jobs'. http://news.bbc.co.uk/2/hi/business/4353423.stm

Benstead AV, Hendry LC and Stevenson M (2021) Detecting and remediating modern slavery in supply chains: A targeted audit approach. *Production Planning & Control* 32(13): 1136–1157.

Benstead AV, Mwesiumo D, Moradlou H and Boffelli A (2022) Entering the world behind the clothes that we wear: Practical applications of blockchain technology. *Production Planning & Control*: 1–18.

Boston Consulting Group (BCG) (2007) Sourcing from China: Lessons from the leaders. 27 July.

Boston Consulting Group (BCG) (2010) Global sourcing in the post downturn era. October.

Bozarth C, Handfield R and Das A (1998) Stages of global sourcing strategy evolution: An exploratory study. *Journal of Operations Management* 16(2–3): 241–55.

Brammer S, Hoejmose S and Millington A (2011) Managing Sustainable Global Supply Chains: A Systematic Review of the Body of Knowledge. Network for Business Sustainability: London & Ontario. Public report.

Brandon-Jones E, Dutordoir M, Neto JQF and Squire B (2017) The impact of reshoring decisions on shareholder wealth. *Journal of Operations Management* 49: 31–36.

Caruana R, Crane A, Gold S and LeBaron G (2020) Modern slavery in business: The sad and sorry state of a non-field. *Business & Society* 60(2): 251–287.

Chakkol M, Johnson M, Karatzas A, Papadopoulos G and Korfiatis N (2023) Making supply chains great again: Examining structural changes to US manufacturing supply chains. *International Journal of Operations & Production Management* 44(5): 1083–1108.

Cooper K (2012) Made in Britain: It's not a dream. *The Sunday Times*, 11 November.

Danish Radio (2024) IKEA loves wood. https://www.dr.dk/drtv/program/ikea-elsker-trae_492719 (accessed 1 July 2025).

Doorey DJ (2011) The transparent supply chain: From resistance to implementation at Nike and Levi-Strauss. *Journal of Business Ethics* 103(4): 587–603.

Downes S (2025) What does Ingka annual report say about IKEA sustainability? *Sustainability Magazine*. https://sustainabilitymag.com/articles/what-does-ingka-annual-report-say-about-ikea-sustainability (accessed 1 July 2025).

Dutzler H, Philips D, Mansson A and Parthasarathy S (2011) Best cost country sourcing: A next generation approach. Strategy& (formerly Booz & company). www.strategyand.pwc.com/media/file (accessed May 2017).

Earthsight (2021) IKEA's house of horrors. https://www.earthsight.org.uk/news/investigations/ikea-house-of-horrors (accessed 1 July 2025).

Ellegaard C, Normann U and Lidegaard N (2022) Intuitive global sourcing – A study of supplier selection decisions by apparel SMEs. *International Journal of Operations & Production Management* 42(2): 151–181.

Faes W, Matthyssens P and Vandenbempt K (2000) The pursuit of global purchasing synergy. *Industrial Marketing Management* 29(6): 539–553.

Fairtrade (n.d.) www.fairtrade.org.uk

Ferreira J and Prokopets L (2009) Does offshoring still make sense? *Supply Chain Management Review 13*(1).

Gray JV, Skowronski K, Esenduran G and Rungtusanatham MJ (2013) The reshoring phenomenon: What supply chain academics ought to know and should do. *Journal of Supply Chain Management* 49(2): 27–33.

Guinipero LC and Monczka RM (1990) Organizational approaches to managing international sourcing. *International Journal of Physical Distribution & Logistics Management* 20(4): 3–12.

Hawranek D (2006) Vexing problems plague Volkswagen. *Der Speigel*. 13 February.

Hool A, Helbig C and Wierink G (2024) Challenges and opportunities of the European critical raw materials act. *Mineral Economics* 37(3): 661–668.

Hruza M (2024) Are we being fooled by IKEA's promise of a greener future? *Modern Times Review*. https://www.moderntimes.review/ikea-the-tree-hunter/

Hultman J, Johnsen R, Johnsen T and Hertz S (2012) An interaction approach to global sourcing: A case study of Ikea. *Journal of Purchasing & Supply Management* 18(1): 9–21.

IKEA (2024) IKEA Sustainability Report FY24

International Labor Organization, Walk Free and International Organization for Migration (2022*) Global Estimates of Modern Slavery: Forced Labour and Forced Marriage*. https://www.ilo.org/global/topics/forced-labour/publications/WCMS_854733/lang--en/index.htm

Lund-Thomsen P and Lindgreen A (2014) Corporate social responsibility in global value chains: Where are we now and where are we going? *Journal of Business Ethics* 123(1): 11–22.

Marques L and Manzanares MD (2023) Towards social network metrics for supply network circularity. *International Journal of Operations & Production Management* 43(4): 595–618.

on a small set of core competencies and access complementary competencies through various forms of business networks such as innovation networks (Powell et al., 1996) and supply networks (Lamming et al., 2000).

The need to source specialized technologies and capabilities is particularly important when companies seek to develop new environmentally-friendly – or green – products and packaging solutions. This is a process that typically requires radical changes to product designs and therefore a need for innovation. Consider how the automotive industry is in the process of transitioning from combustion engine power to electrification: a paradigmatic change that also affects other industries, such as the aerospace and train industries. These are examples of industries that are literally in a race to develop new technological solutions to tackle sustainability challenges (Johnsen et al., 2022: 1). Or the need to design-out toxic materials or to replace non-recyclable materials, which end up in landfill sites, with alternative materials that are easy to recycle.

Developing green innovations creates a need for novel technology and therefore a need to connect with new suppliers. Where existing supply partners used to be the main (upstream) sources of innovation, companies are now looking further afield to scout for new suppliers from outside their existing supply networks in their wider ecosystems.

This chapter begins by introducing the concept of supplier involvement in NPD as the point of departure. We explore how NPD is increasingly driven by the need to develop new sustainable product and service offerings and the need for sourcing – or scouting – new suppliers and to connect with new non-traditional supply chain players, such as startups. This is followed by an examination of the more recently developed concept of early procurement involvement (EPI) (Schiele, 2010), sometimes called early purchasing involvement, which emphasizes the fact that if suppliers need to be involved at an early stage in NPD projects so does procurement.

7.2 SUPPLIER INVOLVEMENT IN NEW PRODUCT DEVELOPMENT (NPD)

In innovation circles the buzzword of the last 25 years or so has been 'open innovation' (Chesbrough, 2003). This implies that instead of developing and protecting technologies and competencies internally, companies choose to connect to these through their business networks. Companies increasingly consider suppliers as critical sources of innovation and try to involve and integrate suppliers of key components or technology into design and development processes. However, not only do suppliers need to be closely involved in NPD projects, but they also need to be involved *early*. The concept of early supplier involvement (ESI) is often used in practice to emphasize the importance of involving suppliers early in the NPD process in order to fully capitalize on suppliers' specialized capabilities.

Since the beginning of research on supplier involvement in NPD the idea has been that it is a key factor in enabling design-for-manufacture (DfM) (Swink, 1999). The logic is clear: with a large part of manufacturing outsourced to suppliers these must be closely involved in the design and development of the products that they will ultimately produce. DfM is a long-established design philosophy that has been followed in more recent times by 'design-for-X' philosophies that dedicated to environmental performance, such as 'design-for-environment' (DfE), or 'design-for-sustainability' (see note 7.1).

Studies have shown that collaborating with suppliers as part of NPD processes may enable companies to improve NPD performance. In particular, the expected performance benefits include reducing time-to-market and development cost (efficiency) and improving product quality (effectiveness). However, positive results should not be taken for granted, indeed first attempts to implement ESI processes may not bear fruit. A recent meta-analysis (Suurmond et al., 2020) showed that extensive involvement rather than early involvement is the key to achieving a positive NPD impact on efficiency and effectiveness. The emphasis on *extensive* rather than *early* supplier involvement complements Johnsen's (2009) study, however, as we discuss towards the end of this chapter the level of technological newness involved is an important factor in understanding when supplier involvement is appropriate.

Note 7.1 Examples of sustainability-related design-for-X (DfX) guidelines

In addition to, for example, production-related DfX concepts such as design for manufacturability, design to cost, design for assembly, or design for supply chain, some DfX concepts specifically concern environmental improvement. Examples include:

- *Design for environmental manufacturing*, including raw material extraction, processing, and manufacturing using non-toxic materials and processes. This includes the minimization of waste and hazardous by-products, air pollution, and energy expenditure.
- *Design for environmental packaging*, ensuring that materials used in packaging are environmentally friendly, materials and also pallets used for transportation are reusable and recyclable, and unnecessary paper and packaging products are eliminated.
- *Design for disposal or reuse*, involving reuse or refurbishing of a product when it reaches its end of life. This relates to the concepts of closed-loop supply chains and product stewardship that will be discussed in depth in Chapter 8.
- *Design for sustainability* is an eco-design concept that expands the focus to include not only the environmental dimension of sustainability but also the social and economic dimensions. Typically, the objectives are to use fewer resources and apply eco-friendly alternatives e.g. in the choice of materials. D4S requires radical product innovations and potentially also innovations in product-service systems, which challenge current consumption and production patterns by completely re-thinking products in light of consumer needs.

7.2.1 Early supplier involvement: why 'early'?

As a rule of thumb many companies estimate that as much as 80 per cent of total product cost is committed or 'locked-in' during the concept and design stages (Handfield et al., 1999). This means that it is in fact much more important to strive to reduce product costs during the NPD process than to reduce costs once a product is in production. Furthermore, it is during the early stages of the NPD process that significant changes can be made to product designs and specifications so effective cost minimization requires early intervention in the NPD process. Figure 7.1 helps to understand the reasons for this:

The NPD process illustrated in Figure 7.1 is typical of high-volume manufacturing industries. The first stage 'idea generation', or 'ideation', is about searching for an idea for a new product so involves creative thinking and exploration of potential ideas and concepts. There is no commitment to solutions at this stage. The following stages gradually involve commitment to particular solutions as these are evaluated from different perspectives e.g.:

- Marketing: is the market sufficient?
- Finance: is it financially viable?
- Engineering: can it be developed?
- Operations/production: can it be produced?
- Procurement/sourcing: who needs to be involved from the supply chain?

As the design and development process progresses the company commits to particular solutions and it becomes both difficult and expensive to make changes, for example, to a different design or use of different materials. The product and process engineering stage requires investment in prototypes and tooling and this is traditionally the stage when companies release product specifications and start to consider who is going to produce the various components. However, as the company has already made significant commitments and investments at this stage it is very difficult and costly to change anything that has already passed the earlier stages of approval.

ESI means involving suppliers of key components (parts or ingredients) as early as possible, i.e. during concept development or early product planning (e.g. as part of feasibility studies). Involving suppliers at this stage enables design for manufacture and helps to prevent, reduce, or introduce earlier costly design changes: it is a 'first time right' method. Design for manufacture (DfM) means that the design (and development) process is carried out with a specific view to putting the product into production. This is by no means a certainty in many companies where the early stages of the NPD process are the domain

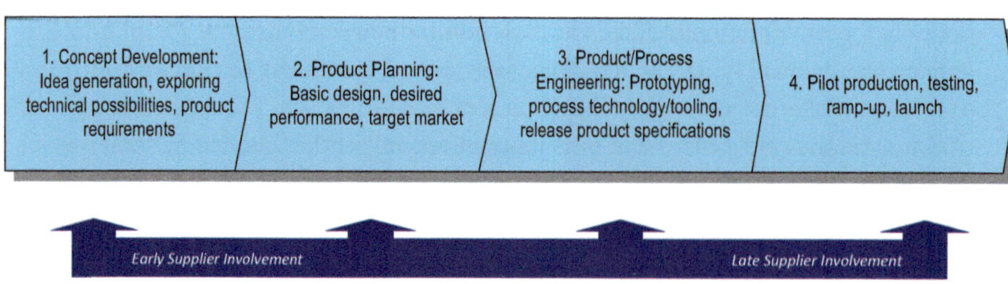

FIGURE 7.1 The new product development process and supplier involvement

of creative people, such as the marketing department, who may have a great feel for what might succeed in the marketplace but do not have the same appreciation of who will end up producing and supplying the product. As Note 2.1 (in Chapter 2) illustrated with the classic example of procurement and engineering collaboration at Harley-Davidson, it is also by no means certain that the technical people in a company will be concerned about the production of products and its parts being developed, in fact, they might even fight against involvement of suppliers at this stage as they may see supplier involvement as a threat.

7.2.2 Different levels of supplier involvement

Successful supplier involvement requires selection of the right suppliers at the right time. Suppliers of high value and complex parts that represent high risk (Kraljic, 1983; Wynstra and ten Pierick, 2000) should be involved early and either assume a black box or grey box responsibility (Le Dain et al., 2010). These strategically important suppliers should not only be selected and evaluated on the basis of cost, quality, and delivery factors, but also, and more importantly, on their innovative capabilities and complementarity with the company (Hartley et al., 1997; Petersen et al., 2005).

Le Dain et al. (2010) proposed a model for identifying and classifying different levels of supplier involvement. Based on Wynstra et al. (1999), their model specifies two dimensions: a) the degree of development risk, which depends on e.g. the number of sub-components used in the 'building block', links between the individual component and other components, and whether it is on the 'critical path'; and b) the appropriate degree of supplier autonomy or responsibility, which depends on e.g. the nature of the supplier's technologies and capabilities vis-à-vis the company's own and supplier availability and interest in working with the company. Different forms of specifications should be provided to suppliers, ranging from entirely customer driven (white box) to supplier driven (black box); the grey box situation requires joint development of specifications. Strategic co-design and development requires close cooperation and extensive exchange of information but a significant amount of responsibility is delegated to the supplier who is viewed as the real expert. In critical co-design and development, specifications need to be jointly developed by the two parties, requiring extensive collaboration. White box collaboration resembles classic sub-contracting or co-ordinated development depending on the degree of development risk; the customer should provide detailed technical specifications to the supplier, leaving as little space as possible for misunderstanding of buyer needs and requirements. This situation involves less intensive collaboration and communication and suppliers can be involved at a later stage in the NPD process.

Successful supplier involvement also requires on-going supplier relationship development and adaptation. For example, the company should provide shared training (Ragatz et al., 1997) and seek to foster mutual trust and commitment (e.g. Song and Benedetto, 2008). Moreover, it is important to have clear arrangements for the sharing of risks and rewards (Ragatz et al., 1997) and agreed performance targets and measures (Petersen et al., 2005; van Echtelt et al., 2008). Supplier representation on the customer's NPD team, for example by inviting key suppliers to share a physical space within the company's premises, can help to create the right form of relationship atmosphere (Petersen et al., 2003).

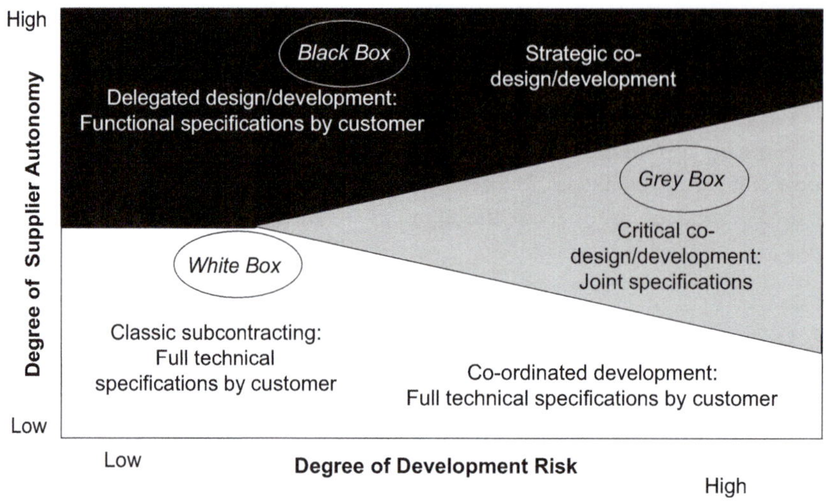

FIGURE 7.2 Forms of supplier collaboration and specifications
Source: Adapted from Le Dain et al. (2010)

An atmosphere of buyer-supplier collaboration is necessary to foster successful supplier involvement projects.

Finally, the internal capabilities of the company need to be adapted to fully benefit from supplier involvement. Top management within the company needs to support and be committed to supplier involvement (Ragatz et al., 1997) and cross-functional coordination between different internal functions, such as procurement, R&D, logistics, production, and marketing is critical (Takeishi, 2001). In particular, departments that are traditionally responsible for technological development (i.e. R&D) need to accept suppliers taking responsibility for activities traditionally handled internally. The same applies to procurement's role in NPD which can be viewed by R&D as a threat. We examine procurement's role in facilitating supplier involvement in the next section.

7.3 PROCUREMENT'S ROLE IN FACILITATING SUPPLIER INVOLVEMENT IN NPD

Procurement plays an important role in facilitating the development of new products because procurement can act as a facilitator between NPD projects and the technologies and capabilities of suppliers (Burt and Soukup, 1985). Through its boundary-spanning role procurement can naturally provide useful insights into the cost, availability, quality, and reliability of supplied components.

However, managing supplier involvement is not solely the prerogative of procurement and as the Harley-Davidson case shows traditional procurement professionals such as buyers or procurement managers are rarely seen as natural internal partners in NPD projects. As discussed in Chapter 2, procurement should have significant input into the product design and development process, in particular in order to avoid the situation where product specifications are purely technical and do not reflect the supply situation. As explained by Wynstra et al. (1999), it is critical that procurement be involved in both individual NPD projects, where for example they can assist in providing input on early product design, and ongoing discussions with suppliers about for example potential future technologies. Table 7.1 provides a framework for managing purchasing involvement in NPD, focused on a set of activities categorized into four groups.

TABLE 7.1 Purchasing involvement in NPD: a framework of activities

Areas	*Activity*
Development management	Determining which technologies to keep/develop in-house and which ones to outsource to suppliers Formulating policies for the involvement of suppliers Formulating policies for purchasing related activities of internal departments Communicating policies and procedures internally and externally
Supplier interface management	Monitoring supplier markets for technological developments Pre-selecting suppliers for product development collaboration Motivating suppliers to build up/maintain specific knowledge or develop certain products Exploiting the technological capabilities of suppliers Evaluating suppliers' development performance
Project management	Planning: Determining specific develop-or-buy solutions Selecting suppliers for involvement in the development project Determining the extent ('workload') of supplier involvement Determining the moment of supplier involvement Execution: Coordinating development activities between suppliers and manufacturer Coordinating development activities between different first tier suppliers Coordinating development activities between first tier suppliers and second tier suppliers Ordering and chasing prototypes
Product management	Extending activities: Providing information on new products and technologies being developed or already available in supplier markets Suggesting alternative suppliers, products, and technologies that can result in a higher quality of the final product Restrictive activities: Evaluating product designs in terms of part availability, manufacturability, lead-time, quality, and costs Promoting standardization and simplification of designs and parts

Source: Wynstra et al. (1999)

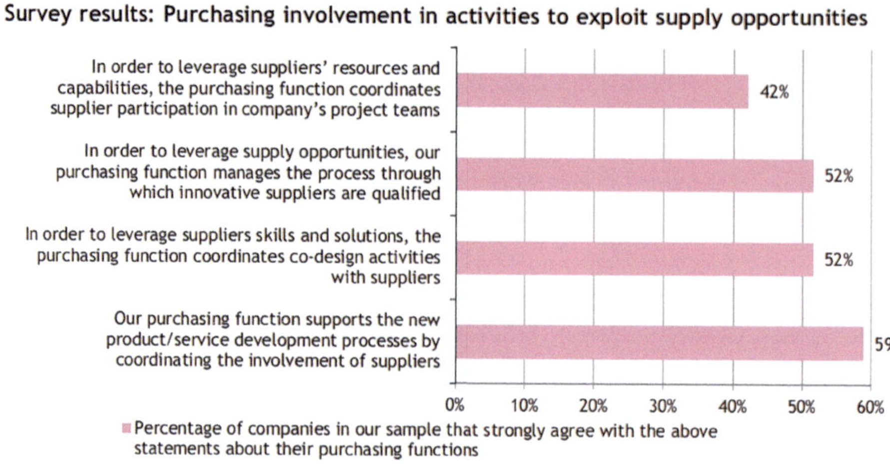

FIGURE 7.3 Procurement involvement in activities to exploit supply opportunities
Source: Adapted from Legenvre and Gualandris (2018)

The idea of procurement involvement in NPD is not new; however, it has not always been very widely practiced. As Figure 7.3 illustrates, procurement in many companies is now not only involved in but actively coordinating supplier involvement projects.

7.4 THE CHALLENGING CASE OF INNOVATION REQUIRING NOVEL TECHNOLOGY: SOURCING NEW SUPPLIERS

Supplier involvement is widely recognized by practitioners and researchers of the field as being a best practice for improving NPD performance. However, where supplier involvement is appropriate for incremental NPD projects, radical or 'discontinuous' innovation requires a different approach. In other words, when companies are dealing with NPD projects that require completely new technologies, as typically the case in green innovations, traditional supplier involvement is no longer the right course of action (Primo and Amundson, 2002).

Research shows that when companies are faced with innovations, which break with existing technological paradigms, new ways of sourcing ideas and knowledge from suppliers are required (Mikkelsen and Johnsen, 2019). Figure 7.4 provides a simple illustration of the concept of discontinuous innovation: as a technology in an industry grows over time it follows an s-curve as it develops from an early embryonic position to maturity and eventually declines; towards the end of this lifecycle a new technology appears from under the radar of the established industry players and ends up partially or completely replacing the existing technology. Consider for example the fate of analogue camera technology, cars and trains powered by the internal combustion engine (ICE) being superseded by electrified alternatives, or bulb technology having shifted from incandescent to LED; many such examples are driven by new environmental regulations that are set to transform entire industries.

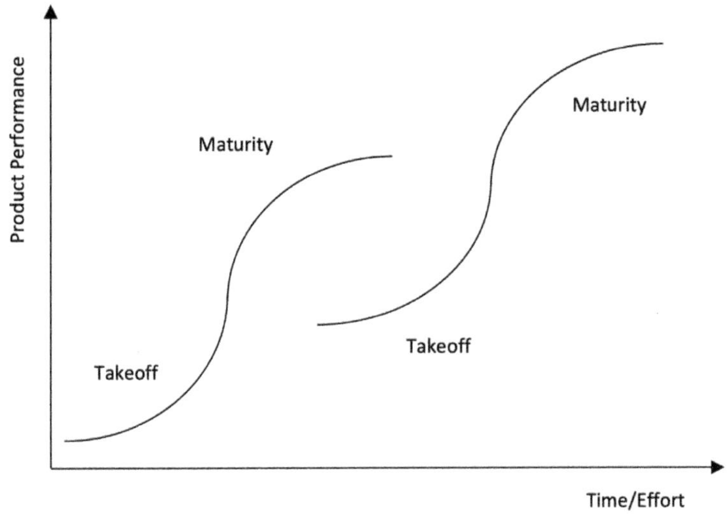

FIGURE 7.4 Discontinuous innovations: s-curve
Source: Adapted from Foster (1986)

Discontinuous innovations are often associated with completely new (to the world) technologies but, in fact, often happen when an existing technology from an entirely different industry is introduced into, and adapted to, an industry where it transforms the existing industry. The incumbents are often reluctant to embrace the innovation as it threatens their business model but face the risk of getting left behind as new players take over control of the industry.

The relevance of this to supplier involvement is that this form of innovation calls for a different way of collaborating with suppliers. Figure 7.5 builds on the seminal typology of innovation by Abernathy and Clark (1985), extended by Phillips et al. (2006), to identify appropriate supplier collaboration across the four quadrants:

1 Regular innovation: exploit existing technological capabilities and supplier relationships for continuous improvement. For example, BMW developing its 7-generation 3-series (G20), which was launched in 2018, to replace the 7-year-old previous generation 3-series (F30).
2 Revolutionary innovation: existing technological capabilities need to be overturned through existing supplier relationships. For example, a car company introducing a new infotainment interface developed in collaboration with existing suppliers.
3 Niche creation: creating new markets using existing technological capabilities through new similar suppliers. For example, entering a new geographical market and establishing a new but similar supply chain with local suppliers (e.g. in China).
4 Architectural/discontinuous innovation: destruction of both existing technological capabilities and markets. For example, smart watches incorporating a range of technologies such as Global Positioning Systems (GPS), touchscreen, and sensors to monitor health and sports performance.

		Technological Capabilities	
		Preserved	Destroyed
Market Capabilities	Preserved	Regular *Co-develop with existing partners*	Revolutionary *Co-innovate with existing supplier*
	Destroyed	Niche *Co-innovate with new similar partners*	Architectural *Co-innovate with new different partners*

FIGURE 7.5 Typology of innovations and supplier relationships
Source: Adapted from Abernathy and Clark (1985); Phillips et al. (2006)

Discontinuous innovation implies that existing technological capabilities and markets become obsolete and are therefore discontinued over time as they are replaced by new technological and market capabilities. As the examples of the four different types of innovation above suggest, many innovations cannot be developed purely through existing suppliers but require new technologies that often stem from new entrants to the industry. Consider the current transition in the automotive industry, forcing car manufacturers to partner with battery technology manufacturers, such as China's CATL, South Korea's LG Energy Solution, and Japan's Panasonic, that were not traditionally major players in the automotive industry.

The risk for companies that excel at collaboration with long-term existing suppliers is that such partnerships may have limited innovative potential (Bessant et al., 2005): if you always only source ideas, knowledge, and technologies from the same old partners this risks reinforcing the old ways of doing things. Naturally, this depends on the ability of those suppliers to stay innovative, notably through R&D investment, making radical changes in technology strategy to ensure that suppliers are not going to lose out to new competitors. Innovating companies can decide to co-develop with its existing suppliers: assuming that these suppliers allocate sufficient resources to invest in R&D, these are still important sources of knowledge provided that technological and market capabilities can be preserved and do not need to be destroyed.

Sourcing innovations from new suppliers is about 'exploring' new relationships. Using the metaphorical language of Lamming and Phillips (2005), this is a process of 'flirting with new partners' as an alternative to nurturing long-term marriages. As illustrated in Figure 7.6, the idea of exploring, or 'flirting' with, unknown potential suppliers involves connecting with suppliers that are typically on the periphery or outside the company's usual innovation search and selection environment and therefore more difficult to detect as they are not part of the company's existing supply network and therefore within its normal field of vision. The term that has gained traction in industry for this form of innovation exploring is 'scouting'.

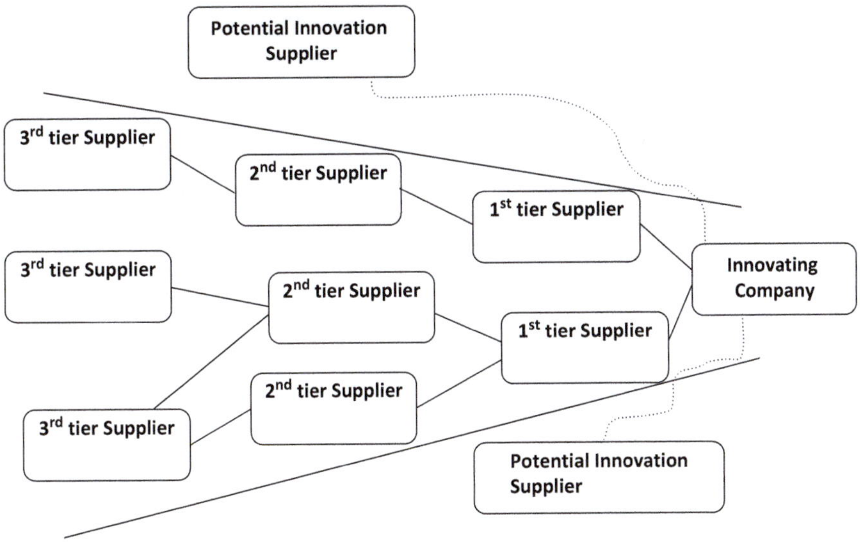

FIGURE 7.6 Exploring (or scouting) sources of innovation outside existing supply networks
Source: Adapted from Johnsen (2022)

7.5 SCOUTING FROM NON-TRADITIONAL SUPPLY CHAIN PLAYERS: THE CASE OF STARTUPS

An increasing number of companies are making significant efforts to scout for new suppliers that can deliver novel solutions that are required to realize new innovations. Such scouting efforts involve exploring new solutions in the wider ecosystem in which the company operates and potentially connecting with suppliers that are not traditionally part of the company's industry. For example, more and more innovative companies interact with innovation clusters, universities, and potential suppliers using trend scouts, incubators, and technology centres. In a survey by Legenvre and Gualandris (2018) 24 per cent of companies scouted for innovations from startups and 'new players', but tellingly 54 per cent of the respondents projected that this would become their future focus when scouting innovation opportunities.

An increasing number of companies use the concept of ecosystem rather than supply chain or networks to describe the collective of heterogeneous yet complementary organizational actors who collectively generate some form of ecosystem-level output (Thomas and Autio, 2020). Whereas supply chains are composed of contractually linked actors, the notion of heterogeneity implies that ecosystems include a wider range of more loosely linked actors, including for example technology providers, competitors, universities, and public research institutions, governmental organizations, etc.

Companies are increasingly making significant efforts to tap into startups, especially because the most promising startups are usually highly sought after. The prevalent model of startup cooperation in recent years has been corporate venture capital and accelerators. These programmes offer startups the advantage of not only capital and coaching, as offered by venture capitalists (VCs), but also clients (Gimmy et al., 2017). Some companies also have startup supplier programmes (Kurpjuweit and Wagner, 2020) under which they may have a range of startup projects. Running a portfolio of startup initiatives allows companies to organize their startup collaborations e.g. according to their stage of development or technology criticality.

For example, BMW established the BMW Startup Garage in 2015 to act as a matchmaker between BMW and startups to ensure that BMW become their venture client. According to their website (https://www.bmwstartupgarage.com/), they engage with startups from over 50 countries, with around 30 startups completing the BMW Garage Programme each year. Connecting with a venture client such as BMW is clearly a major advantage to startups, and increases their market value, but is also critically important to companies in search for the latest innovations that will give them a competitive edge. This may include innovations in in-car user experience, connectivity, automated driving, or circular and sustainable materials. For BMW this is a relatively low risk to gain access to test startup innovation (a 'no strings attached partnership') before making major commitment (and investments). Ultimately, startups are offered the opportunity to become long-term suppliers.

Establishing a startup supplier programme is also a way for companies to engage in a wider startup ecosystem. Startup supplier programmes improve a company's visibility to external startup ecosystems and help firms to participate and exchange more actively with the most important players (Kurpjuweit and Wagner, 2020: 83).

Startups are profoundly different from traditional suppliers: unlike established suppliers, startups are short of resources, fighting for survival, and lack productive routines and track record (Wagner et al., 2017). Interacting with startups therefore presents unique challenges and procurement can play an important bridging role. However, many procurement functions are ill-equipped to engage with startups, because innovation has not been a traditional procurement responsibility. Kurpjuweit et al. (2021) propose a typology of three types of startup buyers:

1. Sceptical buyers: do not adjust their supplier selection process to startups; completely unstructured evaluation process;
2. Opportunistic buyers: partially adjust their supplier selection process to startups; somewhat structured evaluation process;
3. Systematic selectors: fully adjust their supply and selection process to startups; structured evaluation process; predefined startup specific evaluation criteria.

Kurptjuweit et al. (2021) find that *systematic selectors*, such as BMW, try to build a brand around their new venture activities and position themselves as an attractive partner for startups. What is more, they often hire people from VCs, accelerators, or directly from startups to initiate major adaptations in their selection processes and connect with different startup ecosystems.

7.6 PROCUREMENT CONTRIBUTION TO INNOVATION: A CHALLENGING NEW ROLE FOR PROCUREMENT

Although *exploring* – or scouting for – innovation is not a traditional procurement responsibility, we can observe how procurement professionals increasingly see it as part of their responsibility. Such scouting activities are in addition to *exploitation* activities in which procurement supports supplier involvement in NPD projects, coordinating co-design activities, and managing innovative supplier qualification processes.

Supporting this observation, a survey by Legenvre and Gualandris (2018) found a prevalence of activities to actively scout opportunities, for example through attending supplier technology roadmap presentations and innovation workshops. These scouting activities specifically target existing sub-tier and new potential suppliers in the wider ecosystem.

What is becoming clear is that the innovation challenge calls for new ways of working in procurement. As illustrated in Figure 7.8, the effective involvement of procurement in product innovation projects is closely interlinked with procurement process innovation: procurement cannot contribute to product innovations unless it develops new ways of working.

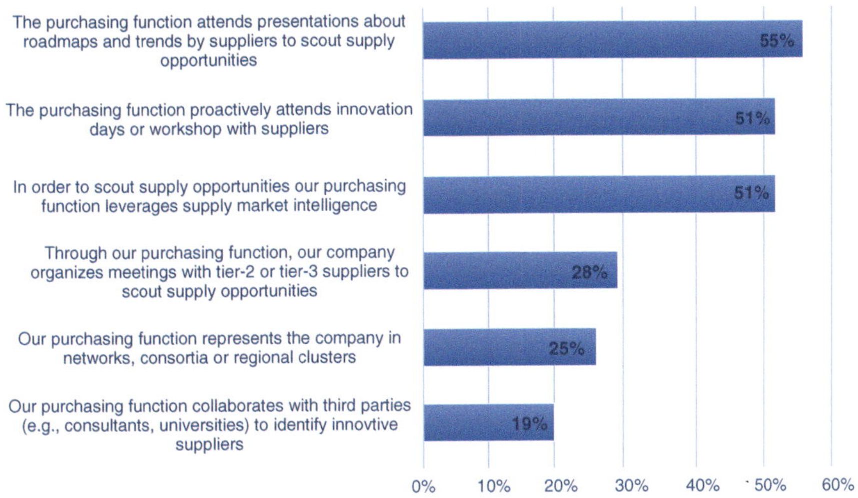

FIGURE 7.7 Survey results: purchasing involvement in activities to explore (scout) supply opportunities
Source: Adapted from Legenvre and Gualandris (2018)

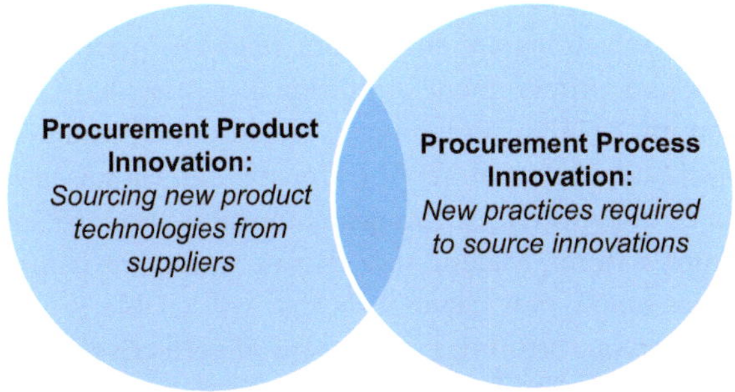

FIGURE 7.8 Interlinked product innovation and process innovations

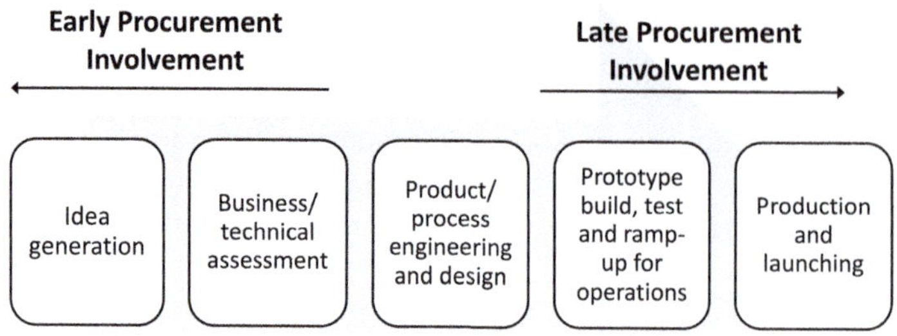

FIGURE 7.9 What is 'early' procurement involvement?
Source: Adapted from Johnsen (2022)

In a similar vein to how companies refer to early supplier involvement (ESI), some companies are beginning to refer to a need for early purchasing (or procurement) involvement. Drawing from research by Picaud-Bello et al. (2019) and based on traditional stages models, Figure 7.9 shows that 'early' means that procurement is involved at least before the product/process engineering stage. The idea of early procurement involvement (EPI) in innovation is that procurement gets involved at such an early stage in innovation projects that allows it to influence really basic product design decisions.

It is one thing for procurement to be able to detect supplier innovations through its scouting activities, but it is quite another to be able to absorb supplier knowledge into the company. This is especially the case when new and uncertain technology is involved. Research has therefore used an absorptive capacity perspective, to investigate how procurement can facilitate the three absorptive capacity processes of exploration, assimilation, and exploitation. Picaud-Bello et al. (2022) has shown the importance of procurement involvement in scanning of new supplier markets, and that procurement can perform a go-between role to facilitate inter-functional knowledge exchange, especially between procurement and R&D, and organize open communication with suppliers.

7.7 AMBIDEXTROUS PROCUREMENT AND POTENTIAL TENSIONS

Many procurement organizations are simply not ready to perform an effective role in innovation sourcing. Many procurement professionals neither have the competences nor the motivation to commit to innovation projects because their traditional remit is focused on delivering savings (Andersen et al., 2021). Constant and Johnsen (2024) recommend that motivations can be enhanced by creating an innovation mindset and designing appropriate KPIs and reward systems. Making sure that procurement is motivated in turn lays the foundation for developing new capabilities that will enable procurement to become more aware of innovation opportunities and contribute effectively to innovation projects and act as a sparring partner with the R&D function.

Rising to the challenge of performing an active role on innovation projects requires new ways of working for procurement but it is a role that is in many ways fundamentally different to traditional procurement activities. It is not a question of shifting from traditional operational procurement activities to new innovation-focused activities. Instead it is about doing both alongside each other. The question here is how companies can manage two such different tasks.

Some forward-thinking companies have developed dedicated units to connect procurement and R&D that work alongside operational procurement. Such a unit or department can act as a sparring partner with R&D. French company Schneider Electric is highly regarded for its focus on innovation: its commitment to green technologies – Schneider is ranked No 7 on the Corporate Knights green ranking index (2024) – pushes the company to connect with promising startup companies; over 690 supplier innovations have been incorporated into Schneider Electric over the last eight years. Its 'Offer Creation Procurement' department works closely with R&D and marketing teams on new product and service offerings and evaluates supplier innovations jointly with R&D. The company has even developed a Purchasing Strategy & Innovation department. These initiatives enable the company to derive many innovations from suppliers with 75 per cent of its innovations now coming from startups (Johnsen, 2022). French personal care company L'Oréal also has an innovation management function within its procurement department which is dedicated to identifying new products from new and unfamiliar suppliers (Maury, 2012).

Creating structural separations within the procurement function is one way to develop an *ambidextrous* procurement organization (Constant et al., 2020). Being ambidextrous means being able to use both the left and the right hand equally well. Derived from this metaphor, the concept of organizational ambidexterity refers to an organization's ability to be efficient in its management of today's business and also adaptable for coping with tomorrow's changing demand. In other words, organizational ambidexterity can be defined as "the ability to simultaneously pursue both incremental and discontinuous innovation ... from hosting multiple contradictory structures, processes, and cultures within the same firm" (Tushman and O'Reilly, 1996: 24). Few procurement professionals are naturally ambidextrous who can master fundamentally different or even conflicting tasks on a day-to-day basis.

The creation of procurement innovation departments can be one way forward but other solutions could be to create new procurement job profiles focused on innovation. Companies like L'Oréal and Faurecia are now employing *innovation purchasers* to take the lead on innovation sourcing. In fact, an analysis of job adverts by Picaud-Bello et al. (2024) reveal that many companies representing from across several sectors have recently advertised for procurement job positions, such as Supply Innovation Manager (BP), Innovation Program Buyer (Faurecia), Advanced Sourcing and Innovation Manager (Johnson & Johnson), Procurement Innovation Manager Raw Materials (Mondelez International), and Chanel advertising for an Assistant Project Manager for Sustainable Purchasing and Eco-Design.

Creating procurement ambidexterity by developing new departments or new job roles is known as structural ambidexterity. An alternative way to develop ambidexterity is known as sequential ambidexterity, where the department supports either exploitation or exploration activities at different points in time. Contextual ambidexterity implies employees

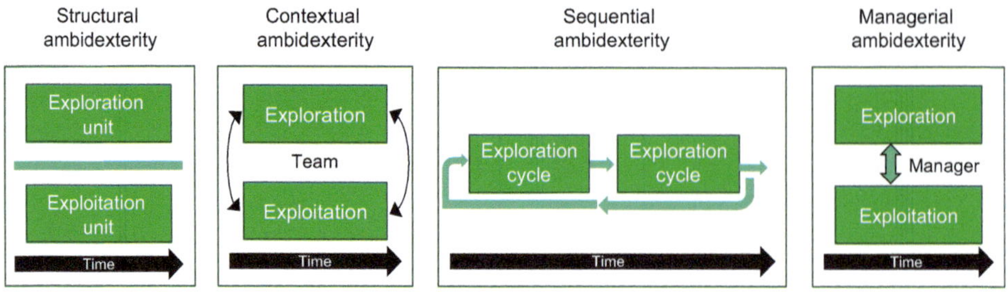

FIGURE 7.10 Organizational ambidexterity design approaches
Source: Adapted from Constant et al. (2020)

participating simultaneously in exploitation and exploration activities in a "double-hat role" (Andersen et al., 2021). Finally, managerial ambidexterity is characterized by management roles that are designed to facilitate ambidextrous activities. Figure 7.10 illustrates the logic of the three ways to create ambidexterity.

Having to balance the two competing tasks of exploitation and exploration inevitably comes at the risk of tensions. Organizational separation may seem like an ideal way to manage tensions but critiques of structural ambidexterity argue that instead of assuming that managers are only capable of managing one type of task, managers may be capable of engaging in paradoxical thinking, fulfilling multiple roles, and conducting multiple tasks outside their formal job descriptions. At least they should be able to manage both exploitative and explorative tasks if these are sequenced over time i.e. across different projects. Constant et al. (2020) argue that where structural separation can be a useful way to create procurement ambidexterity there is a need for contextual ambidexterity (and what they term managerial ambidexterity through managerial skill development) in the long-term.

7.8 CASE STUDY: PROCUREMENT INVOLVEMENT IN INNOVATION AT VOLVO

Founded in 1927 in Gothenburg in Sweden, Volvo is a global icon in the automotive industry, known for its cars (Volvo Cars), as well as the trucks, buses, and even (Penta-branded) boat engines (Volvo Group). Volvo is famous for producing iconic 'boxy' estate cars, such as the 145 launched in 1967 that endured into the early 1990s (as the updated 245), the 740 (1982–1992), and the 900 series of the 1990s.

The early 2000s saw Volvo – somewhat reluctantly – launch its first Sport Utility Vehicle (SUV), the XC90, later than many of its competitors, such as BMW that launched its X5 in 1998. These days its range of SUV models make up most of the product range and the XC60 SUV is the best-selling Volvo in history with 2.7 million examples made (Volvo Cars Global Newsroom, 2025).

Derived from the Latin verb 'volvere' or 'to roll', the Volvo name is synonymous with safety. The company prides itself of having invented a series of safety features, including the three-point safety belt in 1959, the Side Impact Protection System (SIPS), SIPS-airbags, and Whiplash Injury Protection System (WHIPS) in the 1990s, and the Blind Spot Information System (BLIS) in 2003 to mention some of Volvo's most famous innovations.

Safety remains a core value and differentiator in the highly competitive market. Nowadays, Volvos integrate advanced technologies such as high-definitions sensors and radar systems that enable real-time monitoring of hazards in the vehicle's surroundings. Its focus on safety features includes a strong commitment to sustainability, with Volvo aiming to be pioneers in protecting people and the planet by working towards achieving net zero greenhouse gas emissions, embracing the circular economy, addressing our biodiversity footprint, and improving people's lives (Volvo Car Group, 2024: 2).

Like all incumbent automotive companies i.e. the traditional players that have relied on the internal combustion engine (ICE) technology, Volvo's major technological challenge is the transition to electrification. The company set an ambitious target to switch to 100 per cent electric vehicles (EVs) by 2030, phasing out not only pure ICE-powered but also hybridized vehicles that combine ICE technology with electrification i.e. battery technology. Facing slower than expected EV sales, Volvo has recently modified its ambition to allow for 10 per cent mild hybrids. It looks likely that Volvo's future will involve multiple powertrain solutions (including hydrogen power and biogas) but this will hardly simplify its innovation journey.

7.8.1 Organizational structure

Volvo is divided into Volvo Group and Volvo Cars. Volvo Cars is majority owned by Zhejiang Geely Holding (Geely) of China (78.65 per cent). Volvo Cars formed part of Volvo Group until 1999, when the company was taken over by Ford Motor Company. In 2010, Volvo Cars was then acquired by Geely although Volvo maintains autonomy as a standalone legal entity in the Geely ecosystem. Volvo collaborates with other companies in the Geely ecosystem where there are strategic benefits, including for R&D, manufacturing, and procurement (Volvo Car Group Annual and Sustainability Report 2024: 37).

These days there is little more collaboration between Volvo Group and Volvo Cars than with other car companies: "We deal with Volvo Cars as we would with any third party. We collaborate whenever we see a value for us and for them. We do it at arm's length, as we would with any company" (Andrea Fuder, Chief Procurement Officer, Volvo Group).

Volvo Cars annual turnover reached €36.23 billion in 2024 and the company employs 42,600. In comparison, Volvo Group's turnover in the same period was €46 billion and they employ 102,000 people. With sales in over 100 countries and production in ten countries, including e.g. Sweden, Belgium, China, and USA, Volvo Cars is truly a global player. Volvo continues to have a strong base in Sweden with head office, product development, marketing, and administration functions mainly located in Gothenburg.

startup by providing resources and guidance needed to thrive in Volvo Group's open innovation model. Focusing on innovation, co-creation, technology, and business, Volvo Group's purchasing plays an important role because:

> Even though … the mission of CampX is to scout for and to explore new technologies and also new business models the overall ambition is of course to commercialize these initiatives afterwards and then we may need to make sure that we have the proper commercial foundation put in place for the potential next step to come.
>
> (Daniel Heimer, Director, New Technologies & Markets – Group Trucks Purchasing, Volvo Group)

The automotive industry is under pressure to innovate more than ever before and incremental innovations are no longer sufficient. The need for new technological solutions that are required to discontinue ICE technologies is forcing the automotive industry to change its traditional practices for sourcing of innovations. The Volvo case illustrates how automotive companies go beyond collaboration with their long-term supply partners to connect with new suppliers not only within but also beyond the traditional boundaries of the automotive industry.

Shifting towards electrification poses a dilemma as the required batteries are produced using materials, such as lithium, manganese, cobalt, nickel, graphite, aluminium, and copper, that are in short supply. Typically sourced from deposits in countries such as Russia, China, Chile, Brazil, and various African states, there are significant environmental and social sustainability concerns in mining these minerals. In fact, materials sourced from the DR Congo (tin, tungsten, tantalum, and gold) are widely known as conflict minerals due to the highly problematic conditions under which these are mined (OECD, 2016). Automotive manufacturers are exploring opportunities for new approaches to waste management in production and recycling of batteries to cope with this challenge. Considering these sourcing challenges, shifting to battery technology is not simply a task for R&D but very much also for procurement.

7.9 CONCLUSION

Chapter 7 has discussed a range of issues in purchasing that concerns the role of procurement in enabling product innovation through early involvement of key suppliers in new product development (NPD) projects – early supplier involvement or ESI. There is extensive research evidence to suggest that by collaborating with suppliers as part of NPD processes, companies can improve NPD performance, for example, by getting products to market faster, at lower cost and better quality. Chapter 7 explored the role of procurement in facilitating early supplier involvement. By being involved early in NPD projects – giving rise to the term EPI – procurement can act as a boundary spanner, managing the interface between development teams within buying firms, e.g. R&D and suppliers, to ensure that the right cost conditions and supply risks are considered.

Chapter 7 also explored the challenge of discontinuous innovations and how this changes the role of procurement and suppliers: where NPD projects usually call for collaboration with existing suppliers, discontinuous innovations require sourcing of new technologies and capabilities so new supply chain players from wider ecosystems are necessary. One key trend is to connect with startups, which offers opportunities to tap into the latest technological innovations, but also poses challenges due to the different nature and priorities of startups. Discontinuous innovation is particularly important from a sustainability perspective because green products or processes require a fundamental rethinking of products and processes to eliminate environmental impacts at the source.

NOTE

1 Hereafter "Volvo"

REFERENCES

Abernathy WJ and Clark KB (1985) Innovation: Mapping the winds of creative destruction. *Research Policy* 13: 3–22.

Andersen PH, Ellegaard C and Kragh H (2021) How purchasing departments facilitate organizational ambidexterity. *Production Planning & Control* 32(16): 1384–1399.

Automotive Purchasing & Supply Chain Magazine (2018) Volvo Group – A new open-minded approach to supplier partnerships.

Bessant JR, Lamming RC, Noke H and Phillips WE (2005) Managing innovation beyond the steady state. *Technovation* 25(12): 1366–1376.

Burt DN and Soukup WR (1985) Purchasing's role in new product development. *Harvard Business Review* 63(3): 90–97.

Chesbrough HW (2003) The era of open innovation. *Sloan Management Review* 44(3): 35–41.

Clark KB (1989) Project scope and project performance: The effects of parts strategy and supplier involvement on product development. *Management Science* 35(10): 1247–1263.

Constant F and Johnsen T (2024) Purchasing contribution to innovation exploration: Awareness, motivations, and capabilities. *International Journal of Operations and Production Management* 45(2).

Constant F, Calvi R and Johnsen TE (2020) Managing tensions between exploitative and exploratory innovation through purchasing function ambidexterity. *Journal of Purchasing and Supply Management* 26: 100645.

Foster R (1986) *Innovation: The Attacker's Advantage*. New York: Summit Books.

Gimmy G, Kanbach D, Stubner S, Konig A and Enders A (2017) What BMW's corporate VC offers that regular investors can't. *Harvard Business Review Digital Articles* (July): 2–6.

Handfield RB, Ragatz GL, Petersen KJ and Monczka RM (1999) Involving suppliers in new product development. *California Management Review* 42(1): 59–82.

Hartley JL, Zirger BJ and Kamath RR (1997) Managing the buyer-supplier interface for on-time performance in product development. *Journal of Operations Management* 15: 57–70.

Johnsen TE (2009) Supplier involvement in product development and innovation – Taking stock and looking to the future. *Journal of Purchasing & Supply Management* 15: 187–197.

Johnsen T (2022) Towards a framework for early procurement involvement in innovation. *DILFaktuelt* 17 (June): 20–27.

Johnsen TE, LeDain MA, Kiratli N and Schiele H (2022) Purchasing and innovation: Past, present and future of the field of research. *Journal of Purchasing & Supply Management* 28(2): 100768.

Kraljic P (1983) Purchasing must become supply management. *Harvard Business Review* (Sept–Oct): 109–117.

Kurpjuweit S and Wagner SM (2020) Startup supplier programs: A new model for managing corporate-startup partnerships. *California Management Review* 62(3): 64–85.

Kurpjuweit S, Wagner SM and Choi TY (2021) Selecting startups as suppliers: A typology of supplier selection archetypes. *Journal of Supply Chain Management* 57: 25–49.

Lamming RC and Phillips WE (2005) Flirting with new partners. *CPO Agenda* (Summer): 23–26.

Lamming RC, Johnsen TE, Zheng J and Harland CM (2000) An initial classification of supply networks. *International Journal of Operations and Production Management* 20(6): 675–691.

Le Dain MA, Calvi R and Cheriti S (2010) Developing an approach for design-or-buy-design decision-making. *Journal of Purchasing and Supply Management* 16(2): 77–87.

Legenvre H and Gualandris J (2018) Innovation sourcing excellence: Three purchasing capabilities for success. *Business Horizons* 61: 95–106.

Maury M (2012) Responsable innovation: Pour capter les avantages compétitifs. *La Lettre des Achats*. 208: 31–33.

Mikkelsen OS and Johnsen TE (2019) Purchasing involvement in technologically uncertain new product development: Challenges and implications. *Journal of Purchasing & Supply Management* 25(3): 1–11.

OECD (2016) OECD Due Diligence Guidance for Responsible Supply Chains of Minerals from Conflict-Affected and High-Risk Areas. 3rd edn, OECD Publishing, Paris. https://doi.org/10.1787/9789264252479-en

Perkins M (2022) Director of Indirect Procurement EMEA & Global Procurement Volvo, Volvo Cars: A new approach to strategic partnerships. *Procurement Magazine* (September). https://procurementmag.com/company-reports/volvo-cars-a-new-approach-to-strategic-partnerships

Petersen K, Handfield R and Ragatz G (2003) A model of supplier integration into new product development. *Journal of Product Innovation Management* 20(4): 284–299.

Petersen KJ, Handfield RB and Ragatz GL (2005) Supplier integration into new product development: Coordinating product, process and supply chain design. *Journal of Operations Management* 23(3–4): 371–388.

Phillips WE, Lamming RC, Bessant JR and Noke H (2006) Discontinuous innovation and supply relationships: Strategic dalliances *R&D Management* 36(4): 451–461.

Picaud-Bello K, Johnsen TE and Calvi R (2022) Purchasing involvement in new product development: An absorptive capacity perspective. *Industrial Marketing Management* 204: 150–166.

Picaud-Bello K, Johnsen T, Calvi R and Giannakis M (2019) Exploring early purchasing involvement in discontinuous innovation: A dynamic capability perspective. *Journal of Purchasing & Supply Management*. 25(4): 100555.

Picaud-Bello K, Schiele H, Koch V and Francillette M (2024) Innovation through sustainability: Identifying purchaser skills fostering green innovation. *Cleaner Logistics and Supply Chain* 10: 100136.

Powell WW, Koput KW and Smith-Doerr L (1996) Inter-organizational collaboration and the locus of innovation: Networks of learning in biotechnology. *Administrative Science Quarterly* 41(1): 116–45.

Primo MAM and Amundson SD (2002) An exploratory study of the effects of supplier relationships on new product development outcomes. *Journal of Operations Management* 20(1): 33–52.

Ragatz GL, Handfield RB and Scannell TV (1997) Success factors for integrating suppliers into product development *Journal of Product Innovation Management* 14(3): 190–202.

Schiele H (2010) Early supplier integration: The dual role of purchasing in new product development. *R&D Management* 40(2): 138–153.

Song M and Benedetto AD (2008) Supplier's involvement and success of radical new product development in new ventures. *Journal of Operations Management* 26(1): 1–22.

Suurmond R, Wynstra F and Dul J (2020) Unravelling the dimensions of supplier involvement and their effects on NPD performance: A meta-analysis. *Journal of Supply Chain Management* 56(3): 26–46.

Swink ML (1999): Threats to new product manufacturability and the effects of development team integration processes. *Journal of Operations Management* 17: 691–709.

Takeishi A (2001) Bridging inter- and intra-firm boundaries: Management of supplier involvement in automobile product development. *Strategic Management Journal* 22: 403–433.

Thomas LWT and Autio E (2020) Innovation ecosystems in management: An organizing typology. In: R Aldag (ed) *Oxford Research Encyclopaedia of Business and Management*. Oxford University Press.

Tushman ML and O'Reilly CA (1996) The ambidextrous organizations: Managing evolutionary and revolutionary change. *Calif. Manag. Rev.* 38(4): 8–30.

van Echtelt FEA, Wynstra F, van Weele AJ and Duyesters G (2008) Managing supplier involvement in NPD: A multiple-case study. *Journal of Product Innovation Management* 25: 180–201.

Volvo (n.d.) Volvo Cars Tech Fund. https://www.volvocars.com/intl/tech-fund/

Volvo Car Group (2024) Annual and sustainability report 2024. https://www.volvogroup.com/en/investors/reports-and-presentations/sustainability-reports.html

Volvo Cars Global Newsroom (2025) The XC60 is now the best-selling Volvo car of all time. https://www.media.volvocars.com/global/en-gb/media/pressreleases/351319/the-xc60-is-now-the-best-selling-volvo-car-of-all-time (accessed 3 July 2025).

Wagner SM, Kurpjuweit S and Choi T (2017) Managing startup suppliers. CAPS Research.

Wynstra F and ten Pierick E (2000) Managing supplier involvement in new product development: A portfolio approach. *European Journal of Purchasing and Supply Management* 6: 49–57.

Wynstra JYF, van Weele AJ and Axelsson B (1999) Purchasing involvement in product development: A framework. *European Journal of Purchasing and Supply Management* 5(3–4): 129–41.

PART B

Supply chain and network management

CHAPTER 8

Supply chain strategy

LEARNING OBJECTIVES:

At the end of this chapter you should be able to:

- Define supply chain management;
- Discuss the development of supply chain strategy over time from mass production and mass customization, towards more sustainable approaches such as the circular economy;
- Apply lean, agile, and hybrid supply chain strategies to business practice;
- Analyze developments from conventional to closed-loop supply chains;
- Discuss the broader economic implications of sustainability and the circular economy for supply chain strategy.

8.1 INTRODUCTION

Supply chain strategy is the collaborative response to market demand by all firms in the supply chain working together to coordinate the delivery of products and services to the end customer. The strategy adopted by the focal firm is usually driven by the type of product, patterns of demand, customer requirements, and any associated risks which may delay delivery by the supply chain. There are many strategies to choose from, however, including lean, agile, mass customization, as well as sustainable strategies involving closed loop and circular supply chains. This chapter starts by clarifying the concept of supply chain (and supply network) management. We include some background on early production, strategies such as mass production and mass customization, which have helped shape current thinking. We explore how supply chains are increasingly affected by the need to adhere to the United Nation's sustainability development goals over concerns such as waste and pollution, and how the circular economy can help. The chapter concludes with a discussion around closed loop and circular supply chain strategies, and the approach some companies have taken to implement them.

DOI: 10.4324/9781003499602-10

8.2 SUPPLY CHAINS AND NETWORKS

The use of the term 'supply chain' has become common across the business and management community. It is used to describe almost any setting where production requires a staged sequence of processes involving suppliers producing parts or components and building sub-assemblies, delivering them to a focal organization, an assembler or integrator, who then distributes the product to sales outlets. Figure 8.1 provides an illustration of a conventional supply chain comprising a simple flow of raw materials from extraction, through manufacture and customer delivery to 'disposal'.

Basic definitions of supply chain management were provided in Chapter 1. Here it is important to note that the linear or 'stream' aspect of supply chains is an important and well-established aspect of management thinking today: it is derived from the idea of a value stream where goods and services flow towards the customer without impediment (Rother and Shook, 1988; Hines and Rich, 1997; Hines et al., 2000).[1] There are many definitions of Supply Chain Management or 'SCM'. One definition focuses on the process integration:

> The integration of business processes from end user through original suppliers that provides products, services and information that add value for customers.
>
> (Cooper et al., 1997)

Another definition focuses on the importance of connecting supply chain actors through relationships:

> ... the management of upstream and downstream relationships with suppliers and customers to deliver superior customer value at less cost to the supply chain as a whole.
>
> (Christopher, 2005)

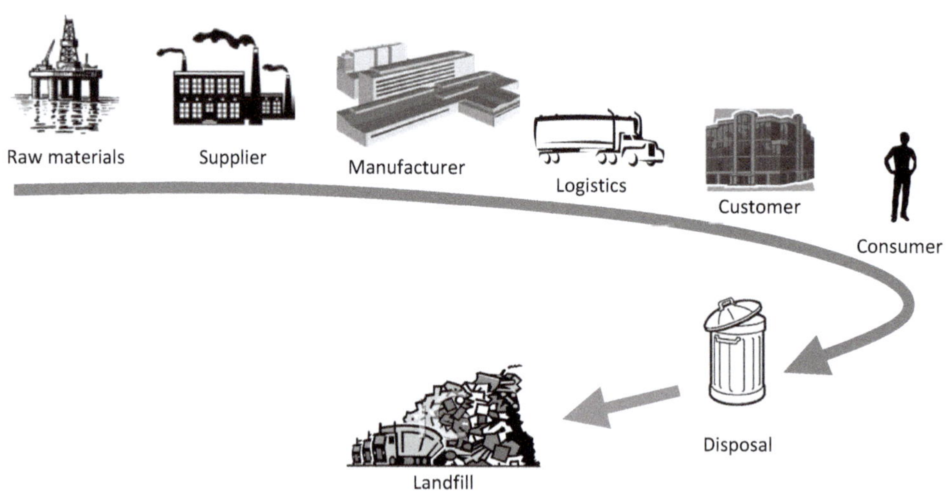

FIGURE 8.1 Conventional supply chain

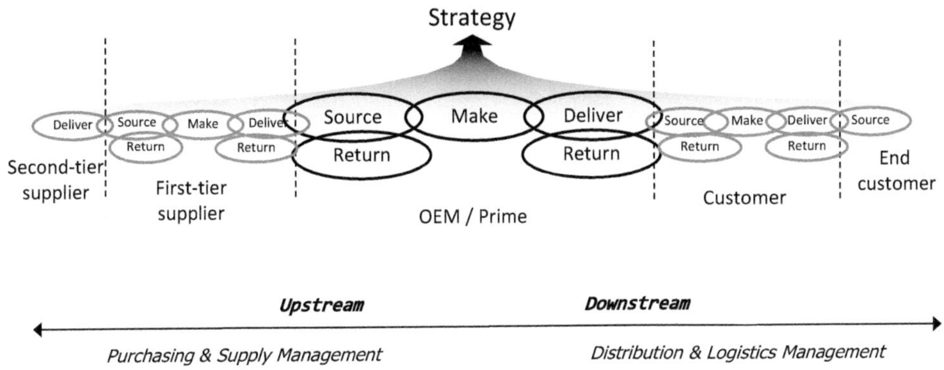

FIGURE 8.2 Supply chain management core processes

More comprehensively, supply chain management can be defined as:

> The management of a network of relationships within a firm and between interdependent organizations and business units consisting of material suppliers, purchasing, production facilities, logistics, marketing, and related systems that facilitate the forward and reverse flow of materials, services, finances and information from the original producer to final customer with the benefits of adding value, maximizing profitability through efficiencies, and achieving customer satisfaction.
>
> (Stock and Boyer, 2009)

The common denominator here is the focus on satisfaction of end customers by maximizing customer value whilst minimizing cost. Building on these definitions and the Supply Chain Operations Reference (SCOR) model developed by the Supply Chain Council, we can depict supply chain management as below.

Figure 8.2 identifies the core processes in supply chain management as source, make, deliver, and return. Integrating these core processes within and across organizations, it is possible to break down barriers or silos that otherwise prevent a smooth flow of supply to end customers. In theory, supply chain management covers all the actors involved in the production of a product and/or service from ultimate raw material extractors to end customers. All the supply chain actors are inter-linked and therefore dependent on each other to satisfy end customers. In practice, few companies have the required visibility over their entire supply chain and many companies focus their supply chain management on the internal supply chain or, at best, their immediate supply chain i.e. with direct first-tier suppliers (Fawcett and Magnan, 2002). The concept of supply chain management as 'end-to-end' is therefore rarely practiced.

The concept of supply chain management has been criticized on a numbered of points, three of which are highlighted here. Firstly, the metaphor of a chain, although useful for emphasizing the importance of inter-dependent supply relationships, suggests that supply structures are simple linear structures, whereas in reality supply structures are much more complex. This has led some authors and companies to use the alternative concept

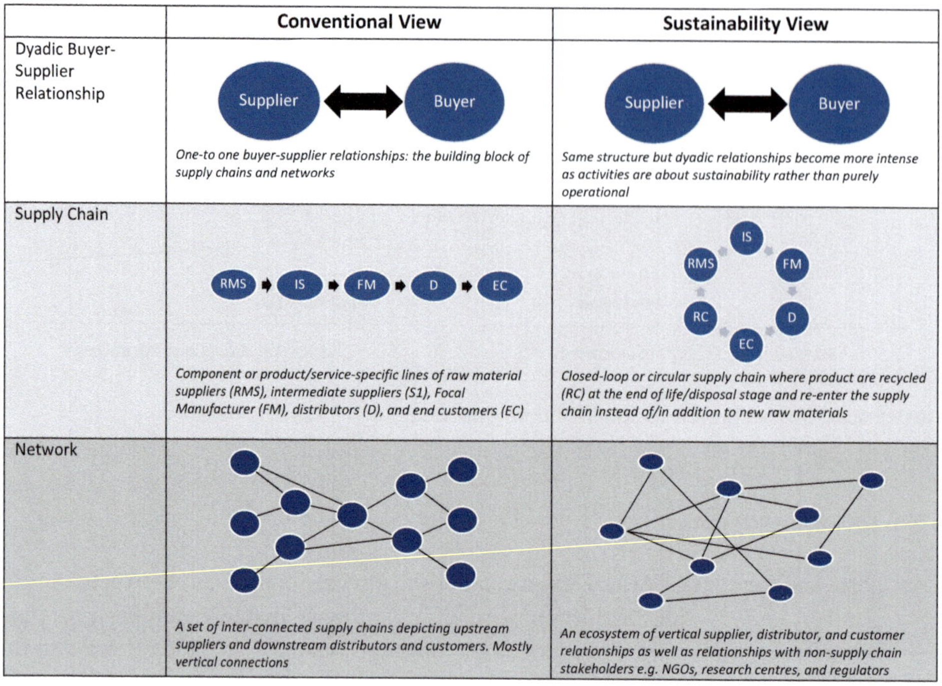

FIGURE 8.3 Levels of analysis (Part B)

of 'supply chain networks' or simply 'supply networks' (Lamming et al., 2000), although 'supply network' in practice tends to refer to only the upstream network of suppliers. As companies rely on global networks of suppliers, the concept of supply chains is an over-simplification of what is, in reality, a highly complex supply system.

Second, supply chain management assumes that all the actors in the supply chain are willing to partner with each other and work towards common objectives. As argued by Cox (1999) this is certainly not always the case and, ultimately, companies are driven by the need to make profit for their own company and not all supply chain actors are willing to collaborate. Supply chain management assumes that the best course of action for actors in a supply chain is to strive towards common goals; although in some cases this may be an accurate assumption, it only works where supply chain actors are highly interdependent and where the focal company exerts a significant amount of influence and power over other supply chain actors (Harland et al., 2001).

Third, the traditional linear supply chain design, which ends with products being disposed of in landfill sites, is being replaced by closed-loop, or circular, supply chains. Dumping in landfill represents one of the ultimate symbols of a wasteful society, meaning whatever has been discarded has either not been designed for disassembly or reuse by the manufacturer, or the systems needed to enable recycling are not in place. Closed-loop supply chains are designed to tackle this problem by finding novel ways to return what was once considered waste, which results from disposed products, back into raw material for the supply chain.

The limitations of traditional supply chain management concepts are therefore exacerbated when adopting a sustainability perspective, underscoring the need for a network or stakeholder perspective (Figure 8.3). As explained in Chapter 1, the theories influencing this book – the Natural Resource-Based View of strategy and the Industrial Marketing and Purchasing Interaction approach – emphasize the role of stakeholders and networks of relationships. As companies seek to incorporate sustainability into their supply chains they need to consider not only their indirect suppliers, who may be located thousands of kilometres away, but also other stakeholders such as non-governmental organizations (NGO) that play an increasingly critical role in e.g. monitoring and auditing suppliers in developing countries.

Figure 8.3 presents the shift in focus from a level of analysis focused on dyadic buyer-supplier relationships, where purchasing is the central issue, to supply chain and network management. This chapter now outlines and discusses some of the most important concepts of traditional supply chain management and strategy that companies can pursue. In order to put this into context, the next section provides a brief overview of how industrial organization has changed over time. We return to the non-linear and complex aspects of supply chains and networks at the end of the chapter and in more depth later in the book.

8.3 BACKGROUND: MASS PRODUCTION AND MASS CUSTOMIZATION

Since the beginning of the Western industrial revolution in the mid 18th century, the focus for development of production was on improving the manufacturing process in terms of cost, performance, and product quality. Very little thought was given towards the social welfare of the workers, product disposal (or 'end-of-life'), or what impact disposal would have on the surrounding environment. The overriding factors driving industrial production at the time were economic growth and profit. Widespread industrial implementation of closed-loop or reverse supply chains designed for product recycling did not emerge until the last quarter of the 20th century, resulting in a prolonged period where economy of scale was considered the over-riding factor in firm competitive advantage. This section reviews the major eras of production to understand how thinking around strategy has evolved from a purely operational focus towards sustainable supply chain management.

The origins of production as a scientific management activity began with the Industrial Revolution (1750–1850) which started in the United Kingdom and spread to Western Europe, North America, and Japan. Improvements in agriculture, manufacturing, mining, and technology heralded an unprecedented period of entrepreneurship and economic growth over the next two centuries, which saw the world's average per capita income increase tenfold. Towards the end of the 1700s, a transition began to occur in the UK's previously manual labour and draft animal-based economy. The shift towards machine-based manufacturing started with the mechanization of the textile industries, development of more refined iron making, and increased use of coal to fuel steam powered engines. While elements of what was later to be termed 'mass production' emerged during the 1800s, such as the division of labour, interchangeable parts, and mechanization (Duguay et al., 1997), the dominant paradigm at the time was craft production. Craft production centres on the skills of the individual who, in a pre-industrialized world, engages in a process of one-off manufacturing and hand-fitting of pieces together without the aid of machine tools (e.g. pottery, cabinet making).

Mass production is probably the most well-known production paradigm in Operations and Supply Management. Traditionally associated with the dominance of the US automobile industry, it was pioneered by Henry Ford's first moving assembly line for his 'Model T' vehicle built in Dearborn, Michigan US in 1913. The early effects of mass production were felt throughout the 1800s driven by successive developments in mechanization and interchangeable parts (Duguay et al., 1997). For example, the Springfield Armoury (1777–1968) was the centre for the manufacture of US military firearms and became the site of a number of technological innovations of global importance, including tooling to enable interchangeable parts and hourly wages. The introduction of lathes and other machine tools enabled high precision and the mass reproduction of identical parts.

Mass production is not only concerned with the process itself but also the organization of production to make work easier to manage. This interest in organization led to the concept of 'Scientific Management' by F.W. Taylor (1865–1915), involving painstaking studies of everyday manual tasks such as assembly, drilling, and shovelling in order to find the most efficient or 'one best way' of execution. The principles of scientific management or 'Taylorism' led to a fragmentation of tasks on the shop floor and an increasing divide between workers and the management controlling them. Workers became almost as interchangeable as the parts used in their products, with the resultant continual hiring and firing of workers becoming a criticism of the narrow efficiency focus of Taylor's technique. The main characteristics of mass producer firms are their concern for reducing costs by increasing volume of production i.e. economies of scale, and an adversarial relationship with suppliers who are "... considered opportunists and are kept at arm's length and are pitted against each other to obtain the best deal" (Duguay et al., 1997: 1185). Mass production reached its peak in the 1960s in the US. The emergence of foreign competition threatened US homeland markets, followed by the oil shock in the early 1970s which forced Western manufacturers to reconsider their predictions over growth.

The term 'mass customization' was coined by Stan Davis in his visionary book *Future Perfect* in 1987 which suggested that there are no truly mass markets anymore, and that each customer represents their own unique requirements who deserves exactly what they want at a price they want to pay. The concept of progressing from mass markets, through segments and niches, to mass customized markets was further developed by Pines (1992) who put forward the idea that companies must recognize this new frontier in production where not only is every customer effectively their own market, but customers may want different offerings at different times under different circumstances. Mass customization is defined as the production of tailored or customized goods and services to meet individual consumers' requirements at near mass production cost. It is enabled by technologies such as computer-aided design and manufacturing, flexible manufacturing systems, and modularization. The concept of mass customization assumes a totally flexible production system where every customer can, in theory, have what they want. The goal for firms of becoming more customer-centric became a useful refocus and competitive differentiator, particularly against traditional mass producers who still compete on price.

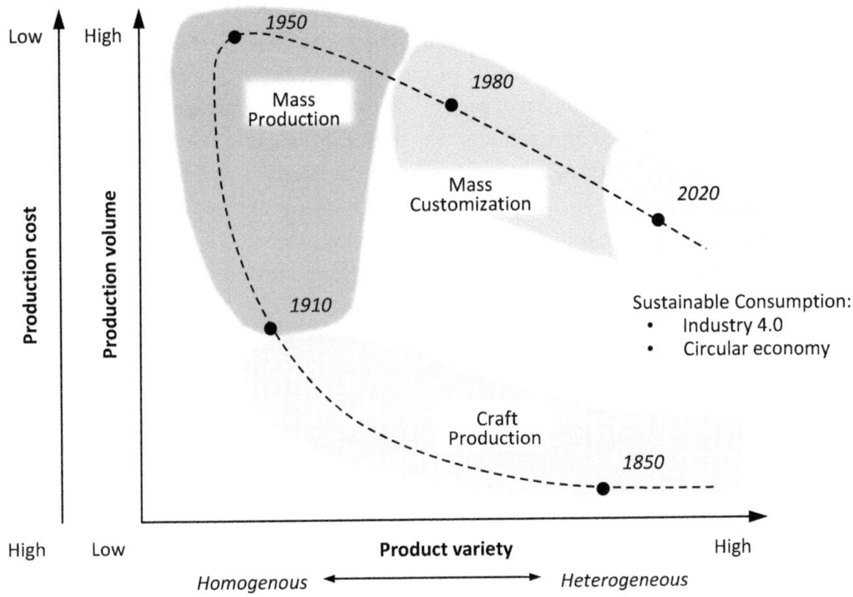

FIGURE 8.4 Evolution of production

Despite the evolution of production from craft, through mass production, to mass customization, it is not correct to say that production is 'returning to its roots' e.g. reviving craft-based manufacture (Figure 8.4). The vision of offering customers *exactly* what they want has never completely materialized because the trade-offs between production cost, volume, and variety have never been fully resolved despite advances in technology and process innovation. Considerable efforts have been made by manufacturers, however, to create a wider range of customer choice available at minimal cost. For example, the developments in modularization and platform-sharing led by Volkswagen in the 1990s, who adopted a system of sharing major structural body components where the same running gear (i.e. suspension, floor pressing, and engine/powertrain) could be used interchangeably in different vehicle models. Using reconfigurable product architecture in this way enabled manufacturers to offer wider product choice, while saving on new vehicle development costs (Salvador et al., 2002). Yet as car-buying customers have become more sophisticated and understand the technologies used in new models, they have also become wary of premium vehicles sold with parts identical to standard vehicles. Considerable effort is expended today by vehicle manufacturers towards protecting their brand values and differentiating their products, often by integrating higher levels of service before and after the vehicle sale. An important supply strategy largely pioneered by the car industry and which represents a major departure from the mass production era is the concept of Building-to-Order (BTO), described in section 8.5 as part of responsive supply chain strategy.

It is interesting to speculate what type of approach to production and supply chain strategy will evolve next. Will the focus continue to shift away from volume and economies of scale, towards a more responsive, customer-orientated approach incorporating environmental and ethical issues? Figure 8.4 indicates the latest thinking to include more information-rich, digitalization of our supply chains, such as Industry 4.0 (Holmström et al., 2016; Bentley, 2017) and the rise of circular economy (Geissdoerfer et al., 2017; Geng et al., 2019). We envision that a new era will emerge altogether that focuses on the broader needs of society and reflects the theme of 'sustainable consumption' rather than our production-driven past, where concerns over product use, longevity, and lifecycle often ceased after departure from the factory. With many of the world's major corporations setting out their sustainable visions for the future, attention is already shifting to concerns over the practical means of supply chain implementation and the extent to which customers and suppliers become motivated and engage with sustainability as an integral element of supply chain strategy.

8.4 LEAN AND AGILE SUPPLY CHAIN STRATEGY

Lean is about doing more with less. The term is generally used in the context of lean manufacturing as part of a 'zero inventory' or just-in-time (JIT) approach to managing the supply chain (see Note 8.2). The use of lean as a supply chain strategy has become legendary in the history of continuous improvement (Womack and Jones, 2003, 2005; Hines et al., 2004). Lean was popularized in 1990 by Womack, Jones, and Roos in the best-selling book *The Machine that Changed the World*, which revealed the staggering 2-to-1 difference in productivity between Japanese and Western automotive manufacturers. Womack and Jones present lean as a practical, step-by-step approach derived from the Toyota Production System, which can be applied in almost any organization context and across the total enterprise or supply chain (Womack and Jones, 1994, 1996, 2003).

The goal of lean is to eliminate all sources of waste or 'muda' in the workplace, a philosophy that emerged from Toyota's resource-starved production halls in Japan after World War II (Monden, 1983; Ohno, 1988; Shingo, 1988). Central to lean thinking is the JIT method of delivery which is used to minimize the accumulation of component stocks (also termed inventory) in the supply chain. Although originally devised to improve manufacturing performance by focusing on material flow, pull, and defining value according to the customer, lean has more recently been applied to eliminate process-related waste such as unnecessary paperwork, movement of equipment and people, and handwritten authorization signatures in the services sector such as insurance, banking, and health (Swank, 2003). Challenged by rival improvement techniques such as Business Process Re-engineering (BPR) and Total Quality Management (TQM), the longevity of lean as a business management tool is attributed to the core principles of value creation, standardization, and putting people at the centre of the operation (Hines et al., 2004). Lean philosophy on production demands that freed up human resources as the result of process improvement exercises are not considered for redundancy or as an opportunity to reduce costs, but must be redeployed to other, more value-adding areas of the business (Womack and Jones, 2003).

A strong following has emerged among practitioners to adopt lean as a supply chain-wide approach which continuously improves the end-to-end customer order fulfilment process (Shapiro et al., 1992; Hines, 1994). Traditionally conceived as a means of production management which controlled the movement of components on the shop floor, it is now applied across multiple firms coordinated as a supply chain. Lean strategies make the distinction between real demand that is 'pulled' from the end customer according to their product requirements, in contrast to forecast-based demand 'pushed' by production which often creates unwanted inventory and serves only to keep the production line running (Monden, 1983). As a reaction against production push mentality the elimination of waste has now become a mantra which can be applied to all firms seeking ways to create changes to the effectiveness and efficiency of their business. Lean is perceived both as a supply chain strategy and a practical tool for daily incremental improvement, applied by shop floor and office staff to ensure any idea for improvement, no matter how small, is considered in terms of potential benefit to the business. As an improvement tool, the principles of lean thinking are used to describe the movement of goods and exchange of information, which are systematically recorded as part of a collaborative team-based exercise often involving key suppliers, before steps are proposed for a more streamlined future state using less stock, effort, and resources (Rother and Shook, 1988).

Note 8.1 Component suppliers deliver just-in-sequence to Volvo Cars, Sweden

Just-in-time delivery is an important element in lean production. In Torslanda, Sweden, the Volvo Car Corporation assembles the XC90 premium family utility vehicle at its final assembly hall just outside the city of Gothenburg. Volvo has assembled its key component suppliers or 'first-tier suppliers' within close proximity of its manufacturing facilities to enable quick delivery of critical vehicle parts such as braking systems, cockpit module, carpets, and glazing to the final assembly line. Volvo runs two or three production shifts a day and requires a delivery of parts and sub-assemblies from each supplier per shift. If any delivery is late, causing the production line to be halted, then the supplier responsible potentially faces a heavy fine, but this is usually a very rare event. Because of the high percentage of passenger vehicles built to specific customer requirements, production schedules at Volvo are incredibly detailed and require a high proportion of suppliers to deliver components not only exactly when needed, but in a specific sequence to match the individual specifications of each vehicle as it passes through the final assembly hall. This has given rise to use of the term 'just-in-sequence' delivery in production management circles.

A lean supply chain requires more collaborative supplier relationships, however, than are traditionally found in many industries. The term 'lean supply partnership' (Lamming, 1993) has entered into the language of supply chain management as part of a shift towards collaborative relationships involving procurement and logistics efficiency and effectiveness (Sako, 1992; Harrison, 1993; Hines, 1994). The rise of the concept of lean supply partnerships implies that the process improvement benefits once exclusively enjoyed by original equipment manufacturers (OEMs), i.e. automotive manufacturers such as Ford and General Motors, are now extended across the supply chain in return for closer, long-term commitment from the supply base. Driven by mutual benefits and trust-based relationships, the idea of partnerships is an opportunity for all firms in the supply chain to contribute and gain from process improvements. Influenced by the uniquely Japanese approach '*keiretsu*', a form of industrial organization similar in principle to the 'extended family', the idea of lean partnerships took off in the West when industry leaders realized the potential of closer buyer-supplier collaboration. Lean supply partnerships offered opportunities for performance improvement not only in terms of supply chain-wide cost reductions through JIT inventory management initiatives, but also reduced new product cycle times gained as a result of closer supplier involvement during new product development programmes.

As one of the most popular management improvement paradigms since the 1980s, lean, however, is not without its critics. Derived from the production-orientated language of the automotive and aerospace industries, concerns over applicability and effectiveness arise when faced with more customer-facing, service-orientated operations where standardization of supplier-customer exchanges may be impractical and inappropriate (James-Moore and Gibbons, 1997). Cultural differences between Eastern and Western working patterns and behaviours have also been suggested as a possible source of social friction in some of the early sites or 'transplants' where firms such as Toyota, Honda, and Nissan set up manufacturing plants outside Japan using hybrid lean production systems, such as in the US and UK (Wickens, 1987). Japanese workers generally tend to have greater respect for authority within the organizational hierarchy and adhere more readily to workplace rules and procedures, leading to suggestions of 'Tayloristic' style management practices by some Western observers (Forza, 1996). Further, as the implementation of lean production creates strategic resources which may in fact aid competitive advantage, the continued focus on incremental improvement over time may "curtail the firm's ability to achieve long-term flexibility" (Lewis, 2000: 959). Nevertheless, since its rise in popularity in the 1980s, lean remains a powerful concept in supply chain strategy particularly where improvement within and between firms is needed and demands closer buyer-supplier participation.

An important question here is: is lean green? Connections have been made between lean thinking and sustainability, i.e. 'lean and green', by scholars making the link between the efficiency paradigm of doing more with less, and minimizing the use of resources and output of industrial emissions to protect the natural environment (e.g. King and Lenoz, 2001; Simpson and Power, 2005; Mollenkopf et al., 2010). While there is evidence for the lean and green concept at a theoretical level, there remains considerable potential for industry to adopt lean and eliminate waste in order to resolve complex operational issues involving sustainability such as the implementation of a low carbon procurement strategy. A further issue is that lean supply chains may no longer be sufficient, or indeed appropriate, in industries facing increasingly turbulent and volatile markets, particularly when facing fluctuating commodity and raw material prices.

The agile supply chain is responsive to the changing needs of the market over time, requiring a high level of manoeuvrability as product life cycles shorten and global economic and competitive forces create uncertainty (Christopher, 2000). Agile supply strategy reflects the interest in time-based competition where responding quickly to specific customer demands is seen as a source of competitive advantage. A considerable distinction is drawn between lean and agile philosophies in management literature, although the 'agile camp' claims that leanness may be an element of agility in certain circumstances! Professor Christopher is a leading exponent of agile supply chain strategy who draws from Webster's dictionary to make the distinction clear: "it defines lean as 'containing little fat', whereas agile is defined as 'nimble'" (Christopher, 2000: 38). A key characteristic of an agile organization or supply chain is flexibility, whose origins as a business concept lie in flexible manufacturing systems (Kidd, 1994; Gunasekaran, 1999). Such systems use state-of-the-art machine technology (e.g. multi-headed computer numerically controlled robotic machines) capable of delivering high levels of product variety to meet customer requirements. There is also likely to be a high level of usage of digital technology to feedback customer requirements to production, making the supply chain more capable of responding to real customer demand rather than forecast-based information. Agile supply chains, therefore, must be market sensitive: able to cope with responding to individual customer requirements in short lead times, as well as coping with the peaks and troughs of demand over time (Christopher and Towill, 2000).

A problem in many supply chains is the restricted visibility of real, customer-based demand. The nature of supply chains today, i.e. extended over large distances, means there are often multiple points at which inventory is stored, meaning supply chain managers have to rely on forecast-driven rather than customer-driven information. The exact position where real demand reaches into the supply chain is called the decoupling point, and represents the meeting of market pull and production push. The issue here is how far real demand in the form of customer orders is made visible to the supply chain, where order information is often distorted and delayed by actions of a third party or an inadequate information system. The decoupling point dictates where inventory should be held, which acts as a buffer between the part of the supply chain directly geared towards satisfying customer orders, and the part based on production planning. This is also the point in the supply chain where real customer orders enter the process and are assigned to individual products or basic sub-assemblies of the product. According to Christopher (2000: 210) "... the aim of the agile supply chain should be to carry inventory in as generic a form as possible, that is, standard semi-finished products awaiting final assembly". He argues that the agile supply chain should hold inventory in a generic form (that is, standard, semi-finished products) awaiting final assembly until the final customer requirements and destination of the order is known. This is known as postponement, or delayed configuration, and is an important supply chain tactic.

The decision over where the customer order enters the production process has implications for sustainability in terms of waste. Supply chains which are capable of building product to customer order, rather than simply keeping production running and piling up inventory in the hope that someone will want to buy the product, will face fewer problems in terms of how to deal with excess stock and wasted resources. Building the perfect agile supply chain has considerable cost implications, however, and while it may seem preferable to adopt a demand driven approach, there are considerable costs involved and a trade-off may have to be reached in terms of how far upstream customer orders can penetrate. Understanding where production meets customer demand in the supply chain means placing inventory 'strategically' so that it assists the order fulfilment process rather than clogging up the process flow. There are also other methods, such as modularization, which can help to alleviate the effects of product variety in production.

An emerging train of thought regarding strategy is that supply chains cannot be thought of as lean or agile in isolation, but instead evolve as a blended or hybrid approach, named by Naylor et al. (1999) as 'leagile'. In the early stages of entering a new market the lean paradigm enables the product to penetrate the market achieved through low-cost production. As the market matures, demand for higher levels of variety grows and the agile paradigm begins to replace it. 'Leagile' strategy or "customized 'leagile' strategy" means the supply chain is agile enough to respond to what is actually selling, with product availability and short delivery lead times supported by information transparency as the critical market winners (Christopher and Towill, 2000: 212). Returning to the respective typical characteristics of supply chain strategy, lean requires the fat to be eliminated, whereas agile must be nimble because lost sales are gone forever. Although important differences exist between the two approaches, for example lean supply chains tend to adopt level scheduling whereas agile supply chains require additional capacity to cope with volatility, there is increasing pressure on firms for lean supply chains to become agile as markets mature and become more customized. Companies such as Zara (see Note 8.2), the high street fashion retailer, are good examples of 'leagile' hybrid supply chain strategy. While not as well-known as either lean or agile, 'leagile' strategy combines elements of both approaches with the concepts of decoupling and the 'information-enriched' supply chain (Mason-Jones et al., 2000).

Note 8.2 Zara: high street fashion meets 'leagile' supply chain strategy

Zara is a highly successful Spanish high street retail company selling fashionable clothes to an international market. It is a good example of a hybrid supply chain strategy in a fiercely competitive environment, combining an agile supply chain which includes many lean characteristics (i.e. leagile). It has developed an effective quick response system which starts with cross-functional teams such as fashion, commercial, and retail specialists all working together at Zara's design department in the company headquarters at La Coruña, Spain. The team's understanding of fashion is guided by regular updates of Electronic Point of Sale data from stores all around the world. Zara's manufacturing systems are similar to other firms, combining the late configuration ideas of Benetton with the cost efficiency of Toyota. Only economies-of-scale operations such as dying, cutting, labelling, and packaging are conducted in-house, with the more labour-intensive finishing stages completed by networks of around 300 small sub-contractors who specialise in one type of garment or process. While the supply chain is designed to be flexible to cope with sudden market changes, production at Zara is kept at a level slightly below sales to keep stock moving through the warehouses to the retail outlets. Having successfully mastered the science of rapid-fire fulfilment (Ferdows et al., 2004), Zara is increasingly under pressure to address how to design an effective 'take back' system across its global supply chain which copes with high quantities of used or discarded clothing that could be reused and given a second life. See Note 8.3 to learn how firms in Brazil address this issue.

Source: Ferdows et al. (2003); Christopher (2000)

8.4.1 Matching the supply chain with the product and the market

Understanding the link between supply chain strategy and product type is crucial to realizing optimum performance. A common mistake is where the supply chain evolves over time to include many different varieties of product line to suit as many different types of customer demand as possible. This results in the supply chain becoming bloated with inventory, sluggish, unable to respond efficiently or effectively to demand, and often clogged with high levels of unwanted finished stock. An important article by Fisher in 1997 on the subject asks: *what is the right supply chain for your product?* This seemingly simple question was the result of years of field research by the US professor who realised that despite the improvements in technology and management thinking, the performance of supply chains had never been worse, with – in some cases – costs rising to unprecedented levels because of adversarial buyer-supplier relationships and poor practices such as overreliance on price promotions leading to heavy discounting.

Fisher established that waste in the affected industries was running into billions of dollars, and yet in many supply chains there was too much of some types of product and not enough of others because of inability to predict demand. He devised a simple framework which started by defining whether the product was functional (i.e. predictable demand, long product life cycle, low variety) or innovative (i.e. unpredictable demand, short product life cycle, high variety).

The second important parameter determines the operating conditions of the supply chain: either physically efficient or market-responsive supply chains. Physically efficient processes are defined as "supply predictable demand efficiently at the lowest possible cost" and market-responsive processes are defined as to "respond quickly to unpredictable demand in order to minimise stock-outs, forced markdowns and obsolete inventory" (Fisher, 1997: 108). By understanding their supply chain in terms of operating environment and market conditions, and matching this with the type of product, managers were better able to devise the ideal supply chain strategy and avoid the possibility of 'mismatch' e.g. functional products delivered by unnecessarily responsive supply chains.

Figure 8.5 develops the ideas of Fisher with the concepts of lean and agile supply chain strategy. It builds on the connection between product and market, and supply chains, by including closely defined characteristics. Lean and agile are positioned diagonally in the matrix, which offers the opportunity to blend particular aspects of both strategies and opt for a leagile approach i.e. positioned in the middle. While initially most managers are likely to adopt either a lean or agile approach, they should definitely avoid the areas of mismatch marked by an 'X' in the opposite corners of the model in Figure 8.5.

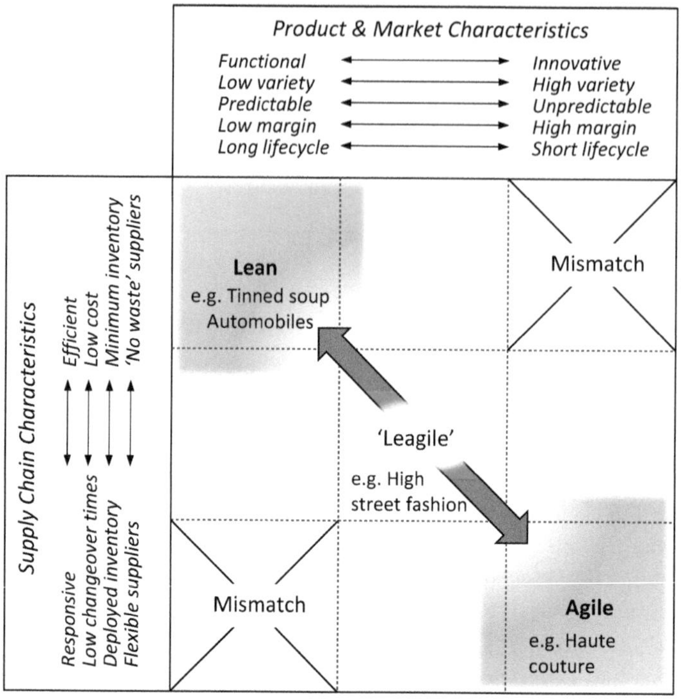

FIGURE 8.5 Lean and agile supply chain strategy

Lean supply chain strategy is characterized by functional, relatively low variety, long life cycle products with predictable but low profit margin type market demand. Lean supply chains are devised around the principle of efficiency and low cost, based on minimum inventory and with suppliers striving towards the goal of 'no waste'. Typical examples of products which are suitable for lean supply chains include tinned soup and family motor cars, although some types of specialist sports vehicle in the premium market segment, such as Aston Martin or Lamborghini, will adopt a more customer-centric and responsive leagile or even agile supply chain approach.

Agile supply chain strategy is characterized by innovative, high variety, and shorter life-cycle products with unpredictable but high-margin market demand. Agile supply chains are designed to be customer responsive, with manufacturers and their suppliers capable of offering the flexibility for low production changeover times. Inventory is often held close to the market in order to respond swiftly to specific customer demands. Examples include the creation of exclusive fashion called 'haute couture' where specialist garments are made or adapted to suit an individual's requirements. Smartphones are another good example, with new models such as the Apple iPhone being updated every year encouraging high levels of turnover and product obsolescence. Although the physical hand units may appear identical at the point of purchase, each customer has the ability to quickly customize to their own preferences by buying aftermarket cases and via built-in or downloadable software applications, offering very high levels of product customization.

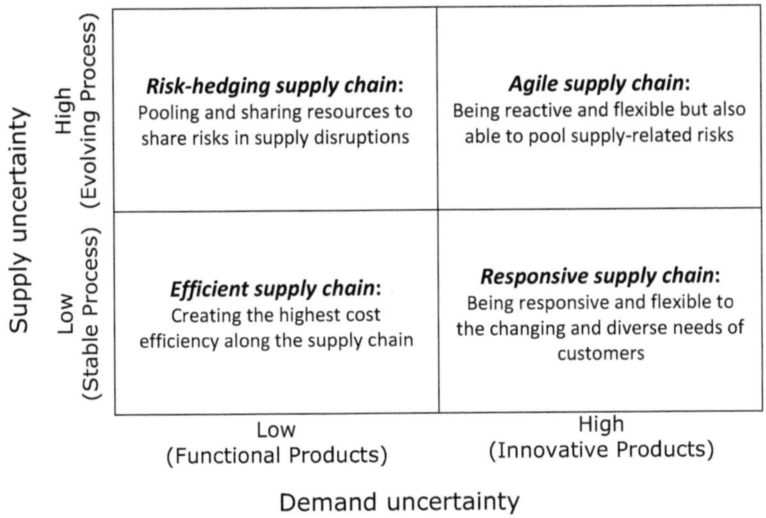

FIGURE 8.6 Lee's supply chain strategy matrix

The concept of agility has also been linked with the mitigation of risk in the supply chain (see 8.5 – Responsiveness and building to order) where supply chain agility is defined as the capability of the firm, both internally and in conjunction with suppliers and customers, to adapt and respond to market changes as well as to potential disruptions (Braunscheidal and Suresh, 2009).

A model developed by Lee (2002) also expands on Fisher's model and the debate on lean and agile supply chain strategies, suggesting a wider range of factors be taken into account when analyzing uncertainty. Lee suggests that it is not only demand uncertainty but also supply uncertainty that creates supply chain challenges. In addition to Fisher's distinction between functional and innovative products, Lee's model distinguishes between low supply uncertainty (stable process) and high supply uncertainty (evolving process). Stable supply processes are characterized by, for example, mature and highly automated manufacturing processes and an established supply base with secure long-term supplier relationships. In comparison, evolving supply processes are immature, with fewer and less reliable suppliers, and technology is still emerging. Lee's matrix in Figure 8.6 suggests four different strategies for managing the different supply and demand uncertainties. Where efficient supply chains are appropriate for low level of demand and supply uncertainty and agile supply chains are required for high demand and supply uncertainty, Lee's framework introduces the concepts of risk-hedging supply chains for situations of low demand uncertainty coupled with high process uncertainty and responsive supply chains for situations of high demand uncertainty but low supply process uncertainty.

Resembling a lean supply chain strategy, the efficient supply chain should seek to create high-cost efficiency along the supply chain. Risk-hedging supply chains focus on managing supply chain process risks through hedging strategies by pooling inventory or other capacity-related resources with other companies or development of new supplier relationships. Responsive supply chains focus on being responsive to changing and diverse customer demands. This can be done through Build-to-Order (BTO) strategies and mass customization strategies. Agile supply chains are both risk-hedging supply and responsive to customer demands: agile supply chains should be truly reactive and flexible hedging the risks of supply shortages or disruptions and be responsive to changing customer demands. In the following section, we explore in more detail the nature of supply chain responsiveness and build-to-order strategies.

8.5 RESPONSIVENESS AND BUILDING TO ORDER

A significant landmark in strategic thinking is the conceptual shift beyond firm level competitiveness towards supply chain responsiveness, where supply chains as a whole compete globally and cope with high degrees of volatility (Handfield and Bechtel, 2002; Ferdows et al., 2004). Responsiveness is about reacting to customer requirements, not just in terms of matching the customer's product or service specifications, but fulfilling the order in the shortest lead-time possible (Holweg and Pil, 2001). As competition increased in the 1990s, with customers becoming more demanding, and developments in information technology helping to improve forecasting and logistics, responsiveness and the ability to build-to-order (BTO) became a new differentiator in supply chain competitive advantage.

One of the first sectors where the importance of supply chain responsiveness emerged was the grocery or Fast-Moving Consumer Goods (FMCG) sector, with the launch of the Efficient Customer Response (ECR) movement in 1994. ECR was a joint trade and industry body working towards making groceries and FMCG more responsive to consumer demand and promoting the removal of unnecessary costs such as excess stock from the supply chain. Characterized by the emergence of collaborative management along the supply chain, it argued that consumers can be served better, faster, and at less cost by firms working together with their trading partners rather than resorting to traditional adversarial tactics. ECR distinguished between the customer, often seen as the most powerful stakeholder (e.g. supermarkets), and the end consumers or 'online shoppers' who expect better choice, service convenience, quality, freshness, and safety from their store.

Advances in information technology (IT) have resulted in an increase in processing power and reduction in the size of computers, allowing Electronic Point of Sale units with barcode scanning technology to be used as standard in all store check-out stations today. This means staff can instantly record the sale of goods in real time and alert the back office to replenish shelves to avoid stock-out of popular items. Developments in the more effective use of information, particularly sharing with logistics operations, has led to companies such as Tesco consolidating several stages of their delivery process and introducing facilities such as the cross-docking warehouse to speed the transfer of goods from in-bound trucks to out-bound delivery to the stores. In the past, non-standardized operational practices and the rigid separation of the traditional roles of supplier and retailer threatened to block the supply chain unnecessarily, and failed to exploit the synergies from new IT and planning tools. ECR and similar concepts such as Collaborative Planning, Forecasting, and Replenishment has enabled firms to create competitive advantage by demonstrating their ability to work with trading partners and add value through superior service (Danese, 2007).

Associated with supply chain responsiveness is the concept of delivery precision: the ability to build a product according to customer specifications and deliver within a short order lead time. The ability to introduce precision into production operations and supply chain management is known as Build-to-Order or 'BTO' (Holweg and Pil, 2001; Gunasekaran and Ngai, 2005) and has its roots in automobile production strategy. In the early days of Henry Ford, vehicle manufacture was about maintaining a high volume of production, where the factory was responsible for pushing out as many products as possible usually with strong market demand. While experiments in production mechanization and interchangeable parts were state-of-the-art during this time, the practice of delivery and supply of the finished product was very basic and based on Make-to-stock. A product supplied from stock means the customer has no choice in its configuration: it is not 'factory fresh' and may have been built many months ago. Today, if the preferred specification is not available within a few days, this means customers haggle with the salesperson for a discount, thereby reducing the firm's opportunity to make a profit. Despite the introduction of initiatives such as lean, and fuelled by constant product segmentation and niche marketing, the production-centric approach employed by many Western carmakers has resulted in huge stockpiles of unsold vehicle inventory worth billions of dollars, a phenomenon that has persisted into the 21st century (Holweg and Pil, 2005). Today, many vehicle manufacturers are rethinking their business strategy in order to reduce stocks by reconnecting with the customer. This means not only considering distribution and supply as playing a central role in the organization, but also how BTO fits strategically with production operations, finance, and marketing.

Implementing a BTO strategy across the enterprise does not, however, happen overnight. All volume vehicle manufacturers in the West since the early 1900s have until recently been operating a system where production takes priority and is generally considered the primary constraint because of the sunk costs and complexity of the process involved. Hence, Material Resource Planning (MRP) systems are geared towards optimizing the highest flow of products through the system, often regardless of the proportion of 'real' customer orders. Conventional practice also involves the vehicle manufacturer sending every dealership a monthly quota of new vehicles to sell, based on past sales, meaning the dealer is forced to sell products that do not always match current market requirements. Car buying customers are becoming increasingly dissatisfied with the traditional ways of negotiation and compromise during the car sales process, and instead are demanding that new products be delivered according to a customized specification, pre-agreed price, and exact delivery date. As the choice of vehicle propulsion is diversifying from petrol and diesel to include electric and hybrid (i.e. combined internal combustion engine and electric motor), the impact of variety is an increasingly significant factor for vehicle manufacturers in terms of how they plan their supply chain.

Understanding product variety and the impact on production costs is an important factor in supply chain strategy (Berry and Cooper, 1999; Salvador et al., 2002). Before vehicle manufacturers fully understood the impact it had on their business, it was assumed that the more choice offered to customers in terms of vehicle specification the better. For example, this meant some automakers offering four different shades of green and ten different types of radio in their vehicle catalogues! Yet the implications upstream in the supply chain, not just in terms of line-side inventory, but also the cost of stock held further upstream by suppliers, was crippling the business. Some customers simply became bewildered by the complexity of vehicle options on offer. As manufacturers such as Toyota began to sell standard equipped vehicles with higher levels of specification than Western equivalents at comparable prices, Western firms began to realise the importance of product standardization (one of the core principles of lean) and the cost benefits it could bring. Rather than arbitrarily reduce choice to the customer, vehicle manufacturers in the 1990s began to make informed decisions over what model configurations and options sold best. This sparked a wave of innovative design and new technology to overcome the cost of complexity to production through techniques such as universal body pressings (i.e. to suit both left and right-hand drive), common 'plug and play' electronics, modularization, and the late configuration of colour-coordinated components such as body trim to minimize disruption in the manufacturing process. Controlling product variety and the resultant impact of complexity in production is an important enabler for manufacturers and their suppliers seeking to develop BTO as an integral element in their supply chain strategy.

Note 8.3 Strategies to reshape the fashion industry in Brazil

The Brazilian fashion industry is one rare case where the full supply chain cycle is available within the same country: abundance of cotton and other raw materials, garment industry, retail competition, and a huge consumer base. Thus, it is not rare to find companies selling millions per year while concentrating on local supply and local market. Within that context, circularity emerges as the next step in Brazilian fashion exploring the three supply chain strategies of narrowing (reduce), slowing (reuse), and closing (recycle).

The first example is **Movin**, a brand that offers a unique way to sell products combining digitalization, minimalism, and circularity. The result is the 'inverted price model', which consists of featuring new products on the website before production occurs. Customers who like a product enter a crowdfunding scheme, which means that they have to pay in advance knowing production only starts once the minimum threshold of 1,000 pieces is met, or else their money is returned. Once this threshold is met, the price increases for future clients, thus opposite to traditional fashion, where the price decreases as the season progresses. The inverted price model offers a true pull strategy where production only occurs after sales, thus reducing unnecessary inventory. This is a clear exemplar of the narrowing (reduce) strategy.

Now meet **Comas**, which aims to produce 'clothes from clothes', i.e. upcycling. Since 2020, Comas has made partnerships with major brands, including the global brand C&A. First initiatives for upcycling came as second-hand stores and informal solutions. These lack scalability and financial support. In a structured upcycling platform such as Comas, the brands play the role of scavengers bringing clothes back to be upcycled and thus implementing the slowing (reuse) strategy.Thirdly, the introduction of recycled cotton in Brazil. This begins with the reverse flow of either textile waste (discarded by industry) or disposed clothes (discarded by final customers). While scavengers operationalize the reverse flow, the Brazilian textile industry has developed a de-fibrillation technology that can decompose textile back into cotton yarn, that can then be re-transformed into new textile patterns. **PG Fios** was the first company to produce recycled yarn in Brazil. Then, garment industry players such as **Cocamar** had to adapt their process to use recycled yarn. And finally, brands such as **Osklen** had to be bold to offer recycled cotton t-shirts to their consumer base, that initially felt less comfortable while technology was improving. Fashion brands adopting recycled cotton also need to adapt their design process as colours are not previously defined any more, but rather accepted as a result of the recycling process. The partnership of these three players offers an example of the closing (recycle) strategy.

Adapted from: Marques and Manzanares (2023)

8.6 INTERMEDIATION AND DISINTERMEDIATION STRATEGY

An intermediary is someone who acts as a link between groups of people, sometimes termed a middleman. In the context of supply chain strategy, intermediation means the link or facilitator between goods manufacturers and customers, requiring a range of knowledge and skills in marketing, operations, and distribution. Free trade and globalized markets have raised the profile of intermediation strategy as goods made in one part of the world can be shipped and delivered to a customer in another, provided the location is served by a network of local offices and warehouses controlled by the intermediary organization which accepts a percentage of the revenue for their services, usually between 5 and 25 per cent (McFarlan and Young, 2002). Original Equipment Manufacturers (OEMs) typically in the auto and aerospace sectors can be considered as the focal firm, who not only profit from product sales but also the lucrative aftermarket in 'OE' parts and components for servicing and fleet repair. As component suppliers seek to increase their margins, usually because of overly harsh contractual pricing agreements, this may tempt them to bypass the OEM and sell parts directly to the customer: a strategy defined as 'disintermediation', with major consequences for the buyer-supplier relationship (Rossetti and Choi, 2005, 2008).

Disintermediation can occur in almost any industry, including capital goods (e.g. aircraft, trucks, passenger vehicles), retail (e.g. books, home computers), or the tourism sector (e.g. hotels, airline flight bookings). Disintermediation often occurs with the emergence of new technology, e.g. the internet which enables new entrants such as Dell, EasyJet, or Amazon to design on-line customer information systems and bypass one or more stages of the supply chain e.g. the retailer's high street store or travel agent (Evans and Wurster, 1997; Chircu and Kauffman, 2000). Today, the rise of what is termed peer-to-peer marketing or the 'sharing economy' means that it is not just disruptive technology which is challenging traditional ways of offering services, but new business models, for example tourist accommodation provided by the likes of Airbnb (Cusumano, 2015).

The Hong Kong trading company Li & Fung had expanded to sales of 2 billion US dollars by the year 2000 and had come a long way from its roots in matching Chinese manufacturers with Western buyers (McFarlan and Young, 2002). However, there was real concern from the company's managing director over the effect of the internet and a third party putting together all the information on buyers and factories on-line: "Would the internet disintermediate us? Would we get Amazoned?" After some business research the company realized that although the internet was indeed a facilitator for the supply chain, it was no substitute for the network of relationships built up over decades by the 5,000 Li & Fung employees with local manufacturers spread across six continents. The key was to have old economy know-how but be open to new economy ideas. Li & Fung decided to launch *Li&Fung.com* in 2000, despite concerns over cannibalization of the core business and uncertainty over the market's response to an internet portal. Today it operates a hybrid system, maintaining internet-based communications with its largest customers including Avon, Coca-Cola, and Disney, with the sophistication of the connection varying with the nature of communications infrastructure available in any specific region. While some firms send digital photos of their product samples to head office, (what is sometimes termed a 'thick connection'), others prefer to do business the more traditional way: if not face-to-face, then by email or telephone.

A prime example of sector-wide disintermediation, or the bypassing and cutting out of once powerful middle players, is the case of the US aerospace industry's parts supply. Rossetti and Choi (2005) describe the strategic blunder of major OEMs in the 1990s such as Airbus, General Electric, and Honeywell where, despite implementing strategic sourcing over the past decade, the supply chain was literally coming apart with suppliers selling their components directly to the buyer's customers. Referring to the phenomenon as "supply chain disintermediation" (46), Rossetti and Choi argue that the core tenets of strategic sourcing, long-term relationships and co-prosperity, had been misapplied, with supplier relationships marked by gamesmanship and deception. At the root of the supplier's motives to bypass its former paymasters was the increasing tendency of the OEMs to offer false promises of long-term contracts simply to gain the lowest component prices and, once the contract was in place, to force suppliers to absorb risks such as holding inventory and cash flow management. As OEM buyers began to rationalize the supply base as part of consolidation to the point where competition disappeared, the resultant effect was unintentionally to create fewer, more powerful suppliers who were able to use their stronger bargaining position in the industry to negotiate more favourable terms. In summing up their observations in terms of the preventative steps against future supply chain disintermediation, Rossetti and Choi recommend:

- Understanding the supply market and supplier's reactions to strategic initiatives;
- Using spend consolidation to increase supplier efficiency and guard against bankruptcy;
- Incorporating broader supply chain metrics that better reflect corporate goals;
- Using long-term agreements to reduce transaction costs and promote co-prosperity based on trust.

Disintermediation can be deployed as a strategy by firms over time to gain control of a project, sector or market. This is particularly the case in restricted markets where there are only a few large suppliers offering specialist services, such as the Western defence sector. The award of a government defence contract for example offers the opportunity of significant revenue and long-term security to OEMs who increasingly offer facility and programme management services as well as platform (i.e. warship, tank, fighter plane) fabrication and engineering. As Western governments such as the UK seek to reduce their commitment in terms of the fixed costs of managing design, construction, maintenance, and support, private multinational firms have stepped in to gain control of almost all stages and stakeholders in the defence commissioning process. These private OEMs therefore have much control over what is meant to be a public sector service i.e. national security. A study of the supply dynamics over time focusing on the management of a government warship design and build contract highlights the disintermediation strategies deployed by powerful suppliers to secure their future in the sector. As a result of extensive outsourcing in the UK by government, one OEM has gained such a level of responsibility that it now assumes the role and influence over major projects formerly adopted by the ministry of defence (Howard et al., 2016).

8.7 CLOSED-LOOP SUPPLY STRATEGY AND THE CIRCULAR ECONOMY

The decision to adopt a closed-loop supply strategy has significant implications for the firm in terms of sustainable supply management. It shows that the organization has begun to consider the issues of environmental management and product lifecycle in terms of the business vision, and can distinguish traditional supply chains from closed loop supply chains (Guide and van Wassenhove, 2003a). Yet introducing a closed loop or 'reverse logistics' supply chain into the business is not simple, particularly as product recycling is rarely considered as a value creating system (Guide and van Wassenhove, 2003b). Closed-loop supply chains require considerable investment in time and resources, initially in understanding the configurations of information flow and parts distribution that serve the product while in use, and then in developing a collection system which takes back or 'harvests' the product at its end-of-life, while integrating the cooperation of customers, suppliers, and not-for-profit organizations (Kumar and Malegeant, 2006).

The process of product disassembly and remanufacturing can be particularly tricky as the condition of used products may vary greatly, can be distributed across the world and, even if retrievable, may have to be discarded if damaged beyond repair. A combination of increasingly stringent government legislation (e.g. European law on vehicle scrapping and disassembly) and manufacturer-led initiatives means most industry sectors today have active recycling schemes in operation e.g. photocopiers, computers, electronics (Spengler and Schröter, 2003). A criticism of some recycling schemes is that they have been retro-introduced at some considerable time after the original plans to design, manufacture, and distribute the product, hence have never been fully integrated into the supply chain. The circular economy however offers a radically different approach as

> an industrial system that is restorative or regenerative by intention and design. It replaces the end-of-life concept with restoration, shifts towards the use of renewable

energy, eliminates the use of toxic chemicals, which impair reuse, and aims for the elimination of waste through the superior design of materials, products, systems, and within this, business models.

(EMF, 2013: 7)

Note 8.4 The rise of the circular economy: strategy, vision, or business model?

While the circular economy could be considered a strategy in its own right, it is often introduced as a business model for individual product lines which operate alongside more traditional approaches such as lean and agile. The circular economy can be described as both a vision of a regenerative industrial system and a business model that is applied to products and components as well as food and chemicals. It follows the concept of producing no waste or pollution from the outset, where material flows of biological nutrients and technical nutrients are designed to circulate within the production system for as long as possible with zero leakages or landfill (EMF, 2013, 2015). Many blue-chip companies are introducing circular economy principles to significant parts of their business, particularly those with potentially high value reusable assets such as batteries, typically representing around 20–30 per cent of total turnover (Zils et al., 2023). However, despite good progress being made with the circular economy, the cost of implementing change to current manufacturing practices means it may be some decades before a whole business or entire sector can claim to be anywhere near 100 per cent circular.

Introducing the circular economy is now of considerable interest across corporations, universities, and parliaments across Europe and beyond (De Angelis et al., 2018; Zils et al., 2023). Given rising sustainability concerns around resource scarcity, pollution, child labour, and carbon net zero, high hopes are being pinned on the circular economy as a strategy which enables firms to transition from a *take-make-waste* linear production model towards alternative modes of production that allow goods to be designed and produced from the outset with reuse, repair, and refurbishment in mind (Figure 8.7). The concept of 'circular business advantage' is used where firms exploit the circular economy concept to create a regenerative production system that achieves limitless growth whilst producing no waste. Such an idea may seem far-fetched, but with the launch of the EU's Circular Economy Package and the 2017 release of British Standard 8001 Framework for Implementing Circular Economy Principles, it may soon become standard practice. Introducing greater circularity into all supply chains is important because the typical nation's resource usage is inefficient and wasteful, with only around 15 per cent of Europe's plastics currently being recycled, and China consuming more aluminium, steel, and cement than the whole of the OECD[2] put together. This imminent crisis in natural resources and the knock-on effect of waste on polluting the land, air, and oceans requires a more radical approach towards resource effectiveness than recycling. A circular economy could help alleviate pressures on mining for high demand minerals such as cobalt, which is commonly associated with child labour abuses. It could also address carbon net zero targets by finding

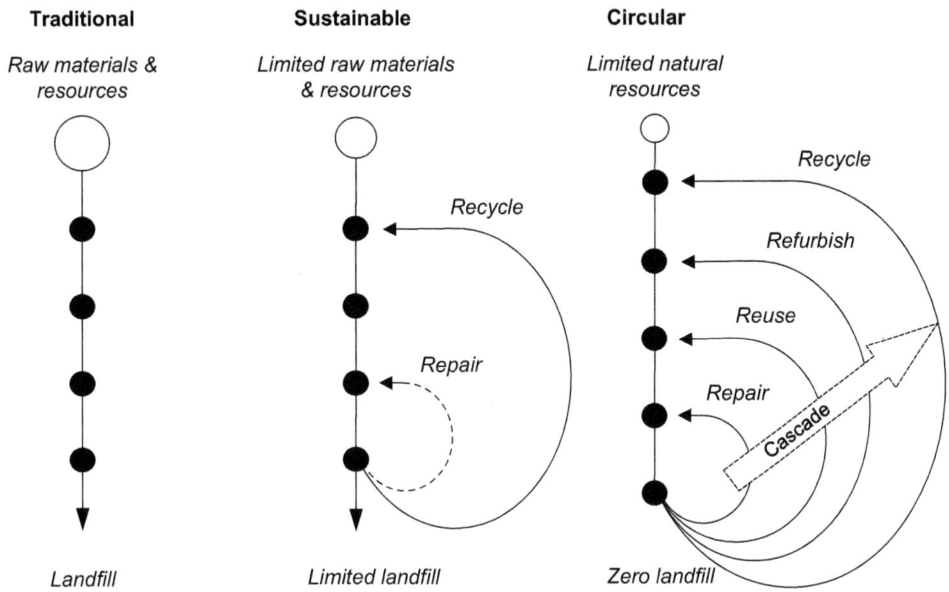

FIGURE 8.7 Transition towards the circular supply chain
Source: Adapted from De Angelis et al. (2018)

ways to harvest and reuse old building materials such as concrete in the construction industry. Adopting a circular approach potentially offers a solution, but with the degree of out-of-the-box thinking, investment, and new regulation required it represents a major challenge to business and society (Howard et al., 2022).

Closed-loop supply chains are challenging in their design and operation, and also have important implications for supply chain strategy (Savaskan et al., 2004). They include traditional forward supply chain activities, but also the additional activities of the reverse supply chain such as the returns process, movements of goods, product testing and sorting, and remarketing (Guide et al., 2003a, b). Although described in detail later, it is worth pointing out here that despite reverse logistics systems being practised since the 1920s (e.g. automotive sector), there is a lack today of the strategic level thinking required to integrate the concept of the closed-loop supply chain into mainstream business activity. Closed loop or reverse systems are typically treated as a silo, isolated from the core business, where common activities are yet to be established and not fully understood in different contexts because of variations in complexity and perceptions in managerial importance. Industry and academia have a tendency to focus on the operational and tactical e.g. how to create a remanufacturing programme, rather than to tackle the broader, more strategic issues of business profitability and the underlying motivations for why the firm has adopted such a scheme in the first place. In the now contentious words of Guide and van Wassenhove (2003a: 3): "… no rational company will invest in environmental measures to save the earth. That's not what companies are for, and legislation is not going to change that".

Before examining the case of a carpet manufacturer who adopted a closed loop supply chain strategy, it is helpful to discuss the work of Pagell and Wu (2009) in the context of sustainable supply chain strategy. In their study of ten exemplar firms seeking to build more sustainable supply chains, they suggest that conventional best practice in supply chain management can be used as a foundation for sustainability. This means that traditional aspects of supply chain management, e.g. proactive stance and commitment, business redefinition, supplier certification, life cycle thinking, and closed loop logistics, can be combined and integrated with newer behaviours such as greater commitment to employees, supply chain integration, sustainable values to help in recruitment, and adding new suppliers to spur sustainable innovation. Pagell and Wu's research also suggests that reconceptualizing the supply chain to include sustainability requires not only "... changing the cognition of managers" but the realization of more intrinsic and long-term benefits, e.g. supplier commitment, employee motivation, customer loyalty, etc., which are derived from the development of sustainable business values and the adoption of closed loop supply chain strategy.

8.8 CASE STUDY: DESSO CARPETS AND CRADLE-TO-CRADLE® CHALLENGE

This case examines the carpet manufacturer Desso, based in the Netherlands, after its decision to adopt Cradle-to-Cradle® or circular principles and the subsequent reframing of the firm's understanding of supply chain management. Although the company had been involved in stand-alone sustainability initiatives such as wind powered energy generation before the management buy-out in 2007, no one in the organization had dared consider incorporating concepts as bold as Cradle-to-Cradle® into the heart of the enterprise.

Cradle-to-Cradle® is a play on the phrase 'cradle to grave' which, in contrast to traditional linear manufacturing models, promotes the use of non-toxic manufacturing systems where products are designed for disassembly using pure materials which can be safely recycled.[3] The concept of Cradle-to-Cradle® or 'C2C®' as it is often abbreviated, was popularized by Braungart and McDonough in their book *Cradle to Cradle: Remaking the way we make things.* Published in 2002, their book is now considered a sustainability classic. Phrases such as 'cradle to grave' allude to a more traditional, linear manufacturing model dating from the industrial revolution, sometimes called a 'take, make, waste' system. While this system has played a role in improving quality of life, it has generated many unintended and undesirable global consequences such as the production of vast amounts of waste and pollution, the depletion of natural resources, and loss of biodiversity. C2C® in contrast promotes non-toxic manufacturing systems where products and materials are designed from the outset to enhance quality-of-life and ensure safe recycling once product life has expired. C2C® takes its design inspiration for products and processes from nature. The model aims to mimic the planet's natural cyclical nutrient flows, its use of solar energy, and its creation of diversity and abundance. In nature for example, there is no such thing as waste. Materials are continuously recycled to nourish new organisms.

Convincing an organization of the need to change represents a challenge, but asking customers and suppliers to change a lifetime of ingrained habits means change at all levels of the enterprise, from strategic vision to daily operations, which doesn't happen overnight. Add to this the challenge for Desso of balancing economic survival in the worst world-wide recession for over 50 years on one hand, with introducing its aspirations for the long-term wellbeing of people and planet on the other. The process of C2C® implementation has gained significant momentum at the firm, with the management team led by CEO Stef Kranendijk (ex-Procter & Gamble) beginning to understand the extent of the complexity involved in changing the organization and supply chain. This includes aspects such as material sourcing, information sharing with suppliers, and a deep commitment to go further on tackling sustainability issues than current legislation requires.

Since the restructuring of the company and announcement of the adoption of C2C®, Desso has steadily increased annual profits in terms of EBIT from one per cent in 2007, to 9.2 per cent in 2011.[4] Traditionally in carpets there is not much money to be made: "... if you make 10 per cent you're doing great!" Stef Kranendijk believes and proves that C2C® is not only good for the environment, but also drives personal health, innovation, and business acumen which leads to higher profits. His ambitious design objectives for the company are to have every product supported by the C2C® vision by 2020: "From the moment we started to publicise C2C, from February 2008 ... and we have been communicating our ideas a lot over the years to end users, architects, CEOs ... people react very positively to it". At the beginning his new management team had to decide which product category from the existing portfolio to start with. They chose carpet tiles: a popular product with commercial customers particularly in busy office environments but composed of around 120 ingredients some of which are toxic though acceptable to the industry and comply with current regulations (such as REACH and CE labelling) and contain elements not allowed by Cradle-to-Cradle® criteria. A major component of the typical carpet tile is the natural material bitumen used as backing. This is the thick residue left after petrochemicals have been removed in the separation process from crude oil. Bitumen contains sometimes unknown and thus difficult-to-control ingredients, adding to the issue of end-of-life treatment which often leads to the dumping of used carpet tiles in landfill sites; a practice that is now forbidden in most countries across Europe.

After Stef Kranendijk got acquainted with Michael Braungart and C2C®, introducing the concept to the site at Desso's production facilities at Waalwijk was not simple. "The people in R&D and Manufacturing got worried and said: 'What is going on?!'" Desso's carpet tile production line was one of the first to start re-thinking its product and production process, and required considerable collaboration with architects, Non-Governmental Organizations (NGOs), and suppliers such as Dow Chemical to decide how best to replace the bitumen used in the backing material. "We have developed together with EPEA[5] and Dow Chemical [the new carpet tile backing] we call EcoBase™ where the polyolefin based layer can be fully and safely recycled at a high level". The EcoBase™ backing is specifically designed for disassembly and recycling in Desso's own production plant. Carpet tiles with DESSO EcoBase® have achieved Cradle-to-Cradle® Silver Certification reaching a level where up to 97 per cent of the materials are positively defined.[6]

A particular challenge for Desso is the 'Take Back' initiative, which the company has offered since 2008. Under this system the company offers to retrieve used carpet tiles from buildings undergoing refurbishment (also termed 'urban mining') and then recycles them at the plant in Waalwijk. Desso's take-back and recycling process is called ReFinity® which separates the post-consumer carpet into its main components, either for recycling into new carpet yarn, or for downcycling into road building materials and for use as secondary fuel in the cement industry.

Encouraging contractors such as the independent carpet fitter to collaborate is one difficult issue, but determining the material used in the tiles which may have been manufactured by a competitor is another. Much of the material is over ten years old and may have a high bitumen content which is the heavy part or stabilizer of the tile and is non-recyclable, traditionally burnt in incinerators or simply landfilled. While Desso is currently exploring the use of incinerated material for use in cement, its objective for carpet tile recycling is to separate the yarn and other fibres from all the other materials for use again, where the tile is typically built up of different layers e.g. polyester, polypropylene, and polyamide. Desso has developed a process of separation which involves shredding and fluffing old carpet. A special colour dye removal process has been developed by a supplier where "… other methods have been tried such as directly extruding the fibre, but this leaves the colour in which is no good for light coloured carpet". Desso's innovative manufacturing and recycling methods mean the white yarn can continuously be re-used, albeit with a certain loss of material with each cycle of the tile at a rate of around 11 per cent. Innovation on the scale envisaged by Desso through the implementation of C2C® requires significant investment in time, resources, and technologies. To develop the yarn recycling process alone, for example, has taken the company two years. In the words of the sustainability director: "It takes guts … it's about challenging the framework, and thinking outside the box".

Adopting a more circular, Cradle-to-Cradle® approach by Desso is complex because it means rethinking traditional supply chain thinking, where once peripheral issues of product end-of-life and disposal become central to the solution. C2C® requires more than an adjustment to supply chain management because rather than outsourcing responsibility to suppliers, under C2C® the prime manufacturer plays a leading role in persuading partners to be receptive to legislation and cooperate through sharing information, process improvement, product design, and materials research. Inter-company relationships become forged by C2C®, recasting traditional notions of 'upstream-downstream' and supply chain hierarchy.

Desso was acquired by Tarkett, a global leader in flooring and sports surfaces in 2015. Stef Kranendijk has now retired from the business, but the vision of transformation he started at the company lives on. Desso has begun implementing

FUTURE RECYCLING PLAN

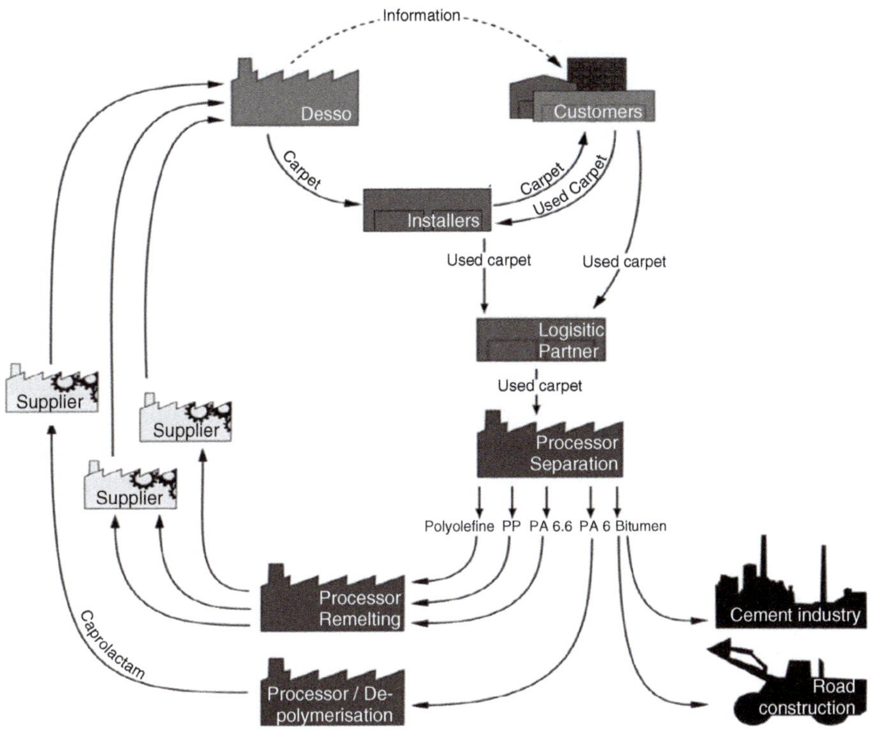

FIGURE 8.8 Desso's closed loop supply chain for carpet tile production
Source: Desso, in Howard et al. (2012)

Cradle-to-Cradle® in its other products such as commercial carpets and sports surfaces and remains one of the top circular exponents in the sector, actively participating in events such as the Davos forum to establish trust across the world business community and build initiatives for cooperation and progress. The concept of the circular economy is even more significant today because it introduces 'new rules of the game' over pricing and incentive structures which requires support from all stakeholders, including NGOs and government. While C2C® is similar in its closed loop approach to reverse logistics and design for disassembly, it redefines thinking around the way recycled materials are treated in terms of upcycle or downcycle, and presents the idea of emulating nature's cycles as the basis for a new industrial model of production and consumption. C2C® reframes our understanding of supply chain strategy, because instead of a linear approach leading to landfill, it adopts the language of circular, closed loop supply systems and repeat material use.

8.9 CONCLUSION

Supply chain strategy is the collaborative response to market demand by firms in the supply chain working together to coordinate the delivery of products and services to the end customer. It is increasingly important today because world markets are being disrupted with many industries facing turbulent and volatile operating conditions particularly from new trading rules and fluctuating raw material prices. As many regions around the world are increasingly disrupted by tariffs, abnormal weather, terrorism, sole commodity ownership (e.g. China), and price volatility (e.g. grain, oil, gas), the traditional practice of supply chains designed exclusively around single narrow strategies may be coming to an end. Supply chain designs should no longer be based on assumptions of a stable operating environment but need to incorporate flexibility and resilience to counter the effects of constant disturbance (Christopher and Holweg, 2011). This means the use of narrow focus strategies which exclusively follow lean or agile may be less effective in the face of current market conditions than a hybrid approach which provides scope to combine elements of sustainable supply chain design e.g. closed loop. The basic principle of controlling an end-to-end process to create a seamless flow of goods must be questioned therefore, where assumptions over long-term stability no longer hold true. Managing supply chains in an age of constant turbulence may mean embracing volatility as an opportunity rather than viewing it as a risk and by trying to understand its true nature and impact. This means reducing the supply chain's exposure to risk by combining different approaches, such as dual sourcing, asset sharing, postponement, flexible labour, and technologies such as additive manufacturing (Holmström et al., 2016).

This chapter has also discussed the implications of sustainability for supply chain strategy and starts by defining common terms such as supply chain and supply network. It applies lean, agile, and hybrid supply chain approaches to industry practice by considering the importance of product and market characteristics. The evolution from mass production to mass customization emphasizes the production-centric nature of past approaches and raises the prospect of a more customer-orientated and responsive approach in future, based on more sustainable consumption using circular models of material supply. Strategy is also about understanding the effects of disintermediation through new digital technology or supplier activity. In shifting from conventional supply chains towards circular supply chain strategy there are considerable challenges in reframing our engagement with customers, suppliers, NGOs, and government, particularly in terms of product redesign, supplier relationships, and the whole end-to-end business implementation side of how to introduce the circular economy. One approach that has proven to be successful is where firms embark on a gradual strategy of circular implementation by picking one product line at a time to redesign and transform, while operating the remainder of the business over the short-term in a conventional linear manner.

NOTES

1 The concept of value stream management is covered in Part C where practical value stream mapping methods are presented.

2 Organization for Economic Co-operation and Development. The mission of the OECD is to promote policies that will improve the economic and social well-being of people around the world – see: www.oecd.org.

3 Cradle-to-Cradle® is the registered trademark of McDonough Braungart Design Chemistry (MBDC). The concept was first used by Stahel and Reday-Mulvey in 1976. See also: Stahel and Reday-Mulvey (1981).

4 These figures refer to the normalized EBIT of the original carpet business. The 'normalization' is defined internally by management.

5 Environmental Protection Encouragement Agency (EPEA) GmbH founded by Professor Dr Michael Braungart who works with clients worldwide to apply the Cradle-to-Cradle® methodology to the design of new processes, products, and services.

6 Positively defined means all ingredients have been assessed as either Green (optimal) or Yellow (tolerable) according to the Cradle-to-Cradle® assessment criteria. As described in the Cradle-to-Cradle® Certification Program Version 2.1.1, prepared by MBDC, September 2008, and updated January 2010.

REFERENCES

APICS / SCOR (2017) Association for Supply Chain Management. https://www.apics.org

Bentley C (2017) The manufacturing industry 4.0 UK Readiness Report. www.themanufacturer.com

Berry W and Cooper M (1999) Manufacturing flexibility: Methods for measuring the impact of product variety on performance. *Journal of Operations Management* 17(2): 163–179.

Braungart M and McDonough W (2009) *Cradle-to-Cradle®: Remaking the way we make things*. UK: Random House.

Braunschiedal M and Suresh N (2009) The organizational antecedents of a firm's supply chain agility for risk mitigation and response. *Journal of Operations Management* 27: 119–140.

Chircu A and Kauffman R (2000) Reintermediation strategies in business-to-business electronic commerce. *International Journal of Electronic Commerce* 4(4): 7–42.

Christopher M (2000) The agile supply chain: Competing in volatile markets. *Industrial Marketing Management* 29: 37–44.

Christopher M (2005) *Logistics and Supply Chain Management: Creating Value Adding Networks*. Harlow UK: Pearson Education.

Christopher M and Holweg M (2011) "Supply chain 2.0": Managing supply chains in the era of turbulence. *International Journal of Physical Distribution & Logistics Management* 41(1): 63–82.

Christopher M and Towill D (2000) Supply chain migration from lean and functional to agile and customized. *Supply Chain Management: An International Journal* 5(4): 206–213.

Cooper MC, Lambert DM and Pagh JD (1997) Supply chain management: More than a new name for logistics. *The International Journal of Logistics Management* 8(1): 1–14.

Cox A (1999) Power, value and supply chain management. *Supply Chain Management: An International Journal* 4(4): 167–175.

Cusumano MA (2015) How traditional firms must compete in the sharing economy. *Communications of the ACM* 58(1): 32–34.

Danese P (2007) Designing CPFR collaborations: Insights from seven case studies. *International Journal of Operations and Production Management* 27(2): 181–204.

Davis S (1987) *Future Perfect*. Reading, Mass: Addison-Wesley.

De Angelis R, Howard M and Miemczyk J (2018) Supply chain management and the circular economy: Towards the circular supply chain. *Production Planning & Control* 29(6): 425–437.

Duguay C, Landry S and Pasin F (1997) From mass production to flexible/agile production. *International Journal of Operations & Production Management* 17(12): 1183–1195.

EMF (2013) Towards the circular economy: Economic and business rationale for an accelerated transition. Cowes, UK: Ellen MacArthur Foundation. https://www.ellenmacarthurfoundation.org

EMF (2015) Growth within: A circular economy vision for a competitive Europe. Cowes, UK: EMF.

Evans P and Wurster T (1997) Strategy and the new economics of information. *Harvard Business Review* (Sept–Oct): 71–82.

Fawcett SE and Magnan GM (2002) The rhetoric and reality of supply chain integration. *International Journal of Physical Distribution & Logistics Management* 32(5): 339.

Ferdows K, Lewis M and Machuca J (2003) Zara – Case study. *Supply Chain Forum: An International Journal* 4(2): 62–67.

Ferdows K, Lewis M and Machuca J (2004) Rapid-fire fulfilment. *Harvard Business Review* (November).

Fisher M (1997) What is the right supply chain for your product? *Harvard Business Review* (March–April).

Forza C (1996) Work organization in lean production and traditional plants: What are the differences? *International Journal of Operations & Production Management* 16(2): 42–62.

Geissdoerfer M, P Savaget NM Bocken and Hultink EJ (2017) The circular economy – A new sustainability paradigm? *Journal of Cleaner Production* 143: 757–768.

Geng Y, Sarkis J and Bleischwitz R (2019) Globalize the circular economy. *Nature* 565(7738): 153–155.

Guide V and van Wassenhove L (2003a) Closed loop supply chains: Practice and potential. Editorial to the special issue, *Interfaces* 33(6): 1–2.

Guide V, Harrison T and van Wassenhove L (2003b) The challenge of closed loop supply chains. *Interfaces* 33(6): 3–6.

Gunasekaran A (1999) Design and implementation of agile manufacturing systems – Editorial. *International Journal of Production Economics* 62: 1–6.

Gunasekaran A and Ngai E (2005) Build-to-order supply chain management: a literature review and framework for development. *Journal of Operations Management*. 23. 423–451.

Handfield R and Bechtel C (2002) The role of trust and relationship structure in improving supply chain responsiveness. *Industrial Marketing Management* 31: 367–382.

Harland CM, Zheng J, Lamming RC and Johnsen TE (2001) A taxonomy of supply networks. *Journal of Supply Chain Management* 37(4): 21–27.

Harrison A (1993) *Just-In-Time Manufacturing in Perspective.* London: Prentice Hall.
Hines P (1994) *Creating World Class Suppliers*. London: Pitman.
Hines P and Rich N (1997) The seven value stream mapping tools. *International Journal of Operations and Production Management* 17(1): 46–64.
Hines P, Holweg M and Rich N (2004) Learning to evolve: A review of contemporary lean thinking. *International Journal of Operations & Production Management* 24(10): 994–1011.
Hines P, Lamming R, Jones D, Cousins P and Rich N (2000) *Value Stream Management: Strategy & Excellence in the Supply Chain*. UK: FT Prentice Hall.
Holmström J, Holweg M, Khajavi SH and Partanen J (2016) The direct digital manufacturing (r) evolution: Definition of a research agenda. *Operations Management Research* 9(1–2): 1–10.
Holweg M and Pil F (2001) Successful build-to-order strategies – Start with the customer. *Sloan Management Review* (Fall): 74–83.
Holweg M and Pil F (2005) *The Second Century: Reconnecting Customers and Value Chain through Build-to-Order. Moving Beyond Mass and Lean in the Auto Industry*. Cambridge, Mass: MIT Press.
Howard M, Jeanrenaud S and Correia F (2012) Desso and the cradle-to-cradle challenge: Rethinking carpet as a closed loop supply system. *European Case Clearing House* 612–031-1.
Howard M, Wu Z, Jia F, Caldwell N and König C (2016) Performance based contracting in the UK defence industry: Exploring triadic dynamics between government, OEMs and suppliers. *Industrial Marketing Management* 59: 63–75.
Howard M, Yan X, Mustafee N, Charnley F, Böhm S and Pascucci S (2022) Going beyond waste reduction: Exploring tools and methods for circular economy adoption in small-medium enterprises. *Resources, Conservation and Recycling* 182: 106345.
James-Moore S and Gibbons A (1997) Is lean manufacture universally relevant? An investigative methodology. *International Journal of Operations and Production Management* 17(9): 899–911.
Kidd P (1994) *Agile Manufacturing – Forging new Frontiers.* Wokingham: Addison Wesley.
King A and Lenoz M (2001) Lean & green? An empirical examination of the relationship between lean production & environmental performance. *Production & Operations Management* 10(3): 455–471.
Kumar S and Malegeant P (2006) Strategic alliance in a closed-loop supply chain: A case of manufacturer and eco-non-profit organization. *Technovation* 26: 1127–1135.
Lamming R (1993) *Beyond Partnership – Strategies for Innovation and Lean Supply*. London, UK: Prentice-Hall.
Lamming RC, Johnsen T E, Zheng J and Harland CM (2000) An initial classification of supply networks. *International Journal of Operations and Production Management* 20(6): 675–691.
Leach A (2013) Supply chain reactions. *Supply Management* 18(2): 14–15.
Lee HL (2002) Aligning supply chain strategies with product uncertainties. *California management review* 44(3): 105–119.
Lewis M (2000) Lean production and sustainable competitive advantage. *International Journal of Operations and Production Management* 20(8): 959–978.

Marques L and Manzanares MD (2023) Towards social network metrics for supply network circularity. *International Journal of Operations & Production Management* 43(4): 595–618.

Mason-Jones R, Naylor B and Towill B (2000) Engineering the leagile supply chain. *International Journal of Agile Management Systems* 2(1): 54–61.

McFarlan F and Young F (2002) Li & Fung: Internet issues. Harvard Business School case study 9–301–009. December.

Mollenkopf D, Stolve H, Tate W and Ueltschy M (2010) Green, lean, and global supply chains. *International Journal of Physical Distribution & Logistics Management* 40(1/2): 14–41.

Monden Y (1983) *Toyota Production System – A Practical Approach to Production Management*. Atlanta, GA: Industrial Engineering and Management Press.

Naylor J, Naim M and Berry D (1999) Leagility: Interfacing the lean and agile manufacturing paradigm in the total supply chain. *International Journal of Production Economics* 62: 107–18.

Ohno T (1988) *The Toyota Production System: Beyond Large-scale Production*. Portland, OR: Productivity Press.

Pagell M and Wu Z (2009) Building a more complete theory of sustainable supply chain management using case studies of 10 examplars. *Journal of Supply Chain Management* 45(2): 37–56.

Pines J (1992) *Mass Customization: The New Frontier in Business Competition*. Boston, Mass: Harvard Business Review Press.

Rossetti C and Choi T (2005) On the dark side of strategic sourcing: Experiences from the aerospace industry. *The Academy of Management Executive* 19(1): 46–60.

Rossetti C and Choi T (2008) Supply management under high goal incongruence: An empirical examination of disintermediation in the aerospace supply chain. *Decision Sciences* 39(3): 507–540.

Rother M and Shook J (1988) *Learning to See: Value Stream Mapping to Create Value and Eliminate Muda*. Cambridge, MA: The Lean Enterprise Institute.

Sako M (1992) *Prices, Quality and Trust*. Cambridge UK: CUP.

Salvador F, Forza C and Rungtusanatham M (2002) Modularity, product variety, production volume, and component sourcing: theorizing beyond generic prescriptions. *Journal of Operations Management* 20(5): 549–575.

Savaskan R, Bhattacharya S and van Wassenhove L (2004) Closed loop supply chain models with product remanufacturing. *Management Science* (50)2: 239–252.

Shapiro B, Rangan K and Sviokla J (1992) Staple yourself to an order. *Harvard Business Review* (July–August): 162–171.

Shingo S (1988) *Non-stock Production: The Shingo System for Continuous Improvement*. Cambridge, MA: Productivity Press.

Simpson D and Power D (2005) Using the supply relationship to develop lean and green suppliers. *Supply Chain Management: An International Journal* 10(1): 60–68.

Spengler T and Schröter M (2003) Strategic management of spare parts in closed-loop supply chains – A systems dynamics approach. *Interfaces* 33(6): 7–17.

Stahel WR and Reday-Mulvey G (1976) The potential for substituting manpower for energy. Report to the Commission of the European Communities, Brussels.

Stahel WR and Reday-Mulvey G (1981) *Jobs for Tomorrow: The Potential for Substituting Manpower for Energy*. New York: Vantage Press. ISBN 533–04799-4.

Stock JR and Boyer SL (2009) Developing a consensus definition of supply chain management: A qualitative study. *International Journal of Physical Distribution & Logistics Management* 39(8): 690–711.

Swank H (2003) The lean service machine. *Harvard Business Review* (October): 123–129.

Wickens P (1987) *The Road to Nissan: Flexibility, Quality & Teamwork*. UK: Macmillan Press.

Womack JP and Jones DT (1994) From lean production to the lean enterprise. *Harvard Business Review* 72(2): 93–103.

Womack JP and Jones DT (1996) Beyond Toyota: How to root out waste and pursue perfection. *Harvard Business Review* (Sept/Oct): 140–144.

Womack JP and Jones DT (2003) *Lean Thinking: Banish Waste and Create Wealth in Your Corporation*. 2nd edn, New York: Free Press, Simon & Schuster.

Womack JP and Jones DT (2005) Lean consumption. *Harvard Business Review* (March): 1–11.

Womack JP, Jones DT and Roos D (1990) *The Machine That Changed the World*. New York: Rawson Associates.

Zils M, Howard M and Hopkinson P (2023) Circular economy implementation in operations & supply chain management: Building a pathway to business transformation. *Production Planning & Control*: 1–20.

FURTHER READING

Gadde LE and Håkansson H (2001) *Supply Network Strategy*. Chichester, UK: John Wiley & Sons.

Harland C, Lamming R and Cousins P (1999) Developing the concept of supply strategy. *International Journal of Operations and Production Management* 19(7): 650–673.

Miemczyk J and Howard M (2008) Managing global auto operations: Supply strategies for build-to-order. *Supply Chain Management – An International Journal* 13(1): 3–8.

CHAPTER 9

Supply chain risk and resilience

LEARNING OBJECTIVES:

At the end of this chapter you should be able to:

- Identify key types of supply chain risks;
- Evaluate risk assessment and mitigation strategies;
- Analyze approaches for building resilient supply chains.

9.1 INTRODUCTION

The most significant recent disruption to supply chains began in early 2020 with the global Covid-19 pandemic. Although the signs of such a large-scale risk event had existed for some time, global economic systems were not adequately prepared. Borders closed, populations were confined to their homes, factories shut down worldwide, hospitals were overwhelmed, and shortages of medical supplies and basic household goods such as toilet paper and pasta became widespread. The pandemic exposed vulnerabilities in global supply chains, prompting major efforts to restore operations to pre-pandemic levels.

Supply chain risk is a well-established field in procurement and supply chain management (e.g. Harland et al., 2003; Chopra and Sodhi, 2004; Christopher and Lee, 2004). While firms have long practiced risk management and contingency planning, the traditional firm-level approach has limited application to complex global supply chains (Manuj and Mentzer, 2008). Managing supply chain risk, or 'vulnerability' (Svensson, 2000), has gained prominence due to several trends: heavy reliance on outsourcing, globalization of markets, dependence on suppliers for specialized capabilities, and increasing use of information technology for coordination and control (Narasimhan and Talluri, 2009). Fan and Stevenson (2018: 210) define supply chain risk management as:

> The identification, assessment, treatment, and monitoring of supply chain risks, with the aid of the internal implementation of tools, techniques and strategies and of

DOI: 10.4324/9781003499602-11

external coordination and collaboration with supply chain members so as to reduce vulnerability and ensure continuity coupled with profitability, leading to competitive advantage.

The adoption of lean supply strategies has contributed to this trend of creating extended supply chains that are susceptible to a stock-out situation. As discussed in Chapter 6, many Western firms have shifted manufacturing to low-cost countries via outsourcing, while also minimizing inventories. In this context, risk assessment becomes essential. The global economy's unpredictability demands supply chain designs that account for demand uncertainty. Zsidisin and Ritchie (2008) note that demand uncertainty poses dual risks: unmet unexpected demand and overestimated demand leading to high inventory costs. Other risks include unreliable vendors, shipment delays, and natural disasters. Kleindorfer and Saad (2005) classify supply chain risks into two main categories:

1. Risks from coordinating supply and demand, such as inventory control and stockouts.
2. Risks from disruption and delay, including natural disasters, civil unrest, and ethical concerns in labour practices.

This chapter focuses primarily on the second category.

It is important not to view supply chain risk solely in terms of negative outcomes however. March and Shapira (1987) argue that risk-taking is inherent to business and essential for realizing positive outcomes. The goal is to understand potential risks, assess their likelihood and impact, and evaluate their significance to the business. While internal issues – such as misinterpretation of data – can cause risks, much of the literature emphasizes the growing exposure of firms to global disruptions and events.

A new and pressing topic in supply chain management is the impact of geopolitical disruptions. This is exemplified by escalating US-China trade tensions and retaliatory tariffs, and highlights how governments increasingly use supply chains as strategic tools, creating a need for new frameworks to guide sourcing and risk management decisions (Carnovale et al., 2025). For example, supply chain research on the impact of nationalist trade policies on supply base structure shows that despite President Trump-era (2014–2020) reshoring pressures, US manufacturers reduced the number of countries they sourced from but became more dependent on foreign suppliers – particularly Taiwan for semiconductors – highlighting unintended consequences of protectionist policies (Chakkol et al., 2025).

9.2 SUPPLY CHAIN RISKS

Understanding the different types of supply chain risks is essential for designing appropriate mitigation strategies and resilience frameworks. Scholars have developed various typologies to categorize supply chain risks based on their origin, frequency, and impact (Kleindorfer and Saad, 2005; Chopra et al., 2007).

Note 9.1 Post Covid effects

The Covid-19 pandemic severely disrupted global supply chains, exposing vulnerabilities in production, logistics, and demand forecasting. Factory shutdowns, especially in China, led to material shortages, affecting industries like electronics, automotive, and pharmaceuticals. Labour shortages and lockdowns further slowed manufacturing and distribution. Logistics bottlenecks, including port congestion and reduced air and sea freight capacity, delayed shipments and increased costs. Just-in-time inventory systems collapsed under unpredictable demand surges, especially for essential goods like medical supplies and groceries. Businesses struggled with sourcing alternatives, while geopolitical tensions and protectionist policies limited trade flexibility. Small and medium enterprises faced financial strain due to disrupted supply chains and shifting consumer behaviours. In response, companies accelerated digital transformation, increased inventory buffers, and explored near-shoring to enhance resilience. The pandemic ultimately highlighted the need for more agile, diversified, and technology-driven supply chain strategies to mitigate future disruptions.

Source: Partly based on Harapko (2023)

A widely accepted distinction is between disruption risks and operational (recurrent) risks. Disruption risks are low-frequency, high-impact events that severely interrupt normal operations, such as the above Covid-19 pandemic example. These include natural disasters, terrorist attacks, pandemics, or large-scale cyber-attacks. Such events are often external to the firm and difficult to predict or control (Kleindorfer and Saad, 2005). In contrast, operational risks are higher-frequency, lower-impact events such as delays, forecasting errors, quality problems, or transportation issues. These tend to originate from within the supply chain and are manageable through routine processes and controls (Chopra et al., 2007).

Bode and Wagner (2006) further classified risks into supply-side, demand-side, internal, and external categories. Supply-side risks include supplier insolvencies or capacity shortages, while demand-side risks stem from forecast inaccuracy or order volatility. Internal risks originate within the focal firm – such as equipment failure or process breakdowns – whereas external risks encompass geopolitical shifts, regulatory changes, and economic crises. Durach et al. (2017) emphasize the interconnectivity of these risk types, noting that disruptions often cascade across supply chain partners, amplifying their effects. This systems-based view reinforces the importance of assessing both direct and indirect risk exposures. In practice, comprehensive risk classification enables firms to prioritize risk management resources, develop tailored mitigation strategies, and enhance overall supply chain resilience.

TABLE 9.1 Types of supply chain risk

Risk Type	*Examples*
Disruption Risks	Natural disasters (e.g. earthquakes, floods), pandemics (e.g. Covid-19), terrorist attacks, large-scale cyber-attacks, political unrest
Operational (Recurrent) Risks	Forecasting errors, delayed shipments, transportation bottlenecks, quality issues, stockouts
Supply-Side Risks	Supplier insolvency, capacity constraints, raw material shortages, delivery unreliability
Demand-Side Risks	Sudden demand fluctuations, inaccurate demand forecasts, changes in customer preferences
Internal Risks	Equipment malfunction, IT system failure, production errors, employee strikes
External Risks	Regulatory changes, currency volatility, trade restrictions, geopolitical conflict
Cascading/ Systemic Risks	Bullwhip effect, multi-tier supplier failure, disruption propagation across supply chain partners

Source: Based on Bode and Wagner (2006); Chopra et al. (2007); Durach et al. (2017); Kleindorfer and Saad (2005)

Note 9.2 Identifying new risks: material scarcity

Rare earth materials refer to a group of 17 chemically similar elements, including neodymium, dysprosium, and terbium, that are essential for producing high-performance magnets, catalysts, and other components in advanced technologies. Despite their name, these elements are relatively abundant but are rarely found in concentrated, economically extractable forms, making their supply complex and geopolitically sensitive. Scarcity of rare earth materials and cobalt presents major risks to global supply chains, particularly in high-tech industries such as electronics, renewable energy, and defence. Rare earths are vital for magnets used in electric vehicles (EVs), wind turbines, and military systems, while cobalt is crucial for lithium-ion batteries that power EVs, consumer electronics, and energy storage. The concentration of rare earth processing in China and over 70 per cent of cobalt supply originating from the Democratic Republic of the Congo (DRC) introduces serious vulnerabilities. Geopolitical tensions, export restrictions, and ethical concerns – such as child labour in the DRC – can trigger supply disruptions, price volatility, and production delays. For instance, EV manufacturers rely on neodymium-based magnets and cobalt for motors and batteries; supply constraints can raise costs and hinder production. Wind turbine makers and defence systems also face risks from rare earth shortages. Cobalt disruptions can slow the clean energy transition, prompting companies like Tesla and Apple to secure long-term contracts or seek alternative sources. To reduce these risks, companies and governments are investing in mining diversification, recycling, and cobalt-free battery technologies. These initiatives aim to strengthen supply chain resilience and reduce dependency on high-risk regions.

Source: Partly based on van den Brink et al. (2020)

9.3 SUPPLY RISK FRAMEWORKS

There are a number of classifications, frameworks, and models which incorporate risk as their focus (for example: Harland et al., 2003; Chopra and Sodhi, 2004), providing a breakdown of the categories and drivers of risk. While some offer ideas for 'risk mitigation', for example adding capacity and inventory, identifying redundant suppliers, and increasing responsiveness and flexibility, it is also accepted that the procurement and supply professional cannot predict every possible future scenario in terms of supply chain disruption. They can however prepare contingency plans for the most likely events, such as considering a multiple sourcing strategy for critical, bottleneck components from suppliers located in remote, geographically exposed or socio-economically unstable areas.

The starting point in any supply chain risk strategy is the identification of risks. This identification is often structured around the drivers or sources of risks which in turn are based on broad categories including environmental, industry, organizational (including decision-maker specific), problem specific issues (Rao and Goldsby, 2009).

In general, supply chain risk management can be seen as a process of four main steps: identification assessment, mitigation, and monitoring. Clearly while this implies a linear sequence the reality is that loops and feedback will occur and each step should be continuously updated as and when new information is available.

9.3.1 Identification

The identification phase of supply chain risks management is primarily related to identifying drivers and sources of risks. Then risks are classified or categorized into different types as mentioned above in the table. According to CIPS (n.d.) these can be organized into micro issues including internal changes within the buying company, change management, new company direction, and strategy or macro issues including environmental risks, economic risks, technology, social, political, legal, ethical, and demographical risks.

Risk drivers are typically those things that make the supply chain more vulnerable and these can lead to either making events more probable or more impactful (Bode and Wagner, 2006). Increasing probability might include efficiency strategies such as just-in-time

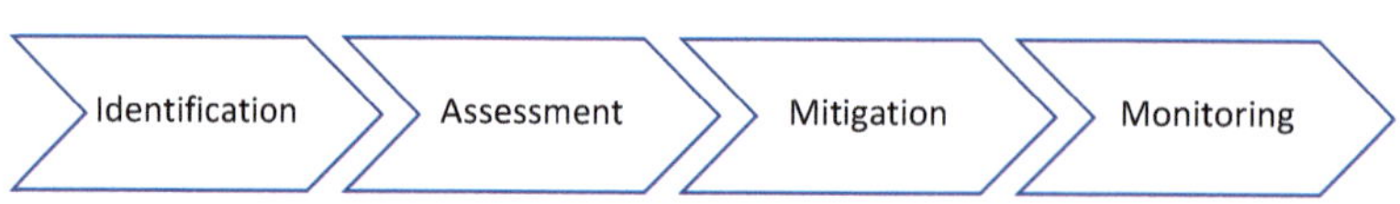

FIGURE 9.1 Main supply chain risk strategies

which might mean less stock is available to cope with an unforeseen event. Drivers that increase the magnitude of impact might include supplier dependence where if a supplier fails there is no alternative supply, for example.

There are numerous supply risk typologies that have been developed, mostly distinguishing between internal and external risks. For example, Christopher and Peck (2004) categorize internal risks to the company related to processes and control mechanisms, risks external to the company but internal to the supply chain related to supply chain demand, and risks external to both stemming from the environment related to socio-political or economic events for example.

Furthermore, a number of approaches can help in the identification of potential SC risks: supply chain mapping, checklists or checksheets, event tree analysis, fault tree analysis, failure mode and effect analysis (FMEA), and Ishikawa cause and effect analysis (Tummala and Schoenherr, 2011). Since Covid-19 for example many companies have put significant resources into mapping their supply chains beyond the tier one level in order to increase their visibility.

An important new development is related to AI. Predictive analytics using AI rely on data on past disruptions, weather patterns, geopolitical events, and supplier performance to identify trends that may lead to future risks. This can include predicting demand spikes of holiday seasons or see supplier delays ahead of time based on historical performance data.

9.3.2 Assessment

Once risk types have been identified it is important to decide which ones to plan for in terms of risk strategies. As in all business this is a question of prioritizing limited resources and so risk assessment is normally a question of evaluation of probability and impact on the company. Below is a typical 2x2 matrix used by companies to allocate risk management resources, based on the levels of supply chain probability (likelihood) and impact (consequences).

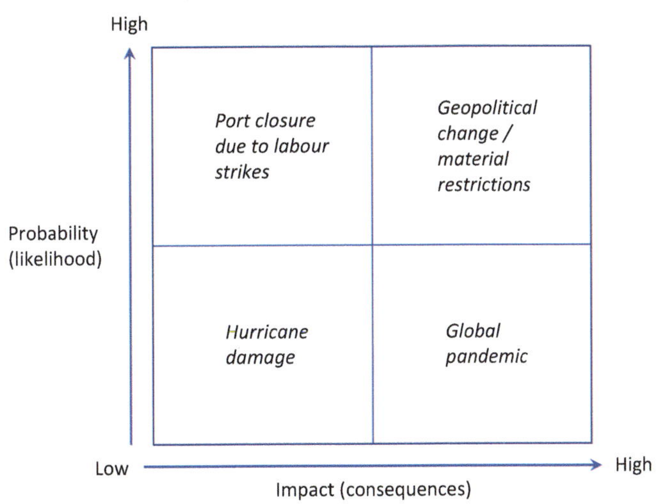

FIGURE 9.2 Risk assessment matrix
Source: Adapted from Sheffi and Rice (2005); Norrman and Jansson (2004)

Supply chain risk probability

Determining the likelihood of specific risk events is a foundational element of effective supply chain risk management. Accurate estimation of probability enables managers to prioritize threats, allocate mitigation resources efficiently, and develop more robust contingency plans (Tang, 2006). Where available, objective data – such as historical performance records, industry benchmarks, or real-time monitoring outputs – can be used to model probability distributions. This data-driven approach is particularly effective in quantifying recurrent risks like forecast inaccuracies, lead-time variability, or equipment failure rates (Tummala and Schoenherr, 2011).

However, in many real-world situations, especially when dealing with low-frequency, high-impact risks, such as natural disasters, geopolitical shocks, or pandemics, reliable historical data may be scarce or non-existent. In such cases, organizations must rely on subjective assessments, incorporating the experience, intuition, and beliefs of domain experts to estimate risk probabilities. These judgement-based approaches often involve the use of structured techniques, such as the Delphi method, which gathers expert opinions through iterative surveys to reach consensus, or expert panels and focus groups, which facilitate interactive discussion and scenario exploration (Zsidisin et al., 2004).

Although subjective, these methods can produce credible risk estimates when managed carefully and supported by a diverse range of perspectives. Furthermore, combining both objective and subjective inputs – through techniques such as Bayesian analysis – can enhance accuracy and flexibility in dynamic risk environments (Harland et al., 2003). Ultimately, a balanced approach to likelihood assessment strengthens the foundation for comprehensive and adaptive supply chain risk management strategies.

Supply chain risk impact and consequences

Risks in supply chains can be evaluated through quantitative or qualitative methods, each offering distinct advantages depending on the availability of data, the complexity of the supply network, and the nature of the risk being assessed. Quantitative techniques often involve statistical modelling, simulation, or probabilistic analysis to assign numerical values to the likelihood and impact of specific events. Tools such as Monte Carlo simulations, fault tree analysis, and scenario planning help organizations estimate financial losses, service level impacts, or recovery times associated with disruptions (Tang, 2006; Tummala and Schoenherr, 2011).

On the other hand, qualitative assessments typically rely on expert judgement, structured interviews, and risk matrices to categorize risks based on their severity and probability. This approach is especially useful when reliable data is scarce, or when risks are emerging and poorly understood, such as geopolitical instability or supplier ethical breaches (Zsidisin et al., 2005).

Increasingly, companies are turning to specialized risk assessment service providers to support their evaluation processes. These organizations provide industry benchmarks, real-time risk intelligence, and decision support tools that help managers identify the most critical risks and allocate mitigation resources effectively. Integrating these assessments into risk governance frameworks supports more resilient and adaptive supply chain strategies (Wieland and Durach, 2021).

Consequences

Supply chain risk consequences are typically divided into tangible and non-tangible categories. Tangible consequences are measurable and often involve increased operational costs, delayed deliveries, or production stoppages. For example, during the 2021 global semiconductor shortage, manufacturers across the automotive and electronics sectors incurred significant losses due to halted assembly lines and expensive alternative sourcing (Ivanov and Dolgui, 2020).

Non-tangible consequences are harder to quantify but potentially more damaging in the long term. These include reputational harm, loss of customer trust, and damage to stakeholder relationships. A prominent case is the Rana Plaza factory collapse in 2013 (more detail at the end of the chapter), which killed over 1,100 garment workers. The disaster exposed unsafe working conditions in the fashion industry and led to intense scrutiny of global brands' supply chains (Kara et al., 2014). Another sustainability-related example is Nestlé's deforestation-linked palm oil sourcing, which led to public backlash, NGO criticism, and the suspension of supplier contracts – demonstrating how environmental non-compliance can escalate into reputational and financial risk (Greenpeace, 2018).

Black swan events – rare, unforeseen disruptions with severe consequences – can amplify both tangible and intangible impacts. The Covid-19 pandemic is a recent example that disrupted global logistics, strained supplier relationships, and highlighted overreliance on limited geographies, forcing firms to reconfigure risk strategies (Taleb, 2007; Wieland and Durach, 2021).

9.3.3 Risk mitigation strategies

TABLE 9.2 Risks mitigation approaches

Mitigation Dimension	*Definition*	*Illustrative Strategies and Actions*
Risk Avoidance	Elimination of activities, products, markets, or relationships that expose the supply chain to unacceptable levels of risk	• Withdrawal from high-risk geographic regions or unstable political environments • Elimination of product lines with chronic sourcing disruptions • Termination of contracts with high-risk suppliers or customers
Risk Reduction	Actions taken to lower either the probability of a risk occurring or the severity of its consequences	• Implementation of quality assurance programs • nvestment in predictive analytics and monitoring systems • Design for robustness and modularity to reduce system fragility

(Continued)

TABLE 9.2 Continued

Mitigation Dimension	*Definition*	*Illustrative Strategies and Actions*
Risk Transfer	Redistribution of risk exposure to third parties, often contractually or financially	• Outsourcing of high-risk activities to specialized providers • Procurement contracts with just-in-time delivery clauses shifting inventory risk to suppliers • Insurance coverage for disruption, cyberattacks, or natural disasters
Risk Sharing	Distribution of risk and reward among supply chain partners through collaboration and contractual mechanisms	• Joint ventures or co-investment in supplier capabilities • Collaborative forecasting and planning with shared service-level agreements • Risk-based contracts (e.g. gainsharing, penalty clauses)
Risk Taking	Acceptance of certain levels of risk when mitigation is infeasible or economically unjustifiable	• Proceeding with sole sourcing in exchange for cost or quality advantages • Entering new markets with limited data but high strategic importance • Reliance on high-risk technologies with potential for competitive gain

Source: Based on Jüttner et al. (2003); Sheffi (2002)

Risk mitigation in supply chains involves a multidimensional set of strategies aimed at anticipating, absorbing, or responding to disruptions and uncertainty. Jüttner et al. (2003) proposed a foundational framework comprising four core categories of mitigation: avoidance, control, cooperation, and flexibility. These strategies are organizational responses to vulnerabilities present in increasingly complex and interconnected global supply networks. However, these categories can be expanded through the integration of additional risk dimensions – risk avoidance, risk reduction, risk transfer, risk sharing, and risk taking – which provide further granularity in managing supply chain risks (Miller, 1992; Sheffi, 2002).

The original category of avoidance aligns directly with the broader concept of risk avoidance. Both entail proactive disengagement from high-risk scenarios, such as exiting volatile geographic markets, terminating partnerships with unreliable suppliers, or withdrawing from product lines vulnerable to supply instability (Miller, 1992; Jüttner et al., 2003). Such strategies are designed to eliminate exposure rather than manage its consequences.

Control refers to strategies that enhance predictability and reduce exposure through mechanisms such as vertical integration, inventory buffering, and contractual enforcement. These directly complement the principle of risk reduction, which focuses on minimizing the likelihood or impact of disruptive events. Tools such as quality assurance systems, process redundancy, and scenario planning support both objectives (Sheffi, 2002; Christopher and Peck, 2004).

Cooperation – defined as joint initiatives between supply chain actors to share risk-related information and co-develop continuity plans – is conceptually aligned with risk sharing. Through collaborative contracts, shared investments, and mutual accountability mechanisms, firms can distribute risk across the supply network and build collective resilience (Braithwaite and Hall, 1999; Jüttner et al., 2003).

Flexibility captures an organization's capacity to adjust rapidly to unforeseen events, typically through design for modularity, multiple sourcing, or localization strategies. This resonates with risk transfer, where companies shift liabilities to third parties – such as insurers, logistics providers, or even customers – via outsourcing, make-to-order models, or contractual clauses (Miller, 1992; Christopher and Lee, 2001).

Finally, risk taking acknowledges the limits of mitigation and embraces calculated exposure to uncertainty. This is particularly relevant in dynamic markets where agility and innovation require firms to accept certain risks as part of strategic opportunity-seeking. Rather than opposing mitigation, risk taking complements the framework by recognizing situations where control or avoidance may be counterproductive (March and Shapira, 1987; Simons, 1999).

The integration of these five dimensions with the original four categories provides a more holistic and strategic toolkit for managing supply chain risks. It highlights not only operational responses but also governance, behavioural, and structural decisions firms must make when confronted with uncertainty. This comprehensive perspective enables managers to align risk strategies with business objectives, sector characteristics, and evolving global challenges. However, other classifications also exist including the distinction between robust and agile supply chains (Wieland and Wallenburg, 2012).

A robust supply chain strategy focuses on building structural strength to absorb and withstand disruptions. One of the most widely used approaches is increasing redundancy in the supplier base. By maintaining multiple or backup suppliers, organizations reduce their dependence on any single source, thereby mitigating risks associated with supply interruptions, such as equipment failures or geopolitical disruptions (Christopher and Peck, 2004; Sheffi, 2005). This redundancy tends to be more cost-effective when applied to high-volume products, where the benefits of continuity outweigh inventory costs. Another robust strategy involves increasing production capacity, which typically demands higher investment and longer lead times. When demand is predictable, firms may decentralize capacity to reduce transportation costs and increase local responsiveness; conversely, in highly volatile markets, centralized capacity can enhance coordination and control (Tang, 2006). Demand pooling – aggregating requirements across regions or business units – is also effective in managing variability. Pooling facilitates economies of scale and enables smoother production planning, helping firms stabilize operations in the face of fluctuating market demand (Fisher, 1997).

In contrast, agile supply chains prioritize responsiveness and flexibility. Agility becomes critical when facing unpredictable demand or supply delays. Strategies such as Efficient Consumer Response (ECR) and Build-to-Order (BTO) help reduce lead times and enhance coordination between manufacturers and suppliers (Lee, 2004). Agility also depends on IT integration, particularly systems like Electronic Point of Sale (EPOS), which provide real-time visibility into inventory and customer demand across the network. Furthermore, agility requires suppliers to switch production rapidly in response to demand changes, especially for low-volume or highly customized products. This flexibility reduces reliance on forecasts and supports a more demand-driven supply chain, enabling firms to respond swiftly to market changes (Swafford et al., 2006; Christopher, 2016).

Note 9.3 Avoiding conflict minerals

Companies avoid conflict minerals in their supply chains by implementing strict due diligence processes, sourcing responsibly, and complying with international regulations like the US Dodd-Frank Act and the OECD Due Diligence Guidance. Conflict minerals – such as tin, tungsten, tantalum, and gold – often originate from regions where mining funds armed conflicts and human rights abuses as exemplified in the film *Blood Diamond* starring Leonardo DiCaprio.

In the jewellery industry, Tiffany & Co. ensures its gold and diamonds are sourced responsibly by working only with suppliers that meet its high ethical standards. The company supports initiatives like the Responsible Jewellery Council1 (RJC) and sources gold from mines that are independently certified as conflict-free. In the electronics industry, Apple has taken significant steps to eliminate conflict minerals from its supply chain. The company conducts third-party audits, requires suppliers to report mineral sources, and removes non-compliant smelters. Apple (2023) publishes an annual Conflict Minerals Report, demonstrating transparency in its sourcing practices.

These efforts, combined with industry-wide collaboration and consumer awareness, help reduce the demand for conflict minerals, promoting ethical sourcing and corporate responsibility. By prioritizing transparency and working with certified suppliers, companies can significantly mitigate their role in funding armed conflicts and human rights violations.

9.3.4 Risk monitoring

Supply chain risk monitoring is the continuous process of observing, evaluating, and responding to risks that could impact supply chain operations and performance. It plays a vital role in enabling proactive management of disruptions and ensuring the relevance and effectiveness of mitigation strategies over time (Christopher and Peck, 2004). Unlike risk identification, which is typically event-driven or periodic, monitoring involves a systematic and ongoing review of both internal and external conditions that influence risk exposure.

There are four principal types of supply chain risk monitoring. Internal monitoring focuses on identifying operational risks within the firm's boundaries, such as equipment failures, quality issues, or capacity limitations. This form of monitoring is supported by Manufacturing Execution Systems (MES), which collect real-time data on machine performance and production rates, enabling early detection of inefficiencies or breakdowns (Sanchoyerto and Campos, 2021).

Supplier monitoring involves assessing upstream partners for delivery reliability, financial stability, and ethical compliance. Advanced Supplier Relationship Management (SRM) systems such as SAP Ariba provide real-time analytics, risk ratings, and performance dashboards that help firms track supplier behaviour and intervene when thresholds are breached (Harland et al., 2003). These tools are especially important for managing exposure in multi-tiered, global supplier networks.

Market and environmental monitoring focuses on macro-level risks, including demand volatility, economic instability, geopolitical tensions, and environmental hazards. Predictive risk platforms like Everstream Analytics or Resilinc gather and analyze real-time data from news sources, government alerts, and weather systems to forecast disruptions and recommend preventive actions (Ivanov and Dolgui, 2020).

Network monitoring examines the entire supply chain structure to identify systemic risks, such as coordination breakdowns or cascading failures. Digital supply chain control towers – integrated platforms that consolidate data from across functions and partners – enhance visibility, simulate scenarios, and alert managers to critical deviations (Wieland et al., 2023). These tools help manage risks such as the bullwhip effect or disruption amplification in interconnected systems.

Together, these types of monitoring – supported by digital technologies – enable supply chain professionals to maintain situational awareness, adapt mitigation strategies, and strengthen resilience in a volatile global environment.

9.3.5 Sustainability risk monitoring

Sustainability risk monitoring focuses on tracking environmental, social, and ethical risks across the supply chain, particularly in relation to compliance, reputational exposure, and long-term viability. Firms increasingly monitor carbon emissions, labour conditions, and resource usage through tools such as EcoVadis and the Higg Index, which assess suppliers' sustainability performance and provide benchmarking data (Busse et al., 2016). Monitoring supports regulatory compliance and responds to rising stakeholder expectations. It is also crucial for identifying risks related to modern slavery, deforestation, and climate change – issues that can disrupt operations and damage brand equity if left unmanaged (Marshall et al., 2016).

Remote sensing plays a vital role in reducing Amazonian deforestation by enhancing transparency in commodity supply chains. Satellite imagery provides objective, high-resolution data to detect land-use change, track agricultural expansion, and verify sustainability commitments. For example, the Soy Moratorium, supported by satellite monitoring, has prevented thousands of square kilometres of deforestation by restricting the purchase of soy grown on newly cleared land. When combined with trade data and Brazil's Rural Environmental Registry, remote sensing enables property-level monitoring of producers. Public platforms such as Global Forest Watch[2] empower governments and civil society to enforce regulations (Ribeiro et al., 2024).

Note 9.4 Supply chain monitoring: modern slavery risks

Modern slavery – encompassing forced labour, child labour, and exploitative working conditions – poses a significant risk to global supply chains, particularly in industries with complex, multi-tiered sourcing networks such as fashion, electronics, agriculture, and mining. These risks are often hidden within subcontracting arrangements, making detection challenging and increasing exposure to reputational damage, regulatory penalties, and operational disruption. Effective risk monitoring is essential to identifying and mitigating modern slavery. This includes continuous assessment of supplier practices, particularly beyond tier one. Technologies such as supply chain mapping tools and third-party audit platforms can enhance visibility. For example, the 2020 Boohoo scandal exposed unsafe conditions and wage violations in UK-based garment factories (Bland and Makortoff, 2020), resulting in severe brand and investor fallout. It highlighted the consequences of insufficient supplier oversight. In the electronics sector, companies like Apple and Tesla face similar risks due to links between cobalt mining in the Democratic Republic of the Congo (DRC) and child labour (BBC News, 2019). Likewise, the seafood industry in Thailand has been criticized for forced labour, prompting stricter import controls. To monitor and manage these risks, companies are increasingly adopting ethical sourcing frameworks and complying with legislation such as the UK Modern Slavery Act. Regular monitoring and transparent reporting are now integral to building responsible and resilient supply chains.

9.4 SUPPLY CHAIN RESILIENCE

Resilience has become a central concept in supply chain management as firms increasingly face unpredictable and large-scale disruptions. Events such as tsunamis, hurricanes, factory fires, and acts of terrorism have exposed the fragility of global supply chains and elevated the urgency of preparing for such shocks. As multinational corporations continue to seek cost efficiencies through global outsourcing, it is not uncommon for supply chains to stretch between 6,000 and 12,000 miles, relying on multi-week transoceanic shipping routes. These extended and interconnected supply networks are inherently more vulnerable to disruption, making resilience a strategic priority.

The concept of supply chain resilience has attracted significant attention from scholars and practitioners alike. Foundational contributions by Rice and Caniato (2003) and Sheffi and Rice (2005) laid the groundwork for understanding how firms can develop resilience capabilities across their supply networks. Christopher and Peck (2004: 4) define resilience as "the ability of a system to return to its original state or move to a new, more desirable state after being disturbed". Within the supply chain context, this suggests a need for flexibility, agility, transparency, and collaboration – requiring not only reactive strategies but also proactive redesigns of sourcing, logistics, and information-sharing practices.

Two dominant conceptualizations of resilience have since emerged: the engineering-oriented and the socio-ecological views. The engineering view sees resilience primarily as the ability to absorb shocks and return to the pre-disruption state as quickly and efficiently as possible (Wieland and Durach, 2021). From this perspective, the speed and effectiveness of recovery influence market competitiveness and financial performance. Sheffi and Rice (2005) detail specific strategies that align with this approach, including dual sourcing, spare production capacity, flexible manufacturing, and the prioritization of critical customer segments during a disruption. Visibility through digital tracking systems and the use of advanced analytics, including artificial intelligence, support timely interventions. Moreover, organizational culture plays a critical role, particularly in enabling frontline employees to respond to early warning signals – what Sheffi and Rice refer to as "weak signals".

In contrast, the socio-ecological view conceptualizes supply chains as complex, adaptive systems embedded within broader social, political, and environmental contexts. This perspective, rooted in ecological systems theory, recognizes that full control over supply chains is often illusory. Instead, resilience is seen as a function of a system's ability to evolve through renewal, reorganization, and transformation in response to discontinuities (Wieland and Durach, 2021; Wieland et al., 2023). Rather than striving to return to a prior equilibrium, firms adopting this view accept non-linearity and aim to build adaptive capacity that allows them to reconfigure in the face of uncertainty.

Both perspectives offer valuable insights. While the engineering view focuses on preserving continuity through control and redundancy, the socio-ecological perspective highlights the importance of systemic learning and adaptation. A comprehensive approach to resilience may therefore require combining both: ensuring preparedness through structural measures while embracing the dynamic nature of disruption through continuous renewal.

Note 9.5 Circular economy as a lever for resilience

Circular economy (CE) practices can significantly enhance organizational and supply chain resilience. For instance, dynamic remanufacturing capacity enables firms to remain flexible and adapt quickly to disruptions. Reducing material inputs or reusing waste – known as narrowing resource loops – and extending product life – slowing loops – can contribute to more stable operations. These strategies have proven especially effective during periods of disruption and within local industrial networks where adaptability is critical. For example, automotive companies that refurbish and reuse parts have been able to continue production during component shortages.

Supplier diversity driven by CE approaches can reduce reliance on limited or high-risk raw materials. However, while diversification enhances resilience, it can also introduce new dependencies. Industrial symbiosis, which involves collaborating with multiple exchange partners, helps manage disruptions through increased redundancy. Yet, this may come with environmental and economic trade-offs. CE practices also show potential to support broader socio-ecological resilience by reducing material use and waste, although rebound effects and unintended sustainability consequences must be considered. A notable example is the Kalundborg Eco-Industrial Park in Denmark, where multiple firms exchange waste and energy flows to minimize risk and environmental impact.

Four main CE themes emerge in building supply chain resilience. First, waste reduction through reuse, recycling, and local sourcing strengthens supply security and reduces environmental impact. For instance, some food retailers now source surplus produce from local farms to avoid reliance on distant supply chains. Second, designing products for modularity and incorporating circular inputs enhances flexibility and supports closed-loop systems. Many electronics manufacturers now design devices for easier disassembly and component reuse. Third, strategic partner selection supports efficient resource use and reverse logistics. Public procurement agencies increasingly select suppliers based on circularity criteria. Finally, technology plays a central enabling role. Companies use blockchain to track recycled materials through their supply chains, ensuring accountability and transparency.

Source: Based on Kennedy and Linnenluecke (2022)

9.5 RANA PLAZA DISASTER

The Rana Plaza disaster, one of the deadliest industrial tragedies in history, occurred on 24 April 24 2013, in Savar, Bangladesh. Rana Plaza, an eight-story commercial building, collapsed, killing over 1,130 people and injuring more than 2,500. Most of the victims were garment workers producing clothing for global fashion brands. The building housed several garment factories supplying companies such as Primark, Benetton, Mango, Joe Fresh, and Walmart. Workers had raised concerns about visible cracks in the building structure the day before the collapse, prompting some businesses in the building to evacuate. However, factory managers forced garment workers to return, under the threat of losing their jobs. It was not just the factory owners ignoring the cracks in the walls, but longstanding issues such as chronic overcrowding (i.e. sweatshop conditions) and pressure from big brand corporate buyers on the company to continue its uninterrupted supply of low-cost garments to the West that led to the building's collapse and high loss of life. The Rana plaza tragedy hit headlines around the world, emphasizing the potential cost of so-called fast fashion and marked a turning point in awareness for the need of equitable treatment of manual workers everywhere in terms of pay, hours, and employment conditions.

The collapse highlighted the extreme exploitation of workers in the global fashion industry, including unsafe working conditions, low wages, and lack of union protections. Investigations revealed that the building had been constructed with substandard materials and lacked proper authorization for the additional floors housing heavy machinery. The tragedy led to global outrage and calls for reforms in supply chain transparency. Initiatives like the Accord on Fire and Building Safety and the Alliance for Bangladesh Worker Safety emerged, aimed at improving factory conditions. However, the disaster remains a stark reminder of the cost of fast fashion and the need for corporate accountability in safeguarding human lives. The Sustainable Apparel Coalition (SAC) has played a critical role in addressing supply chain concerns following the Rana Plaza disaster in 2013. In response, the SAC expanded its initiatives to encompass not only environmental sustainability but also social and labour conditions. A key development was the enhancement of the Higg Index, a standardized tool that measures environmental and social impact in the apparel industry. The Higg Facility Social & Labor Module (FSLM) was introduced to assess factory working conditions, wages, and occupational safety, pushing brands towards higher labour standards. Additionally, SAC has promoted greater supply chain transparency, encouraging major brands such as Nike, H&M, and Patagonia to disclose supplier performance and take accountability for ethical sourcing. The Higg index has come under criticism from consumer watchdogs in Norway stating that data was used selectively and there was a general lack in transparency (Britten, 2022).

The coalition has also worked alongside initiatives like the Accord on Fire and Building Safety in Bangladesh, complementing legally binding agreements with continuous sustainability assessments. This shift has resulted in stronger compliance requirements across the industry, ensuring that brands demand improved safety and labour conditions from suppliers. Increased accountability has also led to better workplace safety, higher wages, and improved chemical management in garment factories. By integrating sustainability and ethical labour practices into business strategies, SAC has influenced a shift towards responsible sourcing. While its approach remains voluntary, it has significantly contributed to preventing future disasters, improving factory conditions, and making sustainability a key driver in global fashion supply chains.

9.6 CONCLUSION

In an era marked by global disruptions, climate change, and shifting stakeholder expectations, managing supply chain risk and building resilience have become critical priorities. This chapter has examined the multidimensional nature of supply chain risks – spanning operational inefficiencies, natural disasters, geopolitical conflicts, resource scarcity, and ethical breaches such as modern slavery. It has also outlined established and emerging frameworks for assessing, mitigating, and monitoring risks within increasingly global and interdependent supply networks.

A key theme throughout the chapter is the transition from reactive risk management to proactive and systemic resilience-building. Risk categorization models and mitigation strategies – from avoidance and reduction to risk sharing and acceptance – are now complemented by sustainability-driven approaches. Firms are not only safeguarding operations but also addressing environmental, social, and governance (ESG) factors to future-proof their supply chains. Tools like EcoVadis and the Higg Index (see Chapter 14) exemplify how environmental and social metrics are embedded into supplier assessments, while circular economy practices enhance both resource security and adaptability. The chapter has also underscored the growing recognition that supply chain resilience is not solely a matter of efficiency or agility. It now includes the capacity to respond to socio-environmental shocks and to operate responsibly in contexts of uncertainty. Circular economy principles, ethical sourcing, and transparency have emerged as resilience enablers, linking operational robustness with long-term sustainability goals.

Ultimately, resilient and sustainable supply chains are built on continuous monitoring, stakeholder collaboration, and strategic foresight. Organizations must integrate resilience and sustainability into core supply chain design and governance – anticipating risks, adapting to disruption, and aligning performance with environmental and social imperatives. As such, resilience and sustainability are no longer separate agendas but interdependent pillars of competitive and responsible supply chain management.

NOTES

1 https://www.responsiblejewellery.com/
2 https://www.globalforestwatch.org/

REFERENCES

Apple (2023) Conflict Minerals Report 2022. https://www.apple.com/euro/supplier-responsibility/l/generic/pdf/Apple-Conflict-Minerals-Report.pdf

BBC News (2019) Top tech firms sued over DR Congo cobalt mining deaths. https://www.bbc.com/news/world-africa-50812616

Bland A and Makortoff K (2020) Boohoo knew of Leicester factory failings, says report. *The Guardian* (25 September). https://www.theguardian.com/business/2020/sep/25/boohoo-report-reveals-factory-fire-risk-among-supply-chain-failings

Bode C and Wagner SM (2006) Contingency planning in supply chain risk management: A conceptual framework. *Journal of Purchasing and Supply Management* 12(6): 339–351.

Braithwaite A and Hall D (1999) Risky business? Critical decisions in supply chain management. *Supply Chain Practice* 1(2/3): 40–58.

Britten F (2022) Fashion brands pause use of sustainability index tool over greenwashing claims. *The Guardian* (28 June). https://www.theguardian.com/fashion/2022/jun/28/fashion-brands-pause-use-of-sustainability-index-tool-over-greenwashing-claims

Busse C, Schleper MC, Niu M and Wagner SM (2016) Supplier development for sustainability: Contextual barriers in global supply chains. *International Journal of Physical Distribution & Logistics Management* 46(5): 442–468.

Carnovale S, Di Mauro C, Moradlou H and Roscoe S (2025) Weaponizing supply chains: (Re)configuring PSM strategies and practices in the era of geopolitical disruptions. *Journal of Purchasing and Supply Management* 31: 101038.

Chakkol M, Johnson M, Karatzas A, Papadopoulos G and Korfiatis N (2025) Making supply chains great again: Examining structural changes to US manufacturing supply chains. *International Journal of Operations & Production Management* 44(5): 1083–1108

Chopra S and Sodhi MS (2004) Managing risk to avoid supply-chain breakdown. *MIT Sloan Management Review* 46(1): 53–62.

Chopra S, Sodhi MS and Taylor M (2007) Mitigating supply chain disruptions: Making the most of insurance. *Harvard Business Review* 85(2): 104–112.

Christopher M (2016) *Logistics and Supply Chain Management*. 5th edn, Harlow: Pearson Education.

Christopher M and Lee H (2001) Supply chain confidence. Working Paper, Cranfield School of Management.

Christopher M and Lee H (2004) Mitigating supply chain risk through improved confidence. *International Journal of Physical Distribution & Logistics Management* 34(5): 388–396.

Christopher M and Peck H (2004) Building the resilient supply chain. *International Journal of Logistics Management* 15(2): 1–13.

CIPS (n.d.) Risk management & analysis in procurement. https://www.cips.org/intelligence-hub/risk-management

Durach CF, Wieland A and Machuca JAD (2017) Antecedents and dimensions of supply chain robustness: A systematic literature review. *International Journal of Physical Distribution & Logistics Management* 47(2/3): 118–137.

Fan Y and Stevenson M (2018) A review of supply chain risk management: Definition, theory, and research agenda. *International Journal of Physical Distribution & Logistics Management* 48(3): 205–230.

Fisher M (1997) What is the right supply chain for your product? *Harvard Business Review* 75(2): 105–116.

Greenpeace (2018) Final countdown: Now or never to reform the palm oil industry. Greenpeace International. https://www.greenpeace.org/international/publication/18455/final-countdown-report-palm-oil/ (accessed 10 July 2025).

Harapko S (2023) How COVID-19 impacted supply chains and what comes next. EY. https://www.ey.com/en_nz/insights/supply-chain/how-covid-19-impacted-supply-chains-and-what-comes-next

Harland C, Brenchley R and Walker H (2003) Risk in supply networks. *Journal of Purchasing and Supply Management* 9(2): 51–62.

Ivanov D and Dolgui A (2020) Viability of intertwined supply networks: Extending the supply chain resilience angles towards survivability. *International Journal of Production Research* 58(10): 2904–2915.

Jüttner U, Peck H and Christopher M (2003) Supply chain risk management: Outlining an agenda for future research. *International Journal of Logistics: Research and Applications* 6(4): 197–210.

Kara S, Ihlwan M and Kim T (2014) The human cost of fast fashion. *BusinessWeek* (May).

Kennedy S and Linnenluecke MK (2022) Circular economy and resilience: A research agenda. *Business Strategy and the Environment* 31(6): 2754–2765

Kleindorfer PR and Saad GH (2005) Managing disruption risks in supply chains. *Production and Operations Management* 14(1): 53–68.

Lee HL (2004) The triple-A supply chain. *Harvard Business Review* 82(10): 102–112.

Manuj I and Mentzer J (2008) Global supply chain risk management. *Journal of Business Logistics* 29(1): 133–155.

March JG and Shapira Z (1987) Managerial perspectives on risk and risk taking. *Management Science* 33(11): 1404–1418.

Marshall D, McCarthy L, McGrath P and Harrigan F (2016) What is your strategy for supply chain disclosure. *MIT Sloan* 57(2): 37–45.

Miller KD (1992) A framework for integrated risk management in international business. *Journal of International Business Studies* 23(2): 311–331.

Narasimhan R and Talluri S (2009) Perspectives on risk management in supply chains. *Journal of Operations Management* 27(2): 114–118.

Norrman A and Jansson U (2004) Ericsson's proactive supply chain risk management approach after a serious sub-supplier accident. *International Journal of Physical Distribution & Logistics Management* 34(5): 434–456.

Rao S and Goldsby TJ (2009) Supply chain risks: A review and typology. *The International Journal of Logistics Management* 20(1): 97–123.

Ribeiro V, De Souza Mendes F, Singh C and Heilmayr R (2024) Leveraging remote sensing for transparency and accountability in Amazonian commodity supply chains. *One Earth* 7(11).

Rice JB and Caniato F (2003) Building a secure and resilient supply network. *Supply Chain Management Review* 7(5), Sept/Oct: 22–30.

Sanchoyerto M and Campos J (2021) Manufacturing execution systems and real-time monitoring: A review of industrial applications. *Journal of Manufacturing Systems* 61: 392–403.

Sheffi Y (2002) Supply chain management under the threat of international terrorism. *International Journal of Logistics Management* 12(2): 1–11.

Sheffi Y (2005) *The Resilient Enterprise: Overcoming Vulnerability for Competitive Advantage*. Cambridge, MA: MIT Press.

Sheffi Y and Rice JB (2005) A supply chain view of the resilient enterprise. *MIT Sloan Management Review* (Fall).

Simons R (1999) How risky is your company? *Harvard Business Review* 77(3): 85–94.

Svensson G (2000) A conceptual framework for the analysis of vulnerability in supply chains. *International journal of physical distribution & logistics management* 30(9): 731–750.

Swafford PM, Ghosh S and Murthy N (2006) The antecedents of supply chain agility of a firm: scale development and model testing. *Journal of Operations Management* 24(2): 170–188.

Taleb NN (2007) *The Black Swan: the Impact of the Highly Improbable*. New York: Random House.

Tang CS (2006) Perspectives in supply chain risk management. *International Journal of Production Economics* 103(2): 451–488.

Tummala R and Schoenherr T (2011) Assessing and managing risks using the supply chain risk management process (SCRMP). *Supply Chain Management: An International Journal* 16(6): 474–483.

van den Brink S, Kleijn R, Sprecher B and Tukker A (2020) Identifying supply risks by mapping the cobalt supply chain. *Resources, Conservation and Recycling* 156: 104743.

Wieland A and Durach CF (2021) Two perspectives on supply chain resilience. *Journal of Business Logistics* 42(3): 315–322.

Wieland A, Stevenson M, Melnyk SA, Davoudi S and Schultz L (2023) Thinking differently about supply chain resilience: What we can learn from social-ecological systems thinking. *International Journal of Operations & Production Management* 43(1): 1–21.

Wieland A and Wallenburg CM (2012) Dealing with supply chain risks: Linking risk management practices and strategies to performance. *International Journal of Physical Distribution & Logistics Management* 42(10): 887–905.

Zsidisin GA and Ritchie B (eds) (2008) *Supply Chain Risk: A Handbook of Assessment, Management, and Performance* (vol 124). Springer Science & Business Media.

Zsidisin GA, Ellram LM, Carter JR and Cavinato JL (2004) An analysis of supply risk assessment techniques. *International Journal of Physical Distribution & Logistics Management* 34(5): 397–413.

Zsidisin GA, Panelli A and Upton R (2005) Purchasing organization involvement in risk assessments, contingency plans, and risk management: An exploratory study. *Supply Chain Management: An International Journal* 10(6): 397–409.

CHAPTER 10

Supply chain transparency and digitalization

LEARNING OBJECTIVES:

At the end of this chapter you should be able to:

- Define key concepts related to corporate transparency and supply chain transparency;
- Understand the drivers and barriers to supply chain transparency;
- Assess the level of maturity of supply chain transparency and persistent unsolved problems in supply chains;
- Evaluate the role of technology and digitalization as an enabler of transparency and sustainability, in particular the extent that blockchain and 'Big Data' can foster traceability and transparency in supply chains.

10.1 OVERVIEW

In the last two decades, society has come to understand that focal firms ought to be liable for damage caused by unsustainable behaviour from suppliers in their globally dispersed supply chains. A number of buying firms have suffered reputational and economic damage as a result of media exposure of the unsatisfactory ethical and/or environmental performance of their suppliers (Hartmann and Moeller, 2014). Examples have emerged particularly since the late 2000s including H&M (Svensson, 2009), Mattel (Sethi et al., 2011), Nike (Lim and Phillips, 2008) and Reebok (Yu, 2008). By 2013, the unforgettable Rana Plaza collapse in Bangladesh described in Chapter 9 exposed not a specific brand, but the whole sector of fashion and garment production. Given the fragmentation of global supply chains, incidents involving sub-suppliers of buying firms, which are often based in low-cost countries, have exposed the lack of managerial tools that buying firms possess to handle such dispersion. In fact, even shorter and local supply chains have been subject to scandals related to environmental contamination and modern slavery such as in Brazil (Marques et al., 2024) or the United Kingdom (Stevenson, 2022). The response to these scandals has been the development of *supply chain transparency* as a core element of supply chain management.

DOI: 10.4324/9781003499602-12

This chapter will discuss the origins of supply chain transparency, rooted in corporate transparency. We present the current stage of development of such initiatives, expose the unsolved issues that persist in local and global supply chains, and reflect on the extent that digitalization can foster traceability and transparency in supply chains. The chapter shows how supply chain transparency has always developed hand-in-hand with advancements in digitalization: from the 1960s electronic data interchange (EDI), to web-based EDI solutions in the late 1990s, to the exponential rise of internet-based solutions from 2000s onward including Internet of Things (IoT), and finally most recently, the emergence of Blockchain technology as a crucial tool for achieving transparency through traceability. We illustrate this challenge with the case of Fairphone, an innovative producer of sustainable, circular, and transparency mobile phones.

10.2 CORPORATE TRANSPARENCY

The concept of *transparency* has been examined in diverse fields including general management, public relations, policy, and finance. This wide-ranging exploration has resulted in a somewhat ambiguous and imprecise understanding of transparency, making it challenging to define precisely. In this book, we adopt the definition by Budler et al. (2023: 2), which defines supply chain transparency as

> the extent of information voluntarily made available in a supply chain concerning, for example, supply chain operations, product origins, and cost analyses, to stakeholders within or beyond the supply chain. These stakeholders may be suppliers, third parties, manufacturers, assemblers, distributors, retailers, governments, NGOs, and/or customers.

The complexity surrounding transparency can lead to unexpected outcomes, such as companies that partially disclose information facing more scrutiny than those that remain completely opaque and share no information at all. These dynamics influence and are influenced by different stakeholders, and the types of disclosure that companies produce – reports, websites, etc. (Albu and Flyverbom, 2019).

Corporate transparency can be a response to regulation or be adopted voluntarily. In both approaches, the aim of corporate transparency is to produce a virtuous cycle where focal firms increase information disclosure, which then is well-perceived by stakeholders such as consumers, NGOs, society more broadly; and as a result, positive feedback incentivizes the focal firms to further disclose. Ultimately, exposed firms perceive stakeholders' positive response and move towards further transparency, thus reinforcing the cycle. On the other front, those firms lagging in terms of transparency may receive negative feedback and be compelled to change. Overall, the virtuous cycle would allow stakeholder behaviour to reward transparency while stimulating competition (Fung et al., 2007).

The notion of *democratic transparency* by Fung (2013) offers four pillars to grade transparency quality. The first one is the availability of information. The second the proportionality between information disclosed and the level of risk involved – i.e. the higher risks a supply chain is exposed to, the higher the level of transparency needed. Thirdly, accessibility of information to interested stakeholders in a comprehensible, accessible manner. And fourthly, the 'actionability' of transparency which means providing the means for stakeholders to take actions based on information disclosed – e.g. change their consumer behaviour, change their investment choices, etc. (Fung, 2013). Regulation related to transparency should consider the above pillars, and clearly define what, when, and how information must be made accessible, and to whom, as well as how the process should be audited to expose or penalize non-compliance (Fung et al., 2007).

One salient challenge for focal firms under transparency scrutiny refers to what extent they disclose information beyond their own data, to include their supply chains.

10.3 SUPPLY CHAIN TRANSPARENCY

Supply chain transparency is as imprecise as the original transparency concept. The predominant view within the supply chain literature takes the standpoint of the focal firm (i.e. buying firm), that is, their control of information along their supply chain. Supply chain transparency can be unpacked as, first, *traceability* which relates to materials and methods applied, *visibility*, which focuses on the level of information the focal firm possesses, and finally *transparency*, which frames how much of such information is disclosed to interested stakeholders. Supply chain transparency is also a controversial topic as some companies might deliberately opt not to disclose information, what Marshall and team defined as a 'secrecy strategy' or 'greenwashing' (Marshall et al., 2016). Some firms might fear that disclosure of negative information might undermine trust, worsening their supply chain relationships, instead of improving it (Egels-Zandén et al., 2015). Moreover, not only focal firms may resist sharing information, but suppliers may also not want to share information about their sub-suppliers, fearing that the focal firm would bypass them and source directly.

Certain regions of the world face higher challenges related to supply chain transparency due to institutional constraints. Take Brazil as an example of a country with poor institutional conditions for transparency. Focal firms in Brazil struggle with transparency initiatives in supply chains because of inadequate infrastructure, prevalent corruption, urgent social challenges, and informal practices, which erode trust (Silvestre, 2015). Marques and colleagues identified a phenomenon they termed 'inhospitable accessibility' in 2021, where governments mandate disclosure from companies but such unfavourable conditions end up obscuring access to information they were supposed to stimulate (Marques et al., 2021). These institutional fragilities can facilitate the secrecy strategy described earlier, wherein firms overwhelm stakeholders with excessive (and non-relevant) data, either unintentionally due to lack of prioritization or deliberately to direct attention to specific practices.

Supply chain transparency can be conceptualized according to Lamming et al.'s (2001) metaphor based on geological properties of how light penetrates substances: opaque (low transparency), translucent (medium transparency), and transparent (high transparency) (see Lamming et al., 2004; Muratore and Marques, 2021). Most recently, a typology has been deployed to discuss the emergent issue of animal welfare in supply chains (see Johnsen et al., 2025). Along this continuum of opacity-transparency, firms may opt for

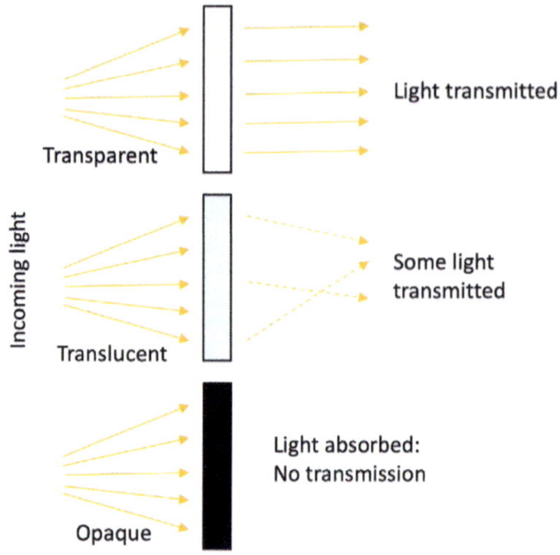

FIGURE 10.1 Conceptualizing types of transparency

opacity (i.e. the secrecy strategy mentioned earlier); translucency (partial disclosure) that includes both intentionally (greenwashing) and unintentionally concealing information that should not be kept secret; and finally, transparency (see Figure 10.1).

The strong resistance by focal firms to advance towards a transparent approach has led the field to look beyond the original focus on supplier information, to also include a reflection of the level of transparency of the focal firms' own purchasing policies and practices that may in fact hurt suppliers (Egels-Zandén et al., 2015). This discussion has evolved into a critical discussion of the lack of transparency of focal firms, exposing practices that are detrimental to suppliers (Muratore and Marques, 2021; Marques et al., 2024). This means that some firms will engage with the transparency agenda by asking suppliers to provide information that stakeholders request, while keeping old practices that hurt supplier profitability. In this sense, suppliers feel double-burdened by both cost and transparency pressures.

When societal pressure increases, and weak regulation does not respond to expectations, non-governmental forces emerge as alternatives to public policy. An outstanding case refers to the NGO Fashion Revolution and their work on the Fashion Transparency Index (FTI). Fashion Revolution was founded in the aftermath of the Rana Plaza disaster in 2013 that killed over 1,000 workers in one single day. The FTI is a compulsory assessment of fashion firms. This means that even firms that refuse to send information to the index survey will be graded zero and appear at the bottom of the rank. Over the years, the FTI expanded from surveying 50 to 250 global fashion brands by 2024. And country level chapters replicate the index in specific countries such as Brazil, India, and Mexico. Over the last years research has shown the positive impact of the FTI in the fashion industry (Brun et al., 2020), but longitudinal data shows slow progress, with 70 per cent of the brands performing poorly (Jestratijevic et al., 2022) and practicing detrimental policies towards suppliers while requesting increasing transparency compliance from them (Muratore and Marques, 2021).

Since the early 1990s, supply chain transparency has slowly evolved based on supplier audits (Stevenson and Cole, 2018). Focal firms may either engage in monitoring themselves and/or resort to third parties to achieve audit capillarity, yet problem detection at the sub-supplier level is limited (Benstead et al., 2018; Nath et al., 2020). Audit schemes tend to work based on annual local visits. Supply chain complexity and dispersion make audit schemes ineffective, making modern slavery practices dynamic and partially hidden (Christ et al., 2020).

For those firms genuinely trying to advance the supply chain transparency agenda, technology, and more specifically digitalization, has emerged as a powerful ally. Next, we revisit the history of digitalization in supply chains, and how current tools can help focal firms.

10.4 THE EVOLUTION OF DIGITALIZATION IN SUPPLY CHAINS

Given the significant number of different terminologies used to describe new or emerging technologies, it is difficult not to get confused. For example, terms such as digital and digitalization are often used interchangeably with electronic and e-business, depending on the context of their application across the organization and supply chain (Swaminathan and Tayur, 2003). Some terms and phrases have also fallen out of fashion, such as the prefix 'electronic' to denote internet-enabled technology in connection to a specific administrative function. In this section we first explore the early developments of information technology (IT) in relation to purchasing and supply, exploring innovations as far as possible in the chronological order of their introductions (See Figure 10.2).

The introduction of information technology in purchasing and logistics began with the emergence of electronic data interchange (EDI) in the 1960s. Described as the beginnings of the 'computerization of business' (Straub et al., 2004), EDI was used by road and rail transport firms who realized the benefit of document standardization and replacing previous paper-based processes with electronic communication (Threlkel and Kavan, 1999). As an early example of digitalization, EDI used bespoke computer hardware and common IT infrastructure (e.g. telephone networks), to send coded information such as goods delivery schedules, dispatch notes, and confirmation of goods received. The integration of EDI

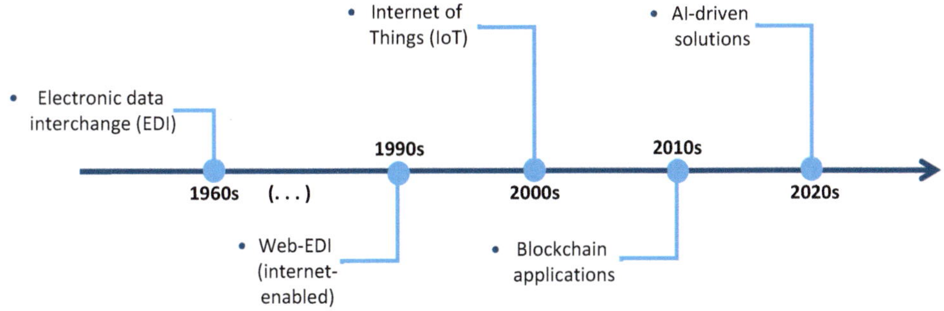

FIGURE 10.2 Chronology of supply chain digitalization

across the supply chain faced a number of difficulties, including high costs of entry, proliferation of electronic protocols, and coercive pressures on suppliers from powerful customers. For instance, the Ford Motor Company in the 1980s developed its EDI network 'Fordnet' in the manner of a competitive weapon, to gain advantage over competitors by locking in suppliers through investment in customized IT systems (Webster, 1995).

The emergence of systems such as web-EDI in the late 1990s offered a low-cost solution for all suppliers seeking connection to their business partners via the internet. Web-EDI also allowed the transition from batch processing to real-time communication between supply chain partners. E-commerce offered on-line development using 'virtual spaces' in which manufacturers and suppliers could collaborate on joint design and development. Hence potential benefits were not only reductions in transaction costs through minimizing delay and uncertainty but also sharing of ideas in new product (or service) development. The explosion in worldwide connectivity has led to a proliferation of electronic-based collaboration, resulting in profound implications for buyer-supplier relationships. Currently, daily shipment instructions can be entered only once into the system and then accessed remotely by suppliers. This solution allows the firm to provide information to suppliers and logistics partners, conducting dialogue within minutes instead of days regarding key aspects such as component scheduling. The primary objectives are typically the creation of a reliable electronic audit trail, elimination of waste and duplicated effort, such as paperwork, faxes, and phone calls, reductions in product delivery lead-time, and an increase in inventory turnover. Such systems also improve supply chain visibility where any product or service quality problems are visible to supply chain partners.

From the 2010s onwards, there has been an exponential rise in the number of computing devices (e.g. smartphones, tablets, laptops, PCs) used for both work and leisure purposes. Each device contains communicating sensors which link to computing intelligence, creating what is called the Internet of Things (IoT) or the Industrial Internet. The IoT is defined as many interconnected physical objects, creating a mesh of devices all producing information about user lifestyle choice and purchasing preferences (Cecchinel et al., 2014). The sensors in these devices in our surrounding environment (e.g. cars, buildings) continuously collect data on our choices as customers which can be invaluable as predictors of future buying trends and for online marketing firms to conduct targeted campaigns on specific consumer groups or individuals. Such is the connective power of the current digital era that terms such as 'smart cities' are now being used to describe the reach and application of digital technology (Li et al., 2016).

The idea of smart cities is based on the integration of urban infrastructures with information and communication technologies (ICT) to enable the development of new operations models. Digitized infrastructures offer opportunities for public and private organizations to design and deliver more customer-centric products or services relating to remote grocery delivery, shared transportation, and access to use of household items (e.g. washing machines) on a pay-per-use basis via online booking and payment systems. The use of IoT data in a domestic setting can also be used by companies to understand patterns of consumption and enable reverse supply chain management. For example, increasing online visibility by the user over all aspects of their purchase, such as experience, consumption, interaction, and depletion, can help service providers predict when to take back used products for reuse, repair, or recycling of valuable components and materials (e.g. electrical items, cardboard, metals), as well as optimizing replenishment levels to match demand (Parry et al., 2016).

Today's business environment is embedded in the internet, meaning digitalization has in many ways positively affected the ways operations are managed where it has encouraged the move away from single firm competition in favour of competitive supply chain networks. As companies are becoming more aware of their competition, this is driving up the levels of adaptation and cooperation necessary in the supply chain, so that digitalization takes on an increasingly critical role. The expectations around digital operational capability required of most suppliers today means the ability to engage in real-time communication between supply chain members, interlocking databases, and 24-hour shipment tracking. The digital know-how therefore has become an essential element in the purchasing and supply chain manager's personal toolkit.

10.5 BLOCKCHAIN IN SUPPLY CHAIN MANAGEMENT

One of the most significant developments affecting the digital supply chain is the introduction of digital currency or 'cryptocurrency'. One of the best-known currencies is Bitcoin (see Note 10.1). Digital currency was created for people to conduct business without the costs or bureaucracy of the banking system. During the purchase, the transaction is recorded in a digital record or ledger called the blockchain which is located across users' computers. Bitcoins are registered to bitcoin addresses and accessed by their owners via their own private passkey. Anyone across the world can dedicate a computer to work verifying blockchain transactions and be rewarded with new bitcoins (or any other crypto coin) in a process known as crypto mining. Despite the lack of centralized banking control, many governments are experimenting with blockchain technology to store information, such as land registry records, while supermarkets are looking at blockchain to help track food through the supply chain, from farmyard to the consumer, as a means of ensuring 100 per cent traceability and avoiding meat processing scandals of the past (e.g. horsemeat in UK burgers).

Note 10.1 What is Bitcoin and where did it come from?

The cryptocurrency Bitcoin was created by an unknown individual or group in 2009. The philosophy behind the payment system's conception is that it is borderless and completely decentralized i.e. owned or controlled by no one individual, bank, or government. In many ways it is a utopian project where users interact with one another and all transactions are recorded and stored forever on a large, secure online public ledger. Like the various currencies which followed it, Bitcoin was seen as an alternative to the traditional economy which at the time in 2009 was going through a financial crisis. Although there are many legitimate uses for cryptocurrency, such as investors and people who don't trust their own country's currency, there are also alleged links with criminal activity and the Dark Web. Criminals can use cryptocurrency to buy drugs, weapons, or internet hacking tools. North Korea for example has been stockpiling Bitcoins to try to circumvent international sanctions. Although such currencies are not anonymous, their air of exclusivity and borderless, password protected accounts can make it difficult for the authorities to trace and claim any tax payments which may be due.

Blockchain technology has emerged as a crucial tool for achieving transparency through traceability. The study of blockchain in information systems began in 2008, with a significant surge in publications occurring in 2016 (Queiroz et al., 2019), and by 2018 the supply chain field saw the introduction of initial theoretical studies and reviews. Initial research on the field proposes 'transaction costs' as a framework to assess blockchain's impact on supply chains, where blockchain would both support supply chain transparency at a systemic level, while reducing transaction costs (see Saberi et al., 2018; Treiblmaier, 2018).

Blockchain is a decentralized system that records and maintains an unalterable, consistent, and linear log of transactions (ledger) among connected supply chain members. Several fundamental principles characterize a blockchain. Firstly, control over information is decentralized: all data is transmitted to every node, eliminating the need for a central authority to validate transactions. Secondly, transaction anonymity is preserved, while network nodes handle authentication, offering a balance of transparency and privacy. Thirdly, once a transaction is recorded in the blockchain, it becomes virtually impossible to modify the ledger. Lastly, it is feasible to create programs, known as smart contracts, which specify the criteria for transaction verification and registration (Tapscott and Tapscott, 2016). Figure 10.3 illustrates how the virtual blockchain can interact with a physical supply chain.

Initially embraced by financial markets, blockchain technology has since been considered for use in various industries, including pharmaceuticals, shipping, forestry, and food production. Blockchain implementations can incorporate real-time tracking capabilities, leveraging technologies such as radio frequency identification, GPS, and the Internet of

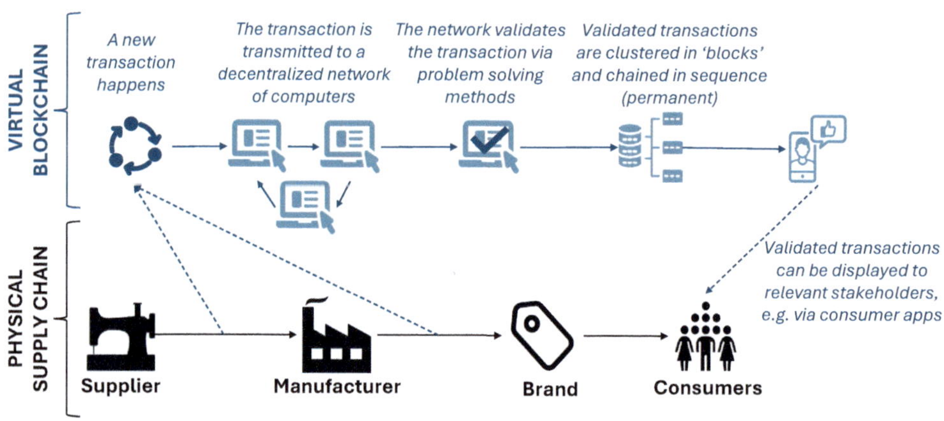

FIGURE 10.3 How blockchain can work for supply chains

Things. These features enable the monitoring of goods in transit and provide visibility into the actions of different entities within various sectors, such as container tracking or supplier oversight. Additionally, blockchain systems can utilize smart contracts to minimize transaction costs and facilitate direct peer-to-peer interactions and collective negotiations (Kshetri, 2018). It has been posited that blockchain can ease transaction costs (Saberi et al., 2018) or even eliminate such costs completely (Tapscott and Tapscott, 2016). Blockchain applications can serve as reputation systems that replace fraudulent rating systems, thus allowing firms to establish the trustworthiness of their suppliers (Efanov and Roschin, 2018). Studies suggest that blockchain can reduce the number of intermediates in a supply chain, and offer conditions for real-time monitoring of suppliers (Shermin, 2017). Beyond transaction costs, it has been argued that blockchain can address core challenges in supply chains such as diminishing the bullwhip effect, improving integration, and offering scalability to monitoring, particularly when supply chains are multi-tiered (Agrawal et al., 2021). Therefore, blockchain has been framed as key to scalable supply chain transparency.

On the issue of working conditions and modern slavery, supply chain transparency can include data about employees clocking in and out of a factory to gauge whether the factory is complying with labour regulations (Stevenson, 2022). Blockchain has been presented as the 21st century's 'shop-lifting camera' providing traceability, decentralization of data collection-validation, and breach-proof confidentiality (Shermin, 2017). However, few empirical studies have addressed the impact of blockchain on social issues in the supply chain (Pournader et al., 2019).

In contrast to the overwhelming number of positive reviews on blockchain, recent studies have exposed the governance challenges and implementation costs, which are neglected by most enthusiasts (see Murray et al., 2021; Pun et al., 2021). A challenging issue relates to costs of third parties hired within blockchain projects. For example, when a dispute between two parties in a blockchain project emerges, the need for third-party arbitration may lead to extra costs. Impartial third-party experts are also hired to design smart contracts and/or to assess data quality. The need to hire these experts (and associated costs) can frustrate those that assume that blockchain is a path to human-free supply chains. Such governance costs are most salient during implementation, and tend to be mitigated by scale, but at this stage, most projects are at a pilot phase, preventing investors from achieving the costs benefits that are dependent on large scale implementations. Ignoring these costs may lead to misjudgements in cost analyses (Pun et al., 2021) and disappointment when inflated expectations are not met (Sodhi et al., 2022).

Besides misjudging unforeseen costs, it is likely that blockchain-based initiatives for improving supply chain transparency will face resistance. Although blockchain aims to reduce human interaction, build technology-based trust, and avoid decoupling, there is evidence of decoupling even after technology is implemented. Firms may resist the adoption of emerging technologies and the change that they provoke (Sodhi et al., 2022), and the greater fairness that may result from transparency (Chen et al., 2022). A recent study has showed that both buying firms and suppliers can resist blockchain implementation. Focal firms will delay adoption, and avoid being the first one, postponing engagement until other competitors start their journey. This creates a systemic effect that paralyzes innovation. Suppliers often have to say yes to buying firms more powerful than them, but can boycott supply chain transparency by hiding information, providing false information, and engaging with fake compliance (Marques et al., 2024).

10.6 A PROCESS PERSPECTIVE OF SUPPLY CHAIN TRANSPARENCY

Figure 10.4 offers a *process perspective* to assess supply chain transparency, depicting three stages: data collection, data analysis, and data disclosure. While the first two stages are significantly affected by technology and digitalization trends, the last stage has gained traction in the last two decades resulting from the emergence of multi-stakeholder disclosure platforms that offer a space for disclosure of supply chain data. Above the data process, the model presents three levels (cumulative) of transparency. And at the bottom, the emerging technologies that can support this process.

In the first level of transparency, companies answer the '*Who*' question: supplier membership lists that simply disclose the names of the suppliers currently supplying to the buying firm, without any further information.

In the second level, companies go beyond the membership list to include the '*Where*' question, also referred to as 'provenance', i.e. specific supplier location, ideally per facility since a supplier might have production in three different facilities. In addition, provenance also includes an audit trail of the flow of raw materials from source to final destination.

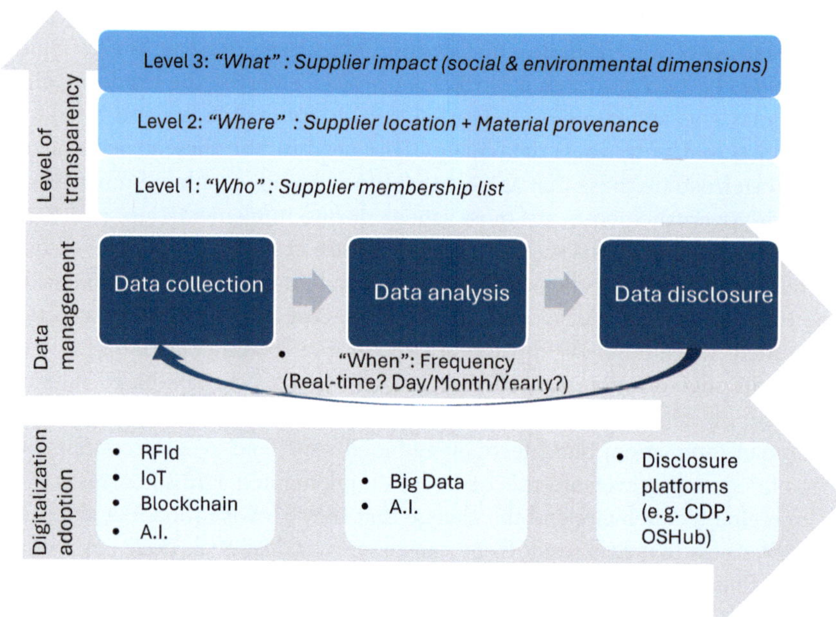

FIGURE 10.4 A process perspective of supply chain transparency: maturity and digitalization

In the third level, besides answering 'Who' and 'Where', companies disclose the '*What*' question which refers to the impact of the supplier base, covering both social and environmental aspects. Here lies most of the complexity. Regarding the social front, companies can disclose basic measures related to number of workers under formal contracts, and other labour related issues and certification. Front runners will also ensure living wave payment for workers in their supplier base, and strong engagement with local communities affected by their supply chains. On the environmental front, disclosure usually starts with the supply chain carbon emissions, which the GHG protocol refers to as *scope 3 emissions*. Often disclosure will be restricted to high-spend suppliers, exploring a pareto approach. More elaborated disclosures will cover the full supply base, and advance beyond carbon to other elements like water consumption and biodiversity. It is not rare to see focal firms resisting to address all these questions, slowly advancing on the 'who' with a simple supply list, then possibly adding the 'where' with supplier addresses, and delaying as much as possible actual disclosure of socio-environmental impact indicators.

The '*When*' [or *how often*] question refers to the frequency of disclosure. While real-time is expected, especially when we discuss the potential of digitalization, the reality is that most firms are dependent on annual local audits to suppliers, and as a result, produce annual reports. Some firms advance to more frequent reports covering partial information at a monthly frequency, and real-time transparency is still a dream to come true. Each stage of the process perspective can benefit from different types of emerging technologies.

Data collection is highly dependent on both hardware and software solutions, even more so if real-time frequency is intended. Barcode and RFId are the usual suspects for data collection, but IoT and blockchain are more recent developments that can support data input. IoT allows large scale and real-time data collection. Estimates indicate that there are close to ten connected devices per person on the planet, so plenty of opportunities for data input. Blockchain can support with decentralized processes that ensure confidentiality, although often a third party will be involved to further ensure anonymity if data shared is sensitive.

Data analysis has reached new levels of complexity with the advancement in Big Data and AI. Big Data analytics can be defined as a field of information science that brings together how to capture, store, organize, process, analyze, disseminate, and manage data and information in high volume, elevated variety, and transacted in high speed (Sanders, 2016). Effective Big Data analytics derives not only from effective data collection but also rapid processing, low level of error, and the quality of data manipulation and visualization (Zhu et al., 2018). Such an approach allows real-time management of the supply chain as well as to rapidly respond to potential risks.

Big Data analytics can be employed through three approaches. Descriptive analytics derives information from significant amounts of data and answers the question of what is happening. At a second stage, predictive analytics in supply chains derives demand forecasts from past data and answers the question of what will be happening. Here, AI can support scenario planning. Finally, prescriptive analytics derives decision recommendations based on descriptive and predictive analytics models and mathematical optimization models. It answers the question of what should be happening (Souza, 2014). Descriptive analytics focuses on ex-post analysis, and it is typically applied for monitoring, reporting, and dashboards activities – which can be restricted to membership and provenance transparency. Predictive analytics entails producing models that help predict the future, detecting patterns in data and generating forecasting. From a sustainability perspective, predictive analytics can assess risk in the supply chain, using a green-yellow-red flagging system. Finally, prescriptive analytics is mostly powered by AI and supports proactive control of the supply chain based on simulation and optimization (Brintrup et al., 2019). From a sustainability perspective, prescriptive analytics can propose action plans to each 'red' supplier-based data pattern, for example.

Data disclosure highly benefits from digitalization trends as well, which offers new ways to tackle supply chain risks related to sustainability and for companies to ensure compliance and transparency across their supply chains. Given the enormity of the challenge for single companies to tackle supply chain risks on their own, more and more companies choose to collaborate with other companies, including their competitors, to jointly manage these challenges. An increasing number of hubs or platform providers are emerging to facilitate the process of supplier monitoring and developmental efforts. The advantage of these platforms is that they provide a way to address supply chain sustainability risks at multiple company or industry level. They are typically run by non-profit consortiums, aimed at establishing standard processes for the sharing of business information between firms (i.e. B2B). Examples include computer and consumer electronics, electronic components, semiconductor manufacturing, telecommunications, and logistics companies, all working to create industry-wide, open e-business process standards. These standards create a common e-business language which helps to connect supply chain partners around the world.

Information sharing hubs are often operated by service providers such as 'Achilles', 'Sedex', 'Ecovadis', and, more recently, the 'Fashion Transparency Index' and the 'Open Supply Hub', and have an increasing role in developing sustainable supply chains, used extensively for sharing sustainability risk data in supply chains for compliance purposes (Note 10.2). The most mature hubs go beyond collecting data through online questionnaires aligned with global standards, typically the Global Reporting Initiative (GRI). For example, these might offer system training and support, audit and embedded system features, such as warnings of incomplete or expired data, and access to third-party data for verification purposes.

Note 10.2 Hub technology for supply chain compliance and auditing

RosettaNet, Sedex, Ecovadis, Open Supply Hub are all examples of application of technology used to promote supply chain sharing of key information. Such information is needed by customers and manufacturers for compliance purposes when seeking to prove a product conforms to legislation, such as the use of harmful substances. Sedex: the Supplier Ethics Data Exchange seeks to "... empower sustainable and ethical supply chains" by encouraging responsible supply chain practice. As a non-profit organization, its core product is a secure, online database which allows members to voluntarily store, share, and report on information on four key areas: labour standards, health and safety, the environment, and business ethics. Similarly, the EcoVadis hub aims at "... improving environmental and social practices of companies by leveraging the influence of global supply chains". EcoVadis claims to operate the first collaborative platform enabling companies to monitor the sustainability performance of suppliers using a system of ratings and easy-to-use monitoring tools. Although the portal operators claim it allows companies to manage risks and drive eco-innovations in their global supply chains, a drawback of all such third-party hubs/portals is the option by unscrupulous suppliers simply not to use them and avoid detection over possible material use, environmental, or human rights infringements. The Open Supply Hub started their activity focused on the fashion industry but has extended to a multi-sector perspective and currently (2025) offers location data covering 1 million suppliers of over 2,000 focal firms.

10.7 MODERN SLAVERY AND THE ROAD AHEAD FOR SUPPLY CHAIN DIGITALIZATION

Supply chain transparency has progressed quite slowly in the last decade, and some issues related to social and environmental impact persist and call for new approaches to the problem. One such issue is modern slavery. Modern slavery increased by 10 per cent from 2016 to 2021 to affect over 49 million people, with over 17 million in the private economy (International Labor Organization et al., 2022). Low-technology and labour-intensive industries tend to concentrate working conditions issues particularly because they offer low entry barriers to new and informal suppliers (Zorzini et al., 2015). Industries where labour outsourcing is common practice can lead to complex supply chains, where a first-tier supplier may outsource part of a contract to a second-tier supplier. The more complexity in the supply chain (e.g. number of tiers), the higher the chances of informal and hidden contracting schemes (Nath et al., 2020; Soundararajan et al., 2021). High levels of outsourcing informality offer fertile ground for modern slavery. Although major scandals tend to attract societal and academic attention, modern slavery persists as a gradual, continuous threat that often finds a home in the multi-tiered nature of supply chains (Tachizawa and Wong, 2015; Busse et al., 2016).

Supply chain digitalization has been slowly gaining ground, particularly since 2000s, including pilot solutions with blockchain, but a large-scale solution for eradication of modern slavery is yet to be seen. The phenomenon that allows firms to hide informal practices even when under scrutiny and with partial adoption of digitalization is called *decoupling*.

Decoupling often occurs due to information asymmetry between firms and their stakeholders. The foundations of decoupling date back to the 1970s. Weick (1976: 4) stated that "intentions are a poor guide for action, intentions often follow rather than precede action, and that intentions and action are loosely coupled". Decoupling is a thoughtful disconnection between organizational structures aiming at legitimacy and daily organizational practices (Meyer and Rowan, 1977). Recent supply chain research has showed decoupling along supply chains (Barratt and Choi, 2007), and investigated decoupling in suppliers' response to pressures related to sustainability (Huq and Stevenson, 2018; Nath et al., 2020). Often, decoupling occurs across the organizational hierarchy: those in charge of policy please external stakeholders, while those in charge of daily activities continue to perform untouched (Barratt and Choi, 2007). If policy adoption alone builds legitimacy without evidence of actual practice, real change can be delayed. Arguments for delaying action include a lack of capacity and the need for time and costs to adapt (Nath et al., 2020). Decoupling also relates to the implementation of policies that have a weak relationship with the intended outcomes (Asif, 2020). The allocation of resources between practices that only aim at legitimacy and core practices disperses energy. Lack of transparency increases the dissociation between policy, practice, and actual results eventually rendering the implementation of sustainability standards impossible (Wijen, 2014).

Persistent issues such as modern slavery are rooted in decoupling, when focal firms transfer responsibility for such issues to their suppliers (Meehan and Pinnington, 2021). In other words, they define policy, but action is 'outsourced' to their supply chain, thereby overburdening suppliers. Suppliers may engage in a concealment strategy, attempting to prevent nonconformity with sustainability practices by deliberately hiding their violations. Alternatively, suppliers may engage in a consensual strategy that entails attempting to implement partial sustainability practices by negotiating with other actors (Nath et al., 2020). As pressures for due diligence increase from policy (both mandatory regulation and voluntary schemes – see Chapter 13 for more on this), effective supply chain digitalization and transparency may reduce information asymmetry and block decoupling (Chen et al., 2022). Yet, scalable solutions for complex supply chains are yet to be developed and implemented.

10.8 CASE STUDY: THE FAIRPHONE

Fairphone's inception in 2010 marked a significant departure from traditional smartphone manufacturers, focusing on creating a more responsible and ethical approach to technology production. The company's origins can be traced back to a collaborative campaign between Dutch associations and Action Aid, an international NGO dedicated to poverty reduction and social justice. Initially, their primary objective was to raise awareness about the extraction of conflict minerals in the Democratic Republic of Congo, highlighting the often-overlooked ethical implications of smartphone production.

By 2013, the organization took a bold step by deciding to manufacture their own mobile phone, aiming to demonstrate that an alternative, more transparent, and ethical approach to sourcing, distribution, and marketing was possible in the smartphone industry. This decision was rooted in a deep understanding of the need for improved supply chain transparency, which became a cornerstone of Fairphone's strategy. The company's commitment to responsible sourcing of minerals, local contracting, and a thorough understanding of the mineral supply chain in Africa set them apart from conventional manufacturers. Despite facing production challenges due to low volumes and high minimum order quantities from suppliers, Fairphone found creative solutions, such as piggybacking on larger orders from industry giants like Apple or Samsung.

Their unwavering commitment to the principles of supply chain traceability and the promotion of transparency within their operations is clearly illustrated through a variety of distinctive and innovative features that set them apart in the industry. First and foremost, they demonstrate an impressive level of transparency by providing full disclosure concerning all of their suppliers, which includes not only the specific geographic locations of these suppliers but also a comprehensive breakdown of the cost of components associated with the materials they source. By the year 2023, they achieved an impressive 76 per cent of full traceability of the total volume sourced from 14 carefully selected materials that they have identified as their primary focus areas. In addition, it is noteworthy that 63 per cent of the factories which they have included in their supply chain have been classified as having a high level of maturity, reflecting their adherence to quality and sustainability standards. Furthermore, the production of the Fairphone 5 in 2023 was powered entirely by renewable energy sources, showcasing their commitment to environmental responsibility and sustainable manufacturing practices.

Fairphone's design emphasizes the principles of modularity, repairability, and circularity. Their pioneering initiative to incorporate recycled materials into their products is grounded on a phone design that features 20 modules which can be independently repaired by users, serving to further underscore their dedication to both sustainability and the empowerment of consumers to take control of their devices. The longevity of their mobile phones has impressively reached an average lifespan ranging between 4.7 and 5.5 years, a remarkable achievement when compared to the typical industry average which generally falls between two to three years for most smartphones on the market. Additionally, they offer a robust five-year manufacturer warranty, which stands as a testament to their confidence in the durability of their products. To complement this, they also provide an extensive eight years of software support, ensuring that users can benefit from the latest updates and security features for a prolonged period. They have demonstrated, for instance, that extending the lifespan of a phone from three years to five years reduces the carbon impact by 28 per cent, while extending the lifespan further from five years to eight years results in an even more significant carbon impact reduction of 46 per cent.

The year 2023 marked a significant decline to the mobile phone market. While this may signal that consumers are using their mobile phones for longer, it led to a flat sales volume for Fairphone from 2022 to 2023, against a target of 50 per cent sales increase. Currently Fairphone faces a number of pressing challenges that must be addressed including determining the most effective strategies to achieve 100 per cent traceability throughout their supply chain, figuring out how to keep pace with technological advancements and consumer expectations without resorting to the frequent launch of new versions, establishing the optimal duration for providing repair support for older versions of their phones, and assessing how profitable – and sustainable – the market for repair parts can be in the long term. Addressing these challenges will require a multifaceted approach that includes collaboration with stakeholders, investment in research and development, and a commitment to sustainable practices that prioritize both environmental impact and consumer satisfaction.

10.9 CONCLUSION

In this chapter, we have presented supply chain transparency starting from its origins in the perspective of corporate transparency. Stretching the notion of transparency from the corporation to the extended supply chain is a complex endeavour. Supply chain transparency was unpacked into questions of who (supplier list), where (supplier location), when (moment and frequency of reporting by the focal firm), and what (specific performance aspects related to social and environmental impact of the suppliers). We have also discussed nuances related to the focal firm's own transparency of their policies and practices. Then, we have reviewed the role of digitalization, showing that as technology advanced to web-based solutions, real-time monitoring has had major implications for supply chain transparency. A closer look into blockchain as a promising, emerging, yet controversial technology for supply chain traceability and transparency has been discussed. Yet, challenges related to the topic still persist. Modern slavery still affects millions of workers in supply chains in food, fashion, electronics, and other industries. Procurement and supply chain experts have e key role in driving supply chain digitalization further – the one path that holds potential to help advancing this agenda. As regulation tightens, all firms will eventually need to advance this agenda. More broadly, the path to supply chain sustainability includes a deep understanding of the possibilities of supply chain digitalization and solutions that help firms map, monitor, and disclose what is happening along their complex supply chains.

REFERENCES

Agrawal TK, Kumar V, Pal R, Wang L and Chen Y (2021) Blockchain-based framework for supply chain traceability: A case example of textile and clothing industry. *Computers and Industrial Engineering* 154: 107130.

Albu OB and Flyverbom M (2019) Organizational transparency: Conceptualizations, conditions, and consequences. *Business & Society* 58(2): 268–297.

Asif M (2020) Supplier socioenvironmental compliance: A survey of the antecedents of standards decoupling. *Journal of Cleaner Production* 246: 1–18.

Barratt M and Choi TY (2007) Mandated RFID and institutional responses: Cases of decentralized business units. *Production and Operations Management* 16(5): 569–585.

Benstead AV, Hendry LC and Stevenson M (2018) Horizontal collaboration in response to modern slavery legislation: An action research project. *International Journal of Operations & Production Management* 38(12): 2286–2312.

Brintrup A, Pak J, Ratiney D, Pearce T, Wichmann P, Woodall P and McFarlane D (2019) Supply chain data analytics for predicting supplier disruptions: A case study in complex asset manufacturing. *International Journal of Production Research* 58(11): 3330–3341.

Brun A, Karaosman H and Barresi T (2020) Supply chain collaboration for transparency. *Sustainability* 12(11).

Budler M, Quiroga BF and Trkman P (2023) A review of supply chain transparency research: Antecedents, technologies, types, and outcomes. *Journal of Business Logistics* 45(1): e12368.

Busse C, Schleper MC, Niu M and Wagner SM (2016) Supplier development for sustainability: Contextual barriers in global supply chains. *International Journal of Physical Distribution & Logistics Management* 46(5): 442–468.

Cecchinel C, Jimenez M, Mosser S and Riveill M (2014) An architecture to support the collection of big data in the internet of things. *In Services, IEEE World Congress*: 442–449.

Chen L, Lee HL and Tang CS (2022) Supply chain fairness. *Production and Operations Management* 31(12): 4304–4318.

Christ KL, Burritt RL and Schaltegger S (2020) Accounting for work conditions from modern slavery to decent work. *Accounting, Auditing & Accountability Journal* 33(7): 1481–1504.

Efanov D and Roschin P (2018) The all-pervasiveness of the blockchain technology. *Procedia Computer Science*, 123: 116–121.

Egels-Zandén N, Hulthén K and Wulff G (2015) Trade-offs in supply chain transparency: The case of Nudie Jeans Co. *Journal of Cleaner Production* 107: 95–104.

Fung A (2013) Infotopia: Unleashing the democratic power of transparency. *Politics and Society* 41(2): 183–212.

Fung A, Graham M and Weil D (2007) *Full Disclosure: The Perils and Promise of Transparency*. New York: Cambridge University Press.

Hartmann J and Moeller S (2014) Chain liability in multitier supply chains? Responsibility attributions for unsustainable supplier behavior. *Journal of Operations Management* 32(5): 281–294.

Huq FA and Stevenson M (2018) Implementing socially sustainable practices in challenging institutional contexts: Building theory from seven developing country supplier cases. *Journal of Business Ethics* 161(2): 415–442.

International Labor Organization, Walk Free and International Organization for Migration (2022) *Global Estimates of Modern Slavery: Forced Labour and Forced Marriage*. https://www.ilo.org/global/topics/forced-labour/publications/WCMS_854733/lang--en/index.htm

Jestratijevic I, Uanhoro JO and Creighton R (2022) To disclose or not to disclose? Fashion brands' strategies for transparency in sustainability reporting. *Journal of Fashion Marketing and Management: An International Journal* 26(1): 36–50.

Johnsen R, Johnsen TE, Beske-Janssen P and Marques L (2025) Animal welfare in fashion: A typology of transparent, translucent and opaque supply chains. *Supply Chain Management: An International Journal* 30(3): 323–338.

Kshetri N (2018) 1 Blockchain's roles in meeting key supply chain management objectives. *International Journal of Information Management* 39: 80–89.

Lamming R, Caldwell ND and Harrison DA (2004) Developing the concept of transparency for use in supply relationships. *British Journal of Management* 15: 291–302.

Lamming R, Caldwell ND, Harrison DA and Phillips W (2001) Transparency in supply relationships: Concept and practice *Journal of Supply Chain Management* 37(3): 4–10.

Li F, Nucciarelli A, Roden S and Graham G (2016) How smart cities transform operations models: A new research agenda for operations management in the digital economy. *Production Planning & Control* 27(6): 514–528.

Lim S-J and Phillips J (2008) Embedding CSR values: The global footwear industry's evolving governance structure. *Journal of Business Ethics* 81(1): 143–156.

Marques L, Erthal A, Schott CSdCM and Morais D (2021) Inhospitable accessibility and blurred liability: Institutional voids in an emerging economy preventing supply network transparency. *Brazilian Administration Review* 18(2): 1–28.

Marques L, Morais D and Terra A (2024) More than meets the eye: Misconduct and decoupling against blockchain for supply chain transparency. *Production and Operations Management* 34(5): 1057–1075.

Marshall D, McCarthy L, McGrath P and Harrigan F (2016) What is your strategy for supply chain disclosure. *MIT Sloan* 57(2): 37–45.

Meehan J and Pinnington BD (2021) Modern slavery in supply chains: Insights through strategic ambiguity. *International Journal of Operations & Production Management* 41(2): 77–101.

Meyer JW and Rowan B (1977) Institutionalized organization: Formal structure as myth and ceremony. *American Journal of Sociology* 83(2): 340–363.

Muratore AP and Marques L (2021) Fashion supply chain transparency: Do as I say not as I do. *International Journal of Productivity and Performance Management* 71(6): 2459–2478.

Murray A, Kuban S, Josefy M and Anderson J (2021) Contracting in the smart era: The implications of blockchain and decentralized autonomous organizations for contracting and corporate governance. *Academy of Management Perspectives* 35(4): 622–641.

Nath SD, Eweje G and Sajjad A (2020) The hidden side of sub–supplier firms' sustainability – An empirical analysis. *International Journal of Operations & Production Management* 40(12): 1771–1799.

Parry GC, Brax SA, Maull RS and Ng IC (2016) Operationalising IoT for reverse supply: The development of use-visibility measures. *Supply Chain Management: An International Journal* 21(2): 228–244.

Pournader M, Shi Y, Seuring S and Koh SCL (2019) Blockchain applications in supply chains, transport and logistics: A systematic review of the literature. *International Journal of Production Research* 58(7): 2063–2081.

Pun H, Swaminathan JM and Hou P (2021) Blockchain adoption for combating deceptive counterfeits. *Production and Operations Management* 30(4): 864–882.

Queiroz MM, Telles R and Bonilla SH (2019) Blockchain and supply chain management integration: A systematic review of the literature. *Supply Chain Management: An International Journal* 25(2): 241–254.

Saberi S, Kouhizadeh M, Sarkis J and Shen L (2018) Blockchain technology and its relationships to sustainable supply chain management. *International Journal of Production Research* 57(7): 2117–2135.

Sanders NR (2016) How to use big data to drive your supply chain. *California Management Review* 58(3): 23–48.

Sethi SP, Veral EA, Shapiro HJ and Emelianova O (2011) Mattel, inc.: global manufacturing principles (GMP) – A life-cycle analysis of a company-based code of conduct in the toy industry. *Journal of Business Ethics* 99(4): 483–517.

Shermin V (2017) Disrupting governance with blockchains and smart contracts. *Strategic Change* 26(5): 499–509.

Silvestre BS (2015) Sustainable supply chain management in emerging economies: Environmental turbulence, institutional voids and sustainability trajectories. *International Journal of Production Economics* 167, 156–169.

Sodhi MS, Seyedghorban Z, Tahernejad H and Samson D (2022) Why emerging supply chain technologies initially disappoint: Blockchain, IoT, and AI. *Production and Operations Management* 31(6): 2517–2537.

Soundararajan V, Wilhelm MM and Crane A (2021) Humanizing working conditions in supply chains: Building a path to decent work. *Journal of Supply Chain Management* 57(2): 3–13.

Souza GC (2014) Supply chain analytics. *Business Horizons* 57(5): 595–605.

Stevenson M (2022) Hidden in plain sight: The bystander effect and the mobilisation of modern slavery whistleblowing. *Supply Chain Management: An International Journal* 27(1): 128–139.

Stevenson M and Cole R (2018) Modern slavery in supply chains: A secondary data analysis of detection, remediation and disclosure. *Supply Chain Management: An International Journal* 12(3): 81–99.

Straub D, Rai A and Klein R (2004) Measuring firm performance at the network level: A nomology of the business impact of digital supply networks. *Journal of Management Information Systems* 21(1): 83–114.

Svensson G (2009) The transparency of SCM ethics: Conceptual framework and empirical illustrations. *Supply Chain Management: An International Journal* 14(4): 259–269.

Swaminathan JM and Tayur SR (2003) Models for supply chains in e-business. *Management Science* 49(10): 1387–1406.

Tachizawa EM and Wong CY (2015) The performance of green supply chain management governance mechanisms: A supply network and complexity perspective. *Journal of Supply Chain Management* 51(3): 18–32.

Tapscott D and Tapscott A (2016) *Blockchain Revolution*. New York: Penguin.

Threlkel M and Kavan CB (1999) From traditional EDI to Internet-based EDI: Managerial considerations. *Journal of Information Technology* 14: 347–360.

Treiblmaier H (2018) The impact of the blockchain on the supply chain: A theory-based research framework and a call for action. *Supply Chain Management: An International Journal* 23(6): 545–559.

Webster J (1995) Networks of collaboration or conflict? Electronic data interchange and power in the supply chain. *Journal of Strategic Information Systems* 4(1): 31–42.

Weick KE (1976) Educational organizations as loosely coupled systems. *Administrative Science Quarterly* 21(1): 1–19.

Wijen F (2014) Means versus Ends in Opaque Institutional Fields: Trading off Compliance and Achievement in Sustainability Standard Adoption. *Academy of Management Review* 39(3): 302–323.

Yu X (2008) Impacts of Corporate Code of Conduct on Labor Standards: A Case Study of Reebok's Athletic Footwear Supplier Factory in China. *Journal of Business Ethics* 81(3): 513–529.

Zhu S, Song J, Hazen BT, Lee K and Cegielski C (2018) How supply chain analytics enables operational supply chain transparency. *International Journal of Physical Distribution and Logistics Management* 48, 47–68.

Zorzini M, Hendry LC, Huq FA and Stevenson M (2015) Socially responsible sourcing: Reviewing the literature and its use of theory. *International Journal of Operations & Production Management* 35(1): 60–109.

Useful websites

- www.ecovadis.com
- www.sedexglobal.com
- www.rosettanet.org
- www.mysourcingteam.com
- www.globalscm.net
- www.esourcingwiki.com
- www.opensupplyhub.org
- www.fashionrevolution.org/fashion-transparency-index

CHAPTER 11

Logistics and distribution

LEARNING OBJECTIVES:

At the end of this chapter you should be able to:

- Explain how transport mode choices impact sustainability and cost efficiency;
- Evaluate inventory and location decisions for environmental trade-offs;
- Analyze reverse logistics practices to support circular supply chains;
- Assess last-mile and city logistics strategies for sustainable urban delivery.

11.1 INTRODUCTION

Logistics and distribution are fundamental components of modern supply chains, enabling the efficient flow of goods from producers to end users. They play a central role in determining both cost competitiveness and customer service levels, but they also exert a profound influence on sustainability outcomes. Transport and distribution activities are among the largest contributors to greenhouse gas emissions in supply chains, while decisions around inventory, facility location, and last-mile delivery can either exacerbate or mitigate environmental impacts (Halldórsson and Kovács, 2010; Edwards and McKinnon, 2009). As global trade intensifies and consumer expectations shift towards speed and flexibility, the challenge of balancing operational efficiency with ecological responsibility has become a defining concern for both firms and policymakers (Wolf and Seuring, 2010).

The chapter explores the interconnections between logistics decisions and sustainability. It begins with transport choices, examining trade-offs between cost, service, and carbon intensity across modes such as road, rail, sea, and air (Piecyk and McKinnon, 2010). Following sections analyze inventory policies and their environmental implications (Bouchery et al., 2012), including the strategic role of location in shaping supply chain efficiency (ReVelle and Eiselt, 2005). The chapter also addresses reverse logistics and the growing importance of circular practices (Carter and Ellram, 1998), the role of logistics service providers in enabling sustainable operations (Kudla and Klaas-Wissing, 2012), and

DOI: 10.4324/9781003499602-13

evolving distribution channel structures (Coughlan et al., 2006). Finally, it considers physical distribution design, last-mile delivery, and urban logistics, highlighting both emerging innovations and continuing challenges (Halldórsson and Wehner, 2020).

11.2 TRANSPORT DECISIONS IN SUPPLY CHAINS

Transport decisions play a pivotal role in logistics operations and have profound implications for environmental sustainability. As logistics revolves around the movement and storage of goods, transport-related energy consumption and greenhouse gas (GHG) emissions have become key concerns. In response, governments have implemented regulations to reduce environmental impacts, shaping both technological innovation and logistical planning.

Progress in the European Union demonstrates a successful decoupling of economic growth from emissions in general but has not been so successful for transport emissions as illustrated in Figure 11.1. This is mostly due to increased freight transport volumes with GDP and it is only since the Covid-19 pandemic that any relative decoupling has been seen.

A critical sustainability and cost consideration is modal choice – selecting the most appropriate transport mode for goods movement. Faster modes such as air and road provide speed and flexibility but come at higher financial and environmental costs. In contrast, rail and sea offer greater energy efficiency, making them attractive for less time-sensitive goods.

Transport planning must balance service level expectations with operational and environmental performance. High service levels require more capacity and frequent shipments, which can lead to suboptimal loads and increased emissions, especially in peak periods. Today, modal decisions increasingly consider flexibility, reliability, and carbon footprint, not just speed and cost.

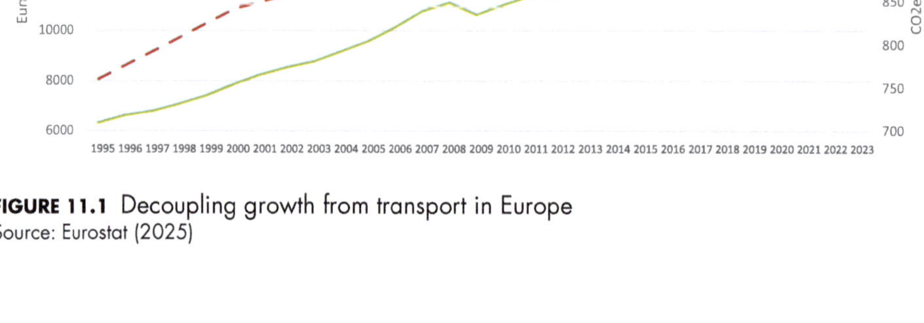

FIGURE 11.1 Decoupling growth from transport in Europe
Source: Eurostat (2025)

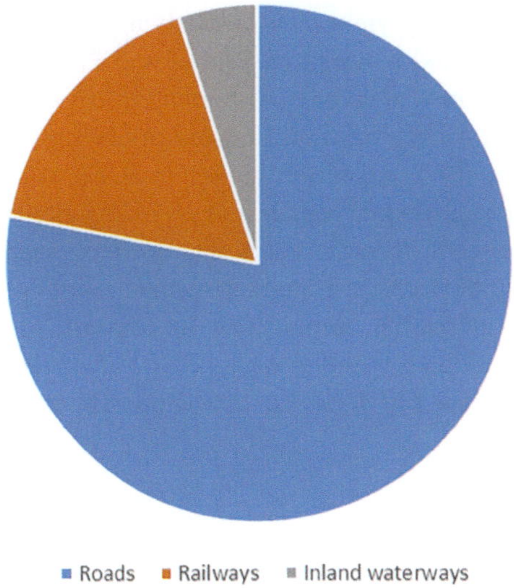

FIGURE 11.2 The proportion of land transport modes used in Europe
Source: Eurostat (2025)

With road transport accounting for more than three quarters of European land freight (Figure 11.2) which has increased in recent years, its decarbonization is central to sustainable logistics strategies.

11.2.1 Road transport

Road transport provides point-to-point flexibility, making it essential in many supply chains. It supports both local and continental deliveries through full truck load (FTL) and less-than-truckload (LTL) services. Despite its versatility, it remains emissions-intensive and heavily reliant on fossil fuels. Vehicle types are governed by specifications and regulations, with specialized trucks required for hazardous or temperature-sensitive cargo. Regulatory frameworks covering emissions, fuel types, and routing practices shape fleet investment and operational models.

Cost structures comprise fixed costs (e.g. depreciation, insurance) and variable costs (e.g. fuel, labour). Sustainability measures – such as carbon taxes and fuel surcharges – aim to internalize environmental externalities and encourage greener practices. Operational efficiencies, including route optimization and improved load factors, reduce emissions and costs. The ton-kilometre (tkm) metric serves as a standard for freight efficiency and environmental benchmarking.

Sustainability efforts focus on technological, operational, and policy innovations. Hybrid and electric vehicles offer significant emissions reductions, though they require high upfront investment. Decades of tightening European emissions regulations have fostered cleaner engine technologies. Nonetheless, smaller carriers face financial barriers to fleet renewal.

Operational optimization can yield measurable benefits. Effective route planning and scheduling reduce fuel use and congestion. Palmer and Piecyk (2010) estimate a 3 per cent CO_2 reduction via off-peak deliveries, although effectiveness depends on traffic conditions. Night deliveries, however, risk noise-related public opposition.

Capacity optimization also contributes. Holter et al. (2010) report that double-deck trailers, while increasing fuel use per vehicle, cut emissions per unit moved, offering theoretical savings of 15 per cent, though practical gains may reach only 3 per cent due to logistical limits. Planning horizons also impact sustainability. Just-in-time (JIT) logistics constrain consolidation, increasing empty runs. In contrast, long-term planning allows higher load efficiency. Halldórsson and Kovács (2010) advocate for integrated planning, while Sanchez-Rodrigues et al. (2010) link planning uncertainty to reactive, high-emission transport activity.

Note 11.1 Autonomous vehicles or 'self driving trucks'

The drive for autonomous vehicles in the freight sector is linked to a number of different trends. Congestion continues to grow in many urban locations, yet at the same time there are fewer people wanting to join the trucking profession. It can be a stressful job and often monotonous and therefore safety is a paramount concern for all road users. Alongside this there are advances in intelligent technologies allowing drivers to use their time differently to just concentrating on the road. Many new entrants in the field, including Google (Alphabet) and Tesla, are trialling new solutions to the trucking industry to capitalize on these advances. At the same time the economics of using trucks is driven not just by the variable costs of drivers but also the total cost of ownership and there are opportunities to reduce this further through automation. The current incumbents such as Daimler and Volvo are actively working on self driving trucks which in theory at least could lead to safer roads and more econ-friendly driving. For example in 2016 six convoys of semi-automated 'smart' trucks arrived in Rotterdam's harbour in an experiment that may revolutionise future road transport on Europe's roads. More than a dozen self-driving trucks made by six of Europe's largest manufacturers arrived in the port in so-called 'truck platoons' which act almost like trains but in the road and not rail. Due to more relaxed regulation autonomous truck are already making deliveries between Dallas and Houston in Texas. While this is just the beginning, technologies are rapidly becoming mature and are likely to have a significant impact on the sustainability of road freight transportation.

Source: Agence France-Presse (2016); Skores (2025)

11.2.2 Sea and inland water transport

Sea freight dominates international logistics by volume, benefiting from economies of scale and low energy intensity per tonne-kilometre. However, its long lead times and sensitivity to disruption limit its suitability for time-critical goods. The introduction of the ISO container standard in the 1970s revolutionized maritime shipping, enabling globalized trade flows.

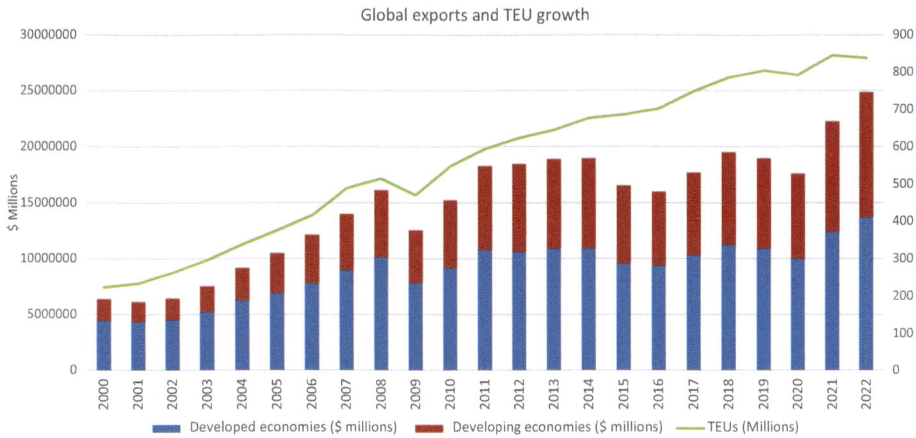

FIGURE 11.3 Global exports and container transport volumes
Source: OECD and World Bank (2025)

Shipping alliances (or conferences) play a critical role in managing capacity and pricing. While this promotes planning stability, critics argue such coordination limits price competition, prompting legal scrutiny under WTO anti-trust provisions.

Stakeholders in maritime logistics include carriers (e.g. Maersk), port agents, and freight forwarders. While sea freight is often the lowest carbon mode, emissions vary widely. Leonardi and Browne (2010) report container ship CO_2 emissions ranging from 19g to 100g CO_2e per tonne-km. Route choices, vessel design, and shipment consolidation all influence this variability. For example, hub-and-spoke models and chartered vessels reduce emissions by 23–28 per cent compared to standard routes.

Incidents such as the Costa Concordia and the Erika oil spill highlight environmental risks beyond emissions. Fuel spills, ballast water discharge, and invasive species are critical concerns in maritime regulation. Inland waterways offer similar benefits for urban freight, providing low-cost, low-emission access to city centres via rivers and canals – though infrastructure limitations remain.

11.2.3 Other transport modes

While road and maritime transport dominate, rail, air, and pipeline also play key roles. Rail offers a more sustainable alternative to long-haul road freight, especially in Europe, but its use is limited by infrastructure rigidity and intermodal transfer requirements. Air freight is used primarily for high-value, time-sensitive goods, despite its high environmental cost. Companies like Zara leverage air freight to maintain responsiveness in fast fashion, prioritizing agility over emissions.

Modal decisions must now consider both traditional performance metrics and environmental consequences. Carbon accounting and emissions reporting are becoming standard components of transport strategy. Companies are increasingly integrating sustainability criteria – such as carbon intensity, noise impact, and air quality – into procurement and network design decisions.

TABLE 11.1 Trade-offs in modal choices (1 = best, 5 = worst)

	Rail	*Road*	*Water*	*Air*	*Pipeline*
Cost	3	4	1	5	2
Speed	3	2	4	1	5
Flexibility	2	1	4	3	5
Volume/ weight limits	3	4	1	5	2
Accessibility	2	1	4	3	5
CO_2 emissions	3	4	1	5	2

Transport planning remains a decisive factor in achieving sustainability objectives. Forward planning improves load consolidation and reduces wasteful trips. Yet, trends towards shorter planning cycles and demand volatility threaten these gains. High uncertainty increases the likelihood of emergency shipments, contributing to excess fuel use and emissions.

Transport planning and modal choices are critical to both operational performance and environmental responsibility. The growing alignment between transport economics and sustainability is reshaping logistics strategy. Cleaner technologies, smarter routing, and forward planning are essential tools, but structural challenges – such as uncertain demand, capital constraints, and regulatory complexity – remain.

As companies strive for **greener, leaner logistics**, the ability to align service performance with sustainability imperatives will be a key differentiator in the global marketplace. The following section turns to inventory management and its relationship with transport planning and carbon reduction.

11.3 INVENTORY DECISIONS IN THE SUPPLY CHAINS

Inventory and transportation decisions in logistics are tightly interlinked. A reduction in inventory levels often necessitates more frequent deliveries, potentially increasing transportation costs and environmental impacts. This section provides a concise overview of inventory-related decisions and their influence on sustainability goals.

Companies hold inventory for several reasons, as outlined by Christopher (1998):

- Insurance against demand uncertainty and forecast errors;
- To offset inflexible production systems (e.g. large batch sizes);
- To seize short-term market opportunities;
- To anticipate future demand and ensure availability;
- To reduce unit costs through larger order sizes;

- To hold stock that appreciates over time (e.g. wine);
- To maintain flow and utilization across processing systems.

Inventory decisions have multiple dimensions, particularly relating to ordering and holding costs. Acquisition price may vary with order size, encouraging bulk buying through quantity discounts. However, if total logistics costs are not considered – including storage, ordering, and transportation – such decisions may result in inefficiency or excess environmental burden. Reliable demand forecasts can reduce required inventory, but uncertainty often leads to buffer stock or more frequent restocking.

Each order incurs not only the purchase cost but also administrative costs (e.g. issuing orders, communication, receiving, and checking). Frequent ordering raises these costs, while high inventory levels increase storage costs – potentially exponentially when considering product handling and space limitations.

11.3.1 Inventory replenishment models

a. Fixed-level ordering (reorder point)

This method triggers a new order when stock reaches a predefined level, based on lead-time and demand rate. The reorder point equals expected usage during lead time plus a safety stock buffer.

b. Fixed-period ordering

Inventory is reviewed at fixed intervals (e.g. weekly) and quantities ordered vary depending on remaining stock. It suits low-value, non-critical items like office supplies.

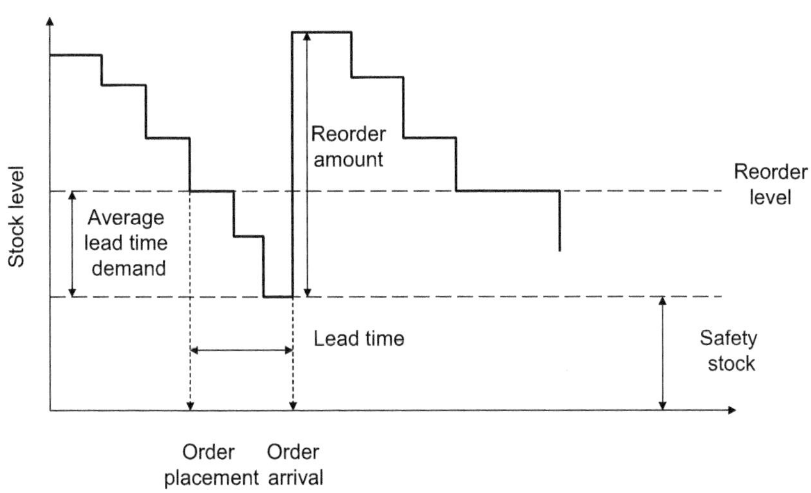

FIGURE 11.4 Reorder point inventory policy

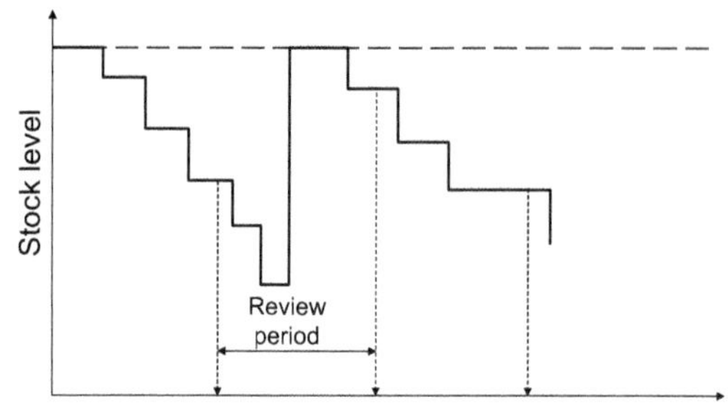

FIGURE 11.5 Fixed-period ordering

c. Economic order quantity (EOQ)

This model balances order frequency with inventory holding costs. The EOQ formula assumes even demand and steady consumption throughout the period.

$$EOQ = \sqrt{(2AS / i)}$$

where A = Annual demand, S = Ordering/setup cost which can include administrative costs for ordering including stock checks and transporting the individual orders, i = Inventory carrying cost which can include obsolescence costs, insurance, and the costs of running a warehouse. While EOQ minimizes internal costs, it may increase external costs such as environmental impacts if reduced batch sizes result in under-utilized transport.

11.3.2 Sustainability implications and trade-offs

Minimizing inventory is a common goal in lean logistics but often comes at the cost of higher transportation frequency. As fuel prices and carbon reduction targets gain prominence, many companies reassess these trade-offs. Some now tolerate higher inventory levels to reduce transportation-related emissions. For instance, Saunier Duval relaxed JIT inventory strategies to hold more stock, reducing transport frequency and emissions.

The EOQ model and similar frameworks are increasingly being adapted to account for environmental costs. Studies by Bonney and Jaber (2011) and Bouchery et al. (2012) explore integrating carbon emissions and other externalities into inventory models.

11.3.3 Summary

Modern logistics strategies often reconcile lean principles with cost efficiency and environmental performance. JIT logistics, while cost-effective, can increase emissions through frequent deliveries. Though EOQ offers theoretical optimization, its assumptions limit real-world applicability and so short-term logistics planning driven by lean philosophies can undermine sustainability (Halldórsson and Kovács, 2010). Moreover, uncertainty in demand and supply increases unplanned transport needs (Sanchez-Rodrigues et al., 2010), leading to inefficiencies and environmental degradation.

Inventory decisions are central to logistics efficiency and environmental sustainability. Balancing ordering costs, stock levels, and transportation impacts is complex – particularly under uncertain demand and tight service level expectations. Emerging research on integrating carbon costs and externalities into inventory models is promising. For now, many companies are adopting hybrid approaches, such as holding more stock strategically, extending planning horizons, or accepting higher inventory costs to lower emissions and enhance resilience.

11.4 LOCATION DECISION-MAKING

One of the key decision variables in logistics planning in addition to transport and inventory is the location of sites in a supply chain. It is clear that transportation costs are directly related to the location of factories, warehouses, and retailers, and ultimately final customers, so one of the options in logistics strategy is to change locations to balance the requirements of costs and service levels (ReVelle and Eiselt, 2005). As mentioned in the next chapter, companies like Amazon are using location advantage to provide new service levels (next day delivery) putting e-commerce retailers in direct competition with traditional sales channels. It is not only the end of the supply chain where location decisions are critical however, these decisions occur throughout, from raw material choices (cement works next to sources of lime) to co-location of suppliers to car manufacturers in supplier parks to reduce logistics costs and improve responsiveness (Howard et al., 2006). Yet, making decisions on location is not straight-forward as there are many variables and constraints to take into account. This section provides a brief overview of the main approaches and how sustainability indicators can be included in these decision models.

At a basic level the choice of locations for a warehouse or factory can be based on the relationship between fixed and variable cost, and the overall volume of demand likely for the location. This is known as breakeven analysis and facilitates the decision on which sites to choose based on each site's specific cost structure and how efficiently the site can process orders. From a sustainability standpoint the fixed costs can include environmental licenses to operate and variable costs can be impacted social charges for personnel, therefore making some sites less favourable because of these additional costs. This has led to the 'pollution haven hypothesis' where companies choose sites because of the lowest cost including environmental costs, which are often in regions and countries with low regulation levels (Smarzynska and Wei, 2001). However, the academic evidence for this is rather weak (Millimet and List, 2004).

A second popular location decision model uses multi-criteria decision making as the core component. This approach improves on breakeven analysis by expanding the comparison from only looking at costs to including other decision variables such as skills and community-based factors. While there are many rigorous methods for this type of analysis, such as analytical hierarchy processes or AHP for short (Alberto, 2000), many companies tend to use a simple weighted factor approach. Selecting factors and allocating importance weights to them is typically done by a cross-functional group of managers who have a stake in the site selection decision – logistics, production, sales, and human resources (Korpela and Lehmusvaara, 1999). Once weights are decided the group then compares scores across a number of preselected/pre-existing locations. While it is possible to add criteria related to environmental laws or social conditions there is no significant research that has reviewed these practices. More recently geopolitical factors are also being considered in such decision-making where the risk of disruption is gaining importance (Bednarski et al., 2025)

The two previous examples of decision-making models for location assume that locations are already known and that managers just need to select between them. In logistics networks this is not always possible especially when setting up a new structure to service multiple customers from multiple suppliers. Thus the centre of gravity method allows a comparison of geographic locations based on optimizing the costs of transport from suppliers to customers through a centralized warehouse location (de la Fuente and Lozano, 1998). As the goal is to minimize transport costs overall, given differing demand levels, one might assume that environmental impacts from emissions are also reduced by the selected location. Again there is very little research that has tested this approach to examine costs and emissions, but of the few studies one at least has shown that there is not necessarily a direct link, where the cost optimum might not be the environmental optimum (Harris et al., 2011). Further, these models are very sensitive to vehicle utilization levels, which is often very difficult to model realistically due to aforementioned problems of short planning cycles and uncertainties. Recent reviews of network design modelling research has shown that sustainability metrics are being included more and more and methods are being proposed to better integrate sustainability into location decision making (Eskandarpour et al., 2015).

11.5 REVERSE LOGISTICS

Reverse logistics refers to the process of moving goods from their typical final destination for the purpose of capturing value or proper disposal. With the rise of e-commerce, companies increasingly face the logistical and financial challenges of handling returns. These reverse movements often exceed the cost and carbon footprint of initial deliveries. Stock (1992) defines reverse logistics as encompassing returns, recycling, repairs, refurbishing, and waste management.

Despite higher costs, reverse logistics can enhance profitability by enabling customer loyalty, creating secondary sales channels, and repositioning unsold stock. Carter and Ellram (1998) note cost-saving opportunities in recovering raw materials from returned goods, reducing dependency on virgin resources. Industries vary in return rates; for instance, publishing has mature systems, whereas online electronics sales still lag behind.

Returns can be classified by their cause. Customer returns arise from unmet expectations, such as incorrect sizing in online clothing purchases. Firms like La Redoute use postal returns to manage this efficiently. Marketing returns occur when goods are in the wrong location or season, often resold via outlet stores. Asset returns include reusable packaging like pallets and stillages, which must be tracked to prevent loss. European packaging regulations encourage reusable designs.

Faulty product returns (recalls) are common in automotive and food sectors, where defective items must be withdrawn swiftly. Tracking ownership of items like cars

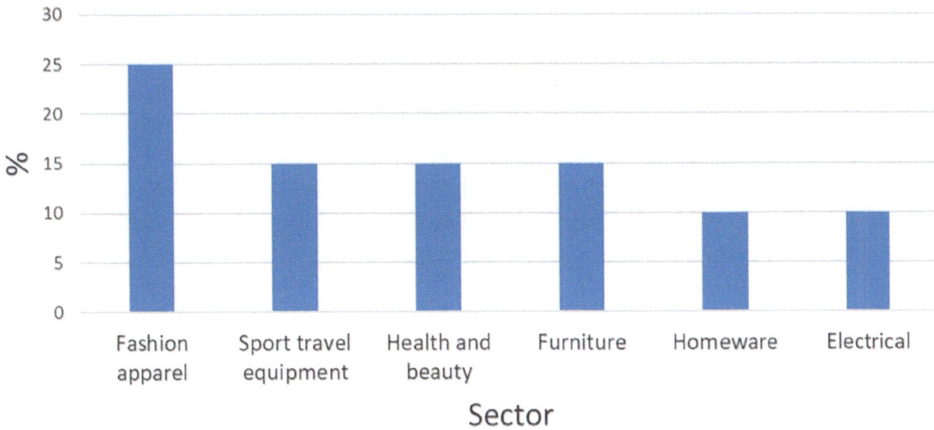

FIGURE 11.6 Sample return rates by industry
Source: Ram (2016)

complicates recall logistics. Environmental returns stem from legislation such as WEEE and ELV directives, which mandate proper disposal of electronics and vehicles to reduce landfill.

Three major challenges in reverse logistics are product acquisition, quality assessment, and disposition. Locating used products is often difficult, especially when ownership has changed. Quality assessment is essential to determine the viability of reuse. Returned items are typically sorted by condition to determine whether to refurbish, remanufacture, recycle, or dispose.

Figure 11.7 outlines possible disposition routes: repair (common for vehicle recalls), reconditioning (e.g. used laptops), remanufacturing (full disassembly and rebuild), or recycling of raw materials. Products unsuitable for recovery are discarded. Each path depends on cost, product structure, and market demand.

The Xerox reverse logistics example demonstrates a sophisticated closed-loop system. Photocopiers, primarily leased not sold, are returned once they become unreliable. Xerox coordinates returns to its Asset Recovery Centre (ARC) using third-party logistics. Returned machines undergo evaluation and are either remanufactured or dismantled for parts recycling. Plastic components like ABS are reprocessed onsite, reducing waste and material transport.

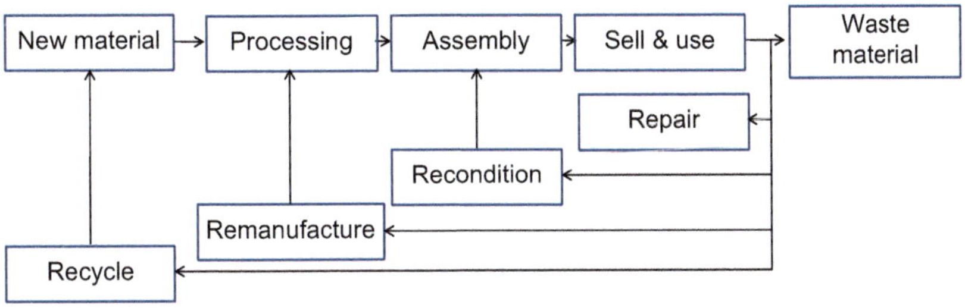

FIGURE 11.7 The various routes for returned products

Xerox's model is effective due to its service-based business model, where availability and uptime are prioritized over ownership. This incentivizes Xerox to maintain efficient reverse flows and reuse assets wherever possible. The system meets European regulatory standards while reducing environmental impact and achieving high material recovery rates.

Reverse logistics, though costly and complex, supports both environmental and financial objectives. With increasing regulatory pressure and consumer expectations around sustainability, companies are investing in better tracking, assessment, and recovery systems to build circular supply chains.

11.6 LOGISTICS SERVICE PROVIDERS

It is worth mentioning here that while logistics is a core element of supply chain management and is the basis for global trade; many companies outsource their logistics processes to specialist service providers. There are many reasons for this but in short companies often have neither the global reach nor the specific competencies to manage the physical flow of goods from suppliers to end customers (Langley et al., 2003). For this reason a huge industry has grown out of the provision of logistics services. The development started with the use of local transport contractors who are able to reach a local population of customers and has now developed into a multibillion dollar sector with large logistics firms such as DHL, UPS, and TNT.

The key reasons for using third-party logistics providers have remained largely constant over the years with cost reduction being the main driver, mainly due to the reduced need for capital investment in transport assets and warehousing. Service level is the second most important reason with expectations on speed and reliability being essential. Flexibility is also seen as important element, probably enabling better service levels, but also from a strategic perspective. Other drivers include change management imperatives and the need to focus on core competences such as manufacturing or managing the customer interface (van Laarhoven et al., 2000).

Part of this argument is the opportunity for economies of scale, whereby the capacity of the provider is shared across a number of customers through consolidation and so the unit costs fall (Wu and Dunn, 1995). This is particularly important in the automotive industry where delivery quantities are low in order to minimize inventory costs driven by lean initiatives. An example of consolidation of logistics flows on the distribution and delivery side is given later in the chapter.

Managers raise numerous concerns about contracting to third-party logistics providers especially during the pre-contract phase of negotiations. Issues such as trust and adequate levels of knowledge are often cited as difficulties, but also the risks of over-dependence and loss of control. During third-party logistics contracts many of these negative perceptions decline although lack of service quality and problems of IT integration often remain in place (van Laarhoven et al., 2000). There are many criteria that can be used to help select logistics service providers. While many of these criteria are common with other supplier selection indicators (as discussed in Chapter 2), there are some that could be considered specific to logistics especially measures of reliability and speed, but also compatibility of planning systems (Razzaque and Sheng, 1998). Today companies are coming to realize that many of their environmental impacts are rooted in the supply chain, and especially the transportation links between customer and suppliers. Therefore sustainability has arisen as an additional criterion for choosing logistics service providers (Wolf and Seuring, 2010). Although criteria related to sustainability are now well used in logistics provider selection (Kudla and Klaas-Wissing, 2012), they are often more for information purposes than really to 'deselect' lower performing providers. In fact the evidence shows that problems persist in that shippers make inconsistent demands and that real cooperation on improving environmental performance with logistics providers can be a challenge (Wolf and Seuring, 2010).

Logistics service providers have started to take on broader roles in supply chain management beyond managing transport and warehousing operations. This increased strategic involvement has led to terms such as 4th Party Logistics Providers (4PLs) or even supply chain orchestrators (e.g. TriVizor). The following table (Table 11.2) shows classifications of LSPs showing that a number of factors influence whether they will take on more complex tasks in the supply chain for their clients. From this the factors of competence, uncertainty, customization, and complexity all play a role in whether LSPs will take on more complex and strategic activities in the supply chain.

TABLE 11.2 The development and scope of logistics services providers

Dimensions	*Roles and services*	*References*
Scope of outsourced activities	Transport Transport and warehousing Transport warehousing and additional services Transport warehousing and additional services, and value add activities 4PL	Fabbe-Costes et al., 2008; Halldórsson and Skjøtt-Larsen, 2004
Competence (and asset specificity) and degree of integration	Market exchange Customized solutions Joint logistics solutions (In house solutions)	Halldórsson and Skjøtt-Larsen, 2004
Based on levels of buyer uncertainty and providers experience	Translating Re-engineering Fine-tuning Developing	Selviaridis et al., 2013
Complexity of distribution collaboration and intensity of collaboration	Transactional 3PL Relational 3PL Problem solving 4PL Collaboration Specialist	Hingley et al., 2011

Source: Based on Michon and Miemczyk (2014)

11.7 CHANNELS TO MARKET

Firms adopt various channels to market depending on strategic objectives such as product availability, customer service levels, cost efficiency, and information feedback. The structure and function of a chosen channel influence a firm's ability to sell effectively, especially when specialized knowledge or technical support is required. Additionally, channels must align with commercial constraints, including order sizes, inventory levels, and delivery expectations.

According to Coughlan et al. (2006), the key functions of marketing channels include carrying inventory, demand generation, physical distribution, after-sales service, and offering customer credit. Each function contributes to operational performance. For example, inventory within the channel helps meet demand quickly (within hours in some cases, see Note 11.2), while reliable physical distribution ensures lead-time targets are met. Likewise, providing credit can widen access to customer segments.

Note 11.2 Amazon's new ways to reach consumers

While Amazon has received plenty of press coverage over its trialling of drones as a means to deliver to customers this is only one of the many of their innovations to distribute better. One of the key investment areas is artificial intelligence (AI, and use of big data) to provide far better predictions of what customers will buy and where these consumers are located. This is even to the extent that Amazon are willing to place certain items on trucks without an order, 'betting' that there will be a customer on the truck's route who needs the product in the next few hours. "When we place a product in the right place ahead of time, before you click buy, it's traveling less distance, which is a win for speed and sustainability". The combination of autonomous vehicles, whether drones or road based vehicles, AI, big data, and connected devices are being heralded to bring a new generation of distribution systems, spearheaded by the likes of Amazon. Generative AI is already being used by their robots in warehouses combined with vision technology to avoid objects. Yet these developments are accelerating faster than the pace of regulation and the question of societal impacts is far from being answered.

Source: Nichols (n.d.); Tarasov (2024)

Selecting an appropriate channel also involves analyzing specific product and market characteristics. Fast-moving consumer goods may require multilayered distribution involving regional and local warehouses, whereas niche or high-value products may be delivered directly. Technical products – such as vehicles – often necessitate specialized retailers to support customer education. Perishable goods or those with 'sell by' dates require short, responsive channels. Hazardous or sensitive goods demand specialized handling and compliance.

Product factors	*Customer factors*
Unit value Product characteristics Replacement rate Gross margin Adjustment Rate of technological change (including fashion changes) Technical complexity Product complexity Product life-cycle stage Volatility of demand Brand positioning on quality Perishability	Frequency of purchase Purchasing effort Rapidity of consumption Significance of purchase Waiting time Searching time Significance of each individual purchase to the consumer Consumer need for service (before, during, or after sale) Frequency of purchase Rapidity of consumption Extent of usage (number and variety of consumers and variety)
Market factors Target focus on mass market Rate of technological change Intensity of competition Geographic concentration of market	*Company factors* Range of products Order size Market share Desire of control Retailer investments Number of support programs Promotion budget Size of the firm

FIGURE 11.8 Channel choice factors

Importantly, channel design decisions have environmental implications. Complex, multi-tiered channels can lead to frequent, low-volume deliveries, raising transport costs and carbon emissions. Channel efficiency must therefore be balanced with sustainability goals, so firms increasingly consider how channel structures influence both customer experience and environmental impact, particularly in response to growing regulatory and stakeholder pressures.

11.7.1 Main channel structures

The aim of channel structures is to organize the link between production and the final customer, often a retailer – although direct links by-passing the retailer are becoming more and more common. The following figure outlines the main possible configurations within distribution channels.

11.7.2 Direct and indirect channels

In modern supply chains, indirect and direct-to-customer channels offer different operational structures and strategic implications. Over time, manufacturer control over logistics infrastructure – such as owning distribution centres (DCs) – has declined. Exceptions like

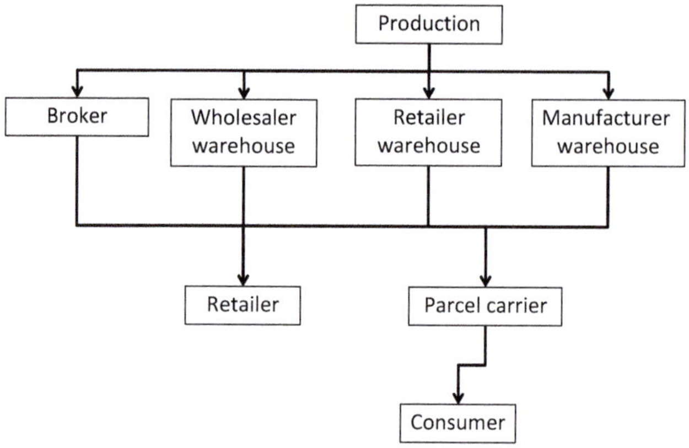

FIGURE 11.9 The main channels to market structures

the brewing industry still retain this model due to specific product handling needs. While retailers often control logistics, designing routes and managing DCs, many now outsource transport and facility operations to third-party logistics providers, while retaining strategic oversight.

Wholesalers remain important in servicing small, independent retailers. They aggregate demand, benefit from volume discounts, and typically own warehousing and transport assets tailored to specific product categories. For instance, Brakes in the UK supports small food businesses by offering specialized cold-chain services as well as providing local food sourcing opportunities (which is not always the most sustainable overall, see box 11.3).

Note 11.3 Reducing food miles – a flawed concept

For a number of years retailers focused on the food miles indicator to show improved sustainability of the food distribution process. However recent studies are beginning to show that this approach is overly simplistic and simply reducing the distance travelled by food does not necessarily equate to better environmental and social implications. For example the assumption that growing vegetables locally to avoid inter-continental transport is not necessarily less carbon intensive when local greenhouses are used to grow food compared with growing outside but overseas. Instead companies are starting to look at carbon footprint of the whole process of growing, delivering, and selling our food – for example one company, G's Fresh, decided to "move salad onion production to Senegal, with the crop freighted by ship rather than being grown and flown from Mexico and Egypt. This reduced greenhouse gas emission by nearly 8000 kg CO_2 per tonne of produce – a reduction of over 90%".

Source: University of Bangor (2014)

Third-party logistics companies have also developed niche channel structures, particularly in sectors like garments or glass, requiring tailored handling. Less common are broker-based channels, which facilitate trade without influencing physical distribution. These structures serve mainly marketing and coordination functions.

Direct-to-customer channels, especially those enabled by the internet, have reshaped retail logistics in recent years. E-commerce giants like Amazon, Shein, and Temu and legacy mail-order firms like La Redoute utilize regional warehouses and third-party parcel services for last-mile delivery. These B2C channels offer wide product ranges and fast delivery, but customers face waiting times, additional delivery charges, and potentially complex reverse logistics.

Retailers have responded with multi-channel or omni-channel models, combining physical stores and online sales. Grocers, in particular, face challenges with time-sensitive goods; for example, Tesco initially managed internet orders via regional DCs but struggled with complexity. The model evolved to 'click and collect' systems, where orders are prepared at local stores for customer pickup. This approach, adopted by Tesco in the UK and Carrefour in France, balances operational control with customer convenience.

11.7.3 Key distribution channel issues

In addition to physical distribution concerns, several strategic issues within marketing channels affect performance, especially in B2B markets where alignment between suppliers and assemblers is essential relating to product ownership, risk-sharing, and the organization of ordering and payment (Coughlan et al., 2006). Ownership timing influences pricing, inventory visibility, and working capital. Models such as vendor-managed inventory (VMI) and consignment stock allow manufacturers to retain control of stock until use, reducing duplication and potentially improving stock efficiency.

Ownership transfers also impacts pricing where multiple handovers through intermediaries can inflate final prices due to added margins. Meanwhile, manufacturers may remain involved post-sale via promotional activities – such as in-store merchandizing – or financial arrangements. For example, automotive manufacturers often provide consumer financing through internal credit divisions, enabling broader market reach while maintaining influence over the customer journey.

Risk-sharing mechanisms also play a key role in balancing inventory-related uncertainties. Manufacturers typically prefer that retailers hold sufficient stock to ensure sales continuity, while retailers aim to minimize overstock and markdowns. Buyback agreements shift some risk back to manufacturers, encouraging higher retail inventory but increasing demand distortion and reverse logistics costs. Revenue-sharing models and quantity flexibility contracts offer more collaborative risk management, especially in volatile sectors like fashion.

These arrangements have important sustainability implications. Poorly coordinated stock ownership and risk-sharing can increase inventory waste, overproduction, and unnecessary reverse logistics – all contributing to environmental harm. In contrast, integrated channel partnerships supported by accurate point-of-sale data and flexible inventory models can minimize waste, reduce returns, and lower carbon emissions. As sustainability becomes a core strategic priority, aligning channel practices with environmental performance is increasingly vital.

11.8 PHYSICAL DISTRIBUTION STRUCTURES

The two central drivers of distribution network design are cost and service levels, particularly inventory and transportation costs. As previously discussed, logistics costs primarily arise from holding stock and moving products across the network. Effective physical distribution structures must, wherever possible, consider the total cost – a combination of inventory and transport costs – while also ensuring service level commitments such as delivery speed and product availability, or even Total Value Contribution (Gray et al., 2020).

From a sustainability perspective, total cost optimization must also account for environmental externalities. These include greenhouse gas emissions from transport, energy use in storage facilities, and waste from excess or obsolete inventory. The strategic placement of stock across a supply network has a significant bearing on not only service performance but also environmental performance. Stock positioning should therefore be understood vertically (proximity to the customer) and horizontally (coverage across locations), factoring in both cost efficiency and carbon reduction goals.

11.8.1 Order fulfilment and the P:D ratio lead-time gap

Order fulfilment and the P:D ratio are closely linked in shaping customer service levels and distribution performance. The P:D ratio – production lead-time to demand lead-time – defines how responsive the supply chain must be, while fulfilment processes determine the speed and efficiency of that response. Together, they influence how well firms can meet delivery expectations sustainably and reliably.

Order fulfilment, or the order management cycle, comprises multiple sub-processes ranging from order generation and processing to inventory retrieval and dispatch (Croxton, 2003; Shapiro et al., 2001). Delays may occur due to manual systems, fragmented workflows, or poor integration across departments. ERP systems have helped streamline these processes, though smaller firms still struggle with spreadsheet-based operations. In e-commerce, fulfilment plays a decisive role in customer satisfaction, where delivery speed, reliability, and flexibility are expected to replicate in-store experiences (Zeithaml et al., 2002; Kawa and Zdrenka, 2024).

Reliability, rather than just speed, is the key driver of satisfaction (Wolfinbarger and Gilly, 2002), and improvements depend as much on organizational learning and responsiveness as on technology (Hult et al., 2002). From a sustainability perspective, fragmented or inefficient fulfilment can lead to excessive expedited shipping, increasing emissions and operational costs.

This pressure is magnified by the lead-time gap. When customer expectations (demand lead-time) are shorter than production capabilities (production lead-time), firms must bridge the gap through inventory buffers or rapid logistics (Mather, 1988). As shown in Figure 11.3, a low P:D ratio is desirable but difficult to achieve for globally sourced, fast-moving items. To compensate, inventory may be positioned closer to market, and flexible, localized fulfilment systems deployed.

Effective physical distribution depends on the alignment of fulfilment capabilities with lead-time expectations. Integrating digital systems, reducing internal inefficiencies, and

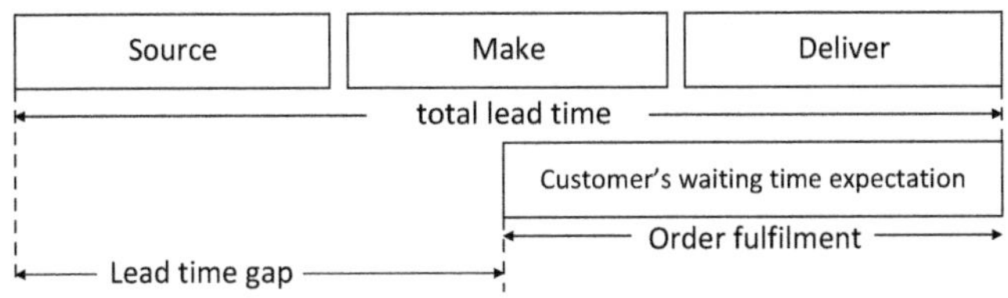

FIGURE 11.10 The P:D ratio and lead-time gap

designing distribution networks that balance speed with sustainability are essential for optimizing service and environmental performance. The following are the main distribution network designs to cope with the above issues.

11.8.2 Manufacturer direct shipments

In this model, finished goods are held at the manufacturer's facility and shipped directly to end customers once orders are received. This structure minimizes inventory costs by aggregating demand and limiting stock duplication across locations. It is particularly beneficial for high-value, low-demand products such as specialized machinery or consumer electronics.

However, this approach can result in higher transportation costs – particularly when using parcel carriers for last-mile delivery – and may also increase emissions due to lack of consolidation. Furthermore, when customers order multiple items from different manufacturers (e.g. a PC and monitor), deliveries may arrive separately, causing customer dissatisfaction and increasing packaging and carbon footprint.

While cost-effective from an inventory standpoint, sustainable application of direct shipments requires measures such as route optimization, carbon-offsetting programmes, and coordination across supply partners to minimize the ecological impact of fragmented deliveries.

11.8.3 Direct shipment to a cross-dock, direct shipment to customer

This hybrid structure, also called merge-in-transit, consolidates shipments from multiple manufacturers at a cross-dock facility before distributing them to customers. Originating from just-in-time (JIT) logistics practices, this model reduces inventory at distribution centres by facilitating near-immediate trans-shipment.

This approach is widely used in sectors like automotive manufacturing, where synchronized inbound deliveries support lean production lines. However, high coordination and data visibility are critical, as misalignment can lead to stockouts or missed delivery windows. In sustainability terms, the reduced need for warehousing can lower energy usage, but increased transportation complexity may raise fuel consumption unless optimally managed.

Efficient cross-docking, supported by digital tracking and shared logistics platforms, can align economic efficiency with environmental stewardship, especially when supported by low-emission transport modes or consolidated vehicle use.

11.8.4 Multiple pick-ups through a consolidation centre with multiple drop delivery

This more traditional model involves collecting small batches from multiple suppliers and consolidating them at a distribution centre (DC) for onward delivery to retailers or consumers. The DC serves as a buffer to match supply and demand variability, making it ideal for perishable or fast-moving goods such as food products.

This structure is especially relevant for large retailers with centralized logistics (e.g. supermarket chains), which require flexibility to serve varied and dispersed demand. For instance, the distribution of yoghurt, with multiple varieties and packaging formats, benefits from centralized control that minimizes waste and ensures product freshness.

However, consolidation centres require sophisticated information systems and incur higher operational costs. From a sustainability standpoint, they offer significant potential. By pooling deliveries and optimizing vehicle loads, they reduce road congestion, fuel usage, and emissions. Coordinated scheduling and load sharing – especially through third-party logistics providers – enable efficient, low-impact delivery systems aligned with circular supply chain principles.

Selecting between direct delivery, cross-docking, or multi-drop consolidation depends on factors such as product value, demand volatility, service expectations, and sustainability goals. As product ranges expand and online orders surge, firms must design physical distribution structures that are both resilient and environmentally responsible. Research studies highlight the trade-offs, for example where a consumer's journey often contributes more carbon than the entire logistics chain and so an alternative to reaching customers is needed (Halldórsson and Wehner, 2020). Hence, the design of physical distribution must consider not only efficiency and responsiveness but also the total environmental footprint. The following section explores how these decisions affect last-mile logistics and the broader challenge of sustainable urban distribution.

11.9 LAST MILE AND CITY LOGISTICS

This section deals with the final delivery portion to the end customer or as in most cases to a final retail location often in urban settings. This is often known as last mile logistics and can be one of the most costly parts of the distribution chain in terms of transport, but also the one where the customer directly experiences the impact of service level especially if things go wrong (Fernie et al., 2010). Related to this is the fact that the majority of 'last mile' operations occur in the urban environment. As urban infrastructure continues to be under pressure from the multitude of users, and is also where populations are most sensitive to damaging effects of pollution and noise and so on, the management of distribution systems takes on a clear social dimension. From this, a strand of logistics has developed known as city logistics which is marked by many successful and failed examples of how a balance can be achieved between competitive priorities and social externalities.

11.9.1 Last mile delivery

Last mile delivery refers to the final leg of a product's journey from manufacturer or distribution centre to the end user. Although typically associated with home deliveries, the last mile may also serve businesses such as retailers or industrial clients.

The structure and efficiency of last mile logistics is largely shaped by the channel to market. The rise of e-commerce has made home delivery an essential part of many retailers' offerings. In this model, products are delivered either from a centralized distribution centre (DC) or local store, or prepared for customer collection. Delivery efficiency varies widely. For example, a DC-based home delivery route may complete 14–18 drops in an eight-hour shift, whereas store-based operations can reach 16–20. In contrast, B2B deliveries – such as those by Staples or OfficeDepot – may handle up to 40 deliveries in a similar timeframe due to concentrated customer locations and broader delivery windows (Boyer et al., 2005).

However, this model presents logistical challenges. Single-item picking, increased handling, and the need for temperature-controlled vehicles (e.g. for fresh food) all add operational complexity and cost. Tesco, for instance, modified vans to deliver frozen, chilled, and ambient items in one journey.

A key sustainability issue in last mile delivery is its environmental impact relative to traditional retail. Research shows that consolidated home delivery can reduce emissions versus individual car trips to stores (Edwards et al., 2011). However, missed deliveries and returns can significantly offset these benefits, as shown in Table 11.2. Failed attempts often require redelivery or alternative arrangements, increasing emissions and undermining efficiency. Cultural and legal differences influence how failed deliveries are handled – ranging from leaving items with neighbours to requiring specific time slots.

TABLE 11.3 Comparison of home delivery options

Shopping activity type	gCO_2	Factor
Bus travel during busy period (five or more items bought)	78	0.43
Standard home delivery drop	**181**	**1.00**
30 per cent first-time delivery failure rate	235	1.30
Trip chain by bus (shopping 25 per cent of distance)	316	1.75
Average shopping trip by bus	1265	6.99
Average shopping trip by car	**4274**	**23.61**
Home delivery drop with consumer return via retailer	4509	24.91
Failed delivery, consumer collection via local warehouse	**5188**	**28.66**

Source: Edwards and McKinnon (2009)

One persistent trade-off in last mile logistics is speed versus sustainability. The increasing demand for responsiveness – faster, more flexible delivery – raises environmental costs when stock is no longer held at retailers (Halldórsson and Wehner, 2020).

In summary, last mile delivery is a critical and increasingly complex part of the supply chain. As e-commerce and consumer expectations evolve, firms must balance delivery flexibility with environmental responsibility. Investments in technology, delivery consolidation, and carbon-efficient routing will be essential to ensure last mile systems are both customer-centred and sustainable.

11.9.2 City logistics

Urban freight distribution, particularly in dense city centres, poses significant sustainability challenges including air pollution, noise, and congestion (O'Connor, 2010). As a response, the field of 'city logistics' has emerged to address the complex trade-offs of delivering goods in urban environments.

There are three main strategies for managing urban deliveries. The first involves delivery rationalization, aiming to reduce the number of trucks entering cities. This is typically achieved by restricting delivery times – often avoiding peak traffic or daytime hours. However, concentrating deliveries in narrow time windows can create freight movement peaks, complicating coordination. Additionally, aligning delivery and pick-up times is difficult, often resulting in empty return journeys. Attempts to coordinate deliveries among retailers face challenges in synchronization and handling complexity, especially across sectors like retail and waste.

The second strategy uses shared freight facilities, such as urban consolidation centres or district-level hubs. These aim to reduce trip frequency and add value through centralized logistics services. While effective in theory, many rely on public subsidies and struggle with financial viability once support ends. The Tenjin project in Fukuoka, Japan, demonstrated success by consolidating routes where over 60 per cent of trucks previously overlapped (Browne et al., 2008).

Note 11.4 City logistics in London

Being the largest city in Europe, London has been at the forefront of urban logistics innovations for many years with the London mayor Sadiq Khan's manifesto commitments including improving air quality, ensuring safety, and tackling congestion.

London is a net importer of goods, where road is the main mode of transport with around 130 million tonnes delivered in 2012 (water – 8.7, rail 6.7, and air 1.6 million tonnes each). Heavy goods vehicles movements have been stable over the years, but light goods vehicles, with nearly 4 billion vehicle Kms in 2012 (Allen et al., 2014), are increasing rapidly. This is partly from growing home delivery services with light goods transport likely to increase by 20% in the next 10 years or so (Mayor of London, n.d.).

One example to is the cross river partnership, where the trial of a zero-emission freight hub at Waterloo Station distributes parcels from vans to electrically-assisted cargo bikes in the final leg. This kind of hub reduces the number of conventional van trips in dense urban areas (Logistics UK, 2025).

Other initiatives in London include timed deliveries to reduce congestion. Transport for London has set itself a target of retiming 500 sites and 4,000 deliveries (currently reaching 144 sites), this also means engaging with over 200 stakeholders to find the right solutions. Working with these stakeholders companies such as McDonalds, Waitrose, Savers and DHL have saved cost, CO_2 impacts and time by shifting to earlier deliveries avoiding the 7am-11am peak (Freight in the City, 2016).

To overcome the issue of missed home deliveries there are now more 'Click and Collect' options creating a network across London where consumers can pick up their online orders without generating more traffic. Service providers include Amazon Locker, Parcelly, CollectPLus, and HubBox, offering an alternative delivery option to retailers.

Source: Mayor of London (n.d.); Logistics UK (2025); Transport for London (n.d.)

The third strategy involves changing delivery modes (Nemoto et al., 2006). Smaller vehicles like vans and bikes offer better access and lower congestion impact, though they require more trips. Mixed-mode systems, such as book deliveries via Seoul's metro, show potential, while others, like Amsterdam's cargo tram, have failed due to cost or integration issues. Most recently during and since the Covid-19 pandemic the rise in food delivery services has raised many social issues linked to worker safety and general employee protections linked to the gig economy and so this has become a contentious issue in many cities (Puram, 2022).

Despite the benefits, all strategies raise unit delivery costs due to extra handling, coordination, and reduced efficiency. Retailers are reluctant to absorb these costs and as environmental externalities – like pollution and health and safety impacts – are not reflected in delivery pricing, they fall on the public. Policy tools such as congestion charges, employment laws, and subsidies may help internalize these costs and promote more sustainable urban logistics.

11.10 CASE STUDY: DHL'S SUSTAINABLE LOGISTICS STRATEGY

In DHL's 2024 environment and energy report Dr Tobias Mayer, DP DHL CEO, reiterated their sustainability ambitions:

> As a logistics company we have a responsibility to make our business cleaner. Which is why we have been a trailblazer in low-carbon logistics, and we will continue to do just that. Not only because it's the right thing to do – but

> also because sustainability offers us an opportunity to grow as we help our customers decarbonize and fulfil their greenhouse reduction commitments. By offering Green Logistics of Choice, we are underscoring our responsibility and our commitment.

The ambitious targets for 2030 and 2050 have been reinforced in recent years with DHL aiming for net zero by 2050 in alignment with the Paris climate goals agreement. By way of an intermediate milestone to net zero DHL commits to reducing scope 1–2 emissions by 42 per cent and scope 3 emissions by 25 per cent by 2030, based on 2021 emission levels. They have already introduced more than 66 per cent of their last mile deliveries by electric transport means and more than 30 per cent of aviation transport uses sustainable aviation fuel.

In a recent interview the head of sustainability made the following observations, regarding the last mile delivery (McKinsey, 2022).

> The biggest challenge is decarbonizing road transportation, and not just for us but for the entire logistics industry. We are probably a couple of years behind passenger EVs, but the technologies are there … In Germany, we run 20,000 electric vehicles [EVs] every day – out of 60,000 total vehicles – to deliver parcels and letters. The fleet of delivery bicycles has been transformed to a fleet of 19,000 e-bikes and e-trikes … also what we try to do is move as much volume as we can from road to rail on our parcel network, which is currently about 6 percent. It might sound like a small number, but that's more than a hundred million parcels every year – a hundred million parcels that used to travel by diesel truck.

The group offers standardized products as well as innovative and tailored solutions – from dialog marketing to industrial supply chains. It is organized into four operating divisions, each of which operates under the control of its own divisional headquarters:

- The EXPRESS division, transport of urgent documents and goods, primarily as time-definite international shipments (TDI).
- The GLOBAL FORWARDING, FREIGHT division handles the carriage of goods by rail, road, air, and sea.
- The SUPPLY CHAIN division is the global market leader in contract logistics, providing warehousing, managed transport, and value-added services at every link in the supply chain for customers in a variety of industries.
- The POST and PARCEL is the only provider of universal postal services in Germany. It delivers mail and parcels throughout Germany and internationally, and proposes press distribution services and electronic services as well.
- The E-COMMERCE division, domestic parcel transport in selected countries in Europe and Asia as well as in the USA. Deferred cross-border services to, from, and within Europe, as well as to and from the United States.

Starting out in 1997, Deutsche Post expanded to the global level, in order to respond to growing customers' demands of a single service provider for all of their domestic and international shipping activities. By 1998 they proposed a European express service, and then expanded its strategy worldwide through acquisitions. Deutsche Post World Net completed the purchase of DHL in 2002 and of Airborne Express in 2003 and integrated it into DHL, which is now known as DHL Express.

For Deutsche Post DHL – and by expansion any company in the logistics industry – there are a wide number of sustainability related influencing factors, as follows.

The transport industry worldwide is one of the top 4 contributors to greenhouse gasses at 14 per cent (Stern, 2007) and Deutsche Post DHL, with a global presence through a both owned and subcontracted fleet (trucks, vans, planes) contributes significantly to that number. According to a recent logistics and transportation survey conducted by Transport Intelligence, 73 per cent of respondents who award logistics contracts include sections on environmental compliance in the contract. Only 46 per cent, though, actually make provision for the extra costs involved. In 2008, two-thirds of Deutsche Post DHL's top customers had concrete reduction targets and expected Deutsche Post DHL to contribute to achieving their targets. Major competitors such as TNT and key industry players like Lufthansa had equally announced corporate climate initiatives. Finally, rising fuels costs are both a threat and an opportunity; it is an opportunity for those who move fast and efficiently as fuel efficient operations can be the source of a sustainable competitive cost advantage while those companies who move too slowly or make sub-optimal choices will be hit with a double cost disadvantage: first of all because the operating costs grow more quickly than those of best-in-class competitors and secondly because legislation is increasingly penalizing fuel-inefficient products and services.

Environmental legislation has been implemented globally – including emerging markets such as China and India – and is becoming increasingly demanding on all stakeholders in the logistics industry. Cost increase from legislation alone could increase cost to €1.3 billion by 2020, reducing EBIT margin by 1 percentage point. Furthermore, cities around the world are attempting to reduce emissions and optimize traffic flows in the city centres. As these initiatives are quite diverse, the impact to DP DHL will vary case-by-case, however very often low-emission vehicles get preferential treatment. At the same time legislation – typically through taxation and subsidization – is lifting the economic barriers that are holding back the introduction to sustainable practices.

As a low-carbon economy will inevitably become reality over the next two decades, carbon-friendly technological innovation is booming. Secondly, the topic of carbon is still high on the agenda of all economic actors – governments, companies, and citizens – reducing the traditional cost and risk barriers associated with the introduction of new technology. That in turn accelerates the general market acceptance of such technology. This means there is considerable technological advancement and new technology is able to compete with traditional technology relatively quickly.

In brief, the forces at work are diverse and impact directly on the basic business fundamentals of DP DHL – and any logistics company.

In 2001 DHL set up a corporate-level Policy and Environment team, part of the newly formed Corporate Public Policy and Environment department, in recognition of the growing importance of environmental issues. The team's initial task was to set the Group's strategy on the environment, and to work with existing divisional teams to implement it. The responsibilities of the corporate team were broadened to include wider sustainability issues, and the development of the Group's global partnerships with the United Nations and other organizations. In 2005, DHL Parcel Germany piloted its Grünes Paket ('Green Parcel'), a carbon-neutral parcel shipping service. With this service, all CO_2 emissions relating to the transportation and handling of each Green Parcel are calculated and offset through climate-protection projects. The Green Parcel is a forerunner for the *GOGREEN* parcel, launched in 2006 which has now be rolled out internationally with customers able to select carbon neutral or 30/50/70 per cent emissions reductions. For these deliveries DHL uses insetting (emissions reduced in the supply chain directly) or offsetting for carbon neutral deliveries. The '*Book and Claim*' option allows customers to select a carbon reduction amount and DHL uses the equivalent renewable energy somewhere in the network and then allocates the reduction in emissions to that customer who can then claim that reduction for their own purposes.

DHL started working on the reduction of CO_2 emissions by following Kyoto protocol recommendations. The key levers of the climate protection programme are the optimization of the air and ground fleets, improved energy efficiency in buildings and plants, the development of innovative technologies, motivating employees, and the involvement of subcontractors.

One of the important milestones in developing their GOGREEN strategy is identifying where the impacts actually come from, in this case DP DHL adopted the Kyoto protocol approach. "Correctly measuring and managing our CO_2 efficiency at the relevant level is extremely important. We are working intensively on this" (Lawrence A. Rosen, CFO, Deutsche Post DHL, 2024).

Scope 1 emissions include direct CO_2 emissions from one's own operations (as classified by the GreenHouse Gas Protocol). Scope 2 emissions are CO_2 emissions corresponding to the electricity, district heating, and cooling purchased. Scope 3 emissions are CO_2 emissions from subcontracted transport, which forms the majority for DHL. Through this analysis DP DHL found that they account for 0.1 per cent of global man-made emissions, which is certainly a call for action.

As mentioned, subcontracted transportation is typically responsible for about 80 per cent of the Group's carbon footprint. In particular, in the area of road freight, transparency and subcontractor engagement is very difficult to achieve due to the high number of subcontractors and limited industry standards. DHL has stated it has worked to help to improve carbon standards and data sources in the logistics industry in general to increase the level of comparability and the engagement of subcontractors.

Capacity utilization is another important lever to improve the CO_2 efficiency. Ideally, trucks should be fully loaded at all times. In reality, an average of 30 per cent of vehicle mileage is empty running, especially on the outward or return leg of local journeys. In 2008, DHL Freight Euronet in Germany determined that the relocation of empty trailers was responsible for nearly 10 per cent of the total empty kilometres. In 2009, an initiative was started to reduce these empty kilometres and the resulting CO_2 emissions. DHL defined clear responsibilities to increase backloads, trained dispatchers to optimize capacity utilization, and installed a real-time information tool to monitor vehicle availability. As a result, there were 7,000 fewer empty runs and the CO_2 efficiency improved from 100 to 70g CO_2 per revenue tonne kilometre.

The following table shows the recent development of carbon emissions at DP DHL. As mentioned before this is one of the largest industrial footprints of any industrial company. The two rows show the internal operations emissions scope 1 and 2 over which DP DHL have direct control and the external emissions of contractors scope 3 over which they have limited control, and which is significantly higher. This is because DP DHL outsources a large proportion of their transportation activities. Hence to have a significant impact on their emissions overall there is a need to work closely with their transport contractors to find ways of reducing the carbon footprint. There was a noticeable increase in the reported scope 3 emissions in 2021 due to a reclassification of upstream transport and distribution to align with the SBTI target setting standards.[1]

While DP DHL still has a long way to go to achieve the target of carbon neutrality, moving from 40 million tonnes in 2021 (for logistics related activities) to <29 million tonnes in 2030 and finally zero in 2050, the first step is to measure how the business is improving on the chosen metrics. From there the company can decide on what innovations and technologies to invest in to achieve their longer-term goals, whether it is electric vehicles, autonomous vehicles, or intelligent planning systems. In reality of course, it is a combination of these that will help create more sustainable logistics solutions.

TABLE 11.4 Total carbon emissions for DP DHL[2]

Total CO_{2e} emissions (million tonnes CO_{2e})	2014	2015	2016	2017	2018	2019	2020	2021	2022	2023	2024
Scopes 1 & 2 emissions	5.66	6.05	6.05	6.34	6.57	6.48	6.78	7.52	8.37	8.30	7.74
Scope 3 emissions	23.36	20.97	29.98	32.03	33.13	31.74	32.19	38.49	34.13	30.85	32.03

11.11 CONCLUSION

Sustainability in logistics and distribution is increasingly recognized as a strategic imperative rather than a peripheral concern. The chapter has shown that transport choices, inventory policies, location decisions, and distribution structures all carry significant environmental implications alongside economic and service considerations. While efficiency gains reduce costs, they often involve trade-offs that may increase emissions or resource consumption if not carefully managed. Reverse logistics and circular practices highlight the potential to recover value while reducing waste, though they remain complex and costly to implement. The role of service providers and evolving channel structures underscores that sustainability is not achieved in isolation but through collaboration across networks. Finally, the challenges of last-mile and urban logistics demonstrate the social as well as environmental stakes of distribution. Integrating carbon reduction, resilience, and innovation across these decisions will be central to achieving both sustainable performance and competitive advantage in the future.

NOTES

1 https://sciencebasedtargets.org/
2 Note: the big jump in 2026 is due to new calculation methods for scope 3 emissions. Most Scope 3 comes from logistics related (so not including commuting, capital goods and so on) activities which is why they have specific targets for this.

REFERENCES

Agence France-Presse (2016) Convoy of self-driving trucks completes first European cross-border trip. *The Guardian*. https://www.theguardian.com/technology/2016/apr/07/convoy-self-driving-trucks-completes-first-european-cross-border-trip

Alberto P (2000) The logistics of industrial location decisions: An application of the analytic hierarchy process methodology. *International Journal of Logistics* 3(3): 273–289.

Allen J, Browne M and A Woodburn (2014) London Freight Data Report: 2014 Update. Report by Univeristy of Westminster for Transport for London, London.

Bednarski L, Roscoe S, Blome C and Schleper MC (2025) Geopolitical disruptions in global supply chains: A state-of-the-art literature review. *Production Planning & Control* 36(4): 536–562.

Bonney M and Jaber MY (2011) Environmentally responsible inventory models: Non-classical models for a non-classical era. *International Journal of Production Economics* 133(1): 43–53.

Bouchery Y, Ghaffari A, Jemai Z and Dallery Y (2012) Including sustainability criteria into inventory models. *European Journal of Operational Research* 222(2): 229–240.

Boyer KK, Frohlich MT and Hult GTM (2005) Extending the supply chain: How cutting-edge companies bridge the critical last mile into customers' homes. AMACOM/American Management Association.

Browne M, Rizet C, Leonardi J and Allen J (2008) Analysing energy use in supply chains: The case of fruits and vegetables and furniture. *Proceedings of the Logistics Research Network Conference.*

Carter CR and Ellram LM (1998) Reverse logistics: A review of the literature and framework for future investigation. *Journal of Business Logistics* 19(1): 85–102.

Christopher M (1998) *Logistics and Supply Chain Management. Strategies for Reducing Costs and Improving Services.* 2nd edn, London: FT Prentice Hall.

Coughlan AT, Anderson E, Stern LW and Ansary AI (2006) *Marketing Channels.* Pearson/Prentice Hall.

Croxton KL (2003) The order fulfillment process. *International Journal of Logistics Management* 14(1): 19–32.

de la Fuente D and Lozano J (1998) Determining warehouse number and location in Spain by cluster analysis. *International Journal of Physical Distribution & Logistics Management* 28(1): 68–79.

DHL (2024) Environment and Energy Report.

Edwards J and McKinnon A. (2009) Comparing the environmental impact of online and conventional shopping: Auditing 'last mile' anomalies. *Retail Digest* (Fall): 10.

Edwards J, McKinnon A and Cullinane S (2011) Comparative carbon auditing of conventional and online retail supply chains: A review of methodological issues. *Supply Chain Management: An International Journal* 16(1): 57–63.

Eskandarpour M, Dejax P, Miemczyk J and Péton O (2015) Sustainable supply chain network design: An optimization-oriented review. *Omega* 54: 11–32.

Fernie J, Sparks L and McKinnon AC (2010) Retail logistics in the UK: Past, present and future. *International Journal of Retail & Distribution Management* 38(11): 894–914.

Gray JV, Helper S and Osborn B (2020) Value first, cost later: Total value contribution as a new approach to sourcing decisions. *Journal of Operations Management* 66(6): 735–750.

Halldórsson Á and Kovács G (2010) The sustainable agenda and energy efficiency: Logistics solutions and supply chains in times of climate change. *International Journal of Physical Distribution & Logistics Management* 40(1/2): 513.

Halldórsson A and Wehner J (2020) Last-mile logistics fulfilment: A framework for energy efficiency. *Research in Transportation Business & Management* 37: 100481.

Harris I, Naim M, Palmer A, Potter A and Mumford C (2011) Assessing the impact of cost optimization based on infrastructure modelling on CO2 emissions. *International Journal of Production Economics* 131(1): 313–321.

Holter A, Liimatainen H, McKinnon A and Edwards J (2010) Double-deck trailers: A cost-benefit model estimating environmental and financial savings. 15th Annual Logistics Research Network Conference, Leeds.

Howard M, Miemczyk J and Graves A (2006) Automotive supplier parks: An imperative for build-to-order? *Journal of Purchasing and Supply Management* 12(2): 91–104.

Hult GTM, Ketchen DJ and Nichols EL (2002) An examination of cultural competitiveness and order fulfillment cycle time within supply chains. *Academy of Management Journal* 45(3): 577–586.

Kawa A and Zdrenka W (2024) Logistics value in e-commerce and its impact on customer satisfaction, loyalty and online retailers' performance. *The International Journal of Logistics Management* 35(2): 577–600.

Korpela J and Lehmusvaara A. (1999) A customer oriented approach to warehouse network evaluation and design. *International Journal of Production Economics* 59(1): 135–146.

Kudla NL and Klaas-Wissing T (2012) Sustainability in shipper-logistics service provider relationships: A tentative taxonomy based on agency theory and stimulus-response analysis. *Journal of Purchasing and Supply Management* 18(4): 218–231.

Langley CJ, Allen GR and Colombo MJ (2003) Third-Party Logistics: Results and Findings of the 2003 Eighth Annual Study. Georgia Institute of Technology, FedEX Supply Chain Services, and Cap Gemini Ernst & Young.

Leonardi J and Browne M (2010) A method for assessing the carbon footprint of maritime freight transport: European case study and results. *International Journal of Logistics: Research and Applications* 13(5): 349–358.

Logistics UK (2025) London logistics takes a greener turn with new zero emission freight hub. https://logistics.org.uk/logistics-magazine-portal/logistics-magazine-features-listing/auto-restrict-folder/03-04-2025/london-logistics-takes-a-greener-turn-with-new-zer

Mather H (1988) *Competitive Manufacturing*. Englewood Cliffs: Prentice Hall.

Mayor of London (n.d.) Investigation into light commercial traffic. https://www.london.gov.uk/moderngov/documents/s52363/Appendix%201%20-%20Light%20Commercial%20Traffic%20views%20and%20information.pdf

McKinsey (2022) DHL on sustainable, customer-centric delivery in the last mile. https://www.mckinsey.com/industries/infrastructure/our-insights/dhl-on-sustainable-customer-centric-delivery-in-the-last-mile

Michon V and Miemczyk J (2014) Logistic pooling as a sustainable solution to reduce logistics cost. Paper presented at the 59th Annual Conference of International Council for Small Business, Dublin, Ireland, 11–14 June.

Millimet DL and List JA (2004) The case of the missing pollution haven hypothesis. *Journal of Regulatory Economics* 26(3): 239–262.

Nemoto T, Browne M, Visser J and Castrp J (2006) Intermodal transport and city logistics policies. Recent Advances in City Logistics. The 4th International Conference on City Logistics.

Nichols MR (n.d.) Amazon wants to use predictive analytics to offer anticipatory shipping. *SmartData Collective*. https://www.smartdatacollective.com/amazon-wants-predictive-analytics-offer-anticipatory-shipping/

O'Connor K. (2010) Global city regions and the location of logistics activity. *Journal of Transport Geography* 18(3): 354–362.

Palmer A and Piecyk M (2010) Time, cost and CO 2 effects of rescheduling freight deliveries. Proceedings of the logistics research network annual conference. University of Leeds, Leeds.

Piecyk MI and McKinnon AC (2010) Forecasting the carbon footprint of road freight transport in 2020. *International Journal of Production Economics* 128(1): 31–42.

Puram P, Gurumurthy A, Narmetta M and Mor RS (2022) Last-mile challenges in on-demand food delivery during COVID-19: Understanding the riders' perspective using a grounded theory approach. *The International Journal of Logistics Management* 33(3): 901–925.

Ram A (2016) UK retailers count the cost of returns. *Financial Times*. https://www.ft.com/content/52d26de8-c0e6-11e5-846f-79b0e3d20eaf

Razzaque MA and Sheng CC (1998) Outsourcing of logistics functions: A literature survey. *International Journal of Physical Distribution & Logistics Management* 28(2): 89–107.

ReVelle CS and Eiselt HA (2005) Location analysis: A synthesis and survey. *European Journal of Operational Research* 165(1): 119.

Sanchez-Rodrigues V, Potter A and Naim MM (2010) The impact of logistics uncertainty on sustainable transport operations. *International Journal of Physical Distribution & Logistics Management* 40(1/2): 61–83.

Shapiro BP, Rangan VK and Sviokla JJ (2001) Staple yourself to an order. *Harvard Business Review* 78(2).

Skores A (2025) The first driverless semis have started running regular longhaul routes. *CNN*. https://edition.cnn.com/2025/05/01/business/first-driverless-semis-started-regular-routes

Smarzynska BK and Wei S-J (2001) Pollution Havens and foreign direct investment: Dirty secret or popular myth? National Bureau of Economic Research.

Stern N (2007) *The Economics of Climate Change: The Stern Review*. Cambridge University Press.

Stock J (1992) *Reverse Logistics*. Oak Brook: Council of Logistics Management.

Tarasov K (2024) Amazon is using generative AI to drive more same-day shipping using smarter robots and better routes. *CNBC*. https://www.cnbc.com/2024/09/17/how-amazon-is-using-generative-ai-to-drive-more-same-day-deliveries.html

Transport for London (n.d.) Rethinking deliveries summary report. London, UK.

University of Bangor (2014) What happened to 'food miles'? https://www.bangor.ac.uk/environmental-sciences-and-engineering/news/what-happened-to-food-miles-20806

van Laarhoven P, Berglund M and Peters M (2000) Third-party logistics in Europe – Five years later. *International Journal of Physical Distribution & Logistics Management* 30(5): 425–442.

Wolf C and Seuring S (2010) Environmental impacts as buying criteria for third party logistical services. *International Journal of Physical Distribution & Logistics Management* 40(1/2): 84–102.

Wolfinbarger M and Gilly M (2002) comQ: Dimensionalizing, measuring, and predicting quality of the e-tail experience. Marketing Science Institute Report (02–100).

Wu H-J and Dunn SC (1995) Environmentally responsible logistics systems. *International Journal of Physical Distribution & Logistics Management* 25(2): 20–38.

Zeithaml VA, Parasuraman A and Malhotra A (2002) Service quality delivery through web sites: A critical review of extant knowledge. *Journal of the Academy of Marketing Science* 30(4): 362–375.

CHAPTER 12

Service-based supply chains

LEARNING OBJECTIVES:

At the end of this chapter you should be able to:

- Define what is meant by service operations, servitization, and service-dominant logic;
- Discuss the role of purchasing and supply in service-based business models;
- Understand the significance of operating models such as Power by the Hour and Contracting for Availability;
- Discuss the implications for buyer-supplier collaboration in outcome-based models involving complex performance;
- Analyze a supply chain in relation to potential for remanufacturing and product recovery;
- Discuss the connection between services, circularity, and the sharing economy.

12.1 INTRODUCTION

This chapter introduces the concept of services to the supply chain as an important source of adding value and as a distinct yet complementary approach to production operations. It is sometimes easy to mistake the supply chain as merely an efficient mechanism for the delivery of goods and indeed many people readily associate fast-moving consumer goods with the term 'supply chain'. The reality today however is that many organizations derive most of their revenue from complex bundles of services delivered downstream from production. This is not to say that products are no longer important (they are). We argue that products and services must be understood as an integrated package that has major implications when it comes to dealing with issues of extended lifecycle, designing product recovery systems, emergent new operating models and how organizations will increasingly engage with suppliers and customers in future to become more circular and sustainable.

DOI: 10.4324/9781003499602-14

12.2 THE RISE OF SERVICE OPERATIONS

Although the concept of service alongside the use of goods has existed since the earliest recorded society, it is only in the last 30–40 years that the orientation and importance of services in their own right, not just in relation to the product, has begun to be seriously examined (e.g. Potts, 1988; Quinn et al., 1990; Oliva and Kallenberg, 2003; Araujo and Spring, 2006). Products and production have tended to dominate thinking in business management not only because their strong physical characteristics have often defined the nature of the enterprise, but also because the majority of a supply chain's resources are committed to product design, manufacture, and delivery. In his seminal paper on the rise of service management, Johnson (1994) describes the origins of production and operations as based on a 300-year evolution of factory and pre-factory craft development, where the core operation in the organization typically accounts for around 70 per cent of manpower and 80 per cent of the total company's assets. It is perhaps no surprise then that management research has traditionally focused on the role played by manufacturing with only limited attention devoted to services and service operations management. Today, services are recognized as the fastest growing source of economic revenue around the world, particularly in areas such as travel, healthcare, and online retailing (Kang and James, 2004). This applies to not just the value represented by support services in the aftermarket, or the potential for new markets using mobile network technology and social media, but the recognition that all industrial sectors are fundamentally affected by services and the quality of their service operations (Roth and Menor, 2003; Corrêa et al., 2007).

A legacy of the dominance of production-orientated thinking is the tendency by scholars to emphasize the *differences* between products and services (e.g. intangibility, heterogeneity, perishability) from either a manufacturing or marketing perspective, instead of highlighting areas of intersection and similarity (Silvestro et al., 1992; van Looy et al., 1998). Such a polarized view makes little sense today given the inexorable slide in the West towards a post-industrial society, where service-based sectors including financial services, healthcare, entertainment, and tourism represent the majority of a developed country's total economic output. Hence current thinking in management literature asks how businesses can integrate products and services to deliver value via 'service-driven supply chains' (Youngdahl and Loomba, 2000). Such business models that incorporate services into the core operation are increasingly being applied in the UK and US, where service industries now account for between 80 to 90 per cent of the total labour force employed (IfM-IBM, 2007). While the role of the product remains significant, the importance of value-added services such as extended warranties, tracking and traceability, 24-hour customer support, and product upgrades are recognized as key to expanding the firm's capability to compete beyond traditional measures of manufacturing competitiveness such as cost, quality, and delivery (Youngdahl and Loomba, 2000). Service-based supply chains, therefore, acknowledge the value of activity at all stages of the product lifecycle, particularly those delivered downstream of production operations, and now involve combinations of in-service support including reverse-loop logistics activities such as product recovery.

Note 12.1 London 2012 Olympics and buying services

The London 2012 Olympics was the first sustainable games with core procurement principles supported by a range of policy documents including a *Sustainable Sourcing Code* and a *Diversity and Inclusion Charter*. Comprising 17 days of competition and involving 205 nations, 10,500 athletes, 70,000 volunteers, and 8 million tickets issued, the London games organizing committee had to get their event planning right first time given the immovable deadline and intense media interest. In terms of buying the necessary goods (e.g. buildings) and services (e.g. catering, media, security), interestingly over 60 per cent of the suppliers were comprised of SMEs. All suppliers of the games were reminded of the need to observe the key themes of the games: **climate change**, **waste**, **biodiversity**, **inclusion**, and **healthy living**. However, while the games were ultimately heralded as a great success, the challenges of buying services for such a large-scale event were demonstrated by the 'G4S fiasco': the British security group who failed to provide enough guards at the London Olympics, costing it around £50 million. G4S Chief Executive Nick Buckles was forced to apologize in a televised session in Westminster for blunders over recruitment which forced the British government to deploy extra troops to guard the London Olympics at the last minute.

Considerable textbook space in the past has been devoted to trying to define the precise attributes of products and services. The result has been an impression where both are easily distinguishable and therefore largely delivered and consumed apart from one another. As research into service operations has developed it is now regarded that there are very few examples of 'pure' goods and services, with almost all business models representing a combination or blended approach. Even a live concert, sporting event, or counselling session involves combining elements of both (Note 12.1). Traditional definitions incorporate concepts around intangibility, heterogeneity, inseparability, and perishability: the 'IHIP' model, which some authors argue only distinguishes products and services from a manufacturing perspective (Vargo and Lusch, 2004). Goedkoop et al. (1999) define a product as a tangible commodity manufactured to be sold and, put simply, as something capable of falling on your toe! Confusingly, a service is sometimes defined by what it is not, i.e. a product (Schemmer, 1995), and the term 'service' can be used to describe the level of performance, as in delivering good service. For the purposes of this chapter services refer to a commercial offering which includes elements such as maintenance, repair, customer support, product upgrade, warranty, and insurance (Baines et al., 2009).

Despite calls for greater integration between products and services during the production and delivery process, it is important to acknowledge the growing body of literature dedicated to the study of services in their own right and the emerging field of service operations management (Oliva and Kallenburg, 2003; Johnson and Clark, 2005; Araujo and Spring, 2006, 2009; Jacob and Ulaga, 2008; Baines et al., 2009). Although it is not possible to review all aspects of services in this chapter, a helpful starting point in understanding

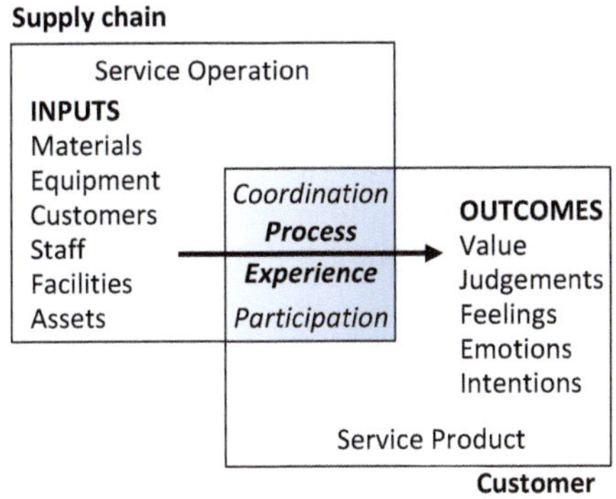

FIGURE 12.1 Managing the service operation
Source: Adapted from Johnson and Clark (2005)

some of the basic service characteristics and how they affect the supply chain is the service operations view of the transformation model (Figure 12.1). The traditional view of operations management involves the transformation model as consisting of inputs i.e. raw materials, which are transformed via production into outputs i.e. finished products. The manufacturing process involves fabrication of components and assembly of parts, and means there is often a considerable *separation* or length of time between manufacturing and the customer actually receiving the goods: an aspect which distinguishes it from service operations which usually requires a high degree of real-time interaction between the customer and supplier.

While the service operations version of the model includes inputs such as materials, technology, and equipment, it also includes customers who undergo their own process experience as part of the transformation, where outcomes involve a 'service product' incorporating a complex combination of value, emotions, judgements, and future intentions (e.g. having your hair cut at a new salon). Presenting the service operation as a simultaneous experience in this way suggests that, unlike more traditional views of manufacturing, "... the customer's experience is an intrinsic part of the operations process" (Johnson and Clark, 2005: 10). The idea of process experience and simultaneity in relation to service operations presents a considerable opportunity and challenge to supply chains in understanding what really represents value in terms of the buyer-supplier relationship: a reoccurring theme in this book. A good example where the service operation is critical to the customer experience is the running of a spa hotel or ski resort (see Note 12.2).

Services pose the idea that unique impressions are formed of the enterprise by both internal and external customers, all of whom are involved with operational and supply chain processes and despite their importance to the performance outcome, cannot be wholly captured or controlled by traditional product-based measures. Figure 12.1 therefore shows a simple representation of managing services and service operations with the process experience of the customer, in conjunction with staff and equipment, forming the central element to the delivery of a desired outcome. Understanding the subtle challenges of service operations, as a distinct departure from production operations, means managers now need to consider how to manage the response from multiple customers in terms of their experiences in real time, co-ordinating different parts of the organization, encouraging innovation, and managing short-term and long-term tasks simultaneously (Johnson, 1994; Johnson and Clark, 2005). Such challenges make a marked change to traditional production-centric concepts such as quality (e.g. physical dimensions, part conformance) and delivery lead time (e.g. logistics and information efficiency), introducing new questions over how to measure and maximize value for the duration of the customer relationship.

Note 12.2 Service supply chains and technology in ski resorts

We usually associate supply chain management with manufacturers that source physical materials into finished products and deliver these to customers. However, supply chains also need to be managed in 'pure' service operations such as the tourism industry. In the case of ski resorts the various actors involved have to make sure operations are managed in order to satisfy (and thrill) customers, and good supply chain management is all part of this.

Ski resort operators, such as hotels and restaurants, clearly have to source a range of materials that will be transformed into finished outputs. For example, they need to source meat and vegetables for food. As nature loving customers increasingly expect sustainable offerings, more and more hotels strive to source local produce as part of their efforts to offer a sustainable and regional culinary experience. Likewise, many hotels work hard to reduce their energy consumption and rely on renewal energy such as solar or hydro power. Many resorts are either car free, allowing only electric buses and taxis, such as Swiss high-end resort Zermatt, that is well-known for its strong sustainability profile (see: https://www.zermatt.ch/en/sustainability).

One critical service supply chain issue concerns the management of capacity. Where product supply chains need to manage capacity to keep lead times short with minimum inventory, service supply chains manage capacity in order to reduce the time customers spend queuing. One particular capacity constraint for ski resorts is lift capacity: 'mile hungry' skiers do not want to waste their time in lift queues but spend as much time as possible on the slopes. Old-fashioned lift systems still hamper some resorts that have struggled to invest in new efficient lift systems, but modern resorts have invested in gondolas or chair lifts with capacities of up to 4,000 or even 5,000 passengers per hour. These transform the customer experience as they greatly reduce the time spent in lift queues.

RFID technology is now widely used to reduce lift queuing. Ski passes contain an RFID tag so that skiers no longer have to take out their card and show it (in the cold...), but can leave the ski pass in their pocket for it to be registered by an RFID card reader as they pass through the lift barrier. RFID technology can also enhance the customer experience by tracking ski or snowboard metrics (e.g. total miles or max speed) and sharing this on social media. North American resort Vail implemented an RFID system in the 2008–2009 season, connecting visitors through a platform called EpicMix, which gives information on snow conditions, live webcams, trail maps, and link experiences via iPhone or Android apps. RFID technology also reduces ski pass fraud and can even help with mountain safety as skier movements through the lift systems are tracked.

Naturally, ski resorts cannot offer their services without snow and with global warming affecting snow falls, snow cannons have become widespread in recent years. This has raised environmental concerns regarding additional pressures on water supplies and energy consumption to operate snow cannons. Usually, water is sourced from reservoirs, streams, or lakes but heavy-treated sewage water is also used in some resorts. With high energy consumption from snow making machines, one option is to install wind turbines to produce the required electricity. Skiing has become big business which many rural regions have come to rely on as a major source of revenue and local employment, but it faces many future challenges that will make service operations and supply chain management ever more important.

A wide range of terminology has grown around the rise in services and service operations literature including terms such as 'servitization' (Vandermerwe and Rada, 1988; Voss, 2008), 'integrated solutions' (Davies et al., 2006), 'service-dominant logic' (Vargo and Lusch, 2004), and 'service science' and 'service innovation' (IfM-IBM, 2007). The increasing influence of supply chain management has played a considerable role in driving the language of services into everyday purchasing and supply business usage (e.g. Lindberg and Nordin, 2008), particularly the involvement of outsourcing decisions requiring managers to consider exactly what type of outcomes are desired and who in the supply chain is responsible for their delivery. Vandermerwe and Rada (1988) were the first to publish their work on what they termed the 'servitization of business' where corporations add value to their corporate offerings through services. "Corporations [are] increasingly offering fuller market packages or bundles of customer-focused combinations of goods, services, support, self-service and knowledge. But services are beginning to dominate" (Vandermerwe and Rada, 1988: 314). They argue that there are three reasons why manufacturing firms should servitize: to lock out competitors, to lock in customers, and to increase the levels of product differentiation. Yet the concept of bundling has proved problematic for some manufacturers used to their production-centric rather than market-centric models which emphasise high volume and repeatability. Creating a 'bundle' is the term used by several leading 20th century strategists to describe the coordination or grouping together of resources, products, services, and knowledge in order to sell it in the most attractive way to the customer (Penrose, 1959; Porter, 1985). An example of bundling is where a smartphone is sold with the capability built in to offer a range of functionality such as fast broadband, video network streaming, social media platforms, remote billing, and other support applications, and where the customer must increasingly pay extra to activate their specific choice of configuration and to de-activate advertising. The limitation of the bundling approach is where the customer no longer wishes to receive all of the attributes offered as part of the standard package, and competitor firms are able to offer different product-service combinations to meet the specific needs of the market.

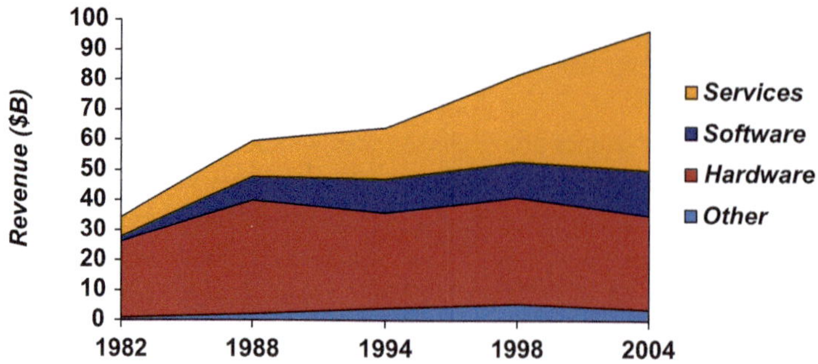

FIGURE 12.2 Business services enabled by advances in IT drive economic growth at IBM
Source: IfM-IBM (2007)

Such differentiation is often achieved by offering various levels of service and designed around a standard core product.

There is some debate, however, over whether servitization genuinely represents new thinking or such a concept has existed alongside the product as a longstanding extension of the delivery process. Voss (2008) argues that servitization and the bundling of goods and services has been with us for some time, with a number of industry sectors already having well established involvement in managing their installed base by incorporating servicing into their core product offering e.g. elevators, mainframe computers, commercial laundry services. IBM has learnt to care about services because it realized in the 1980s that its primary source of growth was coming not from selling hardware due to personal computers quickly becoming commoditized, but focusing on customer-orientated services (Cusumano, 2008) reaching around 50 per cent of total revenue in 2004. IBM's growth depends on the ability to provide what it calls business performance transformation services to its clients. This means not just installing complex computers into the core of their client's business network, but providing a wide range of business-to-business information support and optimization services such as strategic outsourcing, business performance transformation, and customer call centres (Figure 12.2). However they are described or defined, one thing is certain: services have become an essential component to 21st century business practice and will continue to play an increasingly important role across the supply chain in driving performance.

The increasing focus on services integration (Oliva and Kallenberg, 2003) and the blurring between products and services means a new take on competitive strategy, based on the provision of total service or 'integrated solutions' (Davies et al., 2006; Brax and Jonsson, 2009) where preventative maintenance and other support packages are central to the delivery process and included by multinationals such as IBM, Hewlett-Packard, and General Electric. Companies ranging from capital products to janitorial supplies have begun to view the concept of adding services, creating value packages for their new products, and providing '24/7' servicing as not only a significant revenue generator, but also an advantage to getting closer to customers and delaying the margin-eroding characteristic of product commoditization (Oliva and Kallenberg, 2003, Corrêa et al., 2007).

Taken from a customer perspective, why would a customer buy a servitized product? The answer is not always straightforward. In the 1970s, televisions were rented because they were unreliable and rental agreements included servicing which mitigated risk for the user against breakdown (Voss, 2008). A more recent example is the UK's Ministry of Defence whose initiative to develop through-life capability which focused on considering ways of delivering value at all stages of defence equipment's lifecycle (not just cost considerations at the initial purchase stage) as part of a prolonged programme to reduce spending across air, sea, and land forces. This meant outsourcing from the public domain work long associated with the military and being offered to private firms on the basis of competitive tendering.

Given the general trend of manufacturing moving eastwards, gravitating towards low cost countries, the debate in the West over services is about the choices open to public and private organizations in how they manage their installed base of equipment or facilities e.g. generators, trucks, ships, hospitals. This may mean focusing less on new build capital projects and more on leveraging the revenue potential for supporting assets already in use as part of downstream supply chain operations. The high proportion of existing products or equipment in comparison to new sales in the market, known as the 'installed base', makes economic sense for manufacturers to focus on service support packages for the customer (Neely, 2008). Lindberg and Nordin (2008) argue that a new complexity is emerging in procurement, driven by the rise in service-dominant business logic and the associated issues around service intangibility. This means a higher proximity to relational issues between customer and supplier at all stages of the lifecycle, and not simply a case of suppliers meeting the basic contractual obligations at the product's installation. Today, there is a shift towards attempts to evaluate quality of service by suppliers achieving predefined Service Level Agreements or 'SLAs'. The SLA approach involves considering overall performance levels delivered over time often by several organizations, where performance is expressed as an outcome of the whole operation e.g. reliability expressed in hours/days of uptime, flexibility in terms of choice available to the customer, sustainability in terms of reductions in carbon footprint or landfill. SLAs are more effective than traditional short-term target setting, because they can be used to bind supply chain partners together as a means of motivating firms to adopt a sense of collective action towards achieving a desired end result for the whole enterprise.

The recognition of services as a major source of added customer value and revenue means more than just managing customer relationships after a product has been sold. The rise of service operations has prompted a shift in operations and supply chain literature, where emergent product-service thinking now incorporates the dynamics of adapting to structural change, and the potential of services to add value but also risk to the firm, raising serious questions over the role of procurement in the process. In looking beyond manufacturing, procurement affects all stages of the operation, requiring concepts such as product lifecycle to engage with new business models that reframe the way we think about supply chains. Examples of such models include: through-life management, Power by the Hour, and Contracting for Availability; these are examined next.

12.3 PROCUREMENT AND THROUGH-LIFE MANAGEMENT

Procurement has undergone a considerable evolution over the past 30 years particularly in areas such as the commissioning of new equipment (e.g. ships, planes) and construction of complex facilities (e.g. schools, highways, hospitals). Its traditional role, chiefly one of searching the market for the cheapest bid, meant suppliers and contractors were assessed on the basis of price as part of reaching a contractual agreement, with little concern over the longer-term implications for servicing, generally termed Maintenance, Repair, and Overhaul (MRO). Key partners including prime contractors and 'commissioners' (often central government) viewed the success of a project in terms of the platform or facility being built within budget and according to schedule, with concern for downstream support often treated separately and seen as a periphery issue, not a priority.

Possibly as a result of longer than expected life spans of 20th century equipment and facilities, or difficulties in using short-term measures to predict support requirements that spanned several decades or more, the use of contracts alone to retain product maintenance and upgrade services from the supply base has been problematic in the past. The reasons for failure vary considerably, for instance: poor systems of project or programme control, over distinction between product and service elements in the contract, unforeseen union intervention, lack of consistency in government policy, and poor levels of stakeholder collaboration. Generally speaking, however, there is a greater emphasis today on the need of a more central role for procurement (Stremersch et al., 2001; Lindberg and Nordin, 2008). As complex product-service systems such as warships, highways, and hospitals progress through their lifecycle, it is often public procurement that holds operational responsibility and has to make escalating payments to private contractors (who work strictly to the letter of the contract) in order to maintain ageing yet essential national infrastructure. Such arbitrary contractual working practices have now largely ceased thanks to numerous improvement programmes and public-private initiatives emphasizing the need for closer, more joined up industrial collaboration (NAO, 2003, 2007). Yet a period in the UK from the 1970s to 1980s will remain notorious for its typically confrontational and litigious industrial relationships (e.g. automotive, railways, shipyards, and coal production), fuelled by restrictive union practices and the widespread use of 'cost plus' contracts where rigid agreements between the public procurer and private contractor often meant firms could claim additional payments for any construction or maintenance work considered to be outside the terms of the original agreement (Sanderson, 2009).

As the role of procurement and supply has become more prominent in the organization, the value of including a procurement professional in preliminary talks with suppliers before production commences is now recognized as standard practice. It means increasing the chance of reduced costs further down the line by considering lifecycle issues such as service support, disassembly, and product recycling *upfront* at the same time as initial platform or facility design. By using the procurement function to build stronger buyer-supplier relationships at the beginning of a construction programme, and as part of the process of drawing up of working agreements and incentives (e.g. encouraging suppliers to reduce costs, keep to schedule, and continuously innovate), a significant benefit is often shorter and more flexible contracts. Contracts designed with clear incentives enable suppliers to continue working in the event of a problem and, providing appropriate measures are in place to do so, actively seek a solution as part of the customer-supplier team rather than simply stopping work and waiting to consult with a legal representative over contractual responsibilities. Such cohesive buyer-supplier relationships are not easily achieved, and require considerable nurturing, involvement of procurement from day one of project planning, and leadership skills from the prime organization (Brady and Davies, 2011).

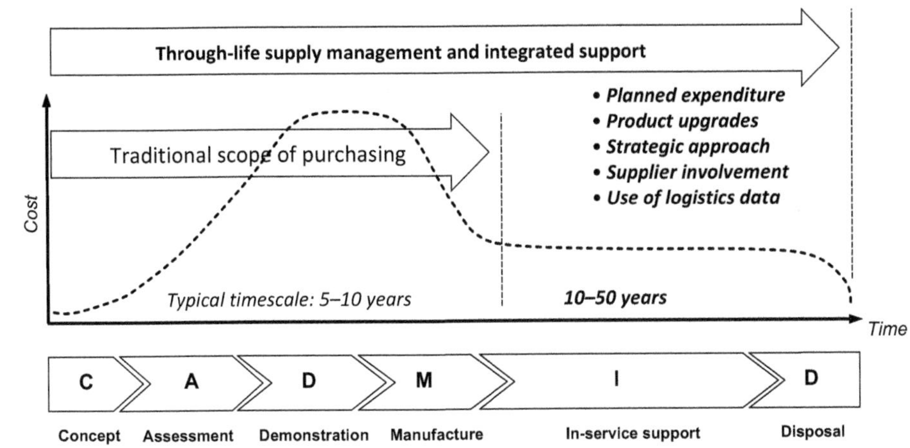

FIGURE 12.3 Through-life supply management and CADMID
Source: Adapted from MoD (2005); Johnsen et al. (2009)

There is always the temptation in large projects involving service support programmes to create distance between firms in an attempt to control them, to outsource responsibility, and ultimately put any blame on the lower and less powerful tiers of the supply chain. The ultimate test of any buyer-supplier relationship, therefore, is when an issue arises between the partners that behaviours do not dissolve into confrontational-type firm territorialism, but the goals of the project or programme are put first and resolution achieved through joint problem-solving, creativity, and innovation.

It is only from the 1990s on that thinking around product lifecycle and through-life management has begun to change the sometimes negative early perceptions of service support as an ancillary activity or even a 'necessary evil' which could be mitigated through the product's disposal and purchase of new equipment. With the rising cost of build programmes making regular new product acquisitions prohibitive, many organizations view the prospect of capturing supplementary services or 'going downstream' (Quinn et al., 1990; Wise and Baumgartner, 1999) and offering 'full service contracts' as one solution to cutting costs and boosting revenue (Stremersch et al., 2001). In order to capitalize on the opportunities offered downstream of the initial design, build, or construction phase, supplier firms must first consider the generic processes associated with the facility or platform lifecycle. To take the defence industry as an example, Figure 9.3 shows the CADMID (Concept, Assessment, Demonstration, Manufacture, In-service support, and Disposal) model as a standardized view of all the major phases military equipment undergoes during its life. It illustrates both the traditional role of purchasing as concerned primarily only with design and build, and the shift towards end-to-end procurement or 'supply management' that recognizes the importance of considering all stages of the product lifecycle. By integrating the requirements of in-service support through planned expenditure, product upgrades, use of logistics data, and supplier involvement, the advantage of the through-life management approach is that it includes the 10 to 50 year lifecycle issues at the same time as the initial project or programme design, enabling long-term planning to be built around projected risk, shared benefit, and overall performance requirements. Such an approach means contracts can be proactively developed to reflect the precise needs of the programme and can also incentivize desired supply chain behaviours from the outset.

One of the most significant changes in the UK defence industry is the shift towards a policy of Smart Acquisition and, more specifically, through-life management (TLM). TLM is broadly derived from product lifecycle management literature and defined in public procurement circles as "an integrated approach to all … acquisition processes, planning and costing activities across the whole system and whole life of a project" (NAO, 2003). The concept has become a driving force in defence procurement policy (MoD, 2005), for example where defence contracts attempt to link all phases of the product-service lifecycle, from conceptualization and design, to manufacture, support, and disposal of products. This requires a new approach towards supply strategy and reveals some important trends where, in the past, the primary focus for industry contractors was to win contracts based on upstream design and manufacturing-based activity because this was where the firm perceived the quickest payback for minimum risk to be.

The concept of TLM fundamentally alters the relationship between the UK Ministry of Defence (MoD) and its strategic suppliers. A UK government white paper titled 'Defence Industrial Strategy' published in 2005 emphasized the need for through-life capability management based on open product architectures, allowing long-term upgrading, and support, reflecting the shift away from successive generations of platform-orientated defence programmes. This new approach requires "leaps of capability with major new procurements", towards "a capability-based approach … a new paradigm centred on support, sustainability and the incremental enhancement of existing capabilities from technology insertions" (MoD, 2005: 17). An extreme example of the extended use of platforms is the B52 bomber used by the US Air Force, originally designed in 1949, but planned to continue to see active service until 2050 by which time it will be a 100-year-old airframe design! This implies that although innovation in the defence industry is considered critical, it will mainly happen through the continuous upgrading of existing technology platforms rather than the development of new stand-alone platform designs. Because of the increasing need to keep product platforms in-service for as many decades as possible (the latest generation of UK aircraft carriers are expected to be used for 50 years), technology insertion – or capability insertion – will be the concept used in the continuous upgrading of platforms with new technologies, such as IT software. In defence terms the concept of TLM is captured in the CADMID lifecycle model (Figure 12.3) which reflects the anticipation that industrial relationships should change to enable the new focus through long-term, strategic, and assured relationships. Through-life *capability* management, therefore, suggests a shift from a contractor's responsibility ending after they have built to the blueprint, towards proactive and participatory relationships involving the MoD 'buying capability' in terms of a supplier's total skill and knowledge, rather than the one-off purchase of a piece of equipment.

The procurement strategy of the UK's Ministry of Defence is to change its stance towards risk and benefit sharing with suppliers. This shift towards strategic alignment emphasizes a new focus on collaboration in relationships between the MoD and key suppliers. The view is that alignment will require industry visibility of the MoD's future plans for resource allocation and the MoD will need visibility of the industry business model: there will be much need for shared processes and partnering, especially as major suppliers gain responsibility for in-service support. There is also a perceived need for a total cost of ownership approach to costing as suppliers are required to guarantee 'end-to-end service provision'. Traditionally, however, there have been disincentives for suppliers to pay for repairs. Consequently, as suppliers take on more responsibility they seek new arrangements for sharing of gains, costs as well as risks: suppliers are dissatisfied with fixed price arrangements. The MoD recognizes that planning needs to be around whole-life costing and capability rather than a simple upfront purchase cost. MoD reports suggest use of incentivization of gain sharing to encourage industry and MoD to improve performance.

Some UK defence suppliers are worried that contractors will find savings to the detriment of aspects such as air safety (Haddon-Cave, 2009) and suppliers are not incentivized to over-maintain military aircraft as has traditionally been the case by armed forces MRO personnel (see Note 12.3). Nevertheless, general policy is to keep markets open, not just rely on one prime contractor. The defence IT and communications market, for example, remains open to all commercial internet providers at present. This shift in supply chain strategy means a fundamental change in the relationship between the MoD and industry. In simple terms it means shifting from singular, static, formal, and one-dimensional relationships, towards multiple, non-linear, dynamic, partnered, and multidimensional relationships. Similar dimensions around purchasing and supply have inspired research into the phenomenon coined 'procuring complex performance', described next.

Note 12.3 Nimrod MRA4 aircraft disaster and the outsourcing of maintenance services

On 2 September 2006, a Royal Air Force Nimrod surveillance aircraft was on a routine mission over Helmand Province in Southern Afghanistan in support of NATO and Afghani ground forces when it suffered a catastrophic mid-air fire leading to the total loss of the aircraft and death of all 14 crew members on board. In the subsequent investigations after the crash, the technical cause of the accident was found to be the escape of fuel after air-to-air refuelling, ignited by exposed elements of faulty electrical equipment. However, an independent review titled 'The Loss of Nimrod XV230: A Failure of Leadership, Culture and Priorities' (Haddon-Cave, 2009) found the causes of the crash to be not just in terms of the aircraft's design flaws, which had failed to be spotted in a number of previous incidents, but a 'general malaise' that had affected the performance of checks carried out by the Integrated Project Team and two private firms acting as maintenance contractor and independent safety advisor. Senior judge Charles Haddon-Cave QC summed up the enquiry by saying that it was organizational causes which played a major part in the loss of the 40-year-old Nimrod XV230. Significant structural changes took place in the MoD during the years when a crucial Nimrod Safety Case was being prepared, between 2001 and 2004. During this time the MoD was being downsized and shifting from functional to project orientated lines, internal organizations were amalgamated into larger more general purpose management structures, and the practice of outsourcing in-service support to industry was increasing.

Source: Haddon-Cave (2009)

12.3.1 Procuring complex performance

Procuring Complex Performance or 'PCP' examines the multiple and often conflicting challenges of managing total supply chain operations during all phases of a major project or programme including design, build, service support, and disposal (Lewis and Roehrich, 2009; Caldwell and Howard, 2011). As an emerging area in business-to-business research based on industry sectors such as building and construction, defence, transportation, and healthcare, PCP seeks to combine theory in the areas of complexity, purchasing and supply, markets, and innovation management. PCP proposes that the traditional combination of hierarchy, linear project management, and high levels of contractual control has increasing difficulty adapting to the dynamics of customer requirements today. This is particularly the case in mega-projects (van Marrewijk et al., 2008) involving capital intensive public-private collaborations where there is an increased risk of oligopolistic market conditions (i.e. limited choice of supplier/manufacturer) and the effects of political interference via government control.

Complex performance means a combination of delivering high value product or platform infrastructure, with long-term (often multi-decade) requirements for in-service support. The complexity element stems from the need for a significant number of operational and supply decisions, such as through-life asset management, product upgrade strategy, cost and risk modelling, new forms of contractual control, and adoption of new business models that emerge over the duration of the lifecycle. The addition of a procurement perspective highlights the need for a more co-ordinated and upfront approach to buying, made necessary by the task being so composed of sub-elements that it cannot be achieved by the sequential or additive achievement of individual transactions: an approach widely applied in the past to production-specific scenarios. The diminished importance of the individual transaction in managing complex performance and the rise of more embedded knowledge in supply relationships create a need for buyer-supplier agreements that focus on outcomes rather than tightly specified inputs or products across organizational boundaries. Put simply, the buying or commissioning of complex performance means going beyond managing the buyer-supplier interface, and involves a mindset shift from production orientated delivery models towards the coordination of long-term assured services (Howard and Caldwell, 2014).

The procuring complex performance approach goes beyond traditional project management techniques such as Gantt chart methodologies that have a tendency to force predefined, sequential steps that conclude at completion of the facility or platform installation. PCP draws on the work known as Complex Product-Systems (CoPS) (Hobday, 1998; Davies and Hobday, 2005; Davies et al., 2006). 'CoPS' involve engineering-intensive products or systems supplied in units of one or small batches, usually tailored to meet the precise requirements of each customer. The creation of CoPS often involves extreme production and innovation complexity. Industries that supply CoPs are usually restricted markets with a few large suppliers facing a few large customers in each country. However, PCP differs from CoPS in four aspects:

- Focus on procurement and supply;
- Customer value is delivered as an integrated product-service (not a product system) where a significant proportion of value is delivered as support services located up and downstream from manufacture/construction;

- The process of co-creation of value between partners involves a greater emphasis on the interplay between inter-firm relationships and contractual governance;
- CoPS are concerned first and foremost with technological progress, while PCP is focused on the sum of performance outcome and economic efficiency.

PCP speaks to the whole-life issues of complex projects, concerned as much with the performance capability to supply sustainable support and maintenance over extended periods, as the initial phases of design and build. There is more similarity between PCP and CoPS in the need for strong co-ordinating roles for the purpose of linking various stages of the project together (Davies and Hobday, 2005), leading Hobday (1998) to see project management and systems integration as the core capability for successful CoPS involving temporary structures consisting of many firms. The extended, multi-decade timeframes typical of the PCP approach maximizes the opportunity to mitigate political interference and the waxing and waning of government policy, see for example the concern with political inspired interference in mega projects (van Marrewijk et al., 2008). Further, PCP suggests that the static world of matrix-based procurement models such as Kraljic (1983) are less suitable for such dynamic and political environments, and require further consideration around the co-creation of value between multiple stakeholders and management of extended, typically 40–50 year lifecycles. Such challenges involving the considerable timescales around service support, remanufacturing, and end-of-life disposal can only be tackled if they are considered upfront at the beginning of the programme or project before the design phase commences (Figure 12.4). This suggests, therefore, that all stakeholders including customers, buyers, suppliers, and NGOs must come to an agreement at the beginning of working together to ensure the optimum outcome throughout the programme's total lifespan.

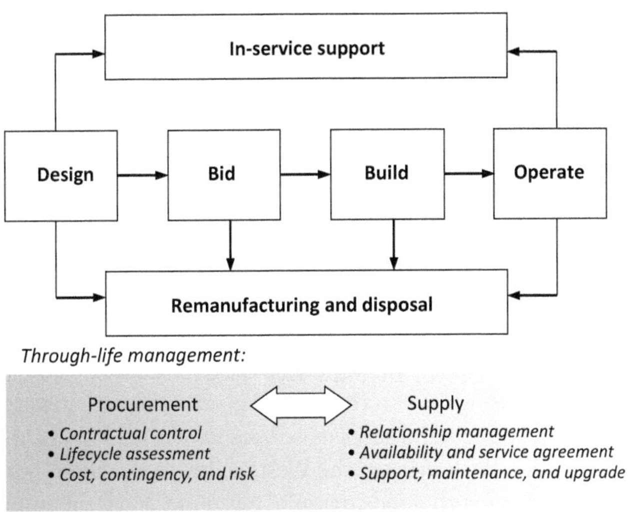

FIGURE 12.4 Managing procurement and supply across the extended lifecycle
Source: Adapted from Caldwell and Howard (2011)

Figure 12.4 presents a vision for integrating the management of procurement and supply which draws from the PCP approach. Rather than show service support, remanufacturing, and product disposal at the end of the process, it shows them as parallel streams of expertise considered upfront at the beginning of a project or programme, which run alongside the more traditional phases of design, bid, build, and operate. The procurement and supply functions are included as separate yet coordinated groups of tasks, focusing initially during the start-up phase on contractual design and control, lifecycle assessment, cost, contingency, and risk, moving increasingly towards longer term issues such as service agreements, product maintenance, repair, and upgrade.

PCP and other new performance-based operating models are similar in some respects to *outcome-based* supply chain thinking proposed by Melnyk et al. (2010). The governance literature has already reached a degree of agreement that a contract cannot, even in simpler contractual arrangements, hope to cover all eventualities and circumstances (Dyer and Singh, 1998; Poppo and Zenger, 2002). Given the necessity of a contract, therefore, under PCP it is likely that there will be a combination of relational and contractual approaches, varying in proportion over time but dominated by relational approaches. There is also a growing need to understand how the customer looks beyond output as a consequence of the purchasing decision, to buying an outcome that includes predefined performance measures (Davies and Brady, 2000; Melnyk et al., 2010). The putting in place of organizational routines and learning processes (Davies and Brady, 2000) explains how suppliers of complex product systems build capabilities based on past performance to develop new lines of business or 'repeatable solutions'. There is a parallel here between solutions and the outcome-based approach where "supply chains ... deliver one or more outcomes" (Melnyk et al., 2010: 34). For example, selected outcomes will include measures scaled in proportion to their importance relative to the project such as cost, responsiveness, security, sustainability, resilience, and innovation, as opposed to traditional delivery mechanisms based around task orientated piecework. Once a blend of outcomes has been selected at the start of the project or programme, it influences critical characteristics in the design and build phase, and continues as a major focus into downstream support and disposal, where delivery responsibly concerns the whole supply chain.

12.4 NEW OPERATING MODELS AND THE SERVITIZED SUPPLY CHAIN

Of all the terms to emerge from recent business research, 'servitization' and the servitized supply chain are probably the most well known by practitioners as a means to improving the manufacturing and industrial sectors performance (Neely, 2008; Baines et al., 2009). The basic premise of the servitized supply chain is "... in order to survive in developed economies manufacturing firms have to move up the value chain, innovating and creating ever more sophisticated products and services, so they do not have to compete on the basis of cost" (Neely, 2008: 103). With firms in the West having to cut costs by an average of 30 per cent in order to compete with goods manufactured in China, the importance of finding ways to differentiate in the global economy is paramount to their survival. Hence minimizing cost and maximizing revenue throughout the product lifecycle is a top priority for firms across European and US industrial sectors. The renewed interest in modes of working such as 'Pay-on-production' (Kuka robots), 'Power by the Hour' (Rolls Royce), and 'Pay-per-print' (Xerox), reflects the shift in emphasis away from product sales, to offering alternative forms of goods and services delivered in ways where customers can choose the method that suits them best. Such operating models demonstrate the need for a greater understanding of lifecycle considerations and the meaning of value to the customer, and have led to a shift in the way many firms contract for products and services. Two of the best-known operating models are reviewed below:

Power by the Hour (PbtH) is a term originally coined in the 1960s to describe a support service provided for engines in the UK business jet aircraft sector. PbtH meant that for a fixed sum per flying hour, a complete engine and accessory replacement service was provided by the manufacturer, allowing the operator to forecast costs with great accuracy, and relieving the purchaser of the need to purchase stocks of engines and accessories. Rolls-Royce Plc re-invented the programme in the 1980s where the key feature of the model is that it undertakes to provide the operator with a fixed engine maintenance cost over an extended period of time. The benefits of the approach mean operators being assured of a smooth cost projection over a fixed period and avoiding unexpected costs associated with breakdowns, hence PbtH has become a popular option for many airlines. Although the term Power by the Hour is commonly used across the industry, it is owned and protected by Rolls-Royce, although other aircraft engine manufacturers such as General Electric and Pratt & Whitney offer similar packages. Unlike extended warranties purchased by consumers for a fixed payment to cover repairs on products like cars or white goods appliances, complex systems such as the engine, flight control, and navigation modules found in aerospace and defence require more sophisticated relationships between buyers and suppliers. In these industries, it is very hard to guarantee product or component availability due to significant uncertainties in product reliability and usage, as well as inherent product complexity, resulting in large risks to both the customer and service provider. Service support in these industries was until relatively recently conducted using fixed-price or cost-plus contracts. Today, manufacturers are recognizing the value of offering product-service packages which offer an assured level of service for an all-inclusive fixed price as part of PbtH and are now actively designing their systems with inbuilt support requirements for easier maintenance and repair.

Contracting for Availability (CFA) was conceived by the UK 'Defence Equipment & Support' (DE&S), a public organization under the control of the Ministry of Defence in response to rising costs of supporting the UK's fleet of aircraft, tanks, surface warships, and submarines. It is based on recent defence industrial strategy (MoD, 2005) where the responsibility for providing platform support services such as engineering, stores, training, IT systems, and equipment upgrade is devolved from the military to selected suppliers. CFA was first conceived for small vessels such as minesweepers and coastal patrol ships, using a transformational staircase model to illustrate to contractors the shift in supply chain practice from 'traditional support', through 'spares inclusive', to 'contracting for availability' and ultimately 'contracting for capability': the ultimate level of service delivery. Although this new style of partnering with industry still requires a full legal contract, considerable emphasis is put on partnering principles such as mutual benefits, openness and trust, exchange of information, innovation, 'no surprises', and value for money.

Above all, the working relationship between the MoD and industry is to emphasize a *no blame* policy, focusing on key performance indicators such as service level, measurement of performance linked to payment, and continuous improvement.

The benefits of outsourcing logistical and repair activities to private contractors adopting CFA principles has been a fixed monthly rate of charter hire for each vessel, a fixed rate of maintenance charges, and a transfer of the majority of risk to the supplier in return for a pre-agreed fee: all of which have resulted in a lower overhead cost per ship. Further, the availability improvement in terms of warships ready to go to sea has increased also. Yet sceptics of these new agreements point out that while this approach may work for purpose-built vessels, supporting the maintenance requirements of older ships suffering from obsolescence issues means difficulties over predictability stemming from equipment unreliability. In other words, CFA support schemes seems to work well on new vessels, but are more problematic on older platforms when the original manufacturer may no longer exist and current suppliers are reluctant to accept the high levels of risk associated with service contracts involving legacy hardware, such as Nimrod aircraft (see Note 12.3).

PbtH and CFA are good examples of new operating models that deploy the servitized supply chain approach. They consider all elements of the product lifecycle in terms of its potential value, where supply chain collaboration is dependent as much on relationship management and incentives as relying purely on contractual obligation. Taking an upfront and outcome-based view of the programme that includes the uncertainties of long-term use helps to ensure accommodation for future performance needs (e.g. IT software upgrades), which even if specifics are not yet known, can still be included as part of the plan for the overall package. Many variations on the PbtH and availability theme that shift from product-based delivery towards assured services have now emerged and include practices which seek to cover legacy scenarios such as the TotalCare® solution for supporting older ship's turbines (Note 12.4).

Note 12.4 The Rolls Royce engines TotalCare® package

The TotalCare® package was introduced in 2005 by Rolls Royce who assumed responsibility for the long-term support of Olympus and Tyne gas turbines engines used in the Royal Navy's older warships in the UK. The £137 million contract was based on similar packages developed for the defence and civil aerospace business, and covered the turbines until they were decommissioned in 2016. A similar scheme is provided for the French, Belgian, and Royal Netherland navies. Under the previous arrangements, the Royal Navy was responsible for all aspects of engine maintenance and repair, with requirements passed to Rolls Royce through rigid, individual contracts. Now Rolls Royce is responsible for all engine maintenance, overhaul, and inventory management, basically ensuring power is available to keep the ships at sea for the duration of the contract with target cost-based prices for engine availability related to the number of running hours. An agreed fee is paid monthly to Rolls Royce by the Ministry of Defence.

Source: Rolls Royce (2006)

12.5 PRODUCT-SERVICE SYSTEMS (PSS) AND PRODUCT RECOVERY

The term product-service systems or 'PSS' has evolved in the literature to describe integrated bundles of customer focused products, services, and knowledge-based activity which increase the value of a core offering (Manzini et al., 2001; Mont, 2002; Aurich et al., 2006). Interest in PSS has steadily increased as industrial firms seek new ways to compete and create value by shifting from production-dominant to service-dominant business models. PSS was initially perceived as part of the expansion of downstream activity such as maintenance, repair, and overhaul, by leveraging value in areas such as customer support services and product upgrade (e.g. Potts, 1988; Quinn et al., 1990). As interest in PSS research grew, new areas and perspectives were adopted, not only product- and service-based, but themes such as complexity, project management, and innovation began to emerge. Related to PSS is the work of Davies and Hobday (2005), who adopt the perspective of complex product systems, seeking to improve understanding of the characteristics and dynamics of innovation in the high technology, high value capital goods sector. A distinctive feature of PSS is the recognition that the 'physical product core' is surrounded by a non-physical service shell, often represented as concentric rings in schematic diagrams of PSS (Figure 12.5) which help to identify precisely where value is added in the delivery process and how these activities enable benefits to the customer (Aurich et al., 2006) as well as the wider environment through remanufacturing.

An important development in the rise of PSS thinking is the recognition that the distinction between product and service is actually unhelpful to business. What really counts is the "nature of producer-user interactions and the institutional structure of production rather than on any essentialist feature of products and services" (Araujo and Spring, 2006: 797). While services are playing a more important role in manufacturing firms, considerably more by way of complexity remains to be discovered through exploring the novel

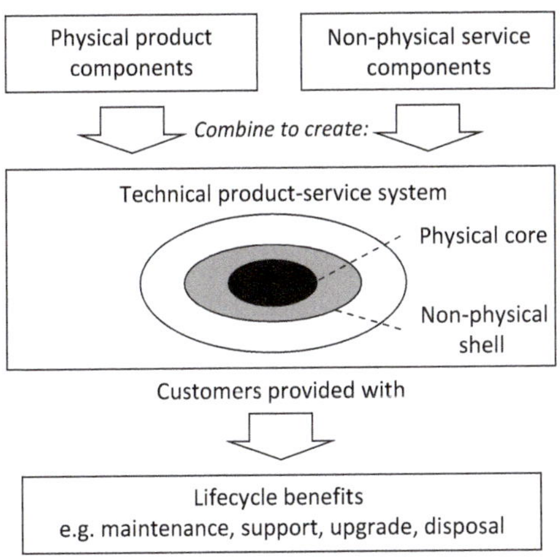

FIGURE 12.5 The structure of product-service systems
Source: Adapted from Aurich et al. (2006)

combinations of customer-supplier interaction, contractual arrangements, and infrastructure which articulate the requirement for high performance outcomes (Lewis and Roehrich, 2009; Caldwell and Howard, 2011).

A theme which has emerged over the past decade or so is the role of PSS in sustainable consumption, where PSS are divided into services providing value into the product lifecycle. In this sense, PSS can be defined as a business innovation strategy offering a marketable mix of products and services jointly capable of fulfilling the client's needs, with the facility to offer higher added value and a smaller environmental impact as desired (Manzini et al., 2001; Mont, 2002). The lifecycle design of technical product-service systems – introducing modularization, ease of maintenance, retrofitting, and refurbishment considerations – means more sustainable production and consumption, offering economic, ecological, and social benefits through improved product differentiation, consideration for the environment, and focus on knowledge and skills from staff (Aurich et al., 2006).

Schweitzer and Aurich (2010: 158) define industrial product service systems as "customer life cycle-orientated combinations of products and services realized in an extended value creation network". In the capital goods industry PSS are typically made up of a complex physical core which is enhanced during its lifecycle by a range of mainly non-physical, complimentary services which deliver value whilst in use (see Figure 12.5). Where traditionally manufacturers have focused on the design, realization, and distribution of products, increasingly their customers are expected to be provided with high quality integrated services which are tailored to individual needs. To support this change, manufactures have realized the merits of becoming service providers, not only keeping up existing product functionalities, but providing additional ones as well as a continuous stream of service options along the whole of the product lifecycle. Manufacturers have now adopted lifecycle orientated PSS that focus on customer solutions, and enabling the closer integration between product and service planning, design, and operations. A particular challenge to continuous improvement of PSS lifecycle management is the process of standardized process descriptions which requires all partners in the extended value network having a common understanding of the necessary design, production, and servicing processes. Typically the process furthest away from the manufacturer are the most difficult to control and yet it is the cooperation and information shared by the customer and contractors, towards the end of the lifecycle, which are the most crucial to boost high rates of return for older product, which may be repairable or capable of disassembly for re-use and remanufacture. Improving the process for new generations of PSS requires the feedback information and return of product which, because of its low perceived economic value, is often the most difficult in terms of incentivizing the supply chain to recover or retain.

The process of product recovery is a key element of downstream sustainable supply chain activity, but one of the last and most difficult to control as it is often conducted many years after production. Remanufacturing then is the disassembly and recovery of modules, sub-assemblies, and (eventually) components from used machines or equipment including automobiles, trucks, computers, and planes. It involves the repair, reconditioning, replacement, and reassembly of worn out components. Any parts which are judged to be sufficiently worn to affect the overall performance or expected life of the whole product are replaced. Where possible, the removed component is either reconditioned or broken down into its constituent material class for recycling. In essence, remanufacturing is a complex form of a product recovery process which differs from other recovery processes in its completeness: a remanufactured machine should match the same customer expectation as a new machine. Other forms of product recovery that can be distinguished from remanufacturing include reuse, repair, refurbishment, and recycling (Note 12.5).

Note 12.5 Product recovery and the '5Rs'

There is more to the subject of product recovery as an important element in sustainable supply chain development than simply introducing terms such as recycling and remanufacture. As we can see from the definitions above, the term remanufacturing is applied only in specific conditions. However, it can be easy to confuse remanufacturing with other methods of product recovery, hence a brief summary of the '5Rs' is provided here:

- **Reuse** – items that are used by a second customer without prior repair operations or as originally designed;
- **Repair** – the process of bringing worn or damaged components back to a functional condition;
- **Refurbish / recondition** – the process of restoring components to a functional state as per their original specification using methods such as resurfacing and repainting;
- **Remanufacture** – part of an industrial process where worn-out products are restored to a like-new condition;
- **Recycle** – the process of taking a component material and processing it to make the same material, or a useful degraded material.

There are a number of definitions for remanufacturing, one of the first being a published report by Lund (1984) who describes remanufacturing as

> … an industrial process in which worn-out products are restored to like-new condition. Through a series of industrial processes in a factory environment, a discarded product is completely disassembled. Useable parts are cleaned, refurbished, and put into inventory. Then the product is reassembled from the old parts (and where necessary new parts) to produce a unit fully equivalent and sometimes superior in performance and expected lifetime to the original new product.

The range of products capable of being remanufactured is very wide and includes aerospace components, air conditioning units, carpet tiles, compressors, defence equipment, excavation equipment, industrial food processing equipment, machine tools, office furniture, pumps, and starter motors.

As the importance of remanufacturing has grown, offering opportunities to turn used products into new ones, so too has the awareness of challenges such as choosing the appropriate reverse channel structure for product collection (Savaskan et al., 2004), the varying condition of used components and means of collection, and imbalances in return and demand rates as part of production control (Guide, 2000). Technically speaking, a remanufactured product can be sold in new product markets, that is, there is no distinction between a remanufactured and a manufactured product. Yet few firms can match the established networks which demand high volume, commodity-type replacement products such as Canon, Hewlett-Packard, or Xerox's ink toner cartridges for example, who boast a saving of 40–65 per cent in manufacturing costs through the reuse of parts and materials. Whilst similar programmes have achieved varying rates of success in sectors such as FMCG packaging, automotive components, and floor coverings, achieving optimal returns appears to favour shorter lifecycle products with relatively low complexity and disassembly implications in order to keep costs of reprocessing to a minimum. Some authors suggest that assumptions around centralized control of reverse loop supply chains in remanufacturing operations needs to be 'relaxed' (Savaskan et al., 2004), in order to engage better with outlying stakeholders in the process such as suppliers and customers, and encourage their participation in returning used goods and being agreeable to adopt new charging models and buying habits (i.e. leasing instead of outright purchase, accepting goods with a percentage of recycled material). In short, the practice of remanufacturing needs to be viewed as core to sustainable supply chain planning, not as something at the periphery or 'end-of-pipeline' (Jayaraman et al., 1999).

12.6 CIRCULARITY AND THE SHARING ECONOMY

There are strong associations between product-service systems, circular practice, and the sharing economy due to firms and their stakeholders collaborating to generate value from new business models (Sosnowski, 2024). Consider for example how networks powered by digital technology meant Airbnb and Uber can threaten traditional hotel accommodation and taxi businesses. Also, how food waste is generally not discarded but collected by local councils and fed into anaerobic digesters whose captured gas generates power. Both examples demonstrate asset or material reuse between collaborating actors. However, while the circular economy (CE) and sharing economy (SE) are connected by the need for a synergistic relationship, there are also some significant differences (Jabbour et al., 2020).

The sharing economy typically involves peer-to-peer (also peer-to-business, business-to-peer, business-to-business) transactions which facilitate collaboration and share the use of idle assets and services (Henry et al., 2021). It is an emerging economic system in which access to assets or services are shared between two or more individuals, either free or for a fee, and using an online platform accessed via the web (Plewnia and Guenther, 2018). SE has not only given rise to businesses such as Airbnb and Uber, but also means that individuals can rent out their car, bike, or Wi-Fi when they are not using them. Sharing assets in this way reflects the closed loop element of the circular economy, which means products are used more and – theoretically speaking – reduces pressure on the planet due to lowering demand on manufacturing and raw material extraction (Aldieri et al., 2021). Yet critics of CE and SE dispute this by pointing to the so-called 'rebound effect' when circular activities, which have lower per-unit-production impacts, also cause increased

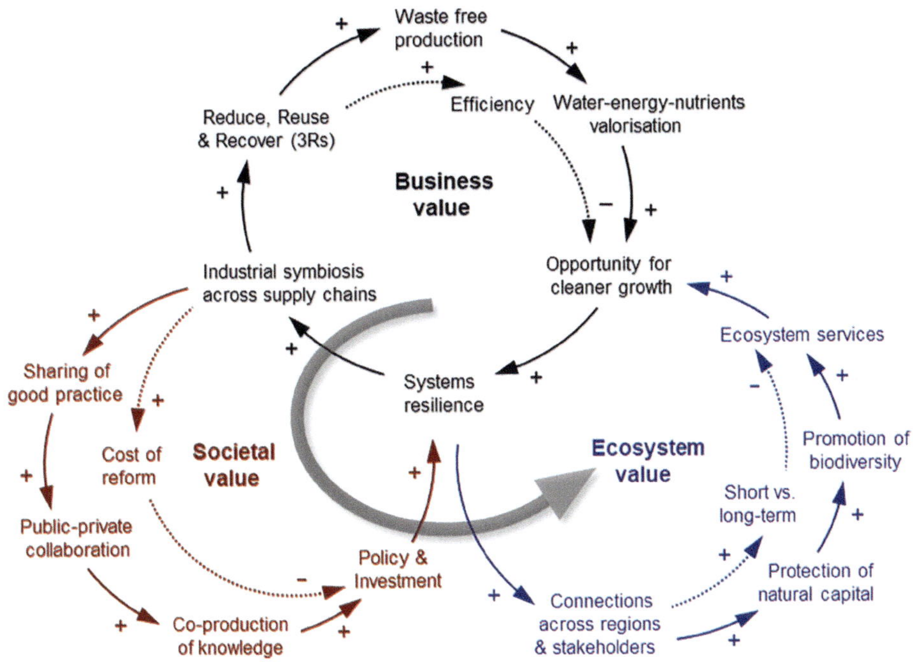

FIGURE 12.6 Systems model of the agri-food sector multilevel tensions and trade-offs in business sustainability across south-west England
Source: Adapted from Howard et al. (2022)

levels of production which reduces their benefit. In other words, an efficiency increase often reduces product or service costs, which in turn can ramp up consumption due to reduced prices, thus partly cancelling out the original savings (Sorrell et al., 2009).

As we have seen in Chapter 8, the circular economy is presented as a powerful vision of a regenerative system based on the principles of value capture and zero waste by design. Yet CE is also criticized for lacking a social perspective and research that focuses on consumption, whereas SE has a strong consumer perspective with social impact discussed at length by scholars (Mont et al., 2002; Henry et al., 2021). SE is typically less advanced than CE in terms of business model development and the interaction with organizational systems. Some recent studies have adopted a hybrid approach where supply chains are explored in the context of a more regional perspective to understand how combining CE and SE can help explore ideas such as systems resilience through business, societal, and environmental value (Howard et al., 2022). Figure 12.6 represents a systems model of the agri-food sector in rural south-west England where multilevel tensions and trade-offs within firms and supply chains can affect overall resilience and sustainability. While the model starts with circularity at firm level, it progresses to the strength of connection with the local community and value placed on the natural environment, also known as 'ecosystem services'. Whether one adopts CE, SE, or a mixed perspective, it is clear that no one model provides all the answers towards achieving a completely sustainable solution. Understanding the strengths and weakness of a particular approach and adopting a hybrid strategy to suit the context of a specific challenge therefore may offer a practical pathway towards implementation where services are fully considered.

12.7 CASE STUDY: ISLABIKES

Islabikes was founded in 2006 in the UK, when former professional cyclist Isla Rowntree decided to change the future of children's bikes forever. Islabikes sells premium children's bikes, and was started by Isla after her sister and other friends said they couldn't find decent bikes for their kids. When Isla looked into it she was appalled at what was available: prevailing bikes were too heavy, with too much material in terms of steel and aluminium, and much stronger than was required. In the 1980s, the mountain bike craze encouraged manufacturers to make kids bikes even bigger, with oversized tubes, 'suspension forks' (which weren't) and triple chain sets: they were just a mass of steel. A child's power to weight ratio is actually very high, but the prevailing bikes were not ergonomically designed. The cranks were too long and standard handlebar fittings meant kids couldn't reach the brakes. So, while they passed safety standards, they were actually dangerous as kids couldn't stop the bike. Isla didn't want kids to have a poor first experience of cycling, and so with Islabikes she had a vision of giving all children a better experience. This has extended not only to designing bikes which are properly scaled for children to ride, but also towards considering what happens when the child grows out of their existing bike and needs a bigger one. Hence the Imagine Project was born.

Islabikes employees around 35 people, based in Bromfield, Ludlow, and with an annual turnover of around £6 million. While their headquarters are in the UK, manufacturing of the bikes is done in Vietnam and then shipped to Ludlow. Islabikes does the final assembly, including 'PDI' or pre-delivery inspection at its site, with the bikes then sold direct to customers who place orders (and their preferences, accessories, etc.) by email, online, or phone. In this way, Islabikes can cut out the retailer and third-party distributor, and go direct to the customer. The worldwide cycle industry has a complex supply chain structure. Taking Specialized, the international brand, as an example: its headquarters are in Morgan Hill, California, where the design, marketing, financing, and human resource functions are based. But the actual manufacturing is carried out by third parties in SE Asia (Taiwan, Vietnam) who make bikes for other brands. These in turn get components made in another tier of specialist third-party suppliers (e.g. saddles, brakes, etc.). The bikes are built and finished to Specialized's specifications and then shipped to another set of third-party distributors, one in each country with the contract to supply Specialized bikes. These distributors have agreements with a specific bike dealer in every town who complete the final assembly.

Islabikes' business model means it has complete control of the PDI and hence the quality of the product as well as the safety of the set-up, and thus the child's experience of cycling. The employees have a rigorous training regime to learn the basic PDI routines with many months of practice and supervision. Depending on the individual, it can quite feasibly take a few years to be 'signed off' on all models. Although not strictly necessary, the company supplements its rigorous internal training with an externally assessed Cytech accreditation which is nationally recognized across the UK. This allows the technician a broader understanding of bicycles beyond the models they work on every day. Isla is very influenced by lean manufacturing principles and ensures that her whole operation is about customer pull, and elimination of all wastes including wasted labour (e.g. wasting time looking for the correct tools for doing the PDI), where the workstations are bespoke designed with everything that the workers need. The stations are also on wheels so they can be moved around when the inventory builds up in the Ludlow warehouse.

The significance of the Imagine Project is that it rethinks the way bicycles will be made and supplied in the future. Its proposition is 'to manufacture and supply children's bikes for rent to the UK market'. Isla believes that the future supply chain will be based on renting the same product multiple times rather than selling it once. The products will be made in small factories close to the market. Ownership will be a thing of the past, and factories will retain ownership. Bicycles therefore will be rented to the user. When they are finished with (either because the owner no longer requires a bike, or has grown out of it) they will be returned to the factory, refurbished and rented to another rider. This will prevent precious raw materials from going into landfill.

Isla argues that "we will have to make bikes that last for much longer than they do now so that we can rent them for as long as possible". The bicycles will be designed so that when they finally reach the end of their lives all raw materials can be separated and reused. This is known as a 'closed loop' or circular supply chain. The aim is that nothing will go into landfill. Indeed, it's anticipated that raw materials will become so precious that business and government will begin mining our landfill sites later this century to recover what was thrown away in the last. Islabikes have always been designed and made with longevity in mind and are renowned as lightweight yet robust and serviceable bikes for children, which can withstand the rigours of use by successive young riders. Unfortunately, as with any bicycle, due to the natural fatigue of the materials they are made from they will eventually reach the end of their useful life. When this happens there is at present no established mechanism to recover and reuse all of the precious materials which are used in their manufacture. In future, therefore, the plan is to transition from the traditional linear 'take, make, dispose' supply of bicycles to an innovative, sustainable circular product and full service-based approach.

12.8 CONCLUSION

This chapter defines what is meant by services and service operations, emphasizing the growing importance of terms such as servitization and the concept of the service-based supply chain. Services offer considerable scope to expand firm revenues particularly in the context of an installed base of existing equipment, but also introduce additional complexity in terms of managing multiple customer and supplier interactions simultaneously as part of a professional service offering. Procurement and supply management has an extremely important role to play in service-based business models, identifying upfront during programme planning the type of support requirements needed, and selecting the best suppliers to deliver defined performance outcomes and continuous innovation as part of long-term maintenance and product upgrade. Perhaps the most difficult task is re-engaging with customers and suppliers at the product, platform, or facility's end-of-life to instigate a product recovery programme which meets all legislative requirements and rewards stakeholders for their participation. This means shifting current business models based on asset ownership, towards leasing and services by the manufacturer for the purpose of extending use and increasing the product lifecycle. Improving downstream supply chain operations through increased collaboration and sharing, and developing models which actively encourage circular activity as a standard component of after-sales customer service are expected to drive the future agenda on sustainability and service-based supply chain innovation. As part of the transition pathway this may mean combining the circular economy and sharing economy as part of a systemic, hybrid approach which recognizes the value and connection between business, society, and the natural environment.

REFERENCES

Aldieri L, Brahmi M, Bruno B and Vinci CP (2021) Circular economy business models: The complementarities with sharing economy and eco-innovations investments. *Sustainability* 13(22): 12438.

Araujo L and Spring M (2006) Services, products, and the institutional structure of production. *Industrial Marketing Management* 35(7): 797–805.

Araujo L and Spring M (2009) Service, services and products: Rethinking operations strategy. *International Journal of Operations & Production Management* 29(5): 444–467.

Aurich J, Fuchs C and Wagenknecht C (2006) Lifecycle orientated design of technical product-service systems. *Journal of Cleaner Production* 14(17): 1480–1494.

Baines TS, Lightfoot HW, Benedettini O and Kay JM (2009) The servitization of manufacturing: A review of literature and reflection on future challenges. *Journal of Manufacturing Technology Management* 20(5): 547–567.

Brady T and Davies A (2011) Learning to deliver a mega-project: The case of Heathrow terminal 5. In: N Caldwell and M Howard (eds) *Procuring Complex Performance: Studies of Innovation in Product-service Management*. NY: Taylor & Francis Group.

Brax SA and Jonsson K (2009) Developing integrated solution offerings for remote diagnostics: A comparative case study of two manufacturers. *International Journal of Operations & Production Management* 29(5): 539–560.

Caldwell N and Howard M (2011) *Procuring Complex Performance: Studies of Innovation in Product-service Management*. NY: Taylor & Francis Group.

Caldwell N and Howard M (2014) Contracting for complex performance in markets of few buyers and sellers: The case of military procurement. In: M Howard and N Caldwell (eds) *International Journal of Operations & Production Management*, Special Issue in Procuring and Management Complex Performance 34(2).

Corrêa H, Ellram L, Scavarda A and Cooper M (2007) An operations management view of the services and goods offering mix. *International Journal of Operations & Production Management*, Special Issue 27(5): 444–463.

Cusumano AM (2008) The changing software business: Moving from products to services. IEEE Computer Society. *Computer* (January): 20–27.

Davies A and Brady T (2000) Organisational capabilities and learning in complex product systems: Towards repeatable solutions. *Research Policy* 29(7–8): 931–953.

Davies A and Hobday M (2005) *The Business of Projects: Managing Innovation in Complex Projects and Systems*. Cambridge Press.

Davies A, Brady T and Hobday M (2006) Charting a path towards integrated solutions. *MIT Sloan Management Review* 47(3): 39–48.

Dyer J and Singh H (1998) The relational view: Cooperative strategy and sources of inter-organizational competitive advantage. *Academy of Management Review* 23(4): 660–679.

Goedkoop M, van Halen C, Te Riele H and Rommens P (1999) *Product Service Systems: Ecological and Economic Basics*. The Hague: VROM.

Guide V (2000) Production planning and control for remanufacturing: Industry practice and research needs. *Journal of Operations Management* 18: 467–483.

Haddon-Cave C (2009) The Nimrod Review – The Loss of RAF Nimrod XV230: A Failure of leadership, culture and priorities. Report HC1025. London Stationary Office, Crown Copyright.

Henry M, Schraven D, Bocken N, Frenken K, Hekkert M and Kirchherr J (2021) The battle of the buzzwords: A comparative review of the circular economy and the sharing economy concepts. *Environmental Innovation and Societal Transitions* 38: 1–21.

Hobday M (1998) Product complexity, innovation and industrial organisation. *Research Policy* 26(6), February: 689–710.

Howard M and Caldwell N (2014) Editorial to the Special Issue in Procuring and Managing Complex Performance. *International Journal of Operations & Production Management* 34(2).

Howard M, Böhm S and Eatherley D (2022) Systems resilience and SME multilevel challenges: A place-based conceptualization of the circular economy. *Journal of Business Research* 145: 757–768.

IfM-IBM (2007) Succeeding through service innovation: Developing a service perspective on economic growth and prosperity. A discussion paper with recommendations for education, business & policy, by University of Cambridge Institute for Manufacturing (IfM) and International Business Machine (IBM).

Jabbour CJC, Camargo Fiorini P, Wong C, Jugend D, Lopes de Sousa Jabbour AB, Seles BMR, Pinheiro MAP and Ribeiro da Silva HM (2020) First-mover firms in the transition towards the sharing economy in metallic natural resource-intensive industries: Implications for the circular economy and emerging industry 4.0 technologies. *Resource Policy* 66.

Jacob F and Ulaga W (2008) The transition from product to service in business markets: An agenda for academic enquiry. *Industrial Marketing Management* 37: 247–253.

Jayaraman V, Guide V and Srivastava R (1999) A closed-loop logistics model for remanufacturing. *Journal of the Operational Research Society* 50: 497–508.

Johnsen T, Howard M and Miemczyk J (2009) UK defence change and the impact on supply relationships. *Supply Chain Management: An International Journal* 14(4): 270–279.

Johnson R (1994) Operations: From factory to service management. *International Journal of Service Industry Management* 5(1): 49–63.

Johnson R and Clark G (2005) *Service Operations Management – Improving Service Delivery*. 2nd edn, Harlow UK: FT Prentice Hall.

Kang GD and James J (2004) Service quality dimensions: An examination of Grönroos's service quality model. *Managing Service Quality: An International Journal* 14(4): 266–277.

Kraljic P (1983) Purchasing must become supply management. *Harvard Business Review* 61(5), September/October: 107–117.

Lewis M and Roehrich J (2009) Contracts, relationships and integration: Towards a model of the procurement of complex performance. *International Journal of Procurement Management* 2(2): 125–142.

Lindberg N and Nordin F (2008) From products to services and back again: Towards a new service procurement logic. *Industrial Marketing Management* 37: 292–300.

Lund R (1984) Remanufacturing. *Technology Review* 87(2), February–March: 19–29.

Manzini E, Vezzoli C and Clark G (2001) Product-service systems: Using an existing concept as a new approach to sustainability. *Journal of Design Research* 1(2).

Melnyk S, Davis E, Spekman R and Sandor J (2010) Outcome-driven supply chains. *MIT Sloan Management Review* (Winter, Special Issue): 33–38.

MoD – Ministry of Defence (2005) *Defence Industrial Strategy*. Defence White Paper. Ref: Cm 6697. London Stationery Office, House of Commons.

Mont O (2002) Clarifying the concept of product-service system. *Journal of Cleaner Production* 10: 237–245.

NAO – National Audit Office (2003) *Through-Life Management*. Report by the Comptroller & Auditor General. London Stationery Office, House of Commons.

NAO – National Audit Office (2007) *Transforming Logistics Support for Fast Jets*. Report by the Comptroller & Auditor General. HC 825 session. London Stationery Office, House of Commons.

Neely A (2008) Exploring the financial consequences of the servitization of manufacturing. *Operations Management Research* 1(2): 103–118.

Oliva R and Kallenberg R (2003) Managing the transition from products to services. *International Journal of Service Industry Management* 14(2): 160–172.

Penrose E (1959) *The Theory of the Growth of the Firm*. Oxford University Press.

Plewnia F and Guenther E (2018) Mapping the sharing economy for sustainability research. *Management Decision* 56(3): 570–583.

Poppo L and Zenger T (2002) Do formal contracts and relational governance function as substitutes or complements? *Strategic Management Journal* 23(8): 707–725

Porter M (1985) *Competitive Advantage: Creating & Sustaining Superior Performance*. NY: Free Press.

Potts G (1988) Exploit your products service life cycle. *Harvard Business Review* (Sept–Oct): 32–36.

Quinn J, Doorley T and Paquette P (1990) Beyond products: Service-based strategy. *Harvard Business Review* (March/April): 58–67.

Rolls-Royce (2006) Service package shifts focus from support to availability. *Indepth Rolls-Royce* (10): 22–23.

Roth A and Menor L (2003) Insights into service operations management: A research agenda. *Production and Operations Management* 12(2): 145–164.
Sanderson J (2009) Buyer-supplier partnering in UK defence procurement: Looking beyond the policy rhetoric. *Public administration* 87(2): 327–350.
Savaskan R, Bhattacharya S and van Wassenhove L (2004) Closed loop supply chain models with product remanufacturing. *Management Science* 50(2): 239–252.
Schemmer RW (1995) *Service Operations Management.* Englewood Cliffs, NY: Prentice-Hall.
Schweitzer E And Aurich JC (2010) Continuous improvement of industrial product-service systems. *CIRP Journal of Manufacturing Science and Technology* 3: 158–164.
Silvestro R, Fitzgerald L, Johnston R and Voss C (1992) Towards a classification of service processes. *International Journal of Service Industry Management* 3(3): 62–75.
Sorrell S, Dimitropoulos J and Sommerville M (2009) Empirical estimates of the direct rebound effect: A review. *Energy Policy* 37(4): 1356–1371.
Sosnowski PC (2024) The role of circular supply chains in sharing economy: Literature review and conceptual framework. *International Journal of Innovation and Sustainable Development* 18(3): 350–379.
Stremersch S, Wuyts S and Frambach R (2001) The purchasing of full-service contracts. *Industrial Marketing Management* 30: 1–12.
Vandermerwe S and Rada J (1988) Servitization of business: Adding value by adding services. *European Management Journal* 6(4): 314–324.
van Looy B, Gemmel P and van Dierdonck (1998) *Services Management: An Integrated Approach.* Harlow UK: FT Prentice Hall.
van Marrewijk A, Clegg SR, Pitsis TS and Veenswijk M (2008) Managing public-private megaprojects. *International Journal of Project Management* 26: 591–600.
Vargo S and Lusch R (2004) The four service marketing myths: Remnants of a goods-based manufacturing model. *Journal of Service Research* 6(4): 324–335.
Voss C (2008) Thoughts on servitization. Presentation at the 1st International Euroma Service Operations Management Forum, University of Exeter, UK.
Wise R and Baumgartner P (1999) Go downstream – The new profit imperative in manufacturing. *Harvard Business Review* 77(5): 133–141.
Youngdahl W and Loomba A (2000) Service-driven global supply chains. *International Journal of Service Industry Management* 11(4): 329–347.

FURTHER READING

Ellram LM, Tate W and Billington C (2008) Offshore outsourcing of professional services: A transaction cost economics perspective. *Journal of Operations Management* 26(2): 148–163.
Howard M and Miemczyk J (2011) Supply management in naval defence. In: N Caldwell and M Howard (eds) *Procuring Complex Performance: Studies of Innovation in Product-service Management.* NY: Taylor & Francis Group.
Vargo S, Maglio P and Akaka M (2008) On value and value co-creation: A service systems and service logic perspective. *European Management Journal* 26(3): 145–152.

PART C

Policy, tools, and implementation

CHAPTER 13

Sustainability policy

Regulatory and voluntary frameworks

LEARNING OBJECTIVES:

At the end of this chapter you should be able to:

- Understand the evolution and role of standards and legislation in procurement and supply chain practices;
- Review standards and legislation related to sustainable procurement and supply chains as well as emerging unvoluntary rankings organized by society and nongovernmental organizations (NGOs);
- Classify the main types of codes of conduct and their uses and limitations.

13.1 INTRODUCTION

The purpose of this chapter is to provide an overview of key legislation, international standards, and guidelines (collectively termed 'policy') affecting sustainability in global trade in general and impacting procurement and supply chain management in particular. In line with the focus of this book, this overview examines those frameworks that are developed to support sustainability imperatives set by international organizations and institutions. In this sense policy can affect any of the three pillars of sustainability i.e. environmental (waste, pollution), social (slavery, child labour), and economic (fair pricing, avoidance of corruption). This chapter does not aim to cover all policies exhaustively but instead identifies those that are most important to procurement and supply chain managers. Thus, this chapter provides insights into how procurement and supply chain decisions may be affected by sustainability-related policy.

Historically, policy relating to sustainability tends to focus on environmental issues such as waste and pollution. Regulations provide a framework of rules within which companies can operate in accordance with the social norms accepted in a region or even globally through multilateral agreements. Typically, these rules are seen as a set of constraints to companies, preventing *laissez faire* free market forces from allowing business practices to harm the environment and society, and so are designed to cope with classical market failures.[1] For example "Globalization critics argue that international trade spurs a race to

DOI: 10.4324/9781003499602-16

the bottom among national environmental standards" (Prakash and Potoski, 2006: 350). As such, suppliers selling into a market or buyers sourcing from a specific region need to be aware of these constraints in order to comply with the legal minimums. Having regulation does not imply that all companies comply though, and it also does not mean that companies meet all societal expectations. Hence, standards and guidelines (codes of practice) have also been developed to provide a framework within which companies can operate, where specific laws are absent (Preuss, 2009), but social norms still exist. In particular, international standards (specifically those developed by ISO) provide further frameworks allowing companies to demonstrate how they deal with specific issues such as environmental management or socially sensitive behaviours and practices. In general these international standards are put in place to provide a minimum level of control (King et al., 2005), so that companies on a global basis can demonstrate how they account for these issues, providing a level playing field. Guidelines and codes of practice tend to be more flexible and more targeted towards specific sectors or practices and are also a way of showing that companies meet certain (minimum) requirements.

Internationally recognized regulation, standards, and guidelines are becoming more important in the domain of procurement and supply chain management characterized by internationalizing operations and global spread of sourcing activities. Moreover, society led by NGOs has slowly moved beyond inviting companies to join voluntary frameworks, to enforcing public transparency rankings as a form of pressure.

This chapter is organized as follows. In the first part, international regulation related to sustainability and affecting supply chains is presented. A timeline is used to denote how regulation becomes increasingly demanding. This mainly focuses on European Directives developed to minimize waste and pollution from chemical products. In particular, the 2023 German Supply Chain Act marks the inclusion of the term 'Supply Chain' in the title of a relevant legislation. An additional part of this section also discusses pertinent international agreements that affect international trade. The second part shifts from mandatory legislation to voluntary frameworks, starting with the International Standards Organization (ISO) as a baseline, and discussing the evolution of codes of conduct. The third section discusses recent advancements where society takes the driver seat to produce unvoluntary rankings that expose companies and pressure them to improve their transparency. Such movements stand in between mandatory public policy and voluntary private schemes. Using the fashion industry as an example, we discuss how the Rana Plaza disaster mentioned in Chapter 9 led to the development of mechanisms to pressure fashion brands to improve supply chain disclosure. The chapter concludes with final reflections on the implications of escalating mandatory and voluntary frameworks on supply chain management.

Note 13.1 The Deepwater Horizon disaster

In 2010 the Deepwater Horizon oil rig explosion killed 11 workers and released nearly five million barrels of oil into the Gulf of Mexico. It devastated marine ecosystems, polluted coastlines, and harmed fisheries. Communities still face health issues, economic losses, and long-term environmental damage, marking it as the worst US offshore oil spill.

If a supplier does not comply with their client's standards, and is exposed in the media, the damage can be significant. Yet simply blaming the supplier may also cause backlash. Consider British Petroleum's (BP) initial response to the 2010 oil spill. BP's internal inquiry into the causes of the disaster provoked immediate criticism from its contractors, as well as US politicians who said the British group was "happy to slice up blame, as long as it gets the smallest piece" (Financial Times, 2010). BP accepted that its engineers should shoulder some of the blame but attempted to pass on the responsibility to its contractors, Transocean, the owner of the Deepwater Horizon drilling rig that exploded, and Halliburton, the company responsible for cementing the Macondo well. The lesson of this accident is that a company cannot simply blame its supplier when something goes wrong and so the responsibility to meet laws, regulations, and standards extends well beyond the company walls and well into the supply chain.

Source: AP News (2025)

13.2 THE EVOLUTION OF THE REGULATORY FRAMEWORK ON SUSTAINABILITY

Historically, social sustainability – especially labour practices – has been limited to international guidelines, such as those developed by the ILO, and not subject to international law. Yet, recent legislation has changed the landscape. A number of new policy developments that emerged since 2010 have significant supply chain relevance notably on supply chain transparency and modern slavery issues (see Figure 13.1). Put together, risks related to social conditions and environmental sustainability are increasingly subject to legislation that includes the request of due diligence procedures to ensure these risks are taken care of along the extended – often global – supply chain. This approach extends the reach of legislation from the country of origin of focal companies to affect their suppliers in other countries if they intend to comply and keep supplying to those focal companies. Environmental sustainability, due to its transboundary nature, is subject to numerous international, multilateral agreements. As a result of this, international trade flows and in particular importation into certain regions, is subject to laws and restrictions with which exporters, importers, and buyers need to comply.

This section does not describe all such policy but instead highlights the types of legislation – with a number of examples – that constrain the free movement of goods in supply chains. The difficulty for businesses is that they need significant investment in skills, compliance personnel, consultancies, and so on to assure compliance, with companies often complaining that "the rules are too complex, they are unclear, they require unreasonable expenditures and they change too often" (Ruhl et al., 2002: 25).

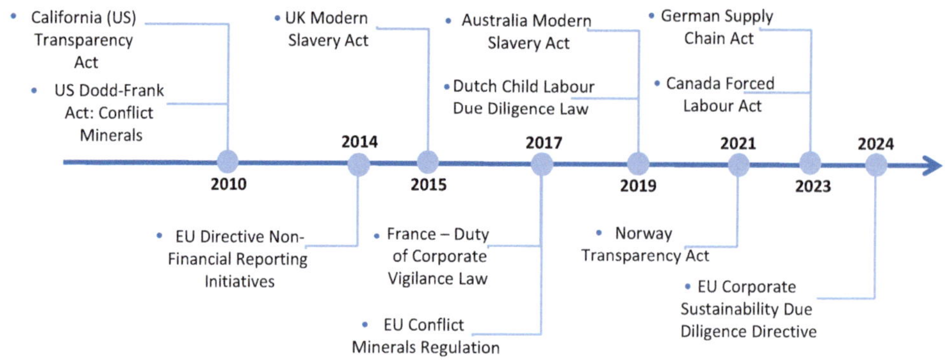

FIGURE 13.1 Timeline of sustainability-related legislation
Source: Adapted and expanded from Marques et al. (2021)

13.2.1 Restricting unsustainable supply inputs

The EU *Restrictions on Hazardous Substances (RoHS) and the Restriction of the use of hazardous substances in electrical and electronic equipment (EEE)* (EC, n.d.a) restrict the use of hazardous substances in electrical and electronic equipment (RoHS Directive 2002/95/EC) and promote the collection and recycling of such equipment (WEEE Directive 2002/96/EC). The legislation provides for the creation of collection schemes where consumers return their used e-waste free of charge. The objective of these schemes is to increase the recycling and/or re-use of such products. It also requires heavy metals such as lead, mercury, cadmium, and hexavalent chromium and flame retardants such as polybrominated biphenyls (PBB) or polybrominated diphenyl ethers (PBDE) to be substituted by safer alternatives.

The aim of the RoHS was also to reduce administrative burdens and ensure coherency with newer policies and legislation covering, for example, chemicals and the new legislative framework for the marketing of products in the EU. A revised RoHS Directive was published in the Official Journal of the European Union on 1 July 2011. The revised RoHS Directive on the restriction of hazardous substances in electrical and electronic equipment continues to ban lead, mercury, cadmium, hexavalent chromium, and so on but has now been extended to all electronic equipment, cables, and spare parts.

Inadequately treated e-waste poses environmental and health risks. In December 2008, the European Commission therefore proposed to revise the directives on electrical and electronic equipment in order to tackle the increasing waste stream of these types of products. The aim is to increase the amount of e-waste that is appropriately treated and to reduce the volume that goes to landfill disposal.

A complementary regulation is the *REACH Regulation (EC) No 1907/2006* that applies to substances in articles (products such as household goods). REACH stands for Regulation on Registration, Evaluation, Authorization and Restriction of Chemicals and entered into force on 1 June 2007. All substances manufactured or imported above 100 tonnes per year have to be registered (EC, n.d.b). Manufacturers and importers of chemicals must identify and manage risks linked to the substances they manufacture and market. For substances manufactured or imported in quantities of one tonne or more per year per company, manufacturers and importers need to demonstrate that they have appropriately done so by means of a registration dossier, which must be submitted to the European Chemicals Agency (ECHA). This can apply to many different types of products ranging from furniture, clothes, vehicles, books, toys, and electronic equipment.

This means that all buyers of products in Europe must obtain a complete chemical inventory of the products they buy within or from outside Europe. Eventually this regulation will be linked to substance restrictions as defined in the ROHS regulation and to further limitations on the types of substances that can be put on sale in Europe.

13.2.2 Producer responsibility (WEEE and ELV Directives)

Other regulations restricting supply chain operations in Europe in particular include those related to producer responsibility. Directives such as the *Directive 2002/96/EC* (EC, 2007) on waste electrical and electronic equipment (but also the *End of Life Vehicle – ELV Directive*) force distributors and manufacturers of products in Europe to take responsibility for the waste generated by the disposal of their products. This implies that companies both restrict certain hazardous substances in their products but also design their products to ensure that they are recyclable. A further element of these laws makes manufacturers responsible for the free (to end users) take back and recycling of these products. Again this implies that suppliers have to take part in design for recycling initiatives with car and electric equipment manufacturers in order to help their customers comply with these new laws.

13.2.3 Supply chain transparency and modern slavery policy

What does Arnold Schwarzenegger have to do with sustainability in supply chains? In 2010, *The California Supply Chain Transparency Act* was one of the first examples of supply chain responsibility being enshrined in law. Signed by Arnold Schwarzenegger this piece of legislation requires companies with a turnover of $100 million or more to disclose how they plan to eradicate slavery and human trafficking from their direct supply chain. Related to this the *UK Modern Slavery Act 2015* requires that companies also disclose the risks of modern slavery and trafficking in their supply chains. In particular they are required to show

> due diligence processes in relation to slavery and human trafficking in its business and supply chains; (d) the parts of its business and supply chains where there is a risk of slavery and human trafficking taking place, and the steps it has taken to assess and manage that risk; (e) its effectiveness in ensuring that slavery and human trafficking is not taking place in its business or supply chains, measured against such performance indicators as it considers appropriate.
>
> (UK Legislation, 2015)

The *French law on Corporate Duty of Vigilance*: this law signed in February 2017 is designed to regulate companies with more than 5,000 employees in the company's direct or indirect French-based subsidiaries and with more than 10,000 employees if including direct and indirect subsidiaries globally. These companies must declare whether they have social sustainability risks such as health and safety violations, human rights, and even environmental risks in their supply chains. In-scope companies must prepare a due diligence plan for these risks and include provisions for mapping supply chain risks and provide evidence of evaluation and an alert system in the case of high risks. Companies could be liable for a €10 million penalty if they cannot provide such a plan and required evidence. This is the first step for any country to create a real supply chain liability policy. Other countries such as the Netherlands and Switzerland have followed closely behind.

The Australian *Modern Slavery Act* came into effect on 1 January 2019 aiming to increase corporate transparency around modern slavery risks in global supply chains. It requires entities with an annual consolidated revenue of at least A$100 million to submit yearly Modern Slavery Statements, detailing the risks and actions taken to mitigate them. These reports are made publicly available on a government registry. While the *Commonwealth Act* does not impose financial penalties, it uses a 'name and shame' approach for non-compliant entities. However, a 2023 statutory review has recommended introducing civil penalties for failing to report, false reporting, or non-compliance with ministerial directions. Separately, New South Wales passed its own legislation with a lower threshold (A$50 million) and potential fines up to A$1.1 million, though it is not yet enforced. The Act has placed Australia among countries promoting responsible business conduct through transparency and accountability.

The German Supply Chain Act (*Lieferkettensorgfaltspflichtengesetz*, or LkSG) came into force on 1 January 2023, initially applying to companies with 3,000 or more employees in Germany. From 1 January 2024 its scope expanded to include companies with at least 1,000 employees. The law requires these companies to ensure that both human rights and certain environmental standards are respected throughout their global supply chains. Under the law, companies must implement risk management systems, conduct regular risk analyses, adopt preventive and corrective measures, establish a complaints mechanism, and document and report their due diligence activities annually. Obligations apply to a company's own operations, direct suppliers, and – in certain cases – indirect suppliers when there is substantiated knowledge of potential violations. Thus, the Act enforces companies to implement due diligence beyond their operations, to their extended supply chains. The law prohibits child labour, forced labour, hazardous working conditions, and serious environmental damage. Oversight can lead to fines of up to 2 per cent of global turnover and exclude non-compliant companies from public procurement – which is of course a major customer for German companies. The German Supply Chain Act marks a major shift towards legally enforceable due diligence.

Recent research has discussed the impact of supply chain-related legislation, such as the German Supply Chain Act. The study by Brandenburg et al. (2024) offers insights into what an EU-wide legislation for SC due diligence could look like. It is relevant to note that, from 2010 to 2023, the threshold for company size has been significantly reduced, putting more companies under scrutiny, included medium-sized ones. It is also worth noting that rigour has increased, and fees and punishment have become institutionalized.

More recently the European Commission has been working on a Europe wide equivalent to these national initiatives. *Directive (EU) 2024/1760 (corporate sustainability due diligence the* CSDDD*)* reshapes supply chains by imposing mandatory human-rights and environmental due diligence across a company's 'chain of activities', covering upstream and selected downstream relationships. Firms in scope – generally those with over 1,000 employees and turnover above €450m – must identify, prevent, mitigate, and remediate adverse impacts; operate grievance mechanisms; and integrate due diligence into policies, risk mapping, and board oversight. Whilst still under negotiation which could lead to watering down compliance requires supply-chain governance beyond disclosure. Companies should: (1) implement risk-based screening and monitoring of suppliers, prioritizing salient impacts; (2) embed contractual clauses, capacity-building, and supplier engagement rather than disengagement; (3) ensure access to remediation and effective grievance channels; (4) execute a climate transition plan aligned with a 1.5°C pathway under Article 15, linking incentives to delivery; and (5) strengthen data systems for traceability and assurance (Reuters, 2024).

A related legislation already in place is the European Union's *Corporate Sustainability Reporting Directive (CSRD)* (in force from January 2023) which substantially extends reporting obligations for companies concerning their environmental, social, and governance (ESG) impacts, inclusive of value chains (upstream and downstream). Supply chain implications include the need to gather granular data from suppliers (including potentially multi-tier suppliers), especially for scope 3 greenhouse gas emissions, labour practices, human rights, resource usage, pollution, and waste. Double materiality (i.e. reporting both how sustainability matters affect the company and how the company's operations affect environment and society) compels companies to assess not just risk but impact across their supply chains (Deloitte, 2025).

13.2.4 Other policy agreements affecting trade

Over the last decades there have been a number of crucial multilateral agreements – between national governments – concerning the environment in particular. The reasoning for this is that environmental issues including pollution do not respect politically agreed boundaries and frontiers and therefore the control of impacts can only be done cooperatively between nation states through multilateral agreements. Therefore, companies have to be constantly vigilant that they meet these requirements if applicable to the products they are either buying or distributing on a global basis. In general these policies have very little impact on global trade overall from an overall cost perspective (Harris et al., 2002), however there are implications for the knowledge levels of supply chain professionals who have to be aware of what is allowed and what it not. Due diligence is now an important part of the supply professional's remit, and compliance to regulation is one important element of this. There are particular challenges to supply chain traceability in this case. The following table outlines some of the key international multilateral agreements affecting global trade and proposing some of the supply chain implications.

TABLE 13.1 Examples of international environmental agreements affecting supply chains

Name	*Main focus*	*Supply chain implications*
Montreal Protocol	Enforced from 1989 this international agreement was put in place to phase out ozone depleting substance such as CFCs to protect the atmospheric ozone layer. Largely replaced by HFCs which are also greenhouse gases which also have negative effects on global warming instead. However the protocol is hailed a success with complete ozone layer recovery by 2050	Companies had to ensure that they produced or sold no products that contained CFCs which required product redesign with the supply base
Stockholm Convention	Effective in 2004, aimed to restrict the use of persistent organic pollutants, POPs, which are used in electrical transformers, capacitors, and in paint and lubricants. These can lead to the release of dioxins which are cancerous	Companies had to ensure their industrial processes phased out POPs and to ensure supplied products, such as industrial paints, did not contain POPs
Basel Convention	This treaty became enforced in 1992 with the aim to control transboundary movement of hazardous waste especially from developed to developing countries. The treaty ensures the restriction of toxic wastes and to help developing countries manage wastes	In order to avoid toxic colonialism, i.e. exporting hazardous wastes to developing countries which could result from current recycling practices in Europe such as export of mobile phones and electronics
Rotterdam Convention	Restricts the imports of hazardous chemicals and pesticides and requires proper labelling and informing purchasers of any hazards	The onus is on exporters but this provides more information to buying companies on the products they source from overseas
Convention on Biological Diversity	From 1993 aims to conserve biodiversity by ensuring ecosystems and biological resources are protected especially if for commercial uses	Many supply chains rely on ecosystem resources such a freshwater, soil timber, and wood fiber and as such this convention ensures the equitable sharing of these resources and by implication the restriction of supply in certain instances
CITES	In 1975, the convention on international trade in endangered species of wild fauna and flora to limit the risk of species survival. Control the trade of these selected species (more than 34,000)	This is a particular challenge to supply chain traceability of certain 'wild' products such as python skins that are used in the luxury fashion sector, where only farmed materials should be used

In summary, there are a burgeoning number of laws and regulations aimed at reducing environmental and social impacts of business activities, which employees involved in international trade need to be aware of. With the growing number of codes of practice and standards being put in place, compliance is the baseline from which to start, but even achieving this can be a huge challenge and it is no wonder companies often claim involuntary non-compliance due to the sheer complexity of these policies (Ruhl et al., 2002). Even high profile legal experts admit that 'slippage' in compliance is almost inevitable (Farber, 1999). Although there are cost implications to noncompliance this is often low compared with the investment required to meet rules. However, the media does not care whether companies willingly break laws or do so 'by accident', the impact on reputation is the same, you are either evil or incompetent!

13.3 THE EXPANSION OF THE VOLUNTARY SUSTAINABILITY FRAMEWORKS

13.3.1 ISO: quality, environment, and social standards

The International Standards Organization (ISO) is the world's largest developer of international standards (existing as a network of national standards bodies, including e.g. BSI in the UK and AFNOR in France). The organization provides a forum for the negotiation of global standards in order to address business and social problems. This forum includes firms, NGOs, and governmental bodies who work to meet the requirements of business and the broader needs of society. ISO has a membership of 163 national standards bodies in all regions of the world, including industrialized and developing economies. ISO has a portfolio of over 18,000 standards which provide business, government, and society with practical tools for the three dimensions of sustainable development: economic, environmental, and social. This section will start by discussing quality standards as these have been used in supplier selection processes for many years and this standard has been the basis for subsequent standards more focused on the environment and social issues.

The main standard developed by ISO is related to quality management: the ISO 9000. While this standard does not link directly to the issues of sustainability (except in the area of product safety perhaps), it has formed the basis of standards linking to environmental management (ISO 14001) and guidance on managing social issues (ISO 26000). The main elements of the ISO 9000 are:

- Top management commitment;
- Establish implementation team;
- Start ISO 9001 awareness programmes;
- Provide training;
- Conduct initial status survey;
- Create a documented implementation plan;
- Develop quality management system documentation;
- Document control;
- Implementation;
- Internal quality audit;

- Management review;
- Pre-assessment audit;
- Certification and registration;
- Continual Improvement.

While these elements were originally planned for quality management systems, they have also formed the basis of the recently developed environmental and social standards. One of the advantages of adopting the ISO series of standards is that they require similar implementation which means they can be combined (i.e. combining document control and audit procedures across quality, environment, safety, and social management systems). The ISO standards can also have different scopes depending on the requirements of the company. For example, with the ISO 9000 series companies can choose to focus the system on just the assembly and testing of products (ISO 9003), include production systems in the scope (ISO 9002), or include all these plus product design, development, installation, and services in the management system (ISO 9001). The main countries in terms of volumes of certifications across the world include China, Italy, UK, Japan, Spain, and the USA.

A number of studies have shown that there are benefits to ISO 9000 related to improved quality awareness, better customer service, greater discipline, improved internal procedures, and even increased organizational efficiency (Johansson et al., 1993; Poksinska et al., 2002). Some researchers have also shown that positive financial performance is often achieved from the first year of certification (Corbett et al., 2005) and in terms of the costs and benefits certification is a worthwhile investment (Lundmark and Westelius, 2006).

However, there have been some criticisms with some commentators stating that ISO 9000 has turned into a pursuit of certificates rather than quality itself, that certification requires a 'mountain' of paperwork, the process is only for documentation, and that it discourages free-thinking (Stevenson and Barnes, 2001). Furthermore the implementation of ISO 9001 in particular can be costly with estimated average costs of $245,200 per certification. Most of this cost relates to employees' time, training, and the use of consultants (the actual registration cost being a rather smaller percentage). However despite these potential downsides – which are more related to the method of deployment than the standard itself – ISO 9000 certification has become a commonly accepted order qualifier for many buying organizations around the world.

While it is important to have an awareness of quality management systems, this chapter focuses on sustainability-related standards. This sub-section reviews the two main environmental management system (EMS) standards ISO 14001 and EMAS. An EMS is one of the tools that an organization can use to implement an environmental policy. It consists of a set of practices that aim to support companies on the road to managing, measuring, and improving the environmental impact of their operations (Welford, 1999).

ISO 14001 is the EMS specification developed by the International Organization for Standardization (ISO) and is part of the ISO 14000 series of environmental management documents. It was issued as both an International and American National Standard in September 1996. The Second Edition of ISO 14001, ISO 14001:2004, was issued as an International Standard in November 2004. There is often confusion over the use of the term ISO 14000 because many people say ISO 14000 when they mean ISO 14001. ISO 14000 refers to the series of voluntary standards and guidelines for environmental management developed by subcommittees of ISO Technical Committee 207 (TC 207); ISO 14001 is one of those standards. Ultimately, TC 207 may develop 15–20 environmental management documents in the ISO 14000 series. This standard is seen as the most widely adopted environmental management system, although there are criticisms that it only provides a minimum level of process control (Prakash and Potoski, 2006).

The main steps to obtain ISO 14001 are as follows:

1. Obtain commitment from top management;
2. Define responsibilities, appoint management representative(s), establish EMS steering committee, develop implementation plan, initial training on EMS;
3. Planning – identify environmental aspects, legal and other requirements; formulate environmental policy; establish environmental objectives and targets and programmes;
4. Implementation and operation – develop documentation and processes;
5. Checking – develop processes for monitoring and measurement and corrective and preventive action;
6. Develop and deliver presentation for awareness of the EMS;
7. Establish internal audit programme, including training; conduct initial internal audit to evaluate conformity to requirements of ISO 14001, including evaluation of compliance;
8. Follow up internal audit with improvements to system;
9. Conduct initial management review of EMS;
10. Implement improvements from management review.

ISO 14001 is designed to be adopted by any type of organization in any industrial sector. Although organizations seeking ISO 14001 can self-declare, there are greater benefits with third-party certification notably in reinforcing the credibility of certifications with customers, regulatory agencies, and the community. Due to third-party certification, ISO 14001 can be more costly than other voluntary codes such as Responsible Care (a US based code for the chemicals industry). The certification costs can vary widely, depending on the size of the company, the type of its operation, and the environmental system already in place. Estimates range from less than \$50,000 for small firms to greater than \$200,000 for larger firms (Watkins and Gutzwiller, 1999). These estimations involve the certification process only and do not take into account the cost of organizational changes that firms may have to carry out to attain the ISO 14001 standard.

One important aspect of ISO 14001 is the idea of *continual* improvement; the difference between continuous and continual is subtle but means companies do not need to show uninterrupted improvement throughout a period for example, only an improvement at the audit date compared to a reference date. This is based on the plan-do-check-act cycle that has been used in quality management systems for many years, again demonstrating the strong link to quality management systems.

Since 1996 ISO 14001 has been developed further to include other standards related to the environmental management systems. These developments include further guidance

TABLE 13.2 Main standards in the ISO 14000 series

Organizational evaluation	*Product evaluation*
Environmental management systems ISO 14001 and ISO 14004	Environmental labeling ISO 14021–1402X
Environmental auditing ISO 14010–14012 and ISO 14015	Life cycle assessment ISO 14040–14043
Environmental performance evaluation ISO 14031	Guide for the inclusion of environmental aspects of product standards ISO Guide 64
Terms and definitions ISO 14050	

on evaluating the company itself such as how to measure performance but have also expanded to include product related issues such as life cycle assessment. The table below provides the main components available as part of the ISO 14001 series standard.

From a procurement and supply chain perspective, the life cycle elements of ISO 14000 are of particular interest as they can provide a standardized way of assessing the sustainability related aspect of products and services bought by companies. Research on ISO 14001 is rather mixed in terms of showing the benefits. Some research shows no economic benefits only awareness and reputation enhancement (Vastag and Melnyk, 2002), whereas other studies have shown that economic benefits of environmental improvements are not realized by smaller suppliers (Nawrocka, 2008), which is not so surprising given the investment costs of such actions.

In 1993, the European Commission adopted the EMAS regulation, which established a voluntary system in which industrial sites could participate by implementing an EMS and pledge to achieve continual improvement in environmental performance (Kollman and Prakash, 2001). Although voluntary, EMAS was established by the European Commission, an executive body composed of members of the European Union countries, rather than from industry or NGOs. The standard requires companies not only to obtain third-party certification but also to issue a public statement with information on their environmental performance (Delmas, 2002). The reporting element of EMAS is particularly interesting for companies to track their suppliers' progress. Like ISO 14001 this type of EMS can also be verified by a third-party audit company, which means the environmental report on performance is checked independently and publicly available.

On the social front, while there have been a number of voluntary developments in the area of social sustainability in the past years (notably SA8000), the most recent and formalized effort is the guidance developed by ISO in the form of ISO 26000. Social standards form the basis for many voluntary codes, guidance notes, and standards relating to social issues. As codes of conduct are covered in the next section, this section will deal only with the recent ISO formulation of social sustainability which will supersede the majority of previous guidance.

From 2005 to 2010, ISO conducted negotiations with its membership of national standards organizations as well as international agencies, governmental bodies, industry groups, and nongovernmental organizations associated with codes of conduct in the domain of CSR. The process of standard negotiation has been studied, showing the stakeholders involved included national bodies e.g. BSI and AFNOR, but also WBCSD, GRI, ILO, UNEP and so on (Helms et al., 2012).

ISO negotiated a consensus on a global definition of CSR and to document what activities constitute appropriate CSR practices. ISO 26000 is not a management system standard however, unlike ISO 14001. It is not intended or appropriate for certification purposes or regulatory or contractual use. Any offer to certify, or claims to be certified, by ISO 26000 would be a misrepresentation of the intent and purpose and a misuse of the Standard. As ISO 26000 does not contain requirements as such, any such certification would not be a demonstration of conformity. According to ISO, social responsibility should be an integral part of core organizational strategy with assigned responsibilities and accountability at all appropriate levels of the organization. It should be reflected in decision making and considered in implementing activities.

The table below outlines the main elements of ISO 26000, with the section reference linked to each section in the guidance.

TABLE 13.3 The main elements of ISO26000

Organizational governance 6.2	
Human rights 6.3	Issue 1 : Due diligence 6.3.3 Issue 2 : Human rights risk situations 6.3.4 Issue 3 : Avoidance of complicity 6.3.5 Issue 4 : Resolving grievances 6.3.6 Issue 5 : Discrimination and vulnerable groups 6.3.7 Issue 6 : Civil and political rights 6.3.8 Issue 7 : Economic, social, and cultural rights 6.3.9 Issue 8 : Fundamental principles and rights at work 6.3.10
Labour practices 6.4	Issue 1 : Employment and employment relationships 6.4.3 Issue 2 : Conditions of work and social protection 6.4.4 Issue 3 : Social dialogue 6.4.5 Issue 4 : Health and safety at work 6.4.6 Issue 5 : Human development and training in the workplace 6.4.7
The environment 6.5	Issue 1 : Prevention of pollution 6.5.3 Issue 2 : Sustainable resource use 6.5.4 Issue 3 : Climate change mitigation and adaptation 6.5.5 Issue 4 : Protection of the environment, biodiversity, and restoration of natural habitats 6.5.6
Fair operating practices 6.6	Issue 1 : Anti-corruption 6.6.3 Issue 2 : Responsible political involvement 6.6.4 Issue 3 : Fair competition 6.6.5 Issue 4 : Promoting social responsibility in the value chain 6.6.6 Issue 5 : Respect for property rights

(Continued)

TABLE 13.3 Continued

Consumer issues 6.7	Issue 1 : Fair marketing, factual and unbiased information, and fair contractual practices 6.7.3 Issue 2 : Protecting consumers' health and safety 6.7.4 Issue 3 : Sustainable consumption 6.7.5 Issue 4 : Consumer service, support, and complaint and dispute resolution 6.7.6 Issue 5 : Consumer data protection and privacy 6.7.7 Issue 6 : Access to essential services 6.7.8 Issue 7 : Education and awareness 6.7.9
Community involvement and development	Issue 1 : Community involvement 6.8.3 Issue 2 : Education and culture 6.8.4 Issue 3 : Employment creation and skills development 6.8.5 Issue 4 : Technology development and access 6.8.6 Issue 5 : Wealth and income creation 6.8.7 Issue 6 : Health 6.8.8 Issue 7 : Social investment

In summary the international standards for quality and environmental management have been taken up by many organizations around the world in order to help harmonize practices in these areas. This has been driven by global trade where finding and assessing suppliers becomes a huge challenge, and so these standards help reduce the impact of this challenge. ISO 26000 was expected to have similar adoption rates as the other standards such as ISO 9001 and ISO 14001 to help companies understand how their suppliers are managing social issues and to compare them on an international basis. However some commentators suggest that as this is only a guidance document among many others the impact may be limited (Moratis and Cochius, 2017).

Note 13.2 TATA Beverages and ISO 14001

"We don't trumpet our standards – they're a business tool, not a marketing tool, there to drive performance. They help achieve consistency in our production processes and drive the right behaviours" says Denise Graham, Technical Manager, Tata Global Beverages. This reinforces the view that, done right, standards can help drive the right processes and performance improvement and not just be a cost to the business. TATA Beverages has plants in the UK, India, and Czech Republic serving more than 250 million cups of tea, including Tetley, and other beverages per day globally. The standard provides a framework on which to drive and formalize business practices and audit processes ensure we're on track and that our policies and procedures are robust: "ISO 14001 provides a framework for our continued attention to environmental issues – we've just reduced water consumption by 20%, for instance". Alongside ISO 14001 they also adopted ISO 50001 which focuses on reducing energy consumption and related impacts. With this standard TATA Beverages have to show year on year improvements in energy use which both reduce the carbon footprint but also the cost of energy. The initial audit showed that 96 per cent of energy in their plant in the north of the UK was electricity, so they focused investments here. Fitting intelligence software to compressors to help them work more efficiently, saw the company make overall savings of £56,000 in the first year, and an additional £28,000 in the second. As a result of ISO standards, the team are qualified auditors who can now also carry out food quality and safety audits at their own suppliers, widening the impact and experience in general.

Source: BSI (2014)

Despite the emergence of alternative frameworks to ISO standards, this quality platform is still relevant, and has managed to evolve over the years, broadening the scope from quality to environmental and social standards as well. Table 13.4 shows the reach of the ISO standards by 2023.

13.3.2 Codes of conduct and sector standards

Alongside increasing sustainability related policies, one of the most significant developments in recent years, particularly regarding self-regulation and corporate responsibility, is the development and adoption of codes of conduct (CoC). There are different types of CoC including specific company codes, industry association codes, multi-stakeholder codes (comprising NGOs and private enterprises), model codes (not adopted directly but serving as guidance such as by Amnesty International on labour practices), and intergovernmental codes such as those developed by the ILO or the UN Global Compact as well as some issue specific codes or agreements (Jenkins and Unies, 2001; Fransen and Kolk, 2007). Some industries are particularly advanced in the development of codes with textiles, clothing, and footwear sectors being the most represented in most studies. This section outlines these main types of codes of conduct and gives examples of each.

TABLE 13.4 The reach of ISO standards in 2023

Standard	*Certifiable?*	*Certificates / Adoption*
ISO 9001	✔ Yes	837,052 valid certificates (2023, ISO Survey)
ISO 14001	✔ Yes	300,410 valid certificates (2023, ISO Survey)
ISO 26000	✖ No	Adopted by 88 countries; used voluntarily – no global certificate count

13.3.3 Company specific codes

These types of codes were among the first to be developed in order to protect companies from exposures to social non-compliance in particular (risk of child labour in the supply chain). Typically these are used for trading relationships and define the terms on which suppliers are dealt with and the requirements (minimum) they must fulfil to engage with the buying company.

In 1991, Levi Strauss & Co. was one of the first companies to establish a code of conduct for dealing with supply chain issues. This was named the Global Sourcing and Operating Guidelines (GSOG).[2] The company explains that the guidelines were developed to help improve the lives of workers manufacturing products, make responsible sourcing decisions, and protect commercial interests. Originally, the guidelines were based on values and standards set by the United Nations, particularly the Universal Declaration of Human Rights and many of the International Labor Organization's (ILO) Core Conventions. Over time, Levi's have modified the GSOG based on the suggestions of NGOs and to reflect what they have learned through experience. These are viewed as a cornerstone of the sourcing strategy and of business relationships with hundreds of contractors worldwide.

The GSOG are made up of two components. Country Assessment Guidelines address large, external issues beyond the control of Levi Strauss & Co.'s individual business partners. Such and approach helps assess the opportunities and risks of doing business in a particular country. The second part of the guidelines is the Business Partner Terms of Engagement (TOE). These deal with issues that are controllable by individual business partners and are an integral part of their business relationships. Levi's employees and their business partners understand that complying with the TOE is not less important than meeting quality standards or delivery times. Overall these actions are believed to help the company use supply chain practices to improve on corporate reputation (Preece et al., 1995).

13.3.4 Professional and industry association codes

Associations which bring together companies in the same sector or individuals from a profession have been prevalent in the development of codes of practice in a number of areas. For example, in the supply management domain associations such as the ISM[3] in the USA and CIPS[4] in the UK have developed codes providing informal rules of ethical behaviour for their members. As sustainability often affects industrial sectors in different ways, associations at the sector level have also developed codes of practice in the sustainability area. Matten and Moon (2008) argue that industry associations are a key feature of the European corporate social responsibility approach giving these actions an 'explicit' rather than internally focused (implicit) nature.

One example is the ICTI code of busness practice which is a toy industry ethical manufacturing programme which aims to ensure adequate working conditions for toy factory workers worldwide.[5] To achieve these goals, ICTI provide education, training, and a single, fair, thorough, and consistent monitoring programme for toy factories. The main focus is on China, Hong Kong, and Macau, where approximately 80 per cent of the world's toys are manufactured.

One argument against these types of codes is that no single company benefits more than another in terms of reputational value, hence where is the competitive value of such approaches? It is clear from the above example that companies do not intend to compete on these issues, but instead enhance reputation at an industrial sector level (Biedermann, 2006).

13.3.5 Multi-stakeholder codes

Multi-stakeholder codes are those "in which several … groups, usually at least business and NGOs, but sometimes also government representatives, work together" (Fransen and Kolk, 2007: 668). The word 'code' is used in a loose sense here because these initiatives are not only a list of requirements but also an approach to dealing with sustainability issues. The Global Reporting Initiative (GRI) and the Ethical Trade Initiative (ETI) are dealt with because they are some of the most prevalent of these types of 'codes'. Some of these codes are also specific to issues of concern, so an example related to palm oil is also discussed here.

The GRI is a significant multi-stakeholder approach, focusing on standardizing reporting metrics and has led to one of the world's most prevalent standards for sustainability reporting.[6] GRI seeks to make sustainability reporting by all organizations as routine as, and comparable to, financial reporting. A sustainability report is a company report that gives information about economic, environmental, social, and governance performance. GRI Guidelines are widely used with more than 4,000 organizations from 60 countries using the guidelines to produce their sustainability reports. GRI Guidelines apply to corporate businesses, public agencies, smaller enterprises, NGOs, industry groups and others. Environmental transparency is one of the main areas of activity under the scope of the GRI. The standardized reporting guidelines concerning the environment are contained within the GRI Indicator Protocol Set. There are 30 environmental indicators ranging from EN1 (materials used by weight) to EN30 (total environmental expenditures by type of investment). Similarly, there are standardized indicators for social, economic, and governance issues. The benefit from a supply chain perspective is that there is a common method for measuring the selected indicators, so that monitoring performance from suppliers can be easier to compare and potentially to aggregate (if used as an input into life cycle assessment).

The Ethical Trading Initiative (ETI) is an alliance of companies, trade unions, and voluntary organizations working in partnership to improve the working conditions of people that make or grow goods.[7] Established in 1998 in the UK with the support of the Department for International Development (DFID), ETI has over 70 member companies with a combined turnover of over £107 billion including John Lewis, ASDA, Tesco, Inditex, and WH Smith.[8] Trade union members represent nearly 160 million workers around the world in every country where free trade unions can operate. NGO members range from large international development charities such as Oxfam and CAFOD, to specialized labour rights organizations such as Anti-Slavery International. Companies that join ETI must adopt the ETI Base Code in full. The ETI Base Code is derived from the standards of the International Labour Organization. They must also sign up to ETI's Principles of Implementation, which set out the approaches to ethical trade that the companies should follow. Member companies must also play an active part in ETI activities alongside their trade union and NGO counterparts, including in members' meetings, supply chain programmes, and working groups. In 2010, ETI member companies' ethical trade activities covered over 9.8 million workers around the world, asking that their suppliers take over 133,000 separate actions to improve workers' conditions.

Other multi-stakeholder codes have focused on specific issues. One example is developed by the Roundtable on Sustainable Palm Oil (RSPO) with the WWF. This code has been developed in answer to many campaigns from NGOs about the impacts of palm oil production.[9] The main issues relate to deforestation – conversion of forest to plantation – which then has an impact on habitats for endangered species such as orangutans particularly in areas such as Borneo and Sumatra. There are other significant impacts on the environment including soil erosion and pollution, and pollution of fresh water sources. In addition to the negative environmental consequences there are also social implications based on land use rights and ownership, and impacts on local community livelihoods. According to this code companies should:

1. Join the RSPO and be an active member;
2. Make a commitment to source 100 per cent RSPO-certified palm oil by 2015 at the very latest;
3. Be transparent about their use of palm oil;
4. Start using certified sustainable palm oil immediately;
5. Start investing in traceable supply chains of certified sustainable palm oil;
6. For retailers, go beyond 'own brand commitments';
7. Raise awareness of the RSPO and certified sustainable palm oil globally.

Certified sustainable palm oil (CSPO) is produced according to the standards established by the RSPO, providing assurance that valuable tropical forests have not been cleared and that environmental and social safeguards have been met during the oil's production.

13.3.6 Codes from international governmental organizations

Probably the best-known code in this category is the United Nations Global Compact (UNGC). This is a United Nations initiative to encourage businesses worldwide to adopt sustainable and socially responsible policies, and to report on their implementation.[10] The Global Compact is a principle-based framework for businesses, stating ten principles in the areas of human rights, labour, the environment, and anti-corruption. Under the Compact, companies are brought together with UN agencies, labour groups, and civil society. The Global Compact is the world's largest corporate citizenship initiative with two objectives: "Mainstream the ten principles in business activities around the world" and "Catalyze actions in support of broader UN goals, such as the Millennium Development Goals (MDGs)". The Compact was announced by the then UN Secretary-General Kofi Annan in an address to the World Economic Forum on 31 January 1999, and was officially launched at UN Headquarters in New York on 26 July 2000.

TABLE 13.5 Main principles of the Global Compact

Human Rights	Principle 1: support and respect the protection of internationally proclaimed human rights
	Principle 2: make sure that they are not complicit in human rights abuses
	Principle 3: the freedom of association and the effective recognition of the right to collective bargaining
Labour Standards	Principle 4: the elimination of all forms of forced and compulsory labour
	Principle 5: the effective abolition of child labour
	Principle 6: the elimination of discrimination in employment and occupation.
Environment	Principle 7: support a precautionary approach to environmental challenges
	Principle 8: undertake initiatives to promote environmental responsibility
	Principle 9: encourage the development and diffusion of environmentally friendly technologies
Anti-Corruption	Principle 10: businesses should work against corruption in all its forms, including extortion and bribery

The Global Compact is not a regulatory instrument, but rather a forum for discussion and a network for communication including governments, companies, and labour organizations, whose actions it seeks to influence, and civil society organizations, representing its stakeholders. Hence, there have been some criticisms of the Global Compact. The compact contains no mechanisms to sanction member companies for non-compliance with the Compact's principles. A company's continued participation is not dependent on demonstrated progress. Some sources have stated that the Global Compact has admitted companies with dubious humanitarian and environmental records in contrast with the principles demanded by the Compact.

In summary, codes of conduct and other voluntary means to monitor and control what happens in supply chains are some of the most important developments in the field of sustainability in recent years. In particular, multi-stakeholder codes of conduct are put in place in response to a lack of formal government or inter-governmental policies, but should not be seen as a replacement of existing legal frameworks (Sobczak, 2003). As an overall observation on these 'codes', there is great variability in the constitution of these stakeholder groups and also the relative involvement of the stakeholders included (Fransen and Kolk, 2007). This means that these approaches also vary in their level of legitimacy.

13.4 BEYOND REGULATION AND VOLUNTARY SCHEMES: WHEN SOCIETY PRESSURES FOR MORE

It should be clear by now that, together, legislation and voluntary frameworks build a complex institutional environment through which companies must navigate. The sum of company specific codes, sector level guidelines, multi-stakeholder standards, plus international standards and policies, leads to a highly complex set of obligations for suppliers with repetition, redundancy, and idiosyncrasies. Yet, there is still frustration spread across society and a general perception that companies are not doing enough. This frustration is captured and operationalized by NGOs that focus on supply chain transparency.

Take the fashion industry as an example. The aftermath of the Rana Plaza disaster cited in Chapter 9 led not only to corporate reactions described earlier, such as (more) rigid codes of conduct and industry-level codes, where companies may voluntarily adhere in their own rhythm, but also enforced standards that push companies to comply and eventually expose those companies that resist engagement. As discussed there, industry-level codes included those by SAC and the Higg index from a voluntary perspective, yet other members of society also reacted to this disaster.

In parallel to this corporate reaction, NGOs led a movement to pressure for further supply chain transparency and sustainability – the clear champion being the NGO Fashion Revolution. Fashion Revolution is a global non-profit activism movement, founded in 2013 by Carry Somers and Orsola de Castro in response to the Rana Plaza factory collapse, currently operating in over 75 countries. Their mission is to increase transparency, accountability, and sustainability in the fashion industry. Key activities include Fashion Revolution Week each April, and campaigns using the hashtag *#WhoMadeMyClothes?* aimed at raising public awareness about garment workers and advocating supply-chain reform. Most importantly, since 2017, the movement has published the annual Fashion Transparency Index (FTI), assessing how much information major fashion brands disclose about their human rights and environmental impact. The FTI began ranking 100 brands in 2017 and expanded to 250 by 2021. Average disclosure scores have increased slowly: from around 24 per cent in 2021, to 26 per cent in 2022, and remaining at 26 per cent in 2023. Notably, in 2023 only two brands (e.g. Gucci and OVS) scored 80 per cent or higher, and disclosure of first-tier supplier lists rose from 32 per cent (in early editions) to over 50 per cent by 2023.

A relevant aspect of the FTI is that brands do not voluntarily engage with the index but are rather selected by the NGO based on their volume and global relevance. If they refuse to provide information to compose the Index, they will be still listed, with a score of zero. In fact, in 2023, 18 brands scored zero in the FTI.

Another relevant aspect is the FTI's focus on supplier transparency, particularly the public disclosure of first-tier manufacturers (where final-stage production occurs). In 2017, only 12.5 per cent of brands disclosed such information; by 2023, that number rose to 52 per cent. However, fewer brands publish information about deeper tiers, such as processing facilities (37 per cent) or raw material suppliers (12 per cent), which are critical for identifying labour and environmental risks.

Originally launched at a global level, focusing on US and European brands, Fashion Revolution has evolved through country specific chapters such as Brazil, Mexico, and India (Note 13.3).

Note 13.3 Fashion revolution country-specific chapters

Fashion Revolution has organized country-specific chapters with two different profiles: consumer countries and producer countries. In producer countries, some chapters have produced an equivalent of the FTI to country-specific brands.

Brazil was the first chapter to implement an FTI that was country specific. Founded in 2014, the Brazilian chapter of Fashion Revolution started to publish their FTI with 20 Brazilian brands in 2018. Every year ten brands were added to the list until 2022 when 60 brands were assessed and ranked. In 2023 they repeated the number of 60 brands, and in 2024 they have decided to consolidate their results, producing a longitudinal analysis of fashion brands' transparency performance in this six-year timeframe. Results unfortunately show a slow progression in transparency, and the challenge to transfer/translate higher transparency to actual sustainability performance in the fashion industry.

Source: Fashion Revolution (2025)

Briefly mentioned in Chapter 10, the most recent endeavour aiming to pressure for supply chain transparency is the Open Supply Hub (OS Hub), a non-profit organization launched in 2019 that operates an open-data platform mapping global production locations – factories, warehouses, and suppliers. Formerly named the Open Apparel Registry, OS Hub transitioned to its current name in November 2022 as part of its expansion. Originally focused solely on mapping garment factories, growing demand for transparency across industries prompted its transformation into a broader platform, which now includes other sectors such as electronics, beauty, consumer packaged goods, automotive, and food and beverage.

OS Hub aggregates and standardizes supply-chain data contributed by over 2,200 organizations, now covering more than 1.4 million production sites across 216 countries, assigning each a unique 'OS ID' for interoperability. The platform enables users – brands, civil society, researchers, and multi-stakeholder initiatives – to share supplier lists, discover overlaps, collaborate on social and environmental improvements, and prepare for due-diligence regulations. In late 2024, OS Hub announced partnerships with four multi-stakeholder initiatives, bringing more than 400 companies into the ecosystem and accelerating transparency at scale. With a vision to map all global production sites and support over 100 million workers, OS Hub is recognized by international bodies such as the World Economic Forum and World Benchmarking Alliance as foundational to responsible sourcing and supply-chain accountability.

Supply chain transparency platforms such as the OS Hub are eventually included within broader frameworks such as the FTI and the GRI guidelines. Over time, these frameworks are integrated, one mentioning the other as criteria, increasing pressure for companies resisting engagement with the topic. Chapter 14 will next discuss how these platforms can support a strategy of supplier compliance.

13.5 CONCLUSIONS

International policies and standards play a central role in guiding purchasers and supply chain managers, shaping how companies control and monitor quality, environmental, and social performance. These frameworks, often linked to international bodies such as the ILO or the UN, provide a basis for comparing management systems across regions. They enable a degree of uniformity and accountability, particularly where legal requirements are inconsistent or absent, thereby helping businesses demonstrate responsible practices i.e. for global sourcing. However, challenges arise when firms develop their own standards or codes of practice independently or at sector level. Without harmonization, suppliers may face multiple audits, reporting formats, and compliance pressures. This fragmentation can create inefficiencies, higher costs, and even disengagement from suppliers who struggle to meet competing demands. The lack of alignment highlights the importance of widely recognized international norms to reduce duplication and improve supply chain collaboration, but also platforms that enable more efficient sharing of information (see digital platforms for supplier sustainability compliance, dealt with in the next chapter).

Compliance with international standards can act as a pre-qualifier for supplier selection, offering minimum assurance levels. Yet, they rarely differentiate suppliers in competitive markets. Traditional selection factors – such as price, quality, and delivery performance – continue to dominate once compliance thresholds are met. As such, many firms remain focused on achieving minimum requirements rather than moving beyond compliance to deliver enhanced value. Central to both mandatory and voluntary compliance frameworks is supplier assessment and auditing. ISO standards such as ISO 14001 offer structured procedures and certified verification, yet voluntary codes are harder to monitor. Auditing suppliers provides assurance beyond self-reporting, though resource constraints require firms to balance monitoring frequency with risk management, making supplier capability building an ongoing requirement.

Opportunities nevertheless exist, particularly in environmental management, where reducing energy use and waste can cut costs and improve efficiency (see supply chain mapping and life cycle analysis in the next chapter). In contrast, raising standards in ethical and social practices is far more complex, as compliance remains underdeveloped across many industries (Brandon-Jones, 2013), meaning higher levels of responsibility in these areas requires long-term investment and cultural change.

NOTES

1 Externalities (pollution), incomplete information (chemical content), property rights (ownership of the ocean and forests), lack of competition (mineral, energy monopolistic, cartels, oligopolistic).

2 https://www.si.edu/object/levi-strauss-1991-terms-engagement-english%3Anmah_1020897

3 https://www.ismworld.org/supply-management-news-and-reports/reports/ism-pmi-reports/

4 https://www.cips.org/employers/services/ethical-services/corporate-code-of-ethics

5 https://toy-icti.org/ICTI/ICTI/about/code-business-practice.aspx?hkey=b225b973-db08–45a5–88ee-d0b60d255004
6 https://www.globalreporting.org/
7 http://www.ethicaltrade.org/about-eti
8 http://www.ethicaltrade.org/about-eti/our-members
9 https://rspo.org/resources/
10 http://www.unglobalcompact.org/AboutTheGC/TheTenPrinciples/index.html

REFERENCES

AP News (2025) 15 years after Deepwater Horizon oil spill, lawsuits stall and restoration is incomplete. *Associated Press*. https://apnews.com/article/01247f5b76c028b09c4ef80d9f982a50

Biedermann R (2006) From a weak letter of intent to prevalence: The toy industries' code of conduct. *Journal of Public Affairs* 6(3–4): 197–209.

Brandenburg M, Warasthe R and Seuring S (2024) Impact pathways: Improving supply chain sustainability by due diligence acts? Insights from a German case. *International Journal of Operations & Production Management* 44(4): 859–874.

Brandon-Jones E (2013) *Institutional and capability perspectives on sustainability in operations and supply management: A dual theoretic analysis of the UK fashion sector.* Unpublished PhD Thesis, University of Bath, Bath.

BSI (2014) BSI Case Study Tata Global Beverages. https://www.bsigroup.com/LocalFiles/en-GB/iso-50001/case-studies/BSI_Tata_220414_WR.PDF

Corbett CJ, Montes-Sancho MJ and Kirsch DA (2005) The financial impact of ISO 9000 certification in the United States: An empirical analysis. *Management Science* 51(7): 1046–1059.

Delmas MA (2002) The diffusion of environmental management standards in Europe and in the United States: An institutional perspective. *Policy Sciences* 35(1): 91–119.

Deloitte (2025) Beyond compliance: Enhancing trust through reporting. https://www.deloitte.com/global/en/issues/climate/mandatory-sustainability-reporting.html

European Commission [EC] (n.d.a) Restriction of Hazardous Substances in Electrical and Electronic Equipment (RoHS). https://environment.ec.europa.eu/topics/waste-and-recycling/rohs-directive_en

European Commission [EC] (n.d.b) REACH Regulation. https://environment.ec.europa.eu/topics/chemicals/reach-regulation_en

European Commission [EC] (2007) The Producer Responsibility Principle of the WEEE Directive. http://ec.europa.eu/environment/waste/weee/pdf/final_rep_okopol.pdf

Farber DA (1999) Taking slippage seriously: Noncompliance and creative compliance in environmental law. *Harvard Environmental Law Review* 23: 297.

Fashion Revolution (2025) Sobre o Índice de Transparência da Moda Brasil – edição comparativa. https://fashionrevolutionbrasil.org/indice-transparencia-moda-brasil/

Financial Times (2010) BP's report sparks backlash from contractors, US. *CNBC* (9 September). https://www.cnbc.com/2010/09/09/bps-report-sparks-backlash-from-contractors-us.html

Fransen LW and Kolk A (2007) Global rule-setting for business: A critical analysis of multi-stakeholder standards. *Organization* 14(5): 667–684.

Harris MN, Konya L and Matyas L (2002) Modelling the impact of environmental regulations on bilateral trade flows: OECD, 1990–1996. *The World Economy* 25(3): 387–405.

Helms WS, Oliver C and Webb K (2012) Antecedents of settlement on a new institutional practice: Negotiation of the ISO 26000 standard on social responsibility. *Academy of Management Journal* 55(5): 1120–1145.

Jenkins R and Unies N (2001) *Corporate codes of conduct: Self-regulation in a global economy*. United Nations Research Institute for Social Development Geneva.

Johansson C, Lindgren M and Lissgard P (1993) Att lyckas med ISO 9000: En ingaende studie av 23 foretag (To succeed with ISO 9000: A thorough study of 23 companies) *Ord & Form AB, Uppsala.*

King AA, Lenox MJ and Terlaak A (2005) The strategic use of decentralized institutions: Exploring certification with the ISO 14001 management standard. *Academy of Management Journal* 48(6): 1091–1106.

Kollman K and Prakash A (2001) Green by choice: Cross-national variations in firms' responses to EMS-based environmental regimes. *World Politics* 53: 399–430.

Lundmark E and Westelius A (2006) Effects of quality management according to ISO 9000: A Swedish study of the transit to ISO 9000: 2000. *Total Quality Management* 17(8): 1021–1042.

Marques L, Erthal A, Schott CSdCM and Morais D (2021) Inhospitable accessibility and blurred liability: Institutional voids in an emerging economy preventing supply network transparency. *Brazilian Administration Review* 18(2): 1–28.

Matten D and Moon J (2008) "Implicit" and "explicit" CSR: A conceptual framework for a comparative understanding of corporate social responsibility. *Academy of Management Review* 33(2): 404–424.

Moratis L and Cochius T (2017) *ISO 26000: The Business Guide to the New Standard on Social Responsibility*. Taylor & Francis. https://doi.org/10.4324/9781351278843

Nawrocka D (2008) Inter-organizational use of EMSs in supply chain management: Some experiences from Poland and Sweden. *Corporate Social Responsibility and Environmental Management* 15(5): 260–269.

Poksinska B, Dahlgaard JJ and Antoni M (2002) The state of ISO 9000 certification: A study of Swedish organizations. *The TQM Magazine* 14(5): 297–306.

Prakash A and Potoski M (2006) Racing to the bottom? Trade, environment, governance, and ISO 14001. *American Journal of Political Science* 50(2): 350–364.

Preece S, Fleisher C and Toccacelli J (1995) Building a reputation along the value chain at Levi Strauss. *Long Range Planning* 28(6): 88–98.

Preuss L (2009) Ethical sourcing codes of large UK-based corporations: Prevalence, content, limitations. *Journal of Business Ethics* 88(4): 735–747.

Reuters (2024) EU parliament approves new business supply chain audit law. https://www.reuters.com/world/europe/eu-parliament-approves-new-business-supply-chain-audit-law-2024-04-24/

Ruhl J, Salzman J, Song K-S and Yu H (2002) Environmental compliance: Another integrity crisis or too many rules. *Nat. Resources & Env't* 17: 24.

Sobczak A (2003) Codes of conduct in subcontracting networks: A labour law perspective. *Journal of Business Ethics* 44(2–3): 225–234.

Stevenson TH and Barnes FC (2001) Fourteen years of ISO 9000: Impact, criticisms, costs, and benefits. *Business Horizons* 44(3): 45–51. https://doi.org/10.1016/S0007-6813(01)80034-3

UK Legislation (2015) Modern Slavery Act 2015. http://www.legislation.gov.uk/ukpga/2015/30/contents/enacted

Vastag G and Melnyk SA (2002) Certifying environmental management systems by the ISO 14001 standards. *International journal of production research* 40(18): 4743–4763.

Watkins RV and Gutzwiller EC (1999) Buying into ISO 14001. *Occupational health & safety* 68(2).

Welford R (1999) *Corporate Environmental Management*. Universities Press.

Core legislation cited in this chapter:

- **California (US) Transparency Act** https://oag.ca.gov/SB657
- **Dodd-Frank Act** https://www.cftc.gov/LawRegulation/DoddFrankAct/index.htm
- **UK Modern Slavery Act** https://www.legislation.gov.uk/ukpga/2015/30/contents
- **French Duty of Corporate Vigilance Law** https://respect.international/loi-2017-399-du-27-mars-2017-relative-au-devoir-de-vigilance-des-societes-meres-et-des-entreprises-donneuses-dordre/
- **Australia Modern Slavery Act** https://www.legislation.gov.au/C2018A00153/latest/text
- **German Supply Chain Act** https://www.bmas.de/DE/Service/Gesetze-und-Gesetzesvorhaben/Gesetz-Unternehmerische-Sorgfaltspflichten-Lieferketten/gesetz-unternehmerische-sorgfaltspflichten-lieferketten.html
- Federal Office for Economic Affairs and Export Control (BAFA), Supply Chain Due Diligence Act https://www.bafa.de/EN/Supply_Chain_Act/Overview/overview_node.html

Useful links and organizations:

- **Directive on Corporate Sustainability Due Diligence (Directive 2024/1760) CSDDD** https://commission.europa.eu/business-economy-euro/doing-business-eu/sustainability-due-diligence-responsible-business/corporate-sustainability-due-diligence_en
- **European Unions Corporate Sustainability Reporting Directive (CSRD)** https://finance.ec.europa.eu/regulation-and-supervision/financial-services-legislation/implementing-and-delegated-acts/corporate-sustainability-reporting-directive_en
- **Fashion Revolution** https://www.fashionrevolution.org/about/
- **Fashion Transparency Index**. 2023 edition. https://www.fashionrevolution.org/fashion-transparency-index/
- **Better Cotton Initiative** www.bettercotton.org
- **Business for Social Responsibility** www.bsr.org

- **Business Social Compliance Initiative (BSCI)** www.bsci-intl.org
- **EICC:** Electronic Industry Citizenship Coalition / GeSI www.eicc.info
- **ETI:** Ethical Trading Initiative www.ethicaltrade.org
- **Fair Factories Clearinghouse** www.fairfactories.org
- **Fair Labor Association** www.fairlabor.org
- **Fair Wear Foundation** www.fairwear.org
- **Global Reporting Initiative** www.globalreporting.org/CurrentPriorities/SupplyChain/
- **GSCP** www.gscpnet.com
- **ICS:** Initiative Clause Sociale www.ics-asso.org
- **ICTI CARE Foundation** www.toy-icti.org
- **IDH** www.idhsustainabletrade.com/en/about-idh
- **ILO**: Declaration on Fundamental Principles and Rights at Work
- **ILO**: Tripartite Declaration of Principles Concerning Multinational Enterprises and Social Policy
- **ISEAL Alliance** www.isealalliance.org
- **OECD**: Guidelines for Multinational Enterprises www.oecd.org/dataoecd/43/29/48004323.pdf
- **OECD**: The Corporate Responsibility to Respect Human Rights in Supply Chains: Discussion Paper
- **Portal for Responsible Supply Chain Management** www.csr-supplychain.org
- **Rainforest Alliance** www.rainforest-alliance.org
- **Sedex** www.sedex.org.uk
- **Social Accountability Accreditation Services (SAAS)** www.saasaccreditation.org
- **Social Accountability International (SAI)** www.sa-intl.org
- **UNHR**: Guiding Principles on Business and Human Rights
- **UNHR**: The Corporate Responsibility to Respect Human Rights, an Interpretive Guide
- **United Nations Global Compact Supply Chain** http://supply-chain.unglobalcompact.org/
- **Worldwide Responsible Accredited Production (WRAP)** www.wrapcompliance.org

CHAPTER 14

Lifecycle analysis, supply chain mapping, and supplier compliance

LEARNING OBJECTIVES:

At the end of this chapter you should be able to:

- Define the links between sustainable supply strategy and policy, assessment tools and implementation;
- Evaluate the use of supply chain mapping and carbon foot-printing;
- Describe the rationale behind lifecycle analysis;
- Reflect on the role of digital platforms to support supplier compliance;
- Describe the challenges of low carbon procurement and the notion of 'carbon net zero'.

14.1 INTRODUCTION

Concerns over the release of increasing quantities of carbon dioxide and other greenhouse gases into the atmosphere from anthropometric (i.e. man-made) activity and its effect on public health and climactic change are being raised with rising urgency. Although carbon dioxide is generated in nature by plants during the process of photosynthesis, it is the vast quantities generated by modern cities, industrial growth, and the spread of transportation networks and the poisonous variants such as carbon monoxide and sulphur dioxide emitted from vehicle tailpipes and factory flues that has produced a wave of legislation seeking to limit emissions. Since 2010, over 200 legislative acts have been passed by EU member states and in the US, associated with managing the reduction of carbon through controlling emission levels. Yet convincing all stakeholders in the supply chain of the urgency and feasibility of emissions reduction is not proving to be straightforward. While many large corporations facing pressure from consumers and government are working together with NGOs to implement low carbon schemes, many suppliers are taking longer to come on board.

This chapter introduces the concepts of scope 1, 2, and 3, supply chain, value chain mapping, and lifecycle analysis as key elements in starting the implementation process

DOI: 10.4324/9781003499602-17

towards a sustainable supply chain: the overarching theme of Part C. While the development of strategy is an important first step towards sustainability, it is often only when firms attempt to put into practice what they have been talking about that the real challenges begin to emerge. It is important, therefore, to understand the links between supply strategy, external policy, enabling tools, and implementation that allows the shift towards sustainability to take root. The first steps in implementing a sustainable supply chain involves more than considerations around organizational change, requiring an in-depth understanding of the types of impact the firm seeks to target as a priority. Figure 14.1 below presents an overview of the major elements involved and are addressed over the coming chapters.

We start therefore by presenting the concept of scope 1, 2, and 3 as a path to link carbon management to procurement and supply chain management. Then, the chapter moves to the evaluative capability of tools such as supply chain mapping, value chain analysis, and lifecycle analysis. The chapter discusses assessment and implementation frameworks that can help firms in being more effective and resource efficient, but also actively engage them in the broader vision of supply chain sustainability. This means considering the views of external policy drivers such as the WWF and implementing practices which are in tune with long-term planetary concerns such as ecological depletion and climate change (Note 13.1). The chapter also includes a discussion of digital platforms that support control of supplier compliance to sustainability, including the case of EcoVadis.

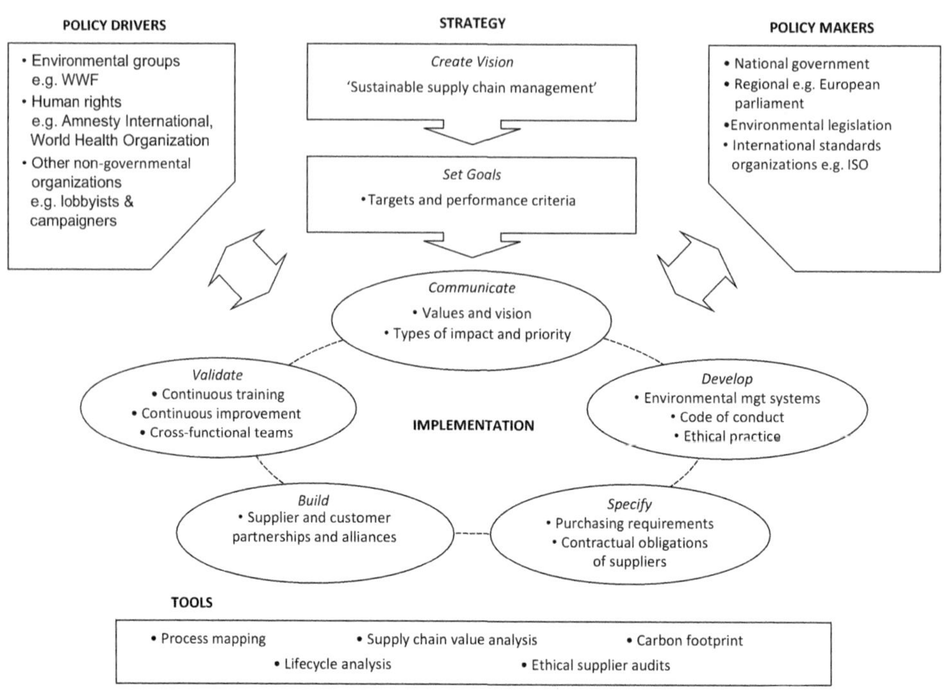

FIGURE 14.1 Framework linking sustainable supply strategy, policy, tools, and implementation

14.2 CARBON FOOTPRINT: SCOPE 1, 2, AND 3

Managing supply chain emissions is the most effective way for firms to meet their commitments to decarbonization. Yet we know that managing supply emissions is essentially voluntary in nature, and an exception rather than the rule (Blanco et al., 2016). Supply chain emissions account for 70 per cent of the total emissions for healthcare products, 95 per cent for cars and mobile phones, and up to 98 per cent for food and beverage products (PRI, 2017). Thus, a product's carbon footprint is mostly out of the focal firm's direct control, as most emissions occur elsewhere in the supply chain (Roemer et al., 2023). Reducing supply chain emissions is the key to achieving significant carbon mitigation. Despite the urgent ethical need to reduce supply chain emissions, industry reports indicate that most companies do not control or report carbon emissions (MIT CTL and CSCMP, 2020; Mallon and De Leener, 2021). And of those that do report, they often restrict their disclosure to emissions from their own operations and energy providers, since they are easier to control and quantify (Blanco et al., 2016).

The technical jargon related to carbon emissions is grounded in the Greenhouse Gas (GHG) Protocol that classifies a firm's carbon emissions into three types: *scope 1* covers emissions within the firm's direct operations. Next, *scope 2* covers specifically emissions from the purchase of energy sources. Finally, *scope 3* are emissions along the firm's supply chain, both upstream and downstream (Blanco, 2021). Thus, we can equate scope 3 emissions to supply chain emissions. Firms are invited to join the global effort of reducing global emissions of carbon dioxide by 50 per cent by 2030, and by 100 per cent by 2050 against a base year of 2000 (IPCC, 2007). Yet in supply chains of consumer goods such as fashion, food and beverage, pharmaceutical, and electronics, scope 3 emissions account for 90–99 per cent of total emissions of a product. Firms are increasingly pressured therefore to move beyond efforts on scope 1 and 2 and engage with their supply chains in the transition to low/net zero carbon. Uncertainty persists however on how to move forward due to the significant challenges associated with scope 3 emissions, despite potential opportunities for first movers (Mishra et al., 2022).

Scope 3 management thus means engaging suppliers and sub-tier suppliers in the process of quantifying and reporting emissions (Villena and Dhanorkar, 2020; Flammer et al., 2021). Supply chain complexity affects how firms manage scope 3, which has so far led even first movers and innovators on this front to have limited product level data, thus carbon targets and progress are often based on estimations (Vieira et al., 2024). The abundance of the use of estimations has led research to call for more transparency on estimation methods (Busch et al., 2022). The challenging nature of scope 3 data includes lack of knowledge regarding the topic, lack of understanding of supply chain structures and over-reliance on estimations as a result (Vieira et al., 2024).

Despite the relevance of supply chain carbon emissions, mandatory regulation is still the exception and ever evolving, as discussed in Chapter 13. In October 2023, California passed a law that requires companies to disclose carbon emissions, including supply chain emissions from 2027 onwards. Globally speaking, weak or absent regulation has provided fertile soil for the emergence of voluntary initiatives (Roemer et al., 2023). Most probably the main voluntary framework for disclosure of carbon emissions is currently found in the

CDP (formerly Carbon Disclosure Project), which started in 2003 with 220 participating companies, and reached over 20,000 by 2024. Yet, among these, only 15 per cent of the reporting companies focus on their supply chain emissions (CDP, 2024). Incipient and limited regulation might explain why some companies advance in this direction voluntarily, while the majority stays unchanged, waiting for regulation or other pressures. In particular, supply chain managers are assigned the task to advance this agenda in a scenario of uncertainty, lack of consensus, and little guidance.

Although improvements in carbon emissions are being realized through efforts by multi-national corporations such as Air France-KLM, Bloomberg, and Dell, upstream supply chain partners are typically lagging behind in their contribution towards managing emissions. In other words, scope 3 management in large corporations lags behind efforts and reported reductions in scope 1 and 2. Many smaller firms find the range of sustainability terminology and legislation confusing and worry that committing to such green engagement might cost them their business.

Research carried out into Low Carbon Procurement (LCP) at the University of Exeter Business School shows the initial reactions of small-medium enterprises to participating in low carbon initiatives often turns from initial reluctance i.e. "… we don't do sustainability here" (Managing Director of anonymous SME), to increasing enthusiasm as they realize the 'win-win' opportunities which simultaneously reduce energy consumption while lowering business costs. Engaging with suppliers requires sensitive handling and strong leadership from their customers, with lead organizations setting targets for carbon and energy reduction but presenting them as part of a longer-term supply chain strategy. Support for firms should be offered in the form of practical training, including the use of carbon tools such as LCA, action learning, and process mapping workshops (Clear About Carbon, 2013).

Procurement has become a powerful force in the efforts to reduce not only greenhouse gas emissions, but on all global sourcing ethical issues and environmental/ecological goals (Walker and Preuss, 2008; Bolton, 2008; Walker and Brammer, 2009). With European countries spending around 16 per cent of the EU's GDP each year on the purchase of goods and services – the UK government alone spends £220 billion – spending on such a scale provides a strong lever in encouraging private industry to adopt proposed changes. Since the Rio de Janeiro summit in 1992 which identified the direct role of procurement in influencing environmental protection, a wide range of initiatives on sustainable public procurement have emerged (UNDESA, 1992).

Implementing a low carbon approach requires a basic level of 'carbon literacy' from firms in understanding terms such as carbon management, foot-printing, and procurement. Carbon management (CM) is defined by Chan (2009: 11) as "… the measurement and management of emissions of carbon dioxide and of the other five greenhouse gases covered by the Kyoto protocol". Carbon foot-printing (CF) is the process of measuring direct and indirect greenhouse gas emissions. Low Carbon Procurement (LCP) is somewhat different again, defined by Correia et al. (2013: 60) as:

> The process whereby organizations seek to procure goods, services, works and utilities with a reduced carbon footprint throughout their lifecycle and/or leading to the reduction of the overall organizational carbon footprint when considering its direct and indirect emissions.

The distinction between direct (scope 1) and indirect (scope 2 and 3) emissions is important because of their implications for firm ownership and boundaries of the firm. In terms of where low carbon procurement fits within the scope of other initiatives, managers need to consider the hierarchical relationship between sustainable, green, and LCP approaches (Correia et al., 2013). The low carbon movement is an element of wider environmental concerns, which in turn are part of the wider sustainability agenda. Procurers will often have to deal with multiple trade-offs between LCP and other complex organizational or political priorities, where there are no clear solutions. For example, trying to meet the challenges of multiple competing agendas such as the 'food vs. fuel' or 'renewable energy vs. habitat loss' dilemma around production and consumption of biofuels. Another is the concept of food miles, where overseas purchases can be used as an argument for local economic protectionism, but at the same time can have a negative impact on poverty eradication efforts in developing countries that are heavily dependent on food exports. Note 14.1 exemplifies how much effort, material, and carbon goes into products that we often do not realize.

Note 14.1 The 1.7 kilogram microchip

As an example of the ecological footprint or rucksack of a product, the analysis done by Williams et al. (2002) shows that the material inputs for a 2g microchip reaches 1.7 kilograms or 850 times the weight of the product itself. For the typical 32MB DRAM chip, the majority of this equivalent weight is from fossil fuels. Looking back into the production chain of the silicon wafers, the researchers found that the purification to chip quality uses 160 times more energy than for other uses of silicon outside of semiconductors, and therefore demonstrates how energy intensive this process really is.

Source: Williams et al. (2002)

14.3 SUPPLY CHAIN MAPPING

Tools such as mapping can help firms achieve a deep level of understanding over processes, information, and cross-organizational activities as a route towards gaining closer collaboration and integration with the supply chain, and management of their scope 3 emissions. It is important to understand the differences between the variety of maps available to the supply chain investigator and their various applications, for example: tactical (i.e. high detail, internal orientation) and strategic (low detail, external orientation). Yet the visualization of supply chains using maps is becoming more complicated as firms pursue outsourcing strategies and delivery systems that are typically more concerned with levels of carbon, pollution, and waste than in the past. As supply chains have become increasingly extended, new evaluative methods are needed to allow for carbon accounting and reducing the risk from potential breaches in corporate social responsibility.

A criticism of mapping is that too often the technique is considered the realm of independent consultants, whereas with a little training, managers, staff, and students are capable of using the tools for themselves. Gardner and Cooper (2003: 37) argue that there need to be well-established processes in place for map building so that knowledge can be transferable and exchangeable between firms. Maps should provide a foundation for the strategic planning process and "… facilitate evaluation of supply chain membership and structure". There are many compelling reasons to create a map of the supply chain, such the need to catalogue and distribute key information for survival in dynamic environments; to provide a communication tool that reaches across firms, functions, and corporate units; to alert managers to possible constraints or problems in the system; to facilitate monitoring of the supply chain integration process; and, crucially, to provide the link between corporate (i.e. firm level) and supply chain strategy to enable change to be implemented.

Note 14.2 The Living Planet Report: 'business as usual' is not an option

The release of the 'Living Planet Report', a joint publication by the World Wildlife Foundation (WWF) and the Organisation for Economic Co-operation and Development (OECD), every two years, serves as a reminder of the urgency of developing greener and more sustainable economies. Using a series of measures which include habitat loss, over-exploitation of species, pollution, and climate change, collectively called the 'ecological footprint', it shows a doubling of our demands on the natural world since the 1960s and a fall of 30 per cent in the health of species that form the totality of our ecosystems. The report provides clear indicators that demonstrate the unprecedented drive for wealth and well-being over the past 40 years is putting unsustainable pressures on the planet. In the words of James Leape, Director General of WWF International:

> The implications are clear. Rich nations must find ways to live much more lightly on the Earth – to sharply reduce their footprint, including in particular their reliance on fossil fuels. The rapidly growing emerging economies must also find a new model for growth – one that allows them to improve the well-being of their citizens in ways the Earth can actually sustain.

Source: WWF (2010)

The use of analysis tools such as charts and maps that incorporate the concepts of process and flow to understand how organizations deliver goods and services has a strong following in management practice (Rother and Shook, 1988; Womack and Jones, 1996a, b; Hines and Rich, 1997; Gardner and Cooper, 2003). One of the earliest examples is the use of simple flowcharts as a diagrammatic representation of manufacturing shop floor operations, providing a step-by-step solution to problems in workstation or machine process sequencing. Developed by US industrial engineer Frank Gilbreth in the 1920s, individual process operations are represented by boxes, and the arrows connecting them represent flow of control. Flowcharts are used in designing and analyzing a process or programme where data flows are not always depicted but are implied by the order of operational steps or activities. Creating a flowchart can aid troubleshooting while enabling managers to visualize what is going on. It helps them to understand a process, find bottlenecks and flaws, and ultimately develop more effective ways of working.

Subsequent developments around 'flow process chart' methods in the 1940s meant the need for standardization of a range of symbols and a capability to reflect the increase in data-processing and associated documentation leading to the use of charts in business improvement programs in corporations such as Proctor & Gamble and IBM. The spread of the use of computers in industry resulted in flowcharts being used to plan computer programs. The planning and coding method of US pioneers Goldstine and von Neumann in their 1947 'electronic computing instruments' is an early illustration of the connection between physical activity and information-based process flows. With process analysis tools capable of representing goods and information, their use in the following decades expanded into general business improvement and more specialist fields such as quality control (e.g. Ishikawa, 1985).

Recognition of the widening role of information technology beyond a common view in the 1960s of computers as back-office data-processors, and the rise of Strategic Information Systems, meant ICT could provide greater organizational control leading to a need for more holistic and systemic representations of firm activity (Ariav and Ginzberg, 1985). Systems theory considers the firm in terms of an open or closed system whose sum of parts is considered as a whole in order to understand the firm's reaction to internal or external stimulus. The origins of systems theory stems from the examination of holistic organizational behaviour and structure, deriving its analysis from comparisons made with the interactions of organisms in nature (von Bertalanffy, 1950). Developments in popular tools such as Soft Systems Methodology (Checkland, 1981) enabled management researchers to represent various information processing activities in the organization as linked variables on a map, drawn as self-reinforcing or balancing loops, similar in approach to the ideas around systems thinking and 'virtuous circles' in the learning organization by Senge (1990).

As the global reach of information systems has increased with the rise of the internet, the advantages of almost unlimited connectivity between customer, buyer, and supplier are offset by the possibility for communication systems to resemble a spaghetti-like mess! There is a compelling need, therefore, to represent process flows in the context of their complex environments, as a juxtaposition of physical production, decision making, and information shared between the individual, department, and firm. One area of development is in business process modelling notation (BPMN), which includes features such as swim lanes, that enable the investigator to capture multiple and overlapping layers of organizational exchange (e.g. White, 2004). Here, process maps are drawn to reflect the unifying nature of information systems as they interact between multiple stakeholder groups showing not only whom or what they interface with, i.e. human or computer, but how the delivery process is supported in complex business settings. Fawcett and Magnan (2002: 351) argue that firms need to go further than using the rhetoric of collaboration, defining how they understand and approach the thorny issue of supply chain integration.

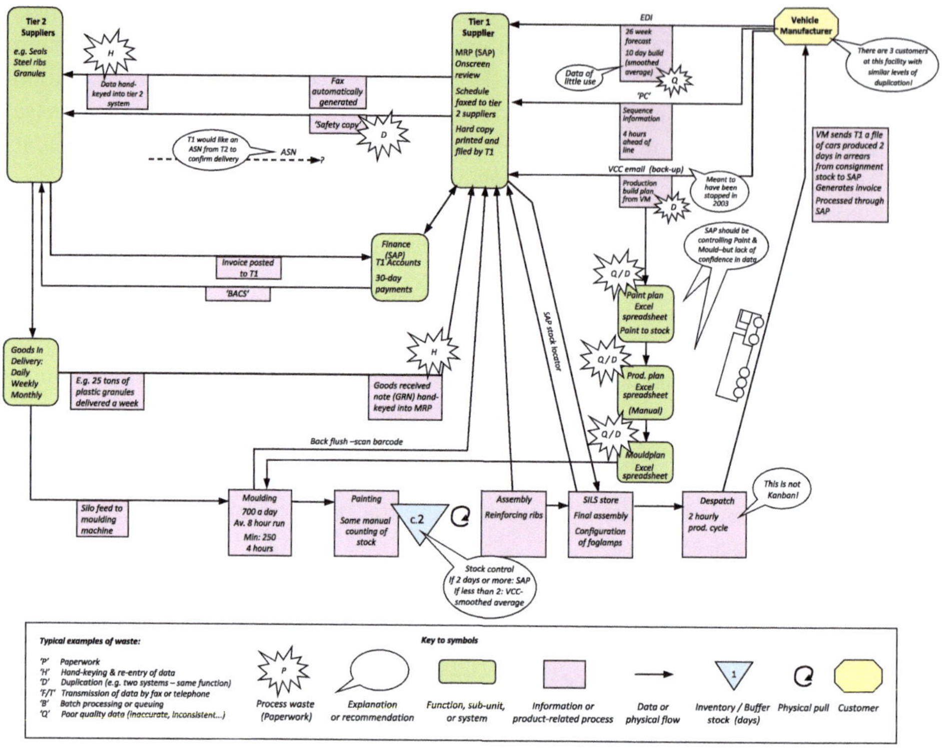

FIGURE 14.2 A supply chain process map: identifying areas of stress, risk, and waste

The reality, however, is often that upstream relationships are 'handed off' to first-tier suppliers through a lack of supply chain knowledge and understanding of evaluative tools such as maps.

The scope of activity and scale over what the process chart, map, or systems diagram tries to convey goes beyond the tactical boundaries set by individual firms. Mapping methodology today is capable of framing the creation of value as a strategic activity, using common notations which provide a connected understanding of the whole supply chain (Gardner and Cooper, 2003). Figure 14.2, for example, shows a supply chain map from the automotive industry which uses universally recognized symbols (i.e. boxes, rectangles, triangles, etc.) to indicate a process or system, connected by arrowed lines to indicate flow of goods or information. It spans upstream from the vehicle manufacturer to include tier 1 and 2 suppliers, illustrating physical process and information flow with comments included to suggest possible sources of bottlenecks in the system (Goldratt and Cox, 1984). Although some production data is omitted for clarity, pinpointing key areas or 'hotspots' using starred symbols to indicate where unnecessary activity or excess inventory can be eliminated enables business performance to be evaluated and improved. Any benefits achieved such as reduced lead-time and cost can then be passed on to the customer in the form of added value. This elimination of wasteful activity has a knock-on benefit for the firm's environmental strategy, for example in the reduction of carbon dioxide emissions and other airborne or water-based pollutants. Process improvement must be seen as both part of a firm level business process and as part of the 'bigger picture' regarding common, supply chain wide practices on sustainability. This means reaching an agreement on specific targets with suppliers in key impact areas such as emissions, water use, remanufacturing, and investment in renewable or so-called clean energy technology (e.g. wind, solar).

Next, we examine established business mapping tools such as Supply Chain Value Analysis (SCVA) and, later, discuss how more environment-orientated tools such as life-cycle analysis and foot-printing can be used in conjunction. Adopting established business process improvement tools for use in sustainability initiatives has the advantage of familiarity when it comes to persuading the 'outliers' in supply chains, such as tier 2 and tier 3 suppliers, of their efficacy. The wide range of tools available to choose from across the business improvement and environmental management spectrum means managers must be clear (and realistic) about what they are trying to achieve before they adopt them. Often, such tools are used as part of a wider corporate change initiative, where the firm selects a particular blend of business and environmental priorities to target specific supply chain outcomes (Melnyk et al., 2010).

14.4 SUPPLY CHAIN VALUE ANALYSIS

The concept of the value chain may already be familiar to readers of this book who are followers of Porter (1980, 1985), whose work champions the search for competitiveness in the marketplace. Porter argues that competitive advantage cannot be understood by looking at firms as a whole, but through understanding each discrete activity. These activities are categorized into primary (i.e. inbound logistics, operations, outbound logistics, marketing, and sales) and support activities (i.e. infrastructure, human resource management, technology development, and procurement). Each activity is then assessed in terms of contribution to the firm's relative cost position and as a basis for market differentiation. If the activity does not create a competitive advantage, then the clear implication is for the firm to consider outsourcing to a partner capable of creating a cost or value advantage.

Christopher (2005: 13) offers an extended view on Porter where "… the supply chain becomes the value chain". As outsourcing has become increasingly prevalent, the value chain extends beyond the boundary of the firm meaning supply chain management is critical to the business. Christopher cites the personal computer firm Dell as one of the first in the internet era to appreciate the importance of achieving a truly integrated supply chain and understanding that it is how a product is sold, i.e. directly to the customer, with minimal waiting and a high rate of inventory turnover that constitutes a unique advantage over conventional businesses.

Having become familiar with the rise of lean thinking and the link between 'lean and green' in Chapter 8, this section discusses the application of associated lean tools such as Supply Chain Value Analysis (SCVA) used in industry for process improvement and change management programmes. Central to the philosophy of all lean tools are the concepts of the 'value stream' and value stream management (Rother and Shook, 1988; Womack and Jones, 1996a, b; Hines and Rich, 1997; Hines et al., 2000). The value stream is the sum of all processes within and between firms required to deliver a product or service from extraction of raw materials to acceptance by the customer. Developing a value stream management approach using lean tools across the supply chain requires starting with an understanding of value and waste, and the value adding (and non-value adding) processes involved throughout. In lean thinking, value is understood to be defined by the customer, and not necessarily what the company thinks it wants to sell to the market.

Womack and Jones (1996a, b) argue there is a need to rethink value as starting from the perspective of the customer and defining the whole product-service package in terms of target cost. Achieving target cost involves the logic of identifying and removing waste (Shingo, 1988; Bicheno, 1994). Using the language of Japanese manufacturing operations, waste or *'muda'* can exist in many forms. The seven traditionally accepted wastes being overproduction, waiting transportation, inappropriate processing, unnecessary inventory, unnecessary motion, and defects (Monden, 1983). Yet the focus on business improvement is shifting away from manufacturing, with new priorities emerging such as supporting the service economy e.g. tourism, retail, health (Swank, 2003). As part of this evolution, lean is beginning to tackle issues with a sustainability focus, such as "... wasted energy, water [and] natural resources" (Bicheno and Holweg, 2009: 25).

Value streams typically cut across functions, hence choosing the appropriate tool to expose wasteful activities in areas such as communication, variation, inventory, and workplace layout is as important as understanding the nature of the business in terms of its production and service orientation. Although there are a number of different SCVA tools designed to target specific types of waste in the organization (Hines and Rich, 1997), the most common starting point is the value stream map. The value stream map (VSM) – an improvement process also known as 'mapping' – is an extremely effective way of quickly getting to the causes of general process related waste in the organization. The underlying ideas which support this mapping technique are the five stages in lean thinking developed by Womack and Jones (1994, 1996a, 1996b):

- **Specify value** (i.e. start with the customer);
- **Identify the value stream** (i.e. draw all related product/service processes and data flows);
- **Flow** (i.e. eliminate 'batch and queue' and other forms of waste);
- **Pull** (i.e. only provide something when the customer asks for it);
- **Perfection** (i.e. continuously improve the process).

Whilst originally devised as an internal tool for use within the firm, VSM is often used today in supply chain settings where several organizations are included as part of an exercise to map product and information-based flows, similar to the process map in Figure 14.2. Process mapping is increasingly being used as a means of highlighting wasteful energy and resource use in the firm, as an indicator of where high levels of carbon dioxide and other greenhouse gases are suspected to reside across the supply chain (CAC, 2013). There is controversy however over adapting original lean tools to meet the aims of sustainability due to the perceived conflict in interests between value-based supply chain economics and the resultant impact on society and the natural environment. Some authors, such as Bicheno and Holweg (2009), argue that adapting lean tools is acceptable especially when able to support sustainable strategy by revealing previously undetected environmental waste using new perspectives which links activities between organizations.

FIGURE 14.3 Value stream mapping workshop

Drawing a map is a good way to start developing ones understanding of the business, whatever type of change or improvements you have in mind. Value stream and general process mapping is usually conducted as a workshop and thus requires a facilitator. Attendees of the workshop should include a range of staff and managers who represent as many of the key functions in the organization as possible e.g. purchasing, operations, finance. The facilitator ensures the group is comfortable with the chosen topic for analysis, such as the order fulfilment process for a product that is known to be troublesome. The facilitator then proceeds to record the current state process guided by workshop participants who have had to use it or have relevant knowledge. As a picture of the full process emerges, the participants are free to alter the positioning of the Post-It™ notes and whiteboard marker lines drawn under the guidance of the facilitator until the map represents as accurate a real-life portrayal of the current business process as is possible (Figure 14.3). A discussion is then held over where the major issues in terms of waste and delay occur in the system. This is usually expressed in terms of the number of stock units held, hour or days of delay/waiting time, staffing levels, and instances of IT system failure. The finished map is then redrawn electronically and distributed to all workshop attendees to reflect on how the current process can be improved. After a minimum period of several weeks, a second workshop is held where the same participants create a future state map (Rother and Shook, 1988), which represents the culmination of all of the recommendations for improvements in waste elimination raised during the first session. Once consensus is reached over the nature and causes of each problem, the facilitator then agrees an action plan with participants to engage them fully in the pathways towards implementation.

The description above in reality often covers a period spanning many months, particularly if there are spending decisions over new equipment to be made involving multiple departments. The facilitator can work with more than one firm, and can join the maps to create a more extended supply chain perspective for further analysis. Where specific problems or constraints are known to occur in the system, such as related to excess product variety, information sharing issues, or data quality (Towill, 1996; Lee et al., 1997), then more specific tools can be applied. Hines and Rich (1997) outline a number of variations of VSM tools found most useful in their work with the automotive, health, and retail sectors. A selection of the most popular are briefly reviewed here:

- **Process activity mapping** has its origins in industrial engineering and is used to eliminate waste, inconsistencies, and irrationalities from the workplace. Based on the study of flow of processes, a detailed recording of all the types of activity involved in the process under consideration is required. After calculating the distance moved, time taken, and people involved, the final table (i.e. a list of activities in order of sequence) can then be used as a basis for further analysis and involvement of the workforce in seeking areas for improvement.
- **Production variety funnel** enables the analyst to understand how underlying complexity in the operation affects the supply chain. As the number of variants increases during the production and assembly process, this is reflected in the widening of the 'funnel' over a given timescale. Different profiles of funnel – for example 'T' or 'V' shaped – reflect the relationship between production process and the accumulation of product variety. The production variety funnel tool can sometimes be used for decisions over the delay or postponement of complexity, enabling product configuration to occur only when really necessary i.e. 'closer' or further downstream towards the customer. It challenges managers to eliminate the costs associated with unnecessary complexity in the production process while maintaining an optimum level of product variety to satisfy customer choice.
- **Demand amplification mapping** is used to capture the effects of information delay, uncertainty, and distortion across the supply chain which can lead to excessive inventory holding by suppliers as they attempt to mitigate the risk of a stock-out situation. In supply chains with poor information sharing capability and excess manufacturing capacity, small changes in demand from the customer can become increasingly exaggerated by the order patterns of successive firms upstream, resulting in many weeks or months of unnecessary stock being held usually at the point furthest from the market. This phenomenon is generally referred to as a 'bullwhip' inventory profile (Lee et al., 1997) or the 'Forrester effect' and is based on the systems dynamics work of Forrester (1958). Demand amplification tools involve plotting actual retail sales data with supplier order data over time to highlight any major areas of fluctuation and mismatch. Ultimately, the sources of tension between firms that are the cause of poor communication and information sharing must be resolved before supply chain inventories can fall and follow a more appropriate level governed by customer demand.

14.5 LIFECYCLE ANALYSIS (LCA): MEASURING ENVIRONMENTAL IMPACT

Lifecycle analysis or lifecycle assessment (LCA) is a management process that evaluates the environmental impact of a product or service throughout its entire lifecycle, from raw material extraction to final disposal. Carbon measuring, often a part of LCA, specifically focuses on quantifying greenhouse gas emissions, typically expressed as carbon dioxide equivalents (CO_{2e}). LCA can also provide a broader perspective on environmental impacts beyond just carbon, while carbon foot-printing focuses on the climate change impact. Overall, the LCA approach helps managers to understand the environmental burden associated with their own and associated firms during different stages of a product's life, such as manufacturing, transportation, use, and end-of-life.

Lifecycle thinking is the consideration of the potential environmental impacts that a product can have during its lifecycle; from extraction and processing of raw materials, through manufacturing, distribution, and use, to recovery or recycling and disposal of any remaining waste. LCA is the process of quantitatively evaluating the environmental impacts of a product over its entire life period. Lifecycle thinking seeks to identify possible improvements to goods and services in the form of lower environmental impacts and reduced use of resources across all lifecycle stages. This begins with raw material extraction and conversion, then manufacture and distribution, through to use and/or consumption. It ends with re-use, recycling of materials, energy recovery, and ultimate disposal.

Note 14.3 Wind turbines and washing machines

The importance of lifecycle thinking can be explained through the example of wind turbines. Here, the use phase of the product's life produces very few impacts especially related to carbon dioxide (CO_2) emissions. Therefore it is important to view the other lifecycle stages such as manufacturing and the end of life. It is during manufacturing in fact where most of the impacts actually reside. In this case companies have established the idea of carbon payback, how long it takes for the renewable energy process to be in operation. This is often between six and nine months of operation, but actions can be taken to reduce this further. For example, the weight of steel turbine towers has been reduced over the last ten years by 50 per cent, reducing the energy used in production and transport.

Another interesting example of balancing different types of impact comes from the household goods sector, specifically washing machines. Lifecycle assessment was carried out on washing machines to demonstrate the difference between detergents that operate in lower temperatures and those that work at normal temperatures. There was suspicion that these low temperature detergents would be more damaging to the water environment through phosphate pollution while saving energy. Results showed that the net impact was improved with these detergents: a solution that also saved consumers money on their electricity bills.

The key aim of lifecycle thinking is to avoid burden shifting. This means minimizing impacts at one stage of the lifecycle, or in a geographic region, or in a particular impact category (e.g. non-renewable energy, carbon dioxide, raw materials), while helping to avoid increases elsewhere. For example: saving energy during the use phase of a product, while not increasing the amount of material needed to provide it. Taking a lifecycle perspective requires a policy developer, environmental manager, or product designer to look beyond their own knowledge and in-house data. It requires cooperation up and down the supply chain. At the same time, it also provides an opportunity to use the knowledge that has been gathered to gain significant economic advantages.

Traditionally, reducing environmental impacts focused on production processes, treatment of waste, and effluent streams. While this remains important, these actions can also help to address issues such as reducing air and water pollution from specific operations. However, this does not necessarily reduce the negative environmental impacts related to the consumption of materials and resources. It also does not account for the shifting of burdens: solving one problem while creating another (see Note 12.2). Solutions therefore may not be optimal and may even be counter-productive, and reflects the emergent nature of the subject, and the relatively early stage thinking with associated lifecycle tools such as carbon footprint (Finkbeiner, 2009). On balance, lifecycle thinking can help to identify opportunities and lead to decisions that help improve environmental performance, corporate image, and economic benefits. This approach also demonstrates that an active responsibility for reducing environmental impacts is being taken by the firm.

Looking at the bigger picture with regards to LCA, businesses do not always consider their supply chains or the 'use' and 'end-of-life' processes associated with their products. Government actions often focus on a specific country or region, and not on the impacts or benefits that can occur in other regions or that are attributable to their own levels of consumption. In both cases, without consideration of the full lifecycle of goods and services (i.e. supply/use/end-of-life), the environment suffers resulting in poorer financial performance and higher potential for reputation damage. There are a number of decision levels regarding lifecycle analysis which need to be addressed:

- *Micro level decision support:* lifecycle-based decision support on micro-level i.e. typically for questions related to specific products. 'Micro-level decisions' are assumed to have limited and no structural consequences outside the decision-context, i.e. they are supposed not to change available production capacity.
- *Meso/macro level decision support:* lifecycle-based decision support at a strategic level (e.g. raw materials strategies, technology scenarios, policy options). 'Meso/macro-level decisions' are assumed to have structural consequences outside the decision-context, i.e. they are supposed to change available production capacity.
- *Accounting:* purely descriptive documentation of the system's lifecycle under analysis (e.g. a product, sector, or country), without being interested in any potential additional consequences on other parts of the economy.
- *Lifecycle thinking:* provides a broader perspective. As well as considering the environmental impacts of the processes within our direct control, attention is also given to the raw materials used, supply chains, product use, the effects of disposal, and the possibilities for re-use and recycling.

Choosing the appropriate LCA tool can be difficult particularly with the 'multiple agendas' presented by the need to transition towards more sustainably aware modes of supply chain management. Note that in the descriptions of types of lifecycle tool below, we include carbon foot-printing because it is both part of LCA as well as carbon management (described in the next section):

***Streamlined lifecycle analysis*:** one example of a streamlined approach is called 'Ecodesign' which draws on a subset of so-called Key Environmental Performance Indicators (KEPIs). The KEPIs are identified through a more detailed ISO LCA and reflect the main considerations or 'hot spots' in the firm or supply chain. The advantages of such an approach is a simplified set of criteria, based on more robust LCAs and other information, which can be used to develop ecolabels. However, care is needed when undertaking a streamlined LCA. Without some baseline knowledge about the product's lifecycle impact, the results may be misleading and might lead to inadvertently shifting the burden to elsewhere in the enterprise or supply chain. Effort could be spent on lifecycle stages that do not have the greatest opportunity for environmental improvement. It is best, therefore, to use streamlined approaches only where solid experience from using ISO LCAs has already been gained.

Carbon foot-printing (CP): involves data on carbon dioxide emissions collected throughout the entire lifecycle at a consistent level of detail as in an ISO LCA, although not all emissions, resources consumed, and impact categories are evaluated. This approach provides a focus on carbon as one of the principal gases whose build up in the earth's lower atmosphere through anthropometric activity is causing a warming effect and climatic change. However, simply focusing on carbon presents the issue of burden shifting: solving one problem while creating another. This can have the effect of unfairly promoting products that do not necessarily have a better overall environmental performance, or environmental footprint.

Ecological foot-printing: this lifecycle approach considers some of the impacts of human activities on the Earth's natural environment. The technique helps to compare the demand placed on eco-systems – the land and the sea that we use and the resources we extract from them – against the Earth's capacity to meet this demand, such as through regeneration of resources and assimilation of waste. Results are presented in planet equivalents, that is, how many planets we would need if the same level of consumption of resources was replicated world-wide. This can build on ISO LCAs but does not consider all impact categories.

Environmental input-output analysis: an economic input-output (I-O) analysis describes the financial inputs and outputs (transactions of goods and services) between given business sectors of the economy within a prescribed geographical area, region, country, or continent. An environmental I-O analysis can help to estimate the impacts of one sector relative to another and highlight significant sectors in terms of their environmental impacts. When combined with environmental data for these sectors, an estimate of the environmental impact per unit value of a sector (for example per euro) can be made. This is often called environmental I-O analysis or I-O LCA. One of the difficulties reported is in economic valuation.

Material flow analysis: a material flow analysis examines the movements of materials through, for example, an industry sector and its supply chain, or a given region. MFAs are used to identify key environmental issues related to the resource efficiency of systems and develop strategies to improve them. The approach links well to other supply chain mapping approaches, such as value stream mapping.

Lifecycle costing (LCC): similar to lifecycle assessment, lifecycle costing (sometimes called 'whole life costing') is an economic application based on lifecycle thinking. This technique takes into account all the costs across the lifetime of a product, including purchase, operation, maintenance, and disposal. Similar approaches are also emerging to estimate social impacts and benefits associated with a product's lifecycle. This information is valuable in understanding the total cost of an investment or ownership. For example, while upfront costs may be greater for an eco model, the overall lifetime cost is lower due to cheaper running costs.

A key point about lifecycle assessment is that not only does it take into account the different life stages of a product, it also considers the wide variety of impact types that can result from the processes at each stage.

Note 14.4 LCA exercise contrasting a 100 km car trip using gasoline vs. electric

Assumptions

- ✓ Manufacturing emissions: gasoline car = 6,000 kg CO_2e; electric car = 10,000 kg CO_2e; lifetime = 200,000 km.
- ✓ Fuel/energy use: gasoline = 6.0 L/100 km, emission factor = 2.77 kg CO_2e/L. EV uses 18 kWh/100 km + 10% charging loss = 19.8 kWh from grid.
- ✓ Grid intensity: 0.50 kg CO_2e/kWh.

Step 1 – Manufacturing allocation (per 100 km)

- ✓ Gasoline car: 6,000 ÷ 200,000 × 100 = 3.00 kg CO_2e.
- ✓ Electric car: 10,000 ÷ 200,000 × 100 = 5.00 kg CO_2e.

Step 2 – Operational emissions

- ✓ Gasoline: 6.0 × 2.77 = 16.62 kg CO_2e.
- ✓ Electric: 19.8 × 0.50 = 9.90 kg CO_2e.

Step 3 – Total life-cycle emissions (100 km)

- ✓ Gasoline: 3.00 + 16.62 = 19.62 kg CO_2e.
- ✓ Electric: 5.00 + 9.90 = 14.90 kg CO_2e.

Sensitivity answers

- ✓ If EV manufacturing goes up to 12,000 kg → 12,000 ÷ 200,000 × 100 = 6.00 kg → Total = 15.90 kg CO_2e (still lower than gasoline).
- ✓ If grid intensity goes up to 0.80 kg/kWh → EV total = 20.84 kg (now worse than gasoline)

Results and reflection

For a 100 km trip, the electric car emits 4.72 kg CO_2e less than the gasoline car under current assumptions. This advantage grows when the grid is cleaner, or the vehicle lifetime is longer but can disappear if the grid relies heavily on coal. The EV benefits are highly dependent on electricity mix, battery production emissions, and driving efficiency. LCA in this case highlights that simply switching technologies is not enough – cleaner grids, efficient driving, and sustainable battery production are crucial for true climate benefit.

Source: International Energy Agency (2023); U.S. Environmental Protection Agency (2022); European Environment Agency (2021)

14.6 DIGITAL PLATFORMS FOR SUPPLIER SUSTAINABILITY COMPLIANCE

A further set of supply chain tools is related to mapping the supply base of companies in order to understand where the main risks lie. One of the key challenges in managing sustainability in the supply chain is that companies will typically deal with many suppliers potentially all over the globe. So far this chapter has dealt with tools that cover single supply chains (mapping tools) or the lifecycle of specific products. However, companies are being asked to assess the impact and risks across their supply base for example where there might be exploitation of labour. The resources to collate sustainability data from many suppliers and then assess where action needs to be taken can be very significant and single buying companies find this extremely challenging. At the same time companies may not have the knowhow to assess the suppliers they have collected information from.

Emerging platforms set up by solution providers provide many advantages to both suppliers and buyers, and there are now many hundreds of such tools available to companies to manage this issue. The Sustainable Purchasing Leadership Council (which comprises purchasing directors from companies such as Microsoft) recently assessed many of these platforms to provide some guidance to purchasing managers on what to look for and which tools might provide the best value. They came up with some key elements worth evaluating before choosing one or other tool (SPLC, 2018). These were as follows:

- Data relevance, and scope covering the main sustainability issues;
- Availability of training for suppliers to provide data;
- Verifying the data provided is trustworthy;
- Converting data into a fair and simple score which can be acted on;
- Benchmarking suppliers against other similar suppliers;
- Linking to corrective actions and feedback.

These types of tools are part of the trend in technology to provide better visibility in supply chains by reducing the costs of sharing data and creating shared formats to allow the tracking of progress and comparability as discussed in the innovation chapter. These tools also support companies in dealing with the burgeoning number of policies and standards that they need to comply with, an issue discussed previously in Chapter 13.

A number of solution providers currently stand out across the globe, namely Sedex, RepRisk, and EcoVadis – and these can be broadly characterized as digital platforms that support supplier assessment and compliance.

Sedex[1] (Supplier Ethical Data Exchange) is a global non-profit organization aimed at improving labour standards across supply chains, with a particular focus on human rights issues such as forced labour. Sedex was founded in 2004 by a group of UK retailers as a not-for-profit membership organization. Its foundation rests on the idea that businesses have both legal and ethical obligations to ensure their operations – and those of their suppliers – are free from coercion, exploitation, and abuse. Sedex works by providing tools, frameworks, training, audits, and data to help companies assess, monitor, and remedy forced labour risks in their supply chains. A central compliance mechanism Sedex offers is its Forced Labour Indicators Tool, which helps companies identify 'red flags' or risk factors – such as retention of identity documents, non-payment of wages, excessive overtime, or abusive conditions – that may suggest forced labour is occurring. These are informed by indicators set by the ILO plus an additional indicator Sedex uses: management systems failure. Compliance is further enforced through audit schemes used to verify conditions on site, self-assessment questionnaires, dashboards, and risk scoring help prioritize where intervention or remediation is needed. Companies must map their supply chains, perform risk assessments (including country-, sector-, and worker-vulnerability-based risk), engage suppliers, track corrective actions, and maintain transparency through reporting. In doing so, Sedex aims to facilitate both prevention and accountability, helping firms comply with laws (such as modern slavery or forced labour legislation) and meet growing expectations from stakeholders around ethical sourcing.

RepRisk[2] is a data-science company founded in 1998 as a Zurich-based consultancy focused on environmental and social risk for the financial sector, later becoming independent, and growing into a global provider of business-conduct risk analytics and metrics. The objective of RepRisk is to provide transparent, timely, external ESG risk and business conduct data that allows organizations – corporates, investors, financial institutions – to identify, monitor, and manage risks such as environmental degradation, human rights violations, corruption, forced labour, and reputational harm. Its methodology is 'outside-in': it relies on public sources (media, NGOs, regulators, etc.), updated daily, with both AI and human analyst input, using a rules-based and transparent framework. For supplier compliance specifically, RepRisk helps by enabling companies to monitor their supply chains (including private and public suppliers) for ESG risk incidents, flag red flags early, benchmark suppliers, and integrate compliance requirements (e.g. on forced labour, child labour, environmental harm) into due diligence. By providing continuous screening, alerts, risk scoring, and metrics mapped to international frameworks (UN Global Compact, SASB, SDGs, etc.), it supports companies in fulfilling regulatory obligations and ethical sourcing policies.

EcoVadis is another major provider of risk assessment of supplier compliance, and the next sub-section offers a detailed case study.

14.7 CASE STUDY: ECOVADIS – A SUPPLIER RATING PLATFORM

EcoVadis is an SME based in Paris that provides sustainability ratings for suppliers, to be used by more than 150 purchasing teams who face complexity in their supply base globally. The large number of standards and reporting formats means that suppliers face complexity and additional costs in responding to buyers' requests for information and reporting requirements.

The benefits for a purchasing department of centralizing this activity into a single service provider includes providing reliable measures, leveraging suppliers, and the use of a collaborative platform and scorecards that can be acted on. On the supplier side the benefits include a reduction in administrative burden, the ability to benchmark within sector, targeted action planning, and the opportunity to demonstrate good CSR performance. EcoVadis works with many global brands worldwide, such as L'Oreal, GSK, Nokia, Air France-KLM, Renault, Henkel, ING, Nestle, and Veolia.

The assessment process by EcoVadis comprises a number of steps. First, supplier companies register on the EcoVadis platform and complete an online questionnaire which is tailored to their company size, industry sector, and geographic location. Figure 14.4 is an example of the survey and some of the initial fields to be completed.

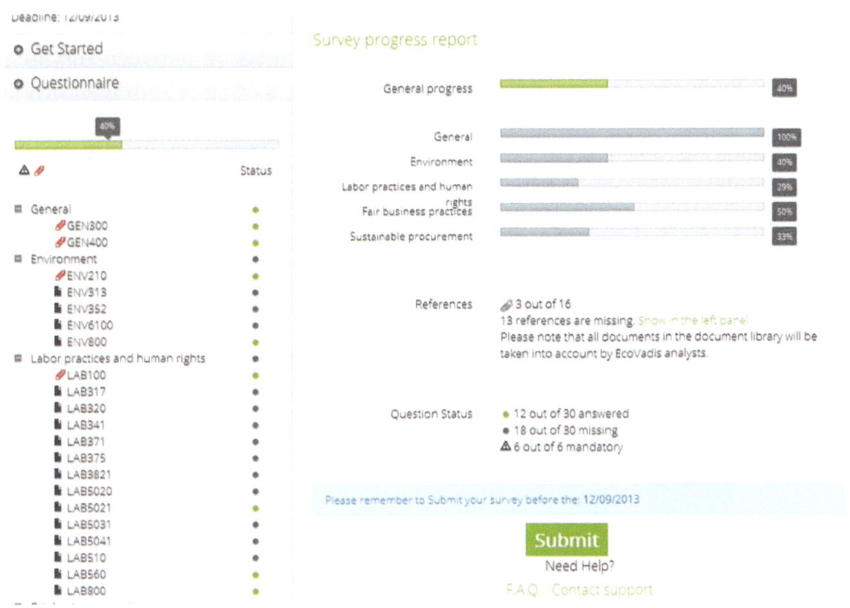

FIGURE 14.4 Example questionnaire fields

Next, documents are uploaded through the portal to provide evidence and answers to their response to the questionnaire. The documents that are collected are secured and guaranteed confidentiality. These might include policies, codes of practice, ISO certificates, and REACH declarations.

A last step at this point is a check by EcoVadis on secondary sources of information to verify the self-report. This includes information and data from more than 2,500 sources including media, governments, trade unions, NGOs, and other business networks. Other sources include Regulatory Datacorp (RDC) watchlists and politically exposed persons (PEPs) databases, China Labor Watch, WWF, and Greenpeace. New sources emerge regularly and EcoVadis scans these to keep up to date.

This information is then verified by EcoVadis CSR experts who check the questionnaire answers and documents that were collected. In total, 21 CSR related criteria are used in the ratings system which are based on the Global Compact, ISO 26000, ILO, and GRI. The themes are grouped into environment, social, ethics, and supply chain issues.

Suppliers are then assessed according to formalized policies and any external endorsements. The actions are also analyzed related to measures, coverage, and certifications and labels. A last part of this evaluation examines the results of these actions (KPIs) and any awards or condemnations. This approach can be seen as broadly based on the plan-do-check-act cycle and is indeed seen as a cyclical evaluation with a continuous improvement vision.

The scoring scale that is then developed allows comparison between suppliers as well as helping focus action plans with suppliers. The scoring system is shown in Figure 14.5.

The purchasing organization can then view a dashboard (Figure 14.6) based on all their suppliers that are registered in the Ecovadis platform. This can show the distribution of scores across the supply base, where the suppliers are based globally, according to their scores, and which sectors are involved and which KPIs the company is doing well and less well on from a supplier perspective.

	CSR Performance	
85 –100	*Outstanding*	• Structured proactive CSR approach • Policies and tangible actions on all topics • Comprehensive CSR reporting on actions & KPIs • Innovative practices and external recognition
65 –84	*Advanced*	• Structured proactive CSR approach • Policies and tangible actions on major topics • Significant CSR reporting on actions & KPIs
45 –64	*Confirmed*	• Structured proactive CSR approach • Policies and tangible actions on major topics • Basic CSR reporting on actions or KPIs
25 –44	*Partial*	• No structured CSR approach • Few tangible actions on selected topics • Partial certification or possible products with eco-labels
0 –24	*None*	• No engagements or tangible actions regarding CSR • Evidence in certain cases of misconduct (e.g. pollution, corruption)

FIGURE 14.5 Example of the scoring system

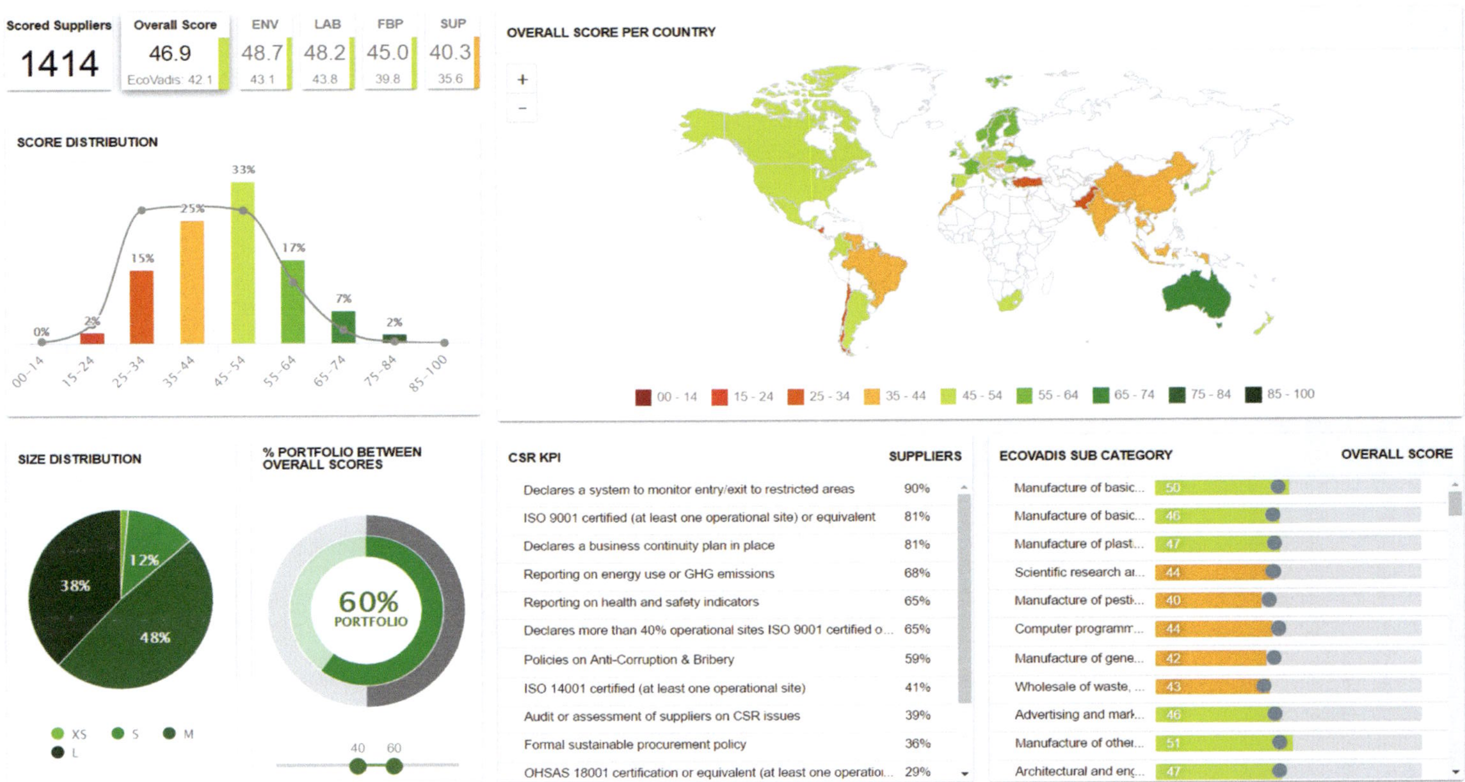

FIGURE 14.6 Dashboard with supplier indicators for the purchasing organization

Suppliers can also obtain tailored reports based on their company size, geographic area, and the industry sector within which they operate, and in this sense can act as a comparison tool. The scorecard then looks as follows (Figure 14.7) for any given supplier.

Based on these elements the EcoVadis supplier ratings tool can be seen as an example of good practice as it covers many of the elements mentioned in the previous section.

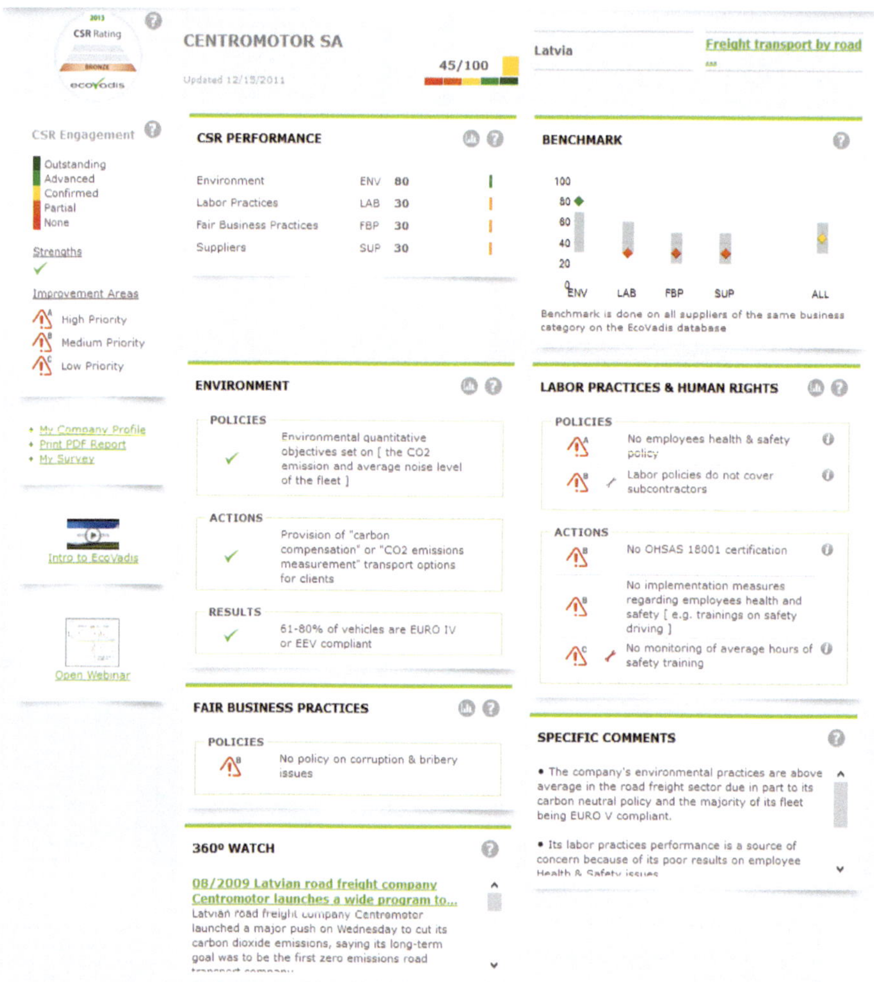

FIGURE 14.7 Example of a supplier scorecard

14.8 CONCLUSION

Moving from the formulation of supply strategy towards engagement and taking action on sustainability through implementation introduces a number of new challenges. Firstly, the aim of reducing the firm's impact on the planet cannot simply be added to existing performance targets in the form of an extended wish list. Considerable thought must be given to the types of impact the firm judges to be the most applicable to target given current policy indicators and the order of priority in which they will be tackled. It is possible that 'win-win' situations may occur through efficiency savings having the knock-on effect of reducing emissions, for example, but this is not always so. A supply chain-wide analysis must be conducted of the whole product or service lifecycle for an in-depth understanding of overall impact. Moreover, once the aim moves from mitigation to the goal of net zero supply chains, the challenge grows larger than win-win short term gains, see Note 14.5.

Note 14.5 Net zero carbon targets

Net zero carbon emissions refer to when the amount of greenhouse gases (GHGs) emitted into the atmosphere is balanced by an equivalent amount of GHGs removed or offset, resulting in no net increase in atmospheric concentrations (IPCC, 2018). Companies calculate progress towards net zero carbon by measuring, reducing, and offsetting greenhouse gas (GHG) emissions across their operations and supply chains. The process begins with a comprehensive GHG inventory aligned with the Greenhouse Gas Protocol, encompassing scope 1 (direct emissions), scope 2 (indirect emissions from purchased energy), and scope 3 (value chain emissions). Net zero is achieved when residual emissions, after all feasible reductions, are balanced by certified carbon removals. To ensure credibility, firms must use transparent accounting frameworks such as the SBTI and commit to time-bound reduction pathways rather than overreliance on offsets (Rogelj et al., 2021).

The Science Based Targets initiative (SBTi) provides the main methodology for setting corporate emission reduction targets in line with climate science. Under SBTi, companies develop near-term targets (5–10 years) and long-term net zero targets consistent with the Paris Agreement's goal of limiting warming to 1.5°C. This involves setting absolute or intensity-based reduction goals, covering at least 95 per cent of scope 1 and 2 emissions, and a significant share of scope 3. Targets are validated by SBTi to ensure ambition and robustness (SBTi, 2021).

Source: IPCC (2018); Rogelj et al. (2021); SBTi (2021)

Once the issues around environmental impact are understood in relation to the business as a whole, the appropriate tools must be selected. Some tools, such as value stream mapping, can be used to gauge not only efficiency and effectiveness, but also potential hotspots or areas in the firm or supply chain where resources are being wasted. Lifecycle analysis data can provide in-depth and accurate analysis of disposal options, as well as the environmental impact of different consumer options. Firms must understand the iterative and often shifting nature of sustainable supply chain implementation, where changes by policy drivers (and makers) may require a response in approach from the market. Purchasing is in the frontline of coping with such changes, where buying products or services with a reduced carbon footprint when compared to alternatives requires extensive knowledge of the process from material extraction to product disposal. This means lead organizations must be better at connecting with all levels of their business, not just tier 1, and communicating the benefits of a coordinated supply chain implementation with all participants: buyers, suppliers, customers, governments, and NGOs.

NOTES

1 Available at *Sedex at a glance*: https://www.sedex.com/sedex-at-a-glance/ (accessed 21 September 2025).
2 Available at *RepRisk AG about*: https://www.reprisk.com/about (accessed 21 September 2025).

REFERENCES

Ariav G and Ginzberg M (1985) DSS design: A systematic view of decision support. *Communications of the ACM* 28(10): 1045–1052.
Bicheno J (1994) *The Quality 50: A Guide to Gurus, Tools, Wastes, Techniques and Systems.* Buckingham, UK: PICSIE Books.
Bicheno J and Holweg M (2009) *The Lean Toolbox: The Essential Guide to Lean Transportation.* 4th edn, Buckingham, UK: PICSIE Books.
Blanco CC (2021) Supply chain carbon footprinting and climate change disclosures of global firms. *Production & Operations Management* 30(9): 3143–3160.
Blanco CC, Caro F and Corbett CJ (2016) The state of supply chain carbon footprinting: Analysis of CDP disclosures by US firms. *Journal of Cleaner Production* 135: 1189–1197.
Bolton P (2008) Protecting the environment through public procurement: The case of South Africa. *Natural Resources Forum* 32(1): 1–10.
Busch T, Johnson M and Pioch T (2022) Corporate carbon performance data: Quo vadis? *Journal of Industrial Ecology* 26(1): 350–363.
CDP (2024) Strengthening the chain: Industry insights to accelerate sustainable supply chain transformation. https://www.cdp.net/pt/insights/strengthening-the-chain
Chan M (2009) Cutting carbon, improving health. *The Lancet* 374(9705): 1870–1871.
Checkland PB (1981) Systems Thinking, Systems Practice. Chichester: John Wiley & Sons Ltd.
Christopher M (2005) *Logistics and Supply Chain Management: Creating Value-Adding Networks.* 3rd edn, Harlow, UK: FT Prentice Hall.

Clear About Carbon [CAC] (2013) Carbon matters: Explorations in low carbon procurement. Internal project report: University of Exeter Business School.

Correia F, Howard M, Pye A, Hawkins B and Lamming R (2013) Low carbon procurement: An emerging agenda. *Journal of Purchasing & Supply Management* 19: 58–64.

European Environment Agency (2021) Monitoring CO_2 emissions from passenger cars. https://www.eea.europa.eu/

Gardner J and Cooper M (2003) Strategic supply chain mapping approaches. *Journal of Business Logistics* 24(2): 37–64.

Goldratt E and Cox J (1984) *The Goal: A Process of Ongoing Improvement.* North River Press.

Fawcett S and Magnan G (2002) The rhetoric and reality of supply chain integration. *International Journal of Physical Distribution & Logistics Management* 32(5): 339–361.

Finkbeiner M (2009) Carbon footprinting – Opportunities and threats. *The International Journal of Life Cycle Assessment* 14(2): 91–94.

Flammer C, Toffel MW and Viswanathan K (2021) Shareholder activism and firms' voluntary disclosure of climate change risks. *Strategic Management Journal* 42(10): 1850–1879.

Forrester J (1958) Industrial dynamics: A major breakthrough for decision makers. *Harvard Business Review* (July–August): 37–66.

Hines P and Rich N (1997) The seven value stream mapping tools. *International Journal of Operations & Production Management* 17(1): 46–64.

Hines P, Lamming R, Jones D, Cousins P and Rich N (2000) *Value Stream Management: Strategy and Excellence in the Supply Chain.* Harlow, England: FT Prentice Hall.

Intergovernmental Panel on Climate Change [IPCC] (2018) Global Warming of 1.5°C. An IPCC Special Report.

International Energy Agency (2023) Global EV outlook 2023. https://www.iea.org/reports/global-ev-outlook-2023

IPCC (2007) Climate Change 2007: Impacts, Adaptation and Vulnerability. Contribution of Working Group II to the Fourth Assessment Report of the Intergovernmental Panel on Climate Change.

Ishikawa K (1985) *What is Total Quality Control? The Japanese Way.* New Jersey: Prentice Hall. ISBN 0–13–952433-9.

Lee H, Padmanabhan V and Whang S (1997) The bullwhip effect in supply chains. *Sloan Management Review* (Spring): 93–102.

Mallon S and De Leener D (2021) Emission possible. ANDE. https://andeglobal.org/publication/emission-possible-a-beginners-guide-to-emission-reporting-that-helps-you-reach-your-climate-goals/

Melnyk S, Davis E, Spekman R and Sandor J (2010) Outcome-driven supply chains. *MIT Sloan Management Review* (Winter, Special Issue): 33–38.

Mishra R, Singh R and Govindan K (2022) Net-zero economy research in the field of supply chain management: A systematic literature review and future research agenda. *The International Journal of Logistics Management* 34(5): 1352–1397.

MIT CTL and CSCMP (2020) State of Supply Chain Sustainability 2020. https://sustainable.mit.edu/state-of-supply-chain-sustainability-report-2020/

Monden Y (1983) *Toyota Production System – A Practical Approach to Production Management.* Atlanta, GA: Industrial Engineering and Management Press.

Porter ME (1980) *Competitive Strategy*. The Free Press.

Porter ME (1985) *Competitive Advantage*. The Free Press.

PRI (2017) Managing ESG risk in the supply chains of private companies and assets. https://public.unpri.org/download?ac=1894

Roemer N, Souza GC, Tröster C and Voigt G (2023) Offset or reduce: How should firms implement carbon footprint reduction initiatives? *Production and Operations Management* 32(9): 2940–2955.

Rogelj J, Geden O, Cowie A and Reisinger A (2021) Net-zero emissions targets are vague: Three ways to fix. *Nature* 591(7850): 365–368.

Rother M and Shook J (1988) *Learning to See: Value Stream Mapping to Create Value and Eliminate Muda*. Cambridge MA: The Lean Enterprise Institute.

Science Based Targets initiative [SBTi] (2021) SBTi Corporate Net-Zero Standard.

Senge P (1990) The Fifth Discipline: The *Art* and *Practice* of the *Learning Organization*. New York: Doubleday.

Shingo S (1988) *Non-stock Production: The Shingo System for Continuous Improvement*. Cambridge MA: Productivity Press.

SPLC (2018) SPLC Insight: Supplier Sustainability Ratings 2018: Landscape and Assessment Framework. www.sustainablepurchasing.org/splcinsight-guide-to-supplier-sustainability-raters/

Swank CK (2003) The lean service machine. *Harvard Business Review* (October): 123–128.

Towill DR (1996) Industrial dynamics modelling of supply chains. *The International Journal of Physical Distribution & Logistics Management* 25(2).

UNDESA (1992) Agenda 21. Section I: Social and Economic Dimensions. Chapter 4: Changing Consumption Patterns. UN Department of Economic and Social Affairs. Division for Sustainable Development. http://www.un.org/esa

US Environmental Protection Agency (2022) Greenhouse gas emissions from a typical passenger vehicle. https://www.epa.gov/greenvehicles/greenhouse-gas-emissions-typical-passenger-vehicle

Vieira LC, Longo M and Mura M (2024) Impact pathways: The hidden challenges of scope 3 emissions measurement and management. *International Journal of Operations & Production Management* 44(13): 326–334.

Villena VH and Dhanorkar S (2020) How institutional pressures and managerial incentives elicit carbon transparency in global supply chains. *Journal of Operations Management* 66(6): 697–734.

von Bertalanffy L (1950) The theory of open systems in physics and biology. *Science* 111 (January): 23–29.

Walker H and Brammer S (2009) Sustainable procurement in the United Kingdom public sector. *Supply Chain Management: An International Journal* 14(2): 128–137.

Walker H and Preuss L (2008) Fostering sustainability through sourcing from small businesses: Public sector perspectives. *Journal of Cleaner Production* 16(15): 1600–1609.

White SA (2004) Introduction to BPMN. IBM Corporation. www.bptrends.com

Williams ED, Ayres RU and Heller M (2002) The 1.7 kilogram microchip: Energy and material use in the production of semiconductor devices. *Environmental Science & Technology* 36 (24): 5504–5510.

Womack JP and Jones DT (1994) From lean production to the lean enterprise. *Harvard Business Review* 72(2): 93–103.

Womack JP and Jones DT (1996a) Beyond Toyota: How to root out waste and pursue perfection. *Harvard Business Review* (Sept/Oct).

Womack JP and Jones DT (1996b) *Lean Thinking: Banish Waste and Create Wealth in Your Corporation.* UK: Simon and Schuster.

Womack JP, Jones DT and Roos D (1990) *The Machine That Changed the World.* New York: Rawson Associates.

WWF (2010) World Wildlife Foundation: The Living Planet Report: Biodiversity, Biocapacity and Development. Private report.

Useful websites:

- Carbon Disclosure Project – www.cdproject.net
- Carbon Trust – www.carbontrust.com
- Clear About Carbon – www.clearaboutcarbon.com
- Department for Environment, Food and Rural Affairs – www.defra.gov.uk
- EcoVadis – www.ecovadis.com/
- RepRisk – www.reprisk.com/
- Sedex – www.sedex.com/
- World Wildlife Fund – www.worldwildlifefund.org

CHAPTER 15

Conclusion

15.1 INTRODUCTION

This final chapter calls attention to the major conclusions and messages of the book for procurement and supply chain management students and professionals. In particular, we highlight the different ways in which sustainability impacts procurement and supply chain management practices. Following this brief summary of key points, we set out what we see as key sustainability challenges for procurement and supply chain management. We conclude by reflecting on recent developments in higher education towards sustainable, or responsible, management in general and, more specifically, procurement and supply chain management education.

15.2 MAIN MESSAGES FOR PROCUREMENT AND SUPPLY CHAIN MANAGEMENT

The following points summarize the major messages and implications of this book for procurement and supply chain management theory and practice, especially those that stem from the need to seize the sustainability challenge:

1. Procurement needs to be managed as a strategic business function. The old-fashioned perception of procurement as a function that primarily aims to buy products at the lowest prices possible is long outdated.
2. Most modern companies have outsourced extensively so that they can focus on core competencies and compete on what they do best; this includes both production and service activities. Consequently the ability of companies to produce products or services that will not only satisfy but delight customers depends heavily on the performance of their suppliers. Without a highly competent and strategically orientated procurement function the company is inhibited in its ability to capitalize on the specialized capabilities offered by its suppliers. This does not mean that procurement is highly competent and strategic in all companies – but it *should* be.
3. The concept of sustainable development includes three dimensions: environment, social, and economic development. These are interlinked and none should be excluded at the

DOI: 10.4324/9781003499602-18

expense of others i.e. traded off each other; if procurement and supply chain management is to be sustainable it requires consideration of all three dimensions.

4 The sustainability trend provides an opportunity for procurement to assume a strategic focus and to make a contribution to the creation of sustainable competitive advantage. Sustainability presents a risk to companies but also an opportunity. Managers might simply seek to ensure compliance, but this would be a missed opportunity for value creation.

5 Companies have outsourced to low-cost countries for years, not least in search of cheap labour costs. This is no longer sustainable in its current form and the sustainability agenda as well as recent geopolitical changes are forcing companies to rethink their global sourcing strategies.

6 The concept of supply chain management assumes a linear industrial system where suppliers at different tiers are linked to, and highly dependent on, each other in satisfying end customer needs and requirements. The chain metaphor was always over-simplistic and the need to create sustainable supply chains makes the chain metaphor completely obsolete. Sustainable supply chains are circular, closed-looped cradle-to-grave structures. Better understood as supply networks or ecosystems, they include actors that are not normally considered as part of the supply chain; these include non-governmental organizations (NGOs) and other stakeholders that play critical roles, for example in monitoring and developing a sustainable supply base.

7 While there is now considerable evidence and literature around the theme of organizations adopting more sustainable ways of operating and including this approach in their overall business strategy, a challenge still remains in implementing new behaviour and practices by suppliers, particularly those furthest upstream.

8 Transparency is critical in supply chain management but is not limited to operational information such as demand, capacity, and inventory. Traceability of product ingredients/materials and supplier processes is the real transparency challenge, but digital technology such as AI and blockchain can significantly aid both traceability and transparency.

9 Products *and* services must be understood as an integrated package that has major implications when it comes to dealing with issues of extended lifecycle, designing product recovery systems, emergent new operating models, and how organizations such as manufacturers will engage with suppliers and customers in future.

10 It is important to understand the linkages between strategy, implementation, external policy, and enabling tools that allow sustainability to take root in the supply chain. Tools such as value chain mapping and lifecycle analysis help firms to be not only resource efficient but actively engage with the broader vision of promoting sustainability.

11 Last but certainly not least, the rise of artificial intelligence (AI) is transforming procurement and supply chain management. Routine tasks are being automated and even more critical tasks such as innovation scouting, spend analysis, and contracting are becoming AI-enabled. Generative AI is transforming the way we live, conduct business, and, consequently, how we procure and manage supply chains. The pace of change is so rapid

that no book or diagram can remain current for long. AI is reshaping how we source and evaluate suppliers, monitor their performance, organize supply chain data, and share this information with stakeholders. It is therefore essential to continue studying the impact of AI on research, business practices, and education in procurement and supply chain management.

15.3 SUSTAINABILITY CHALLENGES FOR PROCUREMENT AND SUPPLY CHAIN MANAGEMENT

Since we published the second edition of our book in 2019, we have realized that the field of procurement and supply chain management has been developing at such a rate that a new edition of our book would soon be required. In the interim time between the second and third editions, we have had the Covid-19 pandemic, the war in Ukraine, disputes in the South China Sea, and the Gaza conflict, and the geopolitical environment has completely changed with free trade being replaced by tariff wars between major economic powers. Global sourcing is no longer seen as a given but a high-risk strategy to manage very carefully.

Although sustainability legislations looked set to raise the requirements for companies to demonstrate due diligence in their monitoring of supply chains, and sustainability reporting, these legislative requirements are now being diluted. Sustainability challenges are now more acute (global temperatures and CO_2 levels continue to rise, material resources are not becoming more circular globally, planetary boundaries continue to be surpassed) and yet are being pushed down the political and corporate agenda. Forward-thinking companies remain committed to sustainability not least as they understand the value of sustainability for their customers. The trend towards circular economy also continues, helped by the fact that circular supply chains can make supply chains significantly more resilient. More recently, ideas of how to build post-growth economies focusing on socio-ecological well-being have arisen including how to downscale sectors that are inherently damaging to that well-being. Regenerative or nature positive approaches have also taken hold where business may actually give back more to the planet than it takes by restoring and improving nature systems. All of which serve as fertile ground to further develop sustainability in procurement and supply chains.

The good news is that in our view both academia (i.e. researchers and educators) and practitioners across industries continue to make great progress in developing sustainable procurement and supply chain management practices. More and more companies have embraced sustainability, including those that were initially reluctant. Coinciding with the release of the second edition of our book, the *Sustainability Pledge* rapidly gained global recognition and today counts over 26,000 ambassadors. In academia, there is still plenty of research on sustainable procurement and supply chain management, addressing current themes such as decarbonization, modern slavery, or the use of AI in sustainability.

We are convinced that the procurement and supply chain management profession is becoming deeply engaged in leading the development towards more sustainable or 'responsible' sourcing practices. Likewise, supply chain management appears to be embracing the sustainability challenge. In the first and second editions of our book we pointed to the risk that sustainability could be viewed as a special theme rather than permeating all the ways in which business is conducted. We pointed to the fact that most supply chain management textbooks have a chapter towards the end dedicated to sustainability (or 'ethical issues') but this is not integrated or viewed as a core supply chain management concern. Sustainable supply chain management has become mainstream.

We believe sustainability should become integrated into companies' fabric: all their processes, including procurement and supply chain management, should take into account the need for sustainability. This was the key procurement and supply chain management challenge we set out to address at the beginning of this book. We hope we have made current and future procurement and supply chain managers really reflect on the ways in which they operate and help them to transform their supply business models.

15.4 THE RISE OF SUSTAINABILITY IN EDUCATION

As we wrote in the preface, this book is intended as a core textbook for procurement and supply chain management courses at universities and business schools. At a higher level our ambition is to inspire the development of future procurement and supply chain management leaders.

This book integrates sustainability into each chapter and each aspect of procurement and supply chain management. Our sincere hope is that the book will play its small part in not only educating, but also changing the mindsets of current and future procurement and supply chain management professionals.

In fact, many programmes at universities and business schools now take sustainability into account. For example, when we began the writing of this book one of our institutions, the University of Exeter, had already launched its 'One-Planet MBA' supported by the WWF. Audencia Business School requires sustainability to be incorporated across all programmes, and ESCP Europe Business School has dedicated specializations and masters programmes in sustainability. Further away from our home institutions, other schools have gone down similar routes, including major league players such as Stanford, Michigan (Ross), Cornell (Johnson), Erasmus (Rotterdam), and MIT (Sloan) to name a few.

Business school and programme rankings focus specifically on sustainability. For example: the 'Beyond Grey Pinstripes' and 'Corporate Knights' rankings. The Financial Times now assesses the extent to which 'carbon net zero topics' are integrated into ranked business school programmes such as MBA and masters in management. Specific business and engineering school sustainability rankings have also emerged such as the Les Echos ChangeNow rankings in France.[1] Education bodies and organizations have emerged that are dedicated to creating more responsible management education including UN PRME (United Nations Principles for Responsible Management Education) and Net Impact.

In our view, there is little doubt that the emphasis on sustainability in higher education is going to continue. We certainly hope so, because education bodies have a responsibility to ensure that the leaders of the future play their part in ensuring that managers are able to challenge established thinking and to think and act differently for the benefit of business, society and our 'one' planet.

NOTE

1 https://www.changenow.world/classement-des-ecoles-2024/

Index